FIFTH EDITION

The Entrepreneur's Guide to
LAW AND STRATEGY

Constance E. Bagley
Yale University

Craig E. Dauchy
Cooley LLP

CENGAGE

Australia • Brazil • Mexico • Singapore • United Kingdom • United States

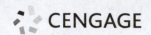

The Entrepreneur's Guide to Law and Strategy, Fifth Edition

Constance E. Bagley and Craig E. Dauchy

Vice President, General Manager, Social Science & Qualitative Business: Erin Joyner

Product Director: Jason Fremder

Senior Product Manager: Vicky True-Baker

Content Developer: Ted Knight

Product Assistant: Christian Wood

Marketing Director: Kristen Hurd

Marketing Manager: Katie Jergens

Marketing Coordinator: Casey Binder

Art and Cover Direction, Production Management, and Composition: Lumina Datamatics, Inc.

Intellectual Property

 Analyst: Jennifer Bowes

 Project Manager: Reba Frederics

Manufacturing Planner: Kevin Kluck

Cover Image: © Flexible and Nanobio Device Lab, KAIST

For product information and technology assistance, contact us at **Cengage Customer & Sales Support, 1-800-354-9706**.

For permission to use material from this text or product, submit all requests online at **www.cengage.com/permissions** Further permissions questions can be emailed to **permissionrequest@cengage.com**.

Library of Congress Control Number: 2016960589

Student Edition:
ISBN: 978-1-285-42849-9

Loose-leaf Edition:
ISBN: 978-1-337-39058-3

Cengage
20 Channel Center Street
Boston, MA 02210
USA

Cengage is a leading provider of customized learning solutions with employees residing in nearly 40 different countries and sales in more than 125 countries around the world. Find your local representative at **www.cengage.com**.

Cengage products are represented in Canada by Nelson Education, Ltd.

To learn more about Cengage platforms and services, register or access your online learning solution, or purchase materials for your course, visit **www.cengage.com**.

Printed at CLDPC, USA, 01-23

To my son Christoph Alexei,
With love and joy.

C.E.B.

To my wife, Sue Crawford,
and to my children, Philip, Winston and Kendra,
Thank you for your support, encouragement, and love.

C.E.D.

Brief Contents

Contents

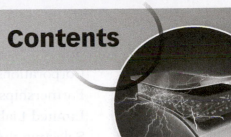

About the Authors

Constance E. Bagley is a Senior Research Scholar at Yale Law School and was formerly Professor in the Practice of Law and Management at the Yale School of Management. Before joining the Yale faculty, she was an Associate Professor of Business Administration at the Harvard Business School, a Senior Lecturer in Law and Management at the Stanford University Graduate School of Business, and a corporate securities partner in the San Francisco office of Bingham McCutchen LLP.

Professor Bagley received Yale's Excellence in Teaching Award in 2013 and 2009. A past president of the Academy of Legal Studies in Business, she is a recipient of its Senior Faculty Award of Excellence.

Professor Bagley served on the Financial Industry Regulatory Authority's National Adjudicatory Council from 2005 to 2009 and was on the faculty of the Young Presidents Organization International Universities for Presidents in Hong Kong and Prague. She is the business school coeditor (with Josephine Nelson) of eshiplaw.org, powered by the Kauffman Foundation and the University of Missouri at Kansas City. Professor Bagley is also the CEO of the Bagley Strategic Consulting Group LLC. Her clients include CVS Health, Microsoft, Prudential Financial, PepsiCo, Colson Associates, and MassMutual Financial.

She has published articles in the *Academy of Management Review*, the *Harvard Business Law Review*, the *Harvard Journal of Law and Technology*, the *American Business Law Journal*, the *Stanford Journal of Law, Business & Finance*, the *University of Pennsylvania Journal of Business Law*, the *Duke Journal of Comparative and International Law*, the *Cornell Journal of Law and Public Policy*, and other journals. Professor Bagley also authored *Managers and the Legal Environment: Strategies for the 21st Century* (8th ed. 2016) and *Winning Legally: How Managers Can Use the Law to Create Value, Marshal Resources, and Manage Risk* (2005). She has contributed to a number of other books, including *The Oxford Handbook of Dynamic Capabilities* (David Teece & Sohvi Leih, eds., 2016), and *General Counsel in the 21st Century: Challenges and Opportunities* (Christoph H. Vaagt & Wolf-Peter Gross, eds., 2015).

She received her J.D., *magna cum laude*, from the Harvard Law School where she was invited to join the *Harvard Law Review*. She received her A.B., with Honors and Distinction, from Stanford University, where she was elected to Phi Beta Kappa her junior year. Lund University in Sweden awarded her an honorary doctorate in economics in recognition of her pioneering work integrating law and management. Professor Bagley is a member of the State Bar of California (inactive) and the State Bar of New York.

Craig E. Dauchy is a partner at Cooley LLP and head of the firm's venture capital practice group. Cooley has 900 lawyers across 12 offices in the United States, China, and Europe. Mr. Dauchy is based in Cooley's Palo Alto office, located in the heart of Silicon Valley.

Since 2005, Cooley has been the most active law firm representing VC-backed companies going public and has ranked as the Number 1 law firm for technology and life sciences IPOs for the past three years. Cooley has represented one-third of the market share of VC-backed IPOs across all industries and has been involved in 375 public offerings in recent years, including some of the nation's most notable securities transactions. Cooley represents more than 350 fund manager organizations, including many of the nation's leading institutional investors, and it has been recognized as the Venture Capital Department of the Year twice by *The Recorder*. For more than 30 years, Mr. Dauchy has represented many of the most active and influential investors, entrepreneurs, and startups in the Bay Area and beyond. His representation of startups ensures they are structured for growth and long-term success. He leads a group of lawyers that has formed more venture capital funds than any other law firm in the world.

Mr. Dauchy is a frequent educator and a distinguished presenter to audiences across the globe on matters relating to securities law, public offerings, mergers and acquisitions, and venture capital. Leading journals such as *Legal 500, Chambers USA* and

Best Lawyers have recognized him as a national leader in investment funds, venture capital and emerging companies; the *Daily Journal* has named him three times in its list of the Top 100 Lawyers in California; and *Super Lawyers* has listed him for 10 consecutive years. In 2010, *Best Lawyers* named Mr. Dauchy Corporate Lawyer of the Year in the San Francisco Bay Area.

He holds a J.D. and an M.B.A from Stanford University, graduated *magna cum laude* with a B.A. in history from Yale University, and is a member of the State Bar of California. He serves on a number of boards of directors and advisory boards.

More information about Mr. Dauchy is available at www .cooley.com/people/craig-dauchy and additional information about Cooley LLP is available at www.cooley.com. Cooley GO, the firm's award-winning free legal resource for startups and those involved in the venture ecosystem, is available at www.cooleygo.com.

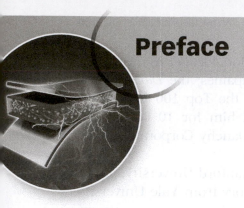

Preface

In a time of multiple "unicorns," private companies with valuations in excess of $1 billion, including Airbnb, Snap and Uber, entrepreneurship offers opportunities to build something enduring, to create good jobs, and to fill unmet financial, social, and material needs. Examples abound of entrepreneurs with extraordinary ideas who need to address legal and strategic issues early on as they seek to translate their vision into a successful business.

Consider Monika Weber, a Ph.D. student at Yale University's School of Engineering and Applied Science, who founded Fluid-Screen, Inc. This biotech startup developed an innovative system for testing water, pharmaceuticals, and other liquids for bacteria and other contaminants. Weber successfully negotiated a licensing agreement with Yale and her doctoral adviser to commercialize the nanotechnology and novel computer chip design that make it possible for customers to obtain accurate testing results in less than an hour. She won the Grand Prize in the NASA Create the Future Design Contest 2011 (1st out of more than 900 projects and 7,000 participants) then proceeded to patent the technology, to raise almost $1 million in grant money and private investments for her startup, and to partner with a major pharmaceutical firm to test her product. Like many entrepreneurs, she now faces many of the issues addressed in this book, including:

> Finding the right venture capitalist to help take her company to the next stage and negotiating the terms of the investment

> Building her firm's human capital by, among other things, providing equity incentives for key employees

> Determining on what terms to license her patented technology

> ➢ Securing additional protection for Fluid-Screen's intellectual property

> ➢ Deciding whether to keep Fluid-Screen independent with hopes of taking it public or selling the company or combining it with another firm.

This book identifies many of the legal challenges inherent in entrepreneurial activities and suggests techniques for meeting those challenges while seizing opportunities and achieving the core business objectives. Chris Dixon, successful serial entrepreneur, angel investor and venture capitalist at Andreessen Horowitz, called the third edition (then-titled *The Entrepreneur's Guide to Business Law*) "perhaps the most useful business book you can ever read."[1] Having our book included in *Business Insider*'s 25 must-read books for entrepreneurs, which includes classics like my former HBS colleague Clay Christensen's *The Innovator's Dilemma*, was a singular honor.[2] We have worked hard to make sure the fifth edition lives up to that legacy.

The Entrepreneur's Guide to Law and Strategy helps entrepreneurs and those who work with them "see around corners," to spot legal issues before they become legal problems, and to practice strategic compliance management. Recent events have highlighted the negative consequences of failing to heed the law. In 2016, the Federal Trade Commission announced that InMobi, a non-U.S. mobile advertising company that provides location-based advertising, would pay $950,000 in civil penalties and implement a comprehensive 20-year privacy program to settle charges that it "deceptively tracked the locations of hundreds of millions of consumers—including children—without their knowledge or consent to serve them geo-targeted advertising."[3]

Yet, staying out of trouble is only part of the picture. The law offers a variety of tools legally astute entrepreneurs advised by strategically astute counsel can use to increase realizable value and grow the business while managing the attendant risks and keeping legal costs under control. Legal astuteness is a managerial capability that enables the top management team to work effectively with counsel to solve complex problems and to protect and leverage firm resources. There are five components: (1) a set of value-laden attitudes, (2) a proactive approach, (3) the exercise of informed judgment, (4) context-specific knowledge of the law and legal tools, and (5) partnering with strategically astute counsel.[4] Table 1.3 in Chapter 1 provides a nonexclusive list of techniques entrepreneurs can use to create and capture value and to manage risk during various stages of business development and indicates the chapters in this book where they are addressed.

PURPOSE AND INTENDED AUDIENCE

The purpose of *The Entrepreneur's Guide to Law and Strategy* is to help future and current founders, managers, investors, and lawyers become more legally and strategically astute so that they can use the law and legal tools to grow the business and manage the firm more effectively. This book is intended not only for entrepreneurs but also for venture capitalists and other investors, lawyers, accountants, consultants, advisers, and board members who work with growing companies.

The Entrepreneur's Guide to Law and Strategy is suitable for undergraduate and graduate courses in colleges, universities, business schools, and law schools. In recognition of the growing demand for undergraduate and graduate courses on entrepreneurship and venture capital, Professor Bagley has made available to instructors the syllabus for her course "Legal Aspects of Entrepreneurship" as well as teaching cases she has authored or co-authored. To access them, instructors will need to register (it's free) for the faculty section of eshiplaw.org, a site powered by the Kauffman Foundation and the University of Missouri at Kansas City. The public section of the site contains additional information for students, faculty and others interested in entrepreneurship. Her cases illustrate various topics addressed in this book. For permission to reproduce or post her Harvard cases, go to hbsp.harvard.edu/product/cases and search under author name "Bagley." Instructor-only teaching notes are available for certain cases. The Academy of Legal Studies in Business also posts a variety of cases on its members-only site, which can be accessed at alsb.org.

The Entrepreneur's Guide to Law and Strategy both provides guidance regarding the legal and strategic issues that entrepreneurs should consider when launching a new enterprise and serves as a reference book and resource for those who are already active in the entrepreneurial world. It is not intended to take the place of an attorney but to help entrepreneurs select one with whom they can work as a strategic partner in an intelligent, informed, efficient, and economical manner.[5]

WHAT DISTINGUISHES THIS BOOK FROM OTHERS

Numerous other self-help and reference books for entrepreneurs cover a host of business and legal issues, and many are quite good. Often, however, the available literature is too general or too technical, impractical, or incomplete. Frequently, the authors are not acknowledged experts in their fields and may have unproven track records. This book satisfies the need for a single definitive source that covers the main legal aspects of starting and growing a business, written in a manner that allows the reader to learn about the relevant law and entrepreneurs' ability to use legal tools to create competitive advantage while at the same time benefitting from practical tips based on the authors' decades of experience.

In particular, *The Entrepreneur's Guide to Law and Strategy* distinguishes itself from the existing literature in the following ways:

> ➤ *Integration of Law, Strategy, and Management.* Much of the relevant literature treats the legal aspects of business as distinct from other aspects, such as the articulation of the value proposition and the identification of the activities in the value chain. Because we see the law as integral to business success, *The Entrepreneur's Guide to Law and Strategy* embeds our discussion in mainstream theories of competitive advantage, including Porter's Five Forces, the resource-based view of the firm, and the dynamic capabilities approach.[6] We interweave the law and its business applications by including real-life business examples that illustrate how in practice the law directly affects business success.

> ➤ *Transactional Approach.* Many legal texts are organized around specific areas of law, such as tax law and securities law. Our book takes a transactional approach, starting with the decision to leave the current employer and culminating

with a business combination or an initial public offering. Readers can easily identify the relevant chapters depending on their stage of development.

➤ *Cutting-Edge Issues that Challenge the Nuances of the Law.* The law is dynamic and it can impact multiple business lines that may, at first blush, not seem to be affected, especially when the laws originate outside the United States. For example, the European Union's General Data Protection Regulation, effective in 2018, gives the EU the ability to impose a fine of up to 20 million euros on companies that do not comply with its provisions surrounding information collected and used by Internet companies, among others.[7] The restrictions may be applied to state-of-the-art artificial intelligence applications incorporating "automated individual decision-making" functions that companies use to target their online advertising.[8] If so, this regulation could significantly affect the way Internet companies in the United States collect, store, and use personal data from individuals abroad.

➤ *From the Trenches.* Throughout this book, a number of examples appear in a boxed feature called "From the Trenches." When the example is based on a reported court case, we have provided the citation to the legal reporter in which the case can be found. However, many examples are drawn from our own practice representing entrepreneurs and venture capitalists. Sensitivity to confidentiality often required us to use fictitious names, but rest assured that the entrepreneurs and companies involved are real and that everything described in "From the Trenches" actually occurred. Our hope is that our readers will both avoid traps others failed to recognize and seize opportunities others missed.

➤ *Running Hypothetical.* A hypothetical presented at the end of each chapter under the heading "Putting It into Practice" follows the progress of Alexei Perlitz and Piper Mao as they leave their former places of employment, start a company in the 3D printing and manufacturing field, face financial challenges, raise money from venture capitalists, acquire another firm, and ultimately take the company public in an initial public offering. Much of working effectively with the law entails knowing the appropriate questions and when to ask them. This hypothetical highlights the key concerns founders need to contemplate as the business progresses. By following the thought processes and progress of these hypothetical entrepreneurs, the reader learns how to identify legal and business opportunities and threats and to "pivot" when necessary to adapt to changes in the regulatory and business environment by marshaling, utilizing, and redeploying firm resources.

➤ *Companion Website.* The companion website for the fifth edition of *The Entrepreneur's Guide to Law and Strategy,* located on CengageBrain.com, contains a variety of useful resources, including Internet sources, a table of cases, a list of information that should be provided to directors so they can perform their jobs effectively, and a summary of legal and other issues relating to franchising. Each resource is keyed in the text to the relevant chapter, so Appendix 6.2, "Information to Be Provided to Directors," relates to the discussion in Chapter 6. To access the companion website on CengageBrain, please follow these instructions: First, use your browser to go to www.CengageBrain.com. Second, if this is the first time you have tried to log into the site, you will need to register. It's free. Click on "Sign Up" in the top right corner of the page and fill out the registration information, making a note of the user name and password you have chosen. Third, after you have registered and logged in for the first time, go to the "Search for Books or Materials" bar and enter the author (Bagley or Dauchy) or ISBN for *The Entrepreneur's Guide to Law and Strategy,* 5th ed. (located on the copyright page in the front of the book). When the title appears, click on it and you will be taken to the companion site. There you can choose among the various folders provided on the Student side of the site. After you have logged in once and identified your book, just enter your user name and password to go directly to the companion site for *The Entrepreneur's Guide to Law and Strategy.* If you are currently using more than one Cengage book, the same user name and password will give you access to all the companion sites for your Cengage titles. After you have entered the information for each title, all the titles you are using will appear in the pull-down menu in the "Search for Books or Materials" bar. Whenever you return to CengageBrain.com, you can click on the title of the site you wish to visit and go directly there.

> ➤ *Getting It in Writing.* A sample independent contractor services agreement appears in a feature called "Getting It in Writing," Appendix 8.1 on this title's companion website at www.CengageBrain.com. Other exemplars, including a venture capital term sheet and a term sheet for an acquisition, are included in the text. In addition, model organizational documents are available at www.cooleygo.com.

CONTENTS

This book is intended to encompass all phases of the entrepreneurial journey. Its 17 chapters follow the progression of a startup and anticipate its legal and strategic concerns from inception to an initial public offering. Each chapter is self-contained and may be read on its own.

We begin with a brief description of the rewards and risks of entrepreneurship and introduce the hypothetical that will be discussed throughout the book. Chapter 2 explores the steps that an entrepreneur who is contemplating leaving an employer can take to make the departure amicable, and it offers guidance regarding the significance of documents (such as a noncompete clause or an assignment of inventions) that the entrepreneur may have signed. Noncompete agreements reportedly affect about 18% of U.S. workers, from senior executives to those in lower-skill jobs, and companies have recently begun increasing enforcement of the agreements through litigation.[9] The chapter also offers insights into the intellectual property issues involved in leaving a company to form a new venture and suggests ways the entrepreneur can safely (i.e., legally) go about recruiting colleagues.

Chapter 3 focuses on the role of an attorney and provides practical tips for selecting and working effectively with counsel. The next two chapters detail the considerations entailed in choosing an appropriate legal form for the business and offer suggestions on how to structure the ownership of the business among the founders and the investors, including problems that can arise when a "forgotten founder" appears, the pros and cons of issuing restricted stock and stock options, and the tax and accounting treatment of equity compensation. Chapter 6 addresses the proper governance structure for an entrepreneurial venture and examines the roles and fiduciary duties of directors. Chapter 7 discusses the pros and cons of different ways of raising money and the steps necessary to comply with federal and state securities laws.

Chapter 8 considers a growing company's relationship with its employees and independent contractors, from hiring to firing. We discuss the pros and cons of hiring employees versus independent contractors in the "gig" economy, as well as implications of misclassification. We address the split in the federal circuit Courts of Appeals over the enforceability under the National Labor Relations Act of mandatory arbitration agreements in employment contracts that include a class or collective action waiver.[10] We also discuss the laws banning employment discrimination and suggest ways to promote compliance.

Chapter 9 explains what constitutes a legally binding agreement and highlights ways entrepreneurs can use formal contracts as complements to trust-building and other relational governance techniques to strengthen business relationships. Chapter 10 highlights special issues associated with the sale of goods and services and electronic commerce, including liability for defective products, as well as consumer privacy. For example, we address the 2016 regulations governing the transfer of data between the European Union and the United States, as well as the European Union's "right to be forgotten." Chapter 11 discusses various business torts and regulatory issues that an entrepreneur may face and suggests ways to manage and insure against certain types of risk. Chapter 12 deals with creditors' rights and provides an overview of bankruptcy and out-of-court workouts. Chapter 13 explores venture capital in depth and highlights the aspects of the term sheet and other venture capital documents of greatest importance to the entrepreneur. Chapter 14 takes an in-depth look at intellectual property, the lifeblood of many entrepreneurial ventures, and issues associated with licensing. As with previous editions, we discuss cutting edge issues, such as the patentability of isolated gene sequences.

Chapter 15 discusses factors to consider when expanding internationally, including tax considerations and employment issues. Chapter 16 explores the processes of buying and selling a business. Sale of a company is a frequent exit strategy for growing firms, and acquisitions are often a way to accelerate growth and increase market share. Chapter 17 concludes the book with insights on another exit strategy, an initial public offering.

NEW TO THIS EDITION

The fifth edition both updates and improves upon its predecessors. It makes explicit the strategic implications of various legal choices and their effect on the sensing and seizing of opportunities and the marshaling, deployment, and redeployment of firm resources.[11] This edition includes significant developments in the legal environment of business and the precepts of business law of particular importance to growing companies. These include amendments promulgated by the Securities and Exchange Commission (*SEC*) in October 2016 to Regulation D and the exemptions from federal securities registration for certain intrastate offerings; the enactment of Regulation Crowdfunding, which allows unregistered offerings to the public of up to $1 million conducted on the Internet through certain broker-dealers or funding portals; and amendments to Regulation A permitting offerings of up to $50 million in a "mini-IPO" subject to SEC qualification (Chapter 7). Chapter 7 also contains a discussion of common terms for the issuance of convertible notes, including so-called SAFE investments. Chapter 8 discusses the 2015 refinement by the National Labor Relations Board of the standard for determining "joint employer status," which can cause temporary staffing agencies and the companies that hire their workers to be jointly responsible for compliance with employment and non-discrimination laws. Chapter 10 includes an expanded discussion of consumer privacy, including new "opt-in" rules for the use and sharing of personal information by broadband Internet service providers adopted by the Federal Communications Commission in October 2016. In light of the many instances of identity theft and computer hacking, Chapter 11 includes new information on data breaches and cyber insurance. Chapter 14 includes the patentability of isolated gene sequences and an expanded discussion of licensing arrangements, which is incorporated into the new running hypothetical "Putting It into Practice."

Many of the "From the Trenches" are new or revised to reflect recent developments in areas ranging from a violation of the Foreign Corrupt Practices Act by a bank that provided student internships to family members of foreign government officials to an employer's duty to make reasonable accommodations for an employee's religious practices to scandals involving product defects at General Motors and Volkswagen.

This edition is supported by MindTap® Business Law, the digital learning solution that powers students from memorization to mastery. It gives instructors complete control over their course—to provide engaging content, to challenge every individual, and to build students' confidence. Empower students to accelerate their progress with MindTap. MindTap: Powered by You.

ACKNOWLEDGMENTS

The authors gratefully acknowledge the guidance, comments, and helpful suggestions provided by a number of academics and practitioners who reviewed this and previous editions of the book. They are identified in Appendix P.1 on the title's companion website accessible at www.CengageBrain.com.

Professor Bagley acknowledges with thanks Christoph Bagley's industry research and his creative contributions to the running hypothetical "Putting It into Practice," the invaluable assistance of research associate Sue Schillaci, and the excellent word-processing support provided by Kaela Heaslip. Mr. Dauchy gratefully acknowledges and thanks Erin Walczewski of Cooley LLP for her superlative editing and Liz Cranford of Cooley LLP for her word-processing support. Mr. Dauchy also gratefully acknowledges and thanks the following Cooley LLP attorneys who helped in writing the fifth edition of this book: Frederick Baron, Leslie Cancel, and Julia Oliver (Chapters 2 and 8); Mark Windfeld-Hansen (Chapter 4); Aaron Velli (Chapter 5); Jodie Bourdet and Stephane Levy (Chapter 7); Mike Stern (Chapter 10);

Bob Eisenbach (Chapter 12); Stephane Levy (Chapter 13); Janet Cullum, Jim Brogan, Marya Postner, David Wittenstein and Brian Focarino (Chapter 14); Julie Wicklund (Chapter 15); Craig Menden and Annie Lieberman (Chapter 16); Charlie Kim, David Peinsipp and Jonie Kondracki (Chapter 17), and he gratefully acknowledges the generous support of Cooley LLP. Both authors would also like to thank Vicky True-Baker, Cengage Senior Product Manager extraordinaire, for her insightful guidance, responsiveness, and grace under pressure.

CONCLUSION

This area of the law is exciting and challenging. Law not only constrains, it also enables successful enterprise development. We have done our best to bring to life the power of the law and the legal and strategic astuteness necessary to make the law work for entrepreneurs and their partners in value creation. We had a lot of fun writing this book, and we hope the reader will have just as much fun using the book as a guide when embarking on the exciting but sometimes perilous journey of entrepreneurship. Please remember, however, that the application of law to a given situation may vary depending on the particular facts and circumstances. As a result, nothing contained in this book is to be considered as the rendering of legal advice for specific cases. Readers are responsible for obtaining such advice from their own legal counsel. This book is intended for educational and informational purposes only, but our hope is that it will help entrepreneurs and venture capitalists work more effectively with counsel as partners in value creation, resource allocation, and risk management.

Taking the Plunge

Individuals start businesses for a number of reasons: to be their own boss, to pursue a passion, to help those who are less advantaged, to achieve financial rewards, to establish a new livelihood after corporate downsizing, to fill an unmet need with an innovative product or service, or to create something enduring. Despite the vast variety of entrepreneurs and their companies, once individuals decide to become entrepreneurs, they will need to address many of the same issues. For example, founders must consider their own strengths and weaknesses and both the resources they currently control and the resources they can reasonably expect to marshal.[1] Thus, important questions include: "How will I raise the financial capital necessary for my business?" "Should I incorporate or use some other form of organization?" "Should I give equity incentives to key employees?" "How can I protect my intellectual property?" "Who should be on my board?" "Should I sell my company or try to take it public?"

1.1 BECOMING AN ENTREPRENEUR

Before starting a business, the would-be entrepreneur should consider the sacrifices—professional, financial, and personal—that will be required. These sacrifices may include accepting years of low pay and long hours in exchange for a large potential payoff later. Although entrepreneurs often work on their venture full time, Patrick J. McGinnis points out that there are ways to be entrepreneurial without quitting your day job.[2] They include being an angel investor or an advisor or board member in exchange for equity in the startup.

Successful entrepreneurship requires a willingness to take risks and the ability to learn from mistakes. As enterprise software pioneer Sandra Kurtzig put it, "Screwing up is part of the process."[3] Most successful entrepreneurs and their backers are not risk *seekers*, however; rather, they are risk *takers* who attempt to manage the risks inherent in pursuing new opportunities by making staged commitments and conducting a series of experiments.[4]

One key to being successful is to make fewer mistakes than your competitors and to build in the flexibility to "pivot"—to change the business plan when new information becomes available or when the original product or service idea fails or turns out to be less attractive than originally contemplated. In other words, it is critically important to learn from each failure and adjust the business plan accordingly.[5]

1.2 DETERMINING WHICH IDEAS CAN BECOME SUCCESSFUL BUSINESSES

A key threshold issue is which products or services to provide to which markets and at what prices, sometimes framed as, "What pain are you alleviating?" or "What hole are you filling?" The answers to these questions will determine the firm's value proposition and the activities in the value chain.

The *value proposition* focuses on customers' needs and the relative price they are willing to pay for a certain feature or service.[6] As Michael Porter explains, "[S]uperior value stems from offering lower prices than competitors for equivalent benefits or providing unique benefits that more than offset a higher price."[7] When selecting an opportunity to pursue, savvy entrepreneurs look for an attractive risk-to-reward ratio, that is, the set of possible negative and positive cash flows, and the likelihood of each possible outcome.[8]

A "novel value proposition often expands the market" and may involve targeting a particular customer class or focusing on the need for a certain feature or service.[9] Steve Jobs of Apple prided himself on creating innovative products, such as iPods and iPhones, that consumers and businesses did not realize they needed until they saw them.

From the **TRENCHES**

In 2005, the founders of the Israeli startup PrimeSense developed a gestural human-computer interface making it possible for individuals to give commands to a computer without having to use a mouse, trackball, touchscreen, or oral commands. Like Tom Cruise in the movie *Minority Report*, users could use their hands and fingers in mid-air to enlarge and shrink images, to turn pages, and to move from one program to another.

Although their invention had obvious military uses, the founders decided to focus first on the entertainment space. Founder Aviad Maizels commented: "The military *used* to be the ones who were pushing the envelope and the frontiers of technology but now in the era that is coming, the newest developments are coming from the entertainment space. Mostly it's in the consumer space where things are cool."

Founders of tech companies often first develop a new technology then form a company to exploit it. "In contrast, the PrimeSense founders first identified the user experience missing from the marketplace then set out to create the innovations needed to *provide* that experience." As Maizels explained, "We first asked, 'What is the value we are creating, the need we are filling? What are the experiences we want consumers to have?'"

Microsoft incorporated PrimeSense's system-on-a-chip and proprietary optics in the Xbox Kinect gaming system. Microsoft then promoted the use of the Kinect technology in everything from operating rooms (to enable surgeons to review patient scans without breaking the sterile field) to automobiles (to sense whether a driver's eyes were drifting off the road). Apple bought PrimeSense in 2013 for roughly $300 million.

Sources: Constance E. Bagley & Reed Martin, PrimeSense, Ltd. (A), Yale Sch. of Mgmt. Case No. 12-023 (2012); Constance E. Bagley & Reed Martin, PrimeSense, Ltd. and the Microsoft Kinect, Yale Sch. of Mgmt. Case No. 13-016 (2013); Shel Israel, *Why Apple Bought PrimeSense*, Forbes (Nov. 25, 2013), http://www.forbes.com/sites/shelisrael/2013/11/25 /why-would-apple-buy-primesense/.

Table 1.1 shows some of the various ways law affects the activities in a firm's value chain, that is, "the activities involved in delivering value to customers."[10]

Entrepreneurs must analyze potential markets to determine whether they are large enough to support the new venture, both providing a living for the entrepreneur and generating the types of returns outside investors will demand. Michael Porter identified "five forces" that determine the attractiveness of an industry: buyer power, supplier power, the power of competitors, barriers to entry, and product substitutes.[11] The most attractive markets are those in which there is weak buyer and supplier power, weak competitors, high barriers to entry, and no substitutes for the company's product or service.[12]

TABLE 1.1 Law and the Value Chain

Support Activities	Firm infrastructure	Limited liability, corporate governance, choice of business entity, tax planning, and securities regulation			
	Human resource management	Employment contracts, at-will employment, wrongful termination, bans on discrimination, equity compensation, Fair Labor Practices Act, National Labor Relations Act, workers' compensation, and Employee Retirement Income Security Act			
	Technology development	Intellectual property protection, nondisclosure agreements, assignments of inventions, covenants not to compete, licensing agreements, and product liability			
	Procurement	Contracts, Uniform Commercial Code, Convention on the International Sale of Goods, bankruptcy laws, securities regulation, and Foreign Corrupt Practices Act			

	Inbound logistics	**Operations**	**Outbound logistics**	**Marketing and sales**	**Service**
	Contracts	Workplace safety and labor relations	Contracts	Contracts	Strict product liability
	Antitrust limits on exclusive dealing contracts	Environmental compliance	Environmental compliance	Uniform Commercial Code	Warranties
	Environmental compliance	Consumer privacy		Convention on the International Sale of Goods	Waivers and limitations of liability
		Strict product liability		Consumer protection laws, including privacy protection	Doctrine of unconscionability
		Process patents and trade secrets		Bans on deceptive or misleading advertising or sales practices	Customer privacy
				Antitrust limits on vertical and horizontal market division, tying, and predatory pricing	
				Import/export controls	
				World Trade Organization	

| **Primary Activities** | | | | | **Margin** |

Sources: Diagram and text in roman type from Michael E. Porter, Competitive Advantage: Creating and Sustaining Superior Performance (1985); text in italic type adapted from Constance E. Bagley, Winning Legally: How to Use the Law to Create Value, Marshal Resources, and Manage Risk (2005), and M.E. Porter & M.R. Kramer, *Strategy and Society: The Link Between Competitive Advantage and Corporate Social Responsibility*, Harv. Bus. Rev., Dec. 1, 2006, at 78.

Of course, markets are not static. As Joseph A. Schumpeter explained, innovation results in "creative destruction," whereby established markets are replaced by new product and service offerings.[13] For example, Polaroid's instant camera and film business was supplanted by digital photography. As Clayton Christensen explains in *The Innovator's Dilemma*,[14] incumbent firms must often decide whether and when to cannibalize sales of legacy products to make room for their substitutes. Mary Barra, CEO of General Motors, announced in 2015 her strategy of investing in ride-sharing services and electric cars,[15] even though they could supplant the gas-guzzling SUVs that generate higher margins as long as the price of oil remains low.

Moreover, firms do not operate in a vacuum. "[T]here is an inherently interactive and symbiotic relationship between the private business organization and the larger society that constitutes its host environment."[16] As shown in Figure 1.2, the top management team is embedded within the dynamic societal context in which firms operate.[17]

It is therefore a "critical managerial task" to anticipate, understand, evaluate, and respond to developments in public policy relevant to the business.[18] As U.S. Supreme Court Justice John Paul Stevens wrote in his dissenting opinion in *Citizens United v. Federal Election Commission*, "[b]usiness corporations must engage the political process in instrumental terms if they are to maximize shareholder value."[19]

Entrepreneurs need to ask, "What regulations govern the proposed business and can I work within them or change them as needed?" It is much easier for a new business to work within existing law, but sometimes a venture can create greater value by lobbying for changes in laws and regulations that affect its business. For example, the hub-and-spoke system FedEx created to move millions of packages efficiently overnight would not have been possible if FedEx had been unable to persuade civil aviation regulators to change their routing regulations.[20]

Resources, especially dynamic capabilities,[21] can provide competitive advantage when they are valuable, rare, not readily substitutable, and difficult to imitate.[22] *Dynamic capabilities* include the capacity "(1) to sense and shape opportunities and threats, (2) to seize opportunities, and (3) to maintain competitiveness through

Figure 1.2   The Systems Approach to Law and Strategy

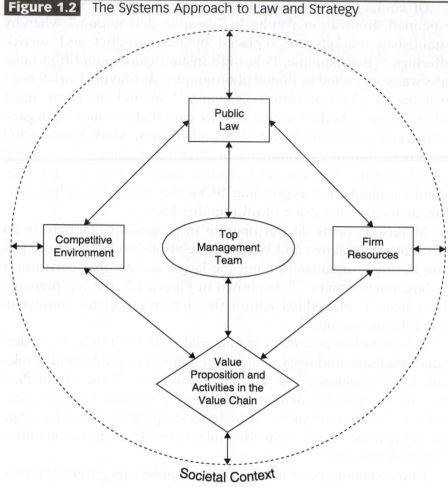

enhancing, combining, protecting, and, when necessary, reconfiguring the business enterprise's intangible and tangible assets."[23] As David Teece explained, sustained competitive advantage requires the ability to "orchestrate" the company's activities and its acquisition, use, and transformation of resources in a unique way.[24]

1.3 LAW, ENTREPRENEURSHIP, AND THE VALUE OF LEGAL ASTUTENESS

The rule of law is fundamental to private enterprise. Absent law and order, secure property rights, and the ability to convert

From the **TRENCHES**

When Joe Gebbia and Brian Chesky learned there was a shortage of hotel rooms in San Francisco because of a conference in 2007, they decided to rent three air-beds on their living room floor, make breakfast for their guests, and charge them $80 a night. They created a website (airbedandbreakfast.com) and booked the space within a week. In 2008, they discovered another shortage of hotel rooms, this time in Denver, where Barak Obama was speaking at the Democratic National Convention. Expansion and multiple financing rounds ensued. By 2016, Airbnb was reportedly valued at more than $25 billion.

Since its founding, the company has worked with a number of regulators. For example, in 2014, Airbnb agreed to collect San Francisco's 14% hotel tax for rentals. In 2015, Airbnb spent almost $8 million to help defeat Proposition F, a San Francisco initiative that would have limited short-term rentals to 75 days a year.

Sources: Jessica Salter, *Airbnb: The Story behind the $1.3bn Room-Letting Website*, TELEGRAPH (U.K.) (Sept. 7, 2012), http://www.telegraph.co.uk/technology/news/9525267/Airbnb-The-story -behind-the-1.3bn-room-letting-website.html; Heather Kelly, *Airbnb Restrictions Shot Down in San Francisco Vote*, CNNMONEY (Nov. 4, 2015), http://money.cnn.com/2015/11/04/technology /san-francisco-prop-f-airbnb-results/; Carolyn Said, *Airbnb to Collect Hotel Taxes for San Francisco Rentals*, SFGATE (Apr. 1, 2014), http://www.sfgate.com/news/article/Airbnb-to -collect-hotel-taxes-for-San-Francisco-5365352.php; Cameron Saucier, *Will There Be an Airbnb IPO in 2016?*, MONEYMORNING (May 5, 2016), http://moneymorning.com/2016/05/05 /will-there-be-an-airbnb-ipo-in-2016/.

"dead capital," such as land, into collateral for loans or working capital, few individuals will be willing to give up what they currently have in hopes of creating something new and potentially more valuable.[25] Law provides the "rules of the game," and "organizations and their entrepreneurs are the players."[26] Failure to comply with the rules can result in crippling lawsuits, devastating fines, and, in egregious cases, the demise of the firm and imprisonment for the individuals involved. Because legal risks are among the most important of the many risks faced by a young company, an entrepreneur can increase the likelihood of success by understanding and managing legal risk, that is, by spotting legal issues before they become legal problems.

Yet overcoming legal challenges and staying out of trouble are only part of the picture. When harnessed correctly, the law and the legal system can be a positive force that helps entrepreneurs create options, including the ability to abandon a path that has proved unprofitable; increase predictability; strengthen relationships; and marshal, leverage, and transform the human and capital resources needed to pursue opportunities.

The law offers a variety of tools legally astute entrepreneurs can use to grow the business and increase realizable value, enhancing the ability of the firm to capture the value it creates while managing the attendant legal *and* business risks and keeping legal costs under control. For example, absent the ability to patent new compositions of matter, the developer of a new drug would be unable to generate revenues sufficient to both (1) recoup the costs of research and development (*R&D*) and commercialization of not only that drug but other compounds that had failed and (2) generate sufficient profit to justify investors' willingness to put their capital at risk.[27]

Legal astuteness is a valuable dynamic capability that enables the top management team to work effectively with counsel to solve complex problems and to protect, leverage, and transform firm resources.[28] There are five components of legal astuteness: (1) a set of value-laden attitudes, (2) a proactive approach, (3) the exercise of informed judgment, (4) context-specific knowledge of the law and legal tools, and (5) advice from strategically astute lawyers who understand the business and work with the management team to help the firm win in the marketplace with integrity. Just as war is too important to leave to the generals,[29] the legal dimensions of business are too important to leave to the lawyers. Legally astute entrepreneurs and managers understand that firms do not have legal issues; they have business issues whose resolution requires knowledge of the law.[30] This book identifies many of the legal challenges and opportunities inherent in domestic and international entrepreneurial activities, and it suggests strategies for meeting those challenges and seizing attractive opportunities in an effective and ethical manner. Table 1.3 provides a nonexclusive list of techniques entrepreneurs can use to create and capture value and to manage risk during various stages of business development and indicates the chapters in this book in which they are addressed.

Each chapter ends with a section called "Putting It into Practice," in which we describe our fictitious entrepreneurs' journey and discuss many of the legal issues and opportunities likely to arise each step of the way.

TABLE 1.3	Legal Tools for Increasing Realizable Value While Managing Risk		
	Stages of Business Development		
Managerial Objectives	**Evaluating the Opportunity and Defining the Value Proposition**	**Assembling the Team**	**Raising Capital**
Create and Capture Value	• Ask whether idea is patentable or otherwise protectable (*Ch. 14*). • Examine branding possibilities (*Ch. 14*).	• Choose appropriate form of business entity and issue equity to founders early (*Chs. 4 & 5*). • Structure appropriate equity incentives for employees (*Ch. 5*). • Secure intellectual property protection and enter into nondisclosure agreements and assignments of inventions (*Ch. 14*).	• Be prepared to negotiate downside and sideways protection and upside rights for preferred stock (*Ch. 13*). • Be prepared to subject at least some founder stock to vesting (*Chs. 5 & 13*). • Sell stock in exempt transaction (*Ch. 7*).
Manage Risk	• Determine whether anyone else has rights to opportunity (*Chs. 2 & 14*).	• Document founder arrangements and subject their shares to vesting (*Chs. 5 & 13*). • Analyze any covenants not to compete or trade secret issues (*Chs. 2 & 14*). • Require arbitration or mediation of disputes (*Chs. 8 & 9*). • Comply with antidiscrimination laws in hiring and firing. Institute antiharassment policy (*Ch. 8*). • Avoid wrongful termination by documenting performance issues (*Ch. 8*). • Caution employees on discoverability of email and provide whistle-blower protection (*Ch. 8*).	• Be prepared to make representations and warranties in stock purchase agreement with or without knowledge qualifiers (*Ch. 16*). • Choose business entity with limited liability (*Ch. 4*). • Respect corporate form to avoid piercing of corporate veil (*Ch. 4*).

Source: Adapted from CONSTANCE E. BAGLEY, WINNING LEGALLY: HOW TO USE THE LAW TO CREATE VALUE, MARSHAL RESOURCES, AND MANAGE RISK 16–17 (2005).

TABLE 1.3 (continued)		
	Stages of Business Development	
Managerial Objectives	**Developing, Producing, Marketing, and Selling the Product or Service**	**Harvesting**
Create and Capture Value	• Protect intellectual property: Implement trade secret policy. Consider patent protection for new business processes and other inventions. Select a strong trademark and protect it. Register copyrights (*Ch. 14*). • Consider entering into licensing agreements. Create options to buy and sell. Secure distribution rights. Decide whether to buy or build, then enter into appropriate contracts (*Chs. 9 & 14*).	• Determine whether employee vesting accelerates on an initial public offering or sale (*Chs. 5 & 17*). • If investor, exercise demand registration rights or board control if necessary to force IPO or sale of company (*Chs. 13 & 17*). • Rely on exemptions for sale of restricted stock (*Ch. 7*). • Negotiate and document arrangements with underwriter or investment banker (*Ch. 17*).
Manage Risk	• Enter into purchase and sale contracts (*Ch. 9*). • Impose limitations on liability and use releases (*Ch. 9*). • Recall unsafe products. Buy insurance for product liability (*Ch. 11*). • Create safe workplace (*Ch. 8*). • Install compliance system (*Ch. 11*). • Conduct due diligence before buying or leasing property to avoid environmental problems (*Ch. 11*). • Avoid antitrust violations: No tying or horizontal price fixing; integrate products; and no illegal tying (*Ch. 11*). • Be active in finding business solutions to legal disputes (*Ch. 3*). • Avoid misleading advertising (*Ch. 11*). • Do tax planning; file tax returns on time; and pay taxes when due (*Ch. 11*).	• When doing an acquisition: be mindful of difference between letter of intent and contract of sale; consider entering into no-shop agreement if buyer; negotiate "fiduciary out" if seller (*Ch. 16*). • Allocate risk of unknown (*Ch. 9*). • Secure indemnity rights (*Ch. 16*). • Disclose fully in prospectus or acquisition agreement (*Chs. 16 & 17*). • Perform due diligence (*Chs. 16 & 17*). • Make sure board of directors is informed and disinterested (*Ch. 6*). • Ban insider trading and police trades (*Ch. 17*).

Putting It into **PRACTICE**

Alexei Perlitz (our fictitious entrepreneur) worked at Empire State Fabrication Inc. (*ESF*), a Delaware corporation headquartered in New York, before taking the plunge to start his own venture. ESF manufactures systems-on-a-chip and other integrated circuits for use in a variety of electronic products ranging from high-precision medical instruments to sensors embedded in palm-sized devices used by law enforcement officers and counter-terrorism agents to detect very low levels of radiation, anthrax, smallpox, Sarin, and nitrates.

Founded in 2006, ESF was the world's second largest producer of the system-on-a-chip used in the counter-terrorism sensors. It had revenues of more than $1 billion in 2015. Even though ESF increased production each year, the relatively high manufacture error rate and the cost of building a second fabrication plant made it impossible for ESF to satisfy customer demand.

Alexei attended Hamilton College as an undergraduate, then earned a double Masters in chemistry and material science from the University of North Carolina in 2010. He began his career in the quality control department at ESF. Although Alexei advanced rapidly, he soon realized he needed more than a technical degree to move into management. At the suggestion of his manager Gianmarco Cavo, Alexei used the company's tuition reimbursement program to attend the Stanford Graduate School of Business from 2013 through 2015. After he earned his MBA, Alexei returned to ESF to oversee the development of chips for the next generation of sensors. He spent the majority of his time supervising a team of engineers designing and testing new materials and configurations in an attempt to find one that would allow the chips to sense more minute quantities of the various substances.

While at the University of North Carolina, Alexei had worked in the laboratory of a professor doing cutting edge work in "additive manufacturing," the manufacture of complex shapes that cannot be manufactured by traditional manufacturing techniques, such as injection molding or milling.[31] Although many such shapes can be created by a 3D printer, it is a very slow process that uses 2D printing processes "over and over again to build up a three-dimensional object."[32] Similarly, manufacturers of transistors and integrated circuits use another 2D technology—lithography—to "build up a structure several times." Alexei learned that nano-fabrication works for integrated circuits less than 10 microns thick, but that the "subtractive techniques" used by the silicon industry to etch wafers "from 10 microns to 1,000 microns, the mesoscale" do not work that well.[33]

While attending his five-year reunion in 2015, Alexei was surprised to see how much progress UNC Professor Joseph DeSimone had made

(continued)

creating a process for fabricating complex shapes in minutes instead of hours. The online pre-reunion packet included a link to a TED Talk Professor DeSimone gave in March 2015, during which he grew in less than 15 minutes before the live audience "a set of concentric geodesic structures with linkages between each one."[34] This reminded Alexei of the hand-carved jade sphere-inside-a-sphere his undergraduate classmate Piper Mao had brought back from Guangzhou, China, during the spring break their senior year at Hamilton College. Professor DeSimone told viewers that he and others in his lab "were inspired by the *Terminator 2* scene for T-1000, and we thought, why couldn't a 3D printer operate in this fashion, where you have an object arise out of a puddle in essentially real time with essentially no waste to make a great object?"[35] He further explained that growing a product continuously instead of layer-by-layer would not only be much faster but would eliminate the defects in mechanical properties caused by traditional 3D printing. "Light can take a resin and convert it to a solid, can convert a liquid to a solid," but "[o]xygen inhibits that process."[36] So by using complex software to control spatially the "oxygen content, the light, the light intensity, the dose to cure, the viscosity, [and] the geometry," it is possible to control the process and "design chemistries that can give rise to the properties you really want in a 3D-printed object," including molecularly smooth surfaces, all at speeds potentially 1,000 times faster than traditional 3D printers.[37] Potential applications ranged from the manufacture of aircraft and car parts with higher strength-to-weight ratios than is attainable with current technology, to sneakers with vibration control and high elasticity, to new drug-delivery techniques and digital dentistry, to customized stents "designed for you, for your own anatomy with your own tributaries, printed in an emergency situation in real time."[38] Alexei was particularly encouraged by Professor DeSimone's closing remark, "I can't wait to see what designers and engineers around the world are going to be able to do with this great tool," which suggested that it might be possible to license what DeSimone dubbed "CLIP": Continuous Liquid Interface Production.[39]

While out for dinner with fellow alumni in Chapel Hill, Alexei bumped into Piper Mao, who had just finished the first year of the MBA program at the Fuqua School of Business at Duke University. When undergraduates, Alexei and Piper had expressed a mutual desire to work for themselves one day. Between college and business school, Piper had worked for Stratasys Ltd., a large U.S. firm that was one of the world's foremost manufacturers of 3D printers. Alexei invited Piper to attend a presentation at the reunion by Professor DeSimone. Afterward, they stayed up half the night talking about the cutting-edge technologies now available for 3D manufacture. They promised to stay in touch and agreed to meet again at Piper's graduation from Duke in 2016.

(continued)

Alexei spent much of his spare time over the next year testing various resins for use in 3D manufacturing. Alexei frequently used Skype to discuss his findings with Piper, and she made several helpful suggestions for tweaking the tests. Alexei was careful not to discuss his outside project with co-workers, but he and Piper agreed that she would join one of her MBA classmates Maren Barillas and an engineering graduate student Steve Asimov to prepare a business plan for a startup that would utilize an innovative process Steve had developed for faster 3D printing. Even though they did not win the business plan competition, Piper gained valuable experience thinking through the process of bringing a new product to market.

By the time Piper graduated from Duke, she and Alexei believed they had a viable design for using several different resins to manufacture a lightweight but highly absorptive bracket for automobile bumpers. They knew that if they were going to take the next step with their product, they would need to test their theoretical design with actual materials and software code. Faced with the prospect of investing money in addition to time, the two decided they should commit their business relationship to writing. So they signed a brief handwritten agreement to form a company to develop what Alexei had taken to calling "Genesis T-2000." The agreement stated that they would "divide any profits fairly."

Alexei took a two-month leave of absence from ESF to thoroughly test their designs in rented laboratory space. He and Piper split the rental cost equally.

While Alexei was testing various resins, Piper prepared a presentation for potential investors and completed plans for commercializing the technology. She estimated that they would need $15 million to purchase the necessary licenses, production equipment and materials, and eventually to hire employees. In addition, they would need to conduct further tests to ensure that the resins could be used to create a wide range of other products.

Alexei wanted to get their new venture underway as soon as possible, and he realized that to do so he would have to leave ESF. For economic and family reasons, Alexei and Piper decided to set up their new business in the San Francisco Bay area.

In preparation for his departure, Alexei asked to review his ESF personnel file to determine what agreements he had signed when he joined ESF. Alexei vaguely remembered being given a stack of papers to sign and return in conjunction with his post-business-school promotion to head of chip development for sensors. In his file he found forms for health insurance and tax withholdings along with a long nondisclosure agreement that he had only skimmed before signing. After reviewing the agreement more carefully, he realized that it contained provisions assigning the rights to his inventions to ESF, a nondisclosure provision, a one-year covenant not to compete, and a no-raid provision prohibiting

(continued)

him from actively hiring ESF's employees. (For a further discussion of these provisions, see Chapter 2.)

Before taking any action, Alexei knew that they needed to investigate these and a number of other crucial issues. Below are some of the questions our founders will confront in the initial and later stages of forming their business and the corresponding chapters of this book that address these questions.

1. Who owns the Genesis T-2000 technology? What rights, if any, can ESF claim to it? (*Chapter 2: Leaving Your Employer*)

2. What can Alexei do to make his departure from ESF amicable? Should he have left sooner? What ongoing obligations does he have to ESF? (*Chapter 2: Leaving Your Employer*)

3. Given their limited budget, can Alexei and Piper afford an attorney? Can they afford not to have one? If they decide to hire counsel, how do they select the right one? (*Chapter 3: Selecting and Working with an Attorney*)

4. What would be an appropriate legal form for the business from a liability and tax standpoint? (*Chapter 4: Deciding Whether to Incorporate*)

5. How should Alexei and Piper approach the issue of splitting the equity in the new venture between them? How should they respond to a claim by Maren Barillas for a stake in the venture based on her work with Piper on the business plan contest at Duke? (*Chapter 5: Structuring the Ownership*)

6. What are the advantages and disadvantages of having an active board of directors? Who should sit on the board, and what should the founders expect the directors to do? (*Chapter 6: Forming and Working with the Board*)

7. What are the founders' options for financing the new venture? (*Chapter 7: Raising Money and Securities Regulation*)

8. Should the company hire workers as employees or independent contractors? Does the company have to pay laboratory technicians the minimum wage and overtime? When is the company required to withhold taxes from their workers' checks and pay Social Security taxes? What accommodations must the company make for workers with physical or mental disabilities? How can the company protect itself against claims of employment discrimination and sexual harassment? (*Chapter 8: Marshaling Human Resources*)

9. What should Alexei and Piper consider before signing a standard-form lease for office, laboratory, or manufacturing space? (*Chapter 9: Contracts and Leases*)

(continued)

10. What warranties are implied when the company sells a product? Can the company disclaim all warranties and limit its liability to replacement of the product or refund of the purchase price? (*Chapter 10: E-Commerce, Sales, and Consumer Privacy*)

11. How should the company resolve a claim for battery and false imprisonment arising out of an altercation with one of the company's employees, and how can the company protect itself against such claims in the future? (*Chapter 11: Operational Liabilities, Insurance, and Compliance*)

12. What happens if the company runs out of cash and cannot pay its debts? (*Chapter 12: Creditors' Rights and Bankruptcy*)

13. If Alexei and Piper seek venture capital financing, how should they approach the venture community? What business and legal provisions in the term sheet and other financing documents should concern them? What is negotiable? Are any of the terms deal breakers? (*Chapter 13: Venture Capital*)

14. How can the company protect its proprietary technology? Does the company need to worry about violating the patents, copyrights, trade secrets, or trademarks of others? Should the company license its technology to a medical device firm interested in using it to make customized stents? If so, on what terms? (*Chapter 14: Intellectual Property and Licensing*)

15. Should the company expand beyond the United States? What are the advantages and disadvantages of going global? (*Chapter 15: Going Global*)

16. What risks are involved in growing the business by acquisition? Is it better to grow the business internally? What factors should entrepreneurs consider when deciding whether to sell their business to a larger competitor? When is franchising a viable option? (*Chapter 16: Buying and Selling a Business*)

17. When is an initial public offering an appropriate exit strategy? What is involved in going public? What obligations are imposed on a public company? (*Chapter 17: Going Public*)

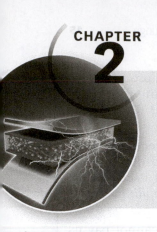

Leaving Your Employer

Sometimes an entrepreneur will start a new business right out of school or while between jobs. More often, a person decides to start his or her own company while still employed by a more established company. The idea for a new business may come from a project the individual was working on for the current employer. Depending on the agreements the entrepreneur has with the current employer, the entrepreneur's position, and the nature of the proposed new business, the entrepreneur may not be free to work on the venture while still employed or for some time thereafter.

The determination of the validity of restrictions varies greatly from case to case—and from state to state—and is very fact-specific. Courts will often apply the statutory or common (judge-made) law of the state where the employee resides or where the employment contract was entered into.

Certain employers require employees to sign an agreement containing a *no-moonlighting clause*, which prohibits the employee from engaging in any business activities (even after-hours activities) unrelated to the employee's job with the employer. A signed nondisclosure (or proprietary information) agreement (discussed in more detail in Chapters 8 and 14) prohibits the entrepreneur from using or disclosing any of the employer's trade secrets (such as a customer list) unless the employer authorizes it. The prohibition against unauthorized use or disclosure of the employer's trade secrets will continue even after the entrepreneur quits, and it may be bolstered by statutory or common law restrictions against misappropriation of trade secrets. In some cases, the entrepreneur may have signed an agreement in which he or she agreed not to compete with the former employer for some period of time after leaving the employer (a *covenant not to compete*). The entrepreneur's ability to recruit former coworkers to join the new enterprise may also be restricted by a *nonsolicitation clause*.

Awareness of these restrictions is crucial. A lawsuit arising out of the entrepreneur's duties to a former employer can be so expensive and occupy so much management time that it sinks the new venture. At a minimum, the new company would be greatly impeded by the threat of a lawsuit by the former employer. The departing employee should review all signed agreements, forms, and materials in his or her personnel file for provisions that may limit future entrepreneurial activities.

This chapter discusses both restrictions that are applicable while a person is still employed by another company and postemployment restrictions, including covenants not to compete. It then presents strategies for leaving on good terms.

2.1 RESTRICTIONS WHILE STILL EMPLOYED

The employer-employee relationship is based on confidence and trust. This gives rise to certain legal duties. For example, the employer has a duty to maintain a good working environment and to compensate employees for their efforts. In return, the employees have a duty to use their best efforts on behalf of the employer and not to act in any way that is adverse to the employer's interests. For example, no employee may use in connection with another venture confidential and proprietary information provided by the current employer to the employee in the course of employment and for the sole purpose of servicing the employer's customers.[1]

The extent of an employee's duties to an employer or former employer depends in substantial part on the position held at the company and whether the new venture will compete with the employer. In addition, the employee needs to consider whether it is permissible to solicit coworkers or former coworkers.

Position with the Company

Absent a covenant not to compete and a no-moonlighting clause, the employee's position will largely determine what he or she can legally do while contemplating starting a new business. In large part, employees' rights and duties depend on whether they are classified as key employees, skilled employees, or unskilled employees. *Key employees* (such as officers, directors, and managers) and *skilled employees* (such as software engineers, marketing specialists, and sales representatives) owe a duty of loyalty to the company. This duty, which exists regardless of whether there is an employment contract, prohibits an employee from doing anything that would harm the employer while the individual is still employed. This includes operating a business that competes with the employer or that usurps any business opportunities that the employer might be interested in exploring. During the period of employment, a key or skilled employee may make plans to compete with an employer but may neither actually compete nor solicit employees to work for the new business.

The duties of *unskilled employees* and other employees not in positions of trust are generally confined to the period of time during which they are actually working. Their off-hour activities are not restricted unless these activities are detrimental to the employer's interests. However, even unskilled employees can be restricted from competing with the company during their non-working hours by a covenant not to compete or a no-moonlighting clause in an employment agreement. Further, in certain states, such as New Jersey, even unskilled employees have a duty not to compete with their employer during the period of employment.[2]

Type of New Venture

The activities in which an employee may engage to further a new venture while still employed also depend on whether the venture will compete with the current employer. If the new enterprise is a noncompeting business, the employee (whether a key employee, skilled employee, or unskilled employee) is essentially free to establish and operate the new venture as long as it does not interfere with current job performance or violate any provisions (such as a no-moonlighting clause) in an employment agreement or the employer's policy manual. An employee may make telephone calls, rent an office, hire employees (but not coworkers, except as explained below), and retain attorneys and accountants for the noncompeting business provided that two conditions are met. First, the employee may not use any of the employer's resources (e.g., the employer's confidential or proprietary information or any telephone, printer, scanner, copying machine, smartphone, laptop or home computer supplied by the employer, or the employer's offices or conference rooms). Second, all activities must be conducted after hours.

What constitutes *after hours* is not always clear. For an employee with specified work hours, defining what is after hours may be easy. It becomes more difficult when the entrepreneur is a key employee whose working hours are not strictly defined and who has a duty to use best efforts to further the interests of the employer. For example, software engineers are famous for doing their best work between midnight and dawn. For them, there may be no clear after hours during the workweek. Instead, vacations may provide the only truly free time to develop an outside venture.

From the **TRENCHES**

When cofounder Steve Jobs left Apple Inc. in 1985, he outraged Apple's board by persuading five top Apple managers to join in starting NeXT, Inc. Jobs had been chair and CEO of Apple but was stripped of the CEO position and control over day-to-day operations in May 1985. Thereafter, he began planning his new company. Five days before resigning as chairman, Jobs gave the newly appointed CEO, John Scully, a list of the five employees who would be joining him at NeXT. Jobs also inquired about the possibility of licensing Apple technology for his new venture. Apple responded by suing Jobs for breach of his fiduciary responsibilities as chair and for misappropriation of confidential and proprietary information. Four months later, Apple agreed to settle the suit in return for Jobs's promise that NeXT would not hire any additional Apple employees for a six-month period and would not solicit Apple employees for a year. NeXT also granted Apple the right to inspect NeXT's products before they were marketed. Apple bought NeXT in 1996 for approximately $400 million and hired Jobs as CEO of Apple in 1997.

Sources: See Scott Ard, *#TBT: Thirty Years Ago, Apple Sues Steve Jobs, Calls Him Nefarious and Secretive,* Silicon Valley Bus. J. (Sept. 24, 2015), http://www.bizjournals.com/sanjose/feature /tbt-heres-how-angry-apple-was-when-steve-jobs.html; Henry Blodget, *Let's Get One Thing Straight—Apple Had No Choice But to Oust Steve Jobs,* Bus. Insider (Sept. 23, 2013), http://www .businessinsider.com/apple-had-no-choice-with-steve-jobs-2013-9; *Steve Jobs: An Extraordinary Career,* Entrepreneur, http://www.entrepreneur.com/article/197538 (last visited Aug. 10, 2016).

If the new venture will compete directly with the current employer, the entrepreneur's actions are significantly more restricted. Key employees and skilled employees may not prepare for or plan the new venture if doing so would interfere with their job responsibilities. Under no circumstances may they be involved in the actual operation of a competing venture while still employed by another. Both the current employees and the new venture they form and operate are jointly and severally liable for the damages suffered by the current employer, meaning that the new venture can be liable for all the damages caused by the employees' wrongful conduct. These can include the net profits of the new venture, punitive damages, and attorneys' fees.[3]

Once plans for the competing business are in place, it is almost always advisable for the would-be entrepreneur to terminate the employment relationship. Although it may be tempting to continue working, the potential liability—and the time required to straighten out any legal or business conflicts that may arise—will probably outweigh the benefit of the extra income.

These rules are summarized in Table 2.1.

TABLE 2.1	Summary of Permissible Activities While Still Employed by Another	
	Type of Venture	
Type of Employee	**Noncompeting Venture**	**Competing Venture**
Key employee or skilled employee	Can prepare for and operate venture as long as it does not interfere with responsibilities or fiduciary duty. If subject to a no-moonlighting clause, the employee cannot operate venture.	Can prepare for venture as long as it does not interfere with responsibilities or fiduciary duty, including duty not to use the employer's confidential or proprietary information. Cannot operate venture.
Unskilled employee	Can prepare for and operate venture as long as it does not interfere with responsibilities or fiduciary duty, including duty not to use the employer's confidential or proprietary information. If subject to a no-moonlighting clause, the employee cannot operate venture.	Can prepare for and, in many jurisdictions, operate venture as long as it does not interfere with responsibilities, including duty not to use the employer's confidential or proprietary information. If subject to a covenant not to compete or a no-moonlighting clause, the employee cannot operate venture.

Solicitation of Coworkers

Solicitation of coworkers to leave their employment and come to work for the new company can be a sensitive issue. If the coworker has an employment contract for a definite term (e.g., two years), the entrepreneur seeking to lure the coworker away may be liable for damages for intentionally and improperly encouraging the coworker to break that contract and leave the employer before the specified term is over. The former employer can sue both the entrepreneur and his or her new firm for intentional interference with contract and prospective business advantage, torts discussed further in Chapter 11.

Even if the coworkers do not have written employment contracts and their employment is terminable *at will* (i.e., at any time, by either party, for any reason)—as is the case with most U.S. employees—an entrepreneur may still be held liable if his or her conduct leads coworkers to violate any applicable restrictive covenants. For example, an entrepreneur may want to hire away a coworker who has access to the company's confidential information or who has developed special expertise that could be of great value to the new business. Doing so, however, may result in the violation of the coworker's nondisclosure agreement or of a covenant not to compete. (As discussed below, even in the absence of a nondisclosure agreement, the entrepreneur and the coworker may be opening themselves up to liability for misappropriation of trade secrets and other forms of confidential and proprietary information.)

In addition, deliberate campaigns to disrupt another company's business by wrongfully inducing its employees to join another firm may constitute tortious intentional interference with prospective economic advantage, which means one party can sue another party for money it lost. For example, after abruptly leaving their former law firm, the founders of a new law firm induced six at-will employees to leave and join their new firm. The founders were liable for $150,000 in damages suffered by their former firm because they mounted a campaign to deliberately disrupt the former firm's business by resigning without notice, not leaving status reports on outstanding matters or deadlines, unlawfully destroying computer files and forms, taking confidential information, improperly soliciting the former firm's clients, and "cultivat[ing]" employee discontent. These purposeful unlawful acts "crippled" the former firm's business operations and caused its personnel to quit.[4]

Often employees are asked to sign an agreement expressly prohibiting them from soliciting coworkers, inducing coworkers to leave, or hiring them for some stated period of time after leaving the former employer. Such a provision is referred to as a *no-raid* or *anti-piracy clause* or as an *employee nonsolicitation provision*. If the entrepreneur has signed such an agreement and solicits or hires in violation of it, the former employer could successfully sue for breach of contract and perhaps even obtain an injunction (or court order) preventing the former coworkers from working for the entrepreneur or the new venture. A distinction is generally drawn between soliciting coworkers and telling them about future plans, however. Even when a no-raid clause prohibits an entrepreneur from soliciting coworkers while still an employee, certain courts would not prevent the entrepreneur from discussing future plans with coworkers. Social networking sites, such as LinkedIn, make it easier for entrepreneurs to make their plans known without fear of violating a no-raid clause. If coworkers are interested, they can contact the entrepreneur later and discuss any potential job opportunities.

Key employees are even more restricted in how they may approach coworkers. Generally, even in the absence of a no-raid clause, a key employee who induces another employee to move to a competitor may be liable for breach of fiduciary duty. Everyone who has participated in or benefited from that breach may be held liable. In one case, several key management employees induced several coworkers to leave their employer and enter into employment with their newly formed competing air-freight forwarding company.[5] The management employees were held liable to the former employer for breach of fiduciary duty, fraud, and interference with contractual relations. The fact that none of the employees had an employment contract was irrelevant.

2.2 POSTEMPLOYMENT RESTRICTIONS AND THE COVENANT NOT TO COMPETE

Once an entrepreneur leaves the former place of employment, he or she may still be restricted by a no-raid clause (discussed above) or by a covenant not to compete (also known as a *noncompete covenant*). A *covenant not to compete* is an agreement between an employer and an employee that is designed to protect the employer from potentially unfair competition from a former employee. Prohibited competition usually includes dealing with or soliciting business from the former employer's customers, using the former employer's confidential business information for the benefit of the new employer, or operating a competing business in the same geographic area where the employee previously worked on behalf of the former employer.

To be binding and legally enforceable, the covenant not to compete must meet certain requirements. It must be ancillary to some other agreement; supported by adequate consideration (i.e., the person agreeing to the covenant must receive something of value from the other party); designed to protect a legitimate interest of the employer; reasonably limited in scope, geography, and duration; and not contrary to the interests of the public. If a court finds that a legally valid covenant has been breached, the court may issue an injunction ordering the entrepreneur to stop the offending activities, award damages, or both. Inducing an employee to violate a valid noncompete covenant can also give rise to a lawsuit against the new employer for tortious interference with contract.

Ancillary to Another Agreement

A stand-alone covenant not to compete is a naked restraint on trade, which, in many states, is *per se*, or by itself, invalid. For a noncompete covenant to be valid, it must be subordinate to some lawful contract that describes the relationship between the parties. A formal employment agreement, a sale-of-business contract, or an agreement dissolving a partnership satisfies this requirement. An Illinois appellate court held that an at-will employment agreement is sufficient even in the absence of a written employment contract to support covenants not to compete, reasoning that "[a]lthough an at-will employment agreement ... might not be considered 'enforceable' in the strictest sense of the term, it is nonetheless an agreement and relationship with numerous legal consequences, imposing rights and obligations on both parties."[6]

Consideration

Like other contracts, a covenant not to compete must be supported by consideration. This can include the payment of money or an exchange of promises. Although certain courts take the position that covenants entered into after employment has commenced are not supported by consideration,[7] others reason that an employer provides consideration when it does not terminate an at-will employment relationship and instead offers continuing employment.[8] An Illinois court held that an at-will employee must have been employed for at least two years for there to be adequate consideration to support a postemployment noncompete covenant,[9] but other courts have declined to adopt a hard-and-fast rule about the length of at-will employment needed to support a covenant not to compete. To ensure consideration, an employer seeking a noncompete covenant from an existing at-will employee should either make an additional payment to the employee (even a nominal amount would suffice) or provide something else of value, such as a stock grant, promotion, or specialized training.[10]

Legitimate Interests

A noncompete covenant may legally protect only legitimate interests of the employer. A general interest in restricting competition is insufficient in most states. For the employer to enforce a restrictive covenant, the employee must generally present a substantial risk either to the employer's customer base or to confidential business information. Employer interests that have been found to be legitimate include protecting trade secrets, customer lists, and other confidential information; preserving long-term, near permanent customer relationships; and protecting the goodwill, business reputation, and unique skills associated with the employer. Courts have also ruled that "the 'efforts and moneys' invested by an employer to provide to its employees specialized training in the methods of the employer's business" qualify as legitimate interests worthy of protection.[11]

Limited in Scope

The restrictions imposed by the noncompete covenant must be reasonably related to the interests protected. To be valid, these restrictions must be limited in time, geographic area, and scope of activities affected. In a dispute, the court will closely scrutinize the restrictions to determine how they relate to the employer's business. If the court finds the restrictions overly broad, it will typically either modify some terms of the covenant to make them reasonable (e.g., shorten the duration) or declare the entire covenant invalid.

With respect to the time restriction, courts have generally found one year or less to be a reasonable limitation. A court would be highly unlikely to enforce a covenant for a period of more than five years, except perhaps in connection with the sale of a business. For example, the Nevada Supreme Court invalidated a noncompete agreement restricting a lighting-retrofitting employee from competing with his former employer within a 100-mile radius of the former employer's site for five years.[12] The duration placed a great hardship on the employee and was not necessary to protect the former employer's interests.

In contrast, a Kansas court upheld a two-year covenant not to compete that prohibited a dermatologist from practicing dermatology within a 30-mile radius of the offices of the doctor for whom he had worked. Two years was considered reasonable to erase from the public's mind any identification of the dermatologist with his former employer's practice and to allow the former employer to reestablish his relationship with patients who had been referred to the dermatologist. The 30-mile radius covered the territory from which the dermatologist's former employer drew most of his patients.[13]

A well-drafted covenant will contain a provision that invites the court to enforce the covenant to the greatest extent possible under applicable law and to modify the covenant as needed to make it enforceable. This is called a *blue-pencilling clause*. States vary on whether they will permit blue-pencilling. For example, Ohio courts tend to revise covenants as needed to make them enforceable, but Nebraska law does not allow courts to modify restrictive covenants to make them reasonable. As a result, a Nebraska court struck down an overly broad noncompete agreement in its entirety.[14] This is an area where less can be more. A more narrowly focused noncompete will have a greater chance of enforcement.

From the **TRENCHES**

Jeffrey Hirshberg was employed in the Buffalo, New York, office of BDO Seidman, a national accounting firm. As a condition to receiving a promotion to the position of manager, Hirshberg was required to sign a "Manager's Agreement," which provided that if, within 18 months following the termination of his employment, Hirshberg served any former client of BDO Seidman's Buffalo office, he would be required to compensate BDO Seidman "for the loss and damages suffered" in an amount equal to one and a half times the fees BDO Seidman had charged that client over the last fiscal year of the client's patronage. After Hirshberg resigned from BDO Seidman, the accounting firm claimed that it lost to Hirshberg 100 former clients who had been billed a total of $138,000 in the year he left the firm.

The New York Court of Appeals ruled that the agreement was reasonable and enforceable except to the extent that it required Hirshberg to compensate BDO Seidman for fees paid by (1) the personal clients whom he had brought to the firm through his own contacts or (2) clients with whom he had never acquired a relationship through his employment at BDO Seidman.

Source: BDO Seidman v. Hirshberg, 712 N.E.2d 1220 (N.Y. 1999).

In certain states, the geographic limitations of a noncompete covenant are only enforced to the extent that they correlate with the employee's territory. One court held that a clause prohibiting an employee from competing with his former employer anywhere within the United States, Puerto Rico, or Canada was excessive because the employee had only worked in Colorado, Kansas, Missouri, Nebraska, and Wyoming. The court modified the clause to cover only those five states.[15]

Interests of the Public

In determining the validity of a noncompete covenant, a court will also look at the interests of the public affected by the covenant. Noncompete covenants can prevent the uninhibited flow of labor necessary for a competitive market so they are disfavored and limited. In addition, there is a basic belief that a person must be able to ply his or her trade to earn a living. Yet, covenants not to compete also help deter unethical and unfair business practices, such as stealing trade secrets. If companies cannot adequately protect legitimate interests, entrepreneurs may be less likely to start new businesses and spend time and money developing and marketing better and cheaper products that increase consumer wealth. The balance struck between these competing public policies varies from state to state and is reflected in each state's legislation and common law.

State Legislation   A number of states have enacted legislation restricting the enforceability of noncompete covenants. Such legislation generally falls into three categories. Some states, such as California, have statutes that, with very limited exceptions, broadly prohibit covenants restraining anyone from engaging in a lawful profession, trade, or business and that prohibit employers from including such restrictions in an ordinary employment agreement. Other states, such as Oregon, have statutes that regulate certain aspects of noncompete covenants without broadly prohibiting them. Texas and a number of other states have taken yet another approach, adopting statutory reasonableness standards that must be satisfied for the covenants to be enforced.

Exceptions to Legislation   Many states with broad prohibitions against covenants not to compete have exceptions permitting such covenants in certain limited circumstances. For example, California has statutory exceptions permitting reasonable restrictions, generally not to exceed five years in duration, when the covenantor sells all of his or her shares in a corporation in a transaction in which the company is sold as a going concern.[16] The covenantor is typically the owner selling the business and, upon the sale, may be restricted from starting a similar business in a certain location. Restrictions are also permissible in the case of a partnership dissolution or the sale of a limited liability company (*LLC*), or a partner's disassociation from a partnership or an LLC member's termination of interest in the LLC. California's statutory exceptions have been further narrowed by judicial rulings that (1) limit restraints against the pursuit of an entire or substantial part of a profession, trade, or business and (2) allow restrictions only to the extent necessary to protect a legitimate business interest. For example, the California Court of Appeal rejected the inevitable disclosure doctrine (discussed below),[17] under which an employee may be barred from taking a position in another firm that would require him or her to use the trade secrets learned at the prior employer.[18] The court reasoned that the doctrine was inconsistent with California's statutory ban on postemployment covenants not to compete.[19]

Common Law   States that do not have special legislation or constitutional provisions governing the use of noncompete covenants usually have common law rules for determining the validity and enforceability of such covenants. Common law is law created by judges in the course of deciding court cases.

Choice of Law   With the high degree of employee mobility in the information economy, it is common for employees to move from state to state for a transfer or a new job. Such moves may affect the enforceability of noncompetition agreements. In particular, some provisions may be enforceable in the state where the employee began working but not in the state to which the employee moves. (The same holds true when an employee moves to another country.) It may be difficult for a company with employees in many different states to use a single noncompetition agreement that will ultimately be enforceable in every state where employees are located.

Companies can use forum selection clauses and *consents to personal jurisdiction*—agreements to litigate any dispute in a specifically named jurisdiction—as well as choice-of-law provisions to achieve more predictability about the enforceability of their noncompetition agreements, but these clauses will not always be honored. In particular, even when an employment agreement specifies that the law of the employer's principal place of business will govern disputes, another state may refuse to enforce a covenant not to compete if the covenant is not consistent with the state's own law or its public policy.

Sometimes, noncompetition disputes involve a "race to the courthouse," in which the person who files the first lawsuit in a jurisdiction with favorable law prevails in the dispute.[20] A court in one state may be reluctant to enjoin proceedings already pending in another.[21] If an employer secures a money judgment against an employee who has consented to jurisdiction in the employer's principal place of business, then the employer may be able to invoke the Full Faith and Credit Clause of the U.S. Constitution to require that the employee's home state court enforce the judgment.

From the **TRENCHES**

Brown & Brown, Inc. hired Theresa A. Johnson as an actuary in 2006. On the day she started working, Johnson signed an employment agreement that included a nonsolicitation covenant prohibiting her from soliciting or servicing (directly or indirectly) any client or account of Brown's New York offices for two years after she was terminated, regardless of whether Johnson had acquired a relationship with such clients. The Agreement included a Florida choice-of-law provision. After Brown terminated Johnson in 2011, she began working at another company. Brown then sued Johnson for violating the nonsolicitation clause, as well as for other causes of action. New York courts typically uphold choice-of-law provisions, underscoring the state's public policy that supports individuals "ordering and deciding" their own interests through contractual arrangements, as long as the chosen law has a reasonable relationship to the parties or the transaction and is not "truly obnoxious" to New York's public policy.

Because Brown was a Florida corporation, Johnson's salary was administered and paid from Florida, and Johnson traveled to Florida for training, the court held that Florida law bore a reasonable relationship to the parties or the transaction, even though Johnson resided in New York. However, the court refused to enforce the choice-of-law provision after finding that Florida law was "truly obnoxious" to New York policy. Unlike New York law, Florida law specifically forbids courts from considering the hardship imposed on an employee when evaluating the reasonableness of a restrictive covenant and further requires that courts review such covenants in favor of the party trying to protect its legitimate business interests. In contrast, a restrictive covenant that imposes an undue hardship on the restrained employee is invalid and unenforceable under New York law. The court refused to use its discretion to grant partial enforcement of the covenant, after finding that Brown had imposed the covenant in bad faith, knowing "full well that it was overbroad."

On appeal in 2015, the Court of Appeals of New York held that the choice-of-law provision was unenforceable in relation to the nonsolicitation provision and that New York law governed. The court also held that there was an issue of fact as to whether the employer had "engaged in overreaching or used coercive dominant bargaining power to obtain the restrictive covenant" and therefore reversed the order of the Appellate Division and remitted for further proceedings.

Source: Brown & Brown, Inc. v. Johnson, 115 A.D.3d 162 (N.Y. App. Div. 2014), *rev'd*, 34 N.E.3d 357 (N.Y. 2015).

Dismissal for Refusal to Sign an Unenforceable Covenant Not to Compete

Sometimes an employer will require an existing employee to sign a covenant not to compete or face termination. The California Court of Appeal held that Playhut, Inc. could not legally discharge an at-will employee for refusing to sign a confidentiality agreement that contained an unenforceable covenant not to compete.[22] Because terminating an employee for refusing to sign an unlawful noncompete covenant violates California public policy, the terminated employee can bring a tortious wrongful discharge claim against the employer. Other jurisdictions have reached the opposite result, arguing that the employee should sign the covenant, then assert its invalidity if later sued by the company for violating the covenant.[23]

Remedies for Breach of a Noncompete Clause

If a court finds that an employee breached a valid noncompete covenant, it will impose liability on the offender. The most common form of relief is an injunction requiring the employee to stop competing against the former employer. In some cases, actual monetary damages may be assessed against an employee in an amount calculated to put the employer in the same position that it would have been in had there been no breach.

2.3 TRADE SECRETS

Most states expressly prohibit the misappropriation of trade secrets by statute or as a matter of common law, regardless of whether the employee signed an agreement prohibiting their use or disclosure. Theft of trade secrets also violates federal law and may be prosecuted as a federal crime. (Trade secrets and programs for their protection are discussed further in Chapter 14.)

Unauthorized use or disclosure of the employer's trade secrets is generally prohibited both during and after employment. Even if a particular state will not enforce a covenant not to compete, courts will generally enforce an agreement by an employee not to disclose or use trade secrets belonging to the former employer. It is critically important for entrepreneurs to ensure that neither they nor any of their employees have misappropriated trade secrets belonging to a prior employer or others.

What Is a Trade Secret?

A *trade secret* is information used in one's business that (1) is neither generally known nor readily ascertainable in the industry and

(2) provides the business owner a competitive advantage over competitors who do not have access to this information. A trade secret can be a formula, pattern, program device, method, technique, process, or customer list.[24] What constitutes a trade secret is not always evident. The two critical factors in determining whether a trade secret exists are (1) the value of the information to the business owner and competitors and (2) the amount of effort made to maintain the secrecy of the information. These two factors are closely related: the more valuable a certain piece of information is to a business owner, the more likely the owner will make efforts to keep it secret.

Misappropriation of Trade Secrets

Most states have passed statutes, such as the Uniform Trade Secrets Act (*UTSA*), that prohibit an employee from disclosing or using trade secrets belonging to the former employer even in the absence of a confidentiality agreement. In those states that have not adopted the UTSA or comparable legislation, judges have developed common law rules that prohibit the misappropriation of trade secrets. In addition, the Defend Trade Secrets Act of 2016[25] provides trade secret owners with a federal civil remedy for trade secret misappropriation. The Act gives federal district courts original jurisdiction to hear such cases, provides whistleblower protection, permits the recovery of damages, and, in extreme situations, allows for a civil seizure remedy.

 From the **TRENCHES**

General Motors Company (GM) became involved in a heated dispute with Volkswagen AG (VW) over the defection of Jose Ignacio Lopez, GM's former purchasing chief, to the German carmaker. GM sued VW, Lopez, and 10 former GM managers, alleging that Lopez and the other former employees took numerous boxes of secret GM documents when they quit GM to join VW. The documents in question allegedly contained confidential GM information about prices for parts, new models, and marketing strategies. The parties settled, with VW agreeing to pay GM $100 million and to buy at least $1 billion worth of GM parts over seven years. Lopez subsequently resigned from VW.

Source: Brian S. Akre, *VW to Pay GM $100 Million to Settle Suit Alleging Theft of Secrets*, Wash. Post, Jan. 10, 1997.

Inevitable Disclosure Doctrine Under the *inevitable disclosure doctrine*, certain courts will enjoin a former employee from working for a competitor firm for a limited period of time if the former employer is able to prove that the employee's new employment will inevitably lead him or her to use the former employer's trade secrets. The leading case involved a former PepsiCo marketing manager who was privy to sensitive, confidential, strategic plans for the marketing, distribution, and pricing of PepsiCo's sports drink All Sport and its ready-to-drink tea products and fruit drinks. The employee left PepsiCo to work for Quaker Oats, seller of market leaders Gatorade and Snapple. The court concluded that the former employee would necessarily rely on his knowledge of PepsiCo's trade secrets when making decisions at Quaker Oats about Gatorade and Snapple. This put PepsiCo "in the position of a coach, one of whose players has left, playbook in hand, to join the opposing team before the big game."[26] The court prohibited him from working at Quaker Oats for a period of six months. As noted earlier, the California Court of Appeal rejected the inevitable disclosure doctrine on the grounds that it violated fundamental California public policy.[27]

Nondisclosure and Proprietary Information Agreements

A prohibition on the use or disclosure of trade secrets and confidential information is usually included in a specialized agreement called a *nondisclosure agreement* (*NDA*) (or a proprietary information agreement). (Such agreements are discussed in more detail in Chapters 8 and 14.) The purpose of an NDA is to put employees on notice that they will be exposed to trade secret information in their work, to inform employees about their duties regarding such information, and to restrict their disclosure or use of trade secrets or other confidential information during or after the termination of their employment. The enforceability of an NDA is conditioned on the existence of the trade secrets it is designed to protect. If trade secrets do exist, then a reasonable NDA will be upheld even in states, such as California, that will not enforce postemployment covenants not to compete.

Criminal Liability

Individuals and firms that misappropriate trade secrets risk not only civil liability but also criminal prosecution under the federal Economic Espionage Act, which prohibits trade secret theft that benefits a foreign entity, as well as theft for the economic benefit of anyone other than the owner of the trade secret.[28] (Certain states, such as California and New York, have enacted legislation making trade secret theft a crime.) For example, in 2014, Walter Liew was convicted of conspiracy to commit economic espionage and trade secret theft by a federal jury and sentenced to 15 years in prison.[29] Liew had formed the company USA Performance Technology and paid former DuPont Co. employees, including engineer Robert Maegerle, for trade secrets relating to titanium dioxide, a pigment used in various products. Liew sold the information provided by Maegerle to Pangang Group, Inc. Liew was also fined $28 million, the amount Pangang paid USA Performance for the information. Maegerle was convicted of conspiring to sell trade secrets, sentenced to two and a half years in prison, and ordered to pay more than $360,000 in restitution to DuPont and to forfeit the $370,000 he earned while employed by Liew.[30]

2.4 INVENTION ASSIGNMENT AGREEMENTS AND WORKS FOR HIRE

Employers often ask their employees to sign an *invention assignment agreement*. This document requires the employee to assign to the employer all inventions conceived, developed, or reduced to practice by the employee while employed by the company. Invention assignment agreements may require disclosure of inventions not only during the period of employment but also within a limited period of time, typically one year, after the termination of employment.

Certain states restrict the scope of such agreements. California Labor Code Section 2870, for example, prohibits the application of such agreements to inventions that the employee developed entirely on his or her own time without using the employer's equipment, supplies, facilities or trade secret information, except when such inventions relate to the employer's business or to current or demonstrably anticipated research and development, or result from any work performed by the employee for the employer. Thus, if an employee subject to an invention assignment agreement with a social media company created a new and improved way to input users' photo files, that new program will belong to her employer even though she created it on her own time and using her own home computer, because it is related to her employer's business.

As explained further in Chapter 14, even if there is no invention assignment agreement, the patent to any invention by a person expressly "hired to invent" belongs, as a matter of law, to the employer. Similarly, as a matter of copyright law, the copyright to any work created by an employee acting within the scope of employment belongs to the employer, even if the employee has not signed an invention assignment agreement. (As discussed in Chapter 8, different rules apply to independent contractors.)

2.5 STRATEGIES FOR LEAVING ON GOOD TERMS

To the extent possible, an employee should try to leave the current employer on good terms. To do this, the employee must be honest with the employer about the real reasons for leaving. The employer is likely to think the worst of former employees who say they are going to set up a noncompeting business but then in fact start a competing company. Such behavior will spark fears of stolen trade secrets and other misdeeds and may make the employer more likely to pursue litigation against the former employee and the former employee's new company.

 From the **TRENCHES**

Two employees of a software company told their employer that they were leaving to start a restaurant. In fact, they founded a competing software company. Their former employer was furious—in part because he had been lied to and in part because he suspected misappropriation of trade secrets—and was successful in getting a court to issue an injunction, preventing the closing of the startup's financing round.

When an employee tells the employer of his or her future plans, it may be advantageous to offer the employer an opportunity to invest in the new venture. The employer will be most likely to invest when the entrepreneur's prospective business will make products that are complementary to the employer's products. Complementary products can increase a product's market share and help establish it as an industry standard. For example, one reason Autodesk's AutoCAD (Computer Aided Design) program has been so successful is that its software code contains "hooks" that allow other software companies to design applications for AutoCAD. The availability of these additional applications helped make AutoCAD an industry standard.

Having the employer invest in the new business offers several benefits. First, it may provide an easy source of funding for the entrepreneur. In addition to money, the employer may contribute technology, commercial expertise, and industry contacts. Second, it generates goodwill between the parties by aligning the interests of the employer with those of the entrepreneur, reducing the likelihood that the employer will try to block the new venture by claiming misappropriations of trade secrets and the like.

This alignment is important because the employer may be a valuable customer or supplier of the entrepreneur's business. Additionally, with an equity interest in the new enterprise, the employer may be more willing to allow the entrepreneur to hire other current employees. The entrepreneur should be careful, however, about how much of an ownership stake and control is given to the former employer. Allowing the former employer to be more than a passive investor may create the same situation that the employee left in the first place—namely, that the entrepreneur will again be working for someone else.

Entrepreneurs should avoid soliciting coworkers while still employed. Active solicitation of employees by a skilled or key employee during employment constitutes a breach of the entrepreneur's duty of loyalty and could lead to an injunction preventing the entrepreneur from hiring anyone from the prior employer. Entrepreneurs may tell fellow employees that they are leaving. If people ask about their future plans, entrepreneurs are permitted to tell them that they plan to start a new business and to give them a phone number or email address where they can be reached. Posting new contact information on sites like LinkedIn is also permitted.

Because Donna Dubinsky, cofounder of Palm Computing, had kept a copy of the emails from coworkers asking her for a job when she left Palm in 1998 to form Handspring, she was able to prove that she had not initiated the contacts with those employees and therefore had not breached her duty to Palm by actively soliciting any Palm employees to leave and join Handspring. She was also successful in negotiating a license for Handspring to use the Palm OS,[31] giving Palm a stake in Handspring's ultimate success. Indeed, Palm bought Handspring in 2003 for $169 million.[32]

 Putting It into **PRACTICE**

Alexei decided that the time had come to inform his boss, Gianmarco Cavo, at Empire State Fabrication Inc. (*ESF*) of his future plans. Before discussing his departure, he contacted Scott Scheinman, a college roommate who had graduated from the Law School at the University of Texas at Austin, for advice on the enforceability of the agreement he had signed. Scott told him that the agreement specified that Texas law governed its interpretation and enforcement. However, Scott believed that a California court would not enforce a posttermination noncompete covenant against a California resident, even though the contract stated that Texas law governed the employment relationship.

Scott told Alexei that he was bound by the provisions covering the assignment of inventions, however, and by the no-moonlighting, nondisclosure, and no-raid clauses. Of the four provisions, the one covering assignment of inventions was potentially the most problematic. Even though Alexei had developed the Genesis T-2000 (GT) technology on his own time, ESF probably owned the technology, because the invention related to ESF's business and Alexei had used some of ESF's resources (namely, his ESF computer and ESF training sessions) when developing it.

Scott explained that the no-moonlighting clause prohibited Alexei from starting his business while employed at ESF. Alexei breached this agreement when he and Piper Mao signed an agreement to develop the GT technology. Although it would have been all right for Alexei to make plans for his new venture before quitting, he should not have begun operating until he left. The nondisclosure provision prohibited Alexei from using or disclosing any confidential information that he learned while working for ESF. The no-raid clause prohibited him from soliciting employees from ESF.

(continued)

He was permitted, however, to hire employees if they contacted him about a potential job. Alexei and Piper did not plan to hire any other employees in the initial phases, so this was not an issue.

Armed with this advice, Alexei went to see his supervisor. After he informed her of his plans, the supervisor told him that he would need to speak to the director of research regarding the rights to the GT technology. A few days later, Alexei and Scott met with the director of research and ESF's corporate counsel. After some negotiating, both parties agreed that ESF would transfer all of its rights to the GT technology to Alexei's new company and release all claims against Alexei and his cofounder Piper in exchange for 15% of the equity.

Satisfied with their agreement, Alexei gave official notice of his resignation. He updated both his LinkedIn profile and his Facebook page to reflect his new role as a cofounder of a new venture. When people asked about his plans, he informed them that he was leaving to start a new business and gave them a cell number and email address where they could reach him.

Alexei realized that if he took any ESF documents, electronic data, or other proprietary items, he could be accused of stealing trade secrets. He returned all non-GT-related documents, flash drives, and concentrator cell raw materials to his supervisor; deleted all non-GT-related information on the storage drives on his office and home computers; and walked out of ESF carrying only his personal effects.

Although Scott had been helpful in advising Alexei about issues related to leaving ESF (and seemed willing to do so for little or no fee), he was not experienced in representing startups. Alexei and Piper next turned their attention to selecting a lawyer for their new venture.

Selecting and Working with an Attorney

Early in the development of the business, the entrepreneur should consider the need for an attorney. A strategically astute attorney can enhance the bottom line of the enterprise by helping craft the best structure for the business, providing sound advice regarding the legality of various possible courses of action and acting as a sounding board for both business and legal issues, thereby helping the management team identify and seize opportunities, marshal and redeploy resources, and manage risk.[1] In assessing when to hire an attorney, an entrepreneur must weigh the financial costs and administrative hassle of finding an attorney against the potential benefits of business and legal advice and document preparation. Although certain law firms may offer reduced rates and deferred-payment plans until the entrepreneur gets started, typically the costs are significant.

Dealing with attorneys and legal issues can be overwhelming and intimidating. This chapter is designed to demystify the process. It explains the need for an attorney and suggests how to choose the right legal counsel for the venture. We address the challenge of deciding when and to what extent to work with an attorney, given the financial constraints of the new enterprise. The chapter summarizes typical billing options and provides suggestions for keeping fees under control. It concludes with a brief description of the attorney-client privilege, which is key to keeping communications with an attorney confidential in the event of a legal dispute with a third party.

3.1 THE NEED FOR AN ATTORNEY

Although there are multiple published legal guides and prefabricated forms, entrepreneurs should not rely on these materials to the exclusion of seasoned legal guidance. The law is often complex and can change quickly, and mistakes are costly. Although an entrepreneur may feel that he or she can turn to published sources for specific answers, often the most valuable service a corporate attorney can perform is pointing out issues that the entrepreneur may not have even considered. Attorneys can also act as information brokers and introduce entrepreneurs to sources of capital, bankers, accountants, and potential board members.

Furthermore, at a certain stage, most startups will encounter matters that require the legal experience and skills that only an attorney can provide, such as the preparation of an opinion of counsel for an investor in the venture. In addition, as the business grows, issues related to real estate, employment, intellectual property, securities, tax, and other areas of specialty may arise. They can be very complicated, and entrepreneurs should delegate them to an outside legal expert so they can focus on the day-to-day running of the business.

3.2 CHOOSING AN ATTORNEY

As with finding the best physician, finding the right attorney is not as easy as running an Internet search. Although any attorney licensed to practice in the state theoretically can fulfill many of the legal requirements of the entrepreneur, only a small percentage of attorneys have the experience and expertise necessary to provide adequate legal guidance for a new venture.

Choosing the right attorney requires diligence. First, entrepreneurs should consider whether they want to work with a large or a small law firm and then identify through referrals several attorneys to investigate. Next, the founders should interview as many attorneys as possible to ensure a good fit, ask for references, and then speak with one or more of the entrepreneurs for whom the final candidates have worked.

Large Firm or Small Firm

Large law firms and small law firms will differ mainly in two significant ways. First, large firms typically employ a variety of specialists, whereas smaller firms often feature generalists. Second, large and small firms differ in their costs and billing procedures.

Large firms typically have many groups of attorneys who focus on discrete areas of law. Smaller firms, on the other hand, typically have practitioners who have a greater breadth of knowledge. However, there are also small boutique firms that practice in a specific area, such as patents. Thus, the trade-off may be seen as depth versus breadth.

In a large firm, however, each attorney has access to the many specialists working at the firm. Consequently, the entrepreneur will have access to an often vast amount of internal knowledge. Also, certain large firms have attorneys who concentrate on representing entrepreneurs so they have the breadth of knowledge usually found in smaller firms. For the young startup with general and common business issues, the difference may be inconsequential. Initially, an entrepreneur may want to focus on finding an attorney who has experience in meeting the entrepreneur's immediate concerns in an efficient and timely manner.

The cost and billing structure of large and small firms may differ greatly. Larger firms tend to charge more per hour but may be better able to accommodate a deferred-payment structure and to

From the TRENCHES

In 2012, two Stanford University undergraduates approached the law firm Cooley LLP seeking help for the first financing of their new company, which allowed smartphone users to share ephemeral photos and videos that disappeared after being viewed. Cooley partners helped the company, called Snapchat, raise its first equity round from the venture firms Lightspeed and Benchmark. Since then, Cooley lawyers have helped the company raise more than $1.1 billion in outside financing, conduct multiple acquisitions, and address the complex intellectual property issues inherent in the use and monetization of user-generated content. By 2015 Snapchat was a worldwide phenomenon and prominent "unicorn," with more than 6 billion videos shared daily worldwide and an estimated value of $15 billion.

Source: Dan Primack, *Snapchat's New Funding Round Is Bigger Than You Think*, FORTUNE (May 29, 2015), http://fortune.com/2015/05/29/snapchats-new-funding-round-is-bigger-than-you-think/.

complete an assignment with fewer billable hours because of their expertise. Larger firms frequently have faster turnaround times because of their staffing structures, and they often offer all-hours availability of their attorneys. In addition, larger firms often employ lower-paid paralegals to complete common tasks, bringing down the overall cost of services. On the flip side, although an entrepreneur may benefit from this cheaper-by-the-hour help, the inefficiencies of involving more persons who are also less experienced may outweigh the benefits.

Referrals

Choosing an attorney is a very personal decision. The choice of the best attorney depends on the type of business involved and the entrepreneur's own business expertise, personality, and skills. One of the best ways to find a good lead is to ask friends, colleagues, and other entrepreneurs in the geographic area who have used a particular law firm and attorney for similar purposes. Venture capitalists can also be a good source of referrals. For example, an entrepreneur starting a high-tech company should find an attorney with prior experience in the high-tech realm. The entrepreneur should find out what others like or do not like about their attorneys and what they consider the most important factors in an effective working relationship. The entrepreneur should also ask what bad experiences, if any, others have had with a particular lawyer or firm.

Community groups or universities may also be able to provide good leads. Local colleges and business schools often hold entrepreneurship classes featuring attorneys as guest speakers. Attorneys who regularly work with startups also often frequent local entrepreneur conventions and meetings. Attending classes, conventions, and meetings offers an opportunity for entrepreneurs to meet and evaluate potential attorneys. Entrepreneurs should also keep an eye on trade journals and reputable online sites for articles written about or by attorneys who have the experience they seek.

The director of the state bar association's continuing legal education program, the local chamber of commerce, accountants, or the local bar committee for business lawyers may also have good suggestions. There are also numerous lawyer referral services and law directories, but these sources are impersonal and often untested.

Shopping Around

It is important to sit down with several attorneys to determine which one best meets the entrepreneur's needs for legal work, understands the business and industry, and has the ability to serve as a potential information broker. Personality and chemistry matter. When first exploring a relationship with an attorney, the entrepreneur should take advantage of any opportunities to have coffee or lunch with members of the law firm to become better acquainted with its attorneys and to obtain some free legal advice. If a person has not worked with an attorney before, it makes sense to bring along someone who has.

Factors many entrepreneurs consider important in deciding which attorney to retain include the following:

> ➤ *Experience.* It is especially important for cash-constrained entrepreneurs to ensure that they select an attorney with broad experience representing startups. For example, experienced counsel will know which provisions are considered "standard" in a venture capital term sheet at any given condition of the market and thus will not waste time and the entrepreneur's money trying to negotiate significant changes in such terms.

> ➤ *Personality.* It is important for the entrepreneur to ensure that there is a good personality fit with the founding team. Most entrepreneurs look for attorneys who are good listeners, communicate well, understand what the entrepreneur wants from the relationship, and are honest and trustworthy.

> ➤ *Role of Junior Attorneys and Paralegals.* Even though an entrepreneur may have spoken initially only to a particular attorney, it is likely that some of the work will be farmed out to others in the firm. As a result, the entrepreneur should ask to meet with any associates, paralegals, or others who will be making significant contributions to ensure a good personality fit with the founding team. As discussed further below, for cost efficiency, typically the associate would do most of the actual drafting and the day-to-day communication with the entrepreneur, and a paralegal would perform certain routine tasks, such as registration of trademarks, state securities filings, and drafting meeting minutes.

➢ *Cost.* Attorneys charge different rates per hour and per task. These rates can appear to differ vastly. Sometimes, however, an attorney who charges less by the hour may take longer to accomplish a given task because he or she is moving up the learning curve on the startup's dime. In that event, the "cheaper" lawyer can end up costing more than the "expensive," but experienced, one. An appropriate way to assess this component is to comparison shop by asking each candidate how much the firm typically charges to do certain basic legal work, such as drafting incorporation documents. The entrepreneur should also ask candidates about their recent experience in drafting such documents and ask how much time they think it will take to create those documents for the new venture. It is important to have an attorney who understands the entrepreneur's budgetary constraints. Having an attorney who watches costs carefully and has a good sense of the appropriate amount of time to spend on a matter is critical.

➢ *Efficient Use of Technology.* Having appropriate computer systems and software and a robust set of sophisticated and customizable forms allows attorneys to rapidly retrieve and modify documents and easily customize standard agreements and forms, thereby creating significant cost savings for the entrepreneur. The entrepreneur should confirm that the firm uses appropriate email security and safeguards to ensure confidentiality. Entrepreneurs often find email a very efficient way to communicate, as attorneys are frequently in meetings and therefore difficult to reach on landlines or mobile phones. Attorneys are often able to respond to email queries more promptly than to long voice messages. Additionally, email provides both entrepreneurs and their attorneys a written document for reference. Particularly sensitive matters may be best discussed by telephone or in person, however. As discussed further below, forwarding an email to a third party can destroy attorney-client privilege.

➢ *Timeliness in Responding to Messages.* Often an entrepreneur needs to resolve a legal question or issue quickly. A timely response from an attorney, ideally within a day, is critical. To some clients, a prompt reply reflects the importance of the entrepreneur to the attorney. If the attorney does not return phone calls or emails promptly, the entrepreneur may conclude that his or her business is not a high priority for the attorney.

➤ ***Business Acumen and Understanding of Industry.*** Although many entrepreneurs view their attorneys solely as legal consultants, legally astute entrepreneurs view them as an important source of business acumen and, in some cases, as coaches or partners in value creation and capture and risk management. For some entrepreneurs, especially those who do not have a business partner, it is important to have an attorney with whom they can discuss ideas and review the business plan. Often the most effective lawyers act as strategic partners with their clients. Rather than simply executing instructions given by the entrepreneur, the most valuable attorneys work with the entrepreneur to determine the best course of action.[2]

Entrepreneurs involved in very technical ventures should search for an attorney who understands the technology and industry involved and is therefore familiar with the technical and industry jargon. Besides such obvious advantages as knowledge of the business field and related law, such an understanding typically implies that the attorney has contacts in the industry and knows how to view the business and how to identify relevant contingencies. On a more practical level, familiarity with the industry jargon helps minimize the legal costs.

➤ ***Information Brokerage and Network.*** Experienced attorneys can serve an important information brokerage function and often have personal and business connections that an entrepreneur can tap. For example, entrepreneurs considering venture capital funding usually find it advantageous to work with a firm that has good relations with the venture capital community.

3.3 THE STRUCTURE OF BILLING COSTS

Most startups monitor their cash outlays and other spending carefully, so it can be daunting for the entrepreneur to be faced with thousands of dollars in legal fees.

The cost of an attorney can be broken into time- and non-time-related costs. Although non-time-related costs can be substantial, the bulk of the costs come from billing for an attorney's or a paralegal's time.

Time-Related Billing Costs

Law firms typically charge for the time spent by attorneys and paralegals on the client's affairs. Firms differ in how they structure fees, and entrepreneurs should insist that the firm provide a written engagement letter that spells out the billing arrangements. Generally, fees fall into one of four categories: hourly fees, flat fees, contingent and deferred fees, and retainers.

Hourly Fees Law firms generally charge on an *hourly* basis. Attorneys record how they spend their time, often in six-minute (one-tenth of an hour) increments, and then the firm bills the individual clients for the attorneys' time. Depending on the firm, its location and the seniority of the attorneys working with the entrepreneur, prices can range from $200 to more than $1,000 per hour.

It is important for the entrepreneur to ask which services are considered billable because billing practices can vary significantly from firm to firm. For example, certain firms will agree that a partner will attend one board meeting of a privately held company each month at no charge. This keeps the attorney abreast of business developments and available for a certain amount of free legal advice. Unless the engagement letter specifies otherwise, any time that an attorney or other staff member spends on the entrepreneur's affairs is generally billable. Thus, for example, the clock may be running for the time spent in meetings or on the telephone, researching a topic or writing a memo or email message, traveling, and discussing matters with other attorneys or paralegals in the firm.

Even though the entrepreneur may have spoken initially only to a particular attorney, it is likely that some of the work will be farmed out to others in the firm. This delegation has positive and negative aspects. Senior attorneys are typically more adept at looking at the big picture and setting up organizational and deal structures, whereas mid-level associates are typically more efficient at preparing documentation. The junior associates gain experience by working on assignments under the supervision of more experienced attorneys. Although this process is beneficial to junior associates, the cash-poor entrepreneur needs to be careful that he or she is not financing this training. The entrepreneur may find junior associates sitting in at meetings and on conference calls. In that case, the entrepreneur should find out whether anyone is unnecessarily involved and, if so, whether the entrepreneur is being charged for that person's presence. The entrepreneur may wish to establish a policy that no new person may be brought in without the entrepreneur's approval. In any event, entrepreneurs should not hesitate to tell the engagement partner if they believe a certain individual should not be on the clock.

Firms typically bill at lower rates for junior attorneys than for more senior attorneys. Many entrepreneurs prefer working with partners because of the prestige and because they believe they are in more knowledgeable hands. However, seniority does not necessarily ensure that the best or ideal person is handling a certain transaction. Junior associates, who are cheaper per hour and usually have more free time to focus on the entrepreneur's concerns and to return phone calls and emails, can be a good or the best choice for working on specific matters as long as they know when to report up a sensitive issue to their superiors.

Sometimes, however, the cheaper per-hour rate is not worth the extra time that a less-experienced person may take. Usually, first-year associates are not cost-efficient unless the billing partner is willing to write off substantial blocks of time as training. Once associates have two or three years' training, they usually will have a level of competency that, coupled with the lower rate, makes them a good choice for drafting and negotiating documents.

Flat Fees   Entrepreneurs can often arrange *flat fees* for discrete tasks, such as drafting a specific contract or registering a trademark. In this case, the attorney will charge a fixed rate, barring unforeseen circumstances, no matter how much time is spent on the matter.

Contingent and Deferred Fees   An attorney may agree to a *contingent fee* structure, whereby the attorney receives a fixed payment or a certain percentage of potential cash flow when a certain event occurs. Although contingent payment structures are most common in trial settings (such as personal injury cases), where, for example, an attorney may receive 40% of the settlement, they can be used in many noncriminal cases.

Alternatively, one popular request among early-stage entrepreneurs is to ask a law firm for a *fee deferral*, whereby the attorney continues to bill at the normal hourly rates but does not expect payment for the bulk of the fee until (and perhaps unless) the business receives venture capital or other investor funding. This type of fee structure may be ideal for entrepreneurs still testing the feasibility of their venture. Because of the risk this arrangement poses to the law firm, most firms will only consider fee deferrals for a startup with a financing event on the near horizon.

An attorney may agree to defer billing but not make payment contingent on financing. For example, one large Silicon Valley law firm gave a startup client a break on the up-front time charged and agreed that the entrepreneur could defer all payments without interest for up to nine months.

Sometimes, a firm will ask for equity in the enterprise or the right to invest at the same price paid by the first outside investors in exchange for deferring its billing. This can create a conflict of interest, however, as the law firm, itself, becomes an investor, so the entrepreneur should proceed cautiously.[3]

Retainers Certain attorneys will request an up-front payment, called a *retainer*, to ensure that they get paid. Because cash is tight in startups, the entrepreneur should resist this arrangement and agree to pay only out-of-pocket costs (such as filing fees) up-front.

Non-Time-Related Costs

Besides charging for the time spent directly on legal matters, law firms typically will bill for other costs the entrepreneur may not expect to pay for separately. Non-time-related costs may include charges for photocopying, online research through legal subscription services, scanning, faxing, long-distance telephone calls, messenger service, travel, and filing fees. Firms usually bill these costs directly to each client rather than absorbing them and raising rates for all clients to cover the added expense. Entrepreneurs should confirm the firm's billing protocols and negotiate how they will be billed for incidental costs. An entrepreneur can try to negotiate better rates or terms—to pay only for faxing and not photocopying, for example—or propose paying a fixed monthly fee or a fee based on a percentage of the professional fees incurred that month.

3.4 WORKING COST EFFECTIVELY WITH AN ATTORNEY

Although many law firms will negotiate a fee arrangement with an entrepreneur, the legal fees are often a significant component of the startup's operating expenses. The entrepreneur can use the attorney more economically, minimize the time the attorney spends on the work, and avoid unpleasant surprises by being organized, preparing an outline for a term sheet, doing a rough draft of certain other documents, meeting the attorney at his or her office, and otherwise remaining proactive in all legal affairs.

Organization

Because firms will bill clients for the time the client spends describing an issue, entrepreneurs should prepare for meetings and phone calls to avoid wasting time. The preparation should include gathering the necessary documents and sketching out the key items to be discussed so the entrepreneur can explain the situation clearly and concisely. By keeping chronological notes on what has been covered with the attorney, entrepreneurs can help avoid omitting important details. Entrepreneurs should also consider minimizing the frequency of interactions by maintaining a running list of questions and being prepared to discuss various issues during one meeting or conversation.

Drafting

Accurately drafting a document to include all the necessary nuances and cover all possible contingencies can be time-consuming. Typically, the entrepreneur knows the company's business issues, and the lawyer knows the legal issues. A thorough understanding of both is critical to drafting certain documents, such as shareholder agreements. No document is so completely standardized that an attorney can simply use a "standard" boilerplate form without some modification.

Entrepreneurs should never sign any agreement without reading it and understanding its terms and their application to the business. Thus, entrepreneurs can spend a significant amount of money for the preparation or explanation of what may seem at first to be a simple document.

Although lawyers can be instrumental in drafting documents, the cash-strapped entrepreneur may want to handle the bulk of the initial drafting. If a firm has standardized documents, such as a certificate of incorporation and bylaws, it may be far more expensive to have the attorney review the entrepreneur's draft than for the attorney to plug the company information into the firm's standard form. Certain firms, such as Cooley LLP, have posted online a variety of forms commonly used to start a business.[4]

When preparing letters of intent, term sheets, contract proposals, portions of patent applications and certain other types of documents, it may make sense for the entrepreneur to prepare a first draft. Counsel should be able to provide model sample forms in electronic form.

Before attempting to customize a form for his or her business, the entrepreneur might want to ask the attorney to quickly summarize the main features of the document. Although the sample forms may include many optional provisions that are not relevant to the entrepreneur's business, crossing out unnecessary terms is much more efficient than possibly forgetting to consider a salient feature. The attorney should review the draft to ensure legal compliance and confirm that all material legal and business issues are adequately covered.

Entrepreneurs can also save money by finalizing standard employment forms, such as offer letters, assignment-of-invention agreements, nondisclosure agreements, and certain stock option agreements. The entrepreneur should obtain the appropriate forms electronically from counsel and then insert the employee's name.

Being Proactive

Although it is important to try to educate one's self before seeing an attorney and to avoid asking unnecessary questions, the client should not be too distant. As with visiting a physician, it is advisable to speak up about any concerns.

It is a good idea to keep the attorney informed of important business issues related to the startup even when they seemingly have insignificant legal implications. Not only might the entrepreneur have failed to recognize the legal implications but also, more important, keeping the attorney informed about the company's progress keeps him or her excited about the client and keeps the entrepreneur's business in the forefront of the attorney's mind.

An entrepreneur can even help keep an attorney current on recent legal developments. For example, an entrepreneur may run across legal issues or precedents relevant to his or her business when scouting industry-specific trade journals. Making a habit of sending relevant articles to the attorney can reduce legal research time.

The Billing Process

Especially when first starting to work with a law firm, the client should ask for a price estimate or upper price limit on the proposed assignment. Although an attorney can never be sure exactly how much time a certain task will take, counsel should be able to provide a reasonable cost estimate, barring unexpected contingencies. Asking for an estimate is important for several reasons. First, as when making any purchase, it is always a good idea to get a sense of how much it will cost. Second, it forces the attorney to work up a reasonable price. To stay competitive, a law firm will not quote an outlandish price for a given transaction. Third, if the task takes longer than anticipated, the law firm may absorb the extra costs rather than charge a higher price than originally quoted.

When first negotiating the fee structure for the business, the entrepreneur should ask to see a sample bill. Ideally, the bill should be detailed enough to show the client for what he or she is being charged. The descriptions of work performed should not be vague, such as "produced documents," but should contain specifics about the types of agreements being drafted. Some firms have a policy of establishing minimum billable hours, whereby they charge a minimum for a certain task, and more if the assignment takes more time. If this method seems inappropriate, the entrepreneur should voice concern. The entrepreneur may desire to pay only for the time actually spent and may ask that work be billed in tenth-of-an-hour increments, the standard for most law firms. The client might also specify that the firm will (1) not bill for telephone calls shorter than a certain number of minutes, (2) not charge for express-mail or air-courier costs unless such services were requested by the client, and (3) provide a detailed description for any charge over a certain number of minutes. All such billing details should be set forth in the engagement letter.

Given that many startups live month to month, the entrepreneur should insist on monthly billing. Although the entrepreneur should keep a written log of incurred legal expenses, if the bill arrives too long after the service, he or she may not be able to recall the work the bill covers.

The entrepreneur should examine each invoice closely. If the amount of time billed for a particular task seems out of line, the entrepreneur should challenge the bill. Firms will often "write down" (or adjust) bills to keep clients happy. Of course, asking the partner on the account to spend an inordinate amount of time delving into billing minutiae may harm the relationship.

3.5 PRESERVING ATTORNEY-CLIENT PRIVILEGE

Communications between a client and a lawyer are generally protected by the *attorney-client privilege* when the client is seeking confidential legal advice. A third party cannot compel the client to disclose privileged communications through discovery or testimony in the event of a legal dispute. As discussed below, in order to qualify as "privileged," a communication has to meet certain requirements, including being between a lawyer and that lawyer's client. Accordingly, when retaining an attorney, it is important to be clear about who the client is.

If the client is a corporation, then the privilege belongs to the corporation and not the officers, other employees, or the directors. The corporate privilege protects the lawyer's communications with any company employee as long as the subject matter of the communication relates to that employee's duties for the employer and the communication is made at the direction of a corporate superior. For example, if a corporation hires a lawyer to do an internal investigation of possible misconduct, and an officer instructs an employee to cooperate in the investigation, then a third party (such as the government or a competitor) cannot compel the disclosure of the communication between the employee and the lawyer over the objection of the corporation. Because the privilege belongs to the corporation, however, the corporation's board of directors may instruct the corporation's lawyers to disclose communications with employees in a case brought by the corporation or the government against an employee. For example, if the CEO of a corporation tells company counsel that the corporation has been booking earnings on sales not yet consummated, then company counsel will be free, if so requested by the board of directors, to testify against the CEO in a criminal prosecution of the CEO. Indeed, under the Sarbanes-Oxley Act, attorneys representing public companies are required to report evidence of a material violation of securities laws or a breach of fiduciary duty to their client's general counsel or CEO.[5] If the informed party does not take appropriate action, then the attorney must bring the evidence to the attention of a board committee comprised solely of independent directors.

Although the founders may initially be the sole representatives of the company, they are usually not considered to be the client. An attorney retained to incorporate a business will normally view the company as the client, at least once it is organized. If a dispute occurs down the road and the board of directors votes to fire a founder, the attorney cannot ethically represent both the founder and the company. The attorney-client relationship should be clearly spelled out in an engagement letter with the attorney.

Attorneys often recommend that each founder retain separate counsel from the outset, especially when structuring the ownership and when negotiating buy-sell agreements. In practice, though, this rarely happens because it is too expensive. A founder should, and usually will, retain separate counsel if there is a dispute or threatened dispute with the company or its board of directors.

Exceptions

The attorney-client privilege applies only to legal advice, not business advice. It also does not protect client communications that are made to further a crime or illegal act. For example, if an entrepreneur asks the attorney the best way to steal a competitor's trade secrets without getting caught, that conversation is not privileged. In addition, attorney-client privilege is lost if the client shares the attorney's advice with outsiders or permits outsiders to listen in on a discussion between the client and the attorney. Although the attorney-client privilege extends to communications with in-house counsel in the United States, that is not true in the European Union.[6]

 Putting It into **PRACTICE**

Because Alexei and Piper thought that an attorney would be useful in the initial structuring of the company and issuance of equity, they decided to find an attorney before officially launching their business. Another entrepreneur had told them that even if you may think you do not need an attorney until you are raising money, an attorney can handle many matters in the beginning, from making sure that stock is issued properly to reviewing a lease for office space. Although Alexei's lawyer friend Scott had been helpful in sorting out Alexei's obligations to Empire State Fabrication Inc. (*ESF*), Scott agreed that Alexei and Piper needed someone experienced in representing high-tech startups as counsel for the new venture.

To find a suitable attorney, Alexei and Piper asked friends and business associates for recommendations, then they pruned their list of prospective attorneys to two: a solo practitioner and a partner in a large national firm. Alexei and Piper made an appointment to talk with both attorneys, who each agreed to meet with them free of charge.

At their meeting with Anjani Sudhir, the solo practitioner, Alexei and Piper learned that he had a general legal practice. Anjani said that he would do all the legal work himself at a rate of $400 per hour. He warned them that his practice was quite busy, so his turnaround time on documents would vary depending on other clients' demands. Anjani explained that he had done a number of projects for startup companies and that, in most cases, he would be able to modify existing documents to meet their needs. He would need to draft certain documents from scratch, however. Anjani had contracted with a local patent firm that would handle any necessary patent applications. He promised that

(continued)

regardless of how busy he was, he would always return phone calls and email the same day. As for a payment plan, Anjani said he could be flexible for a couple of months but ultimately would have to be paid in full.

Alexei's second meeting was with Sarah Crawford, a highly regarded corporate partner in a large national firm. Sarah explained that although she would ultimately be responsible for the startup's legal work, a third-year associate, Aaron Biegert, would actually draft the documents, which Sarah would then review. Sarah said that her billing rate was $845 per hour and that Aaron billed at $530 per hour. Sarah told Alexei and Piper that the firm's resources would allow it to turn around documents as quickly as they needed them. Her firm had several patent counsel who could handle the startup's patent work.

Sarah also explained that the firm had invested heavily in technology and had a computer program that generated customized documents based on input of certain information about a company and its needs. The firm also used state-of-the-art encryption and other security measures to safeguard both the firm's intranet and sensitive email communications. Sarah said that because her schedule entailed significant travel, she might take a day or two to return phone calls. Aaron, however, would be able to respond to calls immediately and would have access to Sarah for advice. In addition, Sarah offered her and Aaron's cell phone numbers to Alexei and Piper and indicated that if time-sensitive issues arose, they should not hesitate to call them on their cells or send an email or text.

Sarah said that her firm would agree to postpone billing until the new company received venture capital or other financing. If the company did not receive financing, the company would still technically be responsible for the legal fees, but Sarah indicated that her firm would not expect the company or the founders to pay the full amount of the fees. Sarah then introduced Alexei and Piper to Aaron, a Stanford School of Engineering and Law School grad who impressed them with his intelligence and enthusiasm.

After the two meetings and calling several of the references provided by Anjani and Sarah, Alexei and Piper decided to hire Sarah. They were particularly impressed by the firm's broad expertise and network of relationships and felt that the improved efficiency would offset the higher billing rates. They also thought they would save money because most work would be done by the associate. Although Sarah might not be accessible at all times, they felt comfortable knowing that they would be able to reach Aaron whenever they had a legal question or concern. Finally, they thought that the law firm would have the attorney resources and sophistication to accommodate the company's growing legal needs both in the United States and globally.

Content with their choice, Alexei called Sarah, told her of their decision, and set up an appointment to discuss which form of legal entity would be best for the new business.

Deciding Whether to Incorporate

B y carefully considering the forms of business entity that are available and then intelligently choosing the most appropriate one, entrepreneurs can reduce exposure to liabilities, minimize taxes, and ensure that the business is capable of being financed and conducted efficiently. In addition, formalizing the business helps prevent misunderstandings among the participants by defining their ownership stakes, roles, and duties in the business.

The primary considerations in the choice of business entity will be the degree to which the founders' personal assets are protected from liabilities of the business; the availability of favorable tax strategies, such as maximizing the tax benefits of startup losses, avoiding double (or even triple) layers of taxation, and converting ordinary income into long-term capital gain, which generally is taxed at lower rates; desirability for potential investors and lenders; availability of attractive equity incentives for employees and other service providers; and costs (startup and ongoing).

This chapter first describes each of the principal business forms and then explores the considerations and strategies involved in making an appropriate selection. The governance of each entity is in most instances determined by the domicile of the entity (e.g., in the case of a corporation, the state in which it is incorporated). The most common requirements are set forth below but they can vary from state to state. We conclude with a discussion of name selection and licensing requirements. Structures for international businesses are addressed in Chapter 15.

4.1 FORMS OF BUSINESS ENTITY

A business may be conducted as a sole proprietorship; a corporation (either a C corporation or an S corporation, which has special flow-through tax attributes but strict limits on the number and types of eligible shareholders); a general, limited, or limited liability partnership; or a limited liability company (*LLC*). A sole proprietorship has little legal significance separate from the individual owner of the business. A corporation is a distinct legal entity owned by its shareholders and managed by a board of directors. Most large business organizations operate as C corporations. A partnership is a separate entity for some purposes and a group of individual partners for others. It does not pay income taxes on its activities; instead, its partners pay income taxes on its activities based on their respective interests in its profits. The LLC attempts to combine the best attributes of the corporation and the partnership. An LLC that has multiple owners is generally taxed the same as a partnership unless it elects to be taxed as a corporation.

A business that expects to raise capital from a venture capital fund will usually be formed as a C corporation—or at least will usually need to convert to C corporation form prior to issuing stock to such a fund—because most venture capital funds raise money from tax-exempt entities such as pension and profit-sharing trusts, universities, and charitable organizations. These nonprofit entities would incur unrelated business taxable income on which the nonprofit must pay tax if the venture capital fund invested in a flow-through entity such as a business organized as a partnership or LLC.

Traditionally, limited partnerships were the entity of choice for activities such as investing in real estate or securities where flow-through tax treatment is desired. In addition to permitting profits and losses to flow through directly to the owners of the business, partnerships can distribute property in kind without incurring tax on the partnership or the partner. Because many investment funds distribute highly appreciated securities to their partners after a liquidity event (e.g., an initial public offering or acquisition by a public company in a tax-free reorganization), each partner can make an individual decision as to when to sell the securities received. The advent of the limited liability company has resulted in many businesses organizing as LLCs instead of as limited partnerships to achieve limited liability for all members, even those who actively participate in the business.

There are other less common forms of business entities that generally are limited to businesses with special characteristics. Some of these more exotic forms are of long standing, such as the Massachusetts business trust, whereas others are of recent origin and have been authorized by only a limited number of states. One example of the newer variety is the *low-profit limited liability company* (*L3C*), which is a form of LLC specifically designed to accommodate the needs of hybrid social ventures that have both financial- and social-betterment goals. Another example is the *benefit corporation* or *public benefit corporation*, which are for-profit corporations that aim to earn profits and at the same time address social and environmental issues. B Lab, a nonprofit corporation, grants *B Corporation* or *Certified B Corporation* status to companies that meet its social, environmental, accountability, and transparency standards; B Lab charges an annual fee based on revenues for such certification.

4.2 SOLE PROPRIETORSHIPS

A *sole proprietorship* is a business owned by one person. It usually requires no governmental filing except a fictitious-business-name statement, which discloses the name under which the business will be conducted and the owner's name and address. The owner reports the income and expenses of the business on a schedule (usually Schedule C) to his or her personal income tax return. Although the sole proprietorship is probably the most prevalent form of small business in the United States, it is often a poor choice because the owner has unlimited liability for the losses of the business, thereby putting all of the owner's personal assets at risk.

4.3 CORPORATIONS

A *corporation* is a distinct legal entity owned by its shareholders. It has an unlimited life and free transferability of ownership, so its existence is not affected by changes in its ownership resulting from transfers of stock by shareholders (or upon a shareholder's death) or the issuance of new shares by the corporation. If an individual shareholder dies, that person's shares are transferred to the shareholder's heirs.

Unlike a partnership, a corporation may be owned by a single person who can be the corporation's sole director and serve as any or all of the required officers (e.g., president, treasurer, and secretary). The shareholders elect the corporation's board of directors but are generally otherwise not active in the management of the corporation. Shareholder approval is required for certain major transactions, however, such as a sale of all the corporation's assets. The board of directors is responsible for appointing the officers, who serve at the pleasure of the board; setting executive compensation; authorizing the sale of stock or the issuance of stock options; approving the corporate strategy; and making other longer-term corporate decisions. Day-to-day management is carried out by the corporation's officers.

A principal advantage of the corporate form—which is a feature it shares with the LLC—is the limited liability it provides to its equity holders: creditors are limited to the assets of the corporation for payment and may not collect directly from shareholders if corporate assets are insufficient to pay all debts and liabilities. Other advantages of the corporate form include its familiarity and well-understood governance laws, its permanence, the ability to transfer corporate stock more easily than partnership or LLC interests (particularly in the public securities markets), and the ease of designing equity incentive plans for employees.

Preserving Limited Liability: Avoiding the Piercing of the Corporate Veil

The proper operation of a corporation limits the liability of the shareholders because the creditors of the corporation usually cannot reach the shareholders' personal assets to satisfy the corporation's obligations. Under the *alter ego doctrine*, however, a court may disregard the corporate entity and hold the shareholders personally liable for the corporation's obligations if the shareholders used the corporation to perpetrate a fraud or promote injustice. In determining whether to *pierce the corporate veil*, that is, whether to disregard the corporate form and make the shareholders directly liable for the corporation's obligations, a court will examine many factors, such as:

1. Was the corporation undercapitalized, given the risks inherent in its business?

2. Were corporate assets used for personal reasons?

3. Were corporate assets commingled with personal assets?

4. Were the corporate and personal books kept separately?

5. Were corporate actions properly authorized by the board of directors or the shareholders?

To preserve limited liability for its shareholders, the corporation should observe at least the following procedures:

1. Start the business with sufficient equity and liability insurance in light of the future capital needs of the business and its inherent risks.

2. Conduct annual shareholders' meetings and regular board meetings.

3. Obtain and record shareholder and board authorization for corporate actions.

4. Prepare accurate minutes of shareholders' and board meetings and maintain as part of the corporate records.

5. Keep corporate funds separate from personal funds.

6. Maintain complete and proper records for the corporation separate from personal records.

7. Make clear in all contracts with others that they are dealing with the corporation, and sign all contracts as shown:

[CORPORATE NAME]

By: _____

_____

[Name and Title of Person Signing]

8. Maintain an arm's-length relationship between the corporation and any principal shareholder. Transactions with any of the directors or principal shareholders (or entities in which they have an interest) must be fair to the corporation and should be

subject to approval by the disinterested members of the board, if any, without the vote of the interested directors, after all facts material to the transaction have been fully disclosed.

Tax Treatment of C Corporations

Unless a corporation elects to be taxed as an S corporation, it is taxed on its net income as a separate legal entity. (A corporation that does not elect S corporation treatment is sometimes referred to as a *C corporation* because it is taxed under Subchapter C of the Internal Revenue Code.) Under federal income tax law in effect on January 1, 2016, a corporation is taxed on its net income (gross income less allowable deductions) at rates ranging from 15% to 35% (e.g., the rate generally is 34% on income greater than $75,000 up to $10 million). The gain on property, other than money, contributed to a corporation (generally equal to the fair market value of the property at the time of transfer less its cost) will generally be subject to tax payable by the contributor unless the person, or group of persons, contributing the property (including persons in the group contributing cash in the same transaction) owns at least 80% of the corporation after the contribution of property. For example, if three individuals contribute a combination of appreciated property and money in exchange for 85% of the corporation's stock, then no tax is due at the time of transfer. When a corporation distributes money or other property to its shareholders in the form of dividends, the shareholders must pay the tax on the fair market value of that dividend income. If the property the corporation distributes to shareholders has increased in value since its acquisition by the corporation, then the corporation also incurs income taxes on that appreciation as if it sold the property for an amount equal to its fair market value then distributed the proceeds to its shareholders.

Although most of the tax aspects of C corporations are generally unfavorable as compared with the forms discussed below, a potential tax benefit of the C corporation form is its ability, depending on the circumstances, to issue *qualified small business stock (QSBS)*. QSBS is generally stock that (1) is acquired by a shareholder directly from the corporation at original issue in exchange for money, property (other than stock, with certain exceptions), or

services and (2) meets various requirements, including most notably that the issuer's aggregate gross assets at the time of issuance
not exceed $50 million. QSBS provides two potentially significant
income tax benefits to holders. First, a sale of QSBS after more
than five years qualifies for partial or full (depending on the year
in which the QSBS was acquired) exclusion of the resulting gain
from taxable income, subject to certain statutory limits. Second,
certain reinvestments of proceeds of sales of QSBS in other QSBS
can qualify for tax-free rollover of the gain. The other forms of business entity discussed below cannot issue QSBS.

Tax Treatment of S Corporations

An S corporation is the same as any other corporation except for
the way it is taxed. The Internal Revenue Code permits certain
shareholders to operate as a corporation while taxing them on the
corporation's net income as individuals. Such corporations, known
as *S corporations* (because they are subject to the tax treatment
under Subchapter S of the Internal Revenue Code), generally do
not pay federal income tax but pass the tax liability for their profits
through to their shareholders. Consequently, profits earned by an S
corporation typically will be taxed only once. Similarly, an S corporation's losses flow through to the shareholders and may be
deducted by the shareholders on their individual tax returns, subject to certain significant limitations, including the inability to use
the S corporation's "passive losses" to offset the shareholders' salary
or other earned nonpassive income. Profits and losses must be allocated based on share ownership for taxation purposes. The shareholders include as individual income their respective shares of the
profits earned by the S corporation regardless of whether any cash
amounts were distributed to shareholders.

A distribution of earnings by an S corporation to its shareholders
is generally not taxed a second time. In contrast, a similar distribution by a C corporation will be taxed twice: the C corporation must
pay federal corporate income tax on profits when earned, and shareholders must treat distributions as dividends subject to tax.

Shareholders generally elect S corporation status when they
expect that the corporation will be profitable and distribute substantially all of its profits to the shareholders, or when the

corporation is expected to incur losses and the shareholders wish to use the loss deductions on their personal income tax returns. The case for S corporation status is weaker when the corporation is owned solely by insiders who work for the company and receive their share of the profits in the form of salary and bonuses, which are normally deductible as expenses by the corporation. The presence of outsiders, who do not receive their share of profits in the form of deductible salary and bonuses, makes the technique of extracting profits by paying salaries and bonuses unavailable and the argument for an S corporation more compelling.

To qualify for S corporation status, the entity must be a domestic (U.S.) corporation and satisfy the following requirements:

1. The corporation must have no more than 100 shareholders.

2. All of the shareholders must be individuals who are U.S. citizens or resident aliens (noncitizens of the United States who hold green cards or otherwise are treated as residents for U.S. tax purposes), certain tax-exempt organizations, or qualifying trusts or estates, so none may be partnerships, limited liability companies, corporations, or nonresident aliens (non-U.S. citizens not entitled to reside and work permanently in the United States).

3. The corporation must have only one class of stock (although options and differences in voting rights are generally permitted).

The requirement that an S corporation essentially have no shareholders other than individuals will prevent any business that intends to raise equity capital from venture capital funds, corporations, or other institutional investors from qualifying as an S corporation after such investors acquire stock. In addition, because an S corporation can issue only common stock, it must issue the stock to founders and employees at the same price paid by the outside investors (unless the stock was sold to the founders and other employees well in advance of the sale to the investors) if the employees are to avoid being taxed on receipt of their "cheap stock." In contrast, when there are two classes of stock, the company will usually issue convertible preferred stock to the outside investors and common stock to founders and other employees. Because the common stock lacks the liquidation, dividend, voting, and other preferences that the preferred stock possesses, the common stock can typically be issued at a cheaper price than the preferred stock without causing the founders and employees to incur any significant tax liability upon receipt of their common stock. Accordingly, the S corporation is most commonly used for family or other closely owned businesses that obtain capital from their individual shareholders or debt from outside sources and do not provide equity incentives to their employees on any significant scale.

A qualified corporation may elect to be taxed as an S corporation by filing Form 2553 with the Internal Revenue Service, together with the written consent of all the shareholders. This election must be filed no more than two months and fifteen days after the beginning of the taxable year of the corporation for which S corporation status is to be effective. If a corporation does not meet all of the S corporation requirements during the entire year, the election will not be effective until the following year, provided that those requirements are met for that year.

4.4 PARTNERSHIPS

A *partnership* is a business carried on by at least two persons. A partnership is generally treated as a distinct legal entity separate from its partners. A partnership can sue and be sued, for example, and can own property in its own name. A creditor of a partner must proceed against that partner's interest in the partnership, rather than directly against the assets of the partnership. Similarly, a creditor of the partnership must first proceed against the assets of the partnership before going after any of the partners individually. For some purposes, however, a partnership is treated as an aggregate of its individual partners. For example, a partnership will dissolve on the death of any partner unless the remaining partners elect to continue the partnership or the partnership agreement provides that the death of a partner does not result in dissolution. As discussed below, however, even if a partnership dissolves, the partnership business need not terminate.

Types of Partnerships

There are three types of partnerships: a general partnership, a limited partnership, and a limited liability partnership. In a *general partnership*, each partner is a general partner with unlimited liability for the debts of the partnership and the power to incur obligations on behalf of the partnership within the scope of the partnership's business. Certain liability concerns, such as potential claims for personal injuries or those resulting from errors or omissions, can be alleviated through insurance. Each general partner acts as an agent for the partnership. As a result of this agency relationship, great care must be exercised in the selection of general partners.

A *limited partnership* has one or more general partners (each of whom has the same liability and power as a general partner in a general partnership) and one or more limited partners. The limited partners' liability is limited to the amount of their capital commitment. Generally, limited partners may not participate in the control of the partnership, or they will be treated as general partners for liability purposes.

A limited liability partnership is a hybrid used by certain professional partnerships (such as law and accounting firms) that are restricted by state law from organizing as limited partnerships. In a *limited liability partnership*, each partner can participate actively in the business and has unlimited personal liability for his or her own actions (such as medical malpractice) but is liable for the misdeeds of other partners only to the extent of the partnership's assets.

Partnership Agreements and Mechanics

Although most states have a general partnership and a limited partnership act, as well as provisions governing limited liability partnerships (many of which are patterned on uniform acts), the partners may generally establish their own business arrangements among themselves by entering into a written partnership agreement. The partners may thereby override most provisions in the state's partnership act both in terms of how a partnership is managed and how profits and losses are allocated and distributed. In the absence of an agreement to the contrary, profits and losses are split evenly among the partners.

Unlike a corporation, a partnership generally will *dissolve* (cease to exist) on the death or withdrawal of a general partner unless the remaining partners elect to continue the partnership. However, a partnership agreement can, and should, provide for alternatives to liquidation after dissolution. For example, the partnership agreement can provide for the buyout of a deceased or withdrawn partner, the election of a new general partner, and the continuation of the business of the partnership by the remaining partners. In a limited partnership, the death of a limited partner typically does not result in the liquidation of the partnership; the limited partnership interest can be passed on to the deceased limited partner's heirs.

General partnerships require few legal formalities. A general partnership does not even require a written agreement; it can be formed with nothing more than a handshake and a general understanding between the partners. For example, students agree to work together on a business plan; a baker and a chef agree to open a restaurant together; or two software programmers agree to collaborate on writing a program. In each case, a partnership of sorts is formed. However, the intention of one party alone cannot create a partnership. There must be a meeting of the minds: each party must intend to establish a business relationship with the other.

Unlike a general partnership, a limited partnership requires a written partnership agreement signed by all the partners. The limited partnership must also file a certificate with the applicable secretary of state.

For the protection of the parties, a detailed written partnership agreement is strongly suggested for both general and limited partnerships. In the absence of a written agreement, state partnership laws will govern the partnership. Some provisions of the laws may lead to unfavorable results. For example, state laws may require partners to share the profits and losses equally regardless of their original capital contributions. A written partnership agreement can prevent future misunderstandings by including the term of the partnership's existence, the division of profits and losses between partners, the allocation of responsibility for any needed capital contributions, the payment of partnership salaries or withdrawals of capital, the duties of the partners, and the consequences to the partnership if a partner decides to sell his or her interest, becomes incapacitated, or dies. The agreement can also provide for a dispute resolution mechanism.

Partnership agreements tend to vary significantly depending on the needs of the parties. As a result, more expense is typically involved in forming a partnership than a corporation because a corporation's governance is largely controlled by statute. Standard, or *boilerplate*, forms should be avoided, because they are not tailored to the particulars of the partners' relationship.

Tax Treatment

A key attraction of a partnership is that it pays no income tax at the entity level. Income or losses of the partnership flow through to each partner and are reported on the partner's individual tax return. Unlike an S corporation, which must allocate income or loss based on stock ownership, a partnership can allocate income and loss flexibly, provided that certain tax law requirements intended to ensure that such tax allocations are generally consistent with the partners' overall economic arrangement are met. For example, income can be allocated differently from losses. In a partnership in which one partner contributes services and another contributes money, the tax losses generated from the expenditure of funds contributed by the cash partner can—and normally must under tax law—be allocated to that partner. In addition, allocations can provide for preferred returns to a certain partner or class of partners and can change over time or as higher profit levels are achieved.

Even though partnership losses flow through to the partners based on the loss-sharing arrangements in the partnership agreement (again, subject to those arrangements complying with tax law requirements to ensure consistency with the overall economic deal among the partners), a number of limitations restrict the partners' ability to deduct these losses on their personal tax returns. For example, the tax law restricts the ability of partners to deduct "passive losses" from salary and other forms of earned nonpassive income. A partner's losses from a partnership generally are passive losses unless the partner materially participates in the partnership's business. A limited partner will rarely be able to treat partnership losses as other than passive. Other tax limitations prevent a partner from deducting losses that exceed his or her *tax basis* (the amount paid for the partner's partnership interest plus his or her share of partnership liabilities, as adjusted over time to reflect allocations to the partner of income and loss). In certain circumstances, a limited partner may not deduct losses attributable to nonrecourse debt, which is debt for which the debtor is not personally liable.

Property can usually be contributed to and distributed from a partnership without being subject to tax. Section 351 of the Internal Revenue Code generally permits a partnership to convert to a corporation without tax if the incorporation is properly structured. Once a partnership converts to a corporation, however, any distribution from the corporation will typically be subject to two levels of tax: a corporate tax and a shareholder tax.

Sources of Capital

Limited sources of operating capital are available to a partnership. It is generally restricted to capital contributed by partners and funds loaned by partners and outsiders. It is uncommon for a partnership to raise capital in a public offering, in part because publicly traded partnerships are taxed as corporations. As noted earlier, most venture capital funds have tax-exempt investors who would receive disadvantaged tax treatment if the fund invested in a partnership. Therefore, a business that expects to attract capital from a venture capital fund generally should not organize as a partnership, or the founders should expect that it may be necessary to convert to a C corporation as a condition to obtaining venture capital financing.

Foreigners (i.e., persons who are not citizens or permanent residents of the United States) are generally disinclined to invest in a partnership that is carrying on an active business because participating as a partner would cause them to be treated as being engaged in a U.S. trade or business. In that case, the foreign investors would have to file U.S. tax returns and pay U.S. tax on any of their U.S. income that is connected with the trade or business. Foreigners generally do not pay tax on income they receive from U.S. corporations in which they have invested.

4.5 LIMITED LIABILITY COMPANIES

A properly structured *limited liability company* (*LLC*) combines the pass-through federal tax treatment of a partnership with the liability protections of a corporation. Thus, an organization that would otherwise organize as a general or limited partnership, or as an S corporation if it met the requirements, will generally derive the most benefit from organizing as an LLC, because it will have limited liability protection while retaining favorable partnership tax treatment. The so-called check-the-box regulations promulgated by the Internal Revenue Service generally allow LLCs and partnerships that are not publicly traded to be taxed as flow-through entities unless they elect to be taxed as corporations.

The owners (referred to as *members*) of an LLC have no personal liability for the obligations of the LLC but, as is also true for corporate directors and officers, members and managers still have personal liability for their individual acts and omissions in connection with the LLC's business. Similarly, the members lose their limited liability for contracts if they fail to make it clear that the contracting party is the LLC. Thus, it is critical for persons acting on behalf of an LLC to make clear the capacity in which they are acting. For example, all stationery and business cards used by managers and members of an LLC should include the name of the LLC and its status as a limited liability company if that is not clear from the name itself. In addition, as with officers

From the **TRENCHES**

Donald Lanham and Larry Clark were managers and also members of Preferred Income Investors, LLC (P.I.I.), a limited liability company organized under the Colorado Limited Liability Company Act. Clark contacted Water, Waste & Land, Inc. (d/b/a Westec) about the possibility of hiring Westec to perform engineering work in connection with the construction of a Taco Cabana fast-food restaurant. In the course of their preliminary discussions, Clark gave representatives of Westec a business card bearing Lanham's address, which was the same address listed as P.I.I.'s principal office and place of business in its articles of organization filed with the secretary of state. Although the name Preferred Income Investors, LLC was not on the business card, the letters "P.I.I." appeared above the address on the card. There was, however, no indication as to what the acronym meant or that P.I.I. was a limited liability company. Although Westec never received a signed contract from Lanham, Clark gave verbal authorization to begin work. When P.I.I. failed to pay for the work, Westec sued P.I.I. as well as Clark and Lanham individually.

Even though P.I.I. had been properly formed, Westec argued that the members had failed to make it clear that they were acting on behalf of an LLC. The Colorado Supreme Court agreed, reasoning that the members were agents acting on behalf of a partially disclosed principal. Under traditional agency principles, agents are personally liable unless they fully identify the person on whose behalf they are acting.

Source: Water, Waste & Land, Inc. v. Lanham, 955 P.2d 997 (Colo. 1998) (en banc).

of corporations, a member or manager of an LLC should execute contracts as follows:

[NAME OF LIMITED LIABILITY COMPANY]

By: _____

_____

[Name and Title of Person Signing]

For all practical purposes, an LLC operates as a limited partnership without the legal requirement of having a general partner who bears ultimate liability for the obligations of the partnership. As discussed above, an S corporation also has both the limited liability and most of the federal tax pass-through features found in the LLC, but ownership of an S corporation is limited to 100 shareholders, all of whom must be individuals, certain tax-exempt organizations, qualifying trusts, or estates, and none of whom may be nonresident aliens; in addition, the S corporation can have only one class of stock. An LLC has none of these restrictions. In addition, unlike a partnership, an LLC can be formed with only one owner.

An LLC has two principal charter documents. The first is a short, one- to two-page document filed with the secretary of state, which sets forth the name of the LLC, its address, its agent for service of process, the term (which may be perpetual), and whether the LLC will be governed by the members or by managers appointed by the members. This document is generally called the *certificate of formation* (Delaware) or *articles of organization* (California).

The second charter document for an LLC is its *operating agreement*, which is analogous to, and closely resembles, a partnership agreement. The operating agreement specifies how the LLC will be governed; the financial obligations of the members (e.g., additional capital calls could be forbidden, voluntary, or mandatory); and how profits, losses, and distributions will be shared. As with a partnership agreement, the operating agreement for an LLC will be tailored to suit the needs of each individual LLC, with the attendant expense of a specialized legal agreement. Again, boilerplate documents should be avoided.

An LLC is generally not the optimal entity form for businesses financed by venture capital funds because of tax restrictions on the funds' tax-exempt and foreign partners. However, an LLC can be very attractive for businesses self-financed by the entrepreneur, financed by corporate investors or, to a lesser extent (because of the passive loss limitations), by wealthy individuals. An LLC is the entity of choice for a startup entity seeking to flow through losses to its investors because (1) unlike a limited partnership, which does not provide limited liability for its general partner, an LLC offers the same complete liability protection to all its members as does a corporation; (2) an LLC can have corporations and partnerships as members (unlike an S corporation) and is not subject to any of the other limitations that apply to S corporations; and (3) losses can be specially allocated entirely to the cash investors (in an S corporation, losses are allocated to all the owners based on share ownership). In addition, an LLC can be incorporated (e.g., by filing a certificate of conversion or by exchanging the LLC interests for the stock of a new corporation), usually on a tax-free basis under Section 351 of the Internal Revenue Code at any time. For example, after the initial startup losses have been allocated to the early-round investors, the LLC could be incorporated to accommodate investment from a venture capital fund in a conventional preferred-stock financing. Alternatively, incorporation could be deferred until a public offering.

4.6   SELECTING THE MOST APPROPRIATE FORM OF ORGANIZATION

Three issues are critical in selecting the form of business entity: (1) Who will be the owners of the business? (2) How does the business expect to distribute its earnings to its owners? and (3) Is the business expected initially to generate losses or profits?

Who Will Be the Owners of the Business?

If a business is owned by a few individuals, then it may be appropriate to form a corporation, partnership, or LLC. If ownership interests in the business will be widely held, however, the C corporation is usually the entity of choice. A corporation has unlimited life and free transferability of ownership, which are both more difficult to achieve in a partnership and, to a lesser extent, an LLC. Investors are also more receptive to offerings of corporate stock than partnership or LLC interests because they are easier to understand. In addition, once interests in a partnership or LLC are publicly traded, they lose their tax advantages and are taxed as C corporations (i.e., there is no flow-through tax treatment). An S corporation is not suitable for a widely held business because of the strict limits on the number and types of eligible shareholders. Moreover, as noted earlier, a business that expects to raise capital from a venture capital fund will usually be formed as a C corporation—or at least will usually need to convert to C corporation form prior to issuing stock to such a fund—to avoid adverse tax consequences for the fund's nonprofit investors.

If ownership interests in the business will be provided to employees, the C corporation will generally be the preferred entity for several reasons. First, stock ownership is easier to explain to employees than equity interests in partnerships and LLCs. Second, creating favorably priced equity incentives is easy to accomplish in a C corporation because ownership can be held through various classes of stock. If properly structured, the common stock can be sold to founders and employees at a discount from the convertible preferred stock issued to investors because of the special rights and preferences of the preferred stock. Although partnerships and LLCs can have similar preferred and common equity structures and thereby permit issuance of cheap equity to service providers (typically through profits interests, which if properly structured can be issued for zero payment with no tax incurred), such arrangements can involve undesirable tax complexities. For example, businesses offering service providers equity ownership in partnerships or LLCs must treat the providers as nonemployees for tax purposes under current Internal Revenue Service guidance, which can create undesirable tax compliance complexities for unsophisticated providers. S corporations, of course, cannot use preferred/common equity structures because they are limited to a single class of stock.

Finally, the tax law gives favorable tax treatment to incentive stock options (*ISOs*) granted by a corporation. As discussed in Chapter 5, the holder of an ISO generally incurs no tax until the shares purchased through an option exercise are sold—other than potential alternative minimum tax upon exercise of the ISO. The recognized gain is taxed at the more favorable long-term capital gains rate, rather than as ordinary income, provided certain holding periods are met. Incentive stock options are available only for corporations, not partnerships or LLCs. When options do not qualify as ISOs, the option holder recognizes ordinary income when the option is exercised and must pay tax on the difference between the exercise price of the option and the fair market value of the underlying stock at the time the option is exercised.

How Does the Business Expect to Distribute Its Earnings to Its Owners?

A business can either distribute earnings currently to its owners or accumulate and reinvest the earnings with the goal of growing the business so that it can either be taken public or sold to another business for cash or marketable stock of the acquiring business. Current earnings distributed to shareholders are taxed as ordinary income, whereas the gain on the sale of stock held by shareholders for more than one year is taxed to individual taxpayers at the more favorable long-term capital gain rate.

If a business intends to distribute earnings currently, a tax flow-through entity (such as a partnership, LLC, or S corporation) is generally the entity of choice because the earnings can be distributed without incurring a second level of tax. If a C corporation is used, earnings can be paid out without being taxed at the corporate level only if they are paid as salary or other reasonable compensation to shareholders who work for the business. (Such compensation is deductible by the corporation against its taxable income.) Distributions of earnings by a corporation to its shareholders, other than as compensation for services, will not be deductible by the corporation and will be taxed as dividend income to its shareholders. Most small businesses that distribute the business's earnings currently and do not have owners who work for the business have a strong incentive to use a tax flow-through entity, such as an S corporation, partnership, or LLC.

Is the Business Expected Initially to Generate Losses or Profits?

If the business is expected initially to generate losses, then a tax flow-through entity, such as a partnership, LLC, or S corporation, is the entity of choice because it offers the potential for the owners to deduct the losses from their taxable income, subject to the

From the **TRENCHES**

Adobe Systems, Inc., a leading desktop publishing software company, was initially organized as a partnership so that its investors, Hambrecht & Quist Investors, and its founders, John Warnock and Charles Geschke, could deduct the losses against their individual taxes. It operated as a partnership for one year, after which its partners traded their interests for stock in the newly formed corporation. Three years after its incorporation, Adobe went public.

various loss limitation restrictions mentioned earlier. For example, biotechnology companies frequently operate at a loss because of the extraordinary costs of developing products, conducting clinical trials, and obtaining the approval of the Food and Drug Administration. Even in the best-case scenario, a biotechnology company will typically experience several years of multi-million-dollar losses before reaching profitability. Depending on the sources of startup funding, use of a flow-through entity may be attractive, as it allows the investors to deduct the startup losses against taxable income.

Otherwise it may be years before the business earns a profit and can use tax loss carryforwards. However, unless the investors will materially participate in the business rather than being simply passive investors, their ability to use those losses may be restricted under the passive loss limitation described earlier (unless they are corporate investors who are not subject to the passive loss rules).

Summary of Pros and Cons of Various Forms of Business Organization

Table 4.1 sets forth the relative advantages and disadvantages of the various forms of business organization.

4.7   CHOOSING AND PROTECTING A NAME FOR A BUSINESS

Proposed names for new corporations, limited partnerships, and LLCs should be precleared through the name-availability section of the office of the secretary of state in the jurisdiction where the entity will be formed before filing documents. Unless the name is precleared or reserved, the business's filing documents may be rejected by the secretary of state because of a name conflict.

TABLE 4.1   Choice of Business Entity: Pros and Cons

The following chart lists the principal considerations in selecting the form of business entity and applies them to the sole proprietorship, C corporation, S corporation, general partnership, limited partnership, and limited liability company. The considerations are listed in no particular order, in part because their importance will vary depending on the nature of the business, sources of financing, and the plan for providing financial returns to the owners (e.g., distributions of operating income, a public offering, or a sale of the business). Other factors that are not listed will also influence the choice of entity. In addition, the "yes or no" format oversimplifies the applicability of certain attributes.

	Sole Propri-etorship	C Corp.	S Corp.	General Partner-ship	Limited Partnership	Limited Liability Company
Limited liability	No	Yes	Yes	No	Yes[a]	Yes
Flow-through taxation	Yes	No	Yes	Yes	Yes	Yes
Simplicity/low cost	Yes	Yes	Yes	No	No	No
Limitations on eligibility	Yes	No	Yes	No	No	No
Limitations on capital structure	Yes	No	Yes	No	No	No
Ability to take public	No	Yes	Yes[b]	No[c]	No[c]	No[c]
Flexible charter documents	Yes	No	No	Yes	Yes	Yes
Ability to change structure without tax	Yes	No	No	Yes	Yes	Yes
Favorable employee incentives (including incentive stock options)	No	Yes	Yes/No[d]	No[e]	No[e]	No[e]
Qualified small business stock exclusion for gains and rollover ability	No	Yes[f]	No	No	No	No
Special allocations	No	No	No	Yes	Yes	Yes
Tax-free in kind distributions	Yes	No	No	Yes	Yes	Yes

a. This limited liability is for limited partners only; a limited partnership must have at least one general partner with unlimited liability.

b. An S corporation would convert to a C corporation upon a public offering because of the restrictions on the permissible number of S corporation shareholders.

c. Although the public markets are generally unavailable for partnership or LLC offerings, a partnership or LLC can be incorporated without tax and then taken public.

d. Although an S corporation can issue ISOs, the inability to have two classes of stock limits favorable pricing of the common stock offered to employees.

e. Although partnership and LLC interests can be provided to employees, they are poorly understood by most employees and require treatment of the recipients of such interests as nonemployees, which involves greater tax compliance complexity for them. Moreover, ISOs are not available.

f. There is a special low capital gains rate for stock of U.S. corporations with not more than $50 million in gross assets at the time stock is issued if the corporation is engaged in an active business and the taxpayer holds his or her stock for more than five years.

Most secretaries of state maintain a consolidated list of the following: (1) the names of all corporations, limited partnerships, and LLCs organized under the laws of that state and in good standing; (2) the names of all foreign corporations, limited partnerships, and LLCs qualified to transact intrastate business in the state and in good standing; and (3) the names reserved for future issuance. Charter documents will not be accepted for filing if the stated name is the same as, resembles closely, or is confusingly similar to any name on the consolidated list.

An organization should also determine whether its preferred name is available for use in other states where it will be conducting business. State laws generally provide for the use of an assumed name in a foreign state when an organization's true name is not available in that state. If a corporate, limited partnership, or LLC name is not available because that name or a similar one is in use, it may still be possible to use that name by obtaining the consent of the entity using the name.

It is important to understand the difference between the actions of a secretary of state in allowing the use of a name and the issues involved in the use of a name or trademark for purposes of identifying a good or service. Approval of a name by a secretary of state merely means that the entity has complied with the state law prohibiting a business from using a name that closely resembles the name of another business organized or qualified to do business in that state. Therefore, the fact that the secretary of state does not object to the use of a particular name as the name of a business does not necessarily mean that other people or entities are not already using the proposed name in connection with similar goods or services. If they are, the law of trademarks (discussed in Chapter 14) will prohibit the new company from using the name. A promising startup business may find its business plan abruptly derailed when it receives a demand to change its name or faces an injunction and penalties for trademark infringement. To prevent this, the entrepreneur should conduct a search of the existing names in the proposed field of use (e.g., automobiles) to determine, prior to its adoption, how protectable a particular name or trademark will be and whether it will infringe the rights of others. As discussed in Chapter 14, certain "famous" trademarks cannot be used even in different fields of use if that use would tend to cause tarnishment or blurring of the famous mark.

Because many companies will want to use their corporate name as their domain name on the Internet (such as Ford.com), entrepreneurs should check with the applicable domain name registry to see what domain names are available before selecting a corporate name. Domain names are granted on a first-come, first-served basis and, as with trademarks, approval of a name by a secretary of state has no bearing on whether a particular domain name is available.

4.8   REGISTERING TO DO BUSINESS IN OTHER STATES AND OBTAINING LOCAL LICENSES

Before commencing operations in other states, the business should determine whether such operations will require it to register as a foreign corporation, partnership, or LLC in those states. Some states impose significant penalties for failure to register properly. Even if it need not register as a foreign business entity, the company may be required to pay income and other taxes (including sales and use taxes) in the states where it operates. If the business has employees in other states, it may be subject to withholding from employees' wages, workers' compensation insurance, and other regulatory requirements in those states. If the business owns real or personal property in other states, it may be required to pay property taxes in those states.

State licensing is required for a wide variety of businesses and professions. Cities, counties, and other municipal agencies require local licenses. Because licensing requirements vary greatly among cities and counties, a business may wish to consider local licensing requirements and taxes before choosing a location for doing business.

 Putting It into **PRACTICE**

Attorney Sarah Crawford outlined the forms of business organization available and their pros and cons. She told Alexei and Piper that they probably had already formed a general partnership by signing the brief handwritten agreement and carrying on joint business activities. No special form of agreement or governmental filing is required to establish a

(continued)

general partnership. Sarah strongly urged them to reorganize their business as an LLC or a corporation to protect themselves from the liabilities of the business. She cautioned that in a general partnership, each partner has unlimited liability for the obligations of the business and the obligations incurred by the other partners in conducting the partnership business. In addition, reorganizing as an LLC or a corporation would formalize their ownership interests by specifying how they would share profits, losses, and distributions and what their respective roles, powers, and obligations would be in the business. (These topics are discussed in more detail in Chapter 5.)

The choice between an LLC and a corporation depended primarily on the expected source of the anticipated $15 million startup funding required and the different tax treatment of LLCs and corporations. Although LLCs offer the same liability protection as a corporation, they are taxed as pass-through entities like partnerships. Because most venture capital funds cannot invest in businesses that are taxed as flow-through entities, Alexei and Piper could only access venture capital by incorporating as a C corporation. Other financing sources, such as corporate investors, wealthy individuals, debt providers, or some combination of these, would find an LLC attractive from a number of perspectives.

An LLC would likely be organized with Alexei and Piper as the managers and with the investors as passive members with such voting and other participation rights as the parties might mutually agree. Because an LLC is a flow-through entity for tax purposes, the LLC operating agreement would allocate startup losses to the LLC members who provided the financing. Corporate investors generally can deduct startup losses allocated to them against other income. Because the law limits the ability of individuals to deduct losses from passive activities, individual investors generally must carry their shares of startup losses forward to use against future income from the LLC. Individuals who have qualifying passive income from other investments can use such losses sooner, however.

An LLC would be the appropriate entity if Alexei and Piper expected to license the Genesis T-2000 technology to another business solely for royalties and would not create their own products for sale. In a royalty-only situation, earnings would be distributed to the owners, rather than retained to grow the business with the view toward selling it or taking it public. Because an LLC is not a separate taxpayer, the royalty income would be taxed only once (although at ordinary income rates). In a C corporation, the royalties would be taxed first at the corporate level, and the shareholders would be taxed again (at dividend rates) on all dividends they received.

Because Alexei and Piper intended to grow the business with a view toward taking it public, they planned to reinvest their earnings in the company and thereby shelter substantial amounts of the business's

(continued)

income. Upon sale of the business or an initial public offering of its stock, the gains of Alexei and Piper would be taxed at the long-term capital gains rate, which for individual taxpayers is lower than the ordinary income rate.

Alexei was contributing the Genesis T-2000 technology to the business for all or part of his equity. As a result, he might want to consider keeping a "string" on it so that the Genesis T-2000 technology would revert to him if the participants elected to dissolve the business. Using an LLC would permit the business to be dissolved and its assets divided among the owners without any tax (either to the entity or to the members). In contrast, if the business were a corporation, Alexei and Piper would be taxed twice if they parted ways and dissolved the business. Sarah pointed out, however, that institutional investors such as venture capital funds would be highly unlikely to permit Alexei to retain any reversionary interest in the Genesis T-2000 technology. With internal financing, such an arrangement is common.

The founders knew they wanted to seek venture capital financing within 12 months. Venture financing would not be available if they organized as a partnership or LLC. Also, organizing as an S corporation was not an option because the new business would have a corporate shareholder, ESF. In addition, Alexei and Piper wanted to issue founders' shares at a fraction of the price to be paid by investors and to be able to issue easily understood and tax-favored employee stock options.

For these reasons, Alexei and Piper decided to organize their business as a C corporation. After checking the name availability of "Genesist" with the secretaries of state in the states where the company expected to do business, doing a trademark search, and acquiring the Genesist.com domain name, they selected the name Genesist, Inc. Having decided to use a C corporation, the founders now turned to understanding the issues involved in incorporating the business and in dividing up the equity.

CHAPTER 5

Structuring the Ownership

After selecting the form of organization best suited to the new business, the entrepreneur's next important step is solidifying the relationship among the founders and structuring the initial ownership of the equity. If done correctly, the resulting structure will protect the rights of each founder, provide incentives for hard work, and divide the rewards fairly. The process also needs to be forward-looking and include considerations, such as whether additional shareholders or new employees will be added in the near future and whether the company will seek venture capital financing. The structure ultimately put in place should anticipate these events and provide the flexibility to deal with them.

The process of structuring the initial, formal relationship is often the first time the founders are forced to sit down and discuss the details of their deal. In the early stages, when the founders may have little more than an idea, their relationship tends to be vague and informal. If the topic is not discussed formally, each participant probably expects to be treated equally and to receive a pro rata share of the equity and control. Even when the relationship is discussed, the result may be nothing more than an oral agreement to "divide any profits fairly." The problem, of course, is that fairness is in the eye of the beholder.

When the time comes to formalize the relationship, hard questions must be addressed to minimize future disputes. They include the following:

➤ Who will own what percentage of the business?
➤ Who will be in the position of control?

➤ What property and how much cash will each participant contribute to the business?

➤ How much time will the participants be required to devote to the business?

➤ What incentives will there be to remain with the company?

➤ What happens if a founder quits?

➤ What protections will a founder have against being forced to leave the company?

➤ If there is a *wayward* or *forgotten founder*—someone who was involved with starting the venture and may have put work into the project, but is no longer actively involved— how is that situation best handled?

➤ What equity incentives will be given to employees?

In some ways, the mechanics of implementing these decisions may appear to be a low priority to entrepreneurs eager to get on with the important tasks of financing their business and developing and marketing a product or service. Nevertheless, thoughtful consideration at this stage will minimize serious problems in the future, problems that can threaten the very survival of the business. An added benefit of carefully planning the initial structure can come when venture financing is sought. A well-planned structure can anticipate the concerns of the venture capitalist, make for smoother venture financings, and provide evidence that the founders "have their act together" and can work through difficult issues as a team.

This chapter describes the basic documents that need to be prepared and the decisions that must be made to get the new business launched, including where to incorporate, how to allocate the equity among the founders, what type of vesting arrangements to impose, and what restrictions to impose on stock transfers. We also discuss stock option plans, which can provide important incentives for employees.

5.1　INCORPORATION

Most entrepreneurs view the formal paperwork of starting a new business as a necessary evil best left to lawyers. Although much of the incorporation paperwork may be boilerplate, entrepreneurs should recognize that careful attention to initial structuring details can help avoid future misunderstandings. On a very basic level, founders should understand the critical terms of the firm's charter documents (the certificate of incorporation and bylaws, discussed below). Although a thorough understanding of all of the details probably is not necessary, a general understanding of the controlling documents is important.

The formal documents required to form a new company will, of course, depend on the type of entity that will be used. Chapter 4 described the various forms of entities available and the pros and cons of each. This section provides a brief description of the documents necessary to legally establish a corporation and set the ground rules by which the owners will deal with each other. It assumes that the founders have decided to form a corporation, rather than a partnership, a limited liability company, or some other entity. Even if a noncorporate entity is used, however, most of the issues discussed must still be addressed.

Where to Incorporate

As a preliminary matter, the founders need to choose the state of formation (also called the *corporate domicile*). Generally, it is best to form the entity either in the state where its principal business will be located or in another state with a well-developed body of corporate law, such as Delaware. The founders should review their choice of state of incorporation with counsel before incorporating.

Delaware is chosen by many companies that are not based in that state because of its favorable and well-developed corporate law, which can, in certain instances, increase the power of management and give the majority shareholders more flexibility in dealing with the minority. Delaware can also be advantageous from an administrative perspective. For example, amendments to the certificate of incorporation and certificates of merger are quickly reviewed and processed in Delaware. This can be critical to timely executing on financings and merger and acquisition transactions. In contrast, certain other states have a prefiling review process that can take several days or more to complete. In addition, Delaware has a specialized and very experienced court (the Court of Chancery) dedicated to the swift resolution of corporate law disputes. In the event of a hostile takeover or other time-critical development, an appeal from a Court of Chancery decision can be heard by the Delaware Supreme Court in a matter of days.

Other areas where state laws differ include the type of consideration that can be used to purchase stock, the enforceability of voting agreements among shareholders, and the ability of the shareholders (1) to act by written consent; (2) to exercise preemptive rights to maintain their pro rata ownership percentage in the event of a financing; (3) to call a special shareholders' meeting; (4) to elect directors for multiple-year terms (and thereby *stagger* the election of directors, which is sometimes preferable because it helps prevent hostile takeovers and provides for institutional continuity); and (5) to demand appraisal rights upon certain events. Choice of domicile also affects the availability of arrangements regarding the indemnification of directors and officers and the ability of directors to adopt certain kinds of *poison pills* and other antitakeover defenses.

Although there are many advantages to incorporating in Delaware, there are also several disadvantages. Incorporating in a state other than the state of the principal place of business usually results in somewhat higher fees and other costs because of the need to comply with certain filing and regulatory requirements in both states. For example, if a corporation operates in a state other than the one in which it is incorporated, it will need to qualify as a foreign corporation and pay a filing fee in each state in which it does business.

The corporations law of California, home to many emerging technology and life sciences companies, has several restrictions worth noting. California requires at least three directors unless there are fewer than three shareholders. A California corporation may buy back shares or pay dividends only to the extent that it meets certain asset coverage or retained earnings tests. Companies that have negative retained earnings are prohibited from paying dividends, repurchasing shares, or making other distributions to shareholders. The penalties for violating this provision are stiff, and the directors are personally liable for any violations of this law. Privately held California corporations must give shareholders the right to vote cumulatively, which may give minority shareholders the opportunity to elect one or more directors. Under *cumulative voting*, each shareholder can cast a total number of votes equal to the number of shares owned multiplied by the number of directors to be elected; the shareholder can allocate those votes to such nominees as he or she sees fit. (We discuss cumulative voting more fully below.) All directors must be elected yearly, so there can be no staggered (*classified*) board.

One of the most significant differences between California and Delaware law is the right of common shareholders in a California corporation to vote as a separate class in the event of a proposed merger of the corporation. A similar right does not exist in Delaware, where a merger must be approved by a majority of all classes of stock, voting together. Although it is customary for the preferred shareholders to negotiate a right to vote as a separate class on significant matters (such as a merger), the right of the common shareholders to approve a merger under California law can give meaningful leverage to the common shareholders.

A corporation is usually subject to the corporate governance laws of only the state where it was incorporated, even if it is not headquartered there. California is perhaps unique in applying its generally pro-shareholder corporate governance laws to corporations that are incorporated elsewhere but are closely linked with California (so-called *quasi-foreign corporations*). In particular, a privately held corporation is subject to California corporate governance laws, regardless of where it incorporates, if more than 50% of its shares are owned by California residents and more than 50% of its business is conducted in California. For this reason, a corporation that will be owned primarily by California residents and will have most of its property, employees, and sales in California may decide to incorporate initially in California and then reincorporate in Delaware in the event of a public offering.

Certificate of Incorporation

The legal steps needed to form a corporation are surprisingly simple. Most state statutes simply require that a very short *certificate of incorporation* (sometimes called *articles of incorporation*) be filed with the secretary of state in the state of incorporation, together with payment of a filing fee. Although laws differ from state to state, the certificate of incorporation normally sets forth the following.

First, the certificate must state the name of the corporation, which typically must include the word "Corporation," "Company," or "Incorporated" (or an abbreviation thereof) and usually cannot contain certain words such as "insurance," "trust," "school," or "bank" unless the corporation satisfies certain other criteria. In some states, a person's name may not be used as the corporate name without adding a corporate ending, such as "Inc.," or some other word or words that show that the name is not that of the individual alone. The corporate name also must not be so similar to an existing name of an entity organized in the state, or authorized to do business therein, as to cause confusion. Additionally, although a state may accept a filing with a name that is dissimilar to others on file in that state, the corporate name must not infringe anyone's trademarks. As noted in Chapter 4, the entrepreneur should do a name search before incorporating.

Second, the business purpose of the corporation must be described. In most states, including California and Delaware, the purpose can be as broad as "engaging in any lawful activity for which corporations can be organized in this state."

Third, the certificate must state the authorized capital of the corporation, including the aggregate number of shares that can be issued, the par value of the shares (if any), and the classes of shares if the shares are divided into classes. If the company expects to seek venture financing, the founders can avoid the need to amend the certificate in connection with future financings by authorizing so-called blank-check preferred stock in the certificate at the outset. To the extent permitted by applicable state statute, *blank-check preferred stock* is authorized by providing in the certificate that classes of preferred stock are authorized and will have such rights, preferences, and privileges as the board of directors sets in board resolutions. This gives the board the authority to negotiate and determine the terms of the preferred stock in the first round of venture financing without the requirement of any further action by the shareholders. This flexibility can be particularly advantageous in young companies that have "angel" or "seed" investors, who are often wealthy individuals who buy common stock. Practically speaking, once the company has venture capital shareholders, the use of blank-check preferred stock will be limited as such shareholders usually require greater control over equity issuances.

Fourth, the certificate must list the name and address of an agent resident in the state for purposes of service of legal process (such as delivery of a summons). Although it is tempting to use an individual who is otherwise involved with the company, this would require promptly amending the company's certificate of incorporation if the individual moves or is no longer in a position to accept service of process on behalf of the company. Otherwise, a court could enter default judgments against the corporation on behalf of plaintiffs who were unable to serve process on the corporation. As a result, it is advisable to use one of the many professional service corporations that perform this service for a small fee rather than naming an individual.

Fifth, while not statutorily required by most states, the certificate should set forth provisions providing indemnification for directors, officers, employees, and other agents and limiting the monetary liability of directors with respect to certain breaches of the duty of care. *Indemnification* means that the company will reimburse the parties indemnified for certain damages and expenses (including attorneys' fees) resulting from their activities on behalf of the corporation.

Certain statutory provisions can be varied only if express language is included in the certificate of incorporation. For example, to impose *supermajority voting requirements*, which require more than a simple majority vote, for shareholder or director actions in California, a provision requiring a supermajority vote must be included in the corporation's articles of incorporation. In Delaware, cumulative voting of shares is permitted only if expressly provided for in the certificate of incorporation.

Certain states give all shareholders preemptive rights unless the certificate of incorporation provides otherwise. *Preemptive rights* give each shareholder the right to participate in future rounds of financing and buy whatever number of shares is needed to maintain the shareholder's percentage ownership interest. This can wreak havoc when the entrepreneur goes out to raise more money in future financings. In Delaware and California, shareholders do not have preemptive rights unless the company's articles or certificate of incorporation or a shareholder agreement so provides.

Bylaws

Although the certificate of incorporation establishes the legal existence of the corporation, it provides little guidance for determining how the shareholders, directors, and officers deal with each other and with third parties. The operating rules of the company generally are set forth in a document called the *bylaws*. However, certain operating rules established by the applicable corporation statute cannot be varied or will apply by default if the bylaws do not provide otherwise. In most cases, the standard bylaws prepared by legal counsel working with the company will both comply with the applicable statute and sufficiently address most issues of concern to the startup company. As corporation statutes impose very few restrictions on what the bylaws can contain, the founders should not hesitate to propose specific provisions needed to effectuate their business deal.

The founders should carefully review the bylaws before they are adopted to confirm that they accurately reflect their intent. Matters deserving particularly close attention include the provisions relating to the number of directors, calling board meetings, and directors' voting rights; the minimum number of directors who must be present at a board meeting to legally transact business (known as a *quorum*); the provisions, if any, for supermajority votes; the term for which directors are elected; the provisions (if any) designating different classes of directors; the process for filling board vacancies and removing directors; and the selection of the chair of the board or the appointment of a lead independent director.[1] Most states permit the bylaws to specify a fixed number of directors or a range (e.g., not fewer than three and not more than five).

The board of directors usually controls all but the most crucial decisions for the company; these decisions, such as a sale of substantially all of the corporation's assets, also require a vote of the shareholders. Thus, even if a founder owns a significant amount of stock, that ownership alone may not guarantee absolute control over all decisions. Instead, each founder should carefully consider whether to insist on a seat on the board and, if so, how to guard against removal or replacement if there are disagreements.

The founders should also review the shareholder voting provisions to make sure that they understand how directors will be elected, which matters will require a vote of the shareholders, whether there will be separate class voting on certain matters, how a quorum for shareholder meetings will be determined, whether the shareholders can act by written consent, and what degree of shareholder approval will be needed for each action. If a founder believes that, by reason of his or her stock ownership, he or she should be ensured a seat on the board or be able to elect more than one director, special attention should be given to how the shareholder votes are counted in the election of directors.

If cumulative voting is either allowed or required, the ability of a relatively small shareholder to elect a director might be surprising. For example, under cumulative voting, if five board seats are being voted on, a shareholder owning as little as 17% of the stock will be able to elect a director. The percentage of stock ownership required to elect one director under cumulative voting can be calculated by taking the number 1 and dividing it by the sum of the number of directors being elected plus 1. The formula to determine the percentage interest necessary to elect one director (x) is

$$x = \frac{1}{\text{number of directors being elected} + 1}$$

Accordingly, if six directors are being elected, a shareholder holding 14.3% of the stock $[1 \div (6 + 1)]$ could elect one director; a shareholder would need to hold at least 28.6% of the stock (14.3% $\times$ 2) to elect two directors. Given the importance of this issue, it is often best to have a separate voting agreement among the shareholders to ensure that the board's composition will be as expected.

When forming the company, the founders typically will have expectations as to who will fill various officer positions, although the actual appointments must be approved by the board of directors. The bylaws will specify the principal duties and responsibilities of the officers, and the founders should confirm that these provisions accurately describe the functions they expect each officer to perform.

Bylaws often contain restrictions on the transferability of shares and may grant a right of first refusal to the corporation or its assignees to purchase shares at the time of a proposed transfer to a third party. Such provisions can be especially important in a new company when it is vital that stock be owned by those individuals and entities that are directly involved in the success of the business. This right should be assignable by the company in case the company itself is not able to exercise the right due to capital constraints or corporate law restrictions on the repurchase of shares.

 ## From the **TRENCHES**

A founder of a California startup who had become unhappy with its management proposed to transfer a large block of stock to a third party. Although the company had a right of first refusal, it was unable to exercise it because it had negative retained earnings. Because the bylaw right of first refusal was assignable, the company was able to transfer its repurchase right to a major shareholder, who purchased the disaffected founder's shares. Later, when the company could legally make the purchase, the major shareholder sold the stock back to the company at cost. The company then used the stock as an incentive for new employees.

In part to attract outside directors, bylaws generally provide for the broadest indemnification of directors, officers, and agents permitted by the controlling state statute. The founders should consider whether such indemnification should be mandatory or permissive and whether it should extend to employees and agents of the company. They should also consider whether the company should be required to advance attorneys' fees if a director, officer, or agent is sued. Often, indemnification agreements are put in place that reflect the indemnification provisions in the certificate of incorporation and bylaws and give those entitled to indemnity a contractual right to an advance of attorneys' fees and the maximum indemnification permitted by applicable law.

Each founder should fully understand the mechanics of amending the bylaws. Including an important provision in the initial bylaws provides little comfort if the provision can easily be deleted or amended later.

Mechanics of Incorporation

Any individual may sign and file the certificate of incorporation; they need not be a founder or attorney. The person signing is called the *incorporator*. In a document generally called the *action by incorporator*, which can be executed as soon as the certificate of incorporation has been filed with the secretary of state of the state of incorporation, the incorporator named in the certificate of incorporation appoints the initial directors, and then resigns. It is possible to name the initial directors in the publicly filed certificate of incorporation, with the incorporator's powers terminating upon the filing of the certificate, but that is unusual. Once appointed, the board of directors then usually adopts the bylaws, elects officers, authorizes the issuance of stock to the founders, establishes a bank account, and authorizes the payment of incorporation expenses. In addition, at its first meeting, the board may adopt a standard form of proprietary information and inventions agreement for use by employees and consultants; a form of restricted stock purchase agreement, which typically imposes vesting and rights of first refusal on employee stock; and an employee stock purchase and/or stock option plan. The board may also select the fiscal year of the corporation and determine whether to elect to be taxed as an S corporation. Written minutes of the meeting should be approved by the board at its next meeting. However, many states permit the board to take actions without a meeting if all directors sign a document approving the action, called an *action by unanimous written consent*. In such states, organizational action by unanimous written consent is common.

A privately held corporation's organizational documents (i.e., the certificate of incorporation, bylaws, and organizational minutes) are largely boilerplate, and standardized organizational documents are readily available for entrepreneurs who desire to incorporate without hiring a lawyer. (For exemplars prepared by Cooley LLP, go to www.cooleygo.com.) Because this documentation is usually straightforward, however, experienced counsel can prepare it inexpensively. Experienced counsel's real value is less in preparing the basic documentation than in providing expert advice on choosing an appropriate capital structure, allocating ownership among the founders, transferring assets to the

From the **TRENCHES**

Four individuals—A, B, C, and D—decided to build a cogeneration power plant. A and B hired a lawyer to prepare incorporation documents. The documents listed his secretary as the incorporator. She signed the articles of incorporation and filed them with the Illinois secretary of state.

A and B then ended their involvement with the project. The two remaining individuals, C and D, proceeded to sign a document they called "Action by Incorporator," in which they purported to adopt bylaws and elect themselves as directors. In their capacity as directors, they issued stock to themselves and elected officers. The corporation subsequently entered into a joint venture with a large Canadian electric company to build the plant.

The construction was financed with a permanent bank loan. When interest rates fell and retail power prices also declined, the company needed to renegotiate the loan to make the plant economically viable. The lender requested an opinion from counsel for the joint venture that the joint venture owned the cogeneration plant. After reviewing the corporation's organizational documents, counsel for the joint venture discovered that the person who had signed the articles of incorporation was different from the persons who had signed the Action by Incorporator appointing the directors. This error created doubt about the legal status of the corporation's directors and the officers they had appointed, and thus their ability to enter into the joint venture.

A and B, the original two parties who had dropped out of the project, learned of the mistake and claimed that they owned 50% of the corporation. The joint venture could not get the refinancing closed without resolving A and B's claim, and the joint venture ended up paying them a substantial sum to get them to relinquish any rights they might have in the venture.

Comment: Although having the wrong person sign the Action by Incorporator designating the directors is a seemingly simple mistake, it created a massive problem, which jeopardized the refinancing and generated very high legal bills. This costly mistake could have been avoided by following the correct legal formalities. It is customary, and indeed critical, for the incorporator to appoint the initial directors immediately following incorporation and then resign.

corporation in the most tax-efficient manner, adopting appropriate equity incentive programs, and generally avoiding pitfalls. In addition, outside investors will usually require the issuer to provide an opinion of counsel regarding proper formation of the entity. It is cheaper for a lawyer to opine on his or her own documents.

5.2 SPLITTING THE PIE

Perhaps the most difficult decision in structuring the new business is how to divide the equity ownership among the founders, which will determine who participates in the financial success of the business and at what level. The participants often avoid this topic initially due to its sensitivity. Delay in working out these details can be disastrous, however. When the time comes to formally structure the ownership of the business, the founders must be forthright in their discussions.

The founders should take into account almost any contribution to the business they believe warrants recognition. Factors commonly considered include the following:

➢ What cash and property will each founder contribute at the outset?

➢ If property is contributed, what is its value, and how was it acquired or developed?

➢ What opportunity costs will each founder incur by joining the business?

In the end, the objective should be to treat each founder as fairly as possible. It is not necessarily in the best interest of an individual to negotiate the best deal possible for himself or herself if it is at the expense of others. Success of the company will depend on the hard work of each member of the team working together over a long period of time. If the business is to grow and be successful, each founder needs to consider the equity allocation fair. If any members feel slighted, they may be tempted to look for opportunities elsewhere or may not be as dedicated to the business as the other founders.

Finally, the founders must address the expectations of individuals who may have contributed to the enterprise during its preincorporation phase, but who are no longer part of the founder group. It can be very harmful to the company if a so-called *wayward* or *forgotten founder* suddenly appears at the time of a venture financing or, worse, at the time of the company's initial public offering and asserts an ownership right. The claim could be based on oral promises by the other founders or, more commonly, on early contributions to, and therefore partial ownership of, the company's underlying technology or other intellectual property. Even if the wayward founder assures the remaining founders upon departure that he or she is not interested in the

From the **TRENCHES**

Two young entrepreneurs received $50,000 from a wealthy individual to finance the test marketing of a new handheld device for consumers. It was the understanding of the parties that the cash would be used to purchase equity in a new entity if the device proved promising but that the money would not have to be repaid if the venture did not proceed. The equity split was not discussed. The test marketing was successful, and the two entrepreneurs incorporated the company. They issued 90% of the company's stock to themselves, 45% each, and proposed issuing the angel investor the remaining 10% of the stock in exchange for his $50,000. The entrepreneurs reasoned that because they conceived of the product concept and would be the driving force behind the company, it was fair to give the angel investor only 10% of the equity. In contrast, the angel investor believed that advancing the initial risk capital for the enterprise entitled him to be an equal partner. After the investor sued the founders and the company, the entrepreneurs offered to pay back the $50,000. The angel refused their offer, insisting that he was entitled to one-third of the equity of this now-promising enterprise. Litigation ensued and the parties settled, with the angel investor receiving 25% of the equity.

Comment: This situation could have been avoided if the parties had either incorporated and issued shares earlier or set forth their deal in writing at the time the $50,000 was advanced.

venture, it is far preferable to solidify and document the parties' understandings about ownership of both intellectual property and equity in the startup company as early as possible. If such persons exist, it is best to resolve their claims at the incorporation stage rather than having to deal with them at a time when the company has increased in value or when their claims could destroy a pending transaction.

Sometimes, the founder group will resist giving any equity to early participants who helped conceptualize a product or service but then moved on, reasoning that they should not have any share of the new enterprise because they will not be helping perform the enormous amount of work still necessary to develop the product or service and make it commercially viable. Yet, if this issue is addressed early on, when the company's prospects are highly uncertain, it is often possible to persuade early participants to accept a modest equity stake (say, 5% of the company) in exchange for any rights they might have in the business. Without such an agreement, an early participant might later claim the right to be an equal partner with the founders who gave up other opportunities to pursue the venture.

From the **TRENCHES**

While Salman Syed and Clinton Grusd were MBA students at the Yale School of Management in 2011, they developed the idea of creating a virtual golf caddy, which would utilize a smartphone app equipped with GPS to track a golf ball equipped with a special device to compile and record the golfer's statistics. Although they never executed a formal written agreement or incorporated the business they called Dolphin Golf, they exchanged numerous text messages and worked together to develop business plans, funding sources, and corporate relationships. After an angel investor introduced Grusd and Syed to the CEO of Callaway Golf Company in August 2011, Syed met with him on a number of occasions in hopes of negotiating a licensing arrangement. At the time, Callaway was developing a similar, competing product so it decided not to do a deal with Dolphin Golf. Nonetheless, Grusd and Syed agreed that Syed would stay in touch with Callaway to continue monitoring its interest in working with Dolphin Golf.

Syed and Grusd worked together on the business until they graduated from Yale in May 2012. That fall, Syed told Grusd that he could no longer afford to work full time on Dolphin Golf and needed to find a paying job. Syed allegedly "asked Grusd to 'hold the fort' and said he would soon return to work on Dolphin Golf." In October 2012, Callaway told Syed that it was abandoning its virtual caddy project and was interested in licensing its technology, which included a device attached to the golf club, to Dolphin Golf. Syed did not tell Grusd about Callaway's offer. Instead, Syed began working with Callaway and raised more than $4 million in financing for a new virtual caddy company he formed called Golfkick. According to *Bloomberg Businessweek*, Syed believed that he did not have an obligation to offer Grusd an opportunity to participate in Golfkick, because Golfkick used a device affixed to the golf club, not the golf ball, which was the idea behind Dolphin Golf.

Grusd did not find out about Golfkick until August 2013, "when Syed updated his LinkedIn profile, indicating that he had been the 'CEO and Co-Founder at Golfkick' since October 2012." Grusd then sued Syed, claiming, among other things, that he and Syed had agreed to be "50-50" partners in the golf business and that Syed had breached his fiduciary duty and contractual obligations by secretly pursuing the opportunity without offering Grusd an equal interest in Golfkick. According to the court's summary of Grusd's complaint, Syed had lied about his need to find a paying job: "Rather than temporarily walking away from developing the golf project to make money doing something else, Grusd claims that Syed was actually moving forward with the golf project on his own, cutting out Grusd and working with the very business partners he and Grusd pursued for Dolphin Golf." Grusd also sued the investors, alleging that they had aided and abetted Syed's wrongful conduct. The court denied the defendants' motion to dismiss the fiduciary duty, contractual, and aiding and abetting claims, reasoning that Grusd had plead sufficient facts that, if proven, showed that Syed and Grusd had created a joint venture or de facto partnership entitling each of them to one half of the equity of Golfkick.

Sources: Grusd v. Arccos Golf LLC, 2014 WL 2531511, No. 653239/2013, slip op. 31471(U) (N.Y. Sup. Ct. June 3, 2014); Louis Lavelle, *Yale MBAs Battle over an Idea for a Golf Business,* Bloomberg Businessweek (Sept. 23, 2013), http://www.businessweek.com/articles/2013-09-23/yale-mbas-battle-over-idea-for-a-golf-business.

Ownership issues often arise when a group of students work together on a business plan for a class. When the groups are pre-assigned by the professor, they may include a mix of individuals who would not work effectively together as a team. In addition, certain students may be unwilling to forgo other employment opportunities after graduation to join a startup but may still expect a share of any venture based on "their" business plan. If the students submit the plan to a business plan contest and win, then what started as a purely academic endeavor can turn into a commercial dispute. Unless the professor or school has provided otherwise, students should consider entering into an agreement at the outset stating that each student (1) has a nonexclusive right to pursue a venture based on the plan (either alone or with one or more team members of their choosing) and (2) grants each other student a nonexclusive right to use the information in or underlying the plan. The students should also try to agree in advance how to allocate the winnings if the plan is submitted to, and wins, a business plan contest. If the plan is based on a proprietary technology, then the inventor may demand an exclusive right to pursue the venture in exchange for either paying the non-inventors for their time, at standard consulting rates, or a predetermined percentage of the equity. Equity may be contingent on a non-inventor's willingness to devote full time to the venture, or made subject to vesting or reduction by the board of directors of the venture after the venture's first external financing event. Such agreement can always be modified later if all the parties agree that a different arrangement would be preferable.

In addition to agreeing on the founders' initial ownership shares, the founders need to determine how they will "split the pie" with future employees. If the management team is incomplete and one or more high-level participants will be recruited, the founders should take into account the dilutive effect of issuing additional stock and its impact on the founders' voting control. For example, if the initial team consists solely of technical people, the company will need a chief executive officer (*CEO*), a chief financial officer (*CFO*) (or controller or vice president of finance), and a vice president of sales/marketing. Depending on the caliber and experience of the individuals recruited, the company may have to issue 5% to 10% of the equity to the CEO and another

7% to 10% to other senior management. Similarly, venture capitalists who invest in the first round of financing could acquire up to 40% to 60% of the company and may require that 10% to 20% of the equity be reserved for employee stock options for key hires as well as rank-and-file employees. The dilutive effect of these potential events should be considered when allocating equity among the founders.

5.3 ISSUING FOUNDERS' STOCK

Once the founders have agreed how to allocate the ownership of the new business, it is time to formally issue stock in the newly formed company. The stock initially issued to the founders (*founders' stock*) is almost always common stock. Founders' stock can usually be issued at a low price without causing the recipients to incur taxable compensation income; it provides the founders certain benefits of direct stock ownership; and it avoids some of the tax drawbacks of stock options. As additional employees are hired and the value of the company increases, it is often desirable to switch from issuing common stock outright to granting employee stock options, which give the option holder the right to acquire common stock in the future at a specified price.

Valuation of Founders' Stock and Taxation of Cheap Stock

The board of directors must have a reasonable basis for determining the fair market value of the founders' stock it issues. A company will often retain an independent appraisal firm to conduct periodic valuations of the company's common stock to support the board's determination. An independent valuation is typically valid for one year or until the company encounters a material event that would affect the value of its stock, such as receiving a term sheet for closing a financing, signing a major contract, or experiencing a significant growth in revenue.

If stock is issued to an individual providing services to the company, the recipient must either pay the fair value of the stock or recognize ordinary taxable income to the extent that the value of the stock exceeds the amount paid. For a newly formed company without significant cash financing, the value of the common stock normally is not an issue. Upon formation, the company's assets usually consist of a limited amount of cash and property. The prospects of the new business are still in doubt. As a result, the value of the company's common stock often is low enough that early participants can afford either to pay fair market value for the stock or to recognize taxable income on the difference between the fair market value at the time of acquisition and the purchase price.

The value of the stock will continue to be low until some event indicates that it should be higher. The valuation event may be undefined (such as advances in product development or increased sales), or it may be more concrete (such as an angel round or venture capital financing in which third parties put a higher value on the business).

If the tax authorities conclude that a service provider received stock worth more than what he or she paid for it (*cheap stock*), then part of the value of the stock may be taxable to the recipient as compensation income. Accordingly, if, at the time of issuance, the common stock has more than a nominal value, the purchase price or the amount recognized as taxable income can be quite high. Consequently, companies whose stock has more than a nominal value normally elect to use employee stock options as a way to allow employees to participate in the growth of the business.

Two-Tier Stock Structure in Venture-Backed Companies

Unlike the founders and other employees, venture capital investors usually acquire preferred, not common, stock. There are two primary reasons for this two-class structure in venture-backed companies: risk management and taxes.

First, the venture investors can reduce their risk by purchasing preferred stock that includes a liquidation preference over the common stock. A *liquidation preference* gives the preferred shareholders first claim on the company's assets in the event that the company is dissolved or is sold. Thus, if the business does not succeed but still owns valuable assets (such as patents or other intellectual property), the preferred shareholders may be able to recoup some or all of their investment. (Liquidation preferences are discussed further in Chapter 13.)

Second, by issuing venture investors stock that has preferential rights over the common stock, the company can properly value the common stock issued to founders and other service providers at a discount from the price paid by the venture investors for their preferred stock. By issuing preferred stock to investors, the company can justify a lower fair market value for the common stock.

In general, the more time that elapses between the issuance of the common to the founders and the issuance of the preferred to investors, the easier it is to defend a larger differential. This is but one reason why it usually makes sense to incorporate and issue founders' stock as early as possible. The more time separating the issuance of the founders' stock from a subsequent event that establishes a higher valuation, the lower the risk that the founders will be treated as having purchased their stock at a discount with resulting taxable compensation income.

Consideration for Stock

The applicable state statute under which the corporation was formed will contain certain restrictions on the types of consideration that can be used to purchase stock. Cash is always acceptable, as are most types of property. Past services are also generally acceptable. Under Delaware law, future services are valid consideration, as are promissory notes in most circumstances. Under California law, future services are not valid consideration and promissory notes are acceptable only in certain cases. Given these restrictions and discrepancies in state law, care must be taken to ensure that each founder provides adequate consideration to purchase his or her allocable portion of the company's stock.

Tax Treatment of Contributions of Property in Exchange for Stock

If any of the founders plans to contribute property to the company in exchange for stock, it is critical to understand the tax consequences. An exchange of appreciated property (i.e., property worth more than its tax basis) for stock in a newly formed corporation will be tax-free only if it qualifies under Section 351 of the Internal Revenue Code. Exchanges not meeting the requirements of Section 351 are subject to tax on the difference between the fair market value and the tax basis of the property.

Section 351 imposes two requirements for tax-free exchanges. First, the property must be transferred solely in exchange for stock (or securities) of the company. If the transferor receives any cash or other non-stock consideration (*boot*) in exchange for the property, then the exchange may still qualify under Section 351, but the transferor will be required to pay taxes on the lesser of the value of the boot and the gain (i.e., the fair market value of all stock and non-stock consideration received minus the transferor's tax basis for the property given up in the exchange). In addition, if the transferor receives stock with a value in excess of the value of the property contributed, the transferor may be taxed on the excess stock value received, usually as compensation income. Second, immediately after the transfer, the transferor(s), including those contributing cash but not those contributing only services, must own both (1) stock possessing at least 80% of the total combined voting power of all classes of stock entitled to vote and (2) at least 80% of the total number of outstanding shares of all other classes of the stock of the corporation.

When there is more than one transferor, the contributions of property do not have to be simultaneous. However, the contributions do need to be part of a single integrated transaction to form the business. When the contributions are not simultaneous, the rights of the parties must have been previously defined, and the execution of the documents necessary to effect the transfer must proceed on a timely and orderly basis. As a result of these rules, if property is contributed by a founder, who alone will not meet the 80% tests, then sufficient other contributions should be made at or around the same time by others so that the contributing group satisfies the 80% tests.

Additionally, the founders should confirm that the person contributing property has the right to do so and that the transfer is complete and binding. If technology or other intellectual property is being contributed and will be improved upon, the founders should be absolutely certain that the company has obtained adequate ownership of the property, so that the company can both use the property in its development efforts and retain and exploit any advances or improvements that it makes.

Sometimes founders who will be contributing intellectual property are reluctant to make the transfer until funding has been assured, or they may wish to license the technology or other intellectual property to the company with a right to terminate the license if funding does not occur or the company fails. Such arrangements must be carefully considered to ensure the contributions are respected for tax purposes as contributions of property under Section 351. Once property has been contributed to the corporation, all shareholders through their stock ownership have a pro rata interest in that property. If the corporation is later dissolved, the corporate property will be distributed among the shareholders in accordance with their stock ownership interests. At the same time, venture capitalists generally expect the founders to transfer all of their rights to the technology or other intellectual property, not just a license. The founders should work closely with legal counsel to establish the optimum timing for their transfers.

From the **TRENCHES**

A young entrepreneur made an informal deal with a retired engineer to exploit proprietary technology owned by the engineer. The entrepreneur formed a company and spent $100,000 to develop and market a product. When the entrepreneur went back to the engineer to negotiate a formal transfer of the technology to the company, the engineer not only refused to complete the transfer but also threatened to sue the company and the entrepreneur for misappropriation of the intellectual property. As a result, the company was never launched, and the entrepreneur lost $100,000.

Comment: This situation could have been avoided if the entrepreneur had required the engineer to transfer the proprietary technology to the new company before spending money to develop or market the product.

Tax Benefits of Direct Stock Ownership

Until the value of the common stock is high enough to cause the purchase price or tax consequences to be prohibitive, direct stock ownership offers a number of tax advantages over stock options. When stock is issued, whether for cash or in exchange for property or services, the stock becomes a capital asset in the hands of the recipient (assuming that the stock is vested or a Section 83(b) election is made, as described below). As a result, any subsequent increase in the value of the stock will be treated as a capital gain when the stock is sold. If the stock is held for more than one year, the gain will be a long-term capital gain, which is taxed at a lower rate than ordinary income. In addition, stock in a domestic C corporation can often be classified as *qualified small business stock* (*QSBS*) under Internal Revenue Code Section 1202. As explained in Chapter 4, depending on the year the stock was acquired and subject to certain limitations, all or a portion of the gain from the sale of QSBS that has been held for at least five years is excluded from taxation. Finally, by owning stock rather than receiving a stock option, a founder can start the holding period both for this exclusion and for purposes of various securities laws, thereby making it easier to sell the stock later.

Vesting

When individuals form a new business based on their own ideas, assets and labor, many founders expect that the stock they acquire will be theirs no matter what happens in the future (i.e., be *fully vested*). After all, the business would not exist but for their initial efforts, so why should their ownership be subject to forfeiture? On the other hand, most founders would also agree that any cofounder who leaves the business shortly after it begins should not continue to own a significant part, or perhaps any part, of a business that will require substantial future efforts to grow and be successful. Because forming the business is only the beginning of the enterprise, the founders and other team members should generally be required to continue working for the company for some period of time to earn the right to participate in the future rewards of the business.

If the founders expect to seek venture capital financing in the future, they should also recognize that the venture investors will have similar concerns. Venture capitalists invest in people as much as in ideas and technologies. The typical venture capitalist will spend considerable time evaluating the team and, before investing, will want to make sure that incentives are in place to keep it intact. If a team member does leave, both the investors and the founders will want to have the ability to allocate the unvested shares to that person's replacement, thereby minimizing the amount of new stock that must be issued to attract the new team member and reducing the dilution of the equity interests suffered by both the remaining founders and the investors. If the founders do not impose restrictions on their stock and the stock issued to other important team members, they can be sure that the venture capitalist will raise this issue before investing. Except in the most unusual situations, a vesting requirement will be imposed before venture capitalists will invest.

Stock subject to vesting is sometimes referred to as *restricted stock*. As discussed below, all recipients of restricted stock should, for tax reasons, consider making an Internal Revenue Code Section 83(b) election, which must be made within 30 days of the date of issuance.

If the owner of restricted stock leaves, whether voluntarily or involuntarily, before becoming fully vested, the company will have the right to repurchase the unvested stock at the lower of the stock's fair market value and the cost of the stock to the shareholder. The purchase price may be paid in cash or, in some cases, the company may be allowed to repurchase the stock with a promissory note. The use of the promissory note alternative is especially important if the purchase price is high and the company is cash poor. The vesting provisions will often permit or require the company to assign its repurchase right to the remaining shareholders in the event the company itself is unable to purchase the stock due to a cash shortage or legal restrictions.

Indeed, it can be a good strategy for founders to self-impose a reasonable vesting schedule up front as a preemptive measure before negotiating with venture capitalists. This approach also helps prevent any one founder from slowing down the financing. In its most common form, vesting occurs if the individual holding the stock continues to be employed by or otherwise performs services for the company over a specified period. A common vesting schedule for founders is to vest a portion of the stock at the time of issuance (especially if the founder has spent considerable time working on the venture before incorporation or has transferred significant assets to the firm) and an additional portion after one year, with the remaining stock vesting monthly over the next 12 to 36 months. Venture capitalists typically will agree to a vesting schedule of this type.

Tax Treatment of Unvested Stock and Section 83(b) Elections

As explained earlier, an individual who receives stock in connection with the performance of services is normally taxed at ordinary income tax rates to the extent that the fair market value of the stock when received exceeds the amount the service provider paid for the stock. If the stock is subject to a substantial risk of forfeiture, however, the taxable event (including the measurement of taxable income and the obligation to pay any tax) is normally delayed until the risk of forfeiture lapses. This is true even if the recipient paid the fair market value for the stock at the time of purchase. In general, a *substantial risk of forfeiture* exists if the recipient's right to full enjoyment of the stock is conditioned upon the future performance of substantial services. Therefore, if stock issued to founders or others is subject to repurchase by the company and/or other shareholders at less than fair market value upon the termination of employment (i.e., the stock is subject to vesting), the stock will be treated as subject to a substantial risk of forfeiture. As a result, if a company issues stock that will vest over a period of time, the founder or other recipient will recognize taxable income on each vesting date equal to the difference (if any) between the fair market value of the shares on the date they become vested and the purchase price paid (the *spread*).

For example, assume that the founder pays $25,000 for 500,000 shares of common stock ($0.05 per share) and that one-fourth of this stock will vest after one year with the balance vesting on a monthly basis for the next three years. Further assume that $0.05 per share was the value of the stock on the date the stock was issued and that the value of the stock increases to $1.00 per share by the end of the first year after purchase. Unless the founder has filed a timely Section 83(b) election, he or she will recognize ordinary taxable income at the end of year one in an amount equal to $118,750 (the value of one-fourth of the stock [$125,000] minus one-fourth of the purchase price [$6,250]). This income will be recognized, and tax will be due and payable in cash, even if the founder still owns the stock and, as is usually the case, the stock is illiquid. Similarly, on each monthly vesting date occurring thereafter, the founder will recognize additional ordinary taxable income measured by the then-current value of the shares that become vested that month minus the amount paid for those shares. In other words, even though the founder may not have sold any stock, the spread will be taxed as if the company had paid the founder cash wages in that amount. If, as is usually the case, the founder is an employee, then the company will be required to deposit the income and employment tax withholding amounts almost immediately after each vesting event. The founder will typically be required to reimburse the company for the withholding tax amount either through additional withholding from the founder's cash salary or through an out-of-pocket cash payment to the company.

As an alternative to recognizing taxable income upon each vesting date, the founder should always consider filing an election under Section 83(b) of the Internal Revenue Code. By filing a timely *Section 83(b) election*, the founder is electing to pay tax at the time the stock is purchased in an amount equal to what would be due if the stock were not subject to vesting.

An 83(b) election must be filed with the Internal Revenue Service within 30 days after the initial purchase of the shares. If an employee "early exercises" an option to acquire unvested stock (discussed further below), then the election must be filed within 30 days of exercising the option.

Thus, if a founder pays full market value at the time he or she purchases restricted stock and files a timely 83(b) election, then no tax will be due when the stock is purchased because the value of the stock on that date will not exceed the purchase price. Once this election is made, subsequent vesting of the stock will also not be taxable. The founder will be required to pay tax only when the stock is ultimately sold, and any gain recognized on the sale will be a capital gain. Thus, the filing of a Section 83(b) election both allows a deferral of tax beyond the vesting dates and enables all appreciation in the stock's value to qualify for capital gains tax treatment.

Filing the election is not always advantageous, however. If the stock subject to vesting is sold to an employee at a discount from its fair market value at the time of sale, then filing a Section 83(b) election will result in the recognition of ordinary income, in the year in which the stock is issued, equal to the spread between the fair market value at the time of issuance and the price paid. For example, assume that an employee pays $10,000 for 200,000 shares of common stock ($0.05 per share) and that one-fourth of this stock will vest after one year with the balance vesting on a monthly basis over the next 36 months. Further assume that the value of the stock on the date the stock was issued was $0.20 per share, and that at the end of the first year, the value of the stock has increased to $1.00 per share. If the employee makes an 83(b) election, then the employee will recognize ordinary income in year one equal to the $30,000 differential between the fair market value of the stock when issued ($40,000) and the price paid ($10,000) and will be required to pay income tax almost immediately on that amount due to the company's withholding obligation. If the employee is terminated before the end of the first year, thereby forfeiting all of his or her stock, then the employee will have paid tax at ordinary income rates on a paper gain of $30,000 that evaporated when all the shares were forfeited. Furthermore, this loss is a capital loss, and so it cannot be used to offset the $30,000 of ordinary income resulting from the 83(b) election. Thus, the tax benefit of this loss may be severely limited. Consequently, the employee will be out of pocket most or all of the taxes paid by reason of the Section 83(b) election. In contrast, if the unvested stock's fair market value when issued is the same as the purchase price, then there usually is no real cost to filing the election. As a result, it is almost always advantageous to file an election when this differential is zero or very small; the decision becomes more difficult only when the differential is substantial.

 From the **TRENCHES**

A number of employees of a software company received stock subject to vesting. By making a Section 83(b) election, they were able to value the shares at the time purchased at a fraction of the value established when the company went public 18 months later. Those who did not make a Section 83(b) election had their shares valued at the public trading price on the date the shares became vested. Because they had paid a fraction of that price for the shares, these employees realized very substantial amounts of ordinary income, and incurred high taxes, as their shares became vested.

Restrictions on Transfer and Repurchase Rights

Privately held companies almost always prohibit or at least restrict the transfer of unvested stock. They may also impose restrictions on the transfer of even vested shares and give the company and/or its shareholders the right to repurchase a departing shareholder's stock. Airbnb, Pinterest, and certain other privately held companies have established programs whereby employees can sell their vested startup shares in "controlled opportunities," thereby making it possible both for employees to "cash out" before the startup goes public or is sold and for the companies to exercise "some control" over potential investors.[2]

5.4 EMPLOYEE STOCK OPTIONS

Although it is usually preferable at the formation stage to issue common stock outright to the founders, as the company matures and the value of its stock increases, employee stock options are used extensively. A *stock option* gives the optionee the right to purchase a defined number of shares of stock, in most cases common stock, at a predetermined purchase price (the *exercise price*). Options provide employees and others the opportunity to participate in the growth of the business without having to put up cash, pay immediate tax, or otherwise put their capital at risk. Moreover, as the number of equity participants increases, stock options may be a preferable way for the founders to retain voting control and for the company to avoid certain corporate and securities law issues created when the number of shareholders exceeds certain thresholds.

In this section, we discuss the most important terms of an option: (1) the number of shares in the option pool, (2) the exercise price and the valuation of the underlying stock, (3) the type of option, (4) the duration, (5) permissible forms of payment, (6) vesting and the availability of early exercise, and (7) restrictions on the transfer of shares. We discuss the tax treatment of employee options in the next section. Given the complexity of the tax code, entrepreneurs should consult with a qualified tax advisor before issuing or exercising options.

Number of Shares in the Option Pool

Typically, a startup business will establish a collective pool of shares under a formal stock option plan approved by the shareholders. The board of directors can then grant options to purchase the company's stock from this pool. For an individual award, the only formal limit is the number of uncommitted shares left in this pool. As a practical matter, however, a business will need to manage its share reserve pool carefully to ensure adequate grants for all employees and other personal service providers (such as nonemployee directors, consultants, and advisors). A reasonable rule of thumb is to earmark about 15% to 20% of a company's shares for issuance to employees and other service providers. In making this calculation, the number of shares in the option pool is included in the total number of shares; convertible securities (such as preferred stock convertible into common and convertible debt) are treated as if they had been converted; and all other outstanding options and warrants are treated as if they had been exercised.

Exercise Price

Options in a startup business are almost always granted at an exercise price equal to 100% of the fair market value of the stock that may be acquired, valued as of the date the option is granted. The grant of options with a lower exercise price (*discounted stock options*) results in accounting charges for the employer, securities law restrictions, and serious adverse tax consequences for optionees unless the option otherwise complies with Section 409A of the Internal Revenue Code. That section generally provides that a discounted stock option may be exercised only on certain permissible payment dates or upon certain events specified under Section 409A. The adverse tax consequences include the imposition of tax payable by the optionee on the spread between the exercise price and the fair market value of the underlying stock at the time of vesting and thereafter until the option is exercised, plus a 20% additional penalty tax and an interest charge. The spread is considered "wages" for tax purposes, and it is subject to income tax withholding and payroll taxes. According to current IRS guidance, the spread must be calculated as of December 31 in the year of vesting, and December 31 of each year thereafter until the option is exercised. The spread for the year of vesting, and any increase in the spread in future years, is subject to withholding and tax reporting for the payroll period ending each December 31. The optionee must also pay the 20% penalty tax and interest charge for any additional spread amount reported each year. As a result of this draconian treatment of discounted stock options, even nonstatutory stock options should generally have an exercise price at least equal to the fair market value of the underlying common stock on the date the option is granted. To satisfy tax and financial accounting rules, the board of directors must have a reasonable basis for its determination of the fair market value of the underlying common stock. By issuing preferred stock in venture financing rounds, a lower common-stock valuation may usually be maintained, resulting in a lower option exercise price for service providers. It should be noted, however, that the pricing of the preferred stock is but one factor, albeit an important one, that must be considered when the board is valuing the common stock. It is typical for a company to retain an independent appraisal firm to conduct periodic valuations of the company's common stock to support the board's determination. An independent valuation is typically valid for one year or until the company encounters a material event that would affect the value of its stock, such as receiving a term sheet for a financing, signing a major contract, or losing a key employee.

If a company discovers after the grant date that an option has a discounted exercise price (because of a later valuation of the company's stock), guidance under Section 409A affords a limited period during which the exercise price can be increased to the value of the stock on the date of grant, thereby making it possible to avoid the adverse consequences of Section 409A. For options granted to officers, directors and 10% shareholders, this period extends until December 31 of the year of grant. For other employees, this period extends for an additional year (December 31 of the year following the grant year).

Backdating options in an attempt to evade these adverse effects may constitute securities, accounting, and/or tax fraud.

Accordingly, the board of directors should ensure that there is a reasonable basis for establishing fair market value on the date of grant and that proper records are kept that reflect accurately the actual date of grant and the fair market value of the stock on that date.

Types of Stock Options

Corporations can grant two types of options to eligible individuals: *incentive stock options (ISOs)* and *nonstatutory stock options (NSOs)*, also called *nonqualified stock options*. As discussed in Section 5.5, the difference between these two types of options relates to the income tax requirements and treatment. ISOs generally receive more favorable tax treatment than NSOs, but ISOs are subject to more restrictive tax requirements. Although a stock option plan may be designed to grant only one type of option, most plans provide for both.

Maximum Duration

Incentive stock options may not be granted with a term longer than 10 years. If, however, an optionee owns more than 10% of the corporation, then the maximum term for incentive stock options is reduced to five years. Although there is no statutory limit on the term of NSOs, most plans limit the terms of both incentive and nonstatutory options to a maximum of 10 years. Many companies have found through bitter experience that five years can be too short a period of time if the business does not develop as rapidly as originally projected. Extending the term of an option due to expire may result in accounting charges for the company and cause the loss of incentive stock option treatment for outstanding options.

A related issue concerns the circumstances under which an option will terminate prior to the expiration of its term. Most plans provide that an option terminates only upon the termination of the optionee's service with the company. Typically, individuals have one to three months after termination of service within which to exercise their options. This period may be extended to

12 months if the termination of service is attributable to disability or to up to 18 months if it is attributable to death (in which case the option is exercisable by the optionee's beneficiary, estate or trustee).

Permissible Forms of Payment

Stock option plans may allow optionees to use four basic forms of payment to purchase stock when exercising their options: (1) cash or cash equivalents, such as checks; (2) shares of the company's stock already owned by the optionee; (3) a "net exercise" or "cashless contribution" as described below; and (4) a promissory note. Most plans permit the use of all four forms of payment, or a combination of those forms, but the standard agreement by which the option is actually granted will typically limit the permissible forms of payment either to cash or cash equivalents or to previously owned shares of the company's stock. In some cases, equity plans of private companies, or individual option awards, contain net exercise provisions. With a *net exercise*, some of the shares that would otherwise be delivered upon exercise are instead retained by the company and used to satisfy the exercise price of the option. A net exercise feature may disqualify an option as an ISO. Plans for publicly traded companies may also permit a so-called *cashless exercise*, whereby option holders engage in a same-day, broker-assisted sale of the stock received upon exercise in the public market (with a portion of the sale proceeds remitted to the company to cover the option's exercise price).

Vesting and Early Exercise

Stock options allow employees to participate in the potential appreciation in the value of the business without putting their capital at risk. However, to ensure the employee earns the right to participate in the financial upside of the company and continues to contribute to value creation, the stock underlying the employee option is typically subject to vesting. The employee is entitled to exercise the option with respect to increasing portions of the stock underlying the option as the employee completes continuous service over a defined period. Shares that are not subject to contractual restrictions in favor of the company are called *vested shares*. Although the precise features of vesting schedules differ among plans, a common vesting schedule for rank-and-file employees is for all stock underlying the option to be completely unvested at the time of issuance, with one-fourth of the underlying stock vesting after one year (*cliff vesting*), and with the remaining stock vesting in equal portions monthly over the next 36 months. Some companies tie vesting to the achievement of performance goals. In all cases, attention needs to be given to the financial accounting treatment of options, especially as the company emerges from its startup phase and generates earnings.

Most stock option plans sponsored by private companies restrict the exercise of options to vested shares. Certain stock option plans, however, contain an *early exercise feature* whereby an individual (often a key employee) may exercise an option immediately, even if the optionee would acquire only unvested shares. The stock purchased pursuant to the early exercise provision is subject to the continuing vesting schedule, with unvested stock subject to repurchase by the company at cost. If an employee "early exercises" an option to acquire unvested stock, then any 83(b) election covering that stock must be filed within 30 days of exercising the option.

The early exercise feature confers upon the optionee the benefit of commencing the holding period for the underlying stock for tax and securities law purposes. If a company's stock becomes publicly traded, immediately exercisable options may therefore provide officers and directors of the company greater flexibility in acquiring and disposing of their stock.

Privately held companies almost always prohibit or at least restrict the transfer of unvested stock acquired upon an early exercise of options. They may also impose restrictions on the transfer of even vested shares and may give the company and/or its shareholders the right to repurchase a departing shareholder's stock. As noted earlier, certain privately held firms have established programs giving their employees "controlled opportunities" to "cash out" before the startup goes public or is sold.

5.5 TAX TREATMENT OF EMPLOYEE STOCK OPTIONS

In this section, we discuss the tax treatment of discounted, incentive, and nonstatutory employee stock options. A *discounted option* is an option with an exercise price less than the fair market value of the underlying shares on the date of grant. To qualify as an *incentive stock option* (*ISO*), the option must be granted to an employee (not other types of service providers, such as nonemployee directors, advisors and consultants, who can receive only nonstatutory options), and the exercise price must be at least 100% of the fair market value of the underlying stock at the date of grant (110% if the grantee is a greater-than-10% owner of the company). Any options that do not meet these requirements are *nonstatutory stock options* (also called *nonqualified stock options*). Of these three types, the most tax disadvantaged are discounted options and the most tax advantaged are incentive stock options.

Receipt of the Option

Because employee options are nontransferable, the optionee must generally exercise the option and sell the underlying stock to realize the value of the option. As a result, the receipt of a stock option by an employee or other service provider is normally not a taxable event. If, however, the company grants an employee or other service provider a discounted option, then the optionee will generally have to pay income taxes, penalty taxes, and interest charges when any of the shares underlying the option vest and thereafter as more shares vest. As discussed earlier, it is critical for the board of directors to ensure that all options, whether they are intended to be incentive or nonstatutory options, be issued with an exercise price not less than the defensible fair market of the underlying stock on the date of grant.

Exercise of Nonstatutory Stock Options

Upon exercise of a nonstatutory stock option, the optionee normally recognizes ordinary taxable income, which, if the optionee is an employee, is subject to income and employment tax with-holding. The optionee must pay tax on the difference between (x) the fair market value of the stock purchased on the date the option is exercised and (y) the amount paid to exercise the option. This is called the *spread*. Appreciation in the value of the stock from the option's grant date through the exercise date is taxed as ordinary income, which results in a lower after-tax return than would be achieved if stock had been issued directly at the outset. When stock acquired upon exercise of a nonstatutory option is sold, the difference between the sale price of the stock and the fair market value of the stock purchased on the date the option is exercised is a capital gain or loss that is long-term or short-term depending on whether the stock was held for more than one year from the date of exercise.

Exercise of Incentive Stock Options

Incentive stock options allow the optionee to avoid recognizing taxable ordinary income at the time the option is exercised (although if the spread is substantial, alternative minimum tax may be due). As a result, no regular income tax is due until the underlying shares are sold. At the time the stock is sold, the optionee recognizes taxable income equal to the difference between (x) the fair market value of the stock on the date it is sold and (y) the option exercise price (the *gain*). The spread between the fair market value of the stock on the date the incentive stock option is exercised and the option exercise price is taxed at capital gains rates only if the optionee has held the stock for more than one year after the date of exercise and more than two years after the date the option was granted. If the stock is disposed of within two years of the grant date or within 12 months after exercise (a *disqualifying disposition*), then the gain (i.e., the sale price minus the option exercise price) is taxed as follows: any gain up to the amount of the spread (i.e., the fair market value of the stock on the date of exercise minus the exercise price) will be ordinary income, and the balance of the gain will be capital gain, which will be long-term or short-term depending on whether the stock was held for more than one year from the date of exercise.

Tax Treatment of Early-Exercise Options

There are several tax benefits associated with taking advantage of a right to exercise an option early, that is, before the underlying shares will be vested. Because the spread on the exercise of an incentive stock option is included for purposes of calculating an individual's alternative minimum tax, an early exercise of an option typically results in a smaller spread that is potentially subject to this tax. In addition, optionees acquiring qualified small business stock within the meaning of Section 1202 of the Internal Revenue Code can generally avoid paying tax on all or a portion of any capital gains recognized upon sale of the qualified small business stock if they have held the stock for more than five years. Early exercise permits the optionee to initiate that five-year holding period sooner. An early exercise also permits the optionee to start both the regular capital gain holding period and the incentive stock option one-year holding period sooner. As noted earlier, an 83(b) election would typically be filed by the employee-shareholder with the Internal Revenue Service within 30 days of "early" exercising the option.

Of course, an option holder must balance the potential tax advantages of an early exercise with the economic reality of having to invest cash in a venture at an earlier time when its success may be far from certain. By exercising early, the option holder both spends what can be limited cash sooner and gives up the valuable right to defer making the investment decision until more information becomes available.

Summary of Tax Consequences of Various Forms of Equity Compensation

Table 5.1 summarizes the federal tax consequences of various forms of equity compensation under the Internal Revenue Code in effect as of January 1, 2016. State taxation may differ. Entrepreneurs, managers, investors, and others should always consult experienced tax advisors. In addition, when choosing a tax-favored business strategy, the decision makers should take into account the nontax features and consequences of various tax-planning alternatives.[3] In addition, the tax preferences of all

TABLE 5.1	Tax Treatment of Restricted Stock Awards, Nonstatutory Stock Options, and Incentive Stock Options	
Event	**Employee Tax Consequences**	**Employer Tax Consequences**
Issuance of stock subject to vesting (restricted stock)	None, until the shares vest unless an 83(b) election was made. If an 83(b) election is filed, employee recognizes ordinary income equal to fair market value of shares at time of issuance minus price paid by employee (the *spread*).	None, unless an 83(b) election was made, in which case the employer (1) can deduct as a compensation expense an amount equal to the spread and (2) must satisfy its employee income tax deposit and payroll tax obligations (assuming founder is an employee).
Vesting of restricted stock	Ordinary income equal to fair market value of the shares on date shares vest minus price paid by employee, unless an 83(b) election was made, in which case no tax is due upon vesting.	Compensation deduction equal to spread (and tax deposit and payroll tax obligations triggered), unless an 83(b) election was made.
Contribution of property (including under certain circumstances intellectual property) to newly formed corporation in exchange for stock	Under Section 351, as long as the contributors (1) contribute property, not services; (2) receive stock in the corporation with a value no greater than the value of the property or cash contributed; and (3) collectively control 80% or more of the corporation after the transaction, the contributors pay no tax on the gain (i.e., the fair market value of the stock and other property received minus the cost basis of the property contributed), unless they receive cash or other non-stock property (*boot*). Contributors receiving boot are taxed on the lesser of their realized gain and the amount of boot.	None.
Contribution by founder of services in exchange for stock issued upon incorporation	Ordinary income equal to the fair market value of the stock received.	Compensation deduction equal to fair market value of stock. Tax deposit and payroll tax obligations triggered (assuming founder is an employee).

TABLE 5.1	(continued)	
Event	**Employee Tax Consequences**	**Employer Tax Consequences**
Grant of nonstatutory stock option (*NSO*) (with an exercise price at least equal to fair market value of the underlying stock at the time of grant)	None.	None.
Grant of incentive stock option (*ISO*)	None.	None.
Exercise of NSO	Ordinary income equal to fair market value of stock on date of exercise minus option exercise price (the spread).	Compensation deduction equal to the spread (and tax deposit and payroll tax obligations triggered).
Exercise of ISO	None, except that the spread will be included as a preference item in calculating the individual's alternative minimum tax (*AMT*), which could trigger AMT for the year in which ISO is exercised. The employee will receive a tax credit for any AMT paid, which can be applied against taxes due in future years.	None.
Sale of stock acquired upon exercise of NSO	Capital gains equal to sale price minus fair market value on date of exercise.	None.
Sale of stock acquired upon exercise of ISO	Capital gains equal to sale price minus exercise price provided that the stock is not disposed of within two years of the grant date or within 12 months after exercise (a *disqualifying disposition*). In the event of a disqualifying disposition, the *gain* (i.e., the sale price minus the exercise price) is taxed as follows: any gain up to the amount of the spread on date of exercise will be ordinary income, and the balance of the gain will be capital gain.	None, unless a disqualifying disposition. If disqualifying disposition, compensation deduction equal to ordinary income recognized by the employee.

a. If the company issues a discounted stock option (i.e., an option with an exercise price below the underlying stock's fair market value on the date of grant), then tax consequences will be different from what is described in this table as a result of the application of Section 409A of the Internal Revenue Code. For example, an optionee would be required to recognize taxable income prior to the exercise of a discounted nonqualified stock option, including associated penalties and interest.

b. Many thanks to Professor Henry B. Reiling of the Harvard Business School for his contributions to earlier versions of this table.

c. In all cases, this table assumes the Section 83(b) election is made in a timely manner.

parties to the transaction should be taken into account. In the context of equity compensation, this means the tax consequences for both the employer and the employee.

5.6 REPURCHASE RIGHTS, RIGHTS OF FIRST REFUSAL, AND OTHER RESTRICTIONS ON THE TRANSFER OF STOCK

It is common for privately held companies to impose certain restrictions on the transfer of both unvested and vested shares. The primary reasons for these restrictions are to keep the ownership of the company with those individuals and entities that are directly involved in the success of the business, to provide liquidity to shareholders in certain situations, to allow other shareholders to participate in transfers of a controlling interest in the company, and to maintain the balance of power among the shareholders. Common provisions include restrictions on the transfer of unvested shares, rights of first refusal, repurchase rights, buy-sell agreements, and co-sale agreements. Although a separate document might be prepared for each of these restrictions and provisions, they also can be reflected in a single agreement among shareholders. Repurchase provisions applicable to shares issued pursuant to employee stock options are typically set forth in the option agreement.

Restrictions on the Transfer of Unvested Shares

Unvested stock acquired outright or through the early exercise of an option normally is not transferable due to restrictions contained in the purchase agreement for the stock or the stock option agreement. The company is usually given the right to acquire the unvested shares upon termination of the shareholder's employment at the lower of the purchase price (or the exercise price in the case of stock acquired through the early exercise of options) and the fair market value of the stock on the termination date. At a minimum, most companies provide for a right of first refusal in favor of the company on unvested shares. This right of first refusal is usually extended to the other shareholders if the company itself does not exercise the right in full.

Right of First Refusal

The most common form of transfer restriction imposed on share-holders of a newly formed company is a right of first refusal. Under a *right of first refusal*, if a shareholder wishes to transfer his or her stock in the company, then the company, its assignees, or the other shareholders (depending on the agreement) must first be given the opportunity to buy the stock pursuant to the terms being offered by the third-party purchaser. Typically, the party or parties with the right have 30 to 60 days to purchase the stock after receiving notice of the pending sale. If they fail to purchase the stock, the selling shareholder is free to sell to the identified third party on the terms presented to the company and the other shareholders within a designated period of time. If the sale to the third party is not consummated within the designated period of time, any subsequent sale may again be made only after applica-tion of the right of first refusal procedures. This type of restriction is so common that in many cases it is contained within the bylaws of the company. Sometimes a more elaborate right of first refusal is contained in a separate agreement among shareholders. It is important to ensure that the terms of the separate agreement are consistent with any provisions in the bylaws.

The primary benefit of a right of first refusal is that it allows the company and other shareholders to prevent transfers to outsi-ders who might be uninterested in, or disruptive to, the business. On its face, a right of first refusal appears to allow an existing shareholder to sell his or her stock at its fair value. As a practical matter, however, the effect of a right of first refusal is to severely limit the transferability of stock. A potential third-party buyer will often be disinclined to negotiate a fair potential purchase because he or she knows that the negotiated terms will then have to be offered first to the company and/or the other shareholders. Even if the right of first refusal is not exercised, the delays caused by the procedures are often enough to dissuade a potential purchaser.

Repurchase Rights

A repurchase right enables a privately held company to restrict transfer of even vested shares issued to current service providers. To repurchase vested shares, the company generally pays the greater of the individual's purchase price (or the exercise price in the case of stock acquired upon the exercise of options) and the stock's fair market value on the date of termination of service. Sometimes, the repurchase of a key employee's shares upon death is funded by a key-person life insurance policy.

Because the event giving rise to the right of repurchase usually does not involve a third-party offer, there often is no arm's-length evidence as to the stock's value, making it difficult to determine the fair market value of the stock to be repurchased. Alternatives for determining value include valuation formulas based on a multiple of earnings or revenues, the use of outside appraisers, a good-faith determination by the board of directors, and a price to be agreed upon by the parties to the transaction. In some agreements, the method for determining or paying the purchase price will vary depending on the event giving rise to the sale. For example, the repurchase of stock triggered by the service provider's voluntary decision to leave the company (without good reason, usually as specified in an employment agreement) or by termination by the company for good cause (again, usually as specified in an employment agreement) might result in a lower purchase price than selling stock as a result of extenuating circumstances (such as death or disability). As a result, it is very important for service providers to understand how key terms in the employment agreement can directly affect their equity rights if they decide to leave or are forced out of the company.

In addition to the challenges of valuing stock subject to repurchase rights, making a determination of the stock's fair market value for such a repurchase may set a benchmark as to the stock's fair market value for other purposes, such as for awarding future stock options. In addition, a repurchase provision for vested shares creates an economic and psychological disincentive for the service provider.

Buy-Sell Agreements

Buy-sell agreements are used to provide some liquidity to shareholders while limiting stock ownership to a small group. Such agreements typically contain three operative provisions. First, the signing shareholder is prevented from transferring his or her shares except as permitted by the agreement. Second, transfers are permitted to certain parties (e.g., family members or controlled entities) or upon certain events (e.g., death), subject in most cases to the transferee's agreement to be bound by the buy-sell agreement. Third, the company or the other parties to the agreement are either granted an option, or are obligated, to purchase at fair value another party's stock and that other party is obligated to sell the stock upon certain events (e.g., termination of employment).

As with repurchase rights applied to vested shares issued to service providers, often the most difficult aspect of a buy-sell agreement is determining the price to be paid for stock purchased under the agreement. Due to their complexity, buy-sell agreements are less common in venture-backed companies than in family and other closely held businesses.

Co-Sale Agreements

Co-sale agreements are routinely used by venture capital investors to allow them to participate in sales by other shareholders. These agreements are especially common when one or more of the founders own a controlling interest in the company. Such a controlling interest could, absent transfer restrictions, be sold to a third party, thereby leaving the venture investors in a minority position in a business that has lost at least one of its key employees. Conversely, a founder concerned that the venture capitalists might sell out to a third party and leave the founder as a minority shareholder could propose a co-sale agreement covering the venture capitalist's shares; however, many venture capitalists are unwilling to agree to such a restriction. We further discuss co-sale agreements in venture capital deals as well as so-called drag-along rights, which give investors the right to force the founders to sell their shares under certain circumstances, in Chapter 13.

5.7 SHAREHOLDER VOTING AGREEMENTS

Although effective control of a business is often tied to the level of equity ownership, this is not always the case, particularly when the company has obtained venture financing and has granted one or more of the investors the right to designate directors through voting agreements. Even before the first venture financing, it may be appropriate to implement a voting agreement to ensure that the composition of the board is defined. Typically, all or a controlling group of the shareholders enter into such an agreement. Under the agreement, the parties commit to vote their shares for designated individuals as directors. The individuals may be named in the agreement, or the agreement may allow one or more of the shareholders to nominate the director at the time of each election. Although shareholders may agree to elect certain named persons as directors, a shareholder agreement purporting to name the officers would be invalid. Only the directors have the legal authority to name and remove the officers.

When the company is being structured initially, the number of shareholders may be small enough that a voting agreement appears to be unnecessary. For instance, if there are three equal shareholders and three board seats, then, if there is cumulative voting, each shareholder will be able to elect himself or herself to the board. Even in these simple cases, however, a voting agreement could still be useful. If, for example, two of the three shareholders are related and are expected to vote together at the board and shareholder levels, then the third shareholder might demand that a fourth board seat be established and that, pursuant to a voting agreement, the third shareholder be entitled to designate two of the board members.

In general, larger venture investors will expect the right to designate one director, and founders should expect that their own board representation will be reduced to one member, or even to just the CEO, over time. When negotiating voting agreements, the parties should consider including a "sunset" clause on board representation that curtails an investor's voting rights if the investor does not continue to invest in the company and is significantly diluted in subsequent rounds of financing. Failure to do so can greatly hinder the company's future financing efforts.

5.8 PROPRIETARY INFORMATION AND INVENTIONS, EMPLOYMENT, AND NONCOMPETE AGREEMENTS

In structuring and forming a new business, the founders should focus not only on equity ownership and control issues but also on the need for individual agreements between the company and the founders and other employees. (Employment agreements and terms of employment are discussed in detail in Chapter 8.)

Proprietary Information and Inventions Agreements

At the very least, all employees (including the founders) should be required to sign a proprietary information and inventions agreement. As discussed further in Chapter 14, the proprietary information (or nondisclosure) provisions will require the employee to keep the company's proprietary information confidential and to use such information only as authorized by the company. Provisions dealing with inventions will effectively assign to the company any inventions that (1) result from work performed for the company, (2) are discovered during company time, or (3) arise from the use of company materials, equipment, or trade secrets.

Employment Agreements

In a company's early stages, employment agreements are uncommon but, in the right circumstances, they can be useful. As explained in more detail in Chapter 8, under the law of most states, employment is considered to be at will unless there is an express or implied agreement to the contrary. *At-will employment* means that the company (or the employee) can terminate the relationship at any time, with or without cause. As a result, the company may have little incentive to implement an employment agreement if it has otherwise obtained a proprietary information and inventions agreement and, if allowed under state law, a noncompete agreement. However, a founder who feels vulnerable to the whims of his or her cofounders may find some comfort in an employment agreement, which can provide for cash severance payments, additional stock vesting, or both if the employee is terminated without good cause. Care should be taken, though, to ensure that any employment agreement is not so restrictive that the employee, including a founder, cannot be terminated even for good reason. If the contract effectively guarantees employment, or imposes substantial costs on the company for terminating employment, venture investors will be concerned. These investors must believe that as the business grows, the company will be able to make necessary personnel changes without having to pay too high a price.

Noncompete Agreements

In states where an agreement not to compete with a previous employer is enforceable, the founders should consider whether such an agreement between themselves and the company is appropriate. Sentiment will probably run against noncompete agreements at this stage of the company's development because all the founders should believe that they will be with the company for a long time. In addition, each founder may want to ensure that he or she is able to establish a competing venture if forced out. Nevertheless, founders should not be surprised if venture investors in the first financing round seek to impose these agreements as yet another way of protecting their investment. (Covenants not to compete were discussed in Chapter 2.)

 Putting It into **PRACTICE**

As a first step in structuring their new enterprise, Alexei and Piper met to discuss their expectations for the business. Their simple agreement to "divide any profits fairly" might have given them some comfort on an informal basis, but they recognized that it was now time for them to be clear and forthright about their expectations as to equity ownership and control. Given that Alexei had developed the initial designs for Genesis T-2000 and had been working on the project longer than Piper, he indicated that he expected a larger piece of the equity. Alexei and Piper concluded that Alexei should be given 50% of the equity and Piper 35%. After consulting with Piper, Alexei had already agreed to give Empire State Fabrication Inc. (*ESF*) a 15% stake in return for licensing critical technology necessary for the development of Genesis T-2000 and releasing any claims to the venture.

After working out their business deal, Alexei and Piper met with their legal counsel, Sarah Crawford and her associate Aaron Biegert, to discuss incorporating the enterprise. Sarah asked them to describe the background regarding the development of the technology and the

(continued)

proposed business and to describe the agreements they had reached and their expectations as to foreseeable events (such as whether they would seek venture capital financing and, if so, when). Alexei said that the new company intended to seek venture capital financing in about six months. Piper indicated that until the company received venture financing, it would be financed by family loans and a modest equity investment by a wealthy family friend. The founders asked Sarah and Aaron what legal documentation was needed to ensure the equity ownership and board structure they had agreed upon. Because they wanted to issue stock with the expectation of continued employment, they inquired about mechanisms to ensure that the stock would remain with the company or the other founder if one of them were to leave. Finally, Alexei told Sarah and Aaron that he wanted to talk about an employment agreement for himself.

Sarah began by outlining the pros and cons of incorporating in Delaware or in California, then suggested that they choose California. She pointed out that for at least the next few years, significant aspects of California corporation law likely would apply to the company no matter where it was incorporated because the company would be privately held and based in California with most of its stock held by California residents.

During the course of the conversation, Piper indicated that one of her MBA classmates named Maren Barillas, an engineering student named Steve Asimov, and she had written a business plan for an innovative process for increasing the speed of 3D printing. Piper told Sarah that Maren had recently inquired about Alexei and Piper's new venture and asked what her stake would be. Sarah brought in an intellectual property colleague to assist in assessing whether Maren, and perhaps Steve, would have a claim to any of the intellectual property underlying the GT technology. While it was determined that such a claim would be very weak, Sarah advised Alexei and Piper that they should at least consider granting Maren and Steve modest equity stakes in the company to foreclose any possibility of a later claim and the disruption that could cause, especially at a time when the company was embarking on a financing or an M&A transaction. Alexei and Piper considered Sarah's advice, but they decided not to lend merit to Maren's or Steve's position and instead to forge ahead as they had initially planned without issuing equity to Maren or Steve. Sarah reminded the founders to be sure not to include any of the text written for the business plan to mitigate the risk that Maren and/or Steve might later assert a claim.

To reflect the agreement regarding equity, Sarah proposed that the company's articles of incorporation authorize 10 million shares of common stock and that 1 million shares of common stock be issued at a

(continued)

price of $0.01 per share, with 500,000 to Alexei, 350,000 to Piper, and 150,000 to ESF. She also suggested the authorization of 1.5 million shares of blank-check preferred stock, based on her prediction that the initial venture investors would seek 40% to 60% of the equity. Sarah explained that to sell 60% of the company's equity to the venture investors, the company would issue 1.5 million shares of preferred stock convertible one-for-one into shares of common stock; thus, after the closing, the 1 million shares held by the founders would represent 40% of the 2.5 million shares outstanding. This capital structure would enable the board of directors to issue convertible preferred stock to venture investors without the need for a shareholder vote and would leave a cushion of shares of common stock available to issue to venture investors upon conversion of their convertible preferred stock and to new employees directly or through options.

Sarah next discussed the board arrangements, pointing out that cumulative voting would apply, as this was a privately held California corporation. Alexei and Piper thought that a four-person board would make the most sense, with Alexei and Piper each having the right to elect two directors. Under this arrangement, neither founder could control the board if disputes arose. Aaron told the founders that with a four-person board, Alexei automatically would be able to elect two directors because he held at least 40% of the stock, and that Piper would be able to elect one of the four directors because she owned at least 20% of the stock. Aaron also advised that it was unlikely that a venture capital investor would agree to a board composition that allowed the founders as a group to elect four directors.

Sarah advised the parties to sign a voting agreement to reflect their decision on board representation. Piper asked Alexei if she could have a veto over Alexei's choice of one director. Alexei agreed, subject to his right to veto any director nominated by Piper.

Aaron indicated that he could include all of these provisions in the proposed voting agreement. He suggested that the agreement expire at the time of the company's initial public offering because the company's investment bankers would insist on this. He also cautioned that the even number of directors could result in a deadlocked board that would be unable to take any action. Alexei said that he would rather have a situation where the directors were forced to agree to an action than either one in which one side could dictate a decision or one in which an outside director would have the swing vote on any important issue. Sarah said that she was not particularly troubled by the deadlock possibility because these voting arrangements would most certainly change once the company received venture capital financing.

(continued)

Aaron then discussed vesting arrangements for the common stock to be issued to the founding group. He started to say that the venture investors would insist on vesting, but Piper interrupted to state that the founders did not need to be persuaded to institute vesting now. Aaron did note that if additional restrictions were imposed on the founders' shares later, after the fair market value of the common stock had increased, then the founders would need to consider filing new Section 83(b) elections and possibly would have to recognize some income on the spread. The founders decided that, for Piper, monthly vesting over four years would be fair and would set an example for future employees, but that vesting for Alexei should be shorter because he had been the driving force behind the project and had been involved for a longer time. The parties agreed to vest one-fourth of Alexei's shares immediately, with the balance to vest monthly over the next three years. Aaron asked whether any credit toward vesting should be given in the event of death, but the founders decided against it because of the need to use unvested shares to attract replacements for key personnel who left the business regardless of the reason. Sarah advised Alexei and Piper to file Section 83(b) elections within 30 days after the date their stock was issued.

Next, Sarah raised the need for controls on the transfer of the shares to be issued to the founders and future shareholders. She pointed out that because the founders' shares were not registered with the Securities and Exchange Commission but were issued pursuant to certain exemptions from registration (namely, Section 4(a)(2) of the Securities Act of 1933 and Regulation D, discussed further in Chapter 7), the shares would be subject to restrictions on transfer. A legend on their stock certificates would provide that the shares could not be sold unless registered under the Securities Act of 1933 or sold in an exempt transaction. In general, for a sale to be exempt from registration under Rule 144, the founders would have to hold their stock for at least six months before sale. Even after six months, they would be unable to sell it publicly unless the company was regularly filing periodic reports with the Securities and Exchange Commission, which normally is not done until the company goes public. In addition to these restrictions, all agreed that it made sense to prevent transfers of shares outside the existing shareholder group. Sarah suggested an assignable right of first refusal in favor of the company with exceptions for estate planning transfers, gifts, and transfers to existing shareholders. Alexei thought that there should be no exceptions to the right, even for gifts to family members. Piper agreed, as long as the board could waive the right of first refusal in particular cases. Aaron said that he would include the right of first refusal, and the ability of the board to waive it, in the company's bylaws.

(continued)

Sarah pointed out that venture investors might not agree to a right of first refusal on their convertible preferred stock, but she suggested that for now the right should apply to all stock of the company.

Finally, Alexei asked about an employment agreement for himself. He was concerned that the venture investors might insist on board control and then use their power to terminate him without compensation. Sarah indicated that employment agreements for executives were uncommon in Silicon Valley startups and that they would probably need to eliminate such an agreement before a venture capitalist would invest. Alexei replied that he would rather face that issue at the time of financing than have nothing in place, and Piper reluctantly agreed. Aaron was instructed to prepare a three-year agreement providing for base compensation of $100,000 per year with a year's severance pay plus an additional 12 months of vesting on Alexei's stock (i.e., vesting the number of shares that would have vested had he remained employed for another 12 months) in the event the company terminated him without good cause. Piper asked Alexei if the commencement of salary payments could be postponed until the company was able to raise capital, and Alexei agreed.

Aaron then sent Alexei and Piper the draft legal documents he had prepared for their review. The founders believed that they had communicated their deal clearly to counsel and initially indicated that they did not plan to review the resulting documents in any detail. Aaron explained, however, that it was much better to discover any differences between what was intended and what the documents said at this early stage rather than in the future, when it might be more difficult to resolve any differences.

Alexei and Piper carefully reviewed the drafts and asked questions about several of the more technical drafting points. With one minor modification, they agreed that the drafts reflected their intentions and then signed the final documents. Having successfully incorporated the venture, divided the ownership and issued stock to the founders, Alexei and Piper turned their attention to selecting the company's board of directors.

Forming and Working with the Board

A corporation is legally required to have a board of directors to protect the interests of the corporation and its equity holders. But there are other reasons to have an active board. A board of directors that brings together people with a variety of strengths and skills can be a valuable asset to a young company and contribute to its success by functioning as a strategic sounding board. Founders often find it challenging to keep an eye on the big picture while being continually concerned with day-to-day operational issues. Effective boards give independent, informed advice to management and challenge the chief executive officer (*CEO*), rather than act as a rubber stamp.

This chapter examines the benefits of having an independent and active board of directors and discusses the factors to consider in structuring the board and selecting its members. It also summarizes directors' legal responsibilities, which include duties of loyalty, good faith, and care. We discuss board compensation, outline the types of information that should be provided to directors, and suggest ways to make effective use of directors' time.

6.1 THE BENEFITS OF HAVING AN INDEPENDENT BOARD

Many startups have filled director positions with agreeable family members or personal friends, rather than establishing an active, outside, and truly independent board. Founders are often hesitant to give up any control of the company they created ("their baby"), fearing that they could be replaced as the firm's leaders or have their vision for the company supplanted by others. Entrepreneurs tend to dislike criticism and resent its sources. In fact, they may go so far as to expel anyone who questions their leadership abilities or experience even when the individual raising questions is merely relaying concerns expressed by potential partners, such as venture capitalists. An entrepreneur may feel uncomfortable revealing confidential information, financial or otherwise. CEOs of family businesses may be even more reluctant to invite outsiders into an enterprise where traditionally only family members have been involved. In addition, many CEOs think that outsiders will not understand their business as well as they do. They may feel that their business is unique and that no one else can assist effectively in long-range planning and strategy development. Founders also may not feel sufficiently organized to deal with an active board and wait before creating one.

In fact, the benefits of an independent board almost always greatly outweigh the drawbacks. Board members can provide a set of complementary skills for the CEO. A company is more likely to achieve its full potential when the CEO can draw on what often amounts to decades of other people's experience and wisdom. Independent directors give the CEO someone to answer to. They can provide a framework for control and discipline and be challenging and objective critics. Gathering and organizing the financial and other information required by an active board can serve as an internal check for the CEO. As Clayton Mathile, CEO of the IAMS pet food company, explained, "Your outside board can be your inside sparring partner who tests your strengths and weaknesses before you get to the main arena—the marketplace."[1]

Directors can fill the CEO's need for a mentor or a coach and give the CEO the emotional support needed for difficult decisions. As one CEO explained, "I need a person on the board with whom I can talk very frankly and not be fearful—someone on the board I can tell, 'I don't know.'"[2]

The board can help top management develop realistic long-range plans and strategies. If the prospective directors have been entrepreneurs, CEOs or venture capitalists in their own right, they are able to provide vision and insight that insiders cannot supply; they also lend an air of credibility to the venture and its value proposition. This credibility is particularly important when the enterprise is trying to raise funds. Board members often are part of valuable business and academic networks and can introduce the founders to potential investors, partners, customers, and advisors. In the case of family corporations, a board of directors with outside perspective and independence from family politics can ease the often difficult generational transitions.

6.2 SIZE OF THE BOARD AND FREQUENCY AND DURATION OF BOARD MEETINGS

The board of directors should be small enough to be accountable and to act as a deliberative body but large enough to carry out the necessary responsibilities. In the earliest stages of a new company, the board may consist of only the founder or founders. Once a company is fully operational, most CEOs find that between five and seven directors is a good, manageable size. Many venture-backed companies have five directors.

The outsiders should outnumber the insiders so the board can reap the benefit of the independent directors. Usually, no more than two insiders should sit on the board, although it is common for officers who are not board members to be invited to make presentations to the board and to sit in on certain board discussions of issues related to their areas of expertise.

The frequency of formal board meetings will be determined in part by how the CEO and board chair envision the role of the board. Boards of venture-capital-backed private companies often meet monthly. But if the board of a private company meets formally only to discuss major issues, less frequent meetings, perhaps quarterly, may be sufficient. Boards at larger companies tend to meet monthly.[3] Typically, regardless of the size of the company, the CEO should be in touch with each board member between the meetings and remember that directors do not like to be surprised at meetings in front of their peers.

The length and location of meetings can affect the quality of decision making. Some boards meet for several hours at a time. Others meet for an entire day, with a break for lunch, which facilitates informal discussions among members. The ideal meeting tends to last between three and five hours, which is long enough to accomplish the necessary work but not so long that the board members cannot continue to give their full attention.

In addition to attending meetings, most effective directors spend at least half a day preparing by examining materials sent to them in advance by the CEO. Also, the directors usually participate in informal discussions with the CEO for a few hours each quarter. They may also serve on committees. Thus, board work for a private-company board that meets quarterly comprises about eight days of a director's year.[4]

Sometimes board members will get together for several days at a time so that they can concentrate on strategic issues without being distracted by the day-to-day aspects of the business. For example, the Hartford financial services group holds yearly two-day off-site meetings with directors and management. Although off-site meetings can be valuable, they can be expensive and are often difficult to schedule because many directors have full-time jobs, such as running their own companies, and they cannot afford to be absent for so long.

6.3 TYPE OF REPRESENTATION DESIRED

There are at least two major aspects to consider when building an independent and active board. The first is the combination of functional skills needed to help the business run smoothly and to bring it to the next level of growth. The second is the mix of personalities and diversity of perspectives. Combining these components, both of which are essential to successfully run the company, is more an art than a science.[5]

Before selecting board members for a startup, the CEO must anticipate the needs of the corporation for the next several years. Questions to consider include the following:

➤ What is the company's value proposition?

➤ What is its competitive advantage? Is it sustainable?

➤ What demands will be placed on the company and its management team over the next few years?

➤ What factors would contribute to the success or failure of the company?

> How much technical expertise is needed to understand the company's products?

> Are changes in current regulations needed to foster the company's growth plans?

> What role does research and development play? Product development? Marketing? Customer service?

> Will the company need to partner with university researchers, industry players, or others to bring its products to market?

> How will the company obtain financing?

By evaluating the resources the company currently controls and anticipating its needs, the CEO will be better equipped to choose a board that will help unlock the company's inherent possibilities.

The Needed Skills

As the Hong Kong Exchanges and Clearing Limited's Corporate Governance Code and Corporate Governance Report states, "The board should have a balance of skills, experience, and diversity of perspectives appropriate to the requirements of the issuer's business."[6] Entrepreneurs need to assess their own strengths and weaknesses and work to fill the gaps with individuals possessing the missing talents. These talents should include industry experience, financial and marketing expertise, startup experience, and technical know-how. Although the ideal board member will be familiar with the product, market and any technologies that may be involved, the entrepreneur should strive to promote breadth and diversity on the board. "Diversity of board members can be achieved through consideration of a number of factors, including but not limited to gender, age, cultural and educational background, or professional experience."[7] Various studies show that companies with female board members generally earn higher returns on investment and returns on sales than all-male boards.[8] If the company is contemplating international expansion, it should consider adding directors who have such experience or who are from countries the firm views as key markets. In a family business, it may be a good idea to have at least one director who is of the same generation as the likely successor to the CEO so that, when the transition takes place, he or she will have a peer on the board.

Although outside representation is important to bring new insights to the company and maintain a truly independent board, the potential benefits of having company insiders on the board are many. Insiders often provide invaluable expertise and perspective in a specific area of management,[9] either as directors or as guests invited to attend the portions of board meetings dedicated to their areas of expertise. Such arrangements give the directors an opportunity to see members of the top management team in action, which can help with successor planning.

The entrepreneur should be wary of filling the board with individuals whose interests may not be aligned with the company's or to whom the company already has access. For example, the interests of the company's commercial banker may not be consistent with the best strategic planning for the company. Although family businesses commonly include corporate counsel or the founder's personal counsel on the board, the result may be the inadvertent waiver of the attorney-client privilege. It is often preferable to have company counsel just sit in on board meetings as an advisor. Consultants of all kinds should be considered carefully, especially when they were hired by the CEO, because they may not feel comfortable challenging the CEO for fear of losing their job. As a result, they are not always appropriate board members.

For companies with venture capital funding, the financing agreement will usually give the investors the right to elect one or more directors. Venture capitalists tend to be very involved and effective board members. They can also be a good source of introductions to other potential board members. As discussed in Chapter 13, under certain circumstances, such as a company's failure to meet its milestones, board control may shift to the investors.

Personality Mix and Board Structure

Individually, board members have no formal power; the board must act as a body. So it is important that the board function cohesively as a group, which means that the board members' personalities must be compatible. Board members need to respect each other. Although a diverse board is ideal, it is important to avoid creating a board that acts like a legislature, with each director focused on championing his or her own constituency. No one

From the **TRENCHES**

David Murdock was Dole Food Co.'s chair, CEO, and owner of 40% of the public company's stock. In 2013, he took the company private in a freeze-out transaction, for which he "primed the market" "by driving down Dole's stock price and undermining its validity as a measure of value." After concluding that Michael Carter, Dole's general counsel, chief operating officer, president and fellow board member, had engaged in fraudulent and manipulative practices to "ruthlessly" carry out Murdock's plans, the Delaware Court of Chancery held both men liable to the other shareholders for more than $148 million in damages for breaches of their duty of loyalty. Delaware Vice Chancellor J. Travis Laster characterized Murdock as "an old-school, my-way-or-the-highway controller, fixated on his authority and the power and privileges that came with it." During the trial, "Murdock testified that he was 'the boss' at Dole, and '[t]he boss does what he wants to do.'" After an outside director questioned Murdock, Murdock forced him off the board. According to Kevin LaCroix, executive vice president of RT ProExec, a management liability insurance intermediary, "The roadside is littered with the carcasses of companies that were headed up by similar domineering personalities."

Sources: In re Dole Food Co., Inc. Stockholder Litig., 2015 WL 5052214, C.A. No. 8703-VCL (Del. Ch. Aug. 27, 2015); Melissa Maleske, *3 Lessons from the Rise and Fall of Dole's GC*, Law360 (Aug. 31, 2015), http://www.law360.com/articles/696619.

person should so dominate the meetings as to preclude others from voicing their opinions. The board chair should be alert to such an exertion of power, including his or her own.

When selecting board members, the entrepreneur should consider the need for a board that is willing to take a hands-on approach to its job. Board members should include individuals with practical experience and business savvy, not just theoretical or technical expertise. At the same time, the board as a whole must understand the difference between inappropriately meddling with the company's management and maintaining a healthy relationship. The goal is to have a board that will be actively involved in the formulation of long-range planning and the selection of key officers, that will scrutinize the budget and actual results compared with plan, and that will question and, when necessary, revise key assumptions.

Several sources, including the National Association of Corporate Directors, the Business Roundtable and the American Bar

Association, provide guidance for creating an effective board and dividing labor among the directors.[10] For instance, it is often desirable to separate the roles of CEO and chair or to appoint a lead director.[11] Boards frequently set up committees to help the board accomplish its work. For example, many private companies set up audit committees consisting of only independent directors as well as compensation and nominating committees comprising solely or primarily independent directors. As discussed in Chapter 17, the Sarbanes-Oxley Act of 2002 (*SOX*), the New York Stock Exchange, and Nasdaq impose additional requirements on public and listed companies. Private companies, particularly those anticipating action that would require compliance with SOX— such as an initial public offering or acquisition by a public company—should consider selectively implementing the SOX mandates. We discuss other SOX requirements in Chapter 17.

6.4   THE RESPONSIBILITIES OF THE BOARD

Legally, the directors are fiduciaries who owe the corporation a duty of loyalty and a duty of care. Their obligations include the duty to act in good faith[12] and the "duty to disclose fully and fairly all material information within the board's control when it seeks shareholder action."[13] Breach of any of these duties can lead to multi-million-dollar liability. For example, in a landmark case, the directors of Trans Union Corp. were held personally liable for $23.5 million ($13.5 million in excess of their directors' and officers' liability insurance) because they approved the sale of company stock at $55 per share without first sufficiently informing themselves of the stock's intrinsic value, which the court decided was substantially higher.[14]

Although shareholder suits involving privately held companies are less common than public company suits, they do occur, particularly in the context of a majority shareholder that has allegedly violated the rights of the minority shareholders. One classic case involved United Savings and Loan Association, a company without actively traded shares. The majority shareholders of the association transferred their association shares to a new holding company, United Financial Corp., and continued to control the association through that holding company. The holding company then went public, and active trading commenced. The majority holders did not permit the association's minority shareholders to exchange their association shares for the holding company's shares. As a result, trading in the association's shares dried up, and the shares lost much of their value. The minority shareholders of the association successfully sued the majority shareholders who set up the holding company for breach of fiduciary duty. The court found that the transaction was not fair because the defendants had misappropriated to themselves the going-public value of the association, to the detriment of the minority shareholders.[15]

Duty of Loyalty and Good Faith

As a fiduciary of the corporation, a director must act in good faith in the best interests of the corporation and should avoid any suggestion of self-dealing. To satisfy their duty of loyalty, directors must subjugate their personal interests, financial and professional, to the interests of the corporation. For example, directors may not usurp an opportunity that is in the corporation's line of business for themselves without first disclosing the corporate opportunity to the other board members and obtaining the board's permission to pursue it.[16]

The duty of loyalty applies to decisions that concern the day-to-day operations of the company, such as executive compensation, as well as strategic decisions, such as a merger. Executive compensation should be set by disinterested directors with no personal interest in the decision. The acquisition of a corporate asset by a director or controlling shareholder should be approved by the disinterested directors.

In determining whether a board of directors is sufficiently disinterested in a decision, a relevant factor in some jurisdictions is whether a majority of the board members are outside directors. The fact that outside directors receive directors' fees but not salaries is viewed as heightening the likelihood that they will not be motivated by personal interest when making decisions affecting the company.

Sometimes it is impossible to have a disinterested vote of the directors. When that happens, all the board can do is to try its best to ensure that (1) the directors are informed, (2) they have access to independent advice, and (3) the transaction is fair to the company and all shareholders. If a transaction approved only by interested directors is challenged, the burden of proof is on them to show that the transaction was fair.

The duty of good faith, which is a component of the duty of loyalty, requires directors to at least make a good faith effort to fulfill their oversight responsibilities.[17] Directors may not passively stand by when they become aware of potentially troubling developments.

Duty of Care and Oversight

The duty of care requires board members to act with the level of care that a reasonably prudent person would use under similar circumstances. To that end, board members should make a reasonable effort to make informed decisions. In most jurisdictions, the general corporation law authorizes directors to rely on reports prepared by officers of the corporation or outside experts such as investment bankers and consultants. However, passive reliance on such reports when the situation warrants further inquiry can lead to an insufficiently informed decision. For example, the directors of SCM Corporation violated their fiduciary duty under New York law when they accepted without question investment bank Goldman Sachs' statement that the option prices for two of SCM businesses were "within the range of fair value," when the directors knew that the two businesses contributed more than half of the firm's total earnings but had been valued by Goldman at less than one-third of SCM's total purchase price.[18]

The duty of care includes a duty of oversight. Directors must use their best efforts to ensure that adequate procedures are in place to prevent violations of law.[19] Under the Sarbanes-Oxley Act, directors of public companies must establish procedures for receiving and acting upon anonymously submitted concerns about accounting and auditing issues.[20] The Business Roundtable also emphasizes the role of directors as monitors.[21] Although directors are not required to search out malfeasance, they must not ignore signs of impropriety.[22]

Limitations on Liability and Indemnification

Many states, including California and Delaware, have adopted legislation that permits shareholders to amend the certificate of incorporation to limit or abolish a director's liability for a breach of duty of care, except for clear cases of bad faith, willful misconduct, or fraud. This can provide a partial substitute for directors' and officers' liability insurance (*D&O insurance*), which is often too costly for private companies. In order to attract well-qualified directors, it is appropriate to reduce the potential liability a director faces by providing in the corporate charter and bylaws for both indemnification and the advancement of expenses to the maximum extent permitted by the law of the state where the corporation is incorporated. Corporations also often enter into agreements that provide for the advancing of legal fees should a director be sued. If it is ultimately found that indemnification is not warranted, the director should be required to reimburse the company for the monies advanced.

Under Delaware law, "grossly negligent conduct, without more, does not and cannot constitute a breach of the fiduciary duty to act in good faith."[23] Liability for failure to monitor requires bad faith, "indolence...so persistent that it could not be ascribed to anything other than a knowing decision not to even try to make sure the corporation's officers had developed and were implementing a prudent approach to ensuring law compliance."[24]

From the **TRENCHES**

Even though Abbott Laboratories, an Illinois corporation, had amended its charter to eliminate director liability for breaches of the duty of care, the directors were still potentially liable after Abbott was fined $100 million by the Food and Drug Administration and required to destroy inventory after six years of quality control violations. The court concluded that there was a "sustained and systematic failure of the board to exercise oversight" that established a lack of good faith. The directors knew that the FDA had repeatedly cited Abbott for FDA violations and yet took no steps to prevent or remedy the situation.

Source: In re Abbott Labs. Derivative S'holders Litig., 325 F.3d 795 (7th Cir. 2003).

Business Judgment Rule

Challenges to the decisions of a corporation's directors are reviewed using the *business judgment rule*, which protects directors from having their business decisions second-guessed. If the directors are disinterested and informed, the business judgment rule requires the plaintiff to prove that the directors were grossly negligent or acted in bad faith before liability for breach of the duty of care will attach. This high burden of proof protects directors from being liable merely for poor decisions.

The business judgment rule reflects the fact that all business decisions have inherent risk, and even reasonable decisions can have poor results. For example, the Delaware Court of Chancery held that the Citigroup directors' failure to anticipate the crash of the subprime mortgage market did not make the directors personally liable for Citigroup's multi-billion-dollar losses. As the court explained, "Business decision-makers must operate in the real world, with imperfect information, limited resources, and an uncertain future. To impose liability on directors for making a 'wrong' business decision would cripple their ability to earn returns for investors by taking business risks."[25]

6.5 COMPENSATION OF BOARD MEMBERS

Individuals usually do not serve on the board of directors for a private company for the monetary compensation alone, as it normally is not very large. Instead, many directors, especially successful entrepreneurs, may see an earlier version of themselves in one or more founders of the company and find it satisfying to advise and contribute to a new venture. There is also prestige associated with sitting on the board of various ventures.

Nonetheless, it is a good idea for entrepreneurs to provide at least some monetary compensation to directors to acknowledge their time and effort. This monetary compensation is more a token of appreciation than a payment to the directors for their time, which many small companies could not afford anyway. Several national executive search firms, including Spencer Stuart, Korn Ferry and Heidrick & Struggles, routinely publish data about trends in director compensation (broken down by company size) and board structure (such as average number of directors, committees, and frequency of meetings). These reports can provide a useful benchmark for an entrepreneur setting up a board for the first time. Typically, the company will also pay some, if not all, of the expenses related to the directors' attendance at meetings, including travel and meals.

As noted above, board work for a private-company board that meets quarterly usually comprises about eight working days of a director's year.[26] Based on the time commitment alone, board tangible compensation could reasonably be set at 2% to 3% of the CEO's annual salary. Yet many small companies cannot afford to pay that amount in cash.

Instead, many companies compensate directors with equity in the company, such as stock options or restricted stock grants. This form of compensation helps to align the directors' incentives with those of the shareholders. If a director (or his or her employer) already owns shares of the company, they may view their involvement on the board as a way to protect their financial investment and be willing to accept less in the way of tangible compensation.

In the more informal advisory board setting, entrepreneurs may not discuss monetary compensation at the outset. Although this approach may be appropriate initially, the entrepreneur should raise the issue before the advisor has made key introductions or performed significant work for the firm to avoid future misunderstandings with the advisor, who may be anticipating some monetary or other compensation.

6.6 TYPES OF INFORMATION DIRECTORS NEED

Before each board meeting, the CEO should ensure that the company provides the directors with an agenda of what will be discussed at the meeting and all relevant information so the directors can prepare effectively.

Agenda

A sample agenda for a board meeting is shown in Table 6.1.

TABLE 6.1   Agenda
XYZ ACADEMIC VENTURES, INC.
Board Meeting
Thursday, January 12, 2017, at 8:00 A.M.

Agenda
- I. Review of May 26, 2016 Board Minutes
- II. Engineering Update
- III. Executive Search
- IV. Food and Drug Administration Approval
  - Strategy
  - Time Lines
- V. Business Development
  - Company X
  - Company Y
  - University Z
- VI. Review Current Financials
- VII. Financing Plans
  - Action Items to Be Completed
  - Lease Line
- VIII. Patent Strategy Review
- IX. Competitive Update
- X. Approval of Option Grant

Information

Members of the top management team should carefully select the facts and figures to be supplied to the directors and present them in a clear and coherent fashion. Excessive amounts of data can bury important information, negating the value of providing the data in advance. The information packet should include general statistics showing how the company is doing so the directors can keep abreast of the company's overall performance and alert management to any potential problems.

Directors should also be given information about the longer-term trends of the company. This should include not just financial information but also information regarding the company's competitive position and organizational health,[27] including executive development and succession planning. Management should do its best to quantify the company's research and development plans and to set goals for the future.

Appendix 6.2—"Information to Be Provided to Directors"—sets forth a nonexclusive list of the types of information directors need to do their job effectively. It is available on this title's companion website at www.CengageBrain.com.

6.7 HOW TO MAKE THE MOST EFFECTIVE USE OF THE BOARD

Management expert Peter Drucker once called the board of directors "an impotent ceremonial and legal fiction."[28] This need not be the case.[29] By revisiting the most important functions of a board, the CEO and board chair (or lead outside director if the CEO is also the board chair) can refine the board's priorities. If the board is spending considerable time on company-related activities that do not fall into one of these categories, the CEO and the board members should take a closer look at that activity and ask, "How was it delegated to the board? Is it a task that could be more effectively or efficiently handled by management?"

A key function of the board is to develop and periodically reevaluate the company's long-term strategic plan[30] and operational implementation of that plan[31] in light of the firm's mission, purpose, and performance. Business author John Ward and others have suggested that directors focus on "big picture" questions such as:

➤ Is the company meeting its potential? Why or why not?

➤ Which is our priority, growth or profit? Or both? How do we attain our objectives?

➤ What are we learning as an organization? How can we learn more?

➤ Are there easy-exit experiments we could run to obtain more information about our market and our products and services? Do we learn from our failures?

➤ Are we empowering our employees and providing the tools, culture, and support they need to succeed?

> ➤ What risks are we currently taking? Do they serve our mission well?

> ➤ Are we prepared for political and economic changes that may come suddenly?

> ➤ How are we positioned for the next two decades? Can we adapt to a changing world?

> ➤ Are we responsible corporate citizens? How can we become more responsible?[32]

Another key responsibility of the board is to evaluate CEO performance on a regular basis (often annually) in light of the long-term strategy and the company's performance, that is, its operational implementation of that strategy. If the board is functioning effectively, the CEO will have a clear set of goals to work toward in managing the company and the freedom and autonomy to achieve these goals in a lawful manner with integrity. As Eugene Zuckert explained:

> [W]e sometimes say that we want a strong board that really runs the business. If pressed, we say that we don't really want the board to run the business because that's a full-time job, and we don't expect the board to operate full time or anything like it. And besides, if we had a board that was too powerful, we probably could not get the strong CEO that we needed.[33]

Directors may find it helpful to include key performance indicators (*KPIs*) in a work plan that supplements the strategic plan so there is a basis against which the CEO is evaluated. These might include not only financial results, such as sales, costs and profits, but also "product and service quality, customer [and employee] satisfaction, and operational excellence," what management guru Jeffrey Pfeffer calls "the not-so-glamorous but essential elements of business process implementation."[34] As a bottom line, the board should be asking, "Is the CEO a good leader?"[35] If the CEO is not treating any employee fairly, then the board will need to step in to ensure that the situation is properly addressed.

By considering the roles and responsibilities of the board and the CEO in this light, some of the tension that can exist between the CEO and the nonexecutive directors on the board is relieved but it is never eliminated entirely, because, as Richard C. Breeden, the former chair of the Securities and Exchange Commission and the court-appointed monitor of MCI-WorldCom, Inc. bankruptcy, explained:

> While the board and the CEO will usually work closely and harmoniously together to further the interests of the company, at times (such as in reviewing compensation issues or in succession planning) the board must be prepared to have an independent perspective at variance from the wishes of the CEO. Boards do not exist merely to rubber-stamp executive decisions, though historically some boards appear to have been unaware of this proposition.[36]

The directors should set the CEO's compensation for the coming year in light of both the executive's and the company's performance.[37] It is also critical for the board to engage in ongoing planning for CEO succession.[38] This requires sensitivity to the tendency of CEOs, especially founder-CEOs, to see themselves as indispensable to the business. One way to bring up what can be a touchy subject is to ask the CEO to consider, "Who should lead the company if you got hit by a bus on the way home tonight?"

Finally, just as the board should formally review the CEO's performance on a regular basis, it should also regularly review its own performance and the performance of all its members. The nominating or governance committee should take the results of these reviews into account when deciding whether to renominate an existing director and selecting new directors to fill vacancies.[39]

 # Putting It into **PRACTICE**

Alexei and Piper were painfully aware of their lack of experience in launching a new venture, so they hoped to find a third director who could not only act as coach and adviser but also bring industry connections, technical expertise, business experience, sound judgment, assistance in predicting future market trends, and, most important, a different perspective from theirs. When Alexei asked Sarah Crawford, counsel for their company Genesist, Inc., whether she had any suggestions, Sarah recommended Keith Tinsley, the former head of a 3D printing research team that had developed specialized software for 3D printing that increased

(continued)

the printing speed by nearly 25%. The major 3D printing manufacturers had recognized the benefits of Keith's software and begun contacting him for advice on how to adapt their manufacturing processes to use his time-saving code. Keith subsequently left the company for which he had worked to start his own company, FastPrint Consulting, which provided 3D printing consulting services. The company had gone public in 2012. Most recently, Keith had taken an advisory role with a company that was trying to develop noncommercial 3D printers for home use. Sarah said that her firm had handled the initial public offering for FastPrint but was not representing the new venture.

Before meeting Keith, Alexei wanted to finalize with Sarah the compensation that the directors would receive for their service. Given the small size of the company and the fact that it might take some time to generate positive cash flow, Sarah suggested that nonemployee directors' compensation reflect an investment in the future of the company. Alexei and Piper agreed. They settled on a package made up of stock options for each year of service and $900 for each board meeting attended. In addition, the company would purchase a D&O liability insurance policy with $3 million of coverage. Genesist's charter already limited directors' liability and the bylaws provided mandatory indemnification and the advancement of expenses to the maximum extent the law allowed.

Sarah then arranged a lunch meeting at Aqua, just up from The Embarcadero in San Francisco, so Alexei and Piper could meet Keith. The meeting went well. Keith was friendly but not afraid to speak his mind. While highlighting the difficulty of taking any new technology to market, Keith was impressed with Alexei's research and its potential for widespread use. He was also enthusiastic about the prospect of helping Alexei and Piper navigate the often difficult waters that had to be crossed to transform a dream into an industry leader.

Alexei and Piper shared their impressions of Keith on the drive back to their office and both readily agreed that Keith would be a great addition to the team. Keith's prior and current experience well positioned him to predict the direction of the 3D manufacturing industry. In addition, his contacts in the industry, particularly with the larger players, would be invaluable. Alexei then called Keith, explained the directors' compensation structure, and asked whether he would be willing to serve as a director. Keith responded with a hearty, "Absolutely."

Even though Keith brought a wealth of entrepreneurial experience to the boardroom, Genesist still needed someone with a background in corporate accounting to help the company avoid financial missteps and maintain a cash flow position that would be attractive to potential investors. Piper immediately thought of her former accounting professor Sue Quinn. Prior to joining the faculty at Duke University, Sue had

(continued)

spent 14 years as CFO of Specialized Manufacture, a large Canadian producer of custom component parts for high-end semiconductor manufacturers. A certified public accountant in both Canada and the United States, Sue had obtained a BA in economics from the University of Waterloo in 1977 and an MBA from the Sauder School of Business at the University of British Columbia in 1983. She was a well-respected and insightful commentator on issues related to accounting and currently served on the board of directors of Swirl Chips, a U.S. semiconductor manufacturer.

Piper had maintained regular contact with Sue after graduating, keeping her apprised of her career developments, including the founding of Genesist. When Piper suggested her, Alexei was excited by the prospect of having such a prominent figure on the company's board. He agreed that Sue would give Genesist's financial reports instant credibility in the eyes of the marketplace, including potential business partners and stakeholders. Happy to assist her former student, Sue readily accepted the invitation to become a Genesist director under the same terms given to Keith.

Having filled the board, Alexei and Piper turned their attention to their biggest challenge yet—raising money to launch their venture.

Raising Money and Securities Regulation

R aising capital for a new or expanding early-stage company with unknown management and no track record may be one of the greatest challenges facing the entrepreneur. It is likely that traditional loans from commercial banks will be unavailable, available only on unacceptable terms, or insufficient for the new company's needs. For these reasons, entrepreneurs often must seek alternative funding sources.

This chapter discusses the advantages and disadvantages of several major alternatives: self-financing and credit from customers and financial institutions; the sale of stock, convertible notes or other debt instruments to individual investors, including "friends and family" and angel investors; venture capital financings; strategic alliances and joint ventures; nondilutive private money grants; and government financing programs. We also briefly discuss the use of equity and debt "crowdfunding" online platforms and placement agents. The chapter then outlines the steps involved in pitching to investors, including preparation of the business plan, and describes common terms in sales of equity and convertible debt. We conclude with a summary of federal and state securities laws that must be complied with when issuing securities. Ignorance of these laws is no defense. As Judge Frank Easterbrook of the U.S. Court of Appeals for the Seventh Circuit famously remarked: "No one with half a brain can offer 'an opportunity to invest in our company' without knowing that there is a regulatory jungle out there."[1]

Chapter 12 discusses borrowing alternatives and issues raised by loan agreements, as well as bankruptcy; Chapter 13 discusses venture capital in detail; and Chapters 16 and 17 discuss the securities laws applicable to business combinations and to public companies, respectively.

7.1   SOURCES OF FUNDS

Each source of funding has advantages and disadvantages, and more than one source of funding may be suitable for a given company. Before making a final decision on which sources to pursue, entrepreneurs should consider the degree of control over the company they wish to retain, the amount of equity dilution (decrease in ownership percentage) they are willing to bear, how long it is likely to take before the company is cash-flow positive, whether the company would benefit from investor representation on the board of directors or involvement in certain aspects of the company's day-to-day business, the available exemptions from registration with the Securities and Exchange Commission (*SEC*) and state securities regulators, and the extent to which a more seasoned company may be interested in a joint venture or other form of strategic alliance with the startup.

One of the most difficult decisions for the aspiring entrepreneur is whether to give up autonomy in exchange for the necessary funding for the startup. Often the entrepreneur has little choice. Losing control of the company may be a prerequisite to financing the cash-starved emerging business. Astute entrepreneurs understand the importance of taking into account not only their slice of the pie but also the size of the pie itself. Having a minority position in a well-financed startup is far preferable to being firmly in control of a venture that never gets traction because it was underfinanced.

Self-Financing and Credit from Customers and Financial Institutions

Some businesses may be able to self-finance—that is, to fund their growth through utilization of their own net income and careful management of their cash resources. This is sometimes called "bootstrapping." For example, a business that sells goods or services may be able to obtain payment within 15 days of shipment rather than the more customary 30 or 45 days. The business may even be able to structure contracts with its customers to require advance payments or deposits, although this feature may require price discounts.

Startups seeking to raise a relatively small amount of money (typically only a few hundred thousand dollars or less) to develop consumer products that can be brought to market relatively quickly may be able to use online product "crowdfunding" platforms to find customers who are willing to fund product development by preordering products, as opposed to making an equity or debt investment. Well-known platforms include Kickstarter and Indiegogo. Product platforms tend not to be useful to companies that will be selling products to other businesses, that are developing complex products with a long research and development time frame, or that have large capital needs. Crowdfunding is discussed in more detail below.

In some cases, a business can negotiate favorable trade credit arrangements with its suppliers whereby the suppliers will not require payment until 60 or 90 days after a shipment is received. In addition, the business may be able to eliminate unnecessary expenses, reduce inventories, or improve inventory turnover. To conserve working capital, an entrepreneur may lease equipment rather than purchase it.

Sometimes a finance company will lend money even to a young company if it has current accounts receivable or readily saleable inventory. The lender takes a security interest in the accounts receivable and inventory, which serve as collateral; the lender has a right to keep or sell the collateral if the loan is not repaid. (We discuss secured borrowing more fully in Chapter 12.) Although entrepreneurs have been known to fund startups with credit card debt, that is rarely sufficient. Moreover, most credit card interest rates are prohibitively high, often 18% to 22%.

Advantages The main advantage of self-financing is that the entrepreneur does not have to share control or the equity of the business. The contractual restrictions and affirmative covenants under an equipment lease, for example, may be less restrictive than the rights granted to holders of preferred stock. An entrepreneur who self-finances will also save time that would otherwise be devoted to vetting and meeting with investors. Finally, if the company self-finances by generating revenue from paying customers, it may make itself more attractive to other funding sources down the road when its capital needs are greater.

Disadvantages Self-financing alone may not generate sufficient funds to cover salaries and other overhead expenses. Customers may object to making advance payments or deposits. Obtaining favorable trade credit terms is more difficult for a new enterprise than for an established business. Lenders and landlords may be more inclined to require personal guarantees from the principal shareholders of a self-financed company than one that has obtained a substantial amount of equity capital from professional investors. Personal guarantees put the guarantor's personal assets at risk (to the extent set forth in the guaranty).

Experience shows that it is difficult to make self-financing work. Self-financing should be attempted only if the company has made realistic projections demonstrating that it can be done successfully.

"Friends and Family"

Particularly in the earliest stages of a company's development, the entrepreneur may want to borrow money from or sell equity in the company to family and friends.

Advantages "Friends and family" financing is often a relatively cheap and quick source of seed capital. It is usually preferable when the management team wants to maintain control and manage the day-to-day business of the enterprise without input from its investors. Friends and family are often as interested in supporting the entrepreneur based on their personal relationship with him or her as they are in a return on their investment, and thus seldom drive a hard bargain in terms of financing terms. Friends and family usually do not seek an active role in the business, board representation, or any other special investor rights.

Disadvantages Friends and family often do not bring any expertise or other strategic value to the company beyond the seed capital they provide. They also are usually unable to invest significant amounts of money, thus providing only a temporary source of growth capital until the business is developed enough to obtain other sources of financing. Finally, the entrepreneur must always consider the risk of harming important personal relationships that is inherent in any financial transaction between friends or family members.

To avoid misunderstandings and to ensure the terms of friends and family financing are not problematic to future sources of financing, an entrepreneur considering friends and family financing should ensure that the documentation relating to the financing is prepared by an experienced securities attorney, just as it would be for a venture capital financing. In addition, as tempting as it may be, entrepreneurs should be careful to refrain from making any commitments or promises to friends and family with regard to their investment outside of the legal documentation.

Angel Investors

Private sales of debt or equity securities directly to individual investors who do not fall into the category of "friends and family" (commonly called *angel investors* or *angels*) may be an appropriate way to raise funds, especially if only modest amounts of money are required and the entrepreneur is acquainted with the persons interested in investing in the startup.

Advantages Angel financing can be a relatively quick source of seed capital. It is usually preferable when the management team wants to maintain control and manage the day-to-day business of the enterprise without significant input from the investors, but wants to raise more capital and obtain more strategic value from the company's investors than "friends and family" financing would provide. Individual angel investors often do not seek an active role in the business. Many angel investors do not insist on board representation or significant approval rights. However, some angel investor groups, such as the Band of Angels and the Angels'

From the **TRENCHES**

Brad Jendersee left Pfizer to form Arterial Vascular Engineering (*AVE*), a company that manufactures and sells coronary arterial stents (metal prostheses designed to hold arteries open) and balloon angioplasty catheters. Because of control and dilution concerns, Jendersee chose not to pursue venture capital financing. Instead, he financed AVE with money from angel investors, many of whom were heart surgeons who understood the need for the company's products. The average price paid by the angels was less than $1 per share. Five years later, AVE went public at a price of $21 per share. The value of the company at $21 per share was $600 million. Jendersee and his two cofounders together owned approximately 25% of AVE's stock at the time of the public offering. Medtronic, Inc., later bought AVE for more than $3 billion.

Forum, operate much more like venture capital funds than typical individual angel investors.

If the startup is a corporation, offerings to angel investors usually take the form of either convertible promissory notes or preferred stock, with the company's founders holding shares of common stock. If the startup is a limited partnership or a limited liability company, convertible promissory notes or equity instruments comparable to preferred stock are often used. (We discussed factors to consider when choosing an appropriate form of business entity in Chapter 4.) The balance of this chapter assumes that the startup is a corporation.

Disadvantages Although certain angel investors bring expertise, talent and connections to the table that are as deep as any top-tier venture capital firm, most do not. Angel investors are also usually unwilling to invest as much money as a venture capital firm would invest and, unlike venture capital funds, they may not have sufficient funds to participate in future rounds of company financing.

Venture Capital Funds and Nontraditional Venture Investors

Venture capital funds are professional investment vehicles formed specifically for investing in new or developing businesses. In deciding whether to invest, venture capital firms differ widely in their preferred technologies, products, industries, size of investment, and stage of development of the company in which the investment is made. In addition, nontraditional venture investors, such as family offices, hedge funds and large money managers, are increasingly participating in late stage financings of startup companies, due in large part to many startup companies delaying decisions to go public.

Venture capitalists are generally not interested in investing in a venture unless the expected return is in the range of at least 40% compounded annually. This is because venture funds are expected to produce at least a 20% compounded annual return for their investors, and not all investments will turn out to be winners. In addition, the venture capitalist must feel that an exit path is likely to be available on attractive terms within the foreseeable future, because most venture capitalists invest through funds with only a 10-year life. An *exit path* is a way for investors to get their money back without liquidating the company, such as through the sale of the company or through an initial public offering of the company's securities.

Advantages   Venture capital firms often have the resources to provide the funds needed to finance research and development and growth in multiple rounds of financing. Many venture capital

From the **TRENCHES**

In February 2004, Mark Zuckerberg, Dustin Moskovitz, Chris Hughes, and Eduardo Saverin launched what is now known as Facebook from their Harvard University dorm room. Facebook received its earliest funding from angel and venture capital funds, including $500,000 in 2004 from angel investor Peter Thiel; $12.7 million in 2005 from Thiel and venture capital firm Accel Partners (reportedly resulting in a valuation of $87.5 million); and $27.5 million in 2006 from Thiel, Accel, and venture capital investors Greylock Partners and Meritech (reportedly resulting in a valuation of approximately $500 million). Facebook went public in May 2012. Its market capitalization was approximately $316 billion as of mid-March 2016 and it had over 1 billion daily active users on average for December 2015.

Sources: JP Mangalindan, *Timeline: Where Facebook Got Its Funding*, FORTUNE (Jan. 11, 2011), http://fortune.com/2011/01/11/timeline-where-facebook-got-its-funding/; Facebook Key Statistics, Y CHARTS, https://ycharts.com/companies/FB/key_stats (updated as of Mar. 16, 2016).

firms work closely with young companies and can assist with formulating business strategy, recruiting additional management talent, assembling a board of directors, and providing introductions in the financial community. They are often able to recommend strategies and approaches that make the company more profitable than it would otherwise be.

Disadvantages Venture capitalists can be expected to negotiate the price paid for equity (or, in the case of a convertible note financing, the conversion cap and discount, which are both discussed below), which may result in greater dilution to the founders than a friends and family or even an angel financing. In addition, most venture capitalists insist on sharing in the control of the company. They usually will want the right to have one or more representatives on the board of directors. If a founder-CEO misses milestones or otherwise fails to perform as expected, the board may be able to force that person to step down. As detailed in Chapter 13, venture capitalists often require a variety of other rights, including veto power over certain important corporate matters and the right to participate in future company financings.

Strategic Alliances and Joint Ventures

A less common source of financing is a collaborative arrangement between a startup and an established company that has complementary needs or objectives. In a joint venture or other form of strategic alliance, the parties commit themselves to sharing resources, facilities or information, as well as the risks and rewards that may accrue from the alliance.

Strategic alliances can take many forms. A strategic alliance may be structured as a joint venture to complete a specific project, such as an automated production line. It may be a minority investment in the young company by the established company, either directly or through the creation of a separate joint venture entity. Alternatively, an established company may agree to fund a young company's research costs in return for the right to market or exploit the product or technology developed. If both parties are required to conduct extensive research, the alliance will often provide that the parties may cross-license each other's technology. With a strategic alliance, the parties generally must accept a substantial loss in autonomy, at least with respect to the project under joint development.

A strategic alliance may be used in any situation in which one party has an essential technology or resource that the other party does not have and cannot readily obtain. For example, if an undercapitalized company is developing a technology that has promising applications in an established company's business, the two companies may agree to collaborate. The established company may provide both financing and access to personnel, equipment, and certain preexisting and future technologies. The young company may correspondingly provide access to its personnel and its preexisting and future technologies.

Advantages   A strategic alliance may provide a young company with less costly financing than a venture capital investor. This advantage is most pronounced when the established company anticipates some synergistic benefit to its existing business from exploiting the new technology. This synergy may cause the established company to place a higher value on the startup than a pure financial investor, such as a venture capitalist, would place on the young company. Not only does the young company often benefit from the more mature company's technical and marketing expertise, but it may earn more from the product through a strategic alliance than it would from a licensing agreement.

Disadvantages   One difficulty with almost any strategic alliance is that the two companies will have to cooperate and agree on the development, marketing and ultimate ownership of a product, a situation that can give rise to management problems. The respective management teams may be unwilling to give up their autonomy to the extent necessary for success. Furthermore, because two parallel management groups will be trying to control the same personnel, it may be difficult to manage the alliance effectively without creating a super-management group. At a minimum, it is critical to align incentives for all participants.

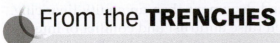
From the **TRENCHES**

Pfizer and other established pharmaceutical companies in the United States and Europe have formed pharmaceutical public-private partnerships with universities and their academic researchers to bridge what Arti K. Rai et al. called the "valley of death" that "separates 'upstream research on promising genes, proteins, and biological pathways' by government-funded academic researchers from 'downstream drug candidates' outside firms fund in hopes of commercializing the researchers' discoveries." Success requires trust-building and other forms of relational governance, long-form contracting, properly aligned incentives, and transparency as well as an intellectual property regime that (1) facilitates "new upstream discoveries and the development of tools of broad application by academic researchers"; (2) gives "the pharmaceutical firms funding commercialization the robust returns necessary to justify the expense of developing and testing multiple compounds and biologics, knowing that only about fifteen percent will ever move past clinical trials to governmental approval"; and (3) provides "university researchers adequate incentives to justify their participation in the commercialization process."

Sources: Arti K. Rai et al., *Pathways Across the Valley of Death: Novel Intellectual Property Strategies for Accelerated Drug Discovery*, 8 Yale J. Health Pol'y L. & Ethics 1, 4 (2008); Constance E. Bagley & Christina D. Tvarnø, *Pharmaceutical Public-Private Partnerships: Moving from the Bench to the Bedside*, 4 Harv. Bus. L. Rev. 373, 386–87 (2014); Constance E. Bagley & Christina D. Tvarnø, *Promoting "Academic Entrepreneurship" in Europe and the United States: Creating an Intellectual Property Regime to Facilitate the Efficient Transfer of Knowledge from the Lab to the Patient*, 26 Duke J. Comp. & Int'l L. 1, 12, 15 (2015).

Another problem with a strategic alliance is that each party may be liable for the other party's wrongdoing. For example, if one company supplies a technology that takes advantage of a third party's trade secret, the other company will be liable for its use of the misappropriated information, regardless of its intent. This risk can be reduced if each party makes certain representations and warranties, and enters into indemnity agreements, regarding the technology it will supply. The established company will usually want absolute representations and warranties concerning infringements of other parties' intellectual property rights. Nevertheless, it may be possible to get the established company to accept a qualified representation and warranty that "to the best of Party A's knowledge" there is no violation of others' intellectual property rights.

Because strategic alliances vary so much in their structure and terms, they can be more expensive, time-consuming, and complicated to negotiate and document than an equity financing. Strategic alliances also often raise antitrust and conflict of interest concerns. The entrepreneur must consider carefully whether a change of strategic direction or personnel at the established company could harm the strategic alliance and thus the young company. The entrepreneur should consult experienced legal counsel before talking with competitors or entering into a joint venture or other form of strategic alliance.

Nondilutive Private Grant Money

Some startups may be eligible for grants or funding from sources that do not require equity in exchange for capital. Examples include prize money from startup pitch competitions (such as TechCrunch Disrupt's Startup Battlefield $50,000 prize), university and business school contests (including the BASES $100K Startup Challenge at Stanford and the $100K Competition at MIT), as well as programs coordinated by startup incubators or accelerators (such as MassChallenge, which awards $3 million in prize money annually to startup companies through its accelerator program). Some private foundations and private companies also offer small grants to entrepreneurs who meet particular eligibility criteria.

Advantages Grant money gives the company funding without diluting the founders' equity stake in the company. Grants that are associated with well-known competitions also may provide prestige or credibility. Some, but not all, competitions provide mentors or other experts that offer some of the same expertise a company could expect from an experienced investor, albeit usually on a smaller scale.

Disadvantages Only certain startups are eligible for grant money from any given competition, and it can be time-consuming to research the possibilities and compete for them. Funding from grants is usually in the $5,000 to $100,000 range and is typically a one-time deal, so it is generally insufficient for a company's ongoing capital needs.

Government Financing Programs

A variety of grants, loans, and subsidies for small businesses are available from the federal government and some state and local governments. For example, the Minority Business Development Agency, which is an agency of the U.S. Department of Commerce, provides grant opportunities for businesses majority-owned by women or minorities. (More information is available at www .mbda.gov.) The U.S. Department of Energy (*DOE*) has invested more than $31 billion to support a wide range of clean energy and technology projects. These investments were made primarily in the form of grants, loans and tax incentives channeled to companies for U.S.-based projects at all stages, from research and development (*R&D*) to demonstration to commercialization. The DOE and other federal agencies have continued to fund clean energy and energy efficiency projects.

Advantages Government grants provide nondilutive financing, and hundreds of companies have secured vital support for advancing their technology to market. Obtaining government financing also can also help companies attract additional private funding. Further, government loans are often issued at favorable interest rates to companies ready to commercialize technology that has already been proven at the pilot and demonstration stages but may still be considered too "high risk" for private commercial lenders.

Disadvantages The government application process can be highly competitive and time intensive, and it often requires granting the government certain rights (e.g., the government may be entitled to certain rights to intellectual property developed with grant funds).

In contrast with angel or venture investing, government funding is generally restricted to expenditures relating to specific projects (rather than use for general operations or expansion), and it often must be matched (called the *company's cost-share*) by non-federal sources of funds. Companies generally provide cost-share through revenue generated by existing operations, an equity contribution, or, if available, state and local grant funds.

The government generally does not accept unsolicited propo-sals but rather issues "funding opportunity announcements" or "solicitations" in specific technology areas. (A database of current opportunities is available at www.grants.gov.)

7.2 USING ONLINE "CROWDFUNDING" PLATFORMS AND PLACEMENT AGENTS

Sometimes startups will use online "crowdfunding" platforms to find private equity or debt investors. More seasoned firms may hire placement agents.

Online "Crowdfunding" Platforms

A variety of online platforms provide an attractive alternative for a startup having difficulty locating equity or debt investors on its own. By providing a way for investors and founders to meet, these platforms may also save the company the time and effort of multiple investor meetings, enabling the management team to focus more on the company's business.

Platforms usually charge a fee, typically a percentage of the proceeds the company raises in the proposed financing. The plat-form may require exclusivity, thereby requiring the company to pay the platform a fee even if the platform is not successful raising money and the company ultimately raises capital elsewhere.

Many investors participating in these platforms tend to be angel investors who cannot individually invest large sums of money. As a result, particularly when using a "crowdfunding" plat-form, companies may find that they need to raise capital from a substantial number of investors to achieve their capital needs. Having a large number of investors can make subsequent transac-tions or shareholder votes more challenging. In addition, if a com-pany (1) has a class of equity securities (other than exempted securities) that is held of record by either (a) 2,000 persons or (b) 500 persons that are not accredited investors and (2) has assets exceeding $10 million, then it will have to register its stock under the Securities Exchange Act of 1934, a very time-consuming and expensive process. Companies intending to raise funds through a crowdfunding platform should seek the guidance of experienced counsel to develop transaction terms that minimize these challenges going forward.

Placement Agents

Sometimes an entrepreneur will engage a broker-dealer as a placement agent to help raise money from individual or institutional investors. A *placement agent* distributes a document (called a private placement memorandum) describing the company and the offering to suitable persons and assists in the private sale of securities. Placement agents are typically used, if at all, in later-stage rounds of financing, such as bridge financings expected to fund the company until its sale or initial public offering. Commissions for placement agents are negotiable and commonly range from 7% to as high as 15% of the amount raised. The commissions often are payable in cash or a combination of cash and equity securities of the company.

Before signing an engagement letter or otherwise making any commitments to a placement agent, entrepreneurs need to do their due diligence. First, the entrepreneur should check the placement agent's references carefully and insist on speaking with a few companies for which the agent has raised capital successfully. In most cases, the entrepreneur should ensure that the placement agent is licensed as a broker-dealer with the Securities and Exchange Commission (*SEC*), the Financial Industry Regulatory Authority (*FINRA*), and any applicable state authorities. The entrepreneur should ask how the placement agent will be making contacts with potential investors. In particular, the entrepreneur should ensure that the placement agent will be calling upon only investors with whom the agent or the company has a substantial preexisting relationship, or else the solicitation could violate the federal securities laws.

Placement agents typically require the company to sign an engagement letter prior to commencement of their services. These letters, which are drafted by the placement agent, set forth the financial terms of the engagement and typically provide for indemnification and limitation of liability of the placement agent. These letters also usually contain a "tail" provision that gives the placement agent the right to be paid for a financing occurring within a specified period of time after the placement agent's services are terminated by the company. These letters are often negotiable, so it is crucial that the entrepreneur use experienced legal counsel to review and assist with the negotiation of any placement agent engagement letter.

7.3 PITCHING TO INVESTORS

Entrepreneurs use various techniques to attract investors.

The Business Plan

A startup's success in attracting funds is determined in part by the care and thought the entrepreneur demonstrates in preparing a business plan[2] or pitch deck (discussed in Chapter 13) and presenting it to potential investors. The entrepreneur and his or her colleagues must effectively communicate the nature of the company and its business, markets, and technology; the qualifications of the key members of the management team; the size of the market that may be addressed by the company's products; the financial goals of the venture; the amount of capital required to achieve these goals; and, in detail, how the required capital will be spent over time. The business plan should also include such information as the competition, the barriers to entry, and any research-based projections. Preparation of a formal business plan will help the initial management team focus its planning efforts and will offer its members the opportunity to discuss goals and set appropriate milestones. Once in place, the business plan will guide management and enable it to measure the company's progress.

When preparing the business plan, the entrepreneur should take care to include all material information about the company, its management and the risks of the investment, because federal and state securities laws prohibit the sale of securities through the use of any misleading or inaccurate information, even if that information is only in a business plan. The business plan should describe all the assumptions on which its projections are based, and it should contain only those projections for which management has a reasonable basis. In addition to mentioning the strengths of the enterprise and its products, it is important to point out any material risks or weaknesses. For example, the product may still be in the development stage; there may be a shortage of a raw material or component required for its manufacture; or another company may produce or be able to produce a competing product. It is important to disclose such facts. Often the entrepreneurs are the only ones who really know these details, and they should volunteer such information to the lawyers or other persons preparing or reviewing the business plan.

The Private Placement Memorandum

Sometimes a company seeking funding through the sale of securities may wish to prepare a more formal offering document (usually called a *private placement memorandum*), especially when offering securities to less sophisticated investors. Although a private placement memorandum is both a selling document and a disclosure document, its primary purpose is to disclose both the benefits and the risks of the investment and to disclose all material information regarding the company, in keeping with the company's obligations under the federal and state securities laws. Consequently, the memorandum may not be as upbeat as the entrepreneur might like.

The content of the memorandum will be determined by the particular exemption from federal securities registration requirements applicable to the offering. Audited financial statements may be required for some offerings. State securities laws may also influence the content and format of a private placement memorandum. Because laws requiring disclosure are technical in nature, the entrepreneur should always consult with an experienced securities attorney before preparing the private placement memorandum and request that the attorney review drafts of it.

In many circumstances, a private placement memorandum is not technically required. Private placement memoranda are not typically used in a venture capital financing or in an angel round when the company already has a direct relationship with the investor. They are often used by placement agents, however. Even if not required by the state or federal securities laws relating to the registration or qualification of securities, however, a company must disclose all material information and risks associated with the enterprise in a business plan, in a private placement memorandum, or in the legal documents pertaining to the financing. Under the antifraud provisions of the federal and state securities laws (which apply even to offerings exempt from registration, qualification, or any other requirement for approval by a federal or state authority), a company is liable if, in connection with the offer or sale of securities, it either makes an untrue statement of a material fact or makes a misleading statement by omitting a material fact. By explaining the company's business and management and the risks of the investment in writing, the entrepreneur can avoid a swearing contest later in court about what oral statements were made to the investor.

7.4   TYPES OF INVESTMENT SECURITIES

As discussed in Chapter 4, many businesses operate as corporations because of their flexibility and limited liability. The investors in a corporation may own shares of one or more classes of stock, and they may also purchase certain debt securities.

Often the type of security to be issued will be determined by the investor. Most investors will desire to purchase preferred stock or some type of convertible debt instrument, such as a promissory note, that can be converted into stock. Some will want *warrants* (options to acquire stock) or at least a right of first refusal to purchase any new securities that may be issued by the company. Most investors will require the company to make extensive representations and warranties about itself in a stock (or note) purchase agreement, and some investments will be conditioned on certain corporate changes, such as expansion of the board of directors or the hiring or resignation of certain key persons.

Generally, investors have greater bargaining power than entrepreneurs because there are more startups competing for funds than investors looking for deals. Investors are also typically more familiar than entrepreneurs with the form and substance of a financing and the points that are typically open to negotiation. The percentage of voting power to be acquired by the investors and the price per share are based on the investors' valuation of the company. The extent of board representation granted to the investor, the type of security purchased, and the rights, preferences, privileges and restrictions afforded to the securities to be purchased are all negotiable. Thus, the entrepreneur needs to know as much as possible about the way a financing works before commencing negotiations. In addition, the entrepreneur should identify the acceptable level of *dilution* (i.e., the amount by which the founders' percentage interests in the company will be reduced); learn the extent to which the principals desire to retain, or relinquish, management and control of the enterprise; identify those persons who will be directors and officers of the corporation; and designate the corporation's accountants, lawyers, bankers, and other advisors.

After the founders and investors reach agreement on the terms of the securities and the investment, these terms are usually memorialized in a term sheet, particularly in equity financings. The *term sheet* allows the parties to agree on the principal terms of the investment before the lawyers proceed to draft a stock (or note) purchase agreement and any necessary amendment to the corporate charter. However, even though the term sheet is designed to be easy for a businessperson to understand, it is important to involve experienced securities counsel in the review and negotiation of the term sheet to ensure that the proposed terms do not present a substantial conflict with the company's existing financing terms and to help management obtain the best terms reasonably available to the company.

Convertible Promissory Notes

Many early-stage companies use convertible debt for their initial fundraising. This section identifies and explains the basic terms of convertible notes commonly used for a startup's initial financing.

A *convertible promissory note* is an instrument with debt-like features that is designed to convert into the company's common or preferred stock in certain circumstances. The holder has the right to be paid back principal plus interest within a stated period of time, unless the holder elects to convert the notes to stock (commonly at a specified discount from the price paid by the equity investors in the next financing round). For most investors, the goal is to convert the note into equity of the company, not to simply get back the principal plus interest. A few variations on convertible notes have recently been introduced, including Y Combinator's "SAFE," the Founder Institute's "convertible equity" and 500 Startups' "KISS," which contain many of the same terms but are designed to be permanent equity, and thus do not have a maturity date.

Principal Amount   The *principal amount* (*face amount*) of an investor's note will typically be equal to the amount of cash invested by the noteholder.

Interest Rate   Usually convertible notes will accrue interest until they have converted or are repaid in full. Interest may be either compounding or simple. Notes may specify that accrued interest can either be repaid in connection with a conversion event, or can be converted into additional shares on the same terms as the principal is converting. (Although low rates of interest between 6% and 8% are common, non-interest-bearing notes are not. There may be adverse accounting and tax consequences if notes are not interest-bearing.) Ultimately, the interest rate is one factor in the investor's return model and should be negotiated as part of the overall economics of the deal.

Maturity Date   The *maturity date* is the date on which the obligation to repay the debt "comes due." Setting the maturity date is a way to set expectations for investors as to the likely outside date for closing the next equity round, so in general a later maturity date is better for the company. Maturity dates vary, but most convertible notes become due not more than two years after issuance. However, notes may include flexible repayment terms that require the holders of a majority of the outstanding principal amount of notes to request repayment before the payment is actually due, or that allow the majority holders to elect to receive stock in lieu of repayment.

When setting the term of promissory notes, entrepreneurs need to ensure they give themselves sufficient "runway" so they have adequate funds (either internally generated or likely to be provided in future financing rounds) to pay off any unconverted notes by the due date. In a worst-case situation, the noteholders could force the company into involuntary bankruptcy if the notes are not paid when due. Because debt must be paid in full before anything is available to the equity holders in bankruptcy, equity can be severely diluted or even wiped out in bankruptcy. In such a case, the noteholders could end up owning all of the assets of the company.

Conversion Terms   The conversion terms of convertible notes typically get the most attention from companies and investors alike. The baseline mechanic is that the principal amount of the notes will automatically convert into shares of the company's capital stock in connection with the company's next round of equity financing. This mechanic is customarily further defined in three main ways:

1. *Qualified Financing.* In most cases an equity financing will trigger an automatic conversion as long as it meets the negotiated definition of a "qualified" financing, which is typically set by reference to a minimum amount of new cash that is raised in the equity financing. The primary goal of setting this floor is to protect the noteholders from having their notes converted to equity in a financing that leaves the company inadequately capitalized. The floor also ensures that the equity financing causing conversion is a "true" financing and not a sham financing designed to force the notes to convert pursuant to unfavorable terms.

2. *Conversion Discount.* In many cases convertible notes provide for a discounted conversion into the company's equity, on the theory that the noteholder should receive a benefit relative to the subsequent equity investors in recognition of the added risk taken by a noteholder who invested earlier in the company's development. For example, a noteholder might be permitted to convert into preferred stock at an effective price equal to 90% of the amount paid by the equity investors.

3. *Conversion Cap.* Another common feature of convertible notes is referred to as a conversion cap. A *conversion cap* is the maximum price per share (typically derived by reference to a valuation of the company as a whole) at which the

convertible debt would convert into equity in the next financing, regardless of the price per share and valuation agreed to by the company and the new equity investors.

Typically a conversion cap and discount operate in the alternative, with the effective conversion price being determined by operation of one or the other based on which results in the lowest conversion price. It is very important for companies to recognize that the size of the convertible note round and the conversion cap are two variables that each can have a significant impact on the ownership position of investors following the conversion of the notes. In addition, if notes convert into preferred stock at a subsequent financing at a steep discount, an unintended consequence may be that the holder receives a liquidation preference that is much larger in dollar terms than the amount of its initial investment. In addition to having an adverse impact on the founders' equity position, these factors can be unattractive to new equity investors paying 100 cents on the dollar for their stock. It is critically important for founders considering a convertible note financing incorporating a conversion cap or discount to perform a sensitivity analysis (1) when determining how much to raise, (2) where to set the cap and discount, and (3) whether to address the liquidation preference impact up front with the note investors. The founders will then need to work with experienced counsel to ensure that the notes are written accordingly.

Repayment Terms The traditional repayment term would require repayment of principal and accrued interest by the company at the maturity date. But the reality for the company is that in most cases if the note has not been converted by the maturity date, then the company probably does not have the money to cover the repayment obligation. And the reality for the investor is that in most cases it is not interested in the prospect of just making its money back with interest; most investors want their note to convert into equity. This has increasingly led to parties taking a more flexible approach, in which at maturity investors can elect repayment or conversion into equity. The conversion price should be agreed to in advance—some companies use the conversion cap but there are no rules here. Also, the parties need to agree in advance whether the notes convert into common stock or preferred stock. Finally, in many cases in which the maturity date occurs before an equity round closes, the company and the investors may agree to extend maturity, or to keep the notes outstanding and "due" but not otherwise take any action to collect or convert.

Amendment Provisions To avoid administrative challenges and "hold-out" problems associated with trying to amend outstanding notes (to extend their maturity date, to renegotiate conversion discounts or caps, or otherwise), notes often include a "majority rules" provision through which the holders of a majority of the principal amount of all outstanding notes may agree to amendments that would be binding on all notes. In some cases investors may require carve-outs to the "majority rules" rule for fundamental changes or for amendments that do not treat all noteholders similarly.

Equity Financings

In the typical case, by the time an equity financing happens, a company will have already issued shares of common stock to its founders in exchange for services, for transferring their rights to technology to the new enterprise, and for modest amounts of cash. The equity financing is then the transaction through which outside investors purchase equity with cash. These equity investors may acquire equity in the form of preferred stock (or, less commonly, common stock) or warrants, or both.

Preferred Stock versus Common Stock If all shares of stock have the same rights, then there is only one class of stock, known as *common stock*. If the company wishes to give all the investors the same rights and restrictions, the company should issue only common stock. In this case, the number of votes per share, the shareholders' rights to vote on various decisions, the dividends to shareholders, and their rights to the corporate assets if the corporation is liquidated will be the same on a share-by-share basis for all shareholders.

Outside investors often require additional rights, such as the right to elect a certain number of directors, to approve major corporate changes, and to receive priority of payment if the corporation is liquidated. Such additional rights can be provided by amending the corporation's certificate of incorporation to authorize a second class of stock, called *preferred stock*, or filing a certificate of determination of preferences if the charter authorizes blank-check preferred stock.

Venture capital firms and institutional investors typically invest in startup companies by paying cash to purchase *convertible preferred stock*, that is, preferred stock that may be converted into common stock at a specified exchange ratio. Issuing convertible preferred stock with greater rights than that of the common stock can often mean that a greater proportion of the company's overall value is allocated to the preferred stock, causing the fair market value of one share of the company's common stock to be lower than that of one share of preferred stock. As discussed in detail in Chapter 5, this disparity in the per-share value of the preferred and common stock may enable the company to grant stock options to employees with a lower per-share exercise price than that paid by the purchasers of the preferred.

Rights of Holders of Preferred Stock

State laws impose few requirements on the creation of preferred stock. California law, for example, requires either a dividend preference or a liquidation preference over common shares, without any requirement as to the type of dividend (cumulative or noncumulative) or the amount of the dividend or liquidation preference. Convertible preferred stock gives investors various rights that, depending on the circumstances and the bargaining positions of the parties, may be structured differently in each transaction. (We will discuss the various rights associated with the preferred stock issued in a typical venture capital financing in Chapter 13.)

Warrants   A *warrant* is a right, for a given period of time, to purchase a stated amount of stock at a stated exercise price. The exercise price, also called the *strike price*, is often equal to the fair market value of the stock when the warrant is issued, permitting its holder to benefit from any increase in the value of the securities. A warrant is similar to a stock option, but whereas stock options are normally granted to the company's directors, employees and consultants in connection with their services to the company, warrants are usually sold to investors. A warrant is sometimes called an *equity sweetener* because, if exercised, it lowers the investor's average price paid per share or allows the investor to purchase a larger share of the company at a fixed price.

Employee Compensation Plans As discussed in Chapter 5, many startup companies find it desirable to have an equity compensation plan, usually in the form of a stock option plan, to attract key technical and executive personnel. Such a plan can be a very significant component of employee compensation because the company's stock will appreciate if the company is successful. Because the equity compensation plan will have tax consequences, legal counsel should be consulted before implementing such a plan.

7.5 FEDERAL AND STATE SECURITIES REGISTRATION AND QUALIFICATION REQUIREMENTS

One responsibility of an entrepreneur is to comply with the federal regulations governing the offer, issuance, and transfer of securities. Largely in response to the stock market crash of 1929 and the Great Depression, Congress adopted the Securities Act of 1933 (the *1933 Act*) to require promoters and issuers to provide potential purchasers of securities adequate information relating to the company, its management, and the offering. The 1933 Act requires promoters of securities offerings to register them with the Securities and Exchange Commission, an agency of the U.S. government, and to provide prospective purchasers with a prospectus containing material information about the company, its management and the offering, unless the security or the type of transaction is exempt from registration.

Most states have enacted their own securities laws (*blue sky laws*) that also require the promoter and issuer to qualify the offering in the state where the company is headquartered (and, if different, the state from which the offers are made) and in each state where any of the offerees lives or is headquartered unless there is an applicable exemption or, as discussed in Sections 7.6 and 7.7, federal law preempts application of state qualification requirements for the particular offering of securities. If an offer is posted on a website, then it is deemed to be made in all 50 states, the District of Columbia, and Puerto Rico. However, several states exempt such an offering from qualification in that state if (1) the offer expressly provides that it is not available to residents of that state and (2) in fact no sales are made to residents of that state.

Fortunately, many states, the District of Columbia and Puerto Rico have adopted the Uniform Securities Act, thereby creating some consistency among state laws. Like the federal statutes, the Uniform Securities Act emphasizes disclosure as the primary means of protecting investors. Other states, including California, have retained their own securities regulatory schemes and authorize the securities administrator to deny a securities selling permit unless he or she finds that the company's plan of business and the proposed issuance of securities are fair, just, and equitable. Even if the state statute does not contain a specific provision to this effect, a state securities commissioner can usually deny registration until he or she is satisfied that the offering is fair. This process is referred to as *merit review*.

In addition, no security may be transferred by its owner to another person unless that transfer is also either registered and qualified or exempt. Thus, the bottom line for entrepreneurs is that any time a company or security holder offers or transfers securities, that transaction has to be either registered with the SEC and qualified in the relevant states or must qualify for an exemption from registration and qualification.

Failure to comply can have disastrous consequences—each purchaser in a nonexempt, non-registered offering has the right to *rescind* (undo) the purchase and get his or her money back or to recover damages. Having to do a rescission offer will almost certainly derail an initial public offering by the company or its sale. In addition to giving purchasers of illegally offered securities what amounts to a put option, failure to comply with federal and state registration requirements is a criminal offence punishable by fines and imprisonment.

Even if an offering is exempt from registration or qualification, all offers and sales of securities are subject to federal and state antifraud rules. For example, Rule 10b-5 under the Securities Exchange Act of 1934 (the *1934 Act*) imposes liability if, in connection with the offer or sale of securities, the company or selling shareholder makes an untrue statement of a material fact or makes a misleading statement by omitting a material fact. Because federal and state registration requirements and antifraud rules are complicated and subject to strict limitations, it is strongly suggested that the entrepreneur consult with an experienced securities attorney before soliciting funds.

What Is a "Security"?

Before discussing exemptions from securities regulation requirements, it is important to consider what constitutes a "security." In most cases it will be obvious that the founders' and the company's fundraising activities involve offering and selling a security. For example, entrepreneurs selling common or preferred stock, issuing options or warrants for stock, or issuing convertible notes are clearly issuing securities. In other cases, the company may need to consult with an attorney to help determine whether a particular activity will likely constitute a security issuance. For example, the company may contemplate pooling investors' money or buying assets, such as citrus trees or electric car charging stations, that are managed collectively by the securities promoter. Such

 From the **TRENCHES**

SG Ltd., a Dominican corporation, operated a website called StockGeneration (SG). The website's virtual stock exchange offered players the opportunity to invest real money in 11 virtual companies, one of which was called the "Privileged Company." The Privileged Company, the website proclaimed, is "supported by the owners of SG, this is why its value constantly rises; on average at a rate of 10% monthly (this is approximately 215% annually)." Approximately 45,000 Privileged Company investors lost a combined $850,000.

The U.S. Court of Appeals for the First Circuit agreed with the SEC's assertion that SG had sold securities, rejecting SG's argument that the website constituted entertainment, not an investment. The parties settled, with SG agreeing to pay over $1.3 million to investors. The StockGeneration website was inoperative at the time of this writing.

Sources: SEC v. SG Ltd., 265 F.3d 42 (1st Cir. 2001); SEC v. SG Ltd., Litigation Release No. 18181, SEC Settles with Internet "Virtual Stock Exchange" Scheme Operators, Recoups Full Amount of Investor Losses, 2003 WL 21310335 (June 9, 2003).

transactions may be deemed the sale of an investment contract, which is a security subject to the 1933 Act and state securities laws. In addition, certain investment pools may constitute an investment company requiring registration as an investment company under the Investment Company Act of 1940. Given the dire consequences of noncompliance, any company in doubt should consult an experienced securities attorney.

7.6 EXEMPTIONS FROM FEDERAL REGISTRATION REQUIREMENTS

Because registered public offerings are very expensive (usually costing more than $1 million in out-of-pocket costs alone), sales of securities to private investors or venture capitalists are almost always structured to be exempt from the federal registration requirements. (Registered initial public offerings are discussed in Chapter 17.) An offering of securities may be exempt from federal registration if it is an offering confined to a single state; a private offering; an offering to the public of up to $5 million; offerings of any amount to accredited investors and a limited number of sophisticated, unaccredited investors; an offering solely to employees, board members, consultants, and advisors; a "crowd-funding" offering of up to $1 million; a public offering of up to $50 million pursuant to an SEC notice of qualification; or an offshore offering. These exemptions are quite technical in nature and must be complied with in full.

Section 3(a)(11) and Rules 147 and 147A: Intrastate Offerings

Section 3(a)(11) of the 1933 Act exempts securities offered and sold by an issuer if the issuer and all the offerees and purchasers are residents of the same state. Rule 147 limits offerings under Section 3(a)(11) to issuers that (1) are incorporated or organized under the laws of the state where the offering is made, (2) have their "principal place of business" in that state,[3] and (3) are "doing business" there.[4] Under SEC Rule 147A, the issuer is not required to be incorporated or organized under the laws of the state where the offering is made, but it must both have its "principal place of business" in that state and be "doing business" there.[5] Rule 147A has no restriction on the domicile of the offerees, but, as with Rule 147, all purchasers must be a resident of the state where the offering occurs or the issuer must have a "reasonable belief" that all purchasers are in-state residents at the time of purchase. Under both Rules 147 and 147A, the issuer must (1) obtain a written representation from each purchaser as to residency and (2) place a legend on the stock certificate stating that the securities have not been registered and may not be resold for six months to a nonresident of the state. All intrastate offerings must comply with the applicable blue sky laws of the state where the offering is made. Finally, certain integration rules apply.

Private Offerings

Section 4(a)(2) of the 1933 Act provides an exemption for private offerings. In a *private offering* (also called a *private placement*), the securities are offered only to a limited number of selected qualified investors who can understand and bear the risk of the investment. A private offering can be consummated more quickly and much less expensively than a public offering. To qualify as a private offering under Section 4(a)(2) (unless qualified under the Regulation D safe harbor, described in more detail below), however, the company must be able to prove that there were a limited number of offerees and that all offerees, even those who did not eventually purchase the securities, had the ability to comprehend and bear the risk of the investment. This proof requires a preoffering qualification process through an offeree questionnaire that includes questions about the potential offeree's education, investment experience, and financial situation.

Offerings made under Section 4(a)(2), unless structured to fall within the Rule 506 exemption under Regulation D discussed below, are not exempted from state blue sky law compliance. Hence, any company seeking to make a private offering under Section 4(a)(2) that does not fall within Rule 506 must ensure that there are available exemptions under the blue sky laws of each applicable state (typically the state in which the company is located and each state in which an investor in the financing is located) or that any applicable state qualification procedures are followed prior to commencement of the offering.

Regulation D Safe-Harbor Exemptions

Regulation D, promulgated by the SEC, provides greater certainty to companies seeking to make public offerings of up to $1 million and limited offerings by providing very specific safe-harbor exemptions from registration. Virtually all venture capital financings are structured to fall within the parameters of Regulation D. A company that fails to comply with all the requirements of the applicable rule may still qualify for an exemption if the transaction meets the conditions of Section 4(a)(2).

Regulation D contains two separate exemptions from registration. These exemptions are outlined in Rules 504 and 506. Before we detail the requirements of those rules, it is important to explain two key concepts: accredited investors and integration of offerings.

Accredited Investors   A key element of Regulation D is the concept of an accredited investor. Offerings to accredited investors are exempted from the registration requirements on the theory that certain investors are so financially sophisticated or well-to-do that they do not need all of the protections afforded by the securities laws and can themselves, or with the assistance of a purchaser representative, obtain the necessary information to make an informed investment decision.

The SEC must review the definition of an accredited investor every four years. The discussion that follows is based on the definition in effect on July 1, 2016. Rule 501 defines an *accredited investor* as any one of the following:

1. Any national bank, savings and loan association, insurance company, registered broker-dealer, registered investment company or licensed Small Business Investment Company, and certain types of employee benefit plans.
2. Any private business development company.

3. Any organization described in Section 501(c)(3) of the Internal Revenue Code, any corporation, business trust or partnership, not formed for the purpose of acquiring the offered securities, with total assets in excess of $5 million.

4. Any director, executive officer, or general partner of the company.

5. Any natural person who had individual income in excess of $200,000 in each of the two most recent years, or joint income with that person's spouse in excess of $300,000 in each of those years, and who has a reasonable expectation of reaching the same income level in the current year.

6. Any natural person whose individual net worth, or joint net worth with that person's spouse, at the time of the purchase exceeds $1 million, excluding the value of the person's primary residence (and reduced by the amount by which the person's primary residence is "underwater," that is, worth less than the outstanding mortgage).

7. Any trust with total assets in excess of $5 million, not formed for the specific purpose of acquiring the securities offered, when the purchase is directed by a financially sophisticated person.

8. Any entity in which all of the equity owners are accredited investors.

Integration of Offerings   In calculating the amount raised in a 12-month period and the number of unaccredited investors, the SEC may combine (*integrate*) certain sales made within a limited period of time; that is, it may deem them to be part of a single transaction. This is most likely to happen when the offerings (1) are part of a single plan of financing, (2) are made at or about the same time, (3) involve the same type of consideration and class of security, and (4) are made for the same purpose.

Rule 502(a) provides an integration safe harbor for Regulation D offerings. Offers and sales made more than six months before the start of a Regulation D offering or more than six months after its completion are not considered part of the Regulation D offering, as long as there are no offers or sales of a similar class of securities during those six-month periods. Offerings to employees and others under Rule 701 (discussed later) are not integrated with offerings under Regulation D.

With the explanations of accredited investors and integration of offerings in mind, we turn now to the details of Rules 504 and 506.

Rule 504: Offerings to the Public of Up to $5 Million Rule 504 exempts offerings of up to $5 million within a 12-month period.[6] There is no limit on the number of purchasers. Because even unsophisticated purchasers may participate in a Rule 504 offering and there is no prescribed information disclosure requirement, Rule 504 is one of the exemptions most frequently relied on for the sale of securities to friends and family and to angel investors in small initial rounds of financing.

General solicitation and advertising is prohibited unless the offering complies with certain state registration and exemption provisions set forth in Rule 504(b)(1).[7] Rule 504 is not available to companies registered under the 1934 Act—known as public reporting companies—or to investment companies such as mutual funds. It is also not available to *blank-check companies*—those that have no specific business except to locate and acquire a currently unknown business. So-called "bad actors," as defined in Rule 506,[8] may not participate in a Rule 504 offering.

Rule 504 may be used to exempt only offerings of up to $5 million in any 12-month period. As a result, companies must be particularly careful to avoid integration problems. When possible, it is best to take advantage of the SEC's integration safe harbor by refraining from making any offers or sales for six months before and after the Rule 504 offering that, if integrated with the offering under Rule 504, would cause the total offered in any 12-month period to exceed $5 million. A notice on Form D must be filed with the SEC, electronically via the SEC's EDGAR system, within 15 days after the first sale of securities. Offerings made under Rule 504 are not exempted from state blue sky law compliance; hence, any company seeking to make an offering under Rule 504 must ensure that there are available exemptions under the blue sky laws of each applicable state or that any state qualification procedures are followed prior to commencement of the offering.

Rule 506: Offerings of Any Amount to Accredited Investors and a Limited Number of Sophisticated, Unaccredited Investors Rule 506 is by far the most common exemption utilized in private offerings of convertible notes and equity securities to venture capital and angel investors. It exempts offerings of any amount to not more than 35 unaccredited investors, provided that the company reasonably believes immediately prior to making any sale that each investor, either alone or with his or her purchaser representative, has enough business experience to evaluate the merits and risks of the prospective investment (i.e., the investor is *sophisticated*). There can be an unlimited number of accredited investors. In Rule 506 offerings, companies must refrain from general solicitation and advertising unless they take "reasonable steps" to verify that all purchasers in the offering are accredited investors. In addition, a company will be unable to rely on Rule 506 if certain "bad actors" (e.g., certain prior violators of securities laws) are participating in the offering.

Rule 506 requires that specified information be provided to purchasers (unless all purchasers are accredited investors) and that purchasers have the opportunity to ask questions and receive answers concerning the terms of the offering. A notice on Form D must be filed with the SEC, electronically via the SEC's EDGAR system, within 15 days of the first sale of securities. Private offerings made in compliance with Rule 506 do not need to be qualified under applicable state blue sky laws; however, the affected states may require notice filings (in some cases accompanied by filing fees and/or consents to service of process) to be made either prior to or after completion of the offering.

Rule 701: Offerings to Employees, Directors, Consultants, and Advisors

Rule 701 exempts offers and sales of securities by privately held companies (1) pursuant to a written compensatory benefit plan for employees, officers, directors, general partners, trustees (if the company is a business trust), consultants, or advisors or (2) pursuant to a written contract relating to the compensation of such persons. If the benefit plan is for consultants or advisors, they must be natural persons and render bona fide services not connected with the offer and sale of securities in a capital-raising transaction. Exempt compensatory benefit plans include purchase, savings, option, bonus, stock appreciation, profit sharing, thrift, incentive, deferred compensation, and pension and similar plans. Rule 701 applies only to securities offered and sold during a 12-month period in an amount not more than the greatest of (1) $1 million, (2) 15% of the total assets of the company, and (3) 15% of the outstanding amount of the class of securities being offered and sold.

Companies relying on Rule 701 must provide each plan participant with a copy of the plan and each contractor with a copy of his or her contract, but no other disclosure document is required by Rule 701 unless more than $5 million of securities are sold pursuant to Rule 701 in a 12-month period. If the aggregate sales price or amount of securities sold during any consecutive 12-month period in reliance on Rule 701 exceeds $5 million, the company must provide the following information a reasonable period of time before the date of sale: (1) if the plan is subject to the Employee Retirement Income Security Act of 1974 (*ERISA*), a copy of the summary plan description required by ERISA; (2) if the plan is not subject to ERISA, a summary of the material terms of the plan; (3) information about the risks associated with investment in the securities sold pursuant to the compensatory benefit plan or compensation contract; and (4) certain financial statements of the company.

Shares issued under Rule 701 are restricted, but they may be resold to the public without registration 90 days after the company completes a registered public offering, without regard to the usual Rule 144 holding periods, provided that the seller is not an officer, director, or controlling shareholder of the company. (The SEC presumes that a person owning at least 10% of the stock is a controlling shareholder.)

Regulation Crowdfunding: Offerings to the Public of Up to $1 Million Conducted on the Internet through Certain Broker-Dealers or Funding Portals

The SEC's "Regulation Crowdfunding" went into effect in 2016. This new regulation makes it possible for a large number of investors, including unaccredited investors, to use the Internet to invest an aggregate of up to $1 million in securities during a 12-month period. Regulation Crowdfunding was promulgated under Section 4(a)(6) of the 1933 Act, which exempts from registration under the 1933 Act a securities offering of up to $1 million on an aggregate basis during a 12-month period, provided that the offering is conducted through certain types of brokers or funding portals. An offering under Regulation Crowdfunding

 ## From the **TRENCHES**

A number of states have passed their own crowdfunding laws. Laws vary, but most state crowdfunding platforms generally provide that money can be raised only from investors within the particular state and limit the amount an individual can invest to $10,000 or less.

MobCraft Beer Inc. is one startup company that used state crowdfunding. MobCraft cofounders Giotto Troia, Andrew Gierczak, and Henry Schwartz were "homebrewing" when Troia learned about crowdsourcing from a college business course. Encouraged by family and friends to grow their business, MobCraft developed a business plan that begins with beer lovers posting beer recipes on its website. Voting by prepaying determines the most popular recipe, which is then brewed and can be picked up at the brewery or shipped to states that allow alcohol shipping. The winning brews are also sold in Wisconsin beer stores.

In November 2013, Wisconsin enacted an equity crowdfunding law that allows investments of up to $10,000. In 2015, Troia used the state's online platform Craftfund.com to try to raise $250,000 in return for 2% of the company's equity, with $525 as the minimum investment. A disclosure document was provided to each potential investor describing the company's history, finances, and business plan; more than half of the document's 13 pages talked about the risk factors involved in the investment.

Although MobCraft raised only $75,000, it considers itself successful. MobCraft moved into a larger facility and plans to increase annual production and open a taproom. In March 2016, CEO Schwartz appeared on "Shark Tank," a television show on which entrepreneurs pitch their business to, and seek funding from, the professional investors who appear weekly on the show, but a deal was not consummated.

Sources: Stacy Cowley, *Tired of Waiting for U.S. to Act, States Pass Crowdfunding Laws and Rules*, N.Y. Times (June 3, 2015), http://www.nytimes.com/2015/06/04/business/smallbusiness/states-pass-crowdfunding-laws-for-small-businesses.html?_r=0; Louis Garcia, *Following the Crowd Leads to MobCraft's Success and Expansion*, Growler (May 22, 2015), http://growlermag.com/following-the-crowd-leads-to-mobcrafts-success-and-expansion/; Robin Shepard, *MobCraft Jumps in the Shark Tank*, Isthmus (Feb. 29, 2016), http://isthmus.com/food-drink/beer/henry-schwartz-to-appear-on-abc-reality-television-series/.

does not need to be qualified under state blue sky laws. As described in more detail below, there are a number of restrictions (in addition to the low $1 million maximum offering limit) in Regulation Crowdfunding that significantly limit its usefulness as a securities law exemption.

As of mid-2016, most "crowdfunding" portals did not rely on Regulation Crowdfunding. Instead, such portals tended to limit their investor participants to accredited investors and to utilize Regulation D (described above) as the exemption from registration. In the balance of this section, "crowdfunding transaction" refers to a transaction under Regulation Crowdfunding, not an online offering exempt under Regulation D.

Eligibility   Certain companies may not use Regulation Crowdfunding, including non-U.S. companies, companies subject to 1934 Act reporting, companies with no specific business plan, and companies that are disqualified due to the involvement of "bad actors."

Investor Limits on Investment Amount   The aggregate amount of securities sold to any investor across all issuers in reliance on Regulation Crowdfunding in a 12-month period may not exceed the greater of $2,000 or 5% of the lesser of the investor's annual income or net worth if either the investor's annual income or net worth is less than $100,000. The aggregate amount sold to an investor whose annual income and net worth are both equal to or more than $100,000 shall not exceed 10% of the lesser of the annual income or net worth, not to exceed an amount sold of $100,000.

Limitations on Transfer   Securities purchased in a crowdfunding transaction cannot be transferred for one year, subject to certain exceptions.

Disclosure Obligations   A company engaged in a crowdfunding transaction is required to file specific disclosures with the SEC (and provide such disclosures to the company's intermediary to make them available to investors) on new SEC Form C. In addition to containing financial and business information regarding the company, it must contain information regarding the funding portal or broker-dealer used for the offering and the compensation paid to the intermediary.

Crowdfunding companies are required to file a report with the SEC annually, no later than 120 days after the end of the most recently completed fiscal year covered by the report. The report also must also be posted to the company's website.

Advertising Companies may not advertise a crowdfunding offering other than publishing notices that advertise the terms of the offering and direct investors to the funding portal or broker. Regulation Crowdfunding describes the acceptable content of such notices, which is fairly limited.

Crowdfunding Requirements for Intermediaries Regulation Crowdfunding also imposes significant requirements on the funding portals and broker-dealers participating in crowdfunding transactions, including that they must register with the SEC on the new Form Funding Portal and become a member of a national securities association (such as FINRA).

Regulation A: Offerings to the Public of Up to $50 Million Pursuant to an SEC Notice of Qualification

As amended in 2015, Regulation A is available for certain "mini-IPOs" raising up to $50 million pursuant to an SEC notice of qualification.

Two Tiers and Limits on Selling Shareholders An offering under Regulation A may be made under one of two tiers:

> **Tier 1** Offerings up to $20 million, including no more than $6 million of securities sold by selling shareholders that are affiliates of the company, in any 12-month period.

> **Tier 2** Offerings up to $50 million, including no more than $15 million of securities sold by selling shareholders that are affiliates of the company, in any 12-month period.

Regardless of the tier, during the company's initial Regulation A offering and for 12 months thereafter, selling shareholders (regardless of whether they are affiliates of the company) may not sell securities worth more than 30% of the aggregate offering price of a particular offering. Additional restrictions apply after this 12-month period has elapsed.

Preemption of State Blue Sky Laws for Tier 2 Offerings   The primary advantage of a Tier 2 offering over a Tier 1 offering, other than the higher maximum offering amount, is that a Tier 2 offering does not have to be registered or qualified under any state blue sky laws. In contrast, Tier 1 offerings must comply with the qualification and registration requirements of all applicable state blue sky laws, which can be costly or even impossible depending on the participants in the offering.

Eligibility   Certain companies may not use Regulation A, including blank-check companies, companies not incorporated in the United States or Canada and companies that are disqualified due to the involvement of "bad actors," such as individuals who have engaged in certain past securities law violations.

Form 1-A Registration Statement   To sell securities under Regulation A, the SEC must issue a "notice of qualification" after it reviews the company's offering materials filed in accordance with the Form 1-A requirements. The Form 1-A ultimately must be publicly filed via the SEC's EDGAR online filing system, but the issuer may initially submit it for SEC review confidentially. Although Form 1-A is a short form when compared with the Form S-1 used for a typical initial public offering, the company must include Form S-1 level disclosure if its securities are to be listed upon qualification on the New York Stock Exchange (*NYSE*) or Nasdaq.

Investment Limitations for Investors in Tier 2 Offerings   Individual investors in a Tier 2 offering may generally not purchase more than 10% of the greater of the investor's (x) annual income and (y) net worth, calculated in a manner consistent with Regulation D. In the case of investors that are not natural persons, the limit is 10% of the greater of (x) annual revenue and (y) fiscal-year end net assets. These investment limitations do not apply to accredited investors or to offerings of securities to be listed on a national securities exchange, such as the NYSE or Nasdaq.

From the **TRENCHES**

Whether the revised Regulation A will be the investment vehicle of choice for eligible companies seeking to raise money is unknown. Some founders, however, find the ability to sell securities to "average investors" attractive; others assert that it can help turn users of a company's products into "brand evangelists" who recommend the products to others. Companies considering using the new Regulation A include Elio Motors, a company developing a three-wheeled, two-seater motor vehicle with high gas mileage; Xreal, a mobile games developer; DietBet, a platform on which users bet and compete with others in a quest to lose weight; and StarShop, an e-commerce mobile app that uses celebrity videos to endorse products.

Sources: Stacy Cowley, *New Rules Let Companies Sell Stakes to Investors of Modest Means*, N.Y. Times (June 18, 2015), http://www.nytimes.com/2015/06/19/business/smallbusiness/new-rules-let-companies-sell-stakes-to-investors-of-modest-means.html; Salvador Rodriguez, *Regulation A+ Round Up: 5 Tech Companies That Might Soon Hold Mini-IPOs*, Int'l Bus. Times (June 19, 2015), http://www.ibtimes.com/regulation-round-5-tech-companies-might-soon-hold-mini-ipos-1975878; *Raising Capital Using a Regulation A+ Mini-IPO*, Seedinvest Blog, https://www.seedinvest.com/blog/raising-capital/raising-capital-reg-a-mini-ipo (last visited Mar. 8, 2016).

Ongoing Reporting Requirements for Tier 2 Offerings Companies conducting Tier 2 offerings are required to file certain periodic reports on EDGAR after the offering: semiannual reports on Form 1-SA, annual reports on Form 1-K, and current reports on Form 1-U. Annual reports must include audited financial statements. These reports are similar to, but may be less extensive than, the quarterly reports registered issuers must file on Form 10-Qs and the annual and current reports they must file on Form 10-K and Form 8-K, respectively.

Regulation S: Offshore Transactions

Regulation S was promulgated by the SEC to address the growing prominence of offshore securities transactions. Rule 901 provides that only offers and sales that occur within the United States are subject to Section 5 of the 1933 Act, and that registration is not required for offers and sales occurring offshore. The regulation creates two nonexclusive safe harbors for both U.S. and foreign companies that conduct offshore transactions. Rule 903 provides a safe harbor for offerings by the company, and Rule 904 provides a safe harbor for resales. Both safe harbors require that the offering or resale (1) be made in an "offshore transaction" and (2) not involve "directed selling efforts" in the United States. In addition to these two requirements, the safe harbors also contain other conditions to protect against *flowback,* or the return of the securities to the United States.

Offshore Transaction To meet the offshore transaction requirement, either (1) at the time of the offer or sale of securities, the buyer must be outside of the United States, or the seller must at least have a reasonable belief that the buyer is outside of the United States; or (2) the transaction must be executed through an established foreign securities exchange or offshore securities market located outside of the United States. Regulation S permits offers and sales to specifically targeted groups of U.S. citizens, such as military personnel, provided that they are abroad at the time the offer or sale is made. It also permits offers and sales in the United States, provided that they are made exclusively to "non-U.S. persons," such as foreign nationals.

No Directed Selling Efforts in the United States The safe harbors also require that no directed selling efforts occur within the United States. Regulation S forbids companies or sellers of securities from engaging in any activity meant to "condition" the U.S. market for the offered securities. This prohibition extends to any activities that could reasonably be expected to condition the market. It includes placing advertisements in publications printed primarily for distribution in the United States or those that have averaged a circulation of more than 15,000 copies per issue in the United States over the preceding 12 months. The prohibition does not apply to advertisements required to be published under U.S. or foreign law, provided that the advertisement (1) does not contain any more information than is required and (2) contains a statement that the securities have not been registered under the 1933 Act and may not be offered or sold in the United States.

Rule 903 Company Offering Safe Harbor Rule 903 classifies company offerings into three categories based on the likelihood that the securities will flow back into the United States and the amount of information available to U.S. investors. *Category 1* offerings are considered to be low risk and are only subject to the offshore transaction and no-directed selling efforts conditions discussed above. *Category 2* securities have a higher risk of flow-back, so certain additional conditions are imposed. *Category 3* is a catchall category for the highest risk offshore offerings (which includes offerings of equity securities by a privately held company incorporated in the United States) and, as a result, Category 3 offerings are subject to the most stringent conditions on the sale or offer of securities. In addition to requiring compliance with all Category 1 and 2 restrictions, Category 3 offerings must also comply with a series of other restrictions mandated by the type of security being offered. For example, for all equity securities sold in a Category 3 offering, there is a one-year distribution compliance period during which no sales or offers of the securities may be made to a U.S. person. The securities must contain legends that transfers are prohibited except in accordance with Regulation S. Purchasers must also certify that they are non-U.S. persons and agree that any resale must be made pursuant to Regulation S or another exemption under the 1933 Act, or be registered.

Rule 904 Resale Safe Harbor   The Rule 904 safe harbor is available for all resale transactions, regardless of whether the original sale was made in an offshore transaction. To meet the safe-harbor requirements, the resale must be made in an offshore transaction with no selling efforts directed at the United States. In addition, persons receiving selling concessions or dealers participating in Category 2 or 3 company offerings cannot knowingly offer or sell to a U.S. person during the applicable distribution compliance period. When officers or directors of the company, or any underwriter, dealer or other person pursuant to a contractual arrangement, sells the securities, only the customary broker's commission may be paid.

Table 7.1 summarizes these federal exemptions as of February 1, 2017.

TABLE 7.1	Key Elements of Certain Federal Exemptions from Registration				
Type of Exemption	**Dollar Limit of the Offering**	**Limits on the Purchasers**	**Purchaser Qualifications**	**Company Qualifications**	**Other Considerations**
Section 4(a)(2): Private Offerings	No limit.	Generally limited to a small number of offerees able to understand and bear risk.	Offerees and purchasers must have access to information and be sophisticated investors.	No limitations.	Blue sky compliance required.
Regulation D, Rule 504	$5 million in 12 months.	No limit.	No requirements.	Not a 1934 Act public reporting company, an investment company, or a blank-check company, or a company (or offering) disqualified under Regulation D's "bad actor" provisions.	Blue sky compliance required. Form D must be filed within 15 days after offering.
Regulation D, Rule 506	No limit.	No limit on the number of accredited investors but limited to 35 unaccredited investors.	Investors (or their representative) must be sophisticated, that is, have sufficient knowledge and experience in financial matters to evaluate the investment.	Not a company (or offering) disqualified under Regulation D's "bad actor" provisions.	Prescribed disclosure must be provided to unaccredited investors. General advertising and solicitation prohibited, or company must take reasonable steps to confirm accredited investor status. Form D must be filed within 15 days after offering.
Rule 701	The greatest of $1 million, 15% of the total assets of the company, and 15% of the outstanding securities of the same class, in any consecutive 12-month period.	No limit on number. Purchasers must be individual employees, directors, or consultants to the company or its affiliates (i.e., no corporations, partnerships, or other entities).	Advisory and consulting services must not be connected with the offer and sale of securities in a capital-raising transaction.	Not a 1934 Act public reporting company or an investment company.	Offering must be pursuant to written compensatory benefit plan or written contract relating to compensation. Blue sky compliance is required. Prescribed disclosure is required if sales exceed $5 million in a 12-month period.

TABLE 7.1 (continued)					
Type of Exemption	**Dollar Limit of the Offering**	**Limits on the Purchasers**	**Purchaser Qualifications**	**Company Qualifications**	**Other Considerations**
Section 4(a)(6) and Regulation Crowdfunding	Up to $1 million in 12 months.	Investors with annual income and net worth of $100,000 or more: investment limited to 10% of lesser of investor's net worth and annual income, up to $100,000. All other investors: investment limited to greater of $2,000 and 5% of lesser of investor's net worth and annual income.	No limitations.	A U.S. company, but not a 1934 Act public reporting company, an investment company, a company (or offering) disqualified under Regulation D's "bad actor" provisions, or a company in breach of its Regulation Crowdfunding reporting requirements.	Must use registered broker or portal. Form C must be filed with the SEC. Ongoing SEC reporting required. Stock generally cannot be transferred for one year.
Regulation A	Tier 1: Up to $20 million, including no more than $6 million of securities sold by selling shareholders that are affiliates of the company, in any 12-month period. Tier 2: Up to $50 million, including no more than $15 million of securities sold by selling shareholders that are affiliates of the company, in any 12-month period. Additional restrictions on selling shareholders also apply.	Tier 1: No limit. Tier 2: Unaccredited individual investors may not purchase more than 10% of the greater of the investor's annual income and net worth (limit for unaccredited non-natural persons is greater of net assets and revenue). The investment limitation does not apply to accredited investors or offerings where the securities are listed on a national securities exchange, such as NYSE or Nasdaq.	No limitations.	A U.S. or Canadian company, but not a 1934 Act public reporting company, an investment company, a blank-check company, a company issuing oil/gas/mineral rights, or a company (or offering) disqualified under "bad actor" provisions of Rule 262.	Tier 1: Blue sky and SEC clearance required. Tier 2: SEC clearance and ongoing SEC reporting requirements.

TABLE 7.1	(continued)				
Type of Exemption	**Dollar Limit of the Offering**	**Limits on the Purchasers**	**Purchaser Qualifications**	**Company Qualifications**	**Other Considerations**
Regulation S[a]	No limit.	No limit.	Purchase must not be by or on behalf of any "U.S. persons."	No limitations.	Local securities law compliance required. The transaction must be an "off-shore transaction," there must be no "directed selling efforts" in the United States, and "offering restrictions" must be limited. The securities must bear a required legend, the purchaser must agree not to distribute the shares except in compliance with federal securities laws, and the company must be obligated not to effect any transfers not in compliance with federal securities laws.

a. Assumes the company is a privately held company incorporated in the United States offering equity securities and thus "Category 3" for purposes of Regulation S.

7.7 BLUE SKY EXEMPTIONS AND FEDERAL PREEMPTION

The availability of state exemptions from qualification often varies depending on such factors as the number of offerees or purchasers, the type of persons who can be solicited, the time period of the offering, the manner of the offering, the aggregate amount of the offering, the types of securities sold or excluded, notice requirements, and the extent to which state blue sky law is preempted as a result of the federal securities law exemption being used. State blue sky exemptions are subject to many limitations and requirements, which are described at greater length in each state's blue sky statutes, regulations, statements of policy, advisories, and interpretations. As a result, a company should consult with securities counsel before relying on any exemption.

To promote the formation of new businesses and reduce regulatory burdens on young firms, Congress has limited the power of the states to regulate certain securities offerings. In the case of offerings exempt pursuant to Rule 506 under Regulation D, all preoffer and presale notice filings and merit review requirements of the states have been preempted. State law is also preempted if the offering is made under Tier 2 of Regulation A or under Regulation Crowdfunding. Federal law similarly preempts state registration requirements and merit review in connection with most initial public offerings registered with the SEC. The law also provides federal preemption for the issuance of securities to "qualified purchasers," a category of investors to be defined by the SEC at a later time. The Securities Litigation Uniform Standard Act of 1998 limits a shareholder's right to bring a securities fraud case involving a public company traded on a national securities exchange in state court and generally preempts the application of state antifraud laws in such cases.

 Putting It into **PRACTICE**

Once Alexei and Piper decided to go forward with Genesist, they needed to determine how to finance it. In choosing a finance structure, they had no hard-and-fast rules to follow—just guidelines. Genesist's attorney, Sarah Crawford, outlined several ways that Alexei and Piper could finance their company.

First, the founders might be able to self-finance the company, which would allow them to continue to develop the business without diluting their equity share. In theory, Genesist might, for example, be able to secure a 50% prepayment from its customers for certain orders. This would help cover the cost of materials. This type of self-financing could work if the founders had a client base that would enable them to identify customers with a prior relationship with them and the necessary confidence to prepay. This financing structure might be beneficial to the customer as

(continued)

well because, with an identified customer, the product could be developed to suit the particular customer's need. But given that they were still developing the technology and were at least six months away from having a prototype, this option did not seem viable. As for using their credit cards, Alexei and Piper were still paying off student loans and were very reluctant to incur any more personal debt.

Second, Alexei and Piper could approach Alexei's prior employer ESF, or another company that might be interested in selling or licensing the new product or the underlying technology, and ask for financial support. This could take the form of an equity investment, a corporate partnership, or as payment for some degree of future access or rights to the product (e.g., a reseller agreement with a guaranteed supply of product or a license to certain of the new company's technology). ESF already owned 15% of Genesist's common stock, and both Alexei and Piper were concerned about giving ESF a larger stake for fear that it might dissuade other investors from investing in future rounds.

Third, Alexei and Piper could approach family and friends. If they could get some short-term support in the form of convertible notes or an equity investment with founder-friendly terms, the founders could obtain the necessary capital to develop their business in the short-term without significant dilution, with the goal of being able to get to a proof of product concept sufficient to command a higher valuation (and thus less dilution to the founders) in a later equity financing.

Fourth, they could try to find angel investors or a venture capital firm willing to make a more significant investment in Genesist in return for an equity stake or convertible notes. However, Alexei and Piper did not have preexisting relationships with either type of investors, and they recognized that trying to meet new potential investors and educate them about the company's business could take up a significant amount of their time, which time they could instead use to further the company's product development. They also recognized that in order to obtain angel or venture capital investment at this very early stage of the company's development,

(continued)

it was likely that they would experience substantial dilution, either through a low valuation and price per share in an equity financing or a low conversion cap in a convertible note financing. They had also heard a horror story about a founder-CEO who had been replaced by the board after the directors selected by the venture capital investors persuaded the independent directors that she lacked the leadership skills to take the company to the next level. She not only lost her job but also all her unvested stock. Although Sarah explained that this was unusual, Alexei and Piper both wanted the opportunity to learn on the job and prove themselves.

Fifth, Alexei and Piper could try to secure a bank loan. Sarah told them that because Genesist did not yet have a product to ship and thus had no accounts receivable or inventory, a bank would not be willing to lend Genesist any substantial amount of money, unless one or both of the founders could demonstrate personal wealth and personally guarantee the loan. In addition, Genesist would not generate cash flow for a while, so it would have no way to pay interest and principal on a bank loan.

Alexei and Piper decided not to approach ESF or other potential resellers of their product for funding because they represented potential competitors of the new company down the line, and Alexei and Piper were uncomfortable with them having any access to information about their product development. Although a medical device company had expressed interest in licensing Genesist's technology to make customized stents, the Genesist founders knew that substantially more R&D was required before they would be in a position to show proof of concept.

Even though Alexei and Piper knew that they wanted to get venture capital financing at some point, they planned to wait until the product was further developed so that they could obtain a higher valuation for the company. They decided to borrow a small sum of money from their family and friends to start the business.

Alexei and Piper finished a business plan, which included five-year projections and the assumptions underlying them. Then, with the help of Sarah, they found an angel investor named Bart Cooperman, a retired executive who was willing to invest $50,000 in exchange for a convertible note. Following various conversations

(continued)

during which Bart argued for no automatic conversion on the convertible note and a very short maturity date of three months, Alexei and Piper were able to agree on terms that afforded the company more flexibility. The convertible note provided for an 18-month maturity, an automatic conversion into a qualified financing (defined as a financing generating proceeds to the company of at least $750,000) and provided for a conversion price reflecting a 20% discount to the price paid by new investors in the qualified financing, subject to a conversion cap of $2,000,000.

Genesist issued a convertible note to Bart pursuant to SEC Rule 506 of Regulation D and the corresponding exemption in California. Because Bart was an accredited investor, Genesist was not required to provide a disclosure document that went beyond the materials Alexei and Piper had provided during Bart's due diligence process. Even so, they were careful to fully disclose to Bart all the risks and uncertainties concerning the venture of which they were aware.

The founders hoped that these funds would be sufficient to support the business's operations for the next six months. They were now ready to focus their attention on building out their management team.

CHAPTER 8

Marshaling Human Resources

H iring and retaining motivated and talented workers are critical to the success of virtually any venture. Failure to appreciate how overlapping federal and state statutes, regulations, and common-law principles affect everything from a company's pre-hiring practices to its decision to terminate an employee can result in time-consuming and expensive litigation and government investigations. This can consume precious cash and divert management's attention from execution of the business plan. Allegations of wrongful conduct can also torpedo a founder's career. In 2016, Fox News founder and CEO Roger Ailes resigned two weeks after a former anchor accused him of sexual harassment, and Fox paid $20 million to settle the case.[1]

In addition to avoiding illegal employment practices, entrepreneurs need to incorporate their human resource strategy into their value proposition and execution of their business plan.[2] For example, a growing number of companies use independent contractors, as well as freelancers, temporary employees, and outsourcing services, to meet changing staffing needs in a cost-efficient way. Such "flexible workplace arrangements" can allow individuals to have more control over the hours they work, but they typically mean less job security and less protection for the workers under federal wage and discrimination statutes.[3] In other firms, it may be preferable to hire full-time employees and provide them a measure of job security and an equity stake in the success of the venture to give them an incentive to make firm-specific investments, such as learning techniques and processes that cannot be readily applied in another firm.[4]

This chapter addresses many of the more prevalent employment laws, which bound the choices available for strategic human resource management.[5] In general, an employer is governed by both federal law and the law of the state and municipality where the individual works, or, if it is more favorable to the employee, the law where the employer is headquartered. Employment laws can vary widely from state to state and from city to city.

Because the application of many employment statutes hinges on the distinction between employees and independent contractors, this chapter begins with a discussion of what differentiates one from the other. We continue with a summary of certain key employment legislation and then discuss employee privacy and employment at will and wrongful discharge. The chapter concludes with an outline of what should be contained in certain key employment documents, a brief discussion of equity compensation (addressed in detail in Chapter 5) and certain common employee benefits, and suggestions for reducing employee-related litigation and for preventing employee fraud.

8.1 EMPLOYEES VERSUS INDEPENDENT CONTRACTORS

Workers may be classified into two general legal categories: employees and independent contractors. The distinction between them is crucial. A worker, such as a painter hired by the owner of an office building, who provides unsupervised, specialized work that is needed only sporadically, is a clear-cut example of an independent contractor. The classification of other types of workers is frequently far less certain.

There is often an inherent struggle surrounding worker classification. The employer may want to classify the worker as an independent contractor to save money. Employers are not required to pay or withhold any federal or state payroll taxes, including Social Security and Medicare taxes, for independent contractors. The company also does not have to provide workers' compensation insurance, unemployment compensation, overtime, or job benefits (such as health insurance and stock-purchase or retirement savings plans) to independent contractors. Often, a worker may try to claim the status of employee to qualify for the legal protections

From the **TRENCHES**

Although it has been estimated that hiring independent contractors instead of employees can save employers about 30% on labor costs, there are countervailing reasons why businesses, including startup ventures, might prefer to hire workers as employees instead of independent contractors. A key reason is superior client service. As the CEO of a delivery-only restaurant in New York City put it, the company's delivery team is "essentially our only point of human contact with customers, so it's a case where who's doing the job and how they are doing it is incredibly important to our success." Employers can train employees in specific and standardized routines or methods for providing service to customers, thereby enhancing both customer satisfaction and trust in the brand. When a stranger arrives to clean a customer's home, serves a customer in a restaurant or performs personal errands, there is comfort in knowing that the individual performing the work has been appropriately trained and that the service level will be consistent, regardless of which individual performs the task. Investing in an employee through training and career opportunities is also likely to keep the individual more committed to the work relationship and the ultimate customer.

Sources: Lydia DePillis, *What We Know About the People Who Clean the Floors in Silicon Valley*, Wash. Post (Mar. 30, 2016), https://www.washingtonpost.com/news/wonk/wp/2016/03/30/what-we-know-about-the-people-who-clean-the-floors-in-silicon-valley/?wpmm= 1&wpisrc =nl_wonk; Sarah Kessler, *In a Backlash to the Gig Economy, Hiring Employees Is Cool Again in Silicon Valley*, Fastcompany.com (June 10, 2015), http://www.fastcompany.com/3047105/a-backlash-to-the-gig-economy-hiring-employees-to-do-work-is-cool-in-silicon-valley-again; Ellen Huet, *Contractor or Employee? Silicon Valley's Branding Dilemma*, Forbes (Nov. 18, 2014), http://www.forbes.com/sites/ellenhuet/2014/11/18/contractor-or-employee-silicon-valleys -branding-dilemma/print/.

and employee benefits afforded employees. Conversely, sometimes "freelancers" prefer quarterly self-employment taxes to employee payroll withholding and resist the employer's more prudent decision to classify the worker as an employee.

The misclassification of workers can create serious legal problems, including audits of the entire workforce by federal and state tax authorities and the imposition of penalties. Both the federal and state governments have ramped up efforts to investigate employee misclassification issues in order to recoup lost revenue through penalties and increased payroll taxes. For example, the U.S. Department of Labor required a company that had misclassified individuals hired to install cable, Internet, and phone service as independent contractors to pay almost $1.5 million in back wages and damages to 250 installers.[6]

A worker's status can also affect the rights of the employer to any copyrightable works or patentable inventions created by the worker. As explained more fully in Chapter 14, the employer generally is deemed to be the author of (and therefore the owner of the copyright for) any works created by an employee acting within the scope of employment, even in the absence of an express assignment of copyright. Similarly, the employer is the owner of any invention created by an employee "hired to invent," even in the absence of an assignment of inventions. In contrast, a company commissioning a work by an independent contractor will not own the copyright unless the company secures either a written contract stating that it is a "work made for hire" or a written assignment of the copyright. Similarly, independent contractors own their inventions (and any patents thereon) absent a written assignment of inventions.

Statutes often do not provide specific guidance for distinguishing employees from independent contractors.[7] For tax purposes, the Internal Revenue Service (*IRS*) guidelines suggest that three criteria generally must be satisfied to characterize a worker as an independent contractor rather than an employee for tax purposes.[8] First, an independent contractor agrees with the client on what the finished work product will be and then the contractor controls the means and manner of achieving the desired outcome. Second, an independent contractor offers services to the public at large, not just to one business, and is responsible for disbursing payments from the client, paying unreimbursed expenses, and providing his or her own tools. Third, the relationship of the parties is often evidenced by a written agreement that specifies that the worker is an independent contractor and is not entitled to employee benefits; the services provided by the worker are not key to the business; and the relationship is not permanent.

None of the IRS suggested guidelines is dispositive. Courts assess and weigh all facets of the worker relationship,[9] including, without limitation, the following:

➢ The nature and degree of control or supervision retained or exercised by the employer

➢ The extent to which the services in question are an integral part of the employer's core business (the more integrated the worker's services are in the employer's day-to-day operations, the less "independent" the worker is deemed to be)

➤ Whether the employer provides the training

➤ The amount of the worker's investment in facilities and equipment

➤ The kind of occupation

➤ Whether services are exclusive, or the worker may pursue other engagements

➤ The worker's opportunities for profit or loss

➤ The method of calculating the payment for the work (by time worked or by the job)

➤ The skill, initiative, and judgment required for the independent enterprise to succeed

➤ The permanence and duration of the working relationship

➤ Whether vacation, sick leave, or other types of leave are given

➤ Whether the worker accumulates retirement benefits or is given medical benefits from the employer

➤ Whether the employer pays Social Security and Medicare taxes

➤ The intention of the parties, including any written agreement between the parties, regarding independent contractor or employee status.

When courts or agencies weigh the interests of relatively low-paid workers against those of employers, the workers' interests usually prevail in close cases. Although no one factor is determinative, workers who are lower paid, are lower skilled, lack bargaining power, have a high degree of economic dependence on their employer, and are subject to regular supervision and control are more likely to be considered employees. In contrast, workers who have "significant entrepreneurial opportunity for gain or loss," and retain direction and control over their work, are more likely to be considered independent contractors.[10]

Establishing Nonemployee Status

Even though an employer can never guarantee that a worker will be legally treated as an independent contractor, the employer can take certain steps to help establish nonemployee status.

From the **TRENCHES**

In February 2016, a class action complaint was filed against Handy Technologies, Inc., a corporation formed in 2012 that "connects individuals looking for independent household service professionals worldwide on demand" through its online platform. The complaint alleges that Handy willfully misclassified the plaintiff cleaners as independent contractors, instead of as employees, to avoid complying with applicable federal and state laws that require payment for all time worked, business expenses, the employer's share of payroll taxes, and mandatory insurance. The plaintiffs allege that they should be classified as employees, under the California Labor Code, because Handy "heavily controlled both the work performed and the manner and means in which the [cleaner plaintiffs] performed their work." The plaintiffs alleged that Handy (1) gave the workers instructions, such as company manuals, as to how to perform their work, including the order and sequence of the work; (2) continuously supervised and trained the workers on matters such as how to take out trash and fold laundry; (3) told the workers which cleaning supplies to take to a customer; (4) controlled and assigned the weekly schedules; and (5) required the workers to wear clothing with the Handy logo. The plaintiffs further alleged that they performed work that was "closely integrated with and essential to" Handy's business of providing cleaning to its customers. As such, the plaintiffs assert they should be classified as nonexempt, hourly employees. The complaint includes counts for unlawful, unfair, and deceptive business practices; failure to pay minimum wage and overtime; and failure to reimburse for certain expenses, such as personal cellphones workers were required to use.

Sources: Easton v. Handy Tech., Inc., No 37-2016-00004419-CU-OE-CTL (Cal. Super. Ct. Feb. 9, 2016). *See also* James Surowiecki, *The Financial Page: Gigs with Benefits*, New Yorker, July 6 & 13, 2015, at 31; Noam Scheiber, *Growth in the 'Gig Economy' Fuels Work Force Anxieties*, N.Y. Times, July 13, 2015, at A1.

Enter into a Written Independent Contractor Agreement   A written independent contractor agreement spelling out the intent of the parties and detailing the worker's duties and the terms and conditions of service will provide some support for finding independent contractor status. The agreement should clearly lay out the responsibilities of the contractor, describing the services to be performed, granting the contractor autonomy and control over how and when to provide and accomplish the services, the time frame in which they will be completed, and the payment that will be given in consideration for these services. The contract should specify what is expected of the contractor (e.g., the contractor will supply all necessary tools, equipment, and supplies). Unless all work must be done by the contractor alone, the contract should give the contractor the right to hire assistants, at his or her own expense. It is also important to make it clear that the independent contractor is free to offer services to other businesses as long as the other work would not result in the violation of trade secret and other intellectual property rights of the client. The contractor should be responsible for carrying his or her own liability and workers' compensation insurance and for paying his or her own taxes and benefits. An example of an agreement between a company and an independent contractor is set forth in "Getting It in Writing: Sample Independent Contractor Services Agreement," Appendix 8.1 on the companion website for this title, available at www.CengageBrain.com. (Before using any form, the entrepreneur should consult with legal counsel to ensure that the form agreement complies with all applicable federal, state, and local legal requirements and meets all of the entrepreneur's needs.) Although independent contractor agreements are helpful, they are not dispositive.[11]

Limit Scope of Work and Employer Supervision   To withstand challenge, an employer should generally not ask independent contractors to perform tasks that are central to the employer's primary or core business. The employer should also give the worker sufficient control and autonomy with respect to the manner and means of his or her performance.

Establish Independent Economic Viability of Contractor   The more the employer can establish the independent economic viability of the worker, the better. Thus, a file should be kept containing, for example, the worker's business card, references, and stationery samples. When feasible, it is best to retain contractors who are incorporated and have their own business offices and equipment. That way, more of the work can be completed off the employer's premises.

Temporary Workers

Sometimes an employer will hire a hybrid type of worker, called a *temporary worker*, often through an employment agency. As of 2014, there were more than 2.87 million U.S. workers employed through temporary personnel agencies.[12] Many companies turn to such agencies for short-term staffing solutions. Because a temporary personnel agency typically hires, fires, pays and provides benefits to the temporary worker, it is likely to be considered an employer of the temporary worker. Unlike the relationship with an independent contractor, however, the client company usually retains the right to direct temporary workers and to manage their duties while they are on-site. Depending on the amount of control the client company and the temporary agency exert over the temporary workers and the work performed, the temporary arrangement may make the client company either a sole or a joint employer of the temporary worker. If found to be joint employers, both the client company and the personnel agency will be held liable for violations of most employment laws, including nondiscrimination laws, wage and hour laws, laws governing employee benefits, and family medical leave laws. If possible, the client company should seek an agreement whereby the temporary personnel agency agrees to indemnify the client firm from all employment-related liabilities.

In 2015, the National Labor Relations Board refined its standard for determining joint-employer status for purposes of the National Labor Relations Act (*NLRA*), which governs, among other things the minimum wage and payment for overtime.[13] Under the decision, two or more entities are joint employers of an individual worker if (1) they are both employers under principles of common law and (2) they share or codetermine those matters that govern the essential terms and conditions of employment. Even if the contract between the hiring company and the staffing agency states that one of them is the "sole employer," both entities may be found to be joint employers if the facts show that both companies have the potential to exercise control over the workers. Importantly, a company that has the "potential" to exercise control over a worker's pay, discipline, hiring, firing, and working conditions may be deemed a joint employer even if the company never actually exercises that control.[14] As a result, certain franchisors can "potentially be held liable for hiring and firing decisions by any of their thousands of individual franchisees."[15]

A joint employer is obligated under the NLRA to negotiate with unions and to permit workers to band together to seek better working conditions. Advocates of the decision maintain that the refined test will help workers "realize their right to meaningful negotiation with their real bosses" and earn better wages; opponents claim that it will reduce the number of individuals who had the option of "being their own bosses while pursuing innovative employment arrangements."[16]

8.2 MAJOR EMPLOYMENT CIVIL RIGHTS LEGISLATION AND THE ROLE OF THE EEOC

A variety of federal, state, and local laws protect workers from discrimination in the workplace. They are designed to ensure that individuals are not excluded from employment or denied equal treatment based on factors not relevant to their ability to perform the job at hand. "Because discrimination involves treatment of individuals based on cues that are unrelated to work performance, it can lead to suboptimal organizational decisions such as the hiring or promotion of less qualified candidates."[17]

Equal Employment Opportunity Commission and State Analogues

The *Equal Employment Opportunity Commission* (*EEOC*) is the federal administrative agency responsible for enforcing federal antidiscrimination statutes. It has work-share agreements with a number of state equal employment agencies, which also enforce state antidiscrimination laws. An individual with a grievance must first follow (*exhaust*) the administrative procedures of the EEOC before filing a lawsuit under Title VII of the Civil Rights Act of 1964 or other federal antidiscrimination statutes. Exhaustion requires an individual to file a sworn document called a *charge of discrimination*, which lists the particulars of the alleged discrimination, harassment, or retaliation. The EEOC (or a state agency with which it has a work-share agreement) then investigates the charge, typically by sending the employer a copy of the charge with a request for a written response and any documentation regarding the allegations in the charge. If the EEOC finds that reasonable cause exists to believe that a violation has occurred, the EEOC may attempt to resolve the charge by the informal process of conciliation and persuasion. If the EEOC is unable to pursue the case due to staff and resource constraints, the agency will provide a right-to-sue letter to the employee. Areas in which the EEOC has been focusing its efforts recently include retaliation; disability, pregnancy, and transgender discrimination; and sexual harassment.[18]

Title VII of the Civil Rights Act of 1964

Title VII of the Civil Rights Act of 1964 (*Title VII*) protects employees from discrimination based on race, color, religion, sex, or national origin. It applies to all businesses, public and private, with 15 or more employees. Title VII bars discrimination based on pregnancy, childbirth or related medical conditions, as well as treating married women differently from married men. Although Title VII does not explicitly ban discrimination against gay, lesbian, bisexual or transgender employees, the EEOC ruled in 2015 that "an allegation of discrimination based on sexual orientation is necessarily an allegation of sex discrimination under Title VII,"[19] and "it interprets and enforces Title VII's prohibition of sex discrimination as forbidding any employment discrimination based on gender identity."[20]

Reasonable Religious Accommodation Title VII imposes a duty on employers to make reasonable accommodation for a prospective or current employee's religious beliefs. This includes "all aspects of religious observance and practice," such as observance of the Sabbath, unless the employer can demonstrate that accommodation would result in undue hardship for the business. An employer can be found liable under Title VII for intentional discrimination based on religion if an adverse employment decision was motivated, at least in part, by the employer's desire to avoid being required to make a reasonable religious accommodation. This is the case even when the job applicant has not requested a religious accommodation and the employer has only an "unsubstantiated suspicion" that an accommodation will be needed.[21]

Many states and some cities have adopted legislation similar to Title VII, some of which is broader in scope and applies regardless of the number of employees employed by the business. Neither

Title VII nor its state or municipal analogues apply to independent contractors; thus, a worker's status can be a contentious point in litigation.

Damages Damages under Title VII include compensation for lost salary and benefits until the date of trial (*back pay*), injunctive relief such as reinstatement, and pay for a period of time in lieu of reinstatement (*front pay*). Compensatory damages (e.g., for emotional distress, damage to reputation, or other nonpecuniary losses) and punitive damages are also available but are subject to caps based on the size of the employer. Specifically, in addition to amounts for back pay and front pay (which are not capped), successful plaintiffs can recover combined compensatory and punitive damages not to exceed $50,000 from employers with between 15 and 100 employees, not to exceed $100,000 from employers with between 101 and 200 employees, not to exceed $200,000 from employers with between 201 and 500 employees, and not to exceed $300,000 from employers with more than 500 employees. A number of states (such as California) do not cap awards for compensatory and punitive damages in employment discrimination cases.

Types of Discrimination Litigation under Title VII has produced four distinct legal theories of discrimination: disparate treatment, disparate impact, harassment, and retaliation.

Disparate Treatment A plaintiff claiming *disparate treatment* must prove that the employer intentionally discriminated by denying employment or a benefit or privilege of employment because of his or her race, color, religion, sex, or national origin.[22] A plaintiff can also establish a claim under Title VII by showing that intentional discrimination based on his or her protected classification was a "motivating factor," even if other factors motivated the employer's decision (*mixed-motive liability*).[23] If, however, the employer demonstrates it would have taken the same action "in the absence of the impermissible motivating factor," the remedies available to the plaintiff are limited.[24]

Even if the plaintiff does not have any direct evidence of discrimination (e.g., a "smoking gun"), the U.S. Supreme Court has established a three-step analysis whereby an employee can prove discrimination through circumstantial or indirect evidence. First, the employee must make a prima facie case by proving that (1) he or she is a member of a class of persons protected by Title VII and (2) his or her employment was terminated or he or she was denied a position or benefit that he or she sought and was qualified for and that was available. Second, if the employee proves this prima facie case, the employer then must present evidence (but need not prove) that it had legitimate and nondiscriminatory business reasons for its decision. Third, if the employer meets this burden of producing evidence, the employee then must prove that the grounds offered by the employer were only a pretext for its actions and that intentional discrimination was the true reason for the adverse employment action. In certain circumstances, if a jury does not believe an employer's explanation or the employer has given shifting reasons for its decision, the jury may, but need not, infer that the employer's true motive was discriminatory.[25]

For example, an employee who is a member of a minority ethnic group might claim that he was fired because of his race. He would do this by showing that he is a member of the ethnic group, that he was fired, and that he possessed at least the minimum qualifications for the job. Some courts may require that he also show that his job was not eliminated, but was filled by someone else after his termination. Once he proves this, his employer might present evidence that the employee was terminated for excessive absenteeism. The evidence might include the employee's attendance records and a supervisor's testimony that the employee's attendance record was unacceptable. To prove his case, the employee then has the burden of proving that his employer fired him because of his race, not because of his attendance record. The employee might show that his employer's claim of excessive absenteeism is false or that his employer's attendance policy requires a written warning about poor attendance before an employee can be terminated on that ground and that he received no such warning. Alternatively, the employee may attempt to prove pretext by showing that nonminority employees with similar attendance records were not fired or that his supervisor uttered racial slurs.

Disparate treatment includes adverse employment decisions, such as not promoting an employee, because they do not conform to stereotypes based on a protected characteristic. In the leading case, the U.S. Supreme Court held that Ann Hopkins, a woman not promoted to partner at the accounting firm Pricewaterhouse-Coopers, had adequately pled a case for sexual discrimination based in part on comments from the promotion committee that she needed to walk, talk, and dress more femininely; have her hair styled; and wear makeup and jewelry. On behalf of the majority, Justice Brennan wrote: "An employer who objects to aggressiveness in women but whose positions require this trait places women in an intolerable and impermissible catch 22: out of a job if they behave aggressively and out of a job if they do not. Title VII lifts women out of this bind."[26]

Disparate Impact   In a *disparate impact* case, it is not necessary to prove intentional discrimination. Instead, the plaintiff needs to prove only that an employment practice, such as testing or other employment selection procedures, although neutral on their face, had a disparate impact on a protected group of which the plaintiff is a member. For example, suppose an employer states that it will hire as security guards only persons who are at least 5 feet 8 inches tall, weigh 150 pounds or more, and can pass certain strength tests. This policy would appear to be neutral. It does not, for example, expressly exclude women or certain Asian males. However, if the number of otherwise qualified women or Asian males who are refused employment is proportionately greater than the number of white males refused employment, then that policy may have a disparate impact. To prove disparate impact, the plaintiff must demonstrate that the specific employment practice, policy or rule, although neutral on its face, has, in a statistically significant way, disproportionately affected a certain protected group and that he or she is a member of that group. The employer then has the burden to produce evidence that the challenged practice, policy, or rule is job-related for the position in question and consistent with business necessity. If the employer shows business necessity, the plaintiff may still prevail if he or she can show there is a less discriminatory alternative.

For example, a Latina applicant who is denied employment because she failed an English-language test may challenge the language requirement. If she has applied for a sales job, the employer

From the **TRENCHES**

International drug manufacturer Novartis agreed to pay more than $150 million to thousands of female employees after a jury concluded that Novartis had discriminated against women by paying them less than men, promoting fewer qualified women, and tolerating a hostile workplace. Although Novartis's employment practices were not overtly intended to discriminate against women, a statistical analysis revealed an explicit practice of sex discrimination.

Sources: Velez v. Novartis Pharm. Corp., 244 F.R.D. 243 (S.D.N.Y. 2007); *see also* Associated Press, *Novartis Deal to Settle Bias Claims*, N.Y. TIMES, July 15, 2010, at B2.

may be able to justify the requirement on the grounds that ability to communicate with customers is an indispensable qualification. On the other hand, if she has applied for a position on the production line, where communication may be a less critical part of the job, that justification may not suffice. As with disparate treatment analysis, the ultimate burden of proof rests with the plaintiff.

Disparate impact analysis applies not only to objective selection criteria, such as tests and degree requirements, but also to subjective bases for decisions, such as interviews and supervisor evaluations. For example, if an employer makes hiring decisions on the basis of interviews alone, and if the percentage of qualified women or African Americans hired differs significantly from the percentage of qualified women or African Americans in the relevant labor pool, then a rejected applicant may claim that this process is unlawful under Title VII. The issue then will be whether the process is justified by business necessity.

Harassment   Employees may bring claims for harassment in violation of Title VII on the basis of sex, race, color, religion, or national origin. Although the most commonly publicized form of harassment is sexual harassment, harassment on the basis of any protected characteristic violates Title VII. For example, racial harassment is considered a form of race discrimination, and harassment based on religion is a form of religious discrimination.[27]

Early on, courts recognized that a specific, job-related adverse action (such as denial of promotion) in retaliation for a person's refusal to respond to a supervisor's sexual advances was a violation of Title VII's ban on discrimination based on sex. Such retaliation is referred to as *quid pro quo harassment*. Quid pro quo harassment also occurs when a supervisor makes submission to sexual conduct a condition for receiving employment benefits.

The creation of a hostile work environment by sexual harassment is also a form of sex discrimination barred by Title VII.[28] An employee can establish a case of *hostile work environment harassment* by showing that (1) he or she was subjected to sexual conduct (such as sexual advances), (2) the conduct was unwelcome, and (3) the conduct was sufficiently severe or pervasive as to alter the conditions of the victim's employment and create an abusive working environment.[29] A hostile work environment can exist even if the employee does not lose a tangible job benefit (e.g., is not terminated).

Both men and women can sue for sexual harassment. For example, Christopher Tarui, an investment adviser at Bridgewater Associates, filed a sexual harassment complaint in 2016 with the Connecticut Commission on Human Rights and Opportunities, alleging that his male supervisor had "repeatedly propositioned him for sex" and talked about sex on work-related trips.[30] Title VII applies to same-sex harassment regardless of whether the conduct is motivated by sexual desire. The critical issue is whether the "members of one sex are exposed to disadvantageous terms or conditions of employment to which members of the other sex are not exposed."[31]

The employer is liable for hostile environment harassment by a supervisor, coworker, or customer if it knew or should have known of the harassment and failed to take prompt and reasonable steps to prevent or remedy it. For example, Pizza Hut was found liable when a rowdy male customer grabbed a waitress and put his mouth on her breast. Before this incident, the waitress had informed the manager that the customer and his companion had made offensive comments to her and pulled her hair, but the manager had ordered her to continue waiting on them saying: "You wait on them. You were hired to be a waitress. You waitress."[32]

Under the *aided-in-the-agency-relation theory*, an employer may also be liable for a supervisor's conduct even when the supervisor was not acting within the scope of employment on the theory that it was the authority that the employer gave the supervisor that made the harassment possible. As the U.S. Supreme Court

From the **TRENCHES**

Manager Teresa Harris sued her former employer for sexual harassment under Title VII, claiming that the company's president, Charles Hardy, had created an abusive work environment. Hardy often insulted Harris because of her gender and subjected her to unwanted sexual innuendos. He asked Harris and other female employees to take coins from his front pants pocket, and he threw objects on the ground in front of Harris and asked her to pick them up. At one point, Hardy suggested that he and Harris "go to the Holiday Inn to negotiate [her] raise."

Eventually, Harris complained to Hardy about his conduct. Hardy claimed he was only joking and apologized. A few weeks later, however, he resumed his insulting behavior. Shortly thereafter, Harris quit and sued the company.

A lower court dismissed the case because the conduct in question was not so egregious as to cause Harris psychological damage. The U.S. Supreme Court reversed the decision, holding that conduct may be actionable under Title VII even if it does not seriously affect the psychological well-being of, or cause injury to, the plaintiff. In the words of the Court, "Title VII comes into play before the harassing conduct leads to a nervous breakdown." Instead, the Court took a middle ground. Although certain offensive behavior would not constitute an abusive work environment, an environment that would be reasonably perceived, and was perceived by the plaintiff, as hostile or abusive does violate Title VII.

Source: Harris v. Forklift Sys., Inc., 510 U.S. 17 (1993).

explained: "When a fellow employee harasses, the victim can walk away or tell the offender where to go, but it may be difficult to offer such responses to a supervisor" with the power to hire, fire, and set work schedules and pay raises.[33]

Under certain circumstances, the employer may be liable for harassment in the workplace even if the employer was not aware of the conduct and had no reason to be aware of it.[34] For example, an employer is automatically liable for a supervisor's quid pro quo sexual harassment. The employer is also automatically liable for a supervisor's hostile work environment harassment—even if the employer had no reason to be aware of the harassment and the supervisor was not acting within the scope of employment—if the supervisor took adverse employment action against the employee, such as discharge, demotion, or undesirable reassignment.

However, when no adverse action is taken against the employee, the employer has an affirmative defense against liability for a supervisor's hostile work environment harassment when the following two requirements are satisfied: first, the employer must have exercised reasonable care to prevent and promptly correct any harassing behavior; and second, the employee must have unreasonably failed to take advantage of any preventive or corrective opportunities provided by the employer or to avoid harm otherwise.[35] Thus, employers should always promulgate and distribute an antiharassment policy, including an effective complaint procedure that specifies company officials other than the employee's direct supervisor to whom complaints can be made. Additionally, the employer should always investigate complaints of harassment, and the investigation should be prompt, thorough, and independent.

Retaliation   Title VII also prohibits employers from retaliating against employees for asserting their Title VII rights, such as by complaining to the employer about a discriminatory practice or filing a discrimination charge with an administrative agency or court. More than 34% of the nearly 89,000 claims filed with the EEOC in fiscal year 2014 included allegations of illegal retaliation under Title VII. To prevail on a retaliation claim under Title VII, the plaintiff employee must show that the employee's protected activity was the "but for" cause of the adverse employment action, and that it was not merely a motivating factor.[36] An employee may prevail on a retaliation claim, even if he or she loses on the underlying discrimination claim, as long as the retaliation claim was made in good faith and the employee reasonably believed that the conduct complained of was discriminatory.

Statutory Defenses under Title VII   Title VII sets forth several statutory defenses to claims of discriminatory treatment. Statutory defenses absolve the employer even if the employee can prove that discrimination occurred. Of these defenses, the one most frequently cited is the bona fide occupational qualification defense.

Bona Fide Occupational Qualification   Title VII provides that an employer may lawfully hire an individual on the basis of his or her religion, sex or national origin if religion, sex or national origin is a *bona fide occupational qualification (BFOQ)* reasonably necessary to the normal operation of that particular business. This is known as the *BFOQ defense*. The BFOQ defense is never available if discriminatory treatment is based on a person's race. Because BFOQ is an affirmative defense, the employer has the burden of showing a reasonable basis for believing that persons in a certain category (e.g., men) excluded from a particular job were unable to perform that job.

Courts and regulators have narrowly construed the BFOQ defense. For example, EEOC regulations provide that gender will not qualify as a BFOQ if a gender-based restriction is based on (1) assumptions of the comparative employment characteristics of women in general (such as the assumption that women have a higher turnover rate than men), (2) stereotyped characterizations of the sexes (e.g., that men are less capable of assembling intricate parts than women), or (3) the preferences of coworkers, employers, or customers for one sex over the other. Gender may, however, be considered a BFOQ if physical attributes are necessary for the position (as with clothing or hair models) or for purposes of authenticity (as with actors) or if a gender-based restriction is necessary to protect the rights of others to privacy (as with rest room attendants).

Sex discrimination suits may be brought by men as well as by women. For example, a group of men successfully sued Southwest Airlines over its policy of hiring only female flight attendants. The court reasoned that the airline could not make gender a BFOQ merely because it wished to exploit female sexuality as a marketing tool. Because the main business of the company was transportation, not entertainment, Southwest Airlines could not bar males from becoming flight attendants.[37] In contrast, Playboy Enterprises was permitted to hire only women to serve as Playboy "bunnies" in Playboy Clubs because the main purpose of the clubs was to provide male entertainment.[38] Several other courts have similarly held that gender, specifically being female, is a BFOQ in some entertainment and fashion jobs.

Seniority and Merit Systems   Under Title VII, an employer can lawfully apply different standards of compensation, or different terms or conditions of employment, pursuant to a bona fide seniority or merit system. A seniority or merit system is considered to be "bona fide" as long as there has not been purposeful discrimination in connection with the establishment or continuation of the system. This is considered an exemption from Title VII rather than an affirmative defense. Consequently, the plaintiff has the burden of proving that the seniority or merit system has a discriminatory intent or illegal purpose. Moreover, although a system's disproportionate impact may indicate some evidence of a discriminatory intent, such an impact is not in itself sufficient to establish discriminatory intent.

Section 1981 of the Civil Rights Act of 1866

Individuals may bring claims of intentional racial discrimination under Section 1981 of the Civil Rights Act of 1866 even if the business has fewer than 15 employees. Such claims are not subject to damage caps. Certain courts have permitted not only employees but also independent contractors to bring intentional racial discrimination claims under Section 1981.

Age Discrimination in Employment Act

The Age Discrimination in Employment Act (*ADEA*) applies to all employers engaged in an industry that affects interstate commerce that have at least 20 employees. (Certain states have adopted comparable legislation that applies regardless of the number of employees employed by the business.) The ADEA prohibits employers, employment agencies, and labor unions from discriminating based on age. Prohibited practices include discharge, failure or refusal to hire, or other discriminatory acts against an individual with respect to his or her compensation, employment terms, and conditions. The Act covers individuals age 40 and older, and it applies to applicants for employment as well as to current employees. Independent contractors are excluded from ADEA coverage.

If an employee age 40 or older suffers a change in the terms and conditions of employment (including discharge) "because of" his or her age, that employee may be able to state a claim under the ADEA even if there is no direct evidence of age discrimination.[39] Such a plaintiff can use circumstantial or indirect evidence to establish a prima facie case by showing that he or she (1) was 40 or older, (2) was qualified for the job or performed the job satisfactorily, (3) suffered an adverse employment action, and (4) was replaced by a significantly younger worker with equal or inferior skills.[40] Once this prima facie case is established, the burden then shifts to the employer to present evidence that it had legitimate and nondiscriminatory business grounds for its decision. The burden then shifts back to the employee to prove that there was discrimination and that the grounds offered by the employer were only a pretext for unlawful discrimination. [41]

ADEA claims generally involve allegations of *disparate treatment* (adverse action "because of" age), but disparate impact claims are also allowable under the ADEA.[42] To prove disparate impact, employees must identify the specific test, requirement, or practice that is responsible for any observed statistical disparities. It is not enough to point to a generalized policy that leads to such an impact. Moreover, even if the employee identifies the relevant practice, the employer has a defense if the employer bases its decision on a *reasonable factor other than age* (the *RFOA defense*).[43] The employer is not required to show business necessity.

Waivers of ADEA Claims   Often an employer will require an employee who is terminated or laid off to waive all employment discrimination claims as a condition to receiving severance benefits (such as severance pay). If the employee is age 40 or older, then an employee release of age discrimination claims will be effective only if the employer meets all the requirements for an ADEA waiver set forth in the Older Workers Benefit Protection Act.

For an ADEA waiver to be valid when *one* employee is discharged, the waiver must (1) be understandable, (2) specifically refer to the employee's rights under the ADEA, (3) not require the employee to waive rights or claims that might arise after the date the waiver is executed, (4) waive rights and claims only in exchange for something of value to which the employee is not otherwise entitled (e.g., additional weeks of severance pay), (5) advise the employee to consult with an attorney prior to signing the waiver, (6) provide the employee with at least 21 days to consider the waiver, and (7) provide the employee with seven days after signing the waiver to revoke his or her consent.

ADEA waiver requirements are similar when *two or more* employees (at least one of whom is protected under ADEA) are offered separation packages at the same time in a program for layoff, reduction in force or termination, except that in these situations the waiver must (1) indicate the decisional unit from which the employees were selected; (2) set forth the eligibility factors for the program and its time limits; (3) contain separate lists of the ages and job titles of all employees in the same organizational or decisional unit who are (a) being retained or (b) being offered the separation program; and (4) provide the employee with at least 45 days (instead of 21 days) to consider the waiver. Employers must strictly comply with these requirements for an ADEA waiver to be effective.[44]

Immigration Reform and Control Act

The Immigration Reform and Control Act of 1986 (*IRCA*) makes it unlawful for an employer with four or more employees to discriminate against applicants or employees on the basis of either their national origin or their citizenship status. The statute protects U.S. citizens, many permanent residents, temporary residents, asylees, and refugees from citizenship-status discrimination. (If the employer has 15 or more employees and is therefore covered by Title VII, charges of national-origin discrimination must be filed under Title VII, not the IRCA.) As discussed below in "Prehiring Practices," the IRCA also prohibits employers of any size from knowingly hiring an individual not authorized to work in the United States.

Americans with Disabilities Act

The Americans with Disabilities Act (*ADA*) covers all employers with 15 or more employees who work at least 20 or more calendar weeks in a year. (Certain states have adopted comparable legislation that applies regardless of the number of employees employed by the business.) The ADA prohibits discrimination against qualified individuals with known disabilities in employee job application procedures, hiring, promotions, training, compensation, and discharge. It also requires the employer to provide reasonable accommodations so that the qualified disabled employee can perform the essential functions of his or her job, unless doing so would constitute an undue hardship for the employer. Available remedies for a violation of the ADA include back pay, reinstatement or hiring, and reimbursement of attorneys' fees and court costs.

The ADA protects only employees and prospective employees, not independent contractors. The choice to use independent contractor services must be made prior to the start of a working relationship, however. Thus, the use of any contractual arrangements to try to circumvent the Act by mischaracterizing workers will be considered an ADA violation if the effect is to screen out qualified individuals with a disability.

Definition of "Disability"   The ADA defines *disability* as (1) a physical or mental impairment that substantially limits one or more of that individual's major life activities, (2) a record of such an impairment, or (3) being regarded as having such an impairment. The definition of "disability" is to be "construed in favor of broad coverage of individuals ... to the maximum extent permitted by the terms of" the statute.[45] Accordingly, the primary focus in ADA cases should be on whether employers "have complied with their obligations, and ... the question of whether an individual's impairment is a disability under the ADA should not demand extensive analysis."[46]

Under the ADA, a *physical or mental impairment* generally includes (1) any physiological disorder or condition, cosmetic disfigurement, or anatomical loss affecting one or more body systems, such as neurological, musculoskeletal, special sense organs, respiratory (including speech organs), cardiovascular, reproductive, digestive, genitourinary, immune, circulatory, hemic, lymphatic, skin and endocrine, as well as (2) any mental or psychological disorder, such as intellectual disability (formerly termed "mental retardation"), organic brain syndrome, emotional or mental distress, and specific learning disabilities. Under the ADA Amendments Act of 2008 (*ADAAA*), correction of myopia with eyeglasses or contact lenses is not deemed a disability, but other impairments are still deemed disabilities even if they can be corrected with medication and other measures.[47] Additionally, an impairment that is episodic (e.g., epilepsy) or is in remission (e.g., cancer) is a disability if it would substantially limit a major life activity when active. Some states (such as California) define disability even more broadly.

Major life activities include, but are not limited to, (1) caring for oneself, performing manual tasks, seeing, hearing, walking and communicating and interacting with others, as well as (2) the operation of a major bodily function, including functions of the immune system, and digestive, bowel, bladder, neurological, and reproductive functions. The statute requires the term "major life activity" to be construed broadly to favor expansive coverage. Accordingly, an activity can be a "major life activity" even if it is not "of central importance to daily life."[48]

An impairment is a disability within the ADA if it "substantially limits" the ability of an individual to perform a major life activity as compared with most people in the general population. To be covered, the impairment does not have to prevent, or significantly or severely restrict, the individual from performing the major life activity.

Employers must exercise caution regarding any employee health issue that might be deemed a disability because the term "disability" is construed very liberally. For example, the U.S. Supreme Court ruled that a woman who was HIV-positive but asymptomatic had a disability within the meaning of the ADA.[49] Even though her HIV-positive status did not preclude her from the major life activity of procreation, it substantially limited her ability and willingness to do so because of the risk of infecting her partner or baby.

Reasonable Accommodation The ADA requires an employer to provide reasonable accommodations for an employee's disability, unless doing so would cause the employer undue hardship. The ADA provides a nonexhaustive list of what might constitute reasonable accommodations, including (1) making work facilities accessible; (2) restructuring jobs or modifying work schedules; (3) acquiring or modifying equipment or devices; (4) modifying examinations, training materials, or policies; and (5) providing qualified readers or interpreters or other similar accommodations for individuals with disabilities. Thus, even if a disability prevents an individual from performing the essential functions of the position, or presents a safety risk to the employee or others, the employer is required to conduct an interactive dialog with the employee or candidate, the objective of which is to identify the possible reasonable accommodations that will permit the individual to perform the essential functions of the job despite the disability. The employer is generally not required to make a reasonable accommodation unless the employee has first requested it, however. Nor is an employer required to make a reasonable accommodation for an employee who is only "regarded as" having a disability. Following the interactive dialog, the employer may select from among the reasonable accommodations the one that best suits the company's interests.

An employer considering disciplining an employee for missing work should ensure that the absences are not related to a disability requiring reasonable accommodation. For example, courts have found that employees with psychological conditions, such as obsessive-compulsive disorder, deserved ADA protection depending on the particular circumstances. At the same time, courts have held that if a person has a disability that makes it impossible for the person to come to work, even with reasonable accommodation, then the person will not be deemed qualified for the job.

Undue Hardship   Reasonable accommodation is not required if it would impose an undue hardship on the employer. The ADA defines *undue hardship* to mean an activity requiring significant difficulty or expense when considered in light of (1) the nature and cost of the accommodation needed; (2) the overall financial resources of the facility, the number of persons employed at the facility, the effect on expenses and resources, or any other impact of the accommodation on the facility; (3) the overall financial resources of the employer and the overall size of the business (with respect to the number of employees and the type, number, and location of its facilities); and (4) the type of operation of the employer (including the composition, structure, and functions of the workforce; the geographic separateness; and the administrative or fiscal relationship of the facility in question to the employer). The employer bears the burden of proving that making the requested accommodation would impose an undue hardship on the employer's business. An employer should not make any determination of undue hardship, or impossibility of accommodation, until after exhausting good faith efforts at an interactive dialog and reasonable research of alternatives.

Direct Threat Defense An employer may lawfully deny employment to or discharge individuals who pose a direct threat that cannot be eliminated or reduced by reasonable accommodation to the health or safety of themselves or others in the workplace. Although employment decisions based on generalizations about a group are prohibited, the U.S. Supreme Court upheld Equal Employment Opportunity Commission regulations that permit an employer to refuse to hire or discharge a candidate if that individual's health and safety would be jeopardized by the requirements of the job, as long as the employer bases the decision on an individual risk assessment and not by paternalistically excluding an entire group.[50] In addition, the determination that an individual poses a direct threat must be based "on a reasonable medical judgment that relies on the most current medical knowledge and/or on the best available objective evidence." For example, an oil company lawfully withdrew a job offer to a candidate with hepatitis C because the company's doctors warned that exposure to toxins in the refinery would degrade his liver. The employer should take into account both the duration of the risk and the severity, nature, likelihood, and imminence of the potential harm.[51] For example, an employer lawfully laid off an HIV-positive dental hygienist whose job included engaging in invasive, exposure-prone activities, such as using sharp instruments to clean teeth.[52] "Direct threat" is an affirmative defense so the employer bears the burden of proof.

Establishing a Nondiscriminatory Reason for Termination An employee with a disability may still be terminated if he or she violates a valid work rule that is applicable to all employees (i.e., if the employer has a legitimate and nondiscriminatory reason for terminating the employee's employment). For example, the city of Chicago lawfully fired a Department of Aviation employee for possessing cocaine, a controlled substance. Although the ADA excludes from ADA protection current illegal drug users, the employee in this case was not automatically disqualified from proceeding with ADA claims because he had completed a rehabilitation program and was not using drugs at the time he was terminated. Nonetheless, the court upheld the city's decision, after concluding that the employee had been fired for breaking a work rule prohibiting illegal drug possession, not because he was a drug addict.[53] Similarly, the

ADA will not protect alcoholics, a group expressly covered, if their behavior violates work rules, such as not being intoxicated at work. An employee cannot avoid the consequences of poor conduct simply because it was caused by alcoholism: "Indeed, in ADA cases involving alcoholism and illegal drug use, courts recognize the distinction between disability-caused conduct and disability itself as a cause for termination."[54]

Other courts have found that absenteeism unrelated to an individual's disability can provide the grounds for disciplinary action up to and including discharge. When an employee's absenteeism is directly related to a disability, however, certain courts have ruled that the employer must suspend its absenteeism policy as a reasonable accommodation.

Family and Medical Leave Laws

The federal Family and Medical Leave Act (*FMLA*) requires employers with 50 or more employees to provide eligible employees up to 12 weeks of unpaid leave per year if such leave is requested in connection with (1) the birth of a child; (2) the placement of an adopted or foster child with the employee; (3) the care of a child, parent, or spouse with a serious health condition; (4) a serious health condition that renders the employee unable to do his or her job; or (5) an urgent need ("qualifying exigency leave," as defined in the FMLA) occurring because the employee's spouse, child or parent in the U.S. Armed Forces, including Reserves and the National Guard, is deployed in support of a "contingency" operation (*family military exigency*). The FMLA also includes a special leave entitlement that permits eligible employees to take up to 26 weeks of leave (cumulative with any weeks of leave taken for purposes listed above) to care for an active duty member of the Armed Forces who (1) has incurred a serious injury or illness in the line of duty (*family military care*) and (2) who is the spouse, child or parent of the employee, or for whom the employee is the next of kin.

To be eligible for FMLA leave, an employee must (1) have worked for the employer for at least 12 months, (2) have worked at least 1,250 hours in the 12 months preceding the leave, and (3) work in a defined proximity to at least 50 other employees of the company. Under certain circumstances, leave may be taken intermittently, in increments of as little as one hour at a time until the 12-week amount is exhausted. Some states have alternative requirements and may require employers with fewer than 50 employees to grant family and medical leave.

Under the FMLA, an employer must expressly designate leave taken by an employee as FMLA leave. The employer must also continue providing health-care coverage for the employee on the same terms as if the employee were actively working.

The Act requires the employer to restore the employee to the same position, or one with equivalent benefits, pay and other terms and conditions of employment, following the expiration of the leave, unless both (1) the employee is a key employee (among the highest paid 10% of all employees and located within a defined proximity) and (2) the employer would suffer substantial and grievous economic injury if required to reinstate the employee. As soon as the employer determines that reinstatement would cause such injury, the employer must notify the key employee that the company intends to deny job restoration and give the employee a reasonable time to return to work. Employees have no right to additional leave or reinstatement if they would have lost their jobs had they not taken leave. For example, if a lay-off occurs during the leave, and an employee would have been included in the layoff, then the employee may be laid off during FMLA leave and would have no reinstatement right.

An employee cannot contract out of his or her right to leave time under the FMLA. However, the employer may require the employee, or an employee may choose, to substitute any or all accrued paid leave for the leave time that is provided for under the Act. The Act should be considered a floor, not a ceiling, as to what employers can provide their employees in terms of a leave option. In addition, the FMLA may interact with other leave laws, such as state pregnancy-leave statutes or state and federal disability discrimination statutes, which may entitle an employee to leave greater than the 12 weeks provided by the FMLA.

Genetic Information Nondiscrimination Act

The Genetic Information Nondiscrimination Act of 2008 covers employers with 15 or more employees. Under Title II, discrimination against employees or job applicants on the basis of genetic information (e.g., genetic tests of the individual and those of the individual's family, as well as family history) is illegal. The law also prohibits harassment and retaliation, and it provides that genetic information must be confidentially maintained in a separate medical file.

Summary of Federal Civil Rights Legislation

Table 8.2 summarizes the major federal statutes barring various kinds of employment discrimination.[55] As noted above, many states have passed their own fair employment acts, which apply to employees working in the state and, in some instances, provide greater protection than their federal counterparts.

TABLE 8.2	Major Pieces of Federal Civil Rights Legislation		
Statute	**Major Provisions**	**Employers Subject to Statute**	**Comments**
Civil Rights Act of 1866 (*Section 1981*)	Prohibits racial discrimination and retaliation by employers of any size in the making and enforcement of contracts, including employment contracts.	All public and private employers	The bar against racial discrimination and retaliation applies not only to hiring, promotion and termination but also to working conditions, such as racial harassment, and to breaches of contract occurring during the term of the contract.
Equal Pay Act of 1963	Mandates equal pay for equal work without regard to gender.	Nearly all public and private employers (including federal, state, and local governments)	
Title VII of the Civil Rights Act of 1964 (*Title VII*)	Prohibits discrimination in employment on the basis of race, color, religion, national origin, or sex. Later amended to provide that discrimination on the basis of sex includes discrimination on the basis of pregnancy, childbirth, or related medical conditions.	All public and private employers with 15 or more employees	

TABLE 8.2 (continued)

Statute	Major Provisions	Employers Subject to Statute	Comments
Age Discrimination in Employment Act of 1967 (*ADEA*)	Protects persons age 40 years and older from discrimination on the basis of age. The ADEA was amended in 1990 by the Older Workers' Benefit Protection Act, which prohibits age discrimination in providing employee benefits and establishes minimum standards for waiver of one's rights under the ADEA.	All public and private employers with 20 or more employees	
The Vietnam Era Veterans' Readjustment Assistance Act of 1974, as amended	Prohibits discrimination and requires affirmative action to employ disabled Vietnam-era and other war veterans.	Employers holding federal contracts of $150,000	Enforced by U.S. Department of Labor.
Rehabilitation Act of 1973	Prohibits discrimination against the physically and mentally disabled and requires affirmative-action efforts.	Employers holding federal contracts of $15,000	Enforced by U.S. Department of Labor. This legislation was the precursor to and guided the development of the Americans with Disabilities Act.
Uniformed Services Employment and Reemployment Rights Act of 1994	Gives employees who served in the military at any time the right to be reinstated in employment without loss of seniority or benefits and the right not to be discharged without cause for one year following such reinstatement.	All public and private employers	An employer is not required to reemploy a person if the employer's circumstances have so changed as to make such reemployment impossible or unreasonable, or employment would impose an undue hardship on the employer.
Immigration Reform and Control Act of 1986 (*IRCA*)	Prohibits discrimination against applicants or employees based on national origin or citizenship status. Prohibits knowingly recruiting or hiring individuals not authorized to work in the United States.	All private employers with four or more employees	If employer has 15 or more employees, plaintiff must file national-origin discrimination claims under Title VII.

TABLE 8.2	(continued)		
Statute	**Major Provisions**	**Employers Subject to Statute**	**Comments**
Americans with Disabilities Act of 1990 (*ADA*), as amended by the ADA Amendments Act of 2008 (*ADAAA*)	Prohibits discrimination in employment on the basis of a person's disability. Also requires businesses to provide "reasonable accommodation" to the disabled, unless such an accommodation would result in "undue hardship" on business operations.	All private employers with 15 or more employees	The ADA is the most sweeping civil rights measure since the Civil Rights Act of 1964.
Civil Rights Act of 1991	Legislatively overruled several parts of prior Supreme Court rulings that were unfavorable to the rights of plaintiffs in employment discrimination cases.	Varies	
Family and Medical Leave Act of 1993 (*FMLA*)	Eligible employees may take off from work up to 12 weeks per year for serious illness or family needs, such as the birth or adoption of a child; care of an ill spouse, child, or parent; exigencies caused by military deployment of a family member; or care of an injured service member in the family. Employees are guaranteed continued health-care benefits and job security during leave.	Private employers with 50 or more employees for at least 20 weeks of the current or previous year	An employer need only give protected leave to eligible employees who work in a facility with at least 50 employees within a 75-mile radius.
Genetic Information Nondiscrimination Act of 2008 (GINA)	Prohibits discrimination based on genetic information.	Employers with 15 or more employees	

Source: Adapted and updated from Constance E. Bagley, Winning Legally: How to Use the Law to Create Value, Marshal Resources, and Manage Risk 190–93 (2005).

8.3 PREHIRING PRACTICES

Various laws affect prehiring practices.

Job Advertisements

Many employers begin the recruitment process by posting or publishing a "Help Wanted" notice. Title VII, the ADEA, and the ADA prohibit employers from publishing or printing job notices that express a preference or limitation based on race, color, religion, sex, national origin, age or disability, unless such specifications are based on bona fide occupational qualifications. These limitations apply to traditional media, such as print or radio advertising, as well as to job openings posted on a company's website or intranet and postings the company authorizes on third-party job sites.

For example, an advertisement for a "waitress" implies that the employer is seeking a woman for the job. If there is no bona fide reason why the job should be filled by a woman rather than a man, the advertisement would be considered discriminatory. Similarly, terms such as "young woman" or "boy" should never be used because they discourage job candidates from applying for positions because of their sex or age.

Employers advertising for jobs should avoid placing advertisements in publications with gender-segregated help-wanted columns. Advertisements should indicate that the employer is an equal-opportunity employer, and employers should use media designed to reach people in both minority and nonminority communities.

Many state laws also prohibit discriminatory advertisements, and certain states may prohibit references to additional protected classifications. For example, Massachusetts and Ohio prohibit references to ancestry, and California prohibits references to sexual orientation.

Word-of-mouth recruiting, whereby current employees inform their family and friends of job openings, can also be discriminatory because it tends to reach a disproportionate number of persons of the same ethnicity as the employer's current employees, thereby potentially perpetuating past discrimination. If word-of-mouth recruiting is used, it should be supplemented with other recruiting activities designed to reach a broader spectrum of people.

Applications and Interviews

Employers use the application and interview process to gain information about an individual's personal, educational, and employment background. Unless there is a valid reason, an employer should avoid making inquiries relating to the protected characteristics of a job candidate on an application form, during a preemployment interview, or in some other manner. For example, employers should not ask applicants to provide photographs of themselves. Although federal laws do not expressly prohibit preemployment inquiries concerning an applicant's race, color, national origin, sex, marital status, religion or age, such inquiries are disfavored because they create an inference that these factors will be used as selection criteria. Indeed, state law may expressly prohibit such inquiries.

Often the line between permissible and impermissible areas of inquiry is not clear. Because the actions of recruiters, interviewers and supervisors can expose an employer to legal liability, it is crucial that they understand which questions should and should not be asked. As a general rule, recruitment personnel should ask themselves, "What information do I really need to decide whether an applicant is qualified to perform this job?," and refrain from questions that go beyond that scope of inquiry.

Following this advice will not only reduce the chances of an illegal hiring practice but also enhance the likelihood that the company is indeed hiring the individual best qualified for the job. Several studies have shown that employers both are less likely to hire applicants with "ethnic," that is, nonwhite, or clearly female, names and are more likely to pay nonwhites and women less than equally qualified, or even less qualified, white male applicants. To enhance diversity and combat even "unconscious bias," major orchestras now audition candidates behind a screen. This practice has led to a significant increase in both female performers and musicians of color.

Gender   Any preemployment inquiry that explicitly or implicitly indicates a preference or limitation based on an applicant's gender is unlawful unless the inquiry is justified by a bona fide occupational qualification. In rare cases, a candidate's gender may be a valid criterion for a job, as in the case of soprano opera singers, actors, actresses, or fashion models. Normally, however, questions concerning an applicant's sex, marital status, or family should be avoided. For example, application forms and interviewers should not inquire about any of the following:

> ➢ Whether an applicant is male or female
> ➢ Whether an applicant is pregnant or plans to become pregnant
> ➢ The number or ages of an applicant's children
> ➢ How an applicant will arrange for childcare
> ➢ The applicant's maiden name
> ➢ Whether a female applicant prefers to be addressed as Mrs., Miss, or Ms.

In addition, an interviewer should not direct a particular question, such as whether the applicant plans to have a family, to only female or only male applicants for the same job.

Some of this information eventually will be needed for benefits, tax and EEOC profile purposes, but it usually can be collected after the applicant has been hired. There are exceptions to this general rule, however. For example, state law may require employers to collect data regarding the race, sex, and national origin of each applicant and the job for which he or she has applied. Certain federal or state government contractors are also obligated to collect applicant-flow data. Such data are collected for statistical and record-keeping purposes only and cannot be considered by the employer in its hiring decision. In general, if an employer is required to collect such data, the employer should ask applicants to provide self-identification information on a form that is separate or detachable from the application form.

Age Application forms and interviewers should not try to identify applicants age 40 and older. Accordingly, job candidates generally should not be asked their age, their birth date, or the date that they completed elementary or secondary school. An employer can inquire about age only if (1) age is a bona fide job requirement, as for a child actor; or (2) the employer is trying to comply with special laws, such as those applying to the employment of minors. The fact that it may cost more to employ older workers as a group does not justify differentiation among applicants based on age.

Race   Employers should not ask about an applicant's race. Questions concerning complexion, skin color, eye color, or hair color should be avoided and, as noted earlier, applicants should not be asked to submit photographs.

National Origin, Citizenship, and Right to Work in the United States

An interviewer should not ask an applicant about nationality or ancestry. Employers cannot discriminate against persons because of their "foreign" appearance or because they speak a foreign language or English with an accent. Nonetheless, because the IRCA makes it unlawful for an employer of any size to knowingly hire an individual not authorized to work in the United States, employers must comply with the correct procedure set forth in the IRCA for determining whether an applicant is authorized to work. Violators can face civil and criminal penalties.

Under the IRCA, any newly hired employee is required to complete the Employment Eligibility Verification (I-9 Form), certifying that he or she is authorized to work in the United States and has presented documentation of work authorization and identification to the employer. After examining the documents presented, the employer must complete the remainder of the form, certifying that the documents appear genuine, relate to the employee, and establish work authorization. Form I-9 must be completed within a prescribed period of time.[56]

Religion   An employer generally should not ask questions regarding an applicant's religion, such as which religious holidays the applicant observes or whether the applicant's religion will interfere with his or her job performance. After an employer has described a job's requirements and the normal work schedule, the employer may ask the applicant if he or she will be able to perform the job, with or without accommodation. Title VII's ban on religious discrimination encompasses more than observance of the Sabbath. It applies to all conduct motivated by religion, such as dress or maintenance of a particular physical appearance. As noted earlier, Title VII imposes a duty on employers to make reasonable accommodation for their employees' religious practices as

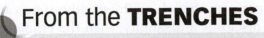

From the **TRENCHES**

Samantha Elauf, a practicing Muslim who wore a headscarf, applied for a job at Abercrombie & Fitch. Although she was qualified for the job, the interviewer was concerned that her headscarf would conflict with the store's Look Policy, which prohibited "caps." At no time did Elauf either tell the prospective employer that she wore the scarf for religious reasons or request a reasonable accommodation. The interviewer raised the issue with the district manager, telling him that she believed Elauf wore the scarf because of her faith. The district manager said the headscarf would violate the Look Policy, as would any type of headwear, and directed that Elauf not be hired. The EEOC sued Abercrombie on Elauf's behalf, claiming a violation of the disparate treatment provision of Title VII.

The U.S. Supreme Court held that an employee or prospective employee can successfully sue for an employer's failure to provide reasonable religious accommodation even if the individual has not requested a reasonable accommodation as long as the adverse employment decision was motivated, at least in part, by the employer's desire to avoid being required to make a reasonable religious accommodation. This is the case even when the employer has only an "unsubstantiated suspicion" that an accommodation will be needed. This contrasts with the Americans with Disabilities Act, which only requires an employer to make reasonable accommodations for the "known" physical or mental limitations of an applicant.

Source: EEOC v. Abercrombie & Fitch Stores, Inc., 135 S. Ct. 2028 (2015).

long as such accommodation will not cause undue hardship to the employer's business.

An employer may only ask about a candidate's religious beliefs when the beliefs are a bona fide occupational qualification. For example, a school that is owned, supported, or controlled by persons of a particular religion may require that its employees have a specific religious belief. In an extreme case, a federal district court ruled that a helicopter pilot could be required to convert to the Muslim religion in order to fly over certain areas of Saudi Arabia that are closed to non-Muslims. The court ruled that the requirement was a bona fide occupational qualification justified by safety considerations because Saudi Arabian law prohibited non-Muslims from entering Mecca, and non-Muslims who did so risked being beheaded if caught.[57]

Disability and Physical Traits   The Americans with Disabilities Act prohibits employers from questioning applicants about their general medical condition or any disabilities. After an employer has described a job's requirements, the employer may ask the applicant if he or she will be able to perform the job, with or without accommodation. If the applicant discloses a disability, then the employer should ask if there is any way to accommodate the applicant's limitation. An applicant may also be told that the offer is contingent on passing a job-related medical exam, provided that all candidates for the same position must also take the exam.

Applicants generally should not be asked questions regarding their height or weight. Height and weight requirements have been deemed unlawful where such standards disqualify physically disabled persons, women and members of certain ethnic or national origin groups, and the employer could not establish that the requirements were directly related to job performance.

Conviction and Arrest Record   Although employers may ask applicants if they have ever been criminally convicted, this question should be followed by a statement that the existence of a criminal record will not automatically bar employment. Because in many geographic areas a disproportionate number of individuals of a given race or national origin are convicted of crimes, automatically excluding applicants with conviction records may have a disparate effect on certain groups and therefore may be unlawful. Some state laws further restrict what an employer may ask concerning criminal convictions.

Consideration of a criminal record generally will be lawful only if the conviction relates to the requirements of the particular job. For example, an employer may be justified in rejecting an applicant convicted of theft for a hotel security position. When a job applicant has been convicted of a crime involving physical violence, the employer may be faced with a delicate problem. In certain cases, courts have held the employer liable where an employee with a record of violent behavior later assaulted another employee or a third party. Liability is based on the theory that the employer was negligent in its duties to protect the health and safety of the injured person by hiring such an employee. If the employer is operating in a jurisdiction that recognizes this *negligent-hiring theory*, a policy against hiring any person with a criminal conviction for a violent act is justified.

Employers generally should not ask applicants if they have ever been arrested. Certain states, such as California, Illinois and

Massachusetts, expressly prohibit or restrict employers from asking applicants about arrests or detentions that did not result in conviction.

Education and Employment Experience Employers may ask applicants questions regarding their education and work experience, but all requirements, such as possession of a high school diploma, must be job related. Inflated standards of academic achievement, language proficiency, or employment experience may be viewed as a pretext for unlawful discrimination or may have a disparate impact on individuals in certain protected classifications. Asking for the date of high school graduation can be interpreted as seeking data reflecting the candidate's age.

Credit References and Reports Rejection of an applicant because of a poor credit rating may be unlawful unless the employer can show that the decision not to hire the applicant was due to business necessity. Because the percentage of members of certain ethnic groups with poor credit ratings is higher than that of other groups, rejection of applicants on this basis can have a disparate impact on certain groups.

The federal Fair Credit Reporting Act requires employers to obtain the prior written consent of the job applicant before retaining a credit-reporting agency to conduct a credit or background check on the applicant. If an employer plans to not hire the applicant based on the report, it must warn the applicant of that fact and provide the applicant with a copy of the report and a specified notice from the Federal Trade Commission. A number of states have passed legislation that prohibits or limits the use of credit reports in hiring and other employment decisions.

8.4 OTHER EMPLOYMENT LEGISLATION

A variety of laws govern other aspects of the employment relationship, such as minimum wage, workers' compensation, and employee benefits.

Fair Labor Standards Act

The federal Fair Labor Standards Act (*FLSA*) regulates employee classification (as either nonexempt or exempt), the minimum wage, overtime pay and the use of child labor by all employers who participate in interstate commerce, regardless of the size of the business or the number of people employed. Independent contractors are not covered by the statute.

All nonexempt employees must be paid a minimum wage, which as of August 1, 2016, was $7.25 per hour. Under the FLSA, private employers[58] must pay nonexempt employees for hours worked in excess of 40 in a workweek at a rate equal to one and one-half times the regular rate of pay. Certain states, including California and Massachusetts and the District of Columbia, and cities (such as Seattle) mandate higher minimum wages for nonexempt employees working there.

Certain types of employees (such as outside salespersons and professional, executive, administrative, and highly skilled computer professional employees) are exempt from the minimum wage and overtime provisions of the FLSA. In general, to be deemed an *exempt employee*, the employee's job responsibilities must include the exercise of discretion and independent judgment, and the employee must also meet other specific statutory criteria, including an annual salary of at least $47,476 as of December 1, 2016, when the Department of Labor's final rule raising the salary threshold for "white-collar" employees from $23,660 takes effect.[59] The salary levels will be adjusted every three years. The FLSA (and analogous state laws) assume that employees are nonexempt, so it is the employer's burden to show that all the requirements for an exemption are met.

Most states and a number of cities have adopted their own provisions regulating wages and overtime pay. Generally, if there is a discrepancy between the federal and state statutes, the employer must abide by the law that is more favorable to the employee. California and certain other states require that overtime be paid to nonexempt employees for work performed in excess of 8 hours in a day and for work performed over 40 hours in a week. Certain states hold managers personally liable for certain violations of the wage and hour laws so entrepreneurs need to ensure that proper processes are in place to ensure that all workers are classified and paid appropriately.

Litigation involving the FLSA has increased substantially over the last decade, with more than 8,800 "wage and hour" cases filed for the year ended September 30, 2015, compared with about 1,900 cases in the year 2000.[60] Misclassification of independent contractors comprises much of the litigation.[61]

Workers' Compensation

Workers' compensation statutes require most employers to obtain insurance for income and medical expenses for employees who suffer work-related accidents or illnesses. These statutes, which generally exclude independent contractors, are based on the principle that the risks of injury in the workplace should be borne by employers. Coverage applies to accidents as well as to gradual onset conditions, such as carpal tunnel syndrome, and illnesses that are the gradual result of work conditions, such as heart disease or emotional illness. The workers' compensation system is no-fault, and an injured employee is entitled to receive insurance benefits regardless of the level of safety in the work environment and the degree to which the employee's carelessness contributed to the incident. In exchange for the no-fault nature of the system, the monetary awards available to employees are generally restricted and lower than those that might be obtained in lawsuits for negligence and other torts.[62] This arrangement is commonly referred to as the *workers' compensation bargain.*

Depending on the jurisdiction, employers may be able to provide workers' compensation insurance in one of three ways. Certain states allow an employer to self-insure by maintaining a substantial cash reserve for potential claims. This is an unrealistic option for many small businesses. Others require an employer to purchase insurance through a state fund. Finally, certain states give the employer the choice of purchasing insurance through a state fund or from a private insurer. State funds and private insurance companies have attorneys who usually determine whether a worker is entitled to coverage.

A properly implemented workers' compensation program provides employers with a basis for arguing that workers' compensation insurance should be the exclusive remedy for workplace injuries and illnesses. If a workers' compensation program is not properly implemented, an injured employee may have a right to claim potentially unlimited damages in a lawsuit against the employer (as opposed to the restricted payments available under the workers' compensation scheme). Additionally, certain states may impose substantial fines or shut down companies that fail to obtain the required workers' compensation insurance. Accordingly, it is very important for entrepreneurs to ensure that their businesses are in full compliance with the applicable workers' compensation statute and that all eligible employees are properly insured.

Occupational Safety and Health Act

Businesses must comply with the federal Occupational Safety and Health Act, known as *OSHA*, as well as its state-law counterparts. OSHA requires employers to establish a safe and healthy working environment for their employees. OSHA applies to all employers engaged in interstate commerce but does not apply to state or federal employees. (A separate program exists for federal employees, and state and local government employees are covered if their state has an OSHA-approved plan.)

An employer governed by OSHA must provide a place of employment that is free from recognized hazards that are causing or are likely to cause death or serious physical harm to employees. What constitutes a recognized hazard is not entirely clear, but its reach is broad and includes anything from sharp objects to radiation. Employers regulated by OSHA are also subject to regulations promulgated by the Occupational Safety and Health Administration (the *OSHA agency*). The OSHA agency is authorized to issue standards regarding a variety of workplace issues, including exposure to hazardous chemicals, first aid and medical treatment, noise levels, protective gear, fire protection, worker training, and workplace temperatures and ventilation.

For example, businesses with 10 or more employees are required to maintain an injury-and-illness log, medical records, and training records. The only types of businesses exempt from these record-keeping requirements are certain low-hazard retail, service, real estate, insurance, and finance businesses. The OSHA agency may conduct surprise inspections at work sites. If a violation is found, the employer must correct the problem immediately. The OSHA agency may seek a court order to ensure compliance. The OSHA agency may also impose fines for more egregious violations. Serious violations resulting in the death of an employee may lead to criminal prosecution of the company's management under OSHA or certain state criminal laws.

National Labor Relations Act

The National Labor Relations Act (*NLRA*) covers most private sector employees but does not protect supervisors or independent contractors.

Union-Related Activities The NLRA requires employers to negotiate with labor unions, protects employees from adverse employment action because of their union activities, and governs employment policies limiting union solicitation. Entrepreneurs sometimes face union organizing among their employees in response to the employer's failure to comply with basic employment regulations, including providing a safe workplace, out of a misguided desire to minimize expenses or streamline operations. Failure to comply with the law or to address employee-relations issues at the outset may cause employees to believe that banding together in a union is the best way to protect themselves. Entrepreneurs facing unwanted union-organizing efforts should consult qualified labor counsel.

Concerted Activities for Mutual Aid or Protection The NLRA also precludes certain employment policies that unduly limit employees' right to engage in *concerted activities* for mutual aid or protection (generally, two or more employees acting together to improve wages or working conditions), regardless of whether a union is involved. For example, an employer may not prohibit an employee from disclosing his or her own salary. Employers must also be careful to ensure that any policies limiting their employees' use of social media or prohibiting employee recordings in the workplace do not infringe upon the employees' rights under the Act to communicate with each other about wages, hours, or other working conditions. In 2015, the National Labor Relations Board cautioned that a blanket policy prohibiting employees from "recording conversations, phone calls, images or company meetings with any recording device (including but not limited to a cellular telephone ... digital camera)" unless prior approval from the supervisor was received (or all parties consented) could reasonably be construed by employees to prohibit their right to engage in concerted activity.[63] The Board ruled that photography and audio or video recordings in the workplace, "as well as the posting of photographs and recordings on social media," are protected activities if employees are acting in concert for their mutual aid and protection and there is no overriding employer interest present.

The NLRA also prohibits employers from taking adverse action against employees engaged in concerted activities, such as signing a petition for better compensation and benefits.[64] The Act provides that an unlawfully discharged employee may be entitled to reinstatement and payment of back pay for the time off work.

8.5 EMPLOYEE PRIVACY, MONITORING OF EMPLOYEE EMAIL, AND LIMITATIONS ON THE USE OF EMPLOYEE HEALTH INFORMATION

Employee privacy issues can arise in a variety of contexts, including employer monitoring of employee email and computer use and employer access to confidential employee medical information.

Computer Use and Email

Employers are increasingly concerned about cyberloafing, employees' spending time "goofing off" online when they should be working.[65] Employers also face potential liability for unlawful, offensive, and defamatory statements sent via the corporate email system or posted by employees to public fora, such as blogs or social networking sites. For example, one court ruled that Continental Airlines could be held liable for hostile environment and sexual harassment if senior management knew or should have known that offensive messages posted on the company email system were part of a pattern of harassment taking place in the workplace and in settings related to the workplace.[66] Disclosure of trade secrets is another concern.

To combat these problems, many employers monitor employee email and employee computer usage to watch for personal use during work hours, visits to inappropriate Internet sites, or even posts to Internet sites that could expose the company to liability. Most courts have upheld the right of private employers to monitor and regulate workplace email and company-computer use, reasoning that employees do not have a reasonable expectation of privacy in workplace emails or computer use.[67] In measuring an employee's expectation of privacy in his or her computer files and email, courts generally consider four factors: (1) does the corporation maintain a policy banning personal or other objectionable use, (2) does the company monitor the use of the employee's computer or email, (3) do third parties have a right of access to the computer or emails, and (4) did the corporation notify the employee, or was the employee aware, of the use and monitoring policies.[68]

To bolster their right to examine employee email, employers should adopt explicit, written policies on the proper and improper use of email and office computers, and they should conduct employee training on the subject. The electronic systems policy should make it clear that the company's computer and electronic systems are the employer's property and that employees have no reasonable expectation of privacy in those systems. It should also reserve to the employer the right to access, review, monitor, disclose and intercept communications, including instant messages, sent or received on those systems.[69] The policy should be carefully worded to ensure it does not prohibit activities related to union organizing or concerted activities that are protected under the NLRA. The NLRB General Counsel Memorandum GC 15-04 provides guidance on employee handbook rules, including email and social media.[70]

Even if a company has an unambiguous policy stating that any electronic files residing on company computers belong to the employer, that policy may not be enforced insofar as it relates to certain communications between the employee and his or her personal lawyer. One state court refused to extend the employer's inspection right to confidential communications between an employee and her lawyer on a personal, password-protected Yahoo email account, even though the account was accessed using the employer's laptop computer.[71] Accordingly, if a review of electronic files on company computers reveals arguably privileged attorney-client communications, the company should either notify opposing counsel or a court for instructions before reading further.[72]

Medical Information

Regulations promulgated by the U.S. Department of Health and Human Services pursuant to the Health Insurance Portability and Accountability Act (*HIPAA*) require virtually all employers that provide health-care coverage to employees and/or their dependents (whether through insurance or a self-insured arrangement) to develop privacy policies and procedures to safeguard protected health information.[73] There is an exception, however, for employers that provide health benefits consisting solely of a group health plan with fewer than 50 participants that is self-administered by the employer that established it. *Protected health information* includes any information relating to an individual's health that (1) was created by a health-care provider, health plan, employer, or health-care clearinghouse and (2) identifies the person to whom the health information relates. For example, employers must establish firewalls to ensure that private health information is used only for purposes of plan administration and not for any other employment-related decisions, such as termination of employment.

8.6 EMPLOYMENT AT WILL AND WRONGFUL DISCHARGE

Employers are generally advised to hire employees working in the United States on an at-will basis. (As discussed in Chapter 15, at-will employment is not available outside the United States.) *At will* means that an employee is not guaranteed employment for a fixed period of time. Rather, both the employee and the employer remain free to terminate the employment relationship at any time for any reason, with or without cause or advance notice. In most of the United States, workers are deemed to be employed at will unless (1) there is an employment agreement setting a specific term of employment, (2) they are covered by a collective-bargaining agreement, or (3) they are public employees subject to a civil service system.

Wrongful Discharge

Judicial decisions and legislation have made significant inroads on the traditional doctrine of employment at will. As a result, employers are usually well advised to consider whether the reasons for any termination will pass muster as good cause.

The Public-Policy Exception Even if an individual is employed on an at-will basis, in most states the person cannot be discharged for a reason that violates public policy. In other words, an employer can discharge an at-will employee for *no* reason but not for a *bad* reason. For example, an employee cannot be lawfully discharged for (1) refusing to commit an unlawful act, such as perjury or price-fixing, at the employer's request; (2) alleging that the company has violated a law (*whistleblowing*); (3) taking time from work to serve on a jury, as a witness in a legal proceeding, or for military leave; (4) exercising a legal right, such as joining a union or filing a workers' compensation claim; or (5) "performing an act that public policy would encourage, or refusing to perform something that public policy would condemn, when the discharge is coupled with a showing of bad faith, malice, or retaliation."[74] An employee terminated in violation of public policy may be able to recover both contract and tort damages, including damages for pain and suffering and, in egregious cases, punitive damages.

Although most states recognize a common-law public-policy exception to at-will employment, several states (including New York, Florida, Alabama, and Louisiana) do not. For example, the New York Court of Appeals refused to create a public-policy exception to the at-will employment doctrine because the court believed that such alterations of the employment relationship were best left to the legislature.[75]

Even in states recognizing a public-policy exception, the courts have shown restraint in defining what constitutes a public policy. For example, courts in California[76] and Pennsylvania[77] have limited the sources of public policy to statutory or constitutional provisions designed to protect society at large. In contrast, the Michigan Supreme Court includes agency regulations as a source of public policy,[78] and the Colorado Supreme Court held that the rules of professional conduct for accountants could be the source of a public-policy wrongful-termination claim by an in-house accountant who was fired.[79]

The judicially created cause of action for discharges in violation of public policy exists alongside a number of federal and state provisions that prohibit certain specified types of retaliatory discharge. For example, the Fair Labor Standards Act prohibits discharge for exercising rights guaranteed by its minimum wage and overtime provisions. The Sarbanes-Oxley Act contains a whistleblower provision that prohibits "any officer, employee, contractor, subcontractor, or agent of" a publicly traded company from retaliating against company employees who provide information regarding conduct the employee reasonably believes violates the federal securities laws, the mail or wire fraud acts, or any other federal laws relating to fraud against shareholders.[80] It also makes it a federal criminal offense for any publicly *or privately held* employer to retaliate against any person for providing truthful information to a law enforcement officer concerning the violation or possible violation of *any* federal criminal statute.[81] The Dodd-Frank Wall Street Reform and Consumer Protection Act includes further whistleblower protections but courts are divided as to whether employees who report violations internally only, and not to the Securities and Exchange Commission, are protected. The 2016 Defend Trade Secrets Act provides immunity to employees and independent contractors for disclosing a trade secret in confidence to government officials or an attorney solely for the purpose of reporting violations of law. Notice of this immunity must be included in all nondisclosure agreements. (For sample language, see Section 4.10 of the "Sample Independent Contractor Services Agreement," Appendix 8.1 on the companion website for this title, available at www.CengageBrain.com.) Also, many states, including New York, have adopted whistle-blower protection statutes that prohibit an employer from discharging or retaliating against an employee who has exercised the right to complain to a government agency about the employer's violation of law.[82]

Implied Contracts   The second judicial exception to the at-will rule arises from the willingness of courts to interpret the parties' conduct as implying a contract limiting the employer's right to discharge without good cause even in the absence of a written contract. Some of the factors that can give rise to an *implied contract* to discharge the employee only for good cause are that (1) the individual had been a long-term employee; (2) the employee had received raises, bonuses, and promotions throughout his or her career; (3) the employee was assured that employment would continue if he or she did a good job; (4) the employee had been assured before by the company's management that he or she was doing a good job; (5) the company had stated that it did not terminate employees at his or her level except for good cause; and (6) the employee had never been formally criticized or warned about his or her conduct. A personnel manual, together with oral assurances, may give rise to a reasonable expectation that an employee will not be terminated except for good cause.

Implied Covenant of Good Faith and Fair Dealing   A third basis for wrongful discharge is breach of an implied covenant of good faith and fair dealing in the employment relationship. In one case, the court found that termination of a 25-year employee without good cause in order to deprive him of $46,000 in commissions was not in good faith and breached this covenant.[83] A startup that fired an employee on the eve of the date his or her stock was due to vest might be found to have violated the implied covenant of good faith and fair dealing. This is one reason why many companies vest stock monthly after some initial period (usually six months to one year).

8.7 THE EMPLOYMENT DOCUMENT

Employers should memorialize the terms of the employment relationship in a written document—either an offer letter or a formal employment agreement. (For ease of discussion, both the offer letter and the employment agreement will be referred to as the *employment document*.) The employment document will clarify the terms and conditions of the employment relationship and serve as an indispensable tool if a dispute later arises concerning the employment or its termination.

Before accepting an offer of employment, individuals should ask to see the entire employment document to ensure that terms often not covered in the offer letter, such as a covenant not to compete or the stock option vesting schedule, are acceptable. An individual's bargaining power goes down dramatically once he or she has accepted the offer and rejected other opportunities.

Although there are numerous terms that an employer may wish to include in the employment document, the following terms are essential.

Duties

The employment document should briefly describe the employee's duties. The description should be general enough that the company retains the flexibility to expand or modify the employee's duties and responsibilities as necessary. If the employee works on an hourly basis (and is therefore eligible for overtime under the wage and hour laws), the regular work schedule should be described. If the employee is salaried and exempt from overtime laws, that fact should be stated in the employment document.

Compensation and Benefits

The employment document should set forth the employee's base salary. If the employee is eligible for a bonus, the employment document should specify the requirements for earning the bonus and provide that the determination of whether the bonus is earned is at the employer's discretion. If earning the bonus is pegged to a specific formula or performance milestone, the formula or milestone should be described in objectively measurable terms to limit future misunderstandings or disputes. The payment date for the bonus, if earned, should also be specified.

The employment document should also briefly describe the benefits an employee may be entitled to receive, such as health, dental, and life insurance; retirement benefits; vacation; sick leave; stock options; and an automobile allowance. It need not provide too much detail, however, as the terms and conditions of coverage should be delineated in separate, formal benefit plan documents. To avoid future confusion and litigation, the employment document should expressly state that the benefits are subject to the applicable plan documents, which are controlling.

The employment document should also provide that the company reserves the right to modify compensation and benefits from time to time in its discretion. This provision helps prevent the company from being locked into certain compensation and benefit levels if circumstances change.

Stock Options and Stock Grants

It is important that the employment document specifically state that (1) any grant of stock or options to purchase stock is subject to the approval of the board, (2) the terms of any stock option grants are subject to the company's stock option plans and a separate stock option agreement, and (3) the stock options are subject to a vesting schedule. This provision helps prevent litigation over whether an outright grant of unrestricted stock was intended, as opposed to a stock option, which is usually subject to forfeiture if the employee leaves before the end of the vesting period. Companies should also consider including clauses in their stock option and stock purchase documents stating that nothing in these documents shall be construed to alter the terms of employment set forth in each employee's employment agreement or in any employment handbook or personnel manual. Chapter 5 discussed employee equity compensation plans in detail.

Duration and Termination of Employment

Employment should be guaranteed for a specified period of time only in extenuating circumstances and only after consultation with legal counsel. If an employer desires to obtain the services of an employee for a specified period of time, the employer should state both the anticipated term of employment and the circumstances under which the employer may terminate the employment relationship prior to the end of the contemplated term. The employer may elect to provide the employee with a severance benefit if it terminates the employment relationship without cause or if the employee quits for good reason (both as defined in the employment document) prior to the end of the contemplated term. Employers often will not want to be obligated to pay severance unless the employee provides a general release of all claims against the company; if this is the employer's intent, then this condition must be set forth in the employment document. An employer cannot force an employee to work (the Thirteenth Amendment to the U.S. Constitution abolished involuntary servitude), but the employer may be able to prohibit an employee subject to a valid employment agreement from working for a competitor before the term of the agreement expires.

Verification of Authority to Work in the United States

As required by federal immigration laws, the employment document should condition employment on the employee's ability, within three days of hire, to verify that he or she has the right to work in the United States. Although citizenship, permanent residency, and a work visa are examples of statuses that will support work authorization,[84] the employer may not require proof in advance, or specify in advance which method of proof, among the methods determined to be acceptable under federal regulations, will be required.

Proprietary Information and Inventions Agreements

The employment document should state that the employee is required to sign the employer's standard proprietary information and inventions agreement, sometimes called a *nondisclosure and inventions assignment agreement*, as a condition of employment. All employees, at all levels of the company, should be required to sign detailed, proprietary information and inventions agreements. As explained in detail in Chapter 14, such agreements prohibit employees from the unauthorized use or disclosure of any of the employer's proprietary information and require them to assign to the company all rights and title that they might have to works and inventions created during the period of employment.

Noncompetition Clauses and Nonsolicitation Provisions

Employers often desire to include noncompetition clauses in employment documents to prohibit an employee from competing with the company both during and for some period of time after the termination of employment. As explained in Chapter 2, although noncompetition covenants are enforceable during the term of employment, the enforceability of postemployment non-competition covenants varies from state to state. Thus, employers should consult legal counsel prior to attempting to preclude a prospective or current employee from engaging in postemployment competitive activities.

Nonsolicitation provisions—under which a former employee agrees not to solicit his or her former employer's employees or customers—are narrower than noncompetition agreements, but they serve a similar purpose of protecting the former employer's business from unfair competition. Because nonsolicitation provisions place fewer restrictions on a former employee's ability to earn a living, such agreements tend to be enforced more frequently than noncompetition agreements. As explained in Chapter 2, the enforceability of nonsolicitation provisions also varies from state to state so consultation with local legal counsel is essential.

Integration Clause

The employment document should contain an *integration clause* stating that the document (and any exhibits attached to the document) constitute the entire agreement with regard to the employment relationship and that the employee is not relying on any prior or contemporaneous oral or written promises that are not delineated in the document. This provision will help a company defeat a later claim that certain promises or commitments were made regarding terms and conditions of employment. Without such a provision, the employee may later claim that the company orally promised a promotion after six months or guaranteed a year-end bonus.

8.8 MANDATORY ARBITRATION OF EMPLOYMENT DISPUTES

Increasingly, employers require employees to sign a document in which the employees agree that they will not sue the company in civil court, but rather will submit all work-related disputes to binding arbitration. Mandatory arbitration protects the employer from the often unpredictable results of a jury trial, and it may provide a faster and less costly way to resolve disputes. A significant drawback is that the appeal rights are limited, and the employer may be bound to an unsatisfactory outcome.

Although mandatory arbitration deprives employees of their day in court before a jury of their peers, arbitration clauses will generally be enforced[85] as long as they do not require the employee to forgo rights afforded by statute.[86] Even agreements mandating arbitration of employment claims based on federal statutes (such as Title VII and the ADEA) are valid[87] unless they are invalidated by general contract defenses, such as duress, fraud, or unconscionability.[88] If the parties have agreed to give the arbitrator exclusive authority to decide whether an agreement is enforceable, then the arbitrator has sole authority to determine whether the agreement taken as a whole is unconscionable.[89] Although arbitration agreements may legally restrict employees from submitting their claims to administrative agencies for adjudication,[90] agencies may still go to court to prosecute firms for violations even if the employee agreed to binding arbitration.[91]

Arbitration awards may be set aside by a court in limited circumstances: when the award was procured by corruption, fraud, or undue means; the arbitrator was demonstrably impartial or corrupt; the arbitrator refused to postpone a hearing when there was valid reason or refused to hear pertinent evidence; and the arbitrator exceeded his or her powers or executed them so poorly that a final decision on the issue put to arbitration was not made.[92]

Employers may require employees to sign an agreement requiring arbitration as a condition of employment. It is not considered duress, and the employer's agreement to hire the employee is adequate consideration for a binding contract. If, however, an existing employee is requested to sign an arbitration agreement, then it is important for the employer to provide some new value, such as a one-time cash bonus, as consideration for the employee's agreement to arbitrate.

Employers should usually include a severability clause in the arbitration agreement, which requests a court to enforce the provision to the full extent permitted by law. Then, if another provision is invalidated as denying a statutory right, the remaining unoffending portions of the contract may still be enforced.[93] Employers should also consider including a provision that arbitrations will be conducted confidentially. Unless agreed to by the parties, an employee might attempt to publicize the fact that arbitration is pending or the result of an arbitration.

Although courts generally enforce mandatory arbitration agreements in employment contracts, there is a split in the circuits regarding the enforceability of clauses purporting to waive an employee's right to bring collective actions under the NLRA.[94] In 2016, the U.S. Court of Appeals for the Seventh Circuit held that an agreement allowing employees to bring wage-and-hour claims against the employer "only through individual arbitration," thereby precluding "collective arbitration or collective action," violated the NLRA.[95] That same year, the Ninth Circuit held that requiring employees to sign an agreement "precluding them from bringing, in any forum, a concerted legal claim" about terms and conditions of employment violated the NLRA, writing that "Section 7's 'mutual aid or protection clause' includes the substantive right to collectively 'seek to improve working conditions through resort to administrative and judicial forums'" and that employers cannot defeat that right by requiring employees to "pursue all work-related legal claims individually."[96] The Second, Fifth, and Eighth Circuits have held that the NLRA does not prohibit class waivers, so the U.S. Supreme Court will ultimately have to resolve this issue.

8.9 FOREIGN NATIONALS WORKING INSIDE THE UNITED STATES AND U.S. CITIZENS AND FOREIGN NATIONALS WORKING OUTSIDE THE UNITED STATES

Special issues must be addressed when a U.S. company has foreign nationals working in the United States or either U.S. citizens or foreign nationals working outside the United States.

Foreign Nationals Working in the United States

Employers considering hiring foreign nationals to work in the United States must comply not only with the U.S. antidiscrimination laws but also with all U.S. immigration laws and procedures prior to hire. In most situations, the employer must file a visa petition with U.S. Citizenship and Immigration Services and obtain approval on behalf of the foreign national desiring employment in the United States. Employment-based visas range from temporary nonimmigrant visas to immigrant visas. Immigration laws are very specific, and at times complex. Federal export control laws may also affect the company's ability to hire individuals from certain countries of origin, if the company's products, services, or intellectual property could be used in a manner adverse to U.S. national security. Thus, employers should consult with an immigration attorney prior to offering employment in the United States to foreign nationals.

Individuals Working Abroad

As discussed in Chapter 15, employment relationships are often heavily regulated by local laws, which vary widely from country to country. Thus, a U.S. company should never blindly rely on a standard American employment document or standard American employment practices when dealing with workers based outside the United States. Instead, companies hiring individuals to work outside the United States should arrange for the employee to sign a detailed employment document tailored by U.S. and local counsel to the location where the employee will be working. Similarly, it is crucial to have local counsel in the relevant country review the company's nondisclosure and inventions assignment agreements to ensure that the worker is both contractually and legally obligated to assign his or her rights to company inventions and to refrain from making unauthorized use or disclosure of the company's proprietary information.

Certain employment laws have extraterritorial application. For example, U.S. antidiscrimination laws apply to all U.S. citizens working outside the United States if the employer is either based in the United States or is controlled by a U.S. employer.

Further, as discussed in Chapter 15, if a U.S. company directly engages a service provider abroad (whether as an employee or a contractor), that act may have foreign law tax consequences for the U.S. company. Accordingly, it is advisable to engage both U.S. counsel and local legal counsel prior to entering into relationships with individuals who will be working outside the United States.

8.10 CASH AND EQUITY COMPENSATION

Compensating employees in a startup company has special challenges and opportunities. Cash is a precious commodity in a startup company, and it is typically best used in product research and development and marketing efforts. Therefore, base salaries are usually significantly lower than the amount that talented individuals could earn doing comparable work for a mature business.

As discussed in Chapter 5, startup businesses generally augment the base cash salary with performance incentives (usually through stock options) to attract and retain good employees. Compensating with stock aligns the interests of employees with those of investors in a collaborative effort to produce value for everyone's stock holdings. It is also an effective signaling device that helps attract individuals who are willing to make shorter-term financial sacrifices in exchange for the opportunity to succeed financially along with the business—the very type of individuals a startup business needs. As a result, meaningful equity compensation helps to reinforce the typical startup company's strategic business objectives of rapid product development for commercial success.

8.11 OTHER EMPLOYEE BENEFITS

At the outset, certain employee benefits, such as health insurance or a retirement package, might not be used to attract and retain employees because, for the most part, purchasing these benefits would require the company to use its cash. As the venture grows, however, broad-based employee benefits are a necessary part of a well-designed, competitive total compensation strategy.

Health Coverage

The broad-based employee benefit that is most important to employees is adequate health insurance. The Patient Protection and Affordable Care Act of 2010,[97] so-called Obamacare, requires employers with more than 50 full-time employees (as defined) to provide health insurance or face a government fine. Employers with fewer than 25 full-time employees (as defined) may be entitled to a tax credit if they purchase insurance for their employees through the Small Business Health Options Program (*SHOP*) and meet certain requirements.[98]

Small businesses generally should not self-insure, so they will typically buy health coverage from an insurance company or health maintenance organization through an insurance broker or consultant. It is important for entrepreneurs to spend time identifying a knowledgeable and responsive broker to help the company select appropriate health coverage.

Under current law, the receipt of health benefits does not create taxable income for the employees (except for partners in a partnership, members of a limited liability company, or greater than 2% shareholders in a Subchapter S corporation). Tax law also creates an incentive for businesses to deliver health-care coverage to their employees by permitting the employer to deduct the cost of employee health coverage as a business expense.

Even with these tax advantages, given the stubborn persistence of rising health-care costs, businesses continue to look for ways to control this expense. As a result, most businesses share the cost of health-care coverage with their employees, particularly the cost of covering an employee's family. A popular way of reducing the after-tax cost of the employee's share of the cost of health-care coverage is for the business to adopt a pretax premium plan that meets IRS criteria. Such a plan allows employees to pay their share of health-care costs with before-tax, rather than after-tax, dollars. Having these costs paid through a pretax premium plan can result in lower withholding taxes and higher take-home pay for the employee. The business can reap tax savings as well, because these payments generally are not subject to payroll taxes such as Social Security taxes.

Retirement Benefits

Startups cannot afford expensive employer-funded benefits, so instead they often offer flexible tax-advantaged plans that permit employees to decide how to split their pay between taxable cash compensation and tax-deferred or tax-exempt employee benefits.

The primary type of retirement plan that couples flexibility with tax advantages is a *Section 401(k) plan*. Such a plan allows employees to authorize the employer to use part of the cash compensation to which the employee would otherwise be entitled to make nontaxable contributions to a special tax-exempt trust account through payroll withholding. Section 401(k) plans offer employees a high degree of flexibility in determining the level of their contributions, subject to an annual maximum (generally $18,000 for calendar year 2016, with an additional $6,000 "catch-up contribution" permitted for employees who are age 50 or older) and certain other legal limitations.[99] The contributions are invested in the trust account and can grow in value without triggering tax liability for the employee until funds are withdrawn. This makes it possible for employees to increase their retirement assets more rapidly than would be the case if they had to pay tax each year on the gain in their account. The employee may withdraw those accumulated assets at a later time (typically upon retirement) and will not incur a tax liability until the time of distribution. Meanwhile, the employer is entitled to take an immediate tax deduction at the time the employee authorizes a contribution to the trust account. For companies with 100 or fewer employees, an even simpler and less expensive 401(k) plan look-alike, known as a *SIMPLE 401(k)*, is available, with 2016 limits of $12,500 and $3,000, respectively.

In the most basic form, a business makes no contributions to the Section 401(k) plan, so its only costs are expenses for establishing and administering the plan. Employees make all contributions through authorized payroll withholding. However, companies may find that plans funded solely through payroll withholding may not pass the nondiscrimination tests imposed by federal tax law, which limit the permissible contributions for the benefit of highly compensated employees in relation to those made for the benefit of all other employees. To safeguard the tax-qualified status of the plan in this situation, companies commonly introduce a matching contribution designed to encourage enough lower-paid employees to authorize sufficient contributions through payroll withholding to enable the plan to pass the nondiscrimination test. For example, a matching contribution might be $0.50 for each $1.00 employee contribution, up to a maximum matching contribution of 2% to 4% of a participant's base pay. The proper matching contribution formula for a particular company's Section 401(k) plan is likely to differ from this example, as the appropriate formula is affected by workforce demographics, actual contribution rates, and other variables. SIMPLE 401(k) plans are not subject to the nondiscrimination rule.

At a later stage in development, some companies also consider making performance-oriented profit-sharing contributions to their tax-qualified retirement plans. Frequently, these contributions take the form of contributing a portion of the company's annual incentive bonus to the plan for the benefit of employees, rather than paying it to them directly in cash. The contribution may also be made in shares of company stock. In deciding whether to divert some of its bonus payout to the plan, the company must consider various additional tax law requirements, such as which employees must be eligible to share in these contributions and how the contributions must be allocated. Cash bonuses paid directly to employees need not satisfy these requirements. Many companies with broad-based profit-sharing plans with contributions based on a formula find that they can make contributions to their retirement plan while preserving the basic integrity of the incentives built into their annual cash-incentive bonus plan. Furthermore, many employees, particularly more highly compensated employees concerned about generating an adequate retirement income, appreciate having a portion of their bonus contributed to the plan instead of having it paid to them directly in cash. To encourage employees to stay with the company, these company contributions may be conditioned on satisfying vesting requirements similar to those imposed on stock options.

Such plans do come with some liability exposure. The employer—in particular, the person or committee overseeing the plan—has a fiduciary obligation under the Employee Retirement Income Security Act of 1974 (*ERISA*) to ensure that the investment choices offered under the plan are prudent ones, even though employees will be selecting their own investments from among those choices. Additional ERISA fiduciary issues are raised if employer stock is the medium of the employer's contribution and employees are restricted in their ability to sell the employer stock in their plan account. The Pension Protection Act of 2006 requires that such a divestment right be provided under certain conditions. Finally, recent litigation over the fees charged to participant 401(k) plan accounts for administration and asset management has underscored the obligation of plan fiduciaries to take due care to ensure both that they understand the nature and amount of such fees and that the fees are in fact reasonable. Employers are subject to certain governmental filings regarding their 401(k) plans, as well as being responsible for distributing certain information about the plan to their employees.

Other Benefits

Even if a young company offers basic health and retirement benefits, it typically will refrain from introducing significant additional benefits so that it can save its cash for other purposes. Of course, some vacation and holiday time off is usually provided from the outset. In addition, many startups offer some basic level of group-term life insurance if only to take advantage of the tax law that allows businesses to provide their employees with up to $50,000 of life insurance coverage without creating any taxable income for the employees.

The next benefit often introduced is disability insurance. Companies may pay for this benefit themselves or arrange for employees to pay for some or all of the cost. If the employer pays the entire premium, the benefits are taxable to the employee. If the employee pays the entire premium with after-tax dollars, the benefits are not taxable. When the premium payment is split, the benefit attributable to the employer paid premium is taxable to the employee; the benefit attributable to the premium portion paid by the employee with pre-tax dollars is taxable, whereas the benefit portion attributable to the premium portion paid with after-tax dollars is not taxable. The use of a pretax premium plan in this fashion gives employees a measure of flexibility in determining the tax treatment of their disability premiums and benefits, at least within the confines of some rather broad nondiscrimination tax requirements governing these types of plans. Several states require employee coverage under a state-operated disability benefits program. In these states, employers should avoid spending resources on what may amount to double coverage by offering a private plan in addition to the government plan.

Eligibility for Benefits

As explained earlier, the misclassification of employees as independent contractors can result in the employer being held liable retroactively for the employee benefits previously denied to such workers. To avoid such unexpected retroactive liability, a company should make sure that its benefit plans (e.g., 401(k), health, life insurance, and disability plans) specifically exclude workers classified by the employer as independent contractors, even if a government agency or court might subsequently reclassify such workers as employees for other purposes.

8.12 EMPLOYER LIABILITY FOR EMPLOYEES' ACTS

An employer is liable for its own negligence in hiring or supervising an employee. In addition, as explained in Chapter 11, the employer may also be vicariously liable for an employee's wrongful acts, even if the employer had no knowledge of them and in no way directed them, when (1) the acts were committed while the employee was acting within the course and scope of employment or (2) the employee was aided in the agency relation. For example, an employer will be liable for an auto accident caused by an employee driving on a work-related errand and for retaliation or discrimination by a supervisor who takes adverse employment action against a subordinate for an unlawful reason. As explained in Chapter 9, an employer is bound by a contract entered into by an individual with actual or apparent authority to enter into it. An individual has *actual authority* when the employer expressly or implicitly authorizes the person to enter into the agreement. Even if an individual does not have actual authority, that person can still bind the employer if the employer engages in conduct (e.g., by giving an employee the title "manager" in a store) that would reasonably lead a third party to believe that the person has authority. This is known as *apparent authority*. To minimize misunderstandings regarding the scope of a worker's authority, employers should make it clear to both workers and third parties when a worker has the authority to bind the employer. For example, an employer might state on a preprinted order form that it is not valid unless signed by a manager.

8.13 REDUCING EMPLOYEE-RELATED LITIGATION RISK

An employer can minimize misunderstandings, decrease the likelihood of work-related disputes or unwelcome union-organizing efforts, and increase the chances of winning a wrongful discharge or discrimination lawsuit by taking certain simple steps.[100] Such steps may also increase productivity and decrease turnover.

Select Employees Carefully

Every employer should exercise care when selecting employees. Companies in a growth mode sometimes fall victim to the tendency to hire individuals quickly to satisfy a compelling need, rather than hiring individuals thoughtfully and deliberately regardless of how long the process may take. Many employment lawsuits stem from a lack of care in hiring. To the extent possible, companies should know whom they are hiring, based on thorough screening, interviewing, and reference checks.[101]

Companies may wish to retain an outside service to conduct comprehensive background checks on candidates for employment. Background checks, while potentially informative, are governed by an array of federal and state laws, including the federal Fair Credit Reporting Act, which requires an applicant's written consent before an employer may obtain an applicant's credit report. A company should retain a reputable consumer-reporting agency if it wishes to conduct background checks, and it should consult employment law counsel to make sure that all applicable legal requirements are met. Offers of employment should be made contingent on the satisfactory results of any such background check.

Document the Relationship

Once the employer decides whether a worker is an employee or an independent contractor, the employer should formalize the working relationship in a written document signed by both the worker and the employer. As discussed earlier, the writing should delineate most, if not all, of the working conditions and benefits. For an employee, this includes job title, duties, and hours; term of employment or at-will language; compensation, benefits, and stock options; the obligation to sign the employer's standard proprietary information and inventions agreement; and the company's right to modify job duties and compensation. For an independent contractor, the document should include the project description and milestones, fees, a recitation of the independent contractor relationship, assignment of inventions and protection of proprietary information, indemnification, and language regarding the contractor's right to control the manner and means of performing the work. An employment or independent contractor agreement should also contain an integration clause that provides that the agreement is the sole and exclusive statement of the parties' understanding and supersedes all prior discussions, agreements, and understandings. It is also advisable to state that the agreement can be modified only by a written agreement signed by both parties.

Implement Good Policies and Practices

Employers should implement good employment policies and practices. Although a lengthy employee handbook is not legally required or even always advisable, every employer should have a few essential written policies, including an at-will employment policy; a policy prohibiting unlawful harassment, discrimination, and retaliation that creates an effective mechanism for employees to report and seek redress for any such conduct; an electronic systems policy to protect the employer's computer and electronic systems against improper or illegal use; a proprietary information and inventions policy; policies governing eligibility for and use of leaves of absence; an insider trading policy; and a policy reserving the company's unilateral right to revise its policies and benefits as it deems appropriate. Employees should also be required to sign an acknowledgment form confirming that they have read and will abide by such company policies. Once the company adopts such policies, it should adhere to and apply them consistently.

Employers should also implement practices that ensure that employees are treated in a fair and nondiscriminatory manner at every stage of the employment relationship. The employer should ensure that all of its recruiting materials accurately describe job requirements and omit non-job-related criteria. The company must then hire or promote the candidate who best fits the criteria for the job, without respect to age, race, or any other protected classification. When evaluating an employee's performance, the supervisor must be timely, honest, specific, and tactful. Evaluation criteria must be objective and job related. A copy of all performance appraisals should be signed by the employee and kept in his or her personnel file. Performance problems should be documented and communicated to the employee as they arise.

If an employee complains about a failure to promote or about harassment or discrimination of any kind, the employer must promptly and thoroughly investigate the circumstances surrounding the claim. Generally, the company may have a duty to investigate, even if the employee wants "nothing done." The company should choose an appropriate investigator—preferably one whom the employee trusts. A supervisor should document the results of the investigation and report the results to the employee. If harassment or discrimination has occurred, immediate and effective action must be taken to remedy the situation and to prevent it from occurring again.

Terminate with Care

If a company has to fire an employee, it should do so with care. The employment document should be reviewed to make sure that all amounts due to the employee are paid within the time required by state law, which in some states is on the last day of work. The employee should be reminded of the obligation to keep the employer's proprietary information and trade secrets confidential and should be required to return all company property and information before leaving. An exit interview may be useful to remind the employee of continuing obligations not to use or disclose confidential information, air the departing employee's grievances, collect all company property, and explain exit compensation and benefits issues.

When a high-level or complaining employee is terminated, it is often desirable to enter into a written separation agreement. Claims against companies often materialize "out of the woodwork" as the filing date for an initial public offering or the closing date for a sale of the company nears. Companies are well advised to recognize and resolve potential claims as early as possible to avoid the actual or perceived leverage that comes with an imminent public filing or sale. Generally, severance should not be paid to the employee without obtaining a signed release of all claims as part of the agreement.

8.14 PREVENTING EMPLOYEE FRAUD

Small- and medium-sized firms are more susceptible to asset misappropriation fraud than larger companies; most fraud is perpetrated by individuals trusted by the business owners or managers.[102] David Sumner and Andrea Fox of PricewaterhouseCoopers recommend a series of steps firms can take to reduce the risk of fraud:

1. Require all accounting personnel to take a vacation during which another employee performs the vacationing employee's duties.

2. Require two signatures for disbursements above a threshold amount and monitor transactions just under this amount as well as multiple transactions with the same vendor.

3. Periodically review the vendor list, including year-to-date spending and addresses, for anomalies.

4. Issue credit cards in the name of the employee not the company and require documentation of the business purpose before reimbursing expenses.

5. Consider using a lock box for customer deposits and ensure that the individual authorized to receive cash receipts and checks is different from the person authorized to write checks on the company's bank accounts.

6. Limit access to the company's bank and investment accounts and keep check stock in a locked space.

7. Create an environment in which employees feel comfortable questioning instructions.

8. Set up an anonymous tip line.

9. Retain an independent third party to audit or review financial statements and deliver them directly to the owner of the business or the board of directors.[103]

Putting It into **PRACTICE**

When Alexei and Piper hired workers to build prototypes utilizing the Genesis T-2000 technology to distribute to potential business partners, they had to decide whether to hire them as independent contractors or employees. From an economic perspective, they preferred to engage contractors, because the contractor, not the employer, is liable for taxes. Classifying workers as independent contractors would also relieve Genesist, Inc. of the need to pay for unemployment insurance, workers' compensation insurance, and other employee-related expenditures. However, Alexei knew that the government favors classifying workers as employees, not independent contractors, and that substantial fines and penalties might be assessed against Genesist for misclassifying workers.

After reviewing the relevant criteria for classifying workers with attorney Aaron Biegert, Alexei and Piper decided to hire them as employees. Although several workers would be using their own computers and working at home, building prototypes was central to Genesist's business and was subject to coordination and supervision by Alexei and Piper. Also, the engineers would be working exclusively for Genesist for a substantial period of time. Although the decision created expense in the short run, the founders hoped to avoid costly liability later on that could even affect the company's attractiveness to investors or an acquirer. Also, they took comfort in knowing that an employer's ownership of the intellectual property developed by employees is much less open to dispute than that developed by independent contractors.

Piper worked with Aaron to prepare a standard at-will employment document, which each of the workers signed. Because the engineers were expected to work more than 40 hours per week, Piper checked with Aaron to confirm that the engineers were exempt employees under the federal Fair Labor Standards Act and the California equivalent. They concluded that the engineers' status as well-paid credentialed professionals doing largely unsupervised tasks over which they had substantial decision-making authority made them exempt from the hourly wage and overtime

(continued)

requirements applicable to nonexempt employees. As a result, the agreement provided for a salary but no extra pay for overtime.

Alexei and Piper were then faced with two more problems. The first involved Subrata Mourobi, a 41-year-old Pakistani employee who had been laid off due to his inability to develop usable resins for the company's prototypes. Although Subrata's resins worked, they performed only 75% as well as those generated by Genesist's other engineers. Subrata had been warned of the need for improvement but, despite extensive review and technical suggestions from fellow employees, his resins were still not acceptable. Finally, he was dismissed for poor job performance.

About three months later, Alexei was served with papers from Subrata's lawyer alleging employment discrimination. The lawsuit claimed that Subrata was fired in violation of Title VII because of his race, national origin, and religion and in violation of the ADEA because of his age. Alexei immediately called Sarah Crawford, who initiated a conference call with Steve Rose, a senior employment litigator in the firm. Steve explained that Subrata could establish a prima facie case by proving that he was a member of a protected group (by means of his race, national origin, religion, and age) and had been fired from a job for which he was arguably qualified. The burden would then shift to Genesist to present evidence that it had legitimate, nondiscriminatory grounds for its decision.

Fortunately, Subrata's poor performance was well documented. Piper had given him timely and honest feedback based on objective and job-related criteria. Copies of all performance appraisals were signed by Subrata and kept in his personnel file. Nevertheless, Steve warned that there was a subjective element to the determination that Subrata had failed to produce usable resins. Subrata might argue that this was a pretext for firing him and try to prove that the real reason he was fired was because he was a 41-year-old Pakistani Muslim.

There was no evidence that Subrata had in fact been intentionally discriminated against (no one had complained of his accent, for example, although a couple of fellow employees had noted that Subrata was often held up longer going through airport

(continued)

security than they were). Steve believed that Genesist would ultimately prevail if the case went to trial, but he told Piper that it would be expensive and time-consuming to litigate Subrata's claims. Steve explained that this was a typical strike suit and that it was likely that Subrata would settle for a small but significant amount of money. Alexei, Piper, and Steve agreed that Steve would contact Subrata's attorney to try to negotiate a settlement.

A week later, Steve called Piper to report that Subrata's attorney had offered to settle all claims for $10,000. Steve recommended that Genesist accept the offer because the legal fees to fight the suit would be a multiple of that amount, and even higher if the case went to trial. Although Piper hated to settle because she knew the company was in the right, Genesist and its managers could not afford the distraction a lawsuit would cause. So she and Alexei decided to simply chalk the settlement up to the cost of doing business.

The second problem was potential sexual harassment of an employee named Bill Rubin by a female supervisor named Millie Meter. Millie, who had just moved from Atlanta, Georgia, frequently called Bill "sweetie" and made comments about his physique. One day when Bill arrived at work wearing a tight-fitting tee-shirt, Millie touched Bill's biceps, and remarked, "Wow! You have definitely been working out. Looking good." After this last incident, Bill came to Alexei to complain.

Bill said that Millie's ongoing behavior embarrassed him and made him feel uncomfortable. He was afraid his coworkers and fiancée might get the wrong idea. He was also concerned that Millie was becoming more aggressive and felt that it was just a matter of time before she propositioned him. Alexei asked Bill if he would like to have a different supervisor, and Bill said that he would.

Alexei thanked Bill for coming to him and assured him that he would take care of the problem. Alexei next spoke with several of Bill's coworkers, who confirmed the incident. Alexei then called Millie into his office to discuss Bill's complaints. Millie's face became flushed, and she said that she had not meant anything by her comments, noting that everyone in her former firm in Atlanta

(continued)

called each other "sweetie." Alexei said that it, nonetheless, was no excuse for inappropriate behavior and that, in California at least, her behavior could create a hostile environment for other employees. Alexei told Millie that a reprimand letter would be placed in her personnel file and warned her that she would be fired if she engaged in similar conduct with Bill or any other employee in the future. Alexei added that the company's policy prohibited retaliation against anyone who complains about such problems or participates in an investigation. Accordingly, she had to be careful not to take any steps that could be interpreted as retaliation. Alexei concluded by telling Millie that Bill would no longer report to her as she was being shifted to a different development group. Millie apologized and assured Alexei that it would never happen again.

After settling the lawsuit with Subrata and resolving Bill Rubin's complaints, Alexei decided that it was time to sit down with Sarah Crawford to go over a lease for additional office and laboratory space and to review the adequacy of Genesist's other contracts.

Contracts and Leases

A *contract* is a legally enforceable promise or set of promises. Contract law makes it possible for parties to create their own "private law" to govern their dealings, which courts will enforce as long as the contract terms do not conflict with the fundamental public policies embodied in the public rules. Contracts enable entrepreneurs to strengthen relationships, increase predictability, create options, expressly allocate risk and reward, and specify the consequences of nonperformance.[1] Without contract law, cofounders could find themselves deadlocked over who owns what percentage of the equity in the new venture. Firms providing services or delivering goods would have no assurance that they would get paid. Investors would be reluctant to invest without an enforceable stock purchase agreement giving them voting rights and protection against dilution of their equity interests. Talented workers might be unwilling to give up their current jobs in exchange for lower pay and stock options if they have no enforceable right to receive the stock underlying the options. Entrepreneurs might find that the fully equipped lab space on which they made a deposit has been stripped of the equipment by the former tenant.

By understanding the principles of contract law, entrepreneurs can read intelligently the agreements drafted by others and, in some cases, create the first drafts of their own agreements. Legally astute entrepreneurs work cooperatively with their counsel as strategic partners to craft contracts that increase realizable value; facilitate the marshaling, deployment, and redeployment of resources; and appropriately allocate both legal and business risk.[2]

In contrast, poorly structured contracts can cause a firm to lose its exclusive right to claim the value of its innovations. While he was the Chief Executive Officer of Apple Computer, John Scully signed a four-page license agreement with Microsoft Corporation that effectively gave away Apple's rights to many aspects of the Apple Macintosh graphical user interface (*GUI*) in exchange for Microsoft's agreement to create a version of Office that would run on the Macintosh computer. After Microsoft released Windows 2.03, which more closely resembled the "look and feel" of the Macintosh GUI than Windows 1.0, Apple sued, claiming that the 1985 agreement was only "a license of the interface of Windows Version 1.0 as a whole, not a license of broken out 'elements' which Microsoft could use to create a different interface more similar to that of the Macintosh."[3] The court rejected this reasoning, stating, "Had it been the parties' intent to limit the license to the Windows 1.0 interface, they would have known how to say so."[4] The court concluded that 179 of the 189 aspects of the Mac GUI at issue were covered by the 1985 agreement. Aside from Apple's use of a trash can for deleted files, the court ultimately held that none of the remaining aspects of the software was protectable under the copyright laws.[5]

This chapter first explains certain basic concepts of contract law, including the elements necessary to form a contract. Next, we discuss the different ways to form a contract and the enforceability of electronic contracts. The chapter identifies general contract terms to consider and provides a checklist for contract analysis. We then outline the remedies that may be available if a contract is breached. We also discuss more limited remedies available under the doctrines of promissory estoppel and *quantum meruit*. The chapter concludes with a description of three types of contracts the entrepreneur is likely to encounter and their special characteristics: leases, contracts for the purchase of real property, and loan agreements.

Chapter 8 outlined key provisions of employment agreements. Chapter 10 discusses contracts for the sale of goods, such as automobile parts, smartphones, and boxes of chocolate. Chapter 14 discusses licensing agreements, and Chapter 16 addresses contracts for the sale or acquisition of a business.

9.1 SOURCES OF LAW

There are two primary sources of contract law in the United States: common law and Article 2 of the Uniform Commercial Code (*UCC*). Most domestic contracts, such as those involving the rendering of services or the purchase of real estate, are governed by common law developed by judges in court cases. Domestic contracts for the sale of goods are governed in every state except Louisiana by Article 2 of the UCC. International sales contracts are governed by the Convention on Contracts for the International Sale of Goods (*CISG*) unless the parties expressly opt out of its provisions. Table 10.1 (on page 319) summarizes key provisions of the common law of contracts, Article 2, and CISG. Unless otherwise specified, the principles of contract law presented in this chapter are generally accepted common law principles.

9.2 NEGOTIATING TERM SHEETS AND OTHER PRELIMINARY AGREEMENTS

Before individuals or firms enter into a significant contract, they will typically engage in negotiations and may draft term sheets or other types of preliminary agreements. All parties should make sure they understand the conditions under which they can "walk away" from the proposed transaction with no responsibility to negotiate further or to perform the terms that have been agreed upon. For example, a preliminary term sheet might include language to the effect that "neither party is under any obligation to negotiate in good faith to reach an agreement" and specifically state that the terms included in the preliminary document are not binding. Simply labeling a term sheet "nonbinding" without including additional disclaimers may not be sufficient to prohibit enforcement of an agreement or imposition of an obligation to negotiate in good faith. Further, if the parties act as if there is a contract by, for example, starting to work together on a project, then a court may find that their conduct is sufficient to prove the existence of a contract and fill any gaps with commercially reasonable terms.

In the infamous case of *Pennzoil v. Texaco*,[6] the court held that a four-page "Memorandum of Agreement" was sufficient to create

From the **TRENCHES**

Two companies entered into a preliminary agreement, marked "non binding," to negotiate in good faith the terms of a licensing agreement for a new drug. Various events occurred during the course of the negotiation that caused the licensor to suffer "seller's remorse." The licensor then proposed terms that were far less favorable to the other party than those in the preliminary term sheet, making it impossible for the parties to reach a final agreement. The Delaware Supreme Court held that the licensor had breached its contractual obligation to negotiate in good faith because it proposed terms that were "drastically different and significantly more favorable" to itself than the terms included in the preliminary term sheet. As a result, the other party was entitled to damages. Note that the court did not find a binding contract to license the drug, only a contract to negotiate such a license in good faith.

Source: SIGA Techs., Inc. v. PharmAthene, Inc., 67 A.3d 330 (Del. 2013).

a contract to sell Getty Oil to Pennzoil. Among other things, the court cited the fact that the parties had shaken hands and exchanged congratulations after the Getty board approved the sale as evidence of intent to be bound.

9.3 TYPES OF CONTRACTS

Contracts can be bilateral or unilateral, explicit or implied, and oral or written.

Bilateral and Unilateral Contracts

A *bilateral contract* involves an exchange of promises by the *offeror*, the person making the offer, and the *offeree*, the person to whom the offer is directed. For example, a seller agrees to deliver component parts by a stated date and the buyer agrees to pay for them within 30 days after delivery. In the case of a *unilateral contract*, the offeror exchanges a promise for the performance of a specified act. Consider, for example, a software company that offers a $500 prize in a contest for the first person to solve a code puzzle. The company promises to pay the prize money, but no one to whom the offer is made is promising to solve the puzzle. The software company is not obligated to pay the prize money until someone solves the puzzle.

Explicit and Implied Contracts

An *explicit contract* is created when the offeror and offeree expressly agree to enter into a contract with stated terms. An *implied contract* is a contract that is not explicitly articulated but is found to exist based on the conduct of the parties or in certain other circumstances. An entrepreneur is most likely to encounter an implied contract in connection with employees who argue that they were promised that they would not be terminated without cause. We discussed implied employment contracts in Chapter 8.

Oral and Written Contracts

Most contracts are enforceable even if they are not in writing. However, the statute of frauds (discussed below) requires certain types of contracts to be in writing to be enforceable.

9.4 CHOICE OF LAW

Each individual state has its own governing body of law that is used to determine whether a contract exists and, if so, what the terms are; whether a breach has occurred; and what remedies are available. As discussed below, a written contract will often include a *choice-of-law provision*, which specifies which state's law will govern the contract. In the absence of such a provision, courts will consider which state has the strongest relationship with the parties and with the substance of the contract, as well as which state has the greatest governmental interest in having its law apply, to determine choice of law. Chapter 2 addressed the application of choice-of-law provisions in noncompete agreements.

9.5 ELEMENTS OF A CONTRACT

There are four basic requirements for a contract: (1) there must be an agreement between the parties formed by an offer and acceptance; (2) the parties' promises must be supported by something of value, known as consideration; (3) both parties must have the capacity and authority to enter into a contract; and (4) the contract must have a legal purpose.

Offer and Acceptance

An *offer* is a statement by the offeror that indicates a willingness to enter into a bargain on the terms stated. In the case of a bilateral contract, *acceptance* occurs when there is an exchange of promises whereby the person to whom the offer was addressed (the offeree) indicates a willingness to accept the offeror's proposed bargain. For example, assume Brian owns a software consulting company. Josephine, a friend who is starting her own travel business, asks Brian to design a smartphone app her clients can use to keep track of their travel arrangements with automatic updates for delayed departures, flight cancellations, and traffic jams and delayed trains or buses en route from the client's home to the station or airport of departure. Brian (the offeror) says he would be willing to design the app for $5,000. Josephine (the offeree), familiar with the high quality of Brian's work, immediately agrees to pay him $5,000 for the software. The agreement, casual though it may seem, incorporates all the basic requirements of a bilateral contract: (1) an offer to design the app for a certain price and acceptance, which includes a promise to pay for the work done; (2) consideration—the exchange of promises by each party, one to design the app and the other to pay; (3) parties who have authority and capacity to enter into a contract—neither is a minor nor is mentally incompetent; and (4) a legal purpose—the creation of the app. Acceptance of a unilateral contract does not occur until the offeree has completed the required act.

If the offeror proposes that something be done, but the offeree does not accept the proposal, then there is no contract. For example, in one case, an individual with insurance coverage asked his insurance agent to increase the coverage limits on his existing policy. The agent, who had no authority to bind the insurer, wrote to the insurer, asking whether it would be willing to increase coverage in the specified amounts. He received no answer. Because there was no express or implied acceptance by the insurance company of the insured's offer to buy increased coverage, the court found that there was no meeting of the minds between the insured and the insurer, and thus no additional coverage.

Duration and Revocation of Offers and Option Contracts   Unless the parties specifically agree otherwise, an offer is usually considered open for acceptance for a reasonable time, unless it is revoked prior to acceptance or becomes void. What is considered reasonable depends on the circumstances and practices in the industry. If the offeree waits beyond a reasonable time to accept an offer, no contract will result.

To keep an offer open for a longer time, parties can enter into a separate agreement, called an *option contract*, which requires the offeree to pay something to the offeror for the privilege of having the offer left open. In most cases, this payment need only be a very small amount in order to create a binding option contract.[7] Option contracts are often used when real estate or businesses are sold. Without a separate option contract, the offer would no longer stand if the offeror revoked it before the offeree had accepted or relied upon it.

Mirror-Image Rule and Intent to Be Bound   Under common law, the acceptance must be the mirror image of what is being offered; otherwise, there is no meeting of the minds. This is called the *mirror-image rule*.

There must also be intent to be bound. Intent is determined by a party's objective intent, which is discerned from that party's statements and conduct. A party's actual intent is irrelevant.[8]

Effect of Counteroffers   If the offeree does not accept the terms specified in the offer but instead offers different terms, that constitutes a *counteroffer*, not an acceptance. No contract is formed unless the initial offeror accepts the different terms proposed by the offeree. A counteroffer extinguishes the original offer so if the counteroffer is rejected, the person making the counteroffer cannot go back and accept the initial offer. Many business negotiations involve several rounds of counteroffers before a contract is formed.

Consideration

Consideration is anything of value that is exchanged by the parties. It can be money, property, doing something a party is not otherwise legally required to do, refraining from doing something a party is otherwise legally permitted to do, or, in the case of bilateral contracts, promising to do something a person is not otherwise legally required to do, or promising to refrain from doing something the person would otherwise be legally entitled to do. Even if the value exchanged is small, there will still be consideration.

In general, the relative value of the promises exchanged is irrelevant to the issue of whether a contract has been formed. For example, in our software example, had Brian offered to design the app for a fee of $10, and had Josephine accepted that offer, a contract would have been formed, despite the wide disparity between the value of the fee and the work done.

Whenever an existing contract is modified, additional consideration must be provided at the time of the modification for it to be enforceable. For example, if a property owner agrees to reduce the rent and the tenant gives nothing in exchange, then the lessor's promise to reduce the rent would be unenforceable by the tenant. Even modest consideration, such as the tenant's agreement to pay $100 in exchange for the reduction in rent, would be enough to make the lessor's promise binding.

Illusory Promises   No contract results when a party makes an *illusory promise*, that is, a promise that in no way restricts the promissor's actions. In a classic case involving a supplier and a distributor, a coal company agreed to sell coal to a lumber company for a certain price regardless of the amount ordered. The lumber company agreed to pay the quoted price for any coal it ordered from this coal company. Because the lumber company was not obligated to buy anything from the coal company, and it retained the right to buy coal from other suppliers, the lumber company's promise was illusory.[9] As a result, there was no contract. At most, the coal company had extended an open offer, which the lumber company could accept by placing orders, with each order creating a new contract. In contrast, if the lumber company had agreed to order all the coal it needed from this coal company, then there would have been adequate consideration to form a contract even if the lumber company wound up needing no coal at all, because the lumber company agreed to refrain from buying coal from another supplier.

A buyer's agreement to purchase all of a specified commodity it needs from a particular seller is called a *requirements contract*.

A seller's agreement to sell all of its output to a particular buyer is an *output contract*. Assuming the other requirements for a contract are met, both requirements and output contracts are enforceable.

Sometimes a unilateral contract may appear at first blush to be unsupported by consideration because an offeree is not bound to do anything (or refrain from doing anything) until the offeree accepts the offer by performing the act specified in the offer. One case involved a pharmaceutical company that had promised participants in a clinical drug trial that they would be given free drug treatments if they remained in the study until its completion. The company subsequently argued that the participants had made an illusory promise because they could leave the trial at any time. The court disagreed, ruling that the participants who remained in the study until the end had entered into a binding unilateral contract.[10]

Capacity and Authority

In general, an individual must have capacity to enter into a contract. Minors and mentally incompetent individuals lack *capacity*. In many jurisdictions, however, an individual who lacks capacity can enter into a binding contract for necessaries, such as food or shelter, often subject to a reasonable dollar amount. Under certain circumstances, such as when a minor reaches adulthood, state law may give minors and mentally incapacitated individuals the right to affirm contracts favorable to them.

When a contract is entered into with an entity, such as a partnership, limited liability company (*LLC*) or corporation, it is important to ensure that the person entering into the agreement has the *authority*, that is, the power, to do so. Normally, a general partner will have the authority to bind a partnership, as will the managing member of an LLC. In the case of an LLC, however, certain major transactions may have to be approved by the members.

Only a duly authorized officer of a corporation (not the board of directors, as some entrepreneurs mistakenly assume) can bind the company to a contract. The chief executive officer (*CEO*) has the authority to enter into most contracts relating to the operation of the business. When dealing with persons besides the CEO, it is prudent to verify their authority, perhaps by requesting a copy of the board of directors' resolution on the subject certified by the secretary of the corporation or the section of the corporation's bylaws that spells out the authority of each officer. Contracts for the issuance of stock or stock options must be authorized by the board of directors before being executed by an authorized officer of the company. Certain contracts, such as an agreement to sell substantially all of the corporation's assets, must be approved by both the board and the shareholders before being executed by an authorized officer.

When entering into a contract with a governmental body, the private party should take special care to ensure that the contract is authorized under state or other applicable law and is signed by the proper official. In addition, it is important to determine whether the governmental entity can be sued if it breaches the contract or has contractual immunity.

Legal Purpose

To be binding, an agreement must have a legal purpose. Thus, a promise to pay a gambling debt in a state where gambling is illegal is void and therefore not enforceable. If a particular activity, such as construction, requires a state license, then the party who promised payment for the services rendered cannot be required to pay the unlicensed contractor even if all the work was up to code.

9.6 ORAL AGREEMENTS AND THE STATUTE OF FRAUDS

Sometimes an entrepreneur will not want to spend the time or money needed to reduce a deal to writing and will instead decide to rely on an oral exchange of promises. Before relying on an oral agreement, it is important to make sure that it will be enforceable in a court of law. Most types of contracts are enforceable even if they are oral and not set forth in writing. However, most states have adopted a type of legislation—called a *statute of frauds*—that requires parties to put certain types of agreements in writing.

The Statute of Frauds

Although the exact requirements vary from state to state, the following types of contracts are usually subject to the statute of frauds and therefore must be in writing to be enforceable:

1. Contracts that cannot be performed within one year

2. Contracts that involve the transfer of interests in real property (including options to purchase real property and leases)

3. Contracts by which a person agrees to guarantee the payment of another person's debt

4. Prenuptial contracts whereby individuals who are going to be married agree how assets are to be allocated if they divorce

5. Contracts for the sale of goods for $500 or more (which are governed by the UCC's statute of frauds, discussed in Chapter 10).

Failure to put a contract in writing in accordance with the statute does not make the contract void, but it will render the contract unenforceable in court if the other party asserts that the contract should have been in writing.

Even if a contract's terms do not clearly indicate that it cannot be performed within one year, a court may still hold that the contract is subject to the statute of frauds. For example, one court refused to enforce an oral employment agreement to sell heavy equipment components after the parties admitted that they had intended the employment relationship to last for longer than one year.[11] To avoid the possibility of having an agreement ruled unenforceable, the parties should put in writing any contract that might take more than one year to perform.

The agreement does not have to be formal to satisfy the requirements of the statute of frauds. In general, all that is required is a writing signed by the party against whom enforcement is sought, setting forth the essential terms as determined from the overall context of the agreement. Initialed notes on the back of an envelope or on a napkin will generally suffice.

If an agent is entering into an agreement that must be in writing to be enforceable, then the agent's authority to sign on behalf of the principal must itself be evidenced by a writing signed by the principal. For example, a real estate agent cannot enter into an enforceable lease on behalf of a tenant unless the tenant has signed a power of attorney or similar document authorizing the agent to sign on the tenant's behalf.

Advantages of Putting a Contract in Writing

Even if a written agreement is not legally required, it is often advantageous to put the terms of a deal on paper so the expectations of all parties are clearly understood. Putting a contract in writing helps prevent later misunderstandings by forcing the parties to articulate their intentions and expectations. A clearly drafted contract provides a written record of the terms agreed to and is more reliable evidence of the parties' intentions than the faded memories of what was said. The act of signing an agreement reinforces the fact that a contract gives rise to legal rights and duties. The drafting process sometimes reveals misunderstandings or unclear points that might otherwise surface only in the event of a later dispute that could lead to an expensive lawsuit. In addition, the process of negotiating a detailed contract, when coupled with trust and other relationship-building techniques, can enhance the value received by each party. For example, researchers found that firms entering into outsourcing arrangements were more likely to express satisfaction with the other party's performance when the parties negotiated a detailed contract *and* established a trusting relationship during the process of negotiation.[12]

Integration, Merger, and Nonreliance Clauses

When negotiations have been drawn out or are complicated, the parties can avoid ambiguity about what they finally agreed to by including a clause to the effect that "this agreement constitutes the entire agreement of the parties and supersedes all prior and contemporaneous agreements, representations, and understandings of the parties." This is called an *integration* or *merger clause*.

The parties can also include an explicit *nonreliance clause*, whereby both parties confirm that they have not relied on any representations or promises that might have been made during the course of the negotiations other than those set forth in the written contract. Such a clause can be helpful in defending a claim of *fraudulent inducement*, when one party claims that its decision to enter into the contract was based on its reliance on oral statements made during the course of negotiations that were not reflected in the written contract. Similarly, the parties can prevent ambiguities with regard to discussions taking place after the contract has been signed by providing that "no supplement, modification, or amendment of this agreement shall be binding unless executed in writing by both parties."

Despite the advantages of having a written contract that clearly sets forth the parties' respective rights and obligations, many individuals find themselves relying on a handshake or signing contracts that are riddled with ambiguities or otherwise do not protect their interests. Many entrepreneurs, after working cooperatively with another party to reach a mutually advantageous agreement, find it awkward and sometimes even impolite to ask the other party to put the deal in writing.

Ironically, this seemingly cooperative approach to doing business may actually increase the likelihood of future disputes. As one lawyer put it, "[I am] sick of being told 'We can trust old Max,' when the problem is not one of honesty but one of reaching an agreement that both sides understand."[13] Studies have shown that individuals tend to be unrealistically optimistic about the future of their personal relationships. Because parties often consider it unlikely that misunderstandings will arise, they may spend little time addressing them in the process of drafting a carefully worded contract. Also, many individuals tend to overestimate the strength of memory. During negotiations, certain issues may seem so obvious that no one even thinks to address them in the contract. As time passes and memories fade, however, the parties to the contract may find themselves differing as to what they thought they had originally agreed on.

9.7 PREPARING WRITTEN CONTRACTS

The strength of contract law lies in carefully drafted written agreements. By using clear, specific language to state their understandings, the parties can often avoid quarrels later. But precise contracts do not come without costs. An entrepreneur must balance the time and expense of having a lawyer draft or review an agreement against the costs of litigating the problems that can stem from a poorly drafted contract and the value of the benefits that might not be attained if the contract does not accurately reflect the entrepreneur's needs.

Drafting Language

Written contracts do not need to be in a particular format or to use stylized language such as "party of the first part." All that is required is a writing signed by all parties that contains such information as the identities of the parties, the subject matter of the agreement, and the basic (what is basic depends on the particular situation) terms and conditions.

Contractual wording is very literal. "All" means everything; "shall" means it must be done; and "may" means it is permitted but not required. "And" means that both elements must be satisfied, whereas "or" means that satisfying either element is sufficient. The term "and/or" should be avoided, as it tends to be ambiguous. The phrase "A and B, or either of them" is clearer.

A careful entrepreneur will be wary of rushing to sign an incomplete or poorly worded contract. The pressure of a deadline is often used as a stratagem by the other party when negotiating a contract. The entrepreneur may feel compelled to sign a contract without understanding it or completely agreeing with it. It is important to resist these pressures.

The contract should set forth all aspects of the relationship or agreement that the entrepreneur believes are important to the needs of the business. For example, a new café owner preparing to negotiate a lease in a strip mall might decide that securing adequate parking for customers and a restriction on other cafés in the strip mall are provisions that justify a higher rent. By carefully considering priorities in advance, the owner minimizes the chances that something important will be excluded in the final agreement.

Form

There are several types of written contracts.

Customized Long-Form Agreements Certain transactions, such as the purchase and sale of substantially all the assets of a business (discussed in Chapter 16), require heavily negotiated, customized agreements prepared by experienced attorneys. The officer signing such agreements should read them before signing and make sure that he or she understands what they mean. It is often useful to ask counsel to prepare a memorandum summarizing the agreement's key terms and flagging any unusual provisions for both the officer and the board of directors.

Letter of Agreement   One format often used to organize a simple agreement between parties is the *letter of agreement*. Typically, one of the parties drafts this letter. The drafter first includes a statement to the effect that the letter constitutes a contract between the parties and will legally bind them, then lists all the important terms and conditions of the agreement. The end of the letter invites the recipient to indicate approval of the terms by signing it, inserting the date after the word "Accepted" typed at the bottom of the page, and returning the signed letter to the drafter. Official acceptance takes place when the letter is mailed or otherwise returned by the offeree to the drafter-offeror.

Standard-Form Contracts   Another commonly used format is a generic printed form (a *standard-form contract*). Standard-form contracts can be used for many business purposes, including leases and promissory notes. If an entrepreneur decides to use one, he or she should obtain an industry-specific sample. Because a standard form will be used frequently, the entrepreneur should have an attorney review it.

A good standard-form contract enhances rather than obscures the understanding between the parties. Therefore, the drafter should write clearly and concisely, using simple language, the active voice and short sentences.

Even with a preprinted contract, many of the terms and conditions remain negotiable. The wise entrepreneur will assess his or her needs and rank them, rather than settling for a cursory review of a preprinted contract. Any changes, modifications, additions, and deletions (which can be handwritten in the margin, if necessary) should be signed or initialed and dated by both parties, so that neither party can later claim that one party made the changes without the assent of the other.

The law generally holds those entering contractual relationships responsible for reading and understanding the contracts they sign. This is known as the *duty to read*. Nevertheless, people sometimes claim that they should not be bound by promises they made in a contract because they were not aware of what they signed. Small print or a crowded format can lend credence to this claim. Besides writing clearly and using a readable type size, entrepreneurs can take other steps to counter this problem. For example, if certain terms and conditions are printed on the reverse side of the page, the drafter can state in bold letters: "This contract is subject to terms and conditions on the reverse side hereof." Requiring the signer to initial key terms or conditions can also help to prove later that the signer was aware of those terms.

Attachments *Attachments* (also called *exhibits*) may also be used to supplement a written agreement. Attachments are ideal when the additional terms are too extensive to note in the margins of the agreement. For example, a caterer might use a general-form contract that contains not only printed terms and conditions but also blank spaces in which the caterer can fill in such information as the quantity of hors d'oeuvres required, the date of the function, and the price. Additional issues not covered in the form contract can be addressed in a simple attachment that both parties sign and date at the same time they sign the main document. To ensure that the attachment is treated as part of the contractual agreement (in other words, that the meeting of the minds incorporates both documents), the drafter should name the attachment (e.g., "Attachment A" or "Exhibit 10.2" for an attachment first referenced in Section 10.2) and include a clause in the main contract clearly stating that the main agreement and the named attachment are incorporated into one contract.

Addenda *Addenda* provide a way for the parties to modify a contract. Whereas attachments are used at the time the main contract is approved by both parties, addenda are used *after* the main contract has been signed by both parties. Typically, the parties note changes to an already approved contract by crossing out words and writing in new ones, then initialing the revisions. If the modifications are extensive, however, an addendum may be drawn up instead.

Each addendum should include an explicit reference to the main contract. For example, "This is an addendum to the lease dated March 10, 2016, between Burns Construction and Kevin Rose for the lease of real property...." The addendum should also spell out the relevant changes and state clearly that, if the terms of the original contract and the addendum conflict, the addendum's terms should prevail. It is also wise to provide that "the parties agree to the above changes and additions to the original contract" and "in all other respects, the terms of the original contract remain in full effect." It is important to ensure that each party gives consideration for the modifications in the addendum. This is not an issue when both parties are giving up rights or assuming new or different duties, but it can arise when one party makes a unilateral concession.

9.8 ELECTRONIC CONTRACTS

In the United States, many contracts executed electronically are given the same legal effect as physical paper contracts.

The Uniform Electronic Transactions Act

Although laws governing electronic transactions vary from state to state, 47 states[14] plus the District of Columbia, Puerto Rico, and the U.S. Virgin Islands have enacted the Uniform Electronic Transactions Act (*UETA*). UETA sets forth four basic rules regarding contracts entered into by parties who agree to conduct business electronically:

1. A record or signature may not be denied legal effect or enforceability solely because it is in electronic form.
2. A contract may not be denied legal effect or enforceability solely because an electronic record was used in its formation.
3. If a law requires a record to be in writing, an electronic record satisfies the law.
4. If a law (such as the statute of frauds) requires a signature, an electronic signature is sufficient.[15]

Almost any mark or process intended to sign an electronic record will constitute an electronic signature, including a typed name at the bottom of an email message, a faxed signature, or a "click-through" process on a computer screen whereby a person clicks on "I Agree" on a website. (Chapter 10 discusses "click-through" contracts in more detail.) Two elements are necessary to create a valid electronic signature: (1) the person must intend the process or mark provided to act as a signature and (2) the electronic signature must be attributed to that person.

The E-Sign Act

In an effort to ensure more uniform treatment of electronic transactions across the United States, Congress enacted the Electronic Signatures in Global and National Commerce Act, more commonly known as the *E-Sign Act*. Consistent with UETA, the E-Sign Act provides that "a signature, contract, or other record ... may not be denied legal effect, validity, or enforceability solely because it is in electronic form." The provisions of the E-Sign Act are very similar to those of UETA. Unlike UETA, however, which applies to intrastate, interstate, and foreign transactions, the E-Sign Act governs only transactions in interstate and foreign commerce. The E-Sign Act expressly preempts all state laws inconsistent with its provisions. For states that have adopted UETA, however, the E-Sign Act does allow state law "to modify, limit, or supersede" its provisions to the extent such variations are not inconsistent with the E-Sign Act. Which variations will ultimately be considered "inconsistent" is not entirely clear and may have to be determined by the courts.

An email from one business to another can constitute an electronic signature and thereby create a binding agreement between the two companies even though neither asked for a written contract.[16] Federal bankruptcy courts have also construed emails as signatures sufficient to establish a contract between a business and its creditors.[17] Mere receipt of an email, however, is not sufficient to establish a contractual relationship. Although parties can give their signatures by email, all the elements of a contract, such as offer, acceptance and consideration, must be present to form a valid contract.[18]

Certain federal agencies have indicated that express written consent can be given via text message. For example, the Federal Trade

Commission, in enforcing the Telemarketing Sales Rule, and the Federal Communications Commission, in enforcing the Telephone Consumer Protection Act of 1991 (both of which deal with telemarketing), have declared that "consent obtained in compliance with the E-SIGN Act will satisfy the requirements [of the relevant rule], including permission obtained via an email, website form, text message...."[19] Whether text messages or instant messaging will be deemed valid signatures in other contexts remains unclear.

Exclusions from UETA and the E-Sign Act

To protect those who choose not to conduct business electronically or do not have access to computers, the E-Sign Act and UETA require that the use or acceptance of electronic records or electronic signatures be voluntary. Moreover, under the E-Sign Act, if a business is legally bound to provide information to a consumer in writing, electronic records may be used only if the business first secures the consumer's informed consent.

Notwithstanding the broad scope of the E-Sign Act and UETA, several classes of documents are not covered by their provisions and thus may not be considered fully enforceable if executed electronically. Both UETA and the E-Sign Act exclude the following documents:

> ➤ Wills, codicils, and trusts
> ➤ Contracts or records relating to adoption, divorce, or other matters of family law
> ➤ Contracts governed by certain provisions of the Uniform Commercial Code in effect in each state.

Unlike UETA, the E-Sign Act additionally excludes the following:

> ➤ Court orders and notices and other official court documents
> ➤ Notices of cancellation or termination of utility services
> ➤ Notices regarding credit agreements secured by, or rental agreements for, a primary residence (e.g., eviction and foreclosure notices)
> ➤ Notices of cancellation or termination of health or life insurance benefits

> Recall notices
> Documents required to accompany the transport of hazardous materials, pesticides, or toxic materials.

Of course, a U.S. national standard governing electronic transactions does not resolve inconsistencies in laws of other countries. As discussed further in Chapter 10, international coordination is necessary to ensure that electronic transactions are consistently enforced across national borders.

9.9   GENERAL CONTRACT TERMS TO CONSIDER

Exactly what should be included in a written contract varies by situation, but without question any contract should include provisions that identify the parties, establish the existence of a contractual relationship, and verify the intent of the parties to be bound by the contract. It is also important to specify the assumptions on which the contract is based, the parties' obligations, conditions to performance, timing issues, the allocation of risk, choice of law, and dispute resolution procedures.

Identification

Contracts should explicitly state the names and addresses of the parties. Corporations, partnerships and other entities should be identified as such, together with an indication of the state under whose laws they were formed.

Signatures

A contract that is subject to the statute of frauds can be enforced only against the party or parties who have signed it. If possible, all parties should sign on the same signature page. If this is not possible (e.g., if one party is located in a different state), then the agreement should expressly provide for the signing of counterparts. When using *counterparts*, each party signs a copy of the signature page, and all signature pages taken together are deemed to be one original.

Sole proprietors may sign on their own behalf, making them personally responsible for fulfilling the terms of the agreement.

A general partner should sign on behalf of a general or limited partnership. This is done by setting forth the name of the partnership and then on a separate line writing the name of the person signing:

[NAME OF PARTNERSHIP]

By _____

_____
[name of person signing]

Its _____
[title]

By making it clear that the contract is being entered into by the partnership, the general partner can require the other party to exhaust the partnership's assets first before going against the general partner's personal assets.

The officer of a corporation or a manager of a limited liability company is not personally responsible for the obligations of the entity as long as the officer or manager makes it clear that he or she is signing only in a representative capacity. This is done by setting forth the name of the corporation or LLC and then on a separate line writing the name of the person signing:

[NAME OF CORPORATION OR LLC]

By _____

_____
[name of person signing]

Its _____
[title]

Ideally, the parties should produce two identical copies of the agreement and sign both copies so that each party has an original, but today this is often not the practice of parties in the United States unless there are special circumstances. Duplicate photocopies, scanned copies, facsimiles, or photographs may be substituted for the original in court unless (1) a genuine question is raised as to the authenticity of the original or (2) circumstances suggest that it would be unfair to admit the duplicate in place of the original; in either case, the *best evidence rule* requires the introduction of an original.

Establishing Intent to Enter into a Contract

Some disputes over contractual relationships center on the question of original intent or even the very existence of a contract.

Existence of a Contract and Intent to Be Bound   Because an arbitrator or court might later have to determine the parties' intentions, it is useful to have an explicit preamble or statement summarizing the parties' intentions (called the *recitals*) drafted at the time the parties enter into the agreement. The recitals are typically placed at the beginning of the contract and often each recital is preceded by the term "whereas." Recitals are not binding, so it is important to use them as orientation for the reader and not as the location for substantive terms of the agreement.

Date   It is important to establish when the meeting of the minds took place. If the parties all sign the agreement on the same date and want it to be effective immediately upon signing, then the agreement should provide: "This Agreement is executed and entered into on [date]." If the parties sign on different days, then the agreement might provide that it is "made and entered into as of the later of the two dates on the signature page." If the agreement is to be effective as of a date other than the date it is signed, then the agreement should provide: "This Agreement is executed and entered into as of [date]."

Terms of the Agreement

The following types of provisions are the heart of the agreement and determine the parties' contractual obligations to one another.

Representations and Warranties   Any key assumptions or understandings upon which the agreement rests should be explicitly stated as *representations and warranties*. For example, "Party A represents and warrants that the ventilation system when installed meets the specifications on Schedule A." If such a representation were not included in the contract, Party A could later claim that it was under the impression that the equipment was to be installed under less stringent specifications or for a different use.

Representations and warranties are also used to contractually guarantee that certain facts are true. For example, an investor will want assurance that the company owns all of its intellectual property and that it is not violating any other person's rights. The investors can sue for breach of contract if it later turns out that someone else—such as a prior employer of the founder or a university where the founder was a graduate student—owns key technology.

Conditions The fulfillment of certain contractual obligations may be conditioned on the occurrence of certain events (called *conditions*), such as the approval of a loan application by a third party, or on the other party's performance of a particular obligation, such as the procurement of insurance. Normally, a party's obligation to perform under a contract is conditional on the representations and warranties being true and correct in all material respects as of both the date the contract is entered into and the date performance is due, such as the closing date for the sale of real property.

The only restriction on the use of conditions is that one party's obligation may not be made conditional upon some occurrence exclusively within the control of that same party (e.g., approval by that party's lawyer). If one party to an agreement has complete control over the occurrence of a condition, that party's obligation will effectively be negated, converting an otherwise valid contract into an unenforceable illusory promise.

Each condition should be stated clearly, using simple, straightforward language, such as "if," "only if," "unless and until," or "provided that." For example, a stock purchase agreement will usually include language to this effect: "The investors shall have no obligation to purchase the Shares and to pay the Purchase Price unless all conditions set forth in Section 4 are satisfied on or prior to the Closing Date."

Logistical Considerations Certain details of performance, such as delivery and installation instructions, should be discussed in advance and included in the written agreement.

Payment Terms Payment terms should specify both when and in what form payment must be made. If payment is to be made in installments, the seller can attempt to deter a buyer from missing payments by including an acceleration clause in the written agreement. An *acceleration clause* specifies that all remaining installments (and interest, if applicable) become immediately due and payable if the buyer is late in paying any installment. Some acceleration clauses take effect automatically upon default, but in many contracts (especially when long-term relationships are a factor), it may be preferable to make the exercise of the acceleration clause optional at the creditor's discretion.

Timing of Performance and Liquidated Damages The contract should specify when each party's obligations must be fulfilled. Special deadlines or time requirements should be stated explicitly. For example, if *time is of the essence* (i.e., if performance being completed on time is especially important), that fact should be noted in the contract. The entrepreneur may want to reserve the right to terminate the contract in the event the other party fails to perform on time. This would be appropriate, for example, when a florist orders a certain number of Easter lilies from a grower in anticipation of filling customers' orders before Easter; lilies delivered a week late will be of no use to the florist, who would have had to find another source.

Another method of discouraging tardiness and other breaches is to build in a specific amount that one party will pay the other party if it does not perform its obligations by the deadline. In drafting such a *liquidated damages* clause, the drafter must take care not to build the wrong incentives into the contract. Finishing the job safely and properly should not be subordinated to finishing it on time. To realign performance with values such as safety and quality, the drafter may want to include a separate clause that, for example, requires a third party's approval of the completed performance before payment is due. This arrangement is often used in construction contracts. In addition, determining the amount to be paid as liquidated damages may be difficult. The amount should reflect the parties' best estimate of the actual damage that would result from the delay in performance. Moreover, the amount should be high enough to influence the party's behavior but not so high as to constitute a penalty. Courts generally are unwilling to enforce penalties in contract cases.

Notice and Opportunity to Cure   It is often helpful to include a provision requiring written notice of a failure to comply with the contract and some opportunity to cure the fault. For example, a company's chief medical officer (*CMO*) might have an employment agreement that requires the CMO to maintain a valid medical license. The CMO should negotiate to add a provision to require the company to provide written notice and a certain period of time for the CMO to renew the license if it lapses or expires. Notice and an opportunity to cure can be even more important in a subjective matter, such as a company subcontracting with a lab for services. If the lab is not performing up to the company's expectations, a requirement for written notification from the company and an opportunity to cure will help clarify both parties' obligations.

Duration and Notice of Termination   The contract should clearly specify the duration of the agreement and the circumstances under which it is terminated. Regardless of the original intent of the parties, contracts lacking a specific duration may be construed later as terminable at will by either party. It is better to avoid this ambiguity by including a clause either stating that the contract is terminable at will or indicating its duration.

Furthermore, a contract terminable at will should be drafted carefully to avoid providing either party with an absolute right of termination, which might cause a court to find an illusory promise and thus no contract. For example, the drafter can stipulate that a party or parties must give notice of intent to terminate the contract a specific amount of time before actual termination is effective. It is also wise to outline specific rules as to how proper notice shall be effected.

Renewability of the Contract   The contract may be automatically renewable, meaning that the contract is automatically extended for a certain period unless one of the parties gives notice of its intention not to renew within a stated period of time before expiration of the contract. Or the contract may be renewable dependent upon prior notice of intention to renew. Either way, the drafter should take care to leave an opportunity for exit so that the contract cannot be construed as perpetual.

Allocation of Risk   The parties to a contract should decide which events would relieve one or more parties of their obligations under the contract. For example, the occurrence of certain natural disasters (known as *acts of God*), such as an earthquake, fire or flood, that make performance impossible or commercially impracticable may release the parties from their contractual obligations. Similarly, an unanticipated governmental action (such as an international embargo), acts of terrorism, computer hacking, or *force majeure* (literally translated as *superior force* but used to designate problems beyond the reasonable control of a party) may excuse the parties from performance if it makes performance impossible or commercially impracticable.

Courts are very reluctant to find *commercial impracticability*, however. The event must have been both unforeseen and unforeseeable, and the party asserting impracticability must not have expressly or implicitly assumed the risk of the occurrence. It is not enough that performance becomes unprofitable or more costly. For example, one case pitted a honey wholesaler against a honey producer that had unilaterally demanded a price nearly 50% above the contracted figure during a particularly dry summer. After the jury considered the weather conditions and the producer's ability to perform its contractual obligations, it concluded that neither the contract's force majeure clause nor commercial impracticability excused the producer's failure to comply with the terms of the contract. In affirming the decision, the appellate court noted, "The *force majeure* clause would allow [the producer] to stop performance if the jury determined a drought occurred. It would not, however, give [the producer] the unilateral right to raise the price of honey under the contract simply because the production of honey was less than expected."[20]

It is often advisable to draft an exculpatory clause listing the many potentially disastrous events that could prevent the party or parties from fulfilling their obligations under the contract. For example:

> Party A will not be liable for any loss, including, without limitation, the loss of Party B's prospective profits, resulting from events outside of Party A's control. Examples of occurrences outside of Party A's control include, but are not limited to, strikes, lockouts, fires, floods, mud slides, hurricanes, earthquakes, machine breakdowns,

lack of shipping space, carrier delays, governmental actions, and inability to procure goods or raw materials.

Although persuading the other party to accept such a wide-ranging exculpatory clause may be a challenge, it is worth the effort to include as many potential problems as possible. Despite the wording "but are not limited to," any events that are not listed in the clause may be subjects of dispute in an action for breach of contract. Also, it is important to keep in mind that including such a clause does not automatically release the party from liability under the circumstances listed. If a court concludes that a contingency could have been reasonably guarded against, for example by shuttering windows before a hurricane, then it may decide not to excuse the party from liability for the resulting loss.

In some instances, the parties may consciously want to shift the risk of certain events occurring to one party. For example, a customer might want its supplier to insure against certain risks, such as fire, that might make delivery impossible or commercially impracticable. Similarly, a customer might want its supplier to buy futures or forward contracts to ensure the supply of raw materials. If this is both parties' intent, then the contract should expressly state that occurrence of the specified events shall not excuse nonperformance. It should also specify when a party is required to procure insurance.

Binding Arbitration Despite the best intentions of both parties, misunderstandings and disputes will arise. One way to avoid the expense, tension, delay and publicity of litigation, as well as the vagaries of a jury trial, is to resolve the issue through arbitration. In arbitration, the parties take their dispute to one or more persons given the power to make a final decision that binds the parties. Unless the parties agree in advance to employ arbitration for conflicts that arise, they are likely to wind up in litigation to resolve competing claims. Often, once a dispute has arisen, one of the parties feels it has a strong case and is unwilling to concede its advantage by seeking an equitable solution through arbitration.

If the parties include an arbitration clause, they may want to specify which arbitration service will be used. Some industries have special arbitration agencies that perform this service for members of their trade; some do not, forcing the parties to rely on a private arbitration firm or a branch of the American Arbitration Association (*AAA*). The AAA suggests inserting a clause similar to this:

> Any controversy or claim arising out of or relating to this contract, or the breach thereof, shall be settled by arbitration administered by the American Arbitration Association in accordance with its Commercial [or other] Arbitration Rules, and judgment on the award rendered by the arbitrator(s) may be entered in any court having jurisdiction thereof.[21]

The parties may also wish to spell out in which jurisdiction the case should be arbitrated and who will pay the resulting fees. If the two parties will be doing business with each other on an ongoing basis, the clause can be drafted to cover all their dealings. Finally, the arbitration agreement should specify what discovery (such as depositions and production of documents), if any, is available and whether the arbitrator has the power to award punitive damages.

As with any other provision in a contract, an arbitration clause will not be enforced if it is *unconscionable*, that is, if it would shock the conscience of the court to enforce it. For example, a court invalidated a mandatory arbitration agreement that required Circuit City's employees to arbitrate all claims but did not require Circuit City to arbitrate any claims against employees. The agreement also restricted the amount of damages available to employees and specified that an employee would have to split the cost of arbitration (including the daily fees of the arbitrator, the cost of a reporter to transcribe the proceedings, and the expense of renting the room where the arbitration would be held), unless the employee prevailed and the arbitrator ordered Circuit City to pay the employee's share of the costs. The U.S. Court of Appeals for the Ninth Circuit concluded that the agreement to arbitrate was an unconscionable contract of adhesion under California law because it "functions as a thumb on Circuit City's side of the scale should an employment dispute ever arise between the company and one of its employees."[22]

In a number of recent cases, the U.S. Supreme Court has strictly limited parties' ability to avoid enforcement of an arbitration clause. For example, in 2011, the U.S. Supreme Court held that the Federal Arbitration Act preempted a state law in

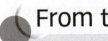

From the **TRENCHES**

A group of merchants entered into an agreement with American Express that required arbitration to resolve disputes and prohibited the arbitration of claims on a class action basis. The merchants instituted a class action antitrust suit against American Express, claiming that American Express had used its "monopoly power" to force them to accept credit cards with fees that were 30% higher than fees for competitors' cards. American Express moved to compel individual arbitration under the Federal Arbitration Act (*FAA*). The merchants tried to invalidate the ban on class arbitration by arguing that the cost of proving their antitrust claims individually would cost at least several hundred thousand dollars while the maximum recovery an individual plaintiff could be awarded under the antitrust laws was about $38,500, assuming treble damages were awarded. The U.S. Supreme Court rejected this argument, explaining that arbitration is a matter of contract so the waiver of class action arbitration was enforceable.

The Court "declined to apply" the "judge-made exception" to the FAA that allows a court to invalidate agreements that prevent the "effective vindication" of a federal statutory right. Here, the merchants asserted that enforcing the waiver of class arbitration would bar effective vindication of their rights under the antitrust laws because they did not have an economic incentive to pursue their antitrust claims individually through arbitration. The Court disagreed. Although the exception would apply to an arbitration provision that forbid a party from asserting certain statutory rights, the exception did not apply here because the "fact that it is not worth the expense in *proving* a statutory remedy does not constitute the elimination of the *right to pursue* that remedy...."

Source: Am. Express Co. v. Italian Colors Rest., 133 S. Ct. 2304 (2013).

California that banned class action waivers in consumer arbitration agreements.[23] Two years later, the Court again held that a class action waiver in an arbitration contract was enforceable even though the amounts recoverable by each potential plaintiff were too low to justify bringing individual arbitration proceedings. (Mandatory arbitration clauses and class action waivers in employment contracts were discussed in Chapter 8.)

In May 2016, the Consumer Financial Protection Bureau (*CFPB*) proposed a rule that would prohibit the use of class action waivers in arbitration agreements between consumers and providers of certain financial products and services.[24] It would also require consumer financial agreements to disclose that the arbitration provisions cannot be used to prevent consumers from filing or participating in a class action. The rules would apply to a variety of products and services, including credit cards, bank accounts, certain types of loans, and consumer agreements involving debt management and collection.

Mediation   Another alternative to litigation to resolve a dispute is mediation. In a mediation, the parties discuss their dispute with each other and a neutral third-party facilitator. The mediator does not have the power to make a final decision, but instead helps guide the parties to a mutually acceptable resolution. Unlike binding arbitration, if the parties fail to reach an agreement in mediation, they are free to go to court. Mediation is typically faster and cheaper than litigation or arbitration, and it is often less contentious. Because mediated settlements require acceptance from both parties, a party cannot be forced into accepting a settlement in a mediation. Parties who are interested in incentivizing each other to try to work out disputes first in a mutually acceptable manner can include a *mandatory mediation clause* in a contract. Such a clause requires the parties to attempt mediation before filing a lawsuit.

Choice of Law and Forum   The contract should specify which jurisdiction's law is to be applied and where disputes are to be adjudicated. It is almost always advantageous for entrepreneurs to require that litigation be commenced in the city and county where they do business. This gives the entrepreneur the home-court advantage and increases the likelihood of finding a sympathetic jury. If local law governs the contract, the entrepreneur's lawyers will not have to learn another jurisdiction's law or hire counsel in the other state. Travel is also minimized, which can be an important factor in a lengthy dispute for both personal and financial reasons. Because a court generally has personal jurisdiction only over persons with at least some minimal contacts with the jurisdiction in which the court sits, the contract should expressly state that all parties submit to the jurisdiction of the courts in the designated locale. As explained in Chapter 2, however, courts may refuse to enforce a choice-of-law provision when the law chosen conflicts with a fundamental public policy of the state where the court deciding the dispute is sitting.

Attorneys' Fees   If the contract does not include a clause requiring the loser to pay the winner's attorneys' fees, then each party must pay its own. Typically, a clause will specify that the losing party shall pay the prevailing party's reasonable attorneys' fees and court costs.

9.10 CHECKLIST FOR ANALYZING A POSSIBLE CONTRACT DISPUTE

The following is a checklist of questions to consider when assessing claims that a contract has been breached or that performance is excused:

> ➤ Is this contract void because it is illegal or violates public policy? A contract to do something illegal is void.

> ➤ Was this contract entered into freely? Unlawful explicit or veiled threats to induce a party to enter an agreement (referred to as *duress*) make it unenforceable.

> ➤ Is this contract unconscionable? Sometimes a contract is unconscionable because onerous terms (such as a limitation of liability or release of claims) are buried in fine print, thereby creating an element of surprise. Other times a party may be aware of the terms but will agree to a totally unfair exchange because he or she lacks bargaining power. For example, a low-income couple may be able to buy appliances on credit only at inflated prices.

> ➤ Has performance become impossible or commercially impracticable? If so, then nonperformance may be excused unless the event making performance impossible or impracticable was foreseeable or one party assumed the risk of its occurrence. Although a several-fold increase in costs usually will not be enough to find commercial impracticability, a 10-fold increase has been held sufficient to excuse performance.

> ➤ Is the contract clearly worded and structured to prevent ambiguity? If a contract is worded so that its terms are subject to different interpretations, it may be voidable by the party who would be harmed by the use of a particular interpretation. This is true only when (1) both interpretations would be reasonable and (2) either both parties or neither party knew of both interpretations when they contracted

with each other. If one (but not both) of the parties knew of the existence of the differing interpretations, a court will generally find in favor of the party who was unaware of the ambiguity. Some courts will resolve any ambiguity by finding against the person who drafted the contract.

➤ Was there a mistake of fact that rendered this contract voidable? A *mistake of fact* occurs when the parties make a mistake about the actual facts underlying the transaction. To determine whether a mistake of fact prevents a meeting of the minds, courts consider three things: (1) whether the mistake had a material effect on one or both of the parties, (2) whether either party allocated the risks of such a mistake to itself, and (3) whether the party alleging mistake did so promptly after discovering it. In determining whether there was a mistake of fact, the courts will often look at the recitals in the beginning of the agreement to determine the intent of the parties. A classic case involved a contract for the purchase of 125 bales of cotton to be brought by the seller from India to England on a ship named *Peerless*. Unbeknownst to the buyer and seller, two ships named *Peerless* were sailing out of Bombay that year. The buyer meant the ship sailing in October, whereas the seller meant the one sailing in December. When the cotton arrived on the later ship, the buyer refused to complete the purchase. The seller then sued for breach of contract. The court found for the buyer, holding that this was a case of mutual mistake of fact so there was no meeting of the minds and thus no contract.[25]

➤ Did a party make a mistake of judgment? A *mistake of judgment* occurs when the parties make an erroneous assessment about the value of some aspect of what is bargained for. Unlike a mistake of fact, a mistake of judgment is not grounds for undoing a contract. A contract to sell a stone for $1 was held enforceable when neither party knew at the time that the stone was in fact a diamond.[26] Another case involved a subcontractor that was awarded a masonry contract as part of a maximum security prison construction project. The subcontractor, which had no experience building complex facilities of this type, estimated that its masons would lay 150 blocks per day, 75% of daily productivity on a typical jobsite. In fact, the company only laid 50 blocks per day. After its request for more time and money was rebuffed, the subcontractor walked off the job, and ultimately the project was completed 180 days late. The court rejected the subcontractor's assertion that it should have been granted an extension and additional compensation, after concluding that the subcontractor had simply grossly underestimated the amount of time and labor necessary to complete the job. "In the end," wrote the court, "while clerical or arithmetic errors are legitimate reasons to obtain relief from an inaccurate bid, mistakes of judgment are not."[27] Distinguishing between mistakes of fact and mistakes of judgment can often be difficult.

➤ Was there a breach of contract by one party that resulted in damages to the other party? Breaches of contract are usually not punished in and of themselves. Some substantial damage to the other party must result for a court to provide a remedy for breach of contract.

➤ Did the party claiming injury *mitigate* (try to lessen) its damages? As explained further below, if the party does not mitigate its damages, a court may order the defendant to pay only the damages that would have occurred had the plaintiff used reasonable efforts to limit the damage resulting from the defendant's breach.

9.11 EFFECT OF BANKRUPTCY

Entrepreneurs should understand what happens if a party to a contract goes into voluntary or involuntary bankruptcy. As explained in detail in Chapter 12, when a party enters bankruptcy, the law provides for an *automatic stay*, which means that creditors are barred from taking any legal action to enforce the contract or to collect money owed under it. A company that has a contract with the bankrupt party (the *debtor*) may neither foreclose on collateral nor stop performing its obligations under the contract without first receiving permission from the bankruptcy court. A provision in a contract that purports to give a party the right to terminate the contract if the other party goes into bankruptcy (a *bankruptcy clause*) is not enforceable.

The penalty for willful violation of an automatic stay is stiff. The debtor may recover lost profits and punitive damages. An entrepreneur who has a contract with a party in bankruptcy, or in danger of entering bankruptcy, should consult with a lawyer before taking any action to enforce or terminate the contract.

In addition to having the benefit of the automatic stay, a debtor may also choose which executory (i.e., ongoing) contracts it wishes to maintain and which it wants to reject. If the debtor rejects a contract, then the other party becomes an unsecured creditor of the debtor for an amount equal to the damage caused by the breach of contract. This often means that the nonbreaching party receives only cents on the dollar or nothing if all of the debtor's assets are mortgaged or otherwise have been used as collateral for secured loans. On the other hand, if the debtor chooses to affirm a contract (as would happen with a lease with a below-market rent or a favorable supply contract in a tight market), then the other party must continue to perform it in accordance with its terms.

9.12 REMEDIES

When a breach of contract occurs, remedies can be monetary or, if financial compensation would not be adequate, they can take the form of specific performance or an injunction. As discussed in Sections 9.13 and 9.14, in certain cases where there is no contract, the courts may grant limited relief under the theory of promissory estoppel or provide compensation for the services rendered under the doctrine of *quantum meruit.*

Monetary Damages

If a party breaches a contract, the nonbreaching party is usually entitled to monetary damages. Damages can take one of three forms: expectation damages, reliance damages, and restitution. Sometimes more than one remedy is appropriate; in that case, the plaintiff may ask for remedies measured by each of the three types of damages. In some cases, consequential and liquidated damages may also be available.

Expectation Damages *Expectation damages* compensate the plaintiff for the amount it lost as a result of the defendant's breach of contract. Expectation damages are calculated to give the non-breaching party the benefit of the bargain, that is, to put that party in the position it would have been in if the contract had been fulfilled. For example, suppose that Brian agrees to design Josephine's app for $2,000 (payable on delivery) and that Josephine has a contract to resell the app for $3,000, which will net her profit of $1,000. If Brian fails to deliver the software for the app, then, subject to the duty to mitigate damages, he will be liable for expectation damages in the amount of $1,000. This is the amount required to put Josephine in the position she would have been in had Brian completed the job.

Reliance Damages A second measurement of damages is *reliance*, which compensates the plaintiff for any expenditures made in reliance on a contract that was subsequently breached. Instead of giving the plaintiff the benefit of the bargain (expectation damages), reliance damages return the plaintiff to the position that he or she was in before the contract was formed. For example, suppose that Ivy agrees to sell Max a refrigeration system, and Max spends money renovating a room to provide an adequate power supply and to allow for proper ventilation of the system. If Ivy then sells the refrigeration system to someone else, Ivy will be required to reimburse Max for the renovation expenses.

Restitution Restitution is similar to reliance damages, but whereas reliance damages look at what the plaintiff has lost, restitution looks at what both parties have gained from the transaction. *Restitution* puts both parties back in the same position they were in before the contract was formed. For example, if Josephine paid Brian $2,000 when she commissioned the app, but Brian never wrote the program, Brian has benefited by receiving the $2,000. Thus, Josephine's restitution damages are $2,000.

Consequential Damages and Liquidated Damages *Consequential damages* are damages that the plaintiff is entitled to as compensation for additional losses that occur as a foreseeable result of a breach. Consequential damages are available only if the breaching party knew, or should have known, that the loss would result from a breach of contract. Thus, consequential damages can include harm resulting from the loss of future business only if the damages were reasonably foreseeable.

The nonbreaching party is entitled to receive consequential damages based on lost future profit only if he or she can demonstrate the amount of profit that would have been earned had the other party not breached the contract. In our software example, Josephine will be entitled to consequential damages only if Brian knew, or should have known, that the successful delivery of the software for the app would allow Josephine to receive a future contract that would have netted Josephine $3,000. This requirement can be a problem for entrepreneurs who seek to recover lost profits for a business that either never got started or ran for only a short time. One way to address this problem is to provide for liquidated damages in the contract.

Duty to Mitigate Damages

As noted earlier, the nonbreaching party is required to make reasonable efforts to minimize damages in the event of a breach. This is called *mitigation of damages*.

Thus, if the supplier fails to deliver goods in accordance with the contract, the buyer must try to procure them elsewhere. Using our app example, if Josephine learns that Brian will be unable to fulfill the contract, Josephine is required to try to find someone else to provide the software for the app. If Josephine is able to hire another programmer to write the code at the cost of $2,200, then Brian will be liable for only $200—the additional amount Josephine was required to pay to get the software written. If Josephine could have hired someone else but elected not to, then a court would most likely award Josephine only $200, which is the additional amount she would have paid had she properly mitigated her damages.

If a company fires an employee in a manner that violates the terms of his or her employment agreement, the employee still has an obligation to try to find comparable work. If the employee fails to take a comparable job in the same city, then (unless the employment contract explicitly provides that the employee has no duty to seek other employment) the employee will be able to recover only the difference between what would have been paid under the employment agreement and what he or she could have earned at the comparable job.

Nonmonetary Equitable Remedies

There are several equitable remedies that may be available in certain cases.

Specific Performance and Other Injunctions Sometimes granting monetary damages to a plaintiff is neither appropriate nor suitable compensation for the defendant's breach of contract. In such cases, the court may exercise its discretionary, equitable powers to grant *specific performance*, that is, to order the defendant to do what it promised. Specific performance is used if (1) the item involved in the contract was unique (e.g., a hand-made sculpture); (2) the contract involved real property, such as a lease or a contract to buy a building; or (3) it is difficult to calculate monetary damages accurately, making money damages inadequate.

Injunctions are court orders to do something or to refrain from doing something. For example, although specific performance by an employee may never be required in a case for breach of an employment contract (individuals may not be forced to work), courts can enjoin the employee from working for the injured party's competitor. Before a case goes to trial, a court sometimes will issue a temporary restraining order (*TRO*) or preliminary injunction to preserve the status quo. Courts usually will not issue a TRO or preliminary injunction unless the plaintiff proves that it will be irreparably damaged if the defendant does not halt certain conduct immediately (e.g., using trade secrets in violation of a nondisclosure agreement).

Rescission In certain situations (such as mistake or misrepresentation) when enforcing the contract would be unfair, a court may exercise its equitable powers and *rescind* (cancel) the contract and order restitution. For example, Gerry, an importer, put down a $7,500 deposit to rent storage space in a building near the dock in West Haven, Connecticut, represented to be well-insulated and secure. In fact, the lessor knew that the roof of the building leaked and that the building had been broken into twice in the last year. Given these facts, a court could rescind the contract, and each party would return the benefit it received up until that point. Gerry would move his goods out of the space in exchange for the return of his $7,500.

9.13 PROMISSORY ESTOPPEL

Under certain circumstances, a court will invoke the equitable doctrine of *promissory estoppel* to give limited relief to a person who has reasonably and foreseeably relied, to his or her detriment, on the promises of another. This is most likely to occur in business settings when a person relies on promises (1) made in the course of negotiations that break down before there is a meeting of the minds on all essential terms, (2) not supported by consideration, or (3) not evidenced by a writing required by the statute of frauds.

To recover under promissory estoppel, a party must meet four conditions: (1) there must be a promise, (2) reliance on the promise must be genuine and justifiable, (3) the actions taken in reliance must be *reasonably foreseeable* to the person making the promise, and (4) grave injustice must result if no relief is given. If all four requirements are met, then the court may require the person who made the promise to pay damages to the person who relied to his or her detriment in an amount equal to the loss the plaintiff suffered by relying on the promise.

For example, in a landmark case, Joseph Hoffman had been negotiating for two years to secure a franchise for a Red Owl grocery store. During this period, Hoffman relied on the promise Red Owl had made that he could get a franchise for a stated price. In reliance on that and other promises, he moved, bought a small grocery store to gain experience, sold a bakery that he had previously owned, and borrowed money from his family. Negotiations broke down when the chain demanded a higher price and insisted that Hoffman's father-in-law sign a document stating that the money he was advancing was an outright gift. Hoffman sued Red Owl for damages based on its failure to keep promises that had induced Hoffman to act to his detriment. The court held that the doctrine of promissory estoppel applied and awarded Hoffman reliance damages equal to the amount he was out-of-pocket because of his reliance on Red Owl's promises.[28]

9.14 *QUANTUM MERUIT*

Quantum meruit can be used to recover the value of products or services provided in the absence of a contract when the products or services clearly were needed but the party receiving the benefit could not agree to purchase them. For example, if Felicity is unconscious on the side of the road, and paramedics pick her up and take her to the emergency room, then Felicity will be required to pay the paramedics, the hospital and the physician treating her the value of the services provided, even though she did not ask for them and did not agree to pay for them. Similarly, suppose that an entrepreneur asks an advertising agency to place an advertisement. The advertising agency contracts with an industry publication to place the advertisement but fails to pay for it. Under the doctrine of *quantum meruit*, the advertising agency's default on payment for the advertisement may render the entrepreneur liable to the publication for the value of the benefit the entrepreneur received (the advertisement). The entrepreneur may have to pay the publication, even though there was no contract between the entrepreneur and the publication.

9.15 LEASES

Entrepreneurs who do not work out of their homes may need to lease a place in which to conduct the business. A *lease* is a contract between the property owner, the *landlord* (also called the *lessor*), and the *tenant* (also called the *lessee*). Usually, the landlord presents a preprinted contract with language favoring its interests. It is then up to the would-be tenant to try to negotiate better terms.

The best way for a potential tenant to approach a lease negotiation is to carefully think through which issues are important and to rank them. By systematically considering all options in advance, the tenant minimizes the possibility that significant interests will be overlooked. For example, when negotiating a lease for a restaurant, securing a good location is the primary concern. It may be more important for Kevin to locate his rotisserie chicken restaurant in the vacant slot next to the anchor tenant, a well-known department store, than to pay $300 per month less in rent for a vacant space at the far end of the mall. Without carefully considering his business's ultimate needs, Kevin might have bargained away thousands of dollars of income each month just to save $300. Kevin might also seek a provision by which the landlord promises not to rent space to another take-out restaurant in the same half of the mall. Other issues to consider include guarantees against environmental hazards and hazardous waste cleanup responsibilities (discussed further below); the landlord's provision of janitorial services; snow and trash removal; maintenance of plumbing and electrical systems; repair, maintenance, or even remodeling of the interior of the rental property; payment of utilities, insurance, and property taxes; indemnification provisions; and maintenance of the building's common areas (such as lobbies, hallways, stairs, and elevators). If the tenant is a startup, it is not uncommon for the landlord to demand a personal guarantee by the major shareholder.

It is also important to make sure that the tenant's contemplated use of the property does not interfere with anyone else's property rights. In one situation, the entrepreneurs' neighbors threatened to sue them for using the alleyway. They claimed that the entrepreneurs were violating their easement. The entrepreneurs ended up having to buy some of the neighbors' space to appease them.

Two important elements that appear in almost every commercial lease merit particular attention: (1) the rental charge and (2) restrictions on subleasing the space or assigning the lease to a third party. Often the rental charge is a flat monthly or yearly rate. Sometimes, however, the landlord may require some percentage of the tenant's gross sales, in addition to the flat rate. For example, Andre might be charged a $3,000 flat rate, plus 7% of his gross sales above $100,000 each year, not to exceed $20,000 per year. In such a situation, Andre would be wise to clearly define what is meant by gross sales and exclude such items as sales tax and tips, which are not really a part of his income.

The right to sublease and assign a lease to a third party are very important issues for entrepreneurs setting up a new business.

Should they find themselves in an unprofitable location or even on the verge of going out of business, they will not want to be responsible for the entire duration of the lease. A landlord may agree to permit the tenant to sublet the space to a responsible third party, if necessary, with the tenant remaining ultimately responsible for the payment of the rent. The landlord may not agree to a tenant's request for the right to assign the remainder of the lease to a third party because an assignment would eliminate the original tenant's involvement completely and potentially leave the landlord in the position of trying to extract rent from an uncooperative or insolvent new tenant.

In fact, landlords often attempt to forestall the possibility of subletting or lease assignment completely by allowing the tenant to sublet the space or assign the lease only with the landlord's prior written consent. In practice, requiring the landlord's consent means that the tenant has no such right. Tenants can even the playing field a bit by negotiating a sentence into the contract that states, "The landlord's [or lessor's] consent shall not unreasonably be withheld." Even when subletting or assignment is permitted, the landlord may require that the tenant share with the landlord any excess rent the subtenant or assignee pays the original tenant over and above the rent specified in the original lease.

9.16 CONTRACTS FOR THE PURCHASE OF REAL PROPERTY

The laws governing the acquisition of real property, such as an empty lot or a building, are highly technical and vary markedly from one state to another. An entrepreneur should never enter into a contract to buy real property without first consulting an experienced real-property lawyer in the state where the property is located.

One particularly dangerous trap for the unwary is liability for the cleanup of hazardous waste. Under the Comprehensive Environmental Response, Compensation, and Liability Act (*CERCLA*), the current owner or operator of real property can be liable for the cleanup of all hazardous waste on the property even if it was dumped there by a previous owner. To avoid liability, the purchaser must be able to prove that it acquired the facility after the hazardous substances were disposed of and without any knowledge or reason to know that hazardous substances had previously been disposed of at the facility. To establish that it had no reason to know that hazardous substances were disposed of at the facility, the purchaser must show that, prior to the sale, it undertook all appropriate inquiry into the previous ownership and uses of the property consistent with good commercial or customary practice.[29] This can be very difficult to prove, and counsel experienced in environmental law should be consulted to help devise an appropriate environmental audit.

9.17 LOAN AGREEMENTS

Loan agreements, which are discussed in more detail in Chapter 12, are usually long, standardized agreements, carefully designed to help ensure that the borrower repays the lender's money. Loan agreements are also characterized by many technical clauses, such as the calculation of interest, interest rates, and special repayment terms. As with all contracts, the parties have a duty to read, and therefore be responsible for, the terms of the agreement. However, this duty is especially important with loan agreements, which may contain substantial obligations for the borrower buried in technical language. An entrepreneur should not sign a loan agreement without first consulting with counsel.

Four particular loan agreement provisions require the borrower's special scrutiny:

1. *Logistical details of receiving the loan*, such as whether the money will be wired or sent by check, and whether the amount will be transferred in full or in installments.

2. *Conditions precedent*, which are all the conditions that must be met by the borrower (or, in some cases, a third party) before the lender is obligated to fund the loan.

3. *Covenants*, which are promises made by the borrower to the lender that, if breached, will result in an event of default and a termination of the loan, usually thereby accelerating payment of all amounts due.

4. *Repayment terms*, including any rights to cure an event of default due to a late or missed payment.

In addition, if the loan is secured by a mortgage or deed of trust on real property or by a security interest in other collateral, it is critical that the borrower understand what happens to the collateral if there is an event of default and whether the creditor has recourse to all assets of the borrower or only the collateral. (Secured lending is discussed in Chapter 12.)

 Putting It into **PRACTICE**

Alexei and Piper knew that they needed to negotiate and sign several contracts to keep Genesist, Inc. on the fast track. The first order of business was renting additional laboratory space. After searching for an appropriate location for several weeks, Piper found one that both met Genesist's needs and was affordable. Unfortunately, the landlord refused to lease the premises to Genesist unless both Alexei and Piper personally guaranteed the payments due under the lease. At first, the founders balked at doing this but, after they checked around, they discovered that a personal guarantee by the key shareholders was customary when startups rented space. They wanted to limit their exposure, though, so they negotiated a two-year lease, with three one-year renewal options.

After reading the proposed lease and going over it with Aaron Biegert, Piper had several other concerns as well. The first issue was employee parking. Because the proposed space was downtown, parking would be both scarce and expensive. Knowing that the landlord owned an adjacent parking lot, she proposed that Genesist be given five free spaces. The landlord balked and countered with an offer of one free space and the guaranteed right to rent an additional space at the lowest available market rate. After some haggling, Piper and the landlord agreed that the lease would provide for two free spaces and the right to rent an additional two spaces at the lowest rate charged any other person.

The second issue was outside lighting. Alexei and Piper and their team were likely to work late many nights, and they were concerned about the lack of lighting in the area. Piper raised the

(continued)

issue with the landlord, who agreed to install several external lights.

The final lease issue was a provision prohibiting an assignment of the lease or the subleasing of the space. The landlord explained that she prohibited lease assignments because the party assuming the lease might not be creditworthy, and she was very selective about the type of tenants allowed. After some discussion, Piper and Alexei agreed to the no-assignment provision in exchange for the right to sublease. In the event of a sublease, Alexei, Piper, and Genesist each agreed that they would be liable for the rental payments if the sublessee failed to make them and that any remaining one-year options would be extinguished.

With the lease for the additional space in hand, Alexei and Piper worked furiously with their team to finish the prototype of the first product utilizing the Genesis T-2000 technology.

CHAPTER 10

E-Commerce, Sales, and Consumer Privacy

E-commerce transactions, as reported by U.S. manufacturers, merchant wholesalers, selected service industries and retailers, amounted to approximately $6.5 trillion in 2014.[1] A one-or-two person firm can now establish a global presence by just creating a website.

The laws governing e-commerce are continuing to evolve. In certain instances, they parallel the rules governing sales in brick-and-mortar establishments. In others, special rules have been developed to address issues such as how electronic contracts are formed, which jurisdiction's law governs online sales, and what rights, if any, consumers have to personal data they provide to online service providers, such as social networking sites.

In Chapter 9, we discussed the principles of contract law applicable to service contracts, contracts for the leasing or sale of real property, and other contracts not involving the sale of goods. We turn now to contracts involving the supply of goods and certain online services.

Well-drafted supply contracts help reduce uncertainty by setting prices and quantity, specifying dates for delivery of the identified supplies and inventory, and ultimately binding the parties and providing remedies for nonperformance. If the supplier is creating something new and innovative for the buyer, the purchaser can use a contract to secure a *right of exclusivity* so the supplier cannot offer the distinctive product or service to others.

When goods delivered pursuant to a contract do not live up to the buyer's expectations, the buyer may sue the seller for breaching an express or implied warranty that the goods sold would have certain qualities or would perform in a certain way. Alternatively, if the product has a defect or did not contain proper warnings, a plaintiff harmed by the defective product may sue in tort for strict product liability, which imposes liability regardless of fault. Multiple data breaches have put pressure on both boards and managers to adopt and implement cybersecurity measures tailored to the firm and the data it generates and collects.

False or misleading advertising erodes the value of a seller's brand and adversely affects the firm's reputation and its attractiveness to customers, employees, and investors. It is also illegal, as is unfair competition.

This chapter begins with a brief discussion of Article 2 of the *Uniform Commercial Code* (*UCC*), which governs the sale of goods in the United States (except in Louisiana), and laws regulating the formation of electronic contracts in the United States and internationally. We then discuss express and implied warranties under the UCC and summarize key provisions of the Convention on Contracts for the International Sale of Goods (*CISG*). Table 10.1 on page 319 identifies some of the key differences between the UCC, the common law of contracts (discussed in Chapter 9), and CISG. The chapter examines strict liability in tort for defective products and describes the important role played by administrative agencies in regulating the advertising and sale of certain products and services. We address online and off-line consumer privacy issues along with laws banning deceptive advertising and unfair competition. The chapter concludes with a discussion of the various jurisdictional and choice-of-law issues associated with sales of goods and services on the Internet. We discuss licensing arrangements in Chapter 14.

10.1 SALES OF GOODS UNDER ARTICLE 2 OF THE UCC

The UCC codified certain aspects of the common law applicable to contracts while freeing those engaging in commercial transactions from some of the more onerous requirements of the common law.

Definition of "Goods"

Article 2 of the UCC governs the sale of goods in every state (except Louisiana), the District of Columbia, and Puerto Rico. Louisiana applies its own statutory rules to the sale of goods and services.

Section 2-105 of the UCC defines *goods* as "all things (including specially manufactured goods) which are movable at the time of identification to the contract for sale." *Identification to the contract* means the designation—by marking, setting aside, or other means—of the particular goods that are to be supplied under the contract. Knowing whether a product is a good is important because it affects both the liability of the seller under the UCC's warranties and the exposure of other firms in the chain of distribution to suits for strict product liability in tort.

Not all arrangements involving the purchase of goods are governed by the UCC, particularly when the agreement covers a combination of goods and services and the sale of goods is only incidental to the transaction. For example, a court held that a consumer could not sue a pharmacy for breach of an implied warranty under the UCC for side effects suffered from use of the oral contraceptive, Yaz. The court ruled that the filling of the prescription was predominantly for the provision of health-care services, not the sale of goods, and, accordingly, the transaction was not governed by the UCC.[2]

Contract Formation

Although the UCC's requirements for contract formation of offer, acceptance, and consideration parallel the common-law contract requirements, the code is more liberal in certain respects.

Missing Terms If the parties act as if they intended to close a deal, such as when a seller ships goods and the buyer pays for them, then the UCC presumes the existence of a contract. This is the case even if material terms are omitted from the offer or acceptance. To determine the terms of a contract with missing terms, a court will (1) examine whatever writings existed between the parties, (2) identify the provisions on which the writings agree, and (3) fill in the rest of the terms based on the circumstances, industry practice, and certain rules set forth in Article 2 (called *gap fillers*).

Additional or Different Terms The UCC abolishes the "mirror-image" rule and provides that a contract can be formed even when the acceptance contains terms that are in addition to, or even in conflict with, those in the offer. Should a party wish to avoid a contract, it should make this explicit by using the language set forth in the UCC: "Acceptance is expressly made conditional on assent to the additional or different terms." Courts have ruled that less direct language does not preclude the finding of a contract.

Additional Terms If there is an acceptance with additional terms, the terms of the contract depend on whether all parties are merchants. A *merchant* is a

> person who deals in goods of the kind [involved in the transaction] or otherwise by his occupation holds himself out as having knowledge or skill peculiar to the practices or goods involved in the transaction or to whom such knowledge or skill may be attributed by his employment of an agent or broker or other intermediary who by his occupation holds himself out as having such knowledge or skill.[3]

If all parties are merchants, then the additions are automatically considered part of the contract unless (1) any of the parties expressly objects to them within a reasonable time, (2) they materially alter the original offer (e.g., substitute a different product), or (3) the original offer contains a clause expressly limiting acceptance to the terms of the offer. If, however, any of the parties is not a merchant, then the additional terms are deemed proposals and are not considered part of the contract unless they are expressly approved by all parties.

Different Terms If the acceptance contains different terms, most courts apply the *knockout rule*, whereby the conflicting terms knock each other out, and a UCC gap filler is substituted in their place.

Approval Clauses When goods or services are being purchased on credit through a sales representative, the seller may afford itself flexibility by including an *approval clause* on the order form specifying that even if the sales order is signed by the sales

From the **TRENCHES**

In an exchange of letters, Reilly Foam Corp. agreed to sell Rubbermaid a quantity of sponges for Rubbermaid's mop business. The terms in Reilly's offer letter and Rubbermaid's acceptance letter varied in certain important respects, however. First, although Reilly sought a contract under which it would supply Rubbermaid with all the sponges it required for two lines of mops, Rubbermaid's acceptance included only one line of mops sold by its subsidiary. Second, Reilly specified in its offer that Rubbermaid would buy a certain quantity of sponges within two years. Rubbermaid's response was silent on the issue of time period.

Because the terms related to types of sponges were not identical, the court applied the knockout rule and discarded the portions of the terms that conflicted and included only those portions on which the offer and acceptance agreed. That meant that Reilly had a requirements contract for only the line of mops produced by Rubbermaid's subsidiary. In contrast, because the two-year time period in the offer was not opposed by any term in the acceptance, the two-year period was held to be part of the contract.

Source: Reilly Foam Corp. v. Rubbermaid Corp., 206 F. Supp. 2d 643 (E.D. Pa. 2002).

representative, it is not a valid contract unless and until it is approved by either the home office or a corporate officer above a specified level. This leaves sales representatives free to take orders without unknowingly binding the company to an uncreditworthy buyer or to unauthorized terms.

Shrink-Wrap Agreements and Other Forms of Acceptance A *shrink-wrap agreement* is formed when a license or other agreement is included inside a shrink-wrapped box that contains a product. Courts will generally enforce shrink-wrap agreements as long as the purchaser is given the right to return the product for a full refund if the purchaser finds the terms of the license unacceptable. Similarly, the contract terms set forth on airline or concert tickets are deemed accepted when the buyer uses the ticket. We discuss click-wrap and other electronic contracts below.

Meeting of the Minds

As under the common law, the UCC requires a meeting of the minds. If there is a mistake of fact, then no contract will result.

From the **TRENCHES**

Spokane Computer Systems was planning to purchase a surge protector to protect its computers from damage caused by electrical surges. The employee in charge of investigating the various products found several units priced between $50 and $200. The employee also contacted Konic International Corp., whose sales representative quoted a price of "fifty-six twenty." The sales representative meant $5,620, but the Spokane employee thought he meant $56.20.

The discrepancy was not discovered until after the equipment was installed and the invoice was received. Spokane then asked Konic to remove the equipment, but Konic refused and sued Spokane for nonpayment.

The court ruled that because both parties attributed a different meaning to the same ambiguous term "fifty-six twenty," there was no meeting of the minds, and thus no contract. The court relieved Spokane of its debt because neither party had reason to believe that the term was ambiguous.

Source: Konic Int'l Corp. v. Spokane Comput. Servs., Inc., 708 P.2d 932 (Idaho Ct. App. 1985).

Consideration

The UCC generally requires the exchange of consideration for a contract to exist, but merchants dealing solely with other merchants may enter into enforceable *option contracts* for periods not to exceed three months without providing consideration. Longer option contracts must be supported by consideration.

Option contracts with nonmerchants must be supported by consideration regardless of their duration. Because a casual seller with no special knowledge or skill peculiar to the goods involved is not a merchant, both the buyer and casual seller will need to provide consideration to enter into an enforceable option contract.

Statute of Frauds

Section 2-201 of the UCC is a *statute of frauds*. It provides that contracts for the sale of goods for $500 or more are unenforceable unless the following three elements are in writing: (1) a *statement* recognizing that an agreement exists, (2) the *signature* of the party against whom enforcement is sought, and (3) an indication of the *quantity of goods* being sold. As long as these elements are in writing, the court will fill in the rest of the terms (including price) based on general tradition and practice within the particular industry. If the contract is between merchants, however, then the contract can still be enforced against the party who has not signed it if the other party sends a written confirmation to which the first party does not respond within 10 days.

10.2 ELECTRONIC CONTRACTS

A variety of statutes and principles govern contracts entered into on the Internet.

The E-Sign Act and the Uniform Electronic Transactions Act

As explained in Chapter 9, the Electronic Signatures in Global and National Commerce Act (*E-Sign Act*) provides, with limited exceptions, that in transactions involving interstate or foreign commerce, "a signature, contract or other record relating to such transaction may not be denied legal effect, validity, or enforceability solely because it is in electronic form." The Uniform Electronic Transactions Act (*UETA*), which has been adopted by 47 states (and by the District of Columbia, Puerto Rico, and the U.S. Virgin Islands), also provides that most electronic contracts may not be denied effect solely because they are in electronic form. The three states that have not adopted UETA—Illinois, New York, and Washington—have passed laws similar to UETA that also prevent nullification of contracts solely because they are in electronic form. As a result, electronic signatures will satisfy the UCC's statute of frauds in most cases.

Almost any mark or process intended to sign an electronic contract or record will constitute a valid electronic signature. These include a name typed at the bottom of an email message. *Digital signatures* add cryptography and other security measures to electronic signatures. These include smart cards, thumbprints, retinal scans, and voice-recognition tests.

If a person to whom an electronic signature is attributed denies "signing" it, UETA requires a party transacting business on the Internet to offer its counterpart the opportunity either (1) to confirm its assent to the terms by other means or (2) to revoke consent if it claims there was a mistake. The E-Sign Act does not expressly address this situation.

"Click-Wrap" Contracts

When a website makes the terms of its licensing agreement readily available and requires the consumer to click on a button, such as "I Accept," before the consumer may have access to the product, an enforceable *"click-wrap" contract* is created when the consumer clicks the appropriate button.[4] Conversely, courts have refused to enforce an agreement when the terms were not readily available or the user was not required to take an affirmative action, such as clicking "I Accept," to indicate acceptance of its terms.[5]

Uniform Computer Information Transactions Act

Maryland and Virginia have adopted the *Uniform Computer Information Transactions Act (UCITA)*, which expressly validates most software license shrink-wrap and click-wrap agreements. It appears unlikely that other states will adopt UCITA.

UNCITRAL's Model Law on Electronic Signatures

The United Nations Commission on International Trade Law (*UNCITRAL*) has promulgated a Model Law on Electronic Signatures.[6] The model law covers signature-related issues, such as how a signature requirement may be met, the conduct of the signatory, and the requirements for service providers that certify electronic signatures. As of mid-2016, 32 jurisdictions across the globe had enacted legislation based on or influenced by the model law, including China, India, Mexico, Thailand, United Arab Emirates, Vietnam, and Zambia.[7]

United Nations Convention on the Use of Electronic Communications in International Contracts

The United Nations Convention on the Use of Electronic Communications in International Contracts (*CUECIC*)[8] addresses such issues as (1) where an electronic contract is created (which can have important implications for jurisdiction and choice of law); (2) where the parties are located (where they have brick and mortar or where their servers are located); (3) how a party expresses consent in an electronic environment; (4) what happens when a party disputes a signature imputed to it or claims that an electronic contract contains errors or mistakes; (5) at what time a contract is formed; and (6) whether displays of goods on a website are offers or just invitations to deal akin to newspaper advertisements. CUECIC entered into force on March 1, 2013.[9] As of August 2016, 18 countries had signed the convention, and 7 had ratified, acceded to, or accepted it.[10] We discuss other UNCITRAL initiatives at the end of this chapter.

10.3 UCC ARTICLE 2 WARRANTIES

There are three types of warranties under Article 2 of the UCC: an express warranty, an implied warranty of merchantability, and an implied warranty of fitness for a particular purpose.

Express Warranty

An *express warranty* is an explicit guarantee by the seller that the goods will have certain qualities. Two requirements must be met to create an express warranty. First, the seller must make a statement or promise relating to the goods, provide a description of the goods, or furnish a sample or model of the goods. Second, such statement, promise, description, sample, or model must become part of the "basis of the bargain," meaning that the buyer must have relied on the seller's statement, promise, description, sample, or model in making the purchase decision. The seller has the burden of proving that the buyer did not rely on the representations. Thus, if a seller has made a representation about the product's qualities that is then relied on by the buyer in choosing to purchase that product, the buyer can sue for breach of express warranty if the product does not live up to that representation. The buyer need not show that the misrepresentation was intentional or even negligent.

An express warranty may be found even if the seller never uses the word "warranty" or "guarantee" and has no intention of making a warranty. For example, the statement "this printer prints 30 color pages per minute" is an express warranty.

Puffing   If, however, a seller is merely *puffing*, that is, expressing an opinion about the quality of the goods, then the seller has not made a warranty. For example, a statement that "this is a great car" is puffing, whereas a factual statement, such as "this car has never been in an accident," is an express warranty. Unfortunately, the line between opinion and fact is sometimes difficult to draw. Much turns on the circumstances surrounding the representation, including the identities and relative knowledge of the parties involved.

If the seller asserts a fact of which the buyer was ignorant, the assertion is more likely to be deemed a warranty. If, however, the seller merely states a view on something about which the buyer could be expected to have formed his or her own opinion and

From the **TRENCHES**

Doug Connor, the president of Doug Connor, Inc., a land-clearing business, purchased a large commercial grinding machine from Proto-Grind, Inc. The brochure for the machine stated that it could grind timber stumps and railroad ties into mulch. During a demonstration of the machine, Connor spoke to George Protos, the president of Proto-Grind, and told him that he needed a machine that would grind palmettos as well as palm and other trees. Protos assured him that the machine was capable of doing this. Connor purchased the machine for $226,000 pursuant to a contract that provided for a two-week trial period to test the machine. Connor waived this trial period in exchange for a discount of $5,500. After Connor had problems with the machine, he sued for breach of express oral warranties that the machine would grind organic materials effectively, that the machine would be free from defects for a period of six months, and that Proto-Grind would fix the machine. Proto-Grind asserted that Connor had waived the express warranties when he waived the trial period.

The Florida District Court of Appeal first ruled that a buyer that refuses an opportunity to inspect the product prior to purchase does not thereby waive any express warranties. The court then found sufficient evidence for a finder of fact to reasonably conclude that the alleged oral promises were more than mere puffing or opinion; the product failed to meet the promise that it was capable of grinding palm trees and palmettos; Connor had relied on these affirmations; and because the deficiency of the product was not cured, Proto-Grind had breached its express warranty.

Source: Doug Connor, Inc. v. Proto-Grind, Inc., 761 So. 2d 426 (Fla. Dist. Ct. App. 2000).

the buyer can judge the validity of the seller's statement, then the seller's statement will most likely be treated as an opinion.

Implied Warranty of Merchantability

The *implied warranty of merchantability* applies to all goods sold by merchants in the normal course of business. The implied warranty of merchantability is implied even if the merchant makes no statements and furnishes no sample or model. As a general matter, it guarantees that the goods are reasonably fit for the general purpose for which they are sold and are properly packaged and labeled. More specifically, it provides that the goods must

(1) pass without objection in the trade under the contract description;

(2) in the case of fungible goods, be of fair average quality within the description;

(3) be fit for the ordinary purposes for which such goods are used;

(4) run, within the variations permitted by the agreement, of even kind, quality and quantity within each unit and among all units involved;

(5) be adequately contained, packaged, and labeled as the agreement may require; and

(6) conform to the promises or affirmations of fact made on the container or label if any.

The key issue when determining merchantability is whether the goods do what a reasonable person would expect of them given the contract description. Goods considered merchantable under one contract may be considered not merchantable under another. For example, a bicycle with a cracked frame and bent wheels is not fit for the ordinary purpose for which bicycles are used, but it will pass under a contract for the sale of scrap metal.

Implied Warranty of Fitness for a Particular Purpose

The *implied warranty of fitness for a particular purpose* guarantees that the goods are fit for the particular purpose for which the seller recommended them. Unlike the implied warranty of merchantability, this warranty does not arise in every sale of goods by a merchant. It will be implied only if four elements are present: (1) the buyer had a particular purpose for the goods; (2) the seller knew or had reason to know of that purpose; (3) the buyer relied on the seller's expertise; and (4) the seller knew or had reason to know of the buyer's reliance.[11] Although a warranty of fitness for a particular purpose can be created by any seller, typically the seller must be a merchant because the seller making the warranty must purport to be an expert regarding the goods and the buyer must have relied on the seller's expertise. A seller may prove that a buyer did not rely on the seller's expertise by showing that (1) the buyer's expertise was equal to or superior to the seller's, (2) the buyer relied on the skill and judgment of persons hired by the buyer, or (3) the buyer supplied the seller with detailed specifications or designs that the seller was to follow.

Limiting Liability and Disclaimers

Subject to certain federal- and state-law restrictions, the seller may limit its liability under any of these three types of warranties. First, the seller need not make any express warranties. This may be difficult to do, however, because even a simple description of the goods may constitute an express warranty. Second, a seller may disclaim any implied warranties of quality if it follows specifically delineated rules in the UCC designed to ensure that the buyer is aware of, and assents to, the disclaimers. A disclaimer of the implied warranty of merchantability must mention merchantability and, if in writing, be conspicuous. A disclaimer of the implied warranty of fitness must both be in writing and be conspicuous. A seller can exclude all implied warranties by using expressions such as "AS IS" or "WITH ALL FAULTS," or other language that in common understanding calls the buyer's attention to the exclusion of warranties and makes plain that there is no implied warranty. (Capital letters are used to fulfill the UCC's requirement that waivers of warranties be prominently displayed.) If this language is used, the buyer assumes the entire risk as to the quality of the goods involved. To avoid creating a warranty of fitness for a particular purpose, the seller can refrain from professing expertise with respect to the goods and can leave the selection to the buyer.

More commonly, the seller limits responsibility for the quality of the goods by limiting the remedies available to the buyer in the event of breach. A typical method is to include a provision limiting the seller's responsibility for defective goods to repair or replacement, often for a specified period of time. It should be noted that certain state laws limit the ability of sellers to sell consumer goods "as is," to disclaim warranties, and to limit remedies in consumer contracts.

From the **TRENCHES**

Jess Mexia purchased a boat manufactured by Rinker Boat Company from a California dealer. Rinker warranted that the boat "will be free from substantial defects in materials and workmanship for a period of one (1) year from the date of purchase."

Two years later, Mexia brought the boat in for repairs because engine corrosion had caused the boat to malfunction. Rinker initially covered the cost of repairs under the warranty, but after similar malfunctions continued to occur, Rinker refused to pay for additional repairs. Mexia then filed a complaint against Rinker alleging breach of the implied warranty of merchantability. Rinker defended by claiming that the suit was banned by the one-year limit on the warranty.

The California Court of Appeal ultimately held that Rinker was liable to Mexia for breach of contract. The court relied on a California consumer protection statute that provides that every retail sale of goods in California includes an implied warranty of merchantability, unless the goods are expressly sold "as is." Because the statute of limitations under the statute is four years, Mexia's filing of the action was timely, notwithstanding the language in the sales contract purporting to limit the manufacturer's liability to just one year.

Source: Mexia v. Rinker Boat Co., 95 Cal. Rptr. 3d 285 (Ct. App. 2009).

10.4 MAGNUSON-MOSS WARRANTY ACT

The Magnuson-Moss Warranty Act is a federal law that protects consumers against deception in warranties. The Act provides that if a seller engaged in interstate or foreign commerce makes an express written warranty to a buyer, then the seller may not disclaim the implied warranties of merchantability and fitness for a particular purpose.

No seller is required to make an express written warranty under this Act. But if the seller does make a written promise or affirmation of fact, then it must also state whether the warranty is a full or a limited warranty. A *full warranty* must satisfy each of the following: (1) the duration of implied warranties is not limited; (2) warranty service is provided to anyone owning the product during the warranty period and is not limited to "first purchasers"; (3) warranty service is free of charge; (4) the consumer may choose either a replacement or full refund if, after a reasonable number of attempts, the product cannot be repaired; and (5) consumers are not required to perform any duty as a precondition for service, other than notification that service is needed. A warranty that does not meet all of the above criteria is a *limited warranty*. The Act also generally prohibits "tie-in sales provisions," which require consumers to buy an item or service from a particular company to maintain the warranty, unless such item or service is provided free of charge under the warranty.

10.5 INTERNATIONAL SALES OF GOODS AND THE CONVENTION ON CONTRACTS FOR THE INTERNATIONAL SALE OF GOODS

The UCC applies only to transactions within the United States; international sales of goods are outside its scope. The Convention on Contracts for the International Sale of Goods,[12] promulgated under the United Nations, governs international sales contracts between merchants in many of the world's largest economies, including Canada, China, France, Germany, Russia, Singapore, and the United States.[13] CISG does not apply to sales of goods bought for personal, family or household use, unless the seller neither knew nor should have known that the goods were for such use.

CISG is the default provision that applies if a sales contract involving merchants from different countries that are signatories to CISG is silent as to applicable law. In other words, CISG will automatically apply to such transactions unless the parties "opt out." Parties can vary the terms of CISG or elect to be governed by another set of laws, but they must expressly agree to do so.

CISG has no statute of frauds provision, so oral contracts for the sale of goods are fully enforceable. CISG also differs from the

UCC in its treatment of the battle of the forms. Under CISG, a reply to an offer that purports to be an acceptance, but contains additional terms or other modifications that materially alter the terms of the offer, is deemed to be a rejection of the offer and constitutes a counteroffer. In such a case, there is no contract. If, however, the modifications do not materially alter the terms and the offeror fails to object in a timely fashion, then there is a contract that will include the terms of the offer with the modifications stated in the acceptance. Price, payment terms, quality and quantity of goods, place and time of delivery, extent of one party's liability to the other, and settlement of disputes are all considered material topics. As a result, as a practical matter, CISG largely applies the mirror-image rule.

Table 10.1 summarizes key differences among the rules established by the UCC, the common law, and CISG.

TABLE 10.1	Comparison of the UCC, Common Law, and CISG			
	Scope	**Battle of the Forms**	**Warranties**	**Statute of Frauds**
UCC	Sale of goods	Contract even if acceptance has additional or different terms	1. Implied warranties of merchantability and fitness for a particular purpose 2. Any express warranties made	Sales of $500 or more
Common Law	1. Provision of services 2. Contracts for sale of land or securities 3. Loan agreements	Mirror-image rule	Any express warranties made	1. Transfer of real estate 2. Contract that cannot be performed within one year 3. Prenuptial agreement 4. Agreement to pay debt of another
CISG	Sale of goods by merchants in different countries unless parties opt out	In practice, mirror-image rule	1. Implied warranties of merchantability and fitness for a particular use 2. Any express warranties made	None

CISG also provides that there shall be regard for the "observance of good faith in international trade," which can limit a party's right to insist on *perfect tender*, that is, the delivery of goods that are exactly in accordance with the contract on the exact date specified. This contrasts with the UCC's perfect tender rule, which entitles a buyer to insist that the delivery of goods meet all the requirements of the contract. For example, under the UCC, a buyer would be entitled to reject goods delivered on June 2 if the contract specified delivery on June 1. Under CISG, if the one-day delay caused no harm to the buyer, then the buyer would be in breach of contract if it rejected the goods on June 2.

CISG holds sellers of goods liable for any express warranties they make as well as for implied warranties of merchantability and fitness for particular use. The implied warranty of merchantability does not attach, however, if the buyer knew that the goods were not fit for ordinary use.

10.6 STRICT LIABILITY IN TORT FOR DEFECTIVE PRODUCTS

Even if the seller makes no warranties, it may still be liable under the theory of strict product liability in tort if a product is defective and causes injuries to persons or property. Product liability generally extends to anyone in the chain of distribution, including manufacturers, wholesalers, distributors, and retailers.

Most states have adopted strict product liability, whereby an injured person does not need to show that the defendant was negligent or otherwise at fault, or that a contractual relationship existed between the defendant and the injured person. The injured person merely needs to show that (1) the defendant was in the chain of distribution of a product sold in a defective condition and (2) the defect caused the injury. For example, a person who is injured by a product purchased from a retail store can sue the original manufacturer, the retail store, or both.

A person injured by a product may also sue for negligence if he or she can prove that the defendant failed to use reasonable care in its design or manufacture. If the defendant made a warranty to the plaintiff, the plaintiff could also sue for breach of warranty. Proving negligence by the defendant allows the plaintiff to receive punitive damages; only compensatory damages are available for claims for breach of warranty or strict product liability.

In the service industries, there is no strict liability (unless the service involves an ultrahazardous activity, such as pile driving or blasting), only liability for negligence. In some cases, it is unclear whether an injury was caused by a defective product or a negligently performed service. For example, a person may be injured by a needle used by a dentist or the hair solution used by a beautician. Certain courts apply strict liability in these situations. Others will not, reasoning the use of the product was incidental to the provision of a service.

Defective Product

An essential element for recovery in strict liability is proof of a defect in the product. The injured party must show that (1) the product was defective when it left the hands of the defendant and (2) the defect made the product unreasonably dangerous. Typically, a product is *unreasonably dangerous* if it does not meet the consumer's expectations as to its characteristics. For example, a consumer expects a stepladder not to break when someone stands on the bottom step.

Certain laws and regulations set minimum safety standards for products. Compliance with a regulatory scheme is not a conclusive defense in a suit for product liability or negligence, however. A product can be defective even if it meets all regulatory standards. On the other hand, failing to comply with regulatory standards is often sufficient to prove that a product was defective and that the defendant was negligent *per se* (i.e., negligent without the need to prove anything else).

Types of Defects A product may be dangerous because of a manufacturing defect; a design defect; or inadequate warnings, labeling, or instructions.

Manufacturing Defect A *manufacturing defect* is a flaw in the product that occurs during production, such as a failure to meet the design specifications. A product with a manufacturing defect is not like the others rolling off the production line. For example, suppose that the driver's seat in an automobile is designed to be securely bolted to the frame. If the worker forgets to tighten the bolts, the loose seat will be a manufacturing defect.

Design Defect   A *design defect* occurs when the product is manufactured according to specifications, but its inadequate design or poor choice of materials makes it dangerous to users. Typically, there is a finding of defective design if the product is not safe for its intended or reasonably foreseeable use. A highly publicized example was the Ford Pinto, which a jury found to be defectively designed because the car's fuel tank was too close to the rear axle, causing the tank to rupture when the car was struck from behind at speeds as low as 25 m.p.h. In certain states, a plaintiff cannot recover damages for a design defect unless he or she can prove that the foreseeable risks of harm posed by the product could have been reduced or avoided by the adoption of a reasonable alternative design.[14]

Failure to Warn   A product must carry adequate warnings of the risks involved in normal use. In the absence of such warnings, the product is defective due to *failure to warn*. For example, the manufacturer of a hair dryer must warn the user of the risk of electrocution if a user taking a bath drops it in the water. A product must also include instructions on its safe use. For example, sellers have been found liable for failing to provide adequate instructions about the proper use and capacity of a hook and the assembly and use of a telescope and sun filter. Certain jurisdictions may require sellers to issue warnings even after the product has been sold, such as when a product is subsequently determined to have been negligently designed and to pose a nonobvious danger.

A warning will not shield a manufacturer from liability for a defectively manufactured or designed product. For example, an automobile manufacturer cannot escape liability for defectively designed brakes merely by warning that "Under certain conditions this car's brakes may fail." In addition, a plaintiff can win a suit for failure to warn even if there was no manufacturing or design defect.

From the **TRENCHES**

A Massachusetts health club was damaged by a fire that started after a member left a towel on the heater in the sauna. Cigna, the health club's insurer, filed suit against the heater manufacturer, Saunatec, for negligently designing the product, negligently failing to warn the club after discovering the defect, and breaching the implied warranty of merchantability.

The court ruled that Saunatec was liable for its negligent design. In contravention of Saunatec's own policy, the heater did not meet Underwriter's Laboratory's safety guidelines, which required a barrier of some sort to prevent combustible materials from coming into contact with any part of the heater that exceeded 536° F. There was a layer of rocks on top of the heater, but that did not keep items away from the heating element. The heater also failed UL's "drape test"—cloth material draped over the heater caught fire.

Saunatec was also liable for failing to warn the club of the defect, because it was not "open and obvious." Although it is generally recognized that a heater carries a risk of fire, it was not readily apparent that leaving a towel on the heater in question would cause a fire in less than 10 minutes. Once Saunatec became aware of the defect, it should have notified prior purchasers and explained how to remedy the problem. Such a warning would have eliminated or reduced the risk of harm.

With regard to the warranty claim, Massachusetts law provides that a negligently designed product is not fit for its ordinary use and therefore violates the implied warranty of merchantability. Nonetheless, the court ruled that Cigna could not recover for breach of warranty, because the club had used the heater unreasonably. The club knew that towels should not be left on the heater and that the heater was defective because the club had already experienced one fire after a towel was left on the heater. Unreasonable use is an affirmative defense to a claim of breach of the implied warranty of merchantability and bars recovery for such a breach.

Source: Cigna Ins. Co. v. Oy Saunatec, Ltd., 241 F.3d 1 (1st Cir. 2001).

Who May Be Liable?

In theory, each party in the chain of distribution may be liable. Manufacturers of component parts are frequently sued as well.

Manufacturers A manufacturer will be held strictly liable for its defective products regardless of how remote it is from the final user of the product. The manufacturer is potentially liable even when the distributor makes final inspections, corrections, and adjustments of the product. The only requirements are that the manufacturer be in the business of selling the injury-causing product and that the product be defective when it left the manufacturer. Occasional sellers, such as a typesetting company selling an unused computer, are not strictly liable.

Wholesalers Wholesalers are usually held strictly liable for defects in the products they sell. In certain states, however, a wholesaler is not liable for latent or hidden defects if the wholesaler sells the products in exactly the same condition that it receives them.

Retailers   In most states, a retailer may also be held strictly liable. A minority of states, however, will not hold a retailer liable if it did not contribute to the defect and played no part in the manufacturing process.

Sellers of Used Goods   Sellers of used goods usually are not held strictly liable because they are not in the product's original chain of distribution. In addition, the custom in the used-goods market is that there are no warranties or expectations relating to the quality of the products (although certain states have adopted rules requiring warranties for used cars). However, a seller of used goods is strictly liable for any defective repairs or replacements that it makes.

Component-Part Manufacturers   A company that makes component parts to the manufacturer's specifications is not liable if the specifications for the entire product are questioned, as this is considered a design defect. For example, if an automaker's specifications for a car's gas pedal prove defective because the pedal can get stuck under the floor mat, the maker of the gas pedal will not be liable. Makers of component parts are liable for manufacturing defects in their components, however.

Successor Liability

As explained further in Chapter 16, a corporation purchasing or acquiring the assets of another is liable for its defective products and other debts if there is (1) a consolidation or merger of the two corporations or (2) an express or implied agreement to assume such obligations. Even if a transaction is structured as a sale of assets with no assumption of liabilities, there may still be successor liability if (1) the purchasing corporation is merely a continuation of the selling corporation or (2) the transaction was entered into to escape liability. Thus, the acquiring corporation may be liable to a party injured by a defect in a product sold by the acquired business prior to the acquisition, making it prudent to purchase appropriate product liability insurance to cover such claims.

Defenses

The defendant in a product liability case may raise the traditional tort defenses of assumption of risk and, in some jurisdictions, a variation of comparative negligence, known as comparative fault. The federal preemption defense may be available in certain failure-to-warn cases, including cases involving certain medical devices approved by the Food and Drug Administration (*FDA*) and generic drugs. In addition, the state-of-the-art defense (explained below) is available in certain jurisdictions. Availability of the following defenses varies from state to state. Usually the law of the state where the injury occurred governs.

Assumption of Risk   When a person voluntarily and unreasonably assumes the risk of a known danger, the manufacturer is not liable for any resulting injury. For example, if a toaster bears a conspicuous warning not to insert metal objects into it while it is plugged in, and a person inserts a metal fork into it anyway to dislodge a bagel and is electrocuted, the toaster manufacturer will not be liable.

Similarly, when the use of a product carries an obvious risk, the manufacturer generally will not be held liable for injuries that result from ignoring the risk. In one case, the court ruled that a manufacturer was not liable when a transmission mast atop a television news truck came into contact with power lines and electrocuted the technician. The mast had operated as expected and the danger of electrocution was well known in the industry.[15]

Courts are often reluctant to find assumption of risk, and certain states have eliminated it as a defense in tort cases except when the injured party contractually agreed to assume the risk. For example, one court found that the manufacturer of a hammer was not entitled to an assumption of risk defense when an alleged manufacturing defect (a "quench crack") caused the claw of its hammer to break off during use and injure the user's eye. The hammer came with a warning that safety goggles should be worn because "tools or struck objects may chip," but because the user was using the hammer to break a metal strap on roofing supplies, he did not expect the tool to chip so did not wear goggles. Because the manufacturer could not show that the user was aware of the specific quench crack defect and voluntarily exposed himself to that condition, the manufacturer could not avail itself of the assumption of risk defense.[16]

Comparative Fault Contributory negligence by the plaintiff is not a defense to liability in a strict liability action. The damages may be reduced, however, by the degree to which the plaintiff's own negligence contributed to the injury. This doctrine is known as *comparative fault*.

Abnormal Misuse of the Product A manufacturer or seller is entitled to assume that its product will be used in a normal manner. The manufacturer or seller will not be held liable for injuries resulting from abnormal use of its product. In contrast, an unusual use or a misuse that is reasonably foreseeable may still result in liability. For example, operating a lawn mower with the grass bag removed was held to be a foreseeable use, and the manufacturer was liable to a bystander injured by an object that shot out of the unguarded mower.[17]

State-of-the-Art Defense The state-of-the-art defense, which is available only in certain states, is based on a manufacturer's utilization of the best available technology (which may or may not be synonymous with the custom and practice of the industry). The *state-of-the-art defense* shields a manufacturer from liability if no safer product design is generally recognized as being possible. Statutes vary in their provisions. For example, the statute in Arizona provides that a defendant is not liable if it can prove that "[t]he defect in the product is alleged to result from inadequate design or fabrication, and if the plans or designs for the product or the methods and techniques of manufacturing, inspecting, testing and labeling of the product conformed with the state of the art at the time the product was first sold by the defendant."[18] The

Tennessee statute makes reference to "scientific and technological knowledge available to the manufacturer or seller at the time the product was placed on the market,"[19] while another provides for a rebuttable presumption that a product was not defective and that the manufacturer or seller is not negligent if the product "conformed to the state of the art, as distinguished from industry standards."[20]

Preemption Under certain circumstances, federal law will preempt claims based on state-law product liability. For certain types of products (such as tobacco and cigarettes), Congress has explicitly preempted state law. In other instances, federal preemption is implied. For example, the U.S. Supreme Court held that a federal statute requiring manufacturers to equip some but not all cars with passive restraints (such as airbags) preempted state-law claims alleging that cars without airbags were inherently defective.[21] The Court also ruled that premarket approval by the FDA of medical devices preempted state-law product liability suits,[22] but that FDA-approved labeling of brand name pharmaceuticals did not preclude state-law failure-to-warn claims, in part because the FDA might not be privy to all the information known by the manufacturers.[23] In a later case, the Court held that state-law failure-to-warn claims for generic drugs were preempted by a federal law requiring generic drugs to bear the same label as their brand-name equivalents.[24]

10.7 THE CONSUMER PRODUCT SAFETY COMMISSION AND OTHER ADMINISTRATIVE AGENCIES

The Consumer Product Safety Commission (*CPSC*) is charged by Congress with protecting the public against unreasonable risks of injury associated with consumer products and assisting consumers in evaluating the comparative safety of such products. To that end, the CPSC is authorized to set consumer product safety standards, such as performance or product-labeling specifications.

It is unlawful to manufacture for sale, offer for sale, distribute in commerce, or import into the United States a consumer product that does not conform to an applicable standard. Violators are subject to civil penalties, criminal penalties, injunctive enforcement and seizure, and private suits for damages or injunctive relief. Monetary fines can reach $100,000 per occurrence and up to $15 million for a related series of violations.

Before implementing a mandatory safety standard, the CPSC must find that voluntary standards are inadequate. Any standards issued by the CPSC must also be reasonably necessary to eliminate an unreasonable risk of injury presented by the regulated product. To determine whether a standard is reasonably necessary, the CPSC weighs the standard's effectiveness in preventing injury against its effect on the cost of the product.

The CPSC can begin a proceeding to develop a standard by publishing a notice in the *Federal Register* inviting any person to submit an offer to develop the standard. Within a specified time limit, the CPSC can then accept such an offer, evaluate the suggestions submitted, and publish a proposed rule. The issuance of the final standard is subject to notice and comment by interested persons. In addition, any interested person may petition the CPSC to adopt a standard and may resort to judicial remedies if the CPSC denies the petition.

Consumers can file a report concerning allegedly defective products on SaferProducts.gov. The CPSC reviews the reports and contacts the manufacturers, who have 10 days to respond. Complaints and responses are generally posted on the website; the CPSC can use its discretion and not publish complaints when a manufacturer claims the report is false or that posting it would reveal a trade secret.

If a product cannot be made free of unreasonable risk of personal injury, the CPSC may ban its manufacture, sale, or importation altogether. The supplier of any already-distributed products that pose a substantial risk of injury may be compelled by the CPSC to repair, modify, or replace the product or refund the purchase price.

The National Highway Traffic Safety Administration has the power to establish motor vehicle safety standards. In 2014, Toyota paid a record $1.2 billion fine to settle U.S. government charges involving "unintended acceleration." Former Attorney General Eric Holder called Toyota's conduct "shameful," stating that it

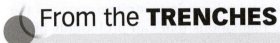

From the **TRENCHES**

General Motors paid $900 million in U.S. criminal fines in 2015 and nearly $600 million in damages to victims and their families as a result of GM's failure to recall cars known to have defective ignition switches linked to at least 124 deaths and almost 400 injuries. General Motor's former general counsel denied knowledge of the ignition switch problem, but other lawyers in his department had been aware of the issues for at least a decade and had used confidential settlement agreements to keep the problems hidden. Mary Barra, who took over as CEO in early 2014, apologized for "putting lives at risk in the company's cars" and fired the employees responsible for fixing the problem. She told employees at a town hall meeting in 2015 that the company had "work to do to restore its reputation for quality and safety," stating that "[a]pologies and accountability don't amount to much if you don't change your behavior."

Sources: Bill Vlasic, *G.M. Chief Is Named Chairwoman, Affirming Her Leadership*, N.Y. Times (Jan. 4, 2016), http://www.nytimes.com/2016/01/05/business/gm-chief-is-named-chairwoman-affirming-her-leadership.html; Jerry Hirsch, *Embattled General Motors General Counsel Millikin to Retire*, L.A. Times (Oct. 17, 2014), http://www.latimes.com/business/autos/la-fi-hy-gm-lawyer-millikin-retires-20141017-story.html ("The automaker knew about the problem for at least a decade but waited until this year to start recalling the cars."); Nathan Bomey & Kevin McCoy, *GM Agrees to $900M Criminal Settlement Over Ignition-Switch Defect*, USA Today (Sept. 17, 2015), http://www.usatoday.com/story/money/cars/2015/09/17/gm-justice-department-ignition-switch-defect-settlement/32545959/.

"showed a blatant disregard for ... the safety of consumers" and that by Toyota's "own admission, it protected its brand ahead of its own customers" constituting a "clear and reprehensible abuse of the public trust."[25]

The Food and Drug Administration monitors the production and sale each year of more than $1 trillion worth of food, drugs, medical devices, and cosmetics. The U.S. Department of Agriculture regulates the slaughtering or processing and the labeling of meat, poultry, and egg products. The Federal Trade Commission has primary responsibility for regulating the packaging and labeling of all commodities other than food, drugs, medical devices, and cosmetics. Broadcasting, telecommunications, and aspects of the Internet are regulated by the Federal Communications Commission. The Consumer Financial Protection Bureau is charged with protecting consumers from deceptive and ill-suited financial products, including credit cards, mortgages, and predatory payday loans.

Congress has given these and other administrative agencies the power to adopt and enforce regulations that can profoundly affect businesses in particular industries. Before enacting regulations, administrative agencies must publish their proposed rules and solicit public comment. When agencies are proposing rules that might affect a company's operations, managers are well-advised to take advantage of the opportunity to participate in the public notice and comment period. Emerging or small companies usually do not have the resources to devote to a government relations function, so it is important for founders and executives to keep abreast of regulatory developments (including enforcement actions) by working with trade associations, chambers of commerce, local lawmakers, and others with the ability to influence the regulatory matters.

10.8 CONSUMER PRIVACY AND IDENTITY THEFT

Virtually all entrepreneurs will encounter consumer privacy issues. The ease with which customer information can be collected online as well as marketers' ability to collect, process and aggregate customer data, have sparked public outrage and tighter government regulations when the public's expectations were not met. For example, in October 2016, the Federal Communications Commission (*FCC*) adopted new rules requiring consumers' express prior consent ("opt-in") before broadband Internet service providers may use or share their sensitive personal information (such as the content of communications and browsing history). The new rules also require prompt notice of data breaches.

The Power of Self-Regulation

Brent Saunders, founder of the Privacy Officers Association and privacy consultant with PricewaterhouseCoopers, points out that certain companies

> see privacy as a market differentiator, as a way of getting and keeping customers. For these companies, it's not just a matter of doing something because they have to or because someone is telling them to. It's more a matter of building a foundation of trust with customers that is crucial to the success of their business.[26]

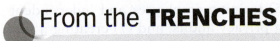

From the **TRENCHES**

In the past, most businesses and private individuals stored sensitive data in locked file cabinets, desk drawers, local computers, and on-premises computers. Because such storage was "within the user's physical possession and control," the government typically had to give notice before accessing such private information. Today, private information is increasingly stored "in the cloud" on remote servers owned and operated by third-party providers.

In 2016, Microsoft Corporation sought a declaratory judgment that Section 2705(b) of the Electronic Communications Privacy Act of 1986 is unconstitutional on its face. According to Microsoft, the government has "exploited" the move to cloud computing by getting information "through a [secret] legal process directed at online cloud providers" while simultaneously preventing the online cloud providers, such as Microsoft, from telling their customers about the government's activity. Under Section 2705(b), courts can order a provider of data storage "in the cloud" to "keep its customers in the dark" when the government seeks their email content or other private information based solely on the government's "reason to believe" that informing the customer could hinder the investigation. Microsoft maintains that the statute violates both (1) its customers' Fourth Amendment right to know when the government is searching or seizing their property and (2) Microsoft's own First Amendment right to be transparent with its customers concerning government investigations.

Sources: Complaint for Declaratory Judgment, Microsoft Corp. v. United States Dep't of Justice, No. 2:16-cv-00538 (W.D. Wash. Apr. 14, 2016), https://www.justsecurity.org/wp-content/uploads/2016/04/Microsoft-v-Lynch-WDWash-Complaint.pdf; Steve Lohr, *Microsoft Sues Justice Department to Protest Electronic Gag Order Statute*, N.Y. TIMES (Apr. 14, 2016), http://www.nytimes.com/2016/04/15/technology/microsoft-sues-us-over-orders-barring-it-from-revealing-surveillance.html; Dina Bass, *Microsoft Sues Justice Department Over Data Gag Orders*, BLOOMBERG (Apr. 14, 2015), http://www.bloomberg.com/news/articles/2016-04-14/microsoft-sues-justice-department-over-client-data-gag-orders; Allison Grande, *Microsoft Fights Gag Orders on Warrants for Customers' Data*, LAW360 (Apr. 14, 2016), http://www.law360.com/articles/784623/microsoft-fights-gag-orders-on-warrants-for-customers-data.

By implementing comprehensive domestic and international privacy policies, businesses can collect relevant personal data and learn how to better serve their customers; assure customers and regulators that personal data are correct and secure; and respond promptly and effectively to contain the harm caused by any data breaches. A number of companies have institutionalized their privacy policies and practices by (1) hiring a professional privacy consultant[27] or appointing a privacy officer;[28] (2) adopting online and off-line privacy policies; (3) conducting periodic privacy risk assessments to evaluate how personal information is used and collected; (4) establishing a formal complaint-resolution program for consumers; (5) training employees and independent contractors; (6) conducting privacy audits; and (7) creating a formal privacy assessment process for new products and services.[29]

Legally astute managers understand that data security is an ongoing process and not a static checklist. As a result, companies must be proactive to protect against emerging threats, including those posed by government hackers, and adapt to changing regulations.

Identity Theft and Other Data Breaches

Identity theft, the illegal access of another's credit and other personal information and its use to the thief's advantage,[30] is rampant, further heightening concerns about the misuse of personal information. Authorities blamed North Korea for an embarrassing data breach at Sony Pictures Entertainment, which was apparently in retaliation for Sony's release of the film *The Interview*, a comedy about a plot to assassinate the leader of North Korea. Sony Pictures Co-Chair Amy Pascal resigned soon thereafter. In an ensuing class action lawsuit, nine Sony employees whose personal identifying information was hacked cited earlier data breaches at Sony and alleged that Sony had made a "business decision to not expend the money needed to shore up its systems, and instead to accept the risk of a security breach."[31]

In 2016, Home Depot agreed to pay a minimum of $19.5 million to settle a consumer lawsuit affecting more than 50 million cardholders who, after using its self-checkout terminals, had payment card data and/or email addresses stolen.[32] The company also agreed to hire a chief information security officer to monitor its progress in improving data security.[33]

California, Utah, and other states have enacted tough privacy legislation, which often applies to any firm shipping products to the state even if the firm has no physical presence there.[34] State attorneys general have successfully prosecuted companies for violating such laws.[35] Private individuals have also sued. For example, plaintiffs filed a class action lawsuit against Shutterfly in 2015 for allegedly violating the Illinois Biometric Information Privacy Act by collecting users' facial recognition data from uploaded Shutterfly photos without users' written consent and for not telling its users how long that information would be stored or used.[36] Most states have also enacted some form of "breach notice laws," which require social media and certain other companies to notify the consumer of a data breach and, in some cases, also require notification to credit agencies and law enforcement.[37]

The Federal Trade Commission (*FTC*) has launched a website to assist individuals with identity-theft issues (IdentityTheft.gov) and another for businesses, which includes FTC guidance on security, tips on setting passwords, information on complying with notification rules, and links to other relevant sites.[38] The agency also offers downloadable materials on how to prevent identity theft that businesses can provide to their customers.

Federal Trade Commission Enforcement Actions

Although Congress has not given the FTC the express authority to require firms to provide data security, the FTC has relied on its broad authority under Section 5 of the Federal Trade Commission Act[39] to prevent "unfair or deceptive acts or practices in or affecting commerce" to protect consumer privacy.[40] At a minimum, if a company publishes a privacy policy, it must abide by its terms. Failures to do so are prosecuted by the FTC.

An infamous case involved the pharmaceutical giant Eli Lilly and its site Prozac.com, which patients taking its antidepressant Prozac could use to manage refills and obtain information about dealing with depression. Lilly sent subscribers emails, which were intended to be addressed to each subscriber individually, and promised subscriber confidentiality. Lilly inadvertently disclosed the email addresses of all the subscribers to its Prozac.com site when an inadequately trained programmer used "reply to all" when sending a message to the subscribers. The Federal Trade Commission brought a successful enforcement action for failure to properly train and oversee employees with access to sensitive consumer data in violation of the firm's own privacy policies. Pursuant to an FTC consent decree, Lilly agreed to:

➢ Designate appropriate personnel to coordinate and oversee the program.

➢ Identify reasonably foreseeable internal and external risks to the security, confidentiality, and integrity of personal information, including any such risks posed by lack of training, and address these risks in each relevant area of its operations, including (a) management and training of personnel; (b) information systems for the processing, storage, transmission, or disposal of personal information; and (c) prevention and response to attacks, intrusions, unauthorized access, or other information systems failures.

➢ Conduct annual written reviews by personnel qualified to monitor and document compliance with the program, evaluate the program's effectiveness, and recommend changes to it.

➢ Adjust the program in light of any findings and recommendations resulting from reviews or ongoing monitoring and in light of any material change to Lilly's operations that affect the program.[41]

Under certain circumstances, failure to protect sensitive consumer information can itself be an "unfair" practice even if the company did not promise to keep the data secure.[42] Since 2002, the FTC has settled more than 50 matters involving failures to abide by stated privacy policies or to implement reasonable data security practices.[43] For example, in 2014, two data brokers agreed to pay fines of $525,000 and $1 million to settle charges they provided reports about consumers to prospective employers and landlords without taking reasonable steps to ensure the reports were accurate or that their users had a permissible reason to obtain them.[44]

Other U.S. Privacy Legislation

A variety of other federal and state statutes are designed to protect consumer privacy.

The Children's Online Privacy Protection Act of 1998[45] prohibits the collection of personal information from children under the age of 13 without first receiving parental consent.[46] "Financial institutions," including banks, debt collectors, credit counselors, retailers that issue credit cards to consumers and certain travel agencies, are required to notify consumers in writing regarding what personal information is being collected, how it is being used, and with whom it is shared.[47] They must also give consumers the opportunity to opt out of having such information shared with other affiliated or unaffiliated entities. The Fair Credit Reporting Act[48] requires credit reporting agencies to put reasonable procedures in place to safeguard confidential information. It also requires all employers to obtain a job applicant's consent before obtaining a credit report as part of the hiring process. A number of states have also enacted legislation that prevents employers from asking employees or job applicants to provide their usernames and passwords for their personal social media accounts. As discussed in Chapter 8, health-care providers and others with personal medical information are required to implement appropriate policies and procedures to ensure that medical information is kept private.[49]

Pursuant to the Do-Not-Call Implementation Act, as amended,[50] the Federal Communications Commission and FTC established the national Do-Not-Call Registry, a registry of persons not wanting to receive unsolicited telemarketing calls. Subject to certain exceptions, companies may not make unsolicited phone calls to consumers who put their names on that registry unless they have done business with the consumer in the recent past. In 2004, the U.S. Court of Appeals for the Tenth Circuit held that the regulations were not unconstitutional restraints on commercial speech, because they furthered important government interests by protecting personal privacy and reducing the risk of telemarketing abuse.[51]

The Controlling the Assault of Non-Solicited Pornography and Marketing (CAN-SPAM) Act[52] prohibits spammers from disguising their identities by using false return addresses and using misleading subject lines. California's Consumer Protection Against Computer Spyware Act prohibits the installation of software that (1) takes control of a computer; (2) modifies a consumer's interaction with the Internet; (3) collects personally identifiable information; (4) prevents without authorization a user's effort to block or disable such software; or (5) removes, disables, or renders inoperative security or antispy software.[53] Certain types of spyware also violate the Electronic Communications Privacy Act,[54] the Computer Fraud and Abuse Act, and Section 5 of the Federal Trade Commission Act.[55]

European Union Privacy Protections

The European Union's Data Protection Directive (95/46/EC) required its Member States to safeguard the privacy of personal data by (1) giving notice to individuals regarding how their information will be used; (2) offering a choice when disclosing information to a third party (with an opt-in consent required for sensitive information); (3) maintaining the security of personal information; (4) ensuring that the data are reliable, accurate, and current; and (5) giving individuals access to examine, correct, and delete information about them. In 2016, the European Union (*EU*) adopted Regulation (EU) 2016/679, which reforms its data protection rules to keep pace with changing technology and the explosion of social media. Member States have until 2018 to comply.[56] For individuals, the rules (1) include clarifying and strengthening the "right to be forgotten," which allows the deletion of personal information under certain circumstances;[57] (2) make it easier to understand how one's data is processed; (3) provide the right to know as soon as possible when data is hacked; and (4) make data protection a priority. For businesses, the provisions include a single, pan-European law for data protection; the establishment of one supervisory authority; and the creation of a "level-playing field" so that all companies, regardless of whether they are established within or outside the European Union, must follow the same rules. Once enacted by the Member States, Regulation (EU) 2016/679 will replace General Data Protection Regulation, Directive 95/46/EC.

The EU prohibits the export of personal information from European Union Member States to countries that do not "adequately" protect personal data. Because existing data protection measures in the United States do not comply with the directive, the EU and the United States formally adopted the EU-U.S. Privacy Shield[58] in July 2016. The EU-U.S. Privacy Shield requires companies to ensure that people's digital information, "from social media posts and search queries to information about workers' pensions and payroll" is not misused.[59] The rules apply to all companies regardless of whether they are a social media platform, a pharmaceutical company, or an industrial conglomerate that are subject to the jurisdiction of the FTC or the U.S. Department of

Transportation.[60] In addition, the United States must provide an annual guarantee that U.S. intelligence agencies will not have "indiscriminate access" to Europeans' digital data when it is sent to the United States.

10.9 ADVERTISING

Three main bodies of law protect consumers against false or deceptive advertising: the common law, statutory law (including the UCC, the Lanham Act, and state consumer protection laws), and administrative law enforced by the FTC.

Common Law

The common law provides two remedies for a consumer who has been misled by false advertising. First, a consumer may be able to sue for breach of contract. Proving the existence of a contract is often difficult, however, because courts usually characterize advertisements as merely offers to deal. A consumer might also sue for the tort of deceit. Deceit requires the proof of several elements, including knowledge by the seller that the misrepresentation is false. The misrepresentation must be one of fact and not opinion, which is a difficult distinction to make in the context of advertising. (We discuss deceit, also called fraudulent misrepresentation, and other business torts in Chapter 11.)

Statutory Law

Both the UCC and the federal Lanham Act may protect consumers from false advertising. As explained earlier, under Article 2 of the UCC, any statement, sample, or model may constitute an express warranty if it is part of the basis of the bargain. Sometimes advertisement of a product may be construed as an express warranty. If so, the buyer can recover for breach of warranty under the UCC. Many states also have their own consumer protection statutes.

The Lanham Act forbids the use of any "false or misleading" description or representation of fact in connection with any goods or services. It provides a claim for any competitor (rather than consumer) who might be injured by any other competitor's false claims. The purpose of the Act is to ensure truthfulness in advertising and to eliminate misrepresentations of quality regarding one's own product or the product of a competitor.

For example, S.C. Johnson & Sons successfully sued the Clorox Company under the Lanham Act for falsely portraying the leakiness of Johnson's Ziploc baggies in a television commercial.[61] The court ruled that Clorox, which manufactures the rival Glad-Lock baggie, impermissibly misrepresented the rate at which liquid exited when a sealed Ziploc baggie was held upside down. The commercial showed water flowing out of the bag when in fact the bag yielded only roughly one drip per second. It also depicted the water level in the bag dropping rapidly and bubbles passing through the water, falsely indicating that water was leaving the bag quickly. The court enjoined Clorox from continuing to run the commercial.

All 50 states and the District of Columbia have statutes offering some level of protection against deceptive trade practices and permitting consumers to bring suits against businesses that attempt to deceive them in commercial transactions. A blatant example of misleading statements involved AT&T's marketing of certain phones that worked only with a cellular technology it had already planned to phase out. AT&T had stated that the phone would provide for its customers' wireless needs for "today and tomorrow" and encouraged customers to enter into two-year service contracts by decreasing the price with the plan. A few months later, AT&T withdrew support for the wireless network the phones used, rendering the units essentially unusable. Several disgruntled customers brought a class action against AT&T. The California Court of Appeal found that offering a two-year contract and claiming it would provide for its customers "today and tomorrow" was sufficient to constitute a cause of action under California's consumer protection laws.[62] In addition to prohibiting intentionally or knowingly deceptive practices, some states allow legal action under their consumer protection laws even if the business acted in good faith with no intention to deceive a customer.[63]

Companies can handle disputes more quickly and inexpensively than litigation by turning to the National Advertising Division (*NAD*) of the Council of Better Business Bureaus, which uses alternative dispute resolution techniques to resolve claims of false or misleading advertising between competitors. This option is particularly attractive to growing companies with limited financial resources. While an NAD decision does not have the enforceability of a judicial decision, its decisions are published and it can refer claims to the FTC for further action. Consumers may also institute complaints.

Regulatory Law: The Federal Trade Commission

As noted above, Section 5 of the FTC Act gives the FTC authority to prevent unfair and deceptive trade practices, including false advertising. *False advertising* occurs when untrue, unsupported, or deceptive claims are made in advertising. Among the areas the FTC has addressed are deceptive quality claims, false or misleading testimonials and mock-ups, and deceptive pricing practices.

Quality Claims   Advertisers should not make quality claims unless they have a reasonable basis for making the claim. Quality claims made without any substantiation are generally deemed deceptive. On the other hand, obvious exaggerations and vague generalities are considered puffing and are not deemed deceptive because consumers are unlikely to rely on them.

False Testimonials and Mock-ups   Testimonials and endorsements in which the person endorsing a product does not, in fact, use or prefer it are deceptive and violate the law. Additionally, it is deceptive for the endorser to imply falsely that he or she has superior knowledge or experience of the product.

It is also illegal to show an advertisement that purports to be an actual product demonstration but is, in fact, a mock-up or simulation. For example, Campbell Soup Co. engaged in false advertising when its ads included photographs of bowls of soup into which clear glass marbles had first been placed to make the solid ingredients rise to the surface, thereby making the soup appear thicker and more appetizing.[64]

FTC Guidance on Endorsements and Testimonials   Besides forbidding false endorsements and testimonials, the FTC has provided guidance to businesses wanting to present genuine endorsements and testimonials to the public.[65] The guidance covers both traditional

From the **TRENCHES**

advertising as well as the use of new media, such as blogs and social networking. Any company running an ad featuring a consumer conveying "exceptional results" must include information that clearly and conspicuously discloses the generally expected performance consumers can expect in similar circumstances.[66]

Deceptive Pricing *Deceptive pricing* includes any practice that tends to mislead or deceive consumers about the price they are paying for a good or service. It is a deceptive pricing practice to offer "free" merchandise with a purchase, or two-for-one deals, when, unbeknownst to the customer, the advertiser is recouping the cost of the free merchandise by charging more than the regular price for the merchandise bought. The FTC also prohibits *bait-and-switch* advertising, which occurs when an advertiser refuses to show an advertised item, fails to have a reasonable quantity of the item in stock, fails to promise to deliver the item within a reasonable time, or discourages employees from selling the advertised item.

10.10 UNFAIR COMPETITION

A number of states have adopted statutes prohibiting unfair competition. *Unfair competition laws* are designed to prevent unlawful, false, deceptive, unfair, and unauthorized business practices, particularly in the areas of sales and advertising. Certain types of unfair competition may also violate federal laws, including the FTC Act and the Lanham Act.

From the **TRENCHES**

The use of terms such as "list price" and "manufacturer's suggested retail price" is a sales tactic used in e-commerce to convince buyers that they are getting a good deal. Recently, however, a number of lawsuits have been instituted claiming that such advertised prices are misleading and that they "exaggerate potential customer savings." In 2014, Overstock.com was fined $6.8 million in a California case for violating the state's false advertising and unlawful business practice laws. Overstock.com had responded to the complaint by saying that pricing laws had become outdated due to e-commerce and that buyers knew the difference between "street, retail and list prices," but the court found that its advertised list prices were "designed to overstate" the amount consumers would save by utilizing its site. The complaint alleged that in one instance Overstock.com advertised a patio set with a list price of $999 and a sales price on its site of $449, but when the customer received the set, a Walmart price tag was attached showing a price of $247.

The former director of the FTC's Bureau of Consumer Protection remarked: "If you're selling $15 pens for $7.50, but just about everybody else is also selling the pens for $7.50, then saying the list price is $15 is a lie. And if you're doing this frequently, it's a serious problem."

The Code of Federal Regulations includes detail with regard to deceptive pricing and list prices. Specifically, because many purchasers believe list price is the price at which an item is "generally sold," an advertised reduction in that price will cause purchasers to believe they are being offered a "genuine bargain." As such, if the list prices do not correspond to the prices at which a "substantial" number of sales of that item are made, advertising the reduction may be misleading. A 2016 news article showed how online retailers market using a Le Creuset skillet as an example. The list or suggested price at four online retailers ranged from $250 to $285, but all four retailers, plus more than 10 other online retailers, were selling the skillet for $200—the same price listed on the Le Creuset site.

Sources: David Streitfeld, *An Online Deal Just for You (Oh, and Everyone Else, Too)*, N.Y. TIMES, Mar. 6, 2016, at A1; Susanna Kim, *Overstock.com Defends Itself After Court's Deceptive Pricing Ruling*, ABC NEWS (Jan. 10, 2014), http://abcnews.go.com/Business/overstock-plans-appeal-courts-deceptive-pricing-ruling/story?id=21479695; 16 C.F.R. § 233.3(a).

Types of Unfair Competition

There are many types of unfair competition. They include false advertising (discussed earlier), passing off, and violations of the right of publicity.

Passing Off *Passing off* involves attempting to fool customers into believing that one's goods are actually those of a competitor. In one case, the publisher of *National Lampoon* successfully sued

ABC when the network used the word *lampoon* in the title of a television series without permission, after unsuccessfully negotiating for permission to use the name. The court held that ABC was trying to improperly exploit the reputation of *National Lampoon* for its own benefit. Passing off often involves improper use of another's trademark or trade name or of a confusingly similar mark or name. As discussed further in Chapter 14, *dilution* occurs when a firm uses another's famous trade name or trademark to promote noncompeting goods and thereby potentially confuses consumers about the true origin of the goods.

Disparagement   *Disparagement* includes making untrue claims about a competitor that would tend to damage its business. It frequently occurs when disgruntled former employees make untrue but damaging statements about their former employer's business.

Right of Publicity   *Right of publicity* is the exclusive right to exploit commercially one's name or likeness. Typically, these cases involve unauthorized attempts to use a sports or entertainment celebrity's name or likeness for commercial gain. For example, singer and actress Bette Midler successfully sued an automobile manufacturer that used a sound-alike singer in television advertising.[67]

Remedies

A victim of unfair competition may be entitled to a court order to stop the activity, as well as actual and punitive damages. Some types of unfair competition also carry criminal penalties.

10.11   RESOLVING E-COMMERCE DISPUTES: JURISDICTION, CHOICE OF LAW, AND ENFORCEMENT OF FOREIGN JUDGMENTS

Although the Internet is inherently global and multijurisdictional, most countries have their own laws regulating electronic commerce. As a result, resolving online disputes can be difficult, especially when there are conflicting public policies underlying the different countries' laws. Key issues include (1) which country (or in the case of disputes between U.S. parties from different states, which state) has the authority to require a defendant to adjudicate a dispute at a particular location (i.e., which court has jurisdiction); (2) what law will govern the dispute (choice of law or conflict of law); and (3) when will a court recognize and enforce a judgment rendered in a foreign jurisdiction.

In Search of Global Rules

A number of international bodies, including UNCITRAL[68] and the Organization for Economic Co-operation and Development,[69] are working to promulgate uniform rules for electronic commerce. The Hague Conference on Private International Law has also commissioned several examinations of electronic commerce issues.[70] The 2005 Hague Convention on Choice of Court Agreement entered into force at the end of 2015. The convention applies to the choice of court agreements in civil or commercial matters and includes provisions relating to enforcement of judgments. Thirty parties are bound by the convention, including most Member States of the European Union. The United States has signed the agreement but has not yet ratified it.[71]

Many jurisdictions permit parties to use private contract law to establish their own set of rules regarding jurisdiction, choice of forum, and choice of law, except in cases involving consumers. Because consumers often lack adequate bargaining power to effectively negotiate the terms proposed in a seller's click-wrap agreement, it seems likely that consumers will be permitted to sue in their home court under local law if the seller shipped products (including bits transmitted electronically) to the consumer's home jurisdiction.

The U.S. Approach to Jurisdiction

As a general matter, a court sitting in a state in the United States cannot require an out-of-state defendant to submit to its jurisdiction unless the defendant either (1) has agreed to do so (e.g., by consenting to jurisdiction in a contract) or (2) has sufficient minimum contacts with the state "such that the maintenance of the suit does not offend 'traditional notions of fair play and substantial justice.'"[72] This generally means that the nonresident defendant must either (1) have done some act or consummated some transaction in the forum in which it is being sued or (2) have purposefully availed itself of the privilege of conducting activities in the forum, thereby invoking the benefits and protections of the forum's laws.

In the case of companies doing business over the Internet, the U.S. courts have generally held that a state does not have personal jurisdiction over a nonresident defendant merely because the defendant has a website accessible to users in that state.[73] On the other hand, a state clearly does have personal jurisdiction over a nonresident defendant that knowingly and repeatedly uses the Internet to transact business in the state.[74] For example, if a corporation based in Arizona intentionally targets Utah users or repeatedly sells products or services to a Utah resident, then the Arizona company can be sued in the Utah courts for breach of warranty or product liability. The Utah resident can then invoke the Full Faith and Credit Clause of the U.S. Constitution to require the courts in Arizona to enforce the Utah judgment. Courts tend to resolve cases between these two extremes, which often involve interactive websites, on an ad hoc basis.[75]

What to Do

Given all this uncertainty, what should an emerging company that plans to use the Internet to sell goods or services do? First, to the extent possible, a company should include in its contracts explicit provisions addressing jurisdiction, choice of forum, and applicable law, while understanding that they may not be enforceable against consumers. Second, a firm should assume that if it regularly sells products or services in a state or country or makes offers directly to persons in a particular state or country, then it will be subject to that jurisdiction's laws and can be required to litigate in that jurisdiction all claims brought by residents of that state arising out of such sales or offers. Finally, a company should keep in mind that any presence in a jurisdiction, other than a passive website accessible there, may be enough to make the company subject to that jurisdiction's laws and answerable in its courts.

Putting It into **PRACTICE**

With its product ready for launch, Genesist enlisted the aid of an advertising agency to create a marketing campaign. The agency produced several 30-second television commercials showing Genesist's product in action. Piper liked the commercials but sensed that something was not quite right with the product demonstration. Although the GT V-Bracket had superior absorptive capacity, the commercial made it look as if a compact car with bumpers secured by the GT V-Bracket could sustain a collision at 55 m.p.h. without sustaining a bent frame. In fact, Genesist's tests showed that any collision at speeds in excess of 40 m.p.h. would bend the frame.

Piper asked the ad's designer about it. "Oh yeah, we wanted to push the concept that the V-Bracket protects drivers even at highway speeds," the designer replied. Piper nodded her head but knew she would have to check with Sarah Crawford to see whether this was all right.

"I'm glad you thought to ask," said Sarah. "The ad must show the brackets working normally and reflect the typical performance a consumer can expect from the product. Otherwise Genesist could be guilty of false advertising and subjected to FTC sanctions." Piper discussed the alternatives with Alexei. After some deliberation, they decided that the ad program should show a car that had stopped at a yellow light rear-ended by a delivery truck.

Piper was also concerned that Genesist might face ruinous liability if it could be held responsible for any damage caused to a consumer's person, property or business if a vehicle equipped with V-Brackets was involved in a collision. She discussed the matter with Aaron Biegert, who suggested that Genesist provide clear installation instructions to the purchasers, explicitly disclaim all implied warranties under the UCC, and expressly limit Genesist's liability to the fullest extent permitted by law. He cautioned, however, that some states curtail a seller's ability to limit its liability. To reduce the chance that any such limitation would be deemed procedurally or substantively unconscionable, he encouraged the

(continued)

founders to be as explicit as possible in the documentation and advertising about the limitations of the V-Brackets. He explained that in most jurisdictions the V-Brackets would be treated as component parts, which would mean that Genesist would only be strictly liable if the brackets themselves were defective. Aaron nonetheless encouraged Piper to ensure that all distributors of Genesist's V-Brackets and all companies incorporating them into their vehicles agree to promptly notify Genesist of any defects or customer complaints. He explained that one reason why there were delays linking the use of Firestone tires on Ford Explorer SUVs with vehicle instability and roll-overs was the failure of the two manufacturers to exchange all accident information.

Aaron then prepared a sales agreement, which Sarah modified slightly, that included the following provisions:

1. **Limited Warranty.** Genesist warrants that the Genesist GT V-Brackets (the "Brackets") will be free from defects for a period of one year from the date of purchase. If defects are present, Genesist's entire liability and Purchaser's exclusive remedy shall be limited to the replacement of the defective product or, at Genesist's option, refund of the purchase price.

2. **No Other Warranties.** The warranties of Section 1 above are the only warranties made by Genesist under this agreement. To the maximum extent permitted by applicable law, Genesist expressly disclaims all other warranties, both express and implied, including but not limited to implied warranties of merchantability and fitness for a particular purpose. Genesist does not warrant that the Brackets will meet Purchaser's needs or the needs of Purchaser's customers.

3. **Limitation of Liability.** To the maximum extent permitted by applicable law, Genesist shall not under any circumstances, including its own negligence, be liable for any incidental, special, exemplary, or consequential damages relating to this agreement or that otherwise result from the operation of the Brackets, whether in contract, in tort, or otherwise, including, without limitation, lost profits, lost sales, or any damage to your property, even if Genesist has been advised of the possibility of such damages.

4. **Indemnification.** Purchaser acknowledges receipt of the Genesist GT V-Bracket installation instructions and shall indemnify Genesist and its agents and assigns from any and all damages,

(continued)

losses, and expenses, including attorney's fees, resulting from the improper installation of the Brackets.

5. **Acceptance of These Terms.** Purchaser's acceptance of delivery of the Brackets shall constitute Purchaser's acceptance of the provisions of this sales agreement and no different or additional terms in any purchase order or other Purchaser form or writing will have any effect.

Alexei then scheduled a meeting with Sarah to discuss Genesist's liability insurance policies and to establish internal procedures designed to ensure compliance with applicable laws and to reduce the risk of operational liabilities.

11

Operational Liabilities, Insurance, and Compliance

C ivil and criminal liability can threaten a fledgling company's viability. By anticipating potential risks and being proactive, legally astute entrepreneurs can reduce the likelihood of violations and better manage problems when they arise. Indeed, effective compliance programs may be a source of competitive advantage, especially when managers are able to convert regulatory constraints into opportunities.[1]

A *tort* is a civil wrong that injures a person, property, or certain economic interests and business relationships. Torts range from strict product liability (discussed in Chapter 10) to negligence to intentional interference with contract. Individuals are always liable for the torts they commit. In addition, employers are vicariously liable for torts committed by employees acting within the scope of their employment.

A company and its managers may also face statutory liabilities stemming from state unfair business practices statutes and a variety of federal statutes imposing both civil and criminal liability for antitrust violations, environmental cleanup costs, bribery, and various types of fraud. Under some circumstances, a supervisor may be held civilly and criminally liable for the misdeeds of subordinates.

This chapter first introduces the tort of negligence, its elements, and its defenses. (We discussed negligence associated with the sale of defective products in Chapter 10.) We then describe a variety of intentional torts that protect people, property, and certain economic interests and business relationships.

Next, we address strict liability for ultrahazardous activities (strict product liability in tort, false advertising, and unfair competition were discussed in Chapter 10). The chapter continues with a discussion of an employer's liability for torts committed by its employees. We then address the antitrust laws (particularly the Sherman Act and its prohibition against horizontal price-fixing), federal environmental liability, bans on bribery under the Foreign Corrupt Practices Act, tax liability, and mail and wire fraud. (We discuss securities fraud in Chapter 17.) The chapter outlines types of insurance, which can cover many types of liability and losses, and concludes with a 10-step program for strategic compliance management.

11.1 NEGLIGENCE

Negligence is conduct that creates an unreasonable risk of causing injury to another person or damage to another person's property. To establish liability for negligence, the plaintiff must show that (1) the defendant owed a duty to the plaintiff to act reasonably under the circumstances; (2) the defendant breached that duty by failing to use the care that a reasonably prudent person would have used; (3) there is a reasonably close causal connection between the defendant's breach and the plaintiff's injury; and (4) the plaintiff suffered an actual loss or injury (*damages*).

Duty

A person with a legal *duty* to another is required to act reasonably under the circumstances to avoid harming the other person. For example, an employer has a duty to use reasonable care protecting the confidentiality of its employees' private data such as Social Security numbers. If the unauthorized transmission of private data results in a pecuniary loss due to identity theft, then the affected employee can sue for negligence. If the release of private information results in severe emotional distress, then the employee may be able to recover damages for negligent infliction of emotional distress. Duty exists in a variety of other contexts.

From the **TRENCHES**

ARCO Alaska, Inc. hired Unicol, Inc., an independent contractor, to perform excavation and install sheet metal piling as part of a bridge construction project. After Unicol had finished its work and turned the property over to ARCO, construction worker William Brent was injured while working on the site when he fell into a hole created by Unicol. The Supreme Court of Alaska found that Unicol was liable under Section 385 of the Restatement (Second) of Torts, writing that it reflects the rule that "a contractor is held to the standard of reasonable care for the protection of third parties who may foreseeably be endangered by his negligence, even after acceptance of the work by the contractee." Section 385 reflects the majority rule adopted by courts that have considered this issue.

Source: Brent v. Unicol, Inc., 969 P.2d 627 (Alaska 1998).

Duty of Landowner or Tenant A landowner or tenant has a legal duty to keep real property reasonably safe and may be liable for injury that occurs outside, as well as on, premises they own or control. For example, a person may be liable if sparks from improperly maintained machinery start a fire on adjacent property. In all jurisdictions, landowners have a general duty to inspect a building on their land and keep it in repair, and they may be liable if a showroom window, a downspout, a screen, or a loose sign falls and injures someone. In a few jurisdictions, landowners have a duty to maintain sidewalks immediately adjacent to their property.

Generally, landowners are not liable for harm caused by natural conditions on their property, such as uncut weeds that obstruct a driver's view, the natural flow of surface water, or falling rocks. Landowners may be liable, however, if they have altered the natural state of the land, for example, by erecting a sign or planting trees that obstruct a motorist's view.

Under traditional analysis, a landowner's duty to a person on its land varied, depending on the person's reasons for being on the property. The duty owed ranged from almost no duty to someone who was a *trespasser* (present on the property without permission) to an affirmative duty to protect a person who entered the premises for business purposes (an *invitee*). Customers are considered invitees and are accordingly owed the highest duty of care. A mere social guest (called a *licensee*) is owed a lesser duty.

In certain states, a business's duty to invitees may include an obligation to protect invitees from criminal conduct by third parties. The New Jersey Supreme Court held a supermarket liable when a 79-year-old woman was abducted from its parking lot and later killed. Even though there had never been an abduction or similar incident on the property, the court ruled that Food Circus was negligent in failing to provide any security or warning signs in its parking lot.[2]

The more modern approach, adopted by a number of states, including New York, is to impose a duty to use reasonable care under the circumstances. Under this standard, courts require all landowners to act in a reasonable manner with respect to entrants on their land, with liability hinging on the foreseeability of harm.[3]

Duty of Employer to Third Parties   As discussed later in this chapter, an employer is liable for any torts committed by employees acting within the scope of their employment, with scope of employment often being liberally defined. Under certain circumstances, employers have a legal duty to protect strangers from injuries caused by their employees even when the employees are off-site and are clearly not acting within the scope of their employment.

For example, the Texas Supreme Court ruled that an employer was potentially liable for an automobile accident in which an intoxicated employee sent home by his supervisor killed someone while driving home.[4] The Tennessee Court of Appeals reached the opposite result in a case with similar facts.[5] An employer may also be responsible for the safe passage home of an employee who is not intoxicated but is tired from working too many consecutive hours.[6] Before sending an impaired employee home, the employer should consider providing a ride home or offering a place where the employee could "sleep it off."

Duty of Professionals to Third Parties   Accountants, lawyers, architects, and other professionals have a duty to their clients to use reasonable care when rendering their services. Failure to do so can result in liability for negligence (commonly referred to in this context as *malpractice*). But under what circumstances can a third party who has relied on the professional's opinion sue the professional for negligence?

Consider an accounting firm that audits financial statements for a retailer that submits them to a bank as part of an application for an unsecured loan. The bank relies on the audited statements when deciding to make a loan on which the borrower subsequently defaults. The bank then discovers that the accountants had negligently failed to require the retailer to write off obsolete inventory. Can the bank hold the accountants liable for negligence? The answer will vary depending on which state's law governs the suit. A few states (including New York) require that there be a contractual relationship (*contractual privity*) between the professional and the person suing for negligence.[7] A few others will permit a third party to sue for negligence if the professional knew that the client intended to give the opinion to a third party whom the professional knew would rely on it when deciding whether and on what terms to enter into a transaction with the client.[8] The most liberal approach, which few jurisdictions have adopted, extends a professional's liability to all persons that the professional should reasonably foresee might obtain and rely on the opinion.

Standard of Conduct

A person is required to act as a reasonable person of ordinary prudence would act under the circumstances. The standard of care is not graduated to consider the reasonable person of low intelligence or the reasonably forgetful person. On the other hand, a person who is specially trained to participate in a profession or trade will be held to the higher standard of care of a reasonably skilled member of that profession or trade. For example, the professional conduct of a doctor, architect, pilot, attorney, or accountant will be measured against the standard of the profession.

The fact that one has complied with the law is not a defense if a reasonably prudent person would have done more than the law required. Thus, for example, a tugboat operator who does not have a radio may still be found negligent even though a radio is not legally required, if a prudent tugboat operator would have installed one. On the other hand, failing to follow the law is a prima facie case of negligence, or negligence *per se*, if the harm that follows is of the type that the law sought to prevent. Suppose, for example, that the law requires a school bus to have side mirrors of a certain size and a bus company fails to repair a broken mirror. If a child walking behind the bus is killed because the broken mirror did not function properly, then the bus company would be negligent *per se*, without the need to prove anything further.

11.2 DEFENSES TO NEGLIGENCE

Certain actors are protected from specific acts of negligence by special statutory provisions. As explained in Chapter 6, many states statutorily permit shareholders to insulate directors from liability for negligence in carrying out certain of their fiduciary duties. Sovereign immunity is another negligence shield, which shelters governmental actors from liability under certain circumstances.

In some jurisdictions, the defendant may absolve itself of all or part of the liability for negligence by proving that the plaintiff was also partly at fault.

Contributory Negligence

Under the doctrine of *contributory negligence*, if the plaintiff was also negligent in any manner, he or she cannot recover any damages from the defendant. Thus, if a plaintiff was 5% negligent and the defendant was 95% negligent, the plaintiff's injury would go unredressed. To avoid such inequitable outcomes, most courts have replaced the doctrine of contributory negligence with that of comparative negligence.

Comparative Negligence

Comparative negligence allows the plaintiff to recover the proportion of his or her loss attributable to the defendant's negligence. For example, if the plaintiff was 5% negligent and the defendant was 95% negligent, the plaintiff can recover 95% of the loss.[9] Some jurisdictions permit plaintiffs to recover for the percentage the defendant is at fault only if the plaintiff is responsible for less than 50% of his or her own injuries. Thus, in these jurisdictions, if the plaintiff is found 51% negligent and the defendant 49%

negligent, the plaintiff cannot recover at all.[10] These are called *modified comparative negligence jurisdictions.*

11.3 INTENTIONAL TORTS

A number of business torts require an intent to harm the plaintiff, the plaintiff's property, or certain economic interests and business relationships. A person *intends* a result when he or she subjectively wants it to occur or knows that it is substantially certain to occur as a result of his or her actions.

A person is automatically liable for their intentional torts without regard to duty. Thus, an accountant who intentionally prepared misleading financial statements would be liable to anyone who relied on those statements.

Torts That Protect Individuals

Several torts protect individuals from physical and mental harm. These include battery, false imprisonment, intentional infliction of emotional distress, defamation, and invasion of privacy. A single set of facts may give rise to claims under more than one theory.

Battery   *Battery* is harmful or offensive contact with the plaintiff's body or something (such as a coat) touching it. Putting poison in a person's food or intentionally releasing toxic waste into a river used for drinking water constitutes battery.

False Imprisonment   *False imprisonment* is intentional restraint of movement, imposed against someone's will by physical barriers, physical force, or threats of force. False imprisonment may occur when the plaintiff's freedom of movement was restricted because of force applied to the plaintiff's property. For example, a court found that when a store clerk confiscated a shopper's baby blanket (believing that it had been shoplifted) and refused to allow the shopper to use the restroom, there was sufficient evidence for a jury to decide whether the store had falsely imprisoned the shopper.[11] Most states have legislation exempting shopkeepers from false imprisonment claims if the shopkeeper acted in good faith and the detention was made in a reasonable manner, for a reasonable time, and was based on reasonable cause.

Intentional Infliction of Emotional Distress The tort of *intentional infliction of emotional distress* protects the right to peace of mind. In most jurisdictions, to prove intentional infliction of emotional distress, a plaintiff must show that (1) the defendant's conduct was outrageous, (2) the defendant intended to cause emotional distress, and (3) the defendant's actions caused severe emotional suffering. Certain jurisdictions also require a physical manifestation of the emotional distress.

When determining outrageousness, courts will consider the context of the tort, as well as the relationship of the parties. For example, in the workplace, the plaintiff can expect to be subjected to evaluation and criticism, and neither criticism nor discharge is in itself outrageous. Merely feeling upset is usually insufficient.

The entrepreneur is most likely to encounter claims of intentional infliction of emotional distress in situations in which an employee complains to a supervisor about racial, sexual, or religious harassment and the employer fails to investigate the claim or take appropriate remedial action.[12] This can also lead to claims of negligent infliction of emotional distress.

Defamation *Defamation* is the communication (often termed *publication*) to a third party of an untrue statement of fact that injures the plaintiff's reputation. *Libel* is written defamation, and *slander* is spoken defamation. Claims of defamation in the business context often arise out of adverse comments about a former employee's performance. Fear of such claims causes many employers to refuse to act as references for former employees other than to confirm dates of employment, title, and salary. Comments on social media can be defamatory, so entrepreneurs should use caution when making statements online about competitors' products or posting product reviews.

Invasion of Privacy Individuals are protected against inappropriate invasions of privacy, including public disclosure of private facts and intrusion. As described in Chapters 8 and 10, the unauthorized disclosure of private information, such as employee or customer Social Security numbers or medical information, may also violate a variety of federal and state privacy laws. In addition, many jurisdictions require the consent of one or both parties to the recording of a telephone call.[13]

Intrusion is objectionable prying, such as eavesdropping or unauthorized rifling through files. For intrusion to be tortious, the plaintiff must have a reasonable expectation of privacy in the object of the intrusion. *Appropriation of a person's name or likeness* may also be an invasion of privacy, such as when a person uses an individual's picture in an advertisement with which he or she has no connection.

Torts to Protect Interests in Property

A number of torts are designed to protect interests in property. These include trespass to land, nuisance, conversion, and trespass to personal property.

Trespass to Land   *Trespass to land* is an intentional invasion of real property without the consent of the owner. For example, a person driving a truck onto land belonging to another person commits trespass even if the land is not injured. The intent required is the intent to enter the property, not the intent to trespass. Thus, a person who intentionally stands on land believing that it is owned by a friend who has given consent is still liable for trespass if the land is, in fact, owned by someone else who has not given consent. The mistake as to ownership is irrelevant.

Trespass may occur both below the land's surface and in the airspace above it. Throwing something, such as trash, onto the land or shooting bullets over it may be a trespass, even though the perpetrator was not standing on the plaintiff's land. Refusing to move something that at one time the plaintiff permitted the defendant to place on the land may also constitute trespass. For example, if the plaintiff gave the defendant permission to leave a forklift on the plaintiff's land for one month, and it was left for two, the defendant may be liable for trespass.

Nuisance   *Nuisance* is a non-trespassory interference with the use and enjoyment of real property, for example, by an annoying odor or noise. *Public nuisance* is unreasonable and substantial interference with the public health, safety, peace, comfort, convenience, or utilization of land. A public nuisance action is usually brought by the government. It may also be brought by a private citizen who experiences special harm different from that suffered by members of the general public. *Private nuisance* is unreasonable and substantial interference with an individual's use and enjoyment of his or her land. Discharge of noxious fumes into the air, the pollution of a stream, or playing loud music late at night in a residential neighborhood can constitute a private nuisance. To determine whether the defendant's conduct is unreasonable, the court will balance the utility of the activity creating the harm and the burden of preventing it against the nature and the gravity of the harm. For example, hammering noise during the remodeling of a house may be easier to justify than playing loud music purely for pleasure. In 2014, a Texas jury awarded almost $3 million to one family, finding that the "offensive noises...odors and smells...offensive sights and light pollution...[and] offensive and abnormal traffic" resulting from an energy company's fracking activities constituted a private nuisance.[14]

Conversion   *Conversion* is the exercise of dominion and control over the personal property, rather than the real property, of another. This tort protects the right to have one's personal property left alone. It prevents the defendant from treating the plaintiff's property as if it were his or her own. Conversion is the tort claim a plaintiff would assert to recover the value of property stolen, destroyed, or substantially altered by the defendant.

The intent element for conversion does not include a wrongful motive. It merely requires the intent to exercise dominion or control over goods, inconsistent with the plaintiff's rights. The defendant need not know that the goods belonged to the plaintiff. For example, if a woman leaves a restaurant and takes another person's coat by mistake and then keeps the coat for three months before discovering the coat is not hers and returning it, that is conversion.[15]

Trespass to Personal Property   When personal property is interfered with but not converted, there is a *trespass to personal property* (sometimes referred to as *trespass to chattels*). No wrongful motive need be shown. The intent required is the intent to exercise control over the plaintiff's personal property. For example, an employer who took an employee's car on a short errand without the employee's permission would be liable for trespass to personal property. However, if the employer damaged the car or drove it for several thousand miles, thereby lowering its value, he or she would be liable for conversion.

Torts That Protect Certain Economic Interests and Business Relationships

Several torts are designed to protect certain economic interests and business relationships. These torts include fraudulent misrepresentation, interference with contractual relations, interference with prospective business advantage, and unfair competition.

Fraudulent Misrepresentation   The tort of *fraudulent misrepresentation,* also called *fraud* or *deceit,* protects economic interests and the right to be treated fairly and honestly. Fraud requires proof that the defendant knowingly and intentionally misled the plaintiff by making a material misrepresentation of fact on which the plaintiff justifiably relied. It also requires that the plaintiff suffer injury as a result of the reliance. For example, if entrepreneurs tell an investor that they developed certain key technology and own all rights to it when, in fact, they know that it belongs to their former employer, that is fraudulent misrepresentation.

Fraud can also be based on the defendant's omission of a material fact when he or she has a duty to speak because of a special relationship of trust with the plaintiff (a *fiduciary duty*). One case involved the owner of an auto dealership, who had relied on a bank for several years for financial advice and then consulted the banker about purchasing a second dealership. The banker recommended that he purchase a certain dealership but failed to tell him that the dealership was in financial straits and owed the bank money. The plaintiff took the bank's advice and bought the troubled dealership. The plaintiff suffered great financial hardship and eventually lost both dealerships after the bank refused to extend financing. The plaintiff successfully sued the bank for fraudulent misrepresentation and won a $4.5 million verdict.

Sometimes, courts will impose a duty to disclose even in the absence of a fiduciary relationship. For example, American Film Technologies, Inc. (*AFT*) convinced an investor to buy warrants that could be used to acquire common stock but failed to reveal that the underlying stock was restricted and could not be freely traded for a period of two years. Upon discovering the omission, the investor sued for fraud. The court held that because AFT had superior knowledge about the restrictions on its securities, it had a duty to reveal those restrictions. Its failure to do so amounted to fraudulent concealment.[16]

Interference with Contractual Relations   The tort of *interference with contractual relations* protects the right to enjoy the benefits of legally binding agreements. It provides a remedy when the defendant intentionally induces another person to breach a contract with the plaintiff. Interference with contractual relations requires that the defendant know that there is a contract.

Perhaps the most famous case involving tortious interference with a contract was *Texaco v. Pennzoil.* A jury assessed Texaco $10.5 billion in damages for interfering with Pennzoil's contract to buy Getty Oil. Texaco offered Getty Oil a better price and agreed to indemnify Getty Oil and its major shareholders if they were sued by Pennzoil for breach of contract.[17] The case was ultimately settled for $3 billion. Texaco could have avoided this outcome if it had made a public tender offer for the Getty stock instead of contracting directly with Getty Oil.

Interference with Prospective Business Advantage   Courts are less willing to award damages for interference with prospective contracts than they are to protect existing contracts. A party still engaged in negotiating a contract has fewer rights not to have a deal disturbed than a party that has already entered into a contract.

To prove *interference with prospective business advantage*, the plaintiff must prove that the defendant unjustifiably interfered with a relationship the plaintiff sought to develop and that the interference caused the plaintiff's loss. The interference usually must be intentional. In rare cases, however, courts have permitted recovery if the defendant was merely negligent.

Interference with prospective business advantage is usually committed by a competitor or at least by one who stands to benefit from the interference. For example, Loral Corp. was liable to the Korea Supply Company for interference with prospective business advantage after Loral's agent offered bribes and sexual favors to key Korean officials to induce them to accept Loral's bid for military radar systems even though MacDonald, Dettwiler, and

Associates' bid was $50 million lower and its equipment was superior. The Korea Supply Company had represented Mac-Donald in the negotiations for the contract and stood to receive a commission of more than $30 million if MacDonald's bid was accepted.[18] It is not a tort to compete fairly, however. Most jurisdictions recognize a privilege to act for one's own financial gain.

Unfair Competition Courts are willing to find certain kinds of anticompetitive behavior actionable if the activities complained of seem egregious and predatory to the court. These cases fall under the rubric of *unfair competition*. The improper use of trade secrets and customer information of prior employers often is found to constitute unfair competition.[19] Also, destroying a business by hiring away all of its employees has been deemed unfair competition.

11.4 STRICT LIABILITY

Strict liability is liability without fault, that is, without negligence or intent. Strict liability is imposed in product liability cases (discussed in Chapter 10) and for ultrahazardous activities.

Ultrahazardous Activities

If the defendant's activity is *ultrahazardous*, that is, so dangerous that no amount of care could protect others from the risk of harm, then the defendant is strictly liable for any injuries that result from the activity. Courts have found the following activities to be ultrahazardous: (1) storing flammable liquids in quantity in an urban area, (2) pile driving, (3) blasting, (4) crop dusting, (5) fumigation with cyanide gas, (6) emission of noxious fumes by a manufacturing plant located in a settled area, (7) locating oil wells or refineries in populated communities, and (8) test firing solid-fuel rocket motors. In contrast, courts have ruled that parachuting, drunk driving, maintaining power lines, and letting water escape from an irrigation ditch are not ultrahazardous. A court is more likely to consider a dangerous activity ultrahazardous when it is inappropriate to the particular location.

Under strict liability, once the court determines that the activity is abnormally dangerous, it is irrelevant that the defendant observed a high standard of care. For example, if the defendant's blasting injured the plaintiff, it is irrelevant that the defendant took every precaution available. Although evidence of such precautions might prevent the plaintiff from recovering under a theory of negligence, it does not affect strict liability. Strict liability for ultrahazardous activities makes it imperative that a company have liability insurance covering such activities.

11.5 TOXIC TORTS

A *toxic tort* is a wrongful act that causes injury by exposure to a harmful, hazardous, or poisonous substance. Modern industrial and consumer society uses these substances in a variety of ways, creating countless opportunities for toxic tort claims.

Potential toxic tort defendants include manufacturers (1) that use substances that may injure an employee, a consumer, or a bystander; (2) whose processes emit hazardous by-products into the air or discharge them into a river; (3) whose waste material goes to a disposal site if the waste could migrate to the groundwater and contaminate nearby wells; and (4) whose products contain or create substances that can injure. Liability is not limited to manufacturers, however. Everyday activities of governmental agencies, distribution services, and consumers may provide a basis for toxic tort claims. Some substances once thought to be safe, such as asbestos, have resulted in ruinous litigation when it was later established that they were harmful. Owners of so-called "sick buildings" have been sued for negligence because of substances present in their buildings that cause headaches, eye or throat irritation, or fatigue. Even financial institutions can be caught in the toxic tort net either by becoming involved in the operations of a company handling hazardous materials or by foreclosing on contaminated land held as collateral and continuing to hold it for an unreasonably long period of time.

Open-ended claims for punitive damages are commonplace in toxic tort cases. When pursuing a toxic tort claim, plaintiffs typically allege intentional torts, such as trespass, intentional infliction of emotional distress, and outrageous or despicable conduct, as well as negligence.

11.6 VICARIOUS TORT LIABILITY AND *RESPONDEAT SUPERIOR*

Under the doctrine of *respondeat superior*—"let the master answer"—an employer is vicariously liable for the torts of employees acting within the scope of their employment. The employer is liable even if the employer had no knowledge of the actions or had instructed the employee not to do the wrongful act. For example, a pizza company will be liable if its delivery person hits someone while speeding to deliver a pizza on time, even if the manager had instructed the employee not to speed.

Scope of Employment

Activities within the scope of employment are activities closely connected to what the employee is employed to do or reasonably incidental to it. Generally, an employee's conduct is considered within the *scope of employment* if it (1) is of the nature that he or she was employed to perform; (2) is within the time and space limitations normally authorized by the employer; and (3) furthers, at least in part, the purpose of the employer. On the other hand, an employer is generally not vicariously liable if an employee commits a tort while engaged in an activity solely for his or her own benefit.

The law draws a distinction between a frolic and a detour. A *frolic* occurs when an employee goes off and does something for himself or herself that is unrelated to the employer's business. A *detour* occurs when an employee temporarily interrupts his or her work to do something for himself or herself. Although the law holds an employer responsible for an employee's torts occurring during a detour, an employer is not responsible for a frolic. For example, if an employee leaves work to run a personal errand and while on the errand hits someone with his or her car, it is a frolic. If, however, the employer sends the employee to drive and pick up something and the employee runs a personal errand along the way, then it is a detour, and the employer will be liable for any torts committed by the employee, including those committed during the portion of the trip relating to the personal matter. Unfortunately, it is often unclear whether the employee's act was entirely outside the employer's purpose so employers should instruct employees not to perform personal errands while on company time or when using company resources, such as a company car or truck.

If an employee intentionally causes injury to the plaintiff or the plaintiff's property, an employer may still be liable if the wrongful act in any way furthered the employer's purpose, however misguided the manner of furthering that purpose. For example, if an employee of a financially troubled company misrepresents the company's financial condition to obtain a bank loan needed for working capital, the employer will be liable for fraud.

Aided-in-the-Agency-Relation Doctrine

Under the *aided-in-the-agency-relation doctrine*, an employer can be vicariously liable for a tort committed by an employee acting outside the scope of employment if the authority of the employer or an instrumentality provided by the employer made it possible for the employee to commit the tort. For example, as discussed in Chapter 8, if a supervisor fires a subordinate because the subordinate rejected the supervisor's sexual advances, then the employer is liable for sexual harassment, even if the employer had no reason to know that the supervisor was harassing the subordinate.

11.7 TORT REMEDIES

Tort damages are intended to compensate the plaintiff for the harm caused by the defendant. In egregious cases, the plaintiff may be able to recover punitive damages as well as compensatory damages. If monetary damages are not sufficient, then a court may impose equitable relief, that is, issue an injunction.

Actual Damages

Actual damages, also known as *compensatory damages*, are based on the cost to repair or replace an item, or the decrease in market value caused by the tortious conduct. When an individual is injured, actual damages may include compensation for medical expenses, lost wages, and pain and suffering.

Punitive Damages

Punitive damages (also called *exemplary damages*) may be awarded to punish the defendant and deter others from engaging in similar conduct. Normally, punitive damages are awarded only in cases of outrageous misconduct. The amount of punitive damages may properly be based on the defendant's wealth and must be reasonably proportional to the actual damages or proportionate to the wrong. The U.S. Supreme Court has ruled that the Fourteenth Amendment's Due Process Clause "prohibits the imposition of grossly excessive or arbitrary punishments on a tortfeasor," establishing a general rule that, except in cases where a particularly

 From the **TRENCHES**

In a well-publicized case that became the poster child for tort reform, an 82-year-old woman was awarded almost $2.9 million by a jury for the third-degree burns she suffered after spilling her McDonald's coffee in her lap while she was a passenger in a car stopped at a McDonald's drive-thru window. The verdict consisted of $160,000 in compensatory damages and $2.7 million in punitive damages. The trial judge subsequently reduced the punitive damages to $480,000.

McDonald's served its coffee at between 180° and 190° on the advice of a coffee consultant, who claimed that coffee tastes best at that temperature. Coffee brewed at home is typically between 135° and 140°. McDonald's acknowledged that its coffee was not fit for human consumption at the temperature served. It had previously received more than 600 complaints of scalding. A juror noted that McDonald's "callous" approach to the suit played a role in the verdict and award. After McDonald's announced its intention to appeal, the parties reached an out-of-court settlement for an undisclosed amount, and McDonald's lowered the temperature of its coffee.

Comment: The plaintiff had offered to settle the case before trial if McDonald's agreed to pay her out-of-pocket medical expenses of $2,500 and to turn down the temperature of the coffee, but McDonald's lawyers responded with a take-it-or-leave-it offer of $800. A legally astute manager might have handled the case differently and at least have apologized to the plaintiff.

Sources: Big Jury Award for Coffee Burn, N.Y. Times, Aug. 19, 1994, at D5; Matthew Kauffman, *Coffee Case a Hot Topic; Facts Cool Debate,* Hartford Courant, Apr. 10, 1995, at A5; Saundra Torry, *Tort and Retort: The Battle over Reform Heats Up,* Wash. Post, Mar. 6, 1995, at F7.

egregious act has caused only a small amount of economic damages, the ratio between punitive and compensatory damages should be in the single digits.[20] Several states have restricted the award of punitive damages to situations in which the plaintiff can prove by clear and convincing evidence that the defendant was guilty of oppression, fraud, or malice.

Equitable Relief

If a money award cannot adequately compensate for the plaintiff's loss, courts may grant *equitable relief.* For example, the court may issue an *injunction,* that is, a court order, prohibiting the defendant from continuing in a certain course of activity or ordering the defendant to do something. For example, a court can order a newspaper found liable for defamation to publish a retraction.

11.8 TORT LIABILITY OF MULTIPLE DEFENDANTS

The plaintiff may name numerous defendants in a tort action. In some cases, the defendants may ask the court to join, or add, other defendants. As a result, when a court determines that liability exists, it may have to grapple with how to allocate the loss among multiple defendants.

Joint and Several Liability

Under the doctrine of *joint and several liability,* multiple defendants are jointly (i.e., collectively) liable and also severally (i.e., individually) liable. This means that once the court determines that multiple defendants are at fault, the plaintiff may collect the entire judgment from any one of them, regardless of that defendant's degree of fault. Thus, a defendant who played a minor role in causing the plaintiff's injury might be required to pay all the damages. This is particularly likely when only one defendant has the financial resources to pay.

Joint and several liability often is imposed in toxic tort cases when a number of companies might have contributed to the contaminated site, such as a landfill or a river, or exposed the plaintiff to hazardous materials, such as asbestos. Frequently, the company with deep pockets ends up having to pay for all the harm done to the plaintiff. Some states have adopted statutes to limit the doctrine of joint and several liability.

Contribution and Indemnification

The doctrines of contribution and indemnification can mitigate the harsh effects of joint and several liability. *Contribution* distributes the loss among several defendants by requiring each to pay its proportionate share (often based on their relative fault) to the defendant that discharged the joint liability to the plaintiff. *Indemnification* allows a defendant to shift its individual loss to other parties whose relative blame is greater. For example, a truck manufacturer might require a seat manufacturer to indemnify it, if a defective seat caused an accident for which the truck manufacturer was found liable. The right to contribution and indemnification is worthless, however, if all the other defendants are insolvent or lack sufficient assets to contribute their share. In such a case, the defendant with money must still pay the plaintiff the full amount of damages awarded, even though the other defendants will not be able to reimburse the solvent defendant for their share of the damages.

11.9 ANTITRUST VIOLATIONS

Section 1 of the Sherman Act provides that "[e]very contract, combination in the form of trust or otherwise, or conspiracy, in restraint of trade or commerce among the several States, or with foreign nations, is declared to be illegal."[21] Although Section 1 appears to prohibit any and all concerted activity that restrains trade, the courts have construed Section 1 to prohibit only those restraints of trade that *unreasonably* restrict competition. Violations of Section 1 may be prosecuted as felonies.[22] In addition, private plaintiffs or state attorneys general acting on behalf of citizens in their states can recover treble damages in civil cases.[23]

A number of financial institutions have paid multi-billion dollar fines for their involvement in currency rigging schemes. For example, in 2015, Citicorp, JPMorgan Chase, Barclays, and the

Royal Bank of Scotland agreed to plead guilty to conspiring to fix prices and rig bids for U.S. dollars and euros exchanged in the foreign exchange spot market and to pay combined criminal fines of more than $2.5 billion.[24] Barclays settled claims with other regulatory bodies for another $1.3 billion.[25] The scheme was described as "brazen," with one Barclays trader writing in an electronic chatroom, "If you aint cheating, you aint trying."[26]

Contract, Combination, or Conspiracy

Agreements can be (1) *horizontal,* that is, between firms that directly compete with one another, such as two automakers, or (2) *vertical,* that is, between firms at different levels of production or distribution, such as a retailer and a manufacturer. In general, courts view horizontal agreements much more harshly than vertical agreements because they reduce *interbrand competition,* that is, competition among manufacturers selling different brands of the same product. As a result, they are more likely to result in higher prices for consumers. In contrast, a vertical restraint, such as a manufacturer's requirement that a distributor sell the manufacturer's products in only a particular geographic location, may limit *intrabrand competition* (i.e., competition among distributors selling the same brand product) but increase interbrand competition (and thereby reduce prices) by creating a stronger distribution network.

Per se Violations of Section 1

Per se analysis condemns practices that are considered completely void of redeeming competitive rationales. This is appropriate when the practice always or almost always tends to restrict competition and harm consumers. Once identified as illegal *per se,* a practice need not be examined further for its impact on the market, and its procompetitive justifications will not be considered. Law and economics scholars have argued that very few practices are inherently anticompetitive.

Horizontal Price-Fixing   The classic example of a *per se* violation of Section 1 is horizontal price-fixing. *Horizontal price-fixing agreements* include agreements between competitors (1) setting prices;

(2) setting the terms of sale, such as customer credit terms; and (3) setting the quantity or quality of goods to be manufactured or made available for sale. *Bid rigging*, agreements between or among competitors to agree in advance which company will submit the winning bid (e.g., by agreeing to bid high on one contract in exchange for a competitor's agreement to bid high on another), is also a form of horizontal price-fixing. The U.S. Department of Justice views price-fixing as "hard crime" to be punished by prison sentences.

Even startups are prohibited from engaging in horizontal price-fixing. It is still illegal *per se* even if none of the parties involved has a significant share of the market.

Horizontal Market Division *Market divisions*, whereby competitors divide up a market according, for example, to a class of consumers or geographic territory, are *per se* violations of Section 1. Market division is prohibited even if it is intended to enable small competitors to compete with larger companies and to foster inter-brand competition.

Group Boycotts An agreement among competitors to refuse to deal with another competitor—a *group boycott*—is also a *per se* violation of Section 1. An agreement between or among competitors that deprives another competitor of something it needs to compete effectively is considered so inherently anticompetitive that no economic motivation may be offered as a defense. For example, manufacturers of different brands of appliances cannot enter into an agreement with a particular distributor's competitors to refuse to sell their appliances to the distributor or to do so at a higher price.

Restraints on Trade Subject to the Rule of Reason

If the plaintiff has not proved that a restraint on trade is a *per se* violation, then the activity will be evaluated under the rule of reason. The objective of the *rule of reason* is to determine whether, on balance, the activity promotes or restrains competition or, to put it differently, whether it helps or harms consumers. In making this determination, the court will consider the structure of the market as well as the defendant's conduct. The court will analyze the anticompetitive and procompetitive effects of the challenged practice. Activity that has a substantial net anticompetitive effect is deemed an unreasonable restraint of trade and hence is unlawful.

Vertical minimum and maximum price-fixing, also referred to as *resale price maintenance,* are subject to the rule of reason.[27] Because minimum prices result in higher costs for consumers, minimum price-fixing is most likely to be upheld when luxury goods are involved and high levels of customer service are an important part of the brand's ability to compete with other manufacturers' products. Geographic vertical restraints, such as exclusive car dealerships, have long been judged by the rule of reason. *Exclusive dealing arrangements,* whereby a party agrees to sell its products only to select buyers, are also subject to the rule of reason. As a general matter, such arrangements are more likely to be upheld if they are of limited duration, do not foreclose a major share of the market, and serve a legitimate business purpose.

From the **TRENCHES**

The Chicago *Daily Herald* sued the *Chicago Tribune* for entering into an agreement with the New York Times News Service, whereby the *Chicago Tribune* was given the exclusive right to publish *The New York Times* crossword and certain other features in the Chicago area for a period of one year. The U.S. Court of Appeals for the Seventh Circuit applied the rule of reason and concluded that the exclusive distributorship arrangement was not an unreasonable restraint of trade. It was of short duration, and other (albeit less famous) crossword puzzles were available to the *Daily Herald*. Exclusive stories and features help newspapers differentiate themselves and thereby better compete with one another. The court noted that the *Herald* had never tried to make a better offer to obtain the right to carry *The New York Times* features and suggested that it "should try to outbid the *Tribune* and *Sun-Times* in the marketplace, rather than to outmaneuver them in court."

Source: Paddock Publ'ns, Inc. v. Chicago Tribune Co., 103 F.3d 42 (7th Cir. 1996).

Monopolization

Section 2 of the Sherman Act prohibits monopolization or attempts to monopolize. A firm does not violate Section 2 merely by having a major share of the market; that may be the result of the firm's superior business foresight, skill, or acumen. To violate Section 2, a firm must have *market power* (generally defined as the ability to raise prices without losing market share) *and* have engaged in anticompetitive acts (such as predatory pricing or exclusive dealing).

Although most young firms do not have sufficient market power to be monopolists, they may well be competing against larger firms that do have market power. Sometimes startups can use the antitrust laws to pry open a market that has theretofore been dominated by a larger player. In its early years, long-distance carrier MCI supported efforts by the U.S. Department of Justice to break up American Telephone and Telegraph so customers could buy cheaper long-distance service from MCI.[28]

After the U.S. Court of Appeals for the District of Columbia Circuit upheld the finding that Microsoft had illegally maintained its monopoly of the Intel-compatible PC operating system market,[29] several of Microsoft's smaller competitors brought private civil antitrust suits, seeking treble damages as well as injunctive relief. Microsoft paid Netscape, creator of Netscape Navigator, the first widely used Internet web browser, $750 million to settle that company's claims. Sun Microsystems, creator of the Java programming language, settled its case against Microsoft in exchange for nearly $2 billion.[30] In total, Microsoft paid more than $4 billion in settlements.

The European Commission is often more aggressive than U.S. regulators in investigating and suing firms for violation of the European Union's competition laws, especially its prohibition on abuse of dominant position. The European Commission fined Intel $1.45 billion in 2009 for "deliberately acting to keep competitors out of the market for computer chips for many years,"[31] thereby preventing open competition and harming European consumers. The U.S. Federal Trade Commission brought similar charges, and it approved a settlement order with Intel in 2010 in order to "open the door to renewed competition and prevent Intel from suppressing competition in the future."[32] Intel also agreed to pay Advanced Micro Devices $1.25 billion in 2009 to settle antitrust litigation and patent cross license disputes.[33]

11.10 ENVIRONMENTAL LIABILITIES

Several federal statutes, and their state analogues, impose liability for the cleanup of hazardous waste. Importantly, a party may be liable even if (1) that person did not generate, transport, or dispose of the waste; (2) the waste was not considered hazardous at the time it was generated, transported, or disposed of; and (3) disposal was done in accordance with all applicable laws in effect at the time. Thus, even if a particular venture will not be using hazardous materials, it may still be liable for cleanup costs if the prior owner of its real property or the prior lessee disposed of hazardous waste improperly.

As one can imagine, an assessment and action by the Environmental Protection Agency (*EPA*) to clean up hazardous waste can be financially crippling to a new venture. To cover the risk of environmental liability, a company contemplating the purchase or lease of real property should seek indemnification from the seller (or lessor in the case of a lease), purchase pollution legal liability insurance, and have an environmental lawyer review the transaction.

Comprehensive Environmental Response, Compensation, and Liability Act

The Comprehensive Environmental Response, Compensation, and Liability Act (*CERCLA*, sometimes called *Superfund*) provides that certain "responsible parties" are strictly liable for the cleanup of hazardous waste. *Potentially responsible parties* include (1) the current owners or operators of a facility, (2) the owners or operators at the time the hazardous substances were disposed of, (3) the transporters of hazardous substances to a facility if the transporter selected the facility, and (4) persons who arranged for treatment or disposal of hazardous substances at a facility. In the absence of any of the defenses outlined below, these parties are liable to the government for response costs, including investigation and cleanup costs, administrative costs, legal costs, and pre-judgment interest. The cleanup liabilities are retroactive, strict (i.e., without fault), and generally joint and several.

Owners include the current fee owners and past owners at the time of disposal. Most importantly, owners can include lessees with attributes of ownership. For example, suppose a startup signs a triple net lease with the owner of a warehouse to rent space in the warehouse. A *triple net lease* requires the lessee to pay all taxes, insurance, and maintenance costs. The lease is sufficient to give the startup the attributes of ownership. If it turns out that the warehouse site contains hazardous substances and the EPA designates the site for cleanup, then the EPA can sue the startup as well as the owner of the building for the response costs and can collect all of them from the startup under joint and several liability.

For CERCLA purposes, an *operator* is "simply someone who directs the workings of, manages, or conducts the affairs of a facility."[34] The term may include lessees with authority to control the facility, but liability extends only to the portion they lease.[35]

Defenses   There are various defenses to CERCLA liability. An otherwise responsible party is not liable if the contamination was caused by an act of God (such as an earthquake) or an act of war. Other defenses include (1) the third-party defense; (2) the contiguous property owner defense; and (3) the bona fide prospective purchaser defense.

To establish the *third-party defense*, also referred to as the *innocent landowner defense*, an owner (or lessee in the case of a triple net lease) must, among other requirements, (1) have acquired the property after the disposal occurred; (2) made "all appropriate inquiry" into the previous ownership and uses of the facility before purchase; (3) have taken reasonable steps to stop and prevent future or continuing releases of hazardous materials; and (4) not know, and have no reason to know, about the hazardous substance when purchasing the property. The *contiguous property owner defense* provides a defense to owners (and lessees) whose property is contaminated from contiguous property when, among other requirements, the owner (or lessee) (1) made "all appropriate inquiry"; (2) did not cause, contribute, or consent to the release of hazardous substances; and (3) takes reasonable steps to stop or prevent future or continuing releases of the hazardous substance.

To encourage the development of *brownfields*, contaminated sites that are eligible for cleaning and reclaiming with assistance from the Superfund, Congress established the *bona fide prospective purchaser defense*. This defense protects an owner (or lessee) who, among other requirements, (1) acquires the property after the disposal occurred; (2) made "all appropriate inquiry"; (3) takes reasonable steps to stop and prevent future or continuing releases of hazardous substances; and (4) fully cooperates with those authorized to conduct response actions.

To comply with the *all appropriate inquiry* requirement, a site assessment must be undertaken by an environmental professional that conforms to ASTM 1527-13 "Standard Practice for Environmental Site Assessments: Phase I Environmental Site Assessment Process."[36] Further testing (Phase II) may be required if potential problems are noted.

Resource Conservation and Recovery Act

The Resource Conservation and Recovery Act (*RCRA*) establishes a system for controlling hazardous waste from the time it is generated until it is ultimately disposed of—"from cradle to grave." The act covers the generators of the waste; the transporters; and the owners and operators of treatment, storage, and disposal facilities.

Personal Liability of Operators under CERCLA and RCRA

Under both CERCLA and RCRA, the individuals responsible for operating a facility that generates hazardous waste (*operators*) are potentially personally liable for violations. This means that they can be fined or even sent to prison for knowing violations. In some cases, courts will apply the *responsible corporate officer doctrine* and hold an officer liable for the misdeeds of a subordinate. This makes appropriate training of personnel and monitoring all the more important.

Clean Air and Clean Water Acts

The Clean Air and Water Acts, and their state analogues, impose liability on generators of waste that release hazardous waste in

From the **TRENCHES**

For 15 years, the Hanlin Group operated a chemical plant in Georgia through its subsidiary, LCP Chemicals-Georgia (*LCP*). LCP had a wastewater treatment system and a Georgia EPD permit to dump treated water into a nearby waterway. Hanlin filed for bankruptcy in 1991. To help turn around the company, Hanlin CEO Christian Hansen brought in his son, Randall, to act as interim CEO of LCP. Randall was soon informed that the plant could not operate in compliance with the environmental laws, because the treatment system could not keep up with the amount of wastewater being produced.

In 1992, the Occupational Health and Safety Administration cited the facility for hazardous conditions created by contaminated water on the plant floor. From that point, environmental law violations related to contaminated water continued to pile up. LCP duly reported the infractions to the state and federal environmental protection agencies, but Randall was unsuccessful in obtaining funds from the bankruptcy court to correct the problems. A potential sale of the plant fell through after the Georgia EPD refused to issue a permit to the new owner unless it committed to clean up not just the waste generated by LCP but the legacy contamination caused by all previous owners. Without money to maintain the equipment or to safely shut the plant down, parts began to break down, causing additional violations.

Without the means to keep the plant operating safely or to shut it down safely, the Hansens and plant manager Alfred Taylor—the corporate officers with authority to control the activity causing the violations—resorted to various methods of handling the excess wastewater issue. In one instance, contaminated water was ordered pumped into underground tanks, which had once been used to store oil despite the fact that once mixed with oil the water could not be put through the treatment system.

LCP was finally forced to close the plant when the Georgia EPD revoked its license in 1993. The U.S. EPA cleaned up the site at a cost of $50 million. A jury found the Hansens and Taylor guilty of violating environmental laws, including RCRA, CERCLA, and the Clean Water Act. Christian Hansen was sentenced to nine years in prison, his son to four years, and Taylor to six and a half years. Their convictions were upheld on appeal.

Comment: This case stands as a stark reminder of the potential criminal liability of managers for criminal violations by their employer.

Sources: United States v. Hansen, 262 F.3d 1217 (11th Cir. 2001); Paul Rosenzweig, *The Over-Criminalization of Social and Economic Conduct*, HERITAGE FOUND. (Apr. 17, 2003), http://www.heritage.org/research/reports/2003/04/the-over-criminalization-of-social-and-economic-conduct.

excess of the mandated limits. In 2013, BP Exploration and Production Inc. pleaded guilty to 14 criminal counts, including felony manslaughter and various environmental crimes, and was sentenced to pay $4 billion in criminal fines and penalties, relating to the 2010 explosion of the Deepwater Horizon oil rig in the Gulf of Mexico.[37] In 2015, BP reached a $20 billion civil settlement with the government, including $4.4 billion in Clean Water Act penalties.[38] As with CERCLA and RCRA, individuals may be criminally liable for their own actions and for the actions of subordinates whom they control.

11.11 BRIBERY AND THE FOREIGN CORRUPT PRACTICES ACT

In free market systems "it is basic that the sale of products should take place on the basis of price, quality, and service. Corporate bribery is fundamentally destructive of this basic tenet."[39] As Secretary of the Treasury Michael Blumenthal testified before Congress: "Paying bribes—apart from being morally repugnant and illegal in most countries—is simply not necessary for the successful conduct of business here or overseas."[40] Because companies paying bribes often try to hide them by falsifying their accounting books and records, bribery also erodes "public confidence in the integrity of the system of capital formation."[41]

Bribes

The Foreign Corrupt Practices Act (*FCPA*)[42] prohibits payments of money or providing anything else of value by a U.S. company or a non-U.S. company controlled by a U.S. company, or its employees or agents, to a foreign government official or a foreign political party for the purpose of improperly influencing government decisions. This antibribery ban applies to all companies, both private and public. Providing gifts or paying for travel and entertainment can be considered payments meant to influence foreign officials. Thus, paying a government medical doctor's travel expenses so the physician can observe a new medical device may come within the definition of seeking to influence a foreign official.

The statute is violated even if a bribe is only offered and is never paid. It is also illegal to make a payment to a private party with actual knowledge, or willful disregard of the fact, that it will be funneled to a foreign government official or a foreign political party.

From the **TRENCHES**

In 2015, the Bank of New York Mellon agreed to pay $14.8 million to settle charges by the Securities and Exchange Commission (*SEC*) that the bank had provided three internships to family members of unnamed officials at an unnamed Middle East sovereign wealth fund. The SEC alleged that the interns were hired "to corruptly win or keep" business with the fund: emails from bank employees characterized the internship positions as an "expensive 'favor,'" noting that the internships could help in "retaining dominant position" and that business would be "jeopardize[d]" if the internships did not materialize.

Sources: Nate Raymond & Sarah N. Lynch, *BNY Mellon to Pay $14.8 Million to Settle Intern Bribery Probe*, REUTERS (Aug. 18, 2015), http://www.reuters.com/article/2015/08/18/us-bny-mellon-sec-corruption-idUSKCN0QN1PJ20150818; Michael J. de la Merced, *Bank of New York Mellon Settles Bribery Case Over Interns*, N.Y. TIMES, Aug. 19, 2015, at B1.

The FCPA includes an exception for payments to low-ranking officials who merely expedite the nondiscretionary granting of a permit or license (*facilitating payments*). A second exception is made for payments to foreign businesses not owned or controlled by the government, subject to the funneling caveat mentioned above. Public companies must still properly account for such payments in their financial statements.

Record-Keeping Requirements

The FCPA requires all public companies that file periodic reports with the SEC under the Securities Exchange Act of 1934, including purely domestic reporting companies that are not engaged in international trade, to keep books and records that accurately and fairly reflect its transactions and dispositions of assets. They must also devise and maintain a system of internal controls sufficient to assure management's control, authority, and responsibility over the firm's assets. These requirements are designed to prevent public companies from setting up a slush fund and then accounting for questionable payments as legitimate business expenses. In 2014, Avon China, a subsidiary of Avon Products Inc., was ordered to pay more than $135 million in criminal and regulatory penalties after it pleaded guilty to conspiring to violate the FCPA's accounting provisions.[43] Failure to maintain the appropriate records is a violation, even if the company never offers or pays a bribe.

Doing Business with State-Owned Enterprises

Both the SEC and the Department of Justice generally consider employees of state-owned enterprises to be "foreign officials" for the purposes of the FCPA. Companies of all sizes are therefore well advised to seek competent legal counsel when doing business with state-owned enterprises.

Because the Chinese government owns or controls many businesses in China, a large proportion of business transactions with Chinese firms involve a foreign official. In 2015, Mead Johnson Nutrition Co. agreed to pay $12 million to settle SEC claims that it violated the FCPA when its distributors in China allegedly paid more than $2 million in bribes over a five-year period to staff at state-owned hospitals so they would promote the company's infant formula to new mothers.[44]

Although China has a centuries-old tradition of gift giving and entertainment (*guanxi*) as an acceptable, and often necessary, means of conducting business, China has stepped up its efforts to combat bribery and corruption. In 2014, the Chinese government fined pharmaceutical giant GlaxoSmithKline (*GSK*) $491.5 million, its largest fine to date, for bribing Chinese physicians and health-care organizations.[45] The head of GSK's Chinese operations pleaded guilty to bribery and was deported. Glaxo apologized in Chinese and English to the Chinese government, people, and medical personnel.[46]

11.12 TAX LIABILITY

Certain violations of the Internal Revenue Code are subject to criminal penalties. The strictest penalties are for violations of Section 7201's prohibition of willful attempts to evade taxes imposed under the code, including employee withholding requirements. Section 7206 forbids any false statements in a tax return and Section 7207 prohibits the willful delivery of a fraudulent return to the Secretary of the Treasury.

Section 6672 imposes a civil penalty equal to the amount of a corporation's unpaid federal employment taxes on those with the power and responsibility for seeing that the taxes withheld from various sources are remitted to the government in a timely fashion. The bottom line for entrepreneurs is that they should never use the taxes withheld from employees' paychecks to meet a cash crunch. The penalties can be severe and personal.

11.13   WIRE AND MAIL FRAUD

The wire and mail fraud statutes prohibit (1) a scheme intended to defraud or to obtain money or property by fraudulent means and (2) the use of the mails or of interstate telephone lines or electronic communication in furtherance of the fraudulent scheme. Conspiring or attempting to commit these same activities is also illegal.[47] "Fraud" includes "everything designed to defraud by representations as to the past or present, or suggestions and promises as to the future."[48]

Almost all white-collar criminal prosecutions include a count for violation of these statutes. This strengthens the plea bargaining power of the government and increases the likelihood of a conviction on at least one count.

11.14   OBSTRUCTION OF JUSTICE AND RETALIATION AGAINST WHISTLE-BLOWERS

During criminal investigations, entrepreneurs and others must be careful to avoid violating other laws that could give the government additional leverage. Any effort to impede a criminal investigation, particularly the alteration or destruction of documents, can result in an obstruction of justice charge.[49] Similarly, it is a federal crime to lie to federal investigators.[50] It is also illegal for any company, public or private, to retaliate against employees who provide truthful information to the government about possible violations of any federal law.[51]

Anyone facing criminal investigation should immediately retain his or her own experienced criminal counsel and be prepared to answer all questions truthfully or to invoke their Fifth

From the **TRENCHES**

Mail and wire fraud charges can be imposed on small and large companies. In 2015, John White was sentenced to 70 months in prison and 5 years of supervised release, and ordered to pay more than $6 million in restitution, after being convicted of conspiracy to commit mail and wire fraud. White had induced U.S. purchasers to buy business opportunities in entities, such as USA Beverages Inc. and Cards-R-Us Inc., under the pretense that purchasers could profitably sell coffee and greeting cards from display racks located at other retail establishments. White and others made false statements to the potential buyers, including that it was likely that purchasers would earn substantial profits; that they would sell a minimum amount of coffee and cards; and that the profits of the companies were partially based on the profits of the business opportunity purchasers, creating the "false impression" that the companies had a stake in the purchasers' success.

On a larger scale, the U.S. Department of Justice charged Toyota with criminal wire fraud in 2014, on the theory that Toyota's "misleading statements about major safety issues constitute wire fraud." This was the first time criminal wire fraud charges had been made in an auto case that focused on concealing safety problems. Toyota agreed to pay a $1.2 billion criminal penalty and admitted that it had misled Americans about two different problems that caused cars to unintentionally accelerate and that it excluded certain vehicles from its recall for cars that had problems with floor mats becoming trapped under the gas pedal. Then-U.S. Attorney General Eric Holder cautioned that this type of settlement may be used as a model for other cases that involve "similarly situated companies." Thus, any manufacturer that hides safety problems (and the responsible employees and supervisors who work for them) runs the risk of criminal prosecution for wire fraud.

Sources: Press Release, Dep't of Justice, U.S. Citizen Pleads Guilty in Connection with Internationally Based Business Opportunity Fraud Ventures (Apr. 29, 2015), http://www.justice .gov/opa/pr/us-citizen-pleads-guilty-connection-internationally-based-business-opportunity-fraud -ventures; Current and Recent Cases, Department of Justice, http://www.justice.gov/civil/current -and-recent-cases (updated Aug. 19, 2015); Aruna Viswanatha, *U.S. Prosecutors Eye New Approach on Company Misconduct after Toyota*, REUTERS (Mar. 25, 2014), http://www.reuters .com/article/2014/03/25/us-usa-autos-accountability-idUSBREA2O09520140325; *U.S. Weighs Charges Against GM Over Ignition Switch Recall: WSJ*, REUTERS (June 9, 2015), http://www .reuters.com/article/2015/06/09/us-usa-gm-doj-idUSKBN0OP1FY20150609.

Amendment right to remain silent. The attorney–client privilege for conversations between an employee and the company's inside or outside lawyers belongs to the company, not the employee, so the board of directors can waive it at the employee's expense. In contrast, communications between an employee under criminal investigation and his or her own counsel are generally privileged. If, however, the communications were made for the purpose of getting advice for the commission or furtherance of a fraud or crime, the crime-fraud exception may be invoked to remove the protective cloak of confidentiality.[52]

11.15 COMPUTER CRIME AND MISAPPROPRIATION OF INTELLECTUAL PROPERTY

Computer fraud is the use of a computer to steal or embezzle funds. This type of theft generally involves improper or unauthorized access to the computer system and the creation of false data or computer instructions.

The Computer Fraud and Abuse Act (*CFAA*)[53] prohibits seven types of activities involving *protected computers*, defined to include not only federal and financial institution computers but also any computers used in or affecting interstate or foreign commerce or communications. Thus, the CFAA applies to anyone using or interfering with a computer connected to the Internet. Offenses include accessing a computer and obtaining information without authorization, or exceeding authorization; accessing a computer to defraud; intentionally causing damage by knowingly transmitting a program, information, code, or command; recklessly causing damage by intentional access; trafficking in passwords; extortion; and obtaining national security information without proper authorization. *Damage* is defined as any impairment to the integrity or availability of data, a program, a system, or information.

Employers have used the CFAA to go after employees who have allegedly stolen trade secrets. There is, however, a split among the federal circuit courts over the meaning of the CFAA term "exceeds authorized access." The U.S. Courts of Appeals for the Second, Fourth, and Ninth Circuits have adopted a narrow construction, whereby an individual exceeds authorized access to a computer "only when he obtains or alters information that he does not have authorization to access for any purpose which is located on a computer that he is otherwise authorized to access."[54] The First, Fifth, Seventh, and Eleventh Circuits have taken a much broader view, holding that an individual exceeds authorized access to a computer when "with an improper purpose, he accesses a computer to obtain or alter information that he is otherwise authorized to access."[55] The broader view could theoretically be interpreted to mean that an employee who uses his or her work computer to look at a baseball score or check a Facebook post could be in violation of the law, resulting in potential criminal penalty. The Fourth Circuit wrote that it did not think Congress intended to impose criminal penalties "for such a frolic."[56] The U.S. Supreme Court or Congress will ultimately have to resolve the conflicting rulings on this issue.

The CFAA makes it illegal to knowingly transmit computer viruses. A *computer virus* is a computer program that can replicate itself into other programs without any subsequent instruction, human or mechanical. A computer virus may destroy data, programs, or files, or it may prevent user access to a computer (*denial-of-service attacks*). The proliferation of computer networks has created millions of entry points for viruses, and they can be quite destructive. Even if a virus is benign or temporary, it is illegal to knowingly transmit one.

Computer piracy is the theft of computer software or its use in violation of the licensing agreement. It is a federal crime to make or post unauthorized copies of software programs, even if the person does not receive any money in exchange. Most states have made the theft of computer software a crime as well. Entrepreneurs should ensure they have purchased the software they use on their networks and are in compliance with any end user licensing agreements.

As discussed further in Chapter 14, the federal Economic Espionage Act of 1996 (*EEA*)[57] made it a crime to misappropriate trade secrets. Congress enacted the Defend Trade Secrets Act of 2016,[58] an amendment to the EEA, to provide a federal civil remedy for the misappropriation of trade secrets. The act, which gave federal district courts original jurisdiction to hear such cases, permits the recovery of damages. In extreme situations, a civil seizure remedy is available as well.

11.16 INSURANCE

The insurance markets have evolved to a point where entrepreneurs can insure against most risks (other than fraud or other intentional wrongdoing) if they are willing to pay a premium to a sophisticated insurer. Insurance can protect the individual participants in a business from personal liability as well as the assets and future retained earnings of the business. Entrepreneurs should make certain that the company's insurance broker adequately understands the risks associated with the business and has provided insurance sufficient to cover those risks. Typical types of coverage for young firms include general liability insurance (including product liability insurance); errors and omissions insurance for directors and officers; fire and casualty insurance; business interruption insurance; key-personnel life and disability insurance; insurance to fund share repurchases upon the death or disability of a major individual shareholder; and workers' compensation insurance.

Insurance is generally divided into two categories: first-party insurance and third-party (liability) insurance. It is prudent for a new business to carry both.

First-Party Insurance

First-party insurance protects the policyholder in the case of damage or loss to the insured or its property. For example, a standard property owner's policy insures against loss due to fire, theft, or flood, but not against structural damage due to termite infestation. Business interruption insurance insures against lost revenues and profits resulting from an earthquake or other event that interferes with the normal conduct of business.

Third-Party (Liability) Insurance

A *third-party*, or *liability*, *policy* typically insures against liabilities to others arising out of the conduct of the business, such as damages arising out of slip-and-fall cases, automobile accidents, or product defects. At a minimum, entrepreneurs should carry third-party insurance for product liability and premises liability. If the company can afford it, it should also obtain commercial general liability (*CGL*) coverage. Other types of coverage vary depending on the industry. For example, the publisher of a newspaper would typically insure against lawsuits for defamation.

Typically, a liability policy will provide that the insurance company will also bear the costs of defending any tort litigation against the insured and will pay damages up to the limits of the policy. As a matter of public policy, however, punitive damages are uninsurable because they are intended to punish a party for its practices.

Even startups may provide directors' and officers' insurance (*D&O insurance*) to protect directors and officers against claims by shareholders and others for breach of fiduciary duty or negligence. Certain claims are often excluded, such as claims under the Employee Retirement Income Security Act of 1974 (*ERISA*), the legislation dealing with employee pension plans. Sometimes special *endorsements* (added provisions in an insurance document) are available, such as coverage for employment-related claims (such as wrongful termination, discrimination, or sexual harassment) or for securities law claims arising out of a public offering.

Liability policies are usually either claims-based or occurrence-based. The distinction can make the difference between coverage and no coverage. Under a *claims-based policy*, the insured must report the claim to the insurance carrier while the policy is still in effect. Claims made after the end of the policy period are not covered. An *occurrence-based policy* covers claims arising out of events that occurred during the policy period even if a claim is not asserted until after the policy has expired. For example, suppose that a customer slipped and fell on an icy sidewalk in front of a store on January 2, 2017, but did not inform the property owner until May 15, 2017. If the property owner had a claims-based policy terminating on May 2, 2017, there would be no coverage. If, however, the property owner had an occurrence-based policy terminating May 2, 2017, there would be coverage because the accident giving rise to the claim occurred before that date. Under certain circumstances, it is possible to purchase *tail coverage*, which extends the period of time during which claims may be asserted. Regardless of the type of insurance, it is always prudent to report a loss to the insurance carrier immediately.

Because insurance documents are often lengthy and confusing, it is imperative that entrepreneurs fully understand their coverage, as well as their rights and duties under the policy, including time limits to report a claim and requirements to mitigate losses. A good insurance broker can help with this.

Product Recall Insurance A product recall can affect a variety of products, including food items, medical devices, consumer goods, and component parts. CGL policies typically do not insure manufacturers against costs associated with a product recall. Recall costs can include the costs of removing the item from the stream of commerce; destroying the product (when necessary); replacing the product; hiring public relations specialists to publish recall notices and manage negative publicity; and retaining legal counsel. Product recall insurance is available for contaminated "consumable products," such as food, beverage, and pharmaceutical products; defective consumer goods; and component parts, when issues of bodily injury or property damage exist (or when there is an imminent danger of such injury or damage).[59] Product recall insurance usually indemnifies the company for the out-of-pocket recall expenses and lost profits, as well as other specified costs. Certain product recall insurance policies may not cover product recalls that are not associated with actual bodily injury or property damage, so care must be taken to understand exactly which events will trigger coverage.

Data Breach and Cyber Insurance Data breaches have become increasingly common, affecting both public data bases and private ones maintained by firms ranging from Target to Goodwill, Dairy Queen, and UPS. One data research organization reported that the total average cost of a data breach is $3.8 million—about $154 per lost or stolen record to correct the breach, provide credit monitoring services to victims, and investigate how the breach occurred.[60] "Mega-breaches," such as those at Home Depot, JPMorgan Chase and Target, cost significantly more. Health-care records are particularly vulnerable to breach because they typically include Social Security numbers, which are "much more useful for identity theft"[61] than other information.

Insuring against the risk of data breaches can be tricky. Although the taking of personal information by hackers is a "publication" that violates a person's right to privacy for which a company's commercial general liability insurance policy generally provides coverage, one court reasoned that there was no coverage because it was the hacker, not the insured company, that caused the publication.[62] Other courts have reached the opposite result.[63]

Certain policies specifically exclude coverage for data breaches and cyberattacks, but a number of insurance companies do offer some type of *cyber liability insurance*.[64] Before issuing such insurance, an insurance company may require a third party to perform a risk assessment of a company's vulnerability to attack, and it may give incentives for risk mitigation programs.[65] Because even well-established companies with "strict cybersecurity policies in place"[66] have been victim to hacking schemes, it is imperative that startup companies mitigate such risks by implementing a comprehensive cybersecurity policy and by evaluating the costs and benefits of obtaining cyber insurance coverage, when available.

Addressing Divergent Interests of Insurance Companies and the Insured

When a plaintiff is suing a company for an amount far greater than the policy limit, the insurance company may have little incentive to settle for an amount at the policy cap because that amount is the maximum it faces anyway. Hence, the insurance company may be inclined to roll the dice and let the case go to trial because, in the event of an adverse verdict, it is liable only up to the policy cap. But the insured is still on the hook for the balance of the damages. Consequently, the interests of the insured and the insurer may diverge during settlement discussions. Most jurisdictions impose on insurance companies an implied duty of good faith and fair dealing. Failure to satisfy that duty can result in punitive damages. Jurisdictions vary in what is considered sufficiently egregious behavior by an insurance company to constitute a violation of this duty. Courts in California are far more likely to find a breach of the duty and award punitive damages to the insured than courts in most other states.

11.17 STRATEGIC COMPLIANCE MANAGEMENT

Failure to ensure compliance with laws can result in significant fines and even endanger the very existence of a firm and the freedom of its founders and other employees. A program of overall risk management is essential to reduce potential tort exposure and regulatory and criminal liability.

Entrepreneurs can promote legal compliance as a source of strategic strength by following the 10-step program discussed in the balance of this chapter.[67] The *first step* is to start with ethics and begin at the top with the founders and the board of directors. Even startups should consider adopting a code of ethics, which will embody the firm's guiding values and the need for not only compliance with the law but also fair and ethical dealings with all constituencies.

The *second step* is to understand duties and exposure to risk. Managers should understand all relevant laws and implement ongoing programs of education and monitoring to reduce the risks of tort and criminal liability. Because torts and crimes can be committed in numerous ways, the programs should ideally cover all possible sources of liability. For example, if a company's management does not respond satisfactorily to an allegation of racial discrimination, the managers may be liable for intentional infliction of emotional distress. Failure to ensure public health and safety can result in criminal liability. Employers should also work to prevent their employees from committing acts of negligence, which can lead to large damage awards against the company. Any tort prevention program must recognize that, under the principle of *respondeat superior*, employers will be held liable for any torts their employees commit within the scope of their employment. Thus, it is crucial to define the scope of employment clearly.

Entrepreneurs should use care to avoid committing torts that wrongfully affect contractual relations. For example, a company may be held liable if it intentionally induces an employee to breach an enforceable covenant not to compete with a prior employer. (We discussed covenants not to compete in Chapter 2.) Although competition itself is permissible, intentionally seeking to sabotage the efforts of another firm is not. Managers should consult counsel when they are unsure whether their proposed activity would cross the line from permissible competition to tortious interference with a prospective business advantage.

Hazardous materials can create risks as can acquiring property on which hazardous waste may have been stored. Companies should adopt a long-term policy to protect employees, customers, and the environment from excess toxic exposure. Before commencing manufacture, they should identify any hazardous toxic substances used in their business activities or products or released into the environment. Sometimes, companies can reduce their possible toxic tort exposure by substituting less hazardous materials and reduce costs in the process. When appropriate, companies should test and monitor to determine levels of exposure. Often it is necessary to obtain an expert assessment of the hazards of toxicity of these substances.

As discussed in Chapter 6, directors must ensure that the company has instituted appropriate mechanisms to prevent and immediately correct violations of the law. Thus, the *third step* is to implement effective internal controls and institute good corporate governance practices to prevent or rectify illegal activities.

It is often desirable to designate one individual to be in charge of risk management. That person will keep track of all claims and determine what areas of company activity merit special attention. The head of risk management should be free to report incidents and problems to the chief executive officer and the board of directors. The same is true for internal auditors. Indeed, it is often prudent for the independent directors to meet at least annually with the risk manager and the internal and external auditors as a matter of course. This protocol enhances independence and reduces the fear of reprisals if the risk manager or auditor blows the whistle on high-ranking officers.

Firms should perform due diligence to uncover potential liabilities and benchmark their liabilities and near misses against industry norms to help expose potential trouble spots. Anonymous hot lines can help protect whistle-blowers, who can be the canaries in the minefield of misconduct.

The *fourth step* is to develop a robust compliance program to prevent securities fraud. As we explain in Chapter 17, companies should disclose material facts fully and carefully to all investors, ban insider trading, and require managers and employees with access to material nonpublic information to preclear trades with counsel. In 2016, Goldman Sachs announced a $5.1 billion settlement in principle to resolve claims related to its securitization, underwriting, and sale of residential mortgage-backed securities, which contributed to the 2008 financial crisis.[68] The settlement requires payment of a $2.385 billion civil penalty; $875 million in cash payments; and $1.8 billion in consumer relief, such as principal forgiveness for certain homeowners and financing for affordable housing.

The *fifth step* is to compete hard but fairly. Managers should be prohibited from engaging in horizontal price-fixing or market division. Resale price maintenance should be precleared with counsel. Any vertical nonprice constraints should be supported by a valid business justification and be reasonable.

The *sixth step* is to consider what innovative business practices or changes in operations might help ensure compliance while reducing costs or increasing value to customers, thereby converting constraints into opportunities. Entrepreneurs should follow the *seventh step* and play it safe in gray areas, however. It is important to evaluate risk/reward in advance and eliminate any unnecessary risk by avoiding red-flag activities until consulting legal counsel. Employees should excuse themselves from a decision if there is even an appearance of self-interest and be instructed to act reasonably to protect others from harm. The *eighth step* is to act responsibly to try to help shape the laws and regulations applicable to the business. Federal Express did this when it lobbied and worked with regulators to change civil aviation rules that would have precluded it from using its innovative hub-and-spoke distribution system to ship packages by air more cheaply and reliably.[69]

The *ninth step* is to educate all employees and distribute written policies on all matters such as insider trading, harassment, discrimination, document retention, and the like. Because even "stray" discriminatory comments by non-decision-making employees may expose an employer to liability for employment discrimination, companies should ensure that all employees understand that inappropriate and potentially harassing or discriminatory comments will not be tolerated. The *tenth step* is to prepare for inevitable compliance failures. They are what Max Bazerman and Michael Watkins call "predictable surprises."[70] It is extremely important to deal with any failures promptly, facing them head-on, and to learn from them in order to prevent future problems of the same type.[71]

☑ Putting It into **PRACTICE**

Alexei was sitting in his office feeling pleased about the positive feedback the company was receiving on its early prototypes and indications of interest from both an automobile manufacturer and a medical device firm specializing in stents. His thoughts were interrupted by a knock on his open door. He turned and saw Patrice Rodriquez, one of Genesist's sales representatives, poke her head into the office. "Do you have a minute?" she asked.

"Sure, what's up?" Alexei replied. He watched Patrice, an ace lacrosse player, sheepishly walk into the office and slouch into a chair. "I messed up," Patrice said. "And now someone is threatening to sue me and the company." "Uh-oh," Alexei muttered. "Start from the beginning, and tell me everything."

Patrice explained that she had been meeting with Alyssa Hu, an employee from AutoPlate Technologies, a small company that was interested in using Genesist's technology in a new line of license-plate holders. The negotiations had been difficult, but Patrice and Alyssa had finally reached an agreement, at which point Alyssa offered to write up the term sheet. After Alyssa gave her the draft term sheet, Patrice discovered that Alyssa had incorporated all of Genesist's concessions but none of AutoPlate's. Enraged, Patrice ripped the term sheet in half and shoved it back across the table, striking Alyssa in the chest. Alyssa rose to leave, but Patrice moved quickly to block her exit.

"No, you don't," Patrice said. "Neither of us is leaving until we write up a term sheet that reflects our agreement." After two hours, both Patrice and Alyssa initialed a revised draft of the term sheet, and Alyssa left without saying a word.

The next day Patrice received a phone call from an attorney representing Alyssa, threatening to sue her and Genesist for battery and false imprisonment. It was at this point that Patrice had gone to talk with Alexei.

As Patrice finished the story, Alexei shook his head and sighed. "Well, thank you for telling me about this," he said. "Let me look into it and we'll talk later." The moment Patrice left his office, Alexei picked up the phone, called Attorney Sarah Crawford, and said, "Sarah, I have a problem." After hearing his story, Sarah replied, "You're right, Alexei, you do." Sarah explained that under the doctrine of *respondeat superior*, Genesist was liable for the actions of its employees as long as they were acting within the scope of employment. Patrice's actions, although misguided, were within the scope of her employment because she was working on Genesist's behalf. As a result, Genesist was probably liable for

(continued)

battery and false imprisonment; the damages could easily reach $100,000 not counting attorney's fees.

Although Genesist had purchased a liability policy that would cover the damages, Alexei preferred not to use it because he knew the premiums would then go up. At the same time, Genesist did not have an extra $100,000 or even the tens of thousands of dollars that would be needed for legal fees if the case went to trial. Sarah suggested that Alexei call Alyssa and invite her to discuss the matter to see whether there was some alternative to litigation.

Alexei called Alyssa and asked whether they could meet at her office the following day. After listening carefully to her story, Alexei told Alyssa that he agreed that Patrice had been way out of line. He then apologized for Patrice's actions. Alexei also assured Alyssa that he would sternly warn Patrice about her behavior and put a memorandum describing the incident into her personnel file. He told Alyssa that he had already assigned a different licensing representative to deal with AutoPlate in the future and offered AutoPlate a 10% discount on its first order. Alyssa appreciated the apology and told Alexei that she was satisfied with the handling of the situation and would drop the matter.

Later that week, Piper walked down the hall to meet with Dave Brady, Genesist's Vice President of Operations. Dave wanted to talk to Piper about potential cost overruns caused by higher than anticipated quantities of waste resins containing potentially toxic substances. Some of the substances required expensive disposal procedures. Genesist had been working with ToxicSafe Enterprises, a reputable disposal service that specialized in hazardous waste. The initial cost was significant but affordable. However, removing waste in excess of the amount called for by the contract would be borderline prohibitive. Dave told Piper that he had carried on some quiet conversations with a few of the laboratory technicians who suggested that Genesist could temporarily avoid the additional cost by hiring a new disposal service that charged only slightly more than it would cost Genesist to haul the waste to the dump. Dave had checked out the new service and discovered that it had no experience dealing with hazardous waste and was charging a fee that was more than 70% less than ToxicSafe and other experienced hazardous waste disposal firms charged. Once Genesist was on more stable financial footing, Dave said, Genesist could go back to using ToxicSafe. Until then, he said, it was the new firm's problem if it could not afford to dispose of the waste safely.

Piper was stunned. As calmly as she could, she explained to Dave that his plan was completely out of the question. Given the bargain prices the new firm quoted, it was almost certain that it would not take the expensive steps necessary to dispose of the resins safely. Genesist

(continued)

could not just turn a blind eye. Aside from the guilt each of them would feel if a toxic substance leaked into the surrounding soil and groundwater, such an event could put the company out of business and land the responsible employees in prison. In addition to being fined, the company would be liable for any injuries suffered by people coming into contact with the substances, including the residents of the neighborhood near the city dump. Genesist would also be responsible for the cost of soil remediation and other cleanup required after a leak. Furthermore, Dave, Alexei, and Piper could be held personally liable and sent to prison for knowingly violating federal and state environmental laws. "It may be expensive to dispose of the substances properly," Piper told Dave, "but doing something like you've suggested is not worth the risk." She instructed Dave to try to negotiate an immediate reduction in the overage fees ToxicSafe was charging now that Genesist had a better sense of the amount of hazardous waste generated by its current operations. Piper also asked Dave to sit down with Genesist's engineers and laboratory technicians to review the entire production cycle in hopes of finding ways to reduce the hazardous waste. "Who knows," Piper said, "a more efficient production process and utilization of less toxic materials could end up saving us money in the long run."

Alexei and Piper then went back to reworking the budget to try to avoid running out of cash before the next round of financing closed. Although they were tempted to draw on the account containing the income tax withheld from employees' salaries, Sarah had warned them not to do so. Because Alexei and Piper were authorized to write checks on that account, they would be personally liable if the employee taxes were not remitted to the Internal Revenue Service on time. Instead, Alexei met with the chief financial officer (*CFO*) to decide which suppliers would continue to ship Genesist's orders, even if Genesist was late paying for them. They agreed that the CFO would reach out to certain suppliers, explain Genesist's short-term cash crunch, and try to negotiate extensions.

Creditors' Rights and Bankruptcy

S tartups are usually funded with equity capital, but sometimes a young firm is able to borrow money from a bank, an angel investor or venture capitalist (often with a convertible promissory note, as discussed in Chapter 7), a seller of goods or services, a trade creditor, or an equipment lessor. Although entrepreneurs hope to raise sufficient capital to weather any financial difficulties, unanticipated events can result in a startup being unable to pay its bills in a timely manner. Unless the enterprise can access additional sources of funding to solve the financial crisis, the company will need strategies for working with creditors and other constituencies. Workouts and bankruptcy are two of those strategies.

The impact bankruptcy may have on the founders personally will be affected by the form of business entity selected for the enterprise and the extent to which the founders have personally guaranteed any of the enterprise's obligations. Although the bankruptcy of a corporation or limited liability company (*LLC*) generally will not put the personal assets of shareholders at risk, a bankruptcy by a general partnership will usually expose each general partner's personal assets to liability for the partnership's debts. In addition, if an individual involved in a corporation or LLC has given a personal guaranty for any of the enterprise's debts, the creditor holding that guaranty may pursue the individual directly if the enterprise is unable to pay.

In this chapter, we first describe the different types of loans available to an entrepreneur then discuss obtaining credit on a secured basis. We then review the types of creditors and others likely to be involved when a firm faces financial difficulties, including tax authorities and employees. After exploring various strategies for responding to a financial crisis, the chapter goes on to discuss workouts and bankruptcy in more detail.

12.1 TYPES OF LOANS

A borrower may require funds to meet everyday working capital needs, to finance an acquisition of assets or a business, to fund a real estate construction project, or for a wide variety of other reasons. These purposes will dictate whether the loan should be a term loan or a revolving loan. Additionally, the borrower may also have to consider the implications of a secured loan.

Term Loans

Funds required for a specific purpose, such as an acquisition or a construction project, are generally borrowed in the form of a *term loan*. The firm borrows a specified amount, either in a lump sum or in installments. It is either to be repaid on a specified date—known as the *maturity date*—or *amortized,* that is, paid off over a period of time. For example, in an acquisition, the buyer may be required to pay the purchase price up front and thus will require a lump-sum loan. By contrast, the borrower of funds for a construction project will require a loan to be disbursed in installments as scheduled progress payments become due. Amounts repaid under a term loan cannot be reborrowed.

Revolving Loans

A borrower may forecast its working capital needs for a given period but want flexibility as to the exact amount of money borrowed at any given time. A *revolving loan* or *revolving line of credit* allows the borrower to borrow whatever sums it requires, up to a specified maximum amount. The borrower may also reborrow amounts it has repaid (hence the term *revolving*). The lender will require a *commitment fee* as consideration for its promise to keep the commitment available because it receives no interest on amounts not borrowed.

Secured Loans

Most startups cannot qualify for a bank loan and instead rely on equity investments from the various sources described in Chapter 7. Nevertheless, understanding the basics of secured lending is critical. Not only will most young companies develop to a point at which a bank loan is sought for additional capital but the many other funding sources that may be available will often seek to invest on a secured note basis in addition to, or as an alternative to, equity. Because secured lenders have the right to foreclose against company assets, they are often at the center of a financial crisis.

In making a loan, the lender relies on the borrower's cash flow, its assets, or the proceeds of another loan as sources of repayment. If the lender relies solely on the borrower's promise to repay the loan, the lender's recourse for nonpayment is limited to suing the borrower. Moreover, even if the lender does sue the borrower, the lender stands in no better position than other *general unsecured creditors* of the borrower (i.e., creditors with no special claim to any specific assets of the borrower as a source of repayment). Because of this risk, many lenders are often unwilling to make loans without something more than the borrower's promise of repayment. Lenders usually require *collateral,* that is, property belonging to the borrower that the lender can sell or retain if the loan is not repaid. A loan backed by collateral in which the lender takes a lien or security interest is known as a *secured loan.* Unsecured loans, if available at all, are priced at a higher rate to reflect the greater credit risk to the lender.

If the borrower fails to repay a secured loan, the lender, in addition to being able to sue for return of the monies lent, may *foreclose* on the collateral (i.e., take possession of it) and either sell it to pay off the debt or keep it in satisfaction of the debt. However, under some *antideficiency* and *one form of action laws,* a lender seeking remedies against real property security may be restricted from suing the borrower personally. Furthermore, when a lender has recourse to the borrower or to other property of the borrower and exercises such rights, the lender may be precluded from foreclosing on real estate mortgaged by the borrower. These laws, some of which date back to the Great Depression, are

From the **TRENCHES**

When one software startup was two months from running out of cash—a "cash cliff"— it returned to its venture capital investors for a further round. The venture capitalists, unwilling to make another investment in return for equity, made the capital infusion in the form of a secured bridge loan. To secure repayment, they required a blanket security interest, including a security interest in the company's intellectual property. The company used the much-needed cash to fund operations and continued to develop its business plan. A year later it paid off the bridge loan with proceeds from a further equity venture round, as a prelude to an initial public offering.

designed to protect borrowers from forfeiting their real estate to overzealous lenders.

12.2 LOAN AGREEMENTS

Given the variety of loans available, the basic structure of loan agreements is surprisingly standard. Lenders are concerned about the administration of the loan, their ongoing relationship with the borrower, and the rights they have if the borrower breaches its promises. At times these concerns must be addressed in specially tailored documentation; however, banks generally use a collection of standard forms, which are distributed to loan officers along with instructions for their use.

12.3 SECURED TRANSACTIONS UNDER THE UCC

Both the mechanics and the consequences of taking a security interest in personal property and *fixtures* (property attached to real property, such as light fixtures and built-in bookcases) are governed by Article 9 of the Uniform Commercial Code (*UCC*), which has been adopted, with certain variations, in every state. Article 9 of the UCC provides a unified, comprehensive scheme for all types of *secured transactions*, that is, loans or other transactions secured by collateral put up by the borrower. With certain exceptions, Article 9 applies to any transaction (regardless of its form) that creates by contract a security interest in personal property or fixtures, including goods, documents, instruments, general intangibles, chattel paper (a record that shows both a monetary obligation and a security interest), and accounts.

Article 9 of the UCC also sets forth the rights of the secured party as against other creditors of the debtor; the rules for *perfecting* a security interest, that is, making it prior to the rights of other creditors of the debtor; and the remedies available to the secured party if a debtor defaults.

Terminology

The UCC uses the single term *security interest* to signify any interest in personal property or fixtures put up as collateral to secure payment or the performance of an obligation. The parties to a secured transaction are the debtor and the secured party. The *debtor* is the person who has an interest in the collateral (other than a security interest or lien) whether or not such person owes payment or performance of the obligation secured. The *secured party* is the lender, seller, or other person in whose favor there is a security interest. A *security agreement* is an agreement that creates or provides for a security interest.

Scope of Article 9

Article 9 provides a single source of reference for most consensual security interests, but some security interests are outside its scope. Article 9 does not apply to liens on real property. Various state and federal laws preempt the UCC in the areas of ship mortgages, mechanic's liens, and aircraft liens. Notices of security interests in trademarks and patents are commonly filed in the U.S. Patent and Trademark Office in addition to being perfected as general intangibles under the UCC. Security interests in registered copyrights are perfected by a filing in the U.S. Copyright Office. Generally speaking, Article 9 does not apply to security interests subject to a landlord's lien, to a lien given by statute or other rule of law for services or materials, or to a contractual right to deduct the amount of damages from the amount of money otherwise due (a *right of setoff*).

Formal Requirements

The UCC also sets forth the formal requirements for creating an enforceable security interest and describes the rights of the parties to a security agreement. If the secured party takes possession of the collateral, an oral agreement is sufficient to create a security interest; otherwise, an authenticated security agreement containing a description of the collateral is required. A security agreement is *authenticated* if it is manually signed or if the parties use some other symbol or process to adopt or accept the agreement (such as executing a record that is stored in an electronic or other medium and is retrievable in perceivable form). For a security interest to be enforceable, value must be given in exchange for it and the debtor must have rights in the collateral. These requirements do not have to be fulfilled in any particular order. When all of the requirements have been met, a security interest is said to have *attached*.

12.4 SECURITY AGREEMENTS

A security agreement identifies the parties and the property to be used as collateral. It may also specify the debtor's obligations and the lender's remedies in case of default.

Parties

Security agreements typically use the UCC terminology to identify the parties. In a loan transaction, the secured party is the lender. The debtor owns the collateral and is also the *obligor* if it owes payment or other performance of the obligation. The debtor also may simply be the owner of property that the obligor is authorized to use for collateral. If a third party acts as a guarantor of the borrower's obligation, he or she may also be referred to as the obligor.

Granting Clause

Unless the security interest is a possessory interest, whereby the lender takes possession of the collateral (traditionally called a *pledge*), the security agreement must be signed or otherwise authenticated by the debtor and must expressly grant a security interest in specified property. The standard operative words are: "The debtor hereby grants to the secured party a security interest in...." The UCC does not require a precise form, but the collateral must be described.

Description of the Collateral

The description of the collateral need not be specific as long as it reasonably identifies the property. Loans to finance the purchase of specific property, such as an equipment loan, will typically be secured by the property purchased, and the security agreement will contain a specific description of the property.

For example, a working capital loan may be secured by receivables and inventory. The inventory may be described as "any and all goods, merchandise, and other personal property, wherever located or in transit, that are held for sale or lease, furnished under any contract of service, or held as raw materials, work in process, supplies, or materials used or consumed in the debtor's business." Frequently, a secured party will take a security interest in all the assets of the debtor—not only fixed assets, inventory, and receivables but also trademarks, trade names, patents, copyrights, licenses, goodwill, books, and records. In such cases, the collateral may be described as "all tangible and intangible property that, taken together, is intended to preserve the value of the debtor as a going concern," or even more simply as "all assets of the debtor." Such a security interest is also known as a *blanket security interest* because it covers all of the debtor's assets.

After-Acquired Property

After-acquired property is property that the debtor acquires after the execution of the security agreement. After-acquired assets may be specified in the security agreement either in addition to, or as replacements of, currently owned assets. A security interest in after-acquired collateral will attach when the debtor acquires rights in the collateral, assuming that the other prerequisites for attachment have previously been met. For example, a lender financing a car dealership's inventory would take a security interest in all cars currently owned by the dealership and all cars acquired later. When a car is sold and a new one purchased, the security interest automatically covers the new car. This feature makes a security interest created under Article 9 a *floating lien.*

Proceeds

The attachment of a security interest in collateral gives the secured party rights to proceeds of the collateral. If the collateral is sold, leased, licensed, exchanged, or otherwise disposed of by the debtor, the security interest continues in the collateral or its proceeds unless the secured party authorized the disposition free of the security interest.

Debtor's Obligations

Under most secured loans, the debtor will be obligated to repay the debt and to pay interest and related fees, charges, and expenses. In addition, the debtor likely will have nonmonetary obligations, such as obligations to maintain prescribed standards of financial well-being, measured by net worth, cash flow, and *leverage* (the ratio of debt to equity). These obligations are typically set forth in detail in a loan agreement or a promissory note, although occasionally they may be found in a security agreement.

Cross-Collateralization

The collateral for one loan may be used to secure obligations under another loan. This is done by means of a *cross-collateralization provision*—sometimes called a *dragnet clause*—in the security agreement. For example, a lender extending an inventory and receivables line of credit to a borrower may insist that the line be secured not only by inventory and receivables but also by equipment owned by the borrower and already held by the lender as collateral for an equipment loan. Thus, if the lender *forecloses on* (sells) the equipment, any proceeds in excess of the amounts owed under the equipment loan will be available to pay down the inventory and receivables line of credit. Likewise, if the equipment loan is cross-collateralized with collateral for the inventory and receivables line of credit, any proceeds realized from foreclosure of the inventory and receivables in excess of what is owed under the line of credit will be available to pay down the equipment loan.

Remedies for Default

The remedies described in a security agreement typically track the rights and procedures set forth in Article 9. After default, the secured party has the right to take possession of the collateral without judicial process, that is, without going to court, if this can be done without breach of the peace. The secured party must then either (1) dispose of the collateral at a public or private sale or (2) propose to retain the collateral in full or partial satisfaction of the debt (sometimes called *acceptance of collateral* or *strict foreclosure*). In all cases, the secured party's disposition of the collateral must be commercially reasonable.

The proceeds from a foreclosure sale must be applied in the following order:

1. To the reasonable expenses of foreclosure and, if provided for in the agreement, reasonable attorneys' fees and legal expenses
2. To the satisfaction of the obligations secured
3. To the satisfaction of any indebtedness secured by a subordinate security interest or to another secured party that is a consignor of the collateral, if an authenticated demand for satisfaction is received in a timely manner.

If there is a surplus from the sale of the collateral, the secured party is required to return the surplus to the debtor. If there is a deficiency, the debtor remains liable for that amount.

The UCC contains guidelines regarding what constitutes a commercially reasonable disposition of collateral by a secured party. The secured party and the debtor are also free to fashion a mutually acceptable standard of commercial reasonableness as long as the standard is not manifestly unreasonable. Security agreements typically contain a description of such standards.

12.5 PERFECTING A SECURITY INTEREST

To protect its rights in the collateral, a lender must ensure that its security interest is *perfected*, that is, prior to (1) the rights of other secured creditors of the debtor; (2) the rights of certain buyers, lessees, and licensees of the collateral; and (3) the rights of a trustee in bankruptcy and other lien creditors of the debtor. (A *lien creditor* includes a creditor that has obtained a lien by attachment, levy, or the like.) The UCC does not define perfection; instead, it describes the situations in which an unperfected security interest will be *subordinated* to, or put below, the rights of third parties. For example, generally speaking, a security interest is subordinate to the rights of a person who becomes a lien creditor before the security interest is perfected. Subordination to lien creditors essentially means that the security interest is not enforceable in bankruptcy. Most security interests can be perfected (1) by possession of the collateral, (2) by filing a financing statement, (3) by taking control of the collateral, or (4) automatically.

By Possession

A security interest in money is perfected only by the secured party's taking possession of the collateral. A security interest in goods may be perfected either by possession or by filing a form known as a *UCC-1 Financing Statement*. For example, when a person goes to a pawnshop and surrenders possession of a smartphone in exchange for a loan, the pawnshop acquires a perfected security interest in the smartphone. A security interest in negotiable documents, instruments, or tangible chattel paper may be perfected either by possession or by filing a financing statement. A security interest in certificated securities may be perfected by taking delivery of the certificates under Article 8 of the UCC.

By Filing

For most other types of collateral, perfection is accomplished by filing a UCC-1 Financing Statement. Standard printed and electronic forms are widely available for this purpose. A centralized filing system gives effective public notice that property in the possession and under the apparent control of the debtor is actually subject to the rights of another.

By Control

A security interest in investment property, letter-of-credit rights, or electronic chattel paper may be perfected by control of the collateral. A security interest in a deposit account must be perfected by control. One way for the secured party to obtain control over a deposit account is to enter into a control agreement with the debtor and the bank with which the deposit account is maintained. Under the control agreement, the parties agree that the bank will comply with instructions from the secured party directing disposition of the funds in the deposit account without further consent by the debtor (often called exercising *exclusive control* over the deposit account).

Automatic Perfection

Certain security interests require neither possession nor filing for perfection. For example, a *purchase-money security interest*—a security interest taken by the seller at the time of sale to secure payment of the purchase price—in consumer goods is automatically perfected. Under certain circumstances, a security interest in certificated securities, instruments, or negotiable documents is temporarily perfected without filing or possession. Automatic perfection of a security interest in such collateral is of limited duration, however, and must be followed by possession or filing if perfection is to survive for a longer period.

12.6   UCC FILING PROCEDURE

Certain types of collateral typically remain in the debtor's possession and control. This happens, for example, when the collateral is intangible (as with accounts receivable) or when possession by the secured party is impractical (as in the case of inventory or equipment).

The UCC filing system enables a prospective creditor to determine whether it will be competing with other creditors if it lends money secured by particular assets. It also enables a purchaser of goods to determine whether the seller's creditors have any claims against the goods. (It should be noted that, under certain circumstances, a purchaser of goods is protected from liens on such goods created by the seller. For example, consumers are protected from inventory liens on a seller's goods.)

What Gets Filed

To perfect a security interest in personal property by filing, a UCC-1 Financing Statement must be filed. The financing statement merely gives notice that a financing transaction is being or is about to be entered into; the statement does not describe the transaction. It need only contain the names of the parties to the transaction, their mailing addresses, and a description of the kinds of collateral in which a security interest has been or may be granted. When a financing statement covers goods that are or are to become fixtures, the UCC also requires a legal description of the land involved. If the debtor does not have an interest of record in the real property, the financing statement must also provide the name of the record owner.

When the Statement Is Filed

A financing statement may be filed in advance of the transaction or the signing of the security agreement. Timing is important because, under the UCC, conflicting perfected security interests rank according to priority in time of filing or perfection. Thus, provided that the security interest has attached, the first secured party to file generally has priority over other parties with security interests in the same property of that debtor. Special priority rules apply to certain transactions, such as a purchase-money security interest in nonconsumer goods, in which the debtor borrows the purchase price from the seller.

Where Filing Is Made

Generally, the proper place to file a financial statement is in the office of the secretary of state in the state where the debtor is located. A corporate debtor is located in the state of its incorporation; a noncorporate debtor is generally located at its chief executive office; and an individual debtor is located at the individual's principal residence. A financial statement granting a security interest in collateral closely associated with real property (such as fixtures, timber, or minerals) must be filed in the office where a deed of trust or mortgage on the real estate would be recorded, usually the county recorder's office in the county where the property is located.

12.7 TYPES OF CREDITORS AND THEIR RIGHTS

An entrepreneurial venture may have various types of creditors. Certain creditors may have priority over others, depending on the nature of the contract or relationship with the debtor.

Secured Creditors

Generally, the first secured creditor to perfect an interest in a piece or type of collateral has priority in payment over all other types of creditors, at least with respect to repayment from its collateral.

Unsecured Trade Creditors

Most of a new company's creditors will be unsecured creditors. *Unsecured creditors* have no security interest in any collateral and only a general claim against the company for payment. If debts remain unpaid, these creditors often first resort to telephone calls, emails, and letters to obtain payment. If these measures are unsuccessful, the claim is usually turned over to a collection agency or an attorney.

If an attorney becomes involved, he or she generally will file a lawsuit on behalf of the creditor. In California and a few other states, the creditor may attempt to obtain a *prejudgment attachment* of the company's assets to secure payment for the claim. If an attachment is allowed before judgment, or if the creditor obtains a judgment against the company, then the creditor has the right to attempt to *levy* on the attachment or judgment. This involves seizing bank accounts and other assets of the company. A creditor that obtains an attachment or judgment also can file a lien similar to a UCC-1 Financing Statement against the company's equipment, inventory, and certain other types of nonreal-estate assets and can record an abstract of the judgment against any real estate the company owns. When creditors take these more aggressive actions, they often precipitate a financial crisis that forces the company to pursue a workout strategy or to file a bankruptcy.

Equipment Lessors

Young companies often need equipment, ranging from computers to manufacturing equipment to printers. Many companies prefer to rent or to finance the equipment rather than use existing capital to purchase it. Although many dealers will offer to lease specific equipment, a separate segment of the financial industry provides equipment financing. Known as *equipment lessors*, these entities finance leases and provide extended financing for the lease or purchase of equipment.

In a *true lease* of equipment, the lessor retains ownership of the equipment. If the company defaults, the lessor is entitled to repossess the leased equipment and has an unsecured claim for the balance of the payments owed. In a bankruptcy, if the payments due under the lease equal the entire economic value of the equipment, then the lease may be recharacterized as a financing arrangement, or *finance lease*, rather than a true lease. In the event of such a recharacterization, the lessor will be treated as an unsecured creditor rather than as the owner of the equipment. To protect themselves against this outcome, equipment lessors commonly require a security interest in the equipment being leased and file a financing statement on the equipment. Taking these steps ensures that the equipment lessor will at least be treated as a secured creditor in bankruptcy should the lease be recharacterized as a financing arrangement.

Taxing Authorities

The Internal Revenue Service (*IRS*) and state taxing authorities have certain special creditors' rights. These include the right to place liens on a taxpayer's property for unpaid taxes and even to seize property. *Withholding taxes* (those taxes required to be withheld from employees' paychecks and paid to the IRS or state taxing authorities) are considered *trust fund taxes* and must be paid on a timely basis. If they are not paid on time, the officers or directors of a corporation may be held personally liable for 100% of the unpaid taxes. Thus, it is advisable to keep current with the taxing authorities and to refrain from ever using funds withheld from an employee's paycheck to pay other company debts or operating expenses. Many companies use a payroll service to ensure that all amounts withheld from their employees are paid to the proper taxing authorities.

Employees

An employee's claim for wages, salary, vacation, or sick leave pay is generally treated as an unsecured claim. In a bankruptcy, however, each employee is given a *priority claim* (entitling him or her to payment after secured creditors but before unsecured creditors) for up to $12,850 of compensation earned but unpaid in the 180 days prior to a bankruptcy filing or the cessation of business, whichever is earlier. State law may give employees additional remedies. For example, in California, the labor commissioner can assist unpaid employees in collecting their wages and may issue fines or penalties against the employer for nonpayment of employees. In addition, an employee with an unsatisfied judgment for wages or salary can petition a court to require the employer to post a bond to pay the employee's wages or be ordered to cease doing business in California.

12.8 PERSONAL GUARANTIES AND LIABILITY OF INDIVIDUAL GENERAL PARTNERS

Certain creditors, such as landlords and banks, may require an enterprise's founder or officers to personally guarantee repayment of the credit extended. A personal guaranty exposes the individual guarantor's house and other assets to the creditor's claim in the event the company does not pay the debt. Indeed, the creditor usually has the right to sue the individual guarantor directly, regardless of whether the creditor has sued the company or whether the company is in bankruptcy. In addition, even though bankruptcy may provide the debtor company with certain benefits (such as capping the extent of a landlord's damages from breach of a lease), those protections may not be available to an individual guarantor.

Not surprisingly, if the company gets into financial trouble, the holder of the guaranty will often demand payment from the guarantor and file a lawsuit to collect. For example, if the company makes a general assignment for the benefit of creditors (discussed below), that will typically trigger personal exposure for the guarantor. For these reasons, an individual should obtain personal legal advice before giving a personal guaranty and whenever the company faces potential financial difficulties.

Similarly, if the enterprise is a partnership and cannot pay its debts, the individual general partners are personally liable for the partnership's debts and may face lawsuits for collection. Again, the individuals involved should seek personal legal advice about their own exposure given the partnership's financial situation.

12.9 STRATEGIES FOR RESPONDING TO A FINANCIAL CRISIS OUTSIDE OF BANKRUPTCY

A young company's specific responses to a financial crisis will depend largely on the nature of the crisis, including the kinds of creditors involved and the amount and type of their claims as well as the company's assets and prospects. In almost every crisis, conserving cash and gaining additional time are critical objectives. A company trying to reorganize needs to be able to use its cash for essential business purposes and requires time to allow its business plan (or revised business plan) to develop. These objectives require methods for restructuring the company's liabilities. Even if liquidation seems inevitable, the company (and its creditors and guarantors) will not want to sell the assets at depressed, "fire sale" prices. Although bankruptcy always remains an option, alternatives for restructuring or *working out* a company's debts short of bankruptcy can be less expensive and buy additional time, even if bankruptcy is ultimately required. The discussion below provides only an overview of several alternative strategies, including out-of-court reorganization and liquidation. Because a financial crisis has many complexities, the company should obtain specific legal advice from an insolvency attorney when deciding how best to respond to a financial crisis.

Role of Turnaround Experts and Intermediaries

As part of a workout strategy, the company should consider hiring a financial consultant or *turnaround expert* who has experience in refocusing business plans, analyzing financial data, and preparing budgets and other reports helpful in persuading creditors that the venture can work its way out of the financial crisis. Retaining a turnaround expert can help build credibility with creditors, an asset often in short supply as payment terms become stretched out or are shifted to a cash-on-delivery (*COD*) basis. In certain cases, the turnaround expert may serve as a management consultant or even as chief executive officer until the company has resolved the crisis. Outside professionals and intermediaries can also help with liquidation of some or all of the company's assets.

Dealing with Secured Creditors

If the company has obtained financing by giving a security interest in some or all of its assets, consideration of reorganization and liquidation options must start with the secured creditor.

Reorganization   If an out-of-court reorganization is desired, the company must reach some form of forbearance or debt restructure agreement with the secured creditor, as the secured creditor has the immediate right to foreclose on its collateral if the company defaults. Secured creditors may be willing to overlook defaults on financial covenants, such as financial ratios, particularly if the company can keep current on its payments. Even if the company is not current, secured creditors often want to avoid the expense and likely financial loss associated with a foreclosure or a potentially prolonged bankruptcy case. As a result, they will evaluate a serious restructuring proposal on its merits.

If the secured creditors are venture capitalists, they may have even more flexibility to work with the company, although they may also demand a greater equity stake. If a forbearance agreement cannot be reached, then a bankruptcy, with its automatic stay of foreclosure efforts, may be the only alternative to liquidation.

Liquidation If management elects to liquidate the company's assets, then the secured creditor may simply prefer to repossess its collateral and foreclose through a public or private sale or by retaining the collateral in satisfaction of the debt. If the secured creditor has a blanket security interest, this may result in the disposal of all of the company's assets. Alternatively, the secured creditor may support a liquidation by the company itself, a liquidation through an intermediary or a general assignment for the benefit of creditors, with the secured creditor receiving a priority distribution of the proceeds from sale of its collateral.

Ability of Unsecured Creditors to Force an Involuntary Bankruptcy

Three or more creditors with unsecured claims aggregating $15,775 that are not contingent or subject to a bona fide dispute can file a petition to try to force the company into an involuntary bankruptcy. (The bankruptcy-related dollar thresholds and other amounts set forth in this chapter are effective as of April 1, 2016.) Although trade creditors frustrated by a lack of payment often threaten to do this, creditors generally shy away from taking such a drastic step because the Bankruptcy Code permits a company to recover damages against creditors that are unsuccessful in forcing it into an involuntary bankruptcy. Moreover, if an out-of-court workout is under way and most creditors are observing a collection-action moratorium, the company may be able to persuade a bankruptcy court to refrain from hearing a petition for involuntary bankruptcy filed by a few dissatisfied creditors. However, the possibility of involuntary bankruptcy can become a major distraction for management and only emphasizes the need to address honestly and aggressively a company's financial problems. (We discuss involuntary bankruptcy more fully below.)

Out-of-Court Reorganizations

One workout method—an *out-of-court reorganization*—involves contacting creditors, individually or as a group, to request a payment or collection-action moratorium or modified payment terms the young company can afford. If a company has only a few large creditors, and they are willing to extend their payment terms, the immediate crisis may be avoided. Because bankruptcy generally means no payments to unsecured creditors for months or years, if at all, unsecured creditors often are willing to accept a credible plan that will pay them on terms more favorable than a bankruptcy is likely to provide.

If the company has lost credibility with its creditors, as often happens when honest promises to pay cannot be fulfilled, the workout may have a better chance of success if an intermediary is used. Credit associations, such as the Credit Managers Association of California (*CMAC*), facilitate workouts by organizing a meeting of creditors at which a creditors' committee is formed to work with the company in trouble. The company and its creditors' committee then enter into discussions in an attempt to negotiate a workout agreement. To convince the creditors to agree to a workout, the company will need to provide the creditors' committee with financial reports and information on its current and projected performance. The company can enter into confidentiality agreements with the creditors' committee members to protect the company's business information.

Once the terms of a workout agreement are hammered out, the intermediary will distribute the proposed agreement with a consent form. The consent form asks each creditor to list the amount of its claim and to agree to abide by the moratorium on collection actions generally provided for in the workout agreement in exchange for the company's agreement to pay the creditors over time. If the consent form is signed, the creditor is contractually bound to honor the moratorium and will receive payments according to the workout agreement. Disputes over the amount of a claim must be worked out between the company and the creditor before the creditor receives any payment, which enhances the company's leverage in resolving the dispute. The workout agreement generally specifies the minimum percentage of creditors that must accept the terms of the agreement before it becomes effective, although the percentage may be adjusted depending on the overall reaction of the creditors. The creditors' committee will thereafter require financial reports from the company, to be discussed at periodic meetings, as well as reports on the company's progress.

The creditors' committee will usually require the company to give the intermediary, acting as a stakeholder on behalf of all creditors, a security interest in all of the company's assets. Any unsecured creditor who obtains an attachment or judgment lien after the intermediary's security interest is perfected will be junior and subject to this security interest. As a result, even if an unsecured creditor refuses to agree to the collection-action moratorium, the intermediary can still invoke its superior rights to prevent an unsecured creditor from levying on the company's assets. If a company has one or more senior secured creditors, it should tell them that it intends to give the intermediary a junior security interest and seek their consent. Even though granting a junior security interest generally violates the terms of the senior creditors' own security agreements, many secured creditors will consent to enable the company to work out its overall financial problems. The company may also attempt to reach a workout agreement without granting the intermediary a security interest.

Out-of-Court Liquidations

When a company has more severe problems, especially when a nonrevenue-generating company cannot raise additional capital, an *out-of-court liquidation* of the company's assets may the only realistic option. Although filing for bankruptcy is one vehicle, a nonbankruptcy liquidation may result in higher payments to creditors. Like an out-of-court reorganization, liquidation can be done by the company itself or with the help of outside professionals or organizations.

By the Company If the company is not faced with creditors obtaining control over its assets by levying on attachments or judgments, it may be able to wind down its business operations over a period of time. This usually involves liquidating its assets, closing its doors, and distributing the proceeds on a pro rata basis according to the legal priorities of its creditors (secured creditors first to the extent of their collateral, then unsecured creditors), often through a formal corporate dissolution. When a company has long-term equipment or facilities leases, it may attempt to negotiate termination of those leases on terms that limit claims for the remaining years on the leases. Because bankruptcy offers the ability to cap a landlord's damages, a company can often use the threat of filing as leverage in these negotiations.

Complications can arise when the company being liquidated is a party to *executory contracts*—agreements under which it has continuing performance obligations other than or in addition to payment. If the other party is unwilling to terminate the company's obligations under the executory contract, management may need to negotiate an assignment of its obligations to an asset purchaser. If, as is often the case, the contract prohibits assignment without the other party's consent, then the company will have to find an assignee acceptable to the counterparty.

With an Intermediary Working at the Direction of the Company
When liquidation is not feasible without an intermediary, management can hire an organization, such as CMAC, that will work at the direction of the company and act as a liquidator. As with the reorganization efforts described above, the intermediary will send a notice to creditors and organize a creditors' meeting where a creditors' committee will be formed and the intermediary will seek a collection-action moratorium. With or without its own counsel, the creditors' committee will oversee the company's liquidation effort and help resolve disputes over creditors' claims. The fees of counsel for the creditors' committee are paid out of the liquidation proceeds. The company may also engage liquidation professionals to replace the officers and directors and undertake the liquidation and/or corporate dissolution.

General Assignment for the Benefit of Creditors If management is willing to cede control over the liquidation of the company to a liquidator it selects, then a second alternative is for the company to make a *general assignment for the benefit of creditors*. In this formal legal procedure, the company appoints an individual or entity to act as assignee and to take possession and control of the company's assets. The assignee then liquidates the assets and distributes the proceeds, much as a bankruptcy trustee does in a liquidation under Chapter 7 of the U.S. Bankruptcy Code. Also,

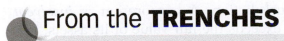

From the **TRENCHES**

When a company ran out of cash and its investors were unwilling to provide additional funds, the company entered into negotiations to sell its principal assets and customer base to another firm. Due to concerns about possible successor liability and fraudulent transfer risks, the purchaser was unwilling to buy these assets directly from the company.

The company instead retained an experienced liquidation professional, who agreed to serve as the assignee for the benefit of creditors. The professional became involved in the sale negotiations and, just before the parties were ready to close the sale, the company made a general assignment for the benefit of creditors to the professional. The professional then finalized the sale agreement with the purchaser, and the sale closed with almost no interruption in service to the customers. The purchase price was paid to the professional in the capacity as assignee for the benefit of the company's creditors. The assignee then wound up the affairs of the company, sending notices to its creditors and administering its remaining assets for their benefit.

like a bankruptcy trustee, the assignee may be able to sue creditors for recovery of preferential payments and fraudulent transfers. If insiders or other creditors have received substantial payments from the company on old debt, they may be subject to such preference lawsuits, as explained more fully below.

Provisions in loans, leases, or other contracts that provide for automatic termination upon the making of an assignment for the benefit of creditors are unenforceable in bankruptcy, but they may be enforced if there is a general assignment for the benefit of creditors, subject to the assignee's right to prevent (*stay*) termination of a lease of real property for up to 90 days by continuing to pay rent. For these reasons, the management team should carefully review the company's operations before choosing this liquidation option.

12.10 FIDUCIARY DUTIES OF THE OFFICERS AND DIRECTORS OF AN INSOLVENT OR BANKRUPT CORPORATION OR A CORPORATION IN THE ZONE OF INSOLVENCY

The scope of fiduciary duties owed to creditors by the officers and directors of an insolvent corporation or a corporation in the zone of insolvency varies by jurisdiction. A corporation is *insolvent* when the sum of its debts exceeds the fair value of its assets; it is in the *zone of insolvency* when insolvency is probable.

When a Delaware company becomes insolvent, the officers and directors of the company owe fiduciary duties to the company and, derivatively, to its creditors, rather than to the shareholders. Creditors of an insolvent Delaware corporation cannot sue for breach of fiduciary duty directly, but they can sue indirectly on behalf of the corporation. In contrast, if a Delaware corporation is only in the zone of insolvency, then there is no shift in the fiduciary duties of its officers and directors, so creditors cannot sue even indirectly for alleged breaches of fiduciary duty.[1]

In contrast, Florida courts have "extended" the fiduciary duties of officers and directors to a Florida corporation's creditors when the corporation becomes insolvent or is "in the 'vicinity of insolvency.'"[2] Thus, when a Florida corporation is in the zone of insolvency, officers and directors must take special care to take into account the interests of both shareholders and creditors to maximize value and must be careful not to approve or take actions that unduly favor shareholders at the expense of creditors or that prefer insiders to noninsider creditors.

Once a bankruptcy is filed, officers and directors are required to act in the best interests of the company's creditors, shareholders, and other parties, subject to the provisions of the Bankruptcy Code. If anything, directors' duty to shareholders after a bankruptcy is filed weakens in comparison with their duty to the creditors because shareholders are last in line in bankruptcy. Balancing the interests of shareholders and creditors can be difficult. Nevertheless, bankruptcy actually provides a forum conducive to resolution of conflicts among competing interests because the contest is judicially supervised. In addition, constituencies can form committees and seek to be represented at the company's expense.

12.11 TYPES OF BANKRUPTCY

Bankruptcy is a final alternative strategy for a company in financial crisis. A company that chooses to file a voluntary bankruptcy petition gains an immediate respite from creditor actions, including foreclosure, by virtue of the automatic stay, as discussed below. By filing under Chapter 11 of the U.S. Bankruptcy Code, a company can retain possession of its assets, propose a plan to restructure its debts to creditors, and, in successful cases, emerge from bankruptcy in better financial shape.

Although bankruptcy gives a company the opportunity to reorganize in an orderly fashion, it also imposes many obligations. The company's finances become an open book: it must file a full schedule of its assets and liabilities, as well as a statement of its financial affairs, soon after the bankruptcy is filed. The company's officers are subject to questioning about every aspect of its business at deposition-style examinations, and approval of the bankruptcy court is required for any business decision outside the ordinary course of business. For these reasons, bankruptcy should be considered a last resort. Nonetheless, its unique benefits may make it the only viable strategy for solving the most severe financial crises.

The following discussion assumes that the company has been organized as a corporation, the most common form of business organization, but it also generally applies to limited liability companies. Enterprises organized as partnerships often raise different issues because individual general partners are liable for a partnership's debts.

Chapter 11 Reorganization Versus Chapter 7 Liquidation

A *Chapter 11* reorganization bankruptcy offers a company the tools to propose a plan for restructuring its debts and emerging from bankruptcy as a going concern. When the financial problems become too severe, the company may file a Chapter 7 liquidation bankruptcy, also known as *straight bankruptcy*. In a *Chapter 7* bankruptcy, a bankruptcy trustee is automatically appointed to liquidate all of the company's assets for ultimate distribution to creditors. The company's management must turn over possession to the bankruptcy trustee, and no reorganization is attempted. A bankruptcy trustee is also under a fiduciary duty to pursue recovery of preferential and fraudulent transfers. Because the goal of most companies in a bankruptcy is to reorganize and maintain ownership of the enterprise, this discussion focuses primarily on Chapter 11 bankruptcy.

Voluntary Versus Involuntary Bankruptcy

When a company chooses to file for bankruptcy, it is known as *voluntary bankruptcy.* When three or more creditors holding claims totaling at least $15,775 jointly petition to force a company into bankruptcy, the result is involuntary bankruptcy. An *involuntary bankruptcy* is started by filing a petition (which is similar to a complaint in regular litigation) that requests the bankruptcy court to order that the company be placed into bankruptcy.

An involuntary bankruptcy can be filed under either Chapter 11 or Chapter 7. An involuntary Chapter 11 filing is often coupled with a request for appointment of a Chapter 11 bankruptcy trustee. If an involuntary bankruptcy petition under Chapter 7 is successful, then a bankruptcy trustee will be appointed automatically. The company can respond to an involuntary bankruptcy petition by (1) objecting to the effort, in which case further litigation will ensue until the bankruptcy court makes its decision; or (2) consenting to the bankruptcy by filing its own voluntary Chapter 11 or Chapter 7 bankruptcy petition.

If the involuntary bankruptcy petition is successful, the company will officially be placed in bankruptcy by an order for relief. An involuntary bankruptcy is more likely in those cases in which creditors suspect a company has engaged in fraudulent activity, is dissipating or concealing its assets, or has announced its inability to pay creditors but has failed to propose a credible workout or liquidation plan. If the involuntary bankruptcy petition fails, then the involuntary case will be dismissed, and the company may be able to recover its costs and attorneys' fees from the petitioning creditors. If the petition was filed in bad faith, the company may even be awarded compensatory and punitive damages. This potential exposure to liability for damages inhibits many creditors from actually filing an involuntary bankruptcy petition.

12.12   THE CHAPTER 11 BANKRUPTCY PROCESS

Chapter 11 of the U.S. Bankruptcy Code is designed to permit a company to reorganize its business by changing the terms on which its debts must be paid. A reorganization is accomplished through a plan of reorganization, which is proposed by the debtor company and considered by the bankruptcy court according to specific substantive requirements set forth in the Bankruptcy Code. Chapter 11 can also preserve the *going-concern* economic value of an operating company, which is the enhanced value of the company's assets functioning together as an ongoing enterprise. This enhanced value is lost when the debtor company is liquidated piecemeal or torn apart by individual creditors foreclosing on security interests or levying on judgments. When a Chapter 11 bankruptcy is filed, the debtor company, through its existing management, generally stays in possession and control of its assets. The company thus serves as a *debtor-in-possession (DIP)* instead of having a bankruptcy trustee appointed to take control of the assets.

 ## From the **TRENCHES**

In 2001, buildings-material manufacturer USG Corp. filed for Chapter 11 bankruptcy. At the time, USG was a financially healthy corporation, but the growing volume of asbestos-related lawsuits threatened to crush what strength remained. CEO William C. Foote, working as a strategic partner with General Counsel Stan Ferguson, recognized that the company needed to definitively limit its exposure to asbestos liability claims in order to move forward. Chapter 11 gave USG a chance.

Foote designated 20 managers to focus on the reorganization, while the rest worked on keeping the business operations humming despite the bankruptcy. On the day USG announced its bankruptcy filing, Foote instructed USG's sales, purchasing, and financial representatives to call each customer, supplier, and creditor to reassure them that USG fully intended to fulfill each order on time and pay each creditor in full, as it had done in the past.

By both aggressively litigating dubious claims and lobbying for legislative reform, USG finally brought the lead plaintiffs' attorneys to the negotiating table. Together, the two parties agreed that USG would establish a multi-billion-dollar trust from which current and future asbestos claimants would draw compensation. To help fund the trust, the company completed a rights offering, backstopped by Warren Buffett's Berkshire-Hathaway Corp. (a major USG shareholder). After almost five years in Chapter 11, USG emerged with the entirety of its debts paid and its shareholders' equity intact. Warren Buffett called it "the most successful managerial performance in bankruptcy that I've ever seen."

Sources: Constance E. Bagley & Eliot Sherman, USG Corporation (A), Harv. Bus. Sch. Case No. 807-090 (2007); Constance E. Bagley & Eliot Sherman, USG Corporation (B), Harv. Bus. Sch. Case No. 807-120 (2007); Constance E. Bagley & Eliot Sherman, USG Corporation (C), Harv. Bus. Sch. Case No. 807-121 (2007).

Costs of Bankruptcy

Aside from the potential negative impact on customer or vendor confidence and the possible stigma associated with filing bankruptcy, a very real cost of bankruptcy is attorneys' and other professional fees. A Chapter 11 bankruptcy for a relatively small company can cost anywhere from $250,000 to $500,000 or more in attorneys' fees; in more complex cases, attorneys' fees can be substantially higher. In addition, given the company's financial condition, most bankruptcy attorneys require all or a substantial part of these funds to be paid up front as a prepaid retainer. When a creditors' committee is active and retains its own attorneys, the company will be required to pay those fees as well. Similarly, if an investment banker, accountant, or other financial advisor is needed, their fees will also be charged to the company. Thus, although bankruptcy can offer significant relief, it can also be very expensive.

Automatic Stay

Immediately upon filing a bankruptcy petition, a company is protected by an *automatic stay* preventing its creditors from pursuing collection of debts. The automatic stay operates as a statutory injunction that prohibits a creditor from continuing or commencing litigation against the debtor (but not against others, such as guarantors), sending dunning notices (notifications of overdue payment), taking other collection steps, or otherwise attempting to exercise control over the debtor's property (e.g., through repossession, foreclosure, or termination of contracts).

Although the automatic stay is one of the most powerful aspects of bankruptcy relief, the bankruptcy court can lift it if either (1) the debtor does not have equity in specific property over and above the claims of secured creditors and its reorganization prospects are doubtful or (2) the court finds that other good cause exists. If the automatic stay is terminated, then certain creditor actions, including foreclosure, become permissible.

Types of Creditor Claims

Every creditor of a company in bankruptcy has the right to file a proof of claim in the bankruptcy case. The *proof of claim* is the creditor's statement of its own claim. A deadline known as a *bar date* is established, and all creditors (with some exceptions) must file their claims by that date or be barred from recovering anything in the bankruptcy. The debtor company must file a schedule of assets and liabilities that lists each creditor and the amount owed according to the company's books. The company then categorizes the creditors' claims as appropriate. A claim is designated *disputed* if the company believes the claim is not valid; *contingent* if the company believes the claim will be valid only if some event does or does not occur; and *unliquidated* if the company believes the amount of the claim has not been established. If the debtor company has designated a creditor's claim as disputed, contingent, and/or unliquidated, then the creditor must file a proof of claim. Otherwise, a creditor in a Chapter 11 bankruptcy may rely on the statement of the claim shown in the debtor company's schedules.

Payment Priority

As seen in Table 12.1, claims in a bankruptcy are paid in an order of priority established by the Bankruptcy Code. A secured creditor holds a *secured claim* to the extent of the value of that creditor's collateral. For example, if a secured creditor is owed $100,000 and its collateral is worth $200,000, then that creditor is *fully secured*. If the same creditor's collateral is worth only $60,000,

---

TABLE 12.1   **Payment Priority of Certain Common Claims**

The Following Claims are Paid in this Order

1. Secured claims
2. Administrative claims
3. Claims of ordinary business creditors arising between an involuntary bankruptcy filing and the decision to put the company in bankruptcy
4. Prepetition claims of employees for unpaid salary and benefits up to $12,850 per employee
5. Consumer deposits for personal and household goods up to $2,850
6. Certain prepetition income and other taxes
7. General unsecured claims (e.g., claims by trade creditors and creditors whose executory contracts or leases have been rejected in bankruptcy, although claims by landlords of nonresidential real property for future rent generally are subject to a cap of the greater of one year's rent or 15% of the total rent reserved under the lease, not to exceed three years' worth of rent)

however, then the creditor is referred to as *undersecured*: the creditor has a secured claim to the extent of the $60,000 value of the collateral and an *unsecured claim* for the $40,000 balance. Secured creditors have the highest priority in a bankruptcy case and are entitled to certain specified favorable treatment.

Certain claims are entitled to priority over claims of other unsecured creditors and thus are called *priority claims.* Creditors that are not secured by any collateral can file priority claims or general unsecured claims, or both, depending on the circumstances. *Administrative claims,* which include the expenses of administering the bankruptcy case and certain postbankruptcy (*postpetition*) claims, receive highest priority after secured creditors. Administrative claims include the claims of the debtor's attorneys and accountants and postpetition claims for business expenses, including employee wages and salaries for work performed postpetition, postpetition raw material and office expenses, and postpetition payments for equipment and facilities leases. In addition, when creditors sell goods to the debtor company in the ordinary course of its business, they are entitled to an administrative claim for the value of goods received by the debtor company within 20 days before the bankruptcy was filed.

Claims of ordinary business creditors that arise in the gap between the filing of an involuntary bankruptcy petition and an order for relief putting a company in bankruptcy get the third priority. Prebankruptcy (*prepetition*) claims of employees for unpaid salaries, wages, severance, vacation, and sick leave, earned within the 180 days prior to the bankruptcy filing, are entitled to a fourth priority to the extent of $12,850 per employee. Other common priority claims include consumer deposits for personal or household goods of $2,850 and certain prepetition income and other taxes.

Creditor claims not entitled to any priority are known as *general unsecured claims.* They include employee claims other than those claims entitled to the $12,850 priority, most trade creditor claims, damage claims in litigation, and claims of creditors whose executory contracts or leases have been rejected in the bankruptcy (discussed below).

If a creditor files a proof of claim but the debtor company (or another party) believes the claim is invalid or in an improper amount, it can file an *objection* to the claim. If the creditor disputes the objection, it will file papers with the bankruptcy court so stating and requesting a hearing on its claim. Ultimately, the bankruptcy court will establish a procedure for resolving the objection to the claim, often by holding a short trial. If the court decides the claim is valid or valid but in a different amount, it will allow the claim in the amount it finds appropriate, and the claim will be paid according to the terms of a plan of reorganization or the Bankruptcy Code. If the court decides the claim is not valid, the claim will be disallowed and will not be entitled to payment in the bankruptcy case.

Treatment of Executory Contracts and Leases

An *executory contract* is an agreement in which both parties to the contract have material continuing obligations to perform. Typical examples include joint development agreements, manufacturing agreements, and licenses in which each party has an ongoing, affirmative performance obligation. In bankruptcy, a debtor company has the right to terminate the active performance obligations in executory contracts by *rejecting* the contracts. The debtor also has the right to terminate unfavorable leases for real property, including stores, facilities, and offices, by rejecting such leases. The rejection is treated as a breach of the contract and must be approved by the bankruptcy court. The court usually defers to management's business decision, however.

The other party to an executory contract or lease that has been rejected has the right to file a proof of claim for its damages caused by the breach, but the claim will be treated only as a prepetition unsecured claim (unless the other party to the contract was granted a security interest). When a lease of real property is involved, the Bankruptcy Code gives the debtor company another benefit: the amount of the landlord's unsecured claim for unpaid rent under the lease is capped at the greater of one year's rent or 15% of the total rent owed, not to exceed three years' worth of rent. This can be a major benefit to a company with a long-term lease at high rental rates. In some cases, a serious threat of bankruptcy can motivate a landlord to renegotiate lease terms.

The debtor company also generally has the right to assume, or to assume and assign to another person, the executory contract or lease regardless of whether the nondebtor party consents. When the company in bankruptcy *assumes* the executory contract or unexpired lease, it expressly agrees to continue to perform all of its obligations under the contract or lease. Before the bankruptcy court will permit a debtor company to assume an executory contract or lease, the debtor must (1) cure any defaults; (2) compensate for any pecuniary losses suffered by the nondebtor party, which may include attorneys' fees incurred in responding to the bankruptcy case; and (3) provide the nondebtor party with adequate assurances of the debtor's ability to perform under the contract or lease in the future. When the debtor company seeks to *assume and assign* an executory contract or unexpired lease, these same three requirements must be met, except that the party taking over the contract or lease from the debtor must itself provide adequate assurances of future performance.

Several types of contracts cannot be assigned to a third party without the nondebtor's consent and, in certain jurisdictions, cannot even be assumed without the nondebtor's consent. These include contracts for personal services and nonexclusive patent licenses when the debtor company is the licensee.

From the **TRENCHES**

After filing for bankruptcy under Chapter 11, an Internet retailer based in New York City recognized that its most valuable asset was an unexpired below-market lease for office space. Market prices for office space in New York had more than doubled from the time the retailer signed the lease to the time the retailer filed for bankruptcy. When the retailer sought to assign its unexpired lease to a media company, the lessor opposed the assignment, knowing that it could lease the space for more money with a new tenant. Even though the lease prohibited assignment without the lessor's consent and further provided that, even if consent were given, the lessee was required to pay over to the lessor any profit realized on the assignment, the bankruptcy court ruled that the retailer had the right to assign the lease over the lessor's objections and to keep the $350,000 profit.

Source: In re Boo.com N. Am., Inc., 2000 Bankr. LEXIS 1559 (Bankr., S.D.N.Y. Dec. 15, 2000).

Preference and Fraudulent Transfer Claims

The Bankruptcy Code provides that the debtor, a bankruptcy trustee if one is appointed or, in some cases, a creditors' committee may pursue recovery of preferential or fraudulent transfers made by the debtor prior to the bankruptcy.

Preferences *Preferences* are transfers made by the debtor, when insolvent, to or for the benefit of a creditor on account of preexisting debt in the 90 days prior to the filing of the bankruptcy petition. The 90-day *reach-back period* means that potentially all payments made to a creditor during the 90 days prior to the bankruptcy filing may be recoverable. The reach-back period is increased to one year in the case of transfers to an *insider* (such as an officer, director, or affiliate of the debtor company). Accordingly, any transfers made to insiders within one year prior to the filing of the bankruptcy petition are recoverable preferences if the debtor was insolvent at the time of the transfer.

Preference payments can be recovered not only from the recipient but also from those for whose benefit the payments were made. When an officer or founder of a company gives a personal guaranty to a bank or other creditor, payments that reduce the company's debt also reduce the individual's exposure on the guaranty. Thus, in a bankruptcy, the debtor company (or more likely a bankruptcy trustee if one is appointed) may sue the guarantor to recover payments made by the company to any lender or other creditor holding a guaranty. Because the guarantor is an insider, the reach-back period is one year, not 90 days. The company or bankruptcy trustee can recover the payments only once, however, but the recipient of the payments will often be sued as well.

The Bankruptcy Code provides creditors with certain defenses, including those for payments made in the ordinary course of business, for cash on delivery, or other contemporaneous exchanges. In addition, creditors can offset against payments the amount of new value provided on an unsecured basis (credit or shipments) after each payment was received. Thus, despite the preference law, creditors may be able to keep certain payments made within 90 days of bankruptcy.

Fraudulent Transfers *Fraudulent transfers* include transfers made by the debtor with actual intent to hinder, delay, or defraud creditors. They also include transfers made by a financially impaired debtor that does not receive reasonably equivalent value in return. Thus, if a debtor company in need of cash sells a major line of its business for substantially less than its market value, the buyer may be subject to a lawsuit by the company, a bankruptcy trustee, or a creditors' committee seeking to *avoid* (i.e., set aside) the transfer or to obtain damages for what is claimed to be the true value of the assets. As a result, a company contemplating the purchase of a firm in financial difficulty should usually ensure that it has an opinion from an investment bank, appraiser, or other valuation expert to justify the adequacy of the purchase price, among other preventative steps. Unlike the 90-day rule for preferences, the reach-back period for fraudulent transfers generally extends to transfers made four years before bankruptcy or even earlier in some circumstances.

Creditors' Committee

The Bankruptcy Code provides for the appointment of a committee of unsecured creditors, which generally should include the debtor's largest unsecured creditors. The United States Trustee, a division of the U.S. Department of Justice, oversees bankruptcy cases. It appoints the committee of unsecured creditors usually within the first month after the case is filed. The committee may employ attorneys and financial advisors. Their fees and expenses are paid out of the debtor's assets (*estate*) as a priority administrative expense. In appropriate cases, committees can also be appointed for bondholders, equity security holders, or others.

12.13 EFFECT OF BANKRUPTCY ON DIRECTOR AND OFFICER LITIGATION AND INDEMNIFICATION

Although the filing of a bankruptcy case immediately protects the debtor from further litigation on prepetition claims due to the automatic stay, there is no stay of litigation against anyone other than the debtor. For example, litigation against the debtor's directors and officers will not be stayed, even if it directly relates to the company's business. Under rare circumstances, a bankruptcy court may issue an injunction prohibiting further litigation against nondebtor officers or directors. This power is rarely used absent a compelling showing that the litigation would be so disruptive to management that, without an injunction, the debtor would not be able to reorganize.

Indemnification claims arising from prepetition services and based on a prepetition contract may be treated as prepetition unsecured claims even if the duty to indemnify arose postpetition. For example, if a director of the debtor company has a prepetition contractual right to be indemnified by the company for any liability arising out of board service, and the director is sued after the bankruptcy petition is filed, his or her claim for indemnification is treated as a prepetition unsecured claim. However, indemnification claims arising from prepetition services (but based on an executory employment contract that the debtor has obtained the bankruptcy court's approval to assume) should constitute postpetition administrative claims. If directors' and officers' (*D&O*) insurance policy proceeds are payable directly to the officer and director beneficiaries, the proceeds likely will not be deemed property of the bankruptcy estate and may be allowed to be paid, but relief from the automatic stay generally is needed to confirm this arrangement. The automatic stay may also prevent insurance companies from canceling a company's D&O policy after a bankruptcy is filed.

12.14 OPERATING A BUSINESS IN BANKRUPTCY

When a company is in bankruptcy, court approval is not necessary for transactions in the ordinary course of business. However, the debtor company must give notice to parties in interest and obtain court approval before, among other things, (1) using, leasing, or selling property of the estate outside the ordinary course of business; (2) borrowing money on a secured or super-priority basis; (3) rejecting or assuming prepetition contracts; or (4) entering into new contracts or settlement agreements that affect property of the estate.

The court will generally defer to the business judgment of the company's management with respect to affairs related to its everyday business operations, such as whether to assume or reject a contract or lease. Business decisions become subject to closer judicial scrutiny, however, as they begin to address core reorganization issues.

Use of Cash Collateral

When a secured creditor's collateral includes cash or cash proceeds of other collateral, the company in bankruptcy may not use the cash collateral unless the company adequately protects the secured creditor or obtains its consent. If a debtor cannot provide the secured creditor with adequate protection or obtain the creditor's consent, then the debtor may not use the cash collateral. Generally, this means the debtor cannot spend any cash and may be forced to close its business. Although a secured creditor will have a security interest in the debtor's prepetition assets, the Bankruptcy Code generally provides that a secured creditor's security interest will not extend to *postpetition assets,* or those assets created after the bankruptcy petition is filed. Thus, adequately protecting a secured creditor often means giving the secured creditor a *replacement lien* on the same type of assets in postpetition collateral as the secured creditor had in prepetition collateral. Adequate protection can take a number of forms, including periodic cash payments, a replacement lien on additional types of assets, or both.

If the value of a secured creditor's collateral more than covers the outstanding debt owed, then the *equity cushion* of collateral value over debt generally will itself provide adequate protection. If the secured creditor is undersecured, however, with the outstanding debt exceeding the value of its collateral, some other form of adequate protection must be provided. This is particularly true for a *junior secured creditor* (a secured creditor whose priority position is behind one or more senior secured creditors), who may be undersecured given the outstanding debt owed a secured creditor with a higher-priority security interest in the same collateral.

Obtaining Postpetition Financing

In many Chapter 11 cases, the debtor will need an additional credit line to continue operations. Under the Bankruptcy Code, a debtor may obtain *postpetition* or *debtor-in-possession financing* (often referred to as *DIP financing*) on such terms as the bankruptcy court approves. Generally, with DIP financing, the new, postpetition lender receives a security interest in the debtor's postpetition assets as well as an administrative claim that is ahead of all other administrative expenses, including attorneys' and other professionals' fees (known as *super-priority administrative expense treatment*). If the value of the debtor's assets is sufficiently high, the bankruptcy court can even approve a *priming* or *first-priority lien*, which gives the DIP lender a first-position lien on all of the debtor's prepetition and postpetition assets, even ahead of an existing prepetition lender.

12.15 CHAPTER 11 PLAN OF REORGANIZATION

When a debtor (or other party) proposes a plan of reorganization, the Bankruptcy Code sets forth the procedure for determining whether the plan will be considered. Along with a plan, the plan proponent must file a disclosure statement. The *disclosure statement* functions much like a prospectus, informing creditors and equity security holders of material financial and business information to be used to evaluate the proposed plan of reorganization. The court must conclude that the disclosure statement contains adequate information before the plan itself can be considered. (Securities offered pursuant to a plan of reorganization approved by a bankruptcy court are generally exempt from registration under the Securities Act of 1933.) Once approved, the disclosure statement is sent to all creditors along with the plan and a ballot for voting on the plan. After the ballots are tabulated, the court holds a hearing on *confirmation* or approval of the proposed plan of reorganization.

Exclusivity Period

During the first 120 days after a bankruptcy petition is filed, the debtor has the exclusive right to propose a plan of reorganization. The bankruptcy court can extend or reduce this period for cause, but it may not extend the exclusive period beyond 18 months from the date the bankruptcy case was filed. The exclusivity period precludes other parties in interest in the bankruptcy case (generally creditors) from proposing a plan that might dispossess the debtor and its management from control.

If exclusivity is terminated or expires, any creditor or party in interest in the bankruptcy case can file a proposed plan of reorganization. Sometimes creditors file plans to liquidate a debtor's assets, force a sale to a third party, or effect a corporate takeover. Thus, a creditor's plan can pose significant risks for a debtor's management, in addition to the potential litigation expense of opposing the plan.

Classification of Claims

Every plan of reorganization must classify creditors by class: secured, general unsecured, or equity security holders. The last group is further classified based on the type of securities held. Depending on the circumstances, debenture holders—parties who hold medium- to long-term debt of the company at a fixed interest rate—who are subordinated may be placed in a separate class or grouped with unsecured creditors if they have no security interest in collateral.

Classes must be designated as impaired or unimpaired, depending on their treatment under the plan. If the plan provides that a particular class will not receive all of its state-law rights (e.g., the plan provides that a secured creditor's loan is to be extended for two years), then the class will be deemed *impaired.* If the plan provides a class all of its state-law rights (e.g., a secured creditor is to receive full payment pursuant to existing terms of a promissory note), then the class will be deemed *unimpaired.* Impaired classes are generally entitled to vote on the plan, but unimpaired classes do not vote and are deemed to have accepted the plan.

Unasserted, Contingent, and Unliquidated Claims

In many cases, a debtor may have creditors or potential creditors that have contingent or unliquidated claims or even unasserted claims. If a creditor has a claim and learns of the bankruptcy (either through formal notice or otherwise) but fails to file a proof of claim when required, then its claim can be barred from any recovery against the debtor and *discharged*, that is, deemed satisfied by the bankruptcy proceeding.

A debtor may have one or more creditors holding a contingent or unliquidated claim, the fixing or liquidation of which would unduly delay reorganization. In such an event, the debtor may seek intervention by the court to estimate the claim for purposes of the bankruptcy case. Thus, a creditor with an uncertain claim, which otherwise might take several years of litigation to establish, may have its claim estimated in a short evidentiary hearing or trial; thereafter, the creditor is limited to the amount of the estimated claim. This procedure enables a debtor company to reorganize even if it faces significant contingent or unliquidated claims.

Plan Voting Requirements

Certain voting requirements must be met before the court can confirm a plan of reorganization. Fundamentally, at least one impaired class must vote to accept the proposed plan of reorganization. If that happens, the plan proponent may attempt to "cramdown" the plan on classes of creditors or equity security holders that oppose it. As discussed further below, in a *cramdown*, the proponent seeks court confirmation of the plan without the consent of all of the classes. In contrast, if all impaired classes vote to accept the plan, confirmation is obtained much more easily. For purposes of meeting these requirements, the votes of the debtor's insiders (such as officers, directors, and large shareholders) are not counted.

For a class to accept the plan, a majority in number of the creditors actually voting on the plan must vote to accept it. In addition, the creditors voting in favor of the plan must hold claims in a dollar amount equal to at least two-thirds of the total claims held by the class members who vote. For example, assume there is a class of creditors with 30 members and $2 million of claims. Only 17 creditors, representing total claims of $1 million, vote. In this case, at least 9 of the 17 creditors voting will have to vote in favor of the plan, and they will have to represent at least $666,667 in claims. If the class vote does not satisfy these requirements, the class will be deemed to have rejected the plan, and the plan proponent will have to attempt to cramdown the plan on that non-accepting class.

If the debtor files an objection to a creditor's proof of claim, then, absent further action, the creditor will not be permitted to vote. The creditor can, however, file a motion seeking temporary allowance of its claim for purposes of voting only, with the actual allowance of its claim being subject to a later determination. The court will determine whether, or in what amount, the claim should be allowed for voting purposes.

Cramdown Issues and the Absolute Priority Rule

If a plan is accepted by at least one impaired class of claims but is rejected by one or more other classes, the plan proponent can seek confirmation of its plan under the cramdown rules. These Bankruptcy Code provisions are designed to provide objecting classes with fair and equitable treatment. Although some variations exist, the plan must provide that a secured creditor retains its lien on its collateral and receives *deferred cash payments* (periodic cash payments over time with an appropriate rate of interest) equal to the creditor's allowed secured claim (i.e., the value of the collateral or the amount of the claim, whichever is less).

For unsecured creditors to be crammed down, (1) they must be paid in full with interest or (2) all junior classes must be precluded from receiving any property on account of their claims or interests. Generally, this means that equity security holders (preferred or common shareholders) may not receive anything by reason of their ownership of shares if unsecured creditors are not being paid in full with interest. Their shares would be canceled under such a plan. This requirement implements the *absolute priority rule* of bankruptcy, which provides that, absent consent, each senior class of creditors must be paid in full before any junior class may receive anything under a plan. Thus, if secured creditors are not being paid in full on their secured claims, unsecured creditors and equity security holders can receive nothing. Or, as just described, if unsecured creditors are not being paid in full, equity security holders cannot retain their stock.

Some courts recognize what is known as a "new value exception" to this absolute priority rule. The *new value exception* permits a junior class, generally shareholders, to retain their shares if they contribute to the debtor substantial new value in the form of money or property that is essential to funding a reorganization. Even when the exception is recognized, satisfying its requirements can be difficult. In particular, equity holders cannot be given an exclusive right to contribute new capital in exchange for equity in the reorganized entity free from competition from other bidders and without the benefit of a market valuation to ensure that the old equity holders pay full value for the new equity.[3]

Instead of relying on the new value exception, equity holders usually work to negotiate a plan of reorganization in which all impaired classes vote in favor of the plan. If all impaired classes vote in favor of the plan, neither the cramdown rules nor the absolute priority rule applies, and equity holders may retain whatever percentage of ownership they are able to negotiate.

Factors to Consider When Crafting and Negotiating a Chapter 11 Plan

Generally, a plan must adhere to the priority scheme of the Bankruptcy Code, including the requirement that the interests of shareholders become subordinated to those of creditors. During the first 120 days, when the debtor has the exclusive right to propose a plan, the debtor's management and board must remember their fiduciary duty to all constituents, including creditors. When the venture's reorganization value is insufficient to pay all creditors in full, favoring equity holders over creditors can pose fiduciary duty problems for officers and directors. The Bankruptcy Code also requires disclosure of which officers, directors, and other insiders will be employed or retained under the plan and the nature of any compensation to be paid to insiders by the reorganized debtor.

Discharge of Claims

A corporate debtor that successfully obtains confirmation of a plan of reorganization and remains in business can receive a discharge of all its debts. This means that creditors must accept the property being distributed under the plan as full satisfaction on their claims and cannot pursue the corporation thereafter on those claims. A discharge injunction, similar to the automatic stay, is issued to prevent creditors from taking action inconsistent with the confirmed plan of reorganization. As discussed above, equity holders will have their interests wiped out unless they have either (1) been able to negotiate a plan in which they retain ownership of some or all of the company's stock or (2) successfully used the new value exception to the absolute priority rule to retain ownership even in a cramdown case.

12.16 PREPACKAGED BANKRUPTCIES AND PLANS OF REORGANIZATION

It can often take a debtor months or years to propose a plan, obtain approval for a disclosure statement, and finally win confirmation of the plan. Consequently, the Bankruptcy Code permits a debtor to prepare a disclosure statement and plan, circulate the statement and plan to its creditors, and actually solicit and complete voting on the plan—all before filing a bankruptcy petition. This process is known as a *prepackaged bankruptcy* (or a *prepack*). When there are enough votes to permit the plan to be confirmed, a prepackaged bankruptcy can speed up a debtor's emergence from bankruptcy.

When a case has been prepackaged, the debtor typically files its disclosure statement, plan of reorganization, ballots, and ballot report on the day it files for bankruptcy. The debtor then seeks an expedited hearing both to approve the adequacy of the information in the disclosure statement and to confirm the plan of reorganization. If the court finds that the disclosure statement is inadequate, a new one must be prepared and sent to creditors along with new ballots for voting. Because many companies filing bankruptcy hope for a quick (and successful) exit from bankruptcy, prepackaged bankruptcy has become popular. Nevertheless, it is very difficult to achieve, particularly for operating companies.

An out-of-court workout can also be structured as a prepackaged bankruptcy, with a disclosure statement and plan instead of simple notices and a workout agreement. If the creditors that support the workout are sufficient for confirmation of a bankruptcy plan, but too many holdouts refuse to consent to the workout to make it practical without a bankruptcy, then a prepackaged bankruptcy can be filed to bind the holdout creditors to the plan. The formality of the required documentation unfortunately adds to the cost of the out-of-court workout. In appropriate cases, however, this approach can be used.

In a variant of the prepackaged bankruptcy, called a *prenegotiated bankruptcy,* the debtor meets with its key creditors and negotiates the terms of the plan of reorganization prior to filing bankruptcy but solicits votes only after the case is filed and the disclosure statement is approved. If the groundwork is laid with the creditor body, the prenegotiated plan can shorten a company's time in bankruptcy. Also, because a formal disclosure statement and plan are drafted only if a bankruptcy case is needed, it involves lower up-front costs.

Although a prenegotiated bankruptcy can be useful for some companies, a true prepackaged bankruptcy is most effective for holding companies with large amounts of public bond or debenture debt that they seek to restructure. This type of bankruptcy also works best for corporations that have few or insignificant disputed, contingent, or unliquidated claims and have no major litigation pending.

12.17 BUSINESS COMBINATIONS THROUGH CHAPTER 11 BANKRUPTCY

It is possible to accomplish a merger between a debtor corporation and another corporation through a Chapter 11 plan of reorganization. Similar to a merger agreement outside bankruptcy, the Chapter 11 plan would set forth the terms of a merger and provide that the stock of the debtor is to be sold to the acquiring corporation, that a new corporation is to be formed into which the debtor and the acquiring corporation are merged, or that some other form of transaction is to be implemented.

The principal disadvantage of a stock merger with a debtor corporation is that the acquiring corporation generally will become liable for all debts of the debtor. In addition, a plan proposing to pay the proceeds to the debtor's shareholders must meet the Chapter 11 plan requirements, potentially including the cramdown and absolute priority rule of bankruptcy. Because creditors have priority over shareholders, it may be very difficult to direct that the debtor's shareholders receive the proceeds of the merger.

An increasingly common alternative is to sell the debtor company's assets, free and clear of liens, with the proceeds to be paid into the bankruptcy estate. Such a sale may be done either through a Chapter 11 plan or as a separate asset sale after notice to creditors and court approval pursuant to Section 363 of the Bankruptcy Code. The acquiring corporation purchases those assets free and clear of existing liens and debts but often assumes selected debts (usually those associated with the ongoing business). The purchase price is distributed in the debtor's bankruptcy pursuant to a Chapter 11 plan or in a Chapter 7 liquidation if the case is converted from Chapter 11, as often happens in smaller cases. If the debtor is insolvent, however, its shareholders will most likely not receive any of the proceeds. These "363 sales" are a regular feature of Chapter 11 bankruptcy cases, both for small companies as well as very large companies (e.g., Chrysler).

 ## From the **TRENCHES**

As with all bankruptcy proceedings, debtor companies selling assets under Section 363 of the Bankruptcy Code must fully disclose all known claims and liabilities to fully protect the postpetition company from prepetition claims. On June 1, 2009, General Motors (*Old GM*) filed for bankruptcy under Chapter 11. The next month, U.S. Bankruptcy Judge Robert E. Gerber approved a 363 sale order whereby a newly created entity (*New GM*) acquired substantially all the assets of the Old GM "free and clear of all liens, claims, encumbrances, and other interests of any kind or nature whatsoever, including rights or claims based on any successor or transferee liability." During the bankruptcy proceeding, Old GM failed to disclose to creditors an ignition switch defect it knew or should have known about as early as 2001. The defect was ultimately linked to at least 124 deaths and 275 injuries. New GM did not start recalling cars with the defective switches until 2014. In 2016, the U.S. Court of Appeals for the Second Circuit ruled that individuals allegedly harmed prior to Old GM's bankruptcy filing could sue New GM for damages because they were not given adequate notice of the defects before the 363 sale.

Sources: In re Motors Liquidation Co., 829 F.3d 135 (2d Cir. 2016); Associated Press, *Appeals Court Lets Suits Over Faulty G.M. Ignitions Proceed*, N.Y. TIMES, July 14, 2016, at B2.

12.18 LOSS OF CONTROL AND OTHER RISKS IN BANKRUPTCY

In a typical Chapter 11 case, a debtor company's management remains in possession and control, subject to replacement by the board of directors. However, creditors or others in a Chapter 11 case can file a motion seeking appointment of an independent Chapter 11 trustee to take possession of all of the debtor's assets. The most common grounds for such a motion are fraud or gross mismanagement by the debtor-in-possession. Even though a debtor's management usually will not be replaced by a Chapter 11 trustee, replacement remains a risk of filing a bankruptcy.

Another risk of filing a Chapter 11 case is that at some point the court may convert the case to a Chapter 7 liquidation, with the accompanying automatic appointment of a Chapter 7 trustee, or the court may decide to dismiss the Chapter 11 case altogether. Conversion or dismissal can be ordered for cause, including inability to effectuate a plan of reorganization, unreasonable delay prejudicial to creditors, failure to meet any court-imposed deadlines for filing a plan, or other failure to comply with court orders.

12.19 BANKRUPTCY PROS AND CONS

Obviously, filing or not filing bankruptcy can be a life-or-death decision for a company. Although bankruptcy offers significant and often unique advantages, there are major risks. Table 12.2 lists some of the major advantages and disadvantages of filing bankruptcy.

TABLE 12.2 Pros and Cons of Filing Bankruptcy	
Advantages	**Disadvantages**
● Automatic stay of creditor actions	● Expensive
● Power to reject unfavorable executory contracts and limit damages on leases	● Court approval required for all decisions outside the ordinary course of business
● Power to force restructure of debts on nonconsenting creditors	● Potential loss of customer or vendor relationships
	● Employee uncertainty and potential adverse effect on employee morale
● Ability to recover preferences and fraudulent transfers	● Possible loss of control through conversion to Chapter 7 or appointment of trustee
	● Preference for cash, making equity a less common acquisition currency
● Opportunity to preserve going-concern value of company	● Risk that shareholders' equity position and employee stock options will be wiped out in favor of creditors

Putting It into **PRACTICE**

Although things started out well for Genesist, the company began experiencing an increasingly serious shortfall in cash. At first, Alexei and Piper were able to pay rent and other operating expenses by delaying certain payments to less critical vendors. As the cash flow problems worsened, payments to certain more important creditors were delayed even further. Calls from creditors increased, and several threatened legal action if they were not paid. One of the company's key suppliers threatened to stop providing goods if not paid in full. Alexei and Piper paid the most vocal creditors but lacked the cash to pay them all. Eventually, two vendors sued Genesist for breach of contract. After Alexei and Piper decided Piper would be the point person for dealing with the crises, Piper called Sarah Crawford for advice.

Sarah involved her insolvency partner, Rebecca Bishop, who filed answers on Genesist's behalf to the two complaints and asked Piper for a package of financial information on the company. After reviewing it, Rebecca asked Piper for her most conservative projections of Genesist's financial situation and an assessment of its business plan in light of the current financial problems. Rebecca pressed Piper to be certain that these projections were realistic, and she warned that a failure to keep the renegotiated promises to creditors could further damage Genesist's credibility if the situation worsened.

With Rebecca's help, the founders concluded that Genesist needed the ability to stretch out payments to its creditors for another three months or so. If the creditors agreed, Genesist could probably avoid a more formal workout effort.

Piper made a list of the largest creditors, the amounts owed each, and how delinquent Genesist was on payments. She then personally called each of the major creditors and explained Genesist's financial condition. She asked that Genesist be allowed to pay 20% of the normal payment for the next two months, at which point Genesist projected it would be able to resume ordinary payment terms. Piper told these creditors that Genesist would completely catch up on payments within six months.

Although several creditors rejected these terms, most accepted Piper's proposal, with the proviso that Genesist be caught up within five months. Building on the progress made with some of Genesist's largest creditors, Piper again called the creditors who had not agreed. She named some of Genesist's creditors that had agreed to the terms and again asked for cooperation. After several more rounds of discussions, Piper was finally able to work out a less favorable, but still feasible, arrangement. Fortunately, the next few months proved to be close to

(continued)

Piper's projections, and the company was able to work its way out of the immediate crisis. The litigation with the two vendors continued during this period, and the company later settled both cases by paying the full debt owed but without additional interest or attorneys' fees.

After several more months of successful operations, Alexei and Piper felt it was time to seek additional financing. Having no desire to repeat their experience with near insolvency, they decided it was time to seriously consider seeking venture capital financing.

Venture Capital

Although the most common sources of early capital for startup companies are the entrepreneur, the entrepreneur's family and friends, and angel investors, venture capitalists (*VCs*) have helped to grow some of the nation's leading companies, including Alphabet (parent company to Google), Amazon, Apple, Cisco, eBay, Facebook, Genentech, Intel, Microsoft, and Uber. In 2015, startup companies raised almost $59 billion in 4,380 VC financings, according to a report from PricewaterhouseCoopers and the National Venture Capital Association.

As discussed in Chapter 7, very early-stage financings (generally under $2 million) are often done through the issuance of convertible notes and, occasionally, SAFEs. A *Simple Agreement for Future Equity (SAFE)* is similar to a convertible note, but without a maturity date and interest.[1] Convertible notes enable a startup company and its early investors to not get bogged down on negotiating and papering a more complex preferred equity financing, including determining a set valuation for the company at its very early stages. Investors in convertible note financings often do not expect many of the control rights they have come to expect in preferred stock financings, instead focusing on ensuring they have the right to participate in future rounds and receive adequate information on the company while they hold the note. They also obtain a certain degree of "price protection" that they otherwise would not have been entitled to if they invested in preferred stock, because they will always get a price lower than that paid by investors in the next preferred stock financing round.

Because these instruments are generally used only in the very early stages of a startup company, this chapter focuses on traditional venture capital transactions, which are more complex and far more common. This chapter first discusses the pros and cons of seeking venture capital, then outlines strategies for finding it and provides tips for preparing pitch decks to present to venture capitalists. We then highlight factors to consider when selecting a venture capitalist. The chapter then discusses how the parties in a preferred stock financing reach agreement on a valuation for the company, and thus the percentage of the company's equity the venture capitalists will receive in exchange for their investment. We then analyze the rights and protections typically given to venture capitalists buying preferred stock. The chapter concludes with a brief description of the vesting requirements normally imposed on founders by venture capitalists and their expectations with respect to the granting of employee stock options.

13.1 DECIDING WHETHER TO SEEK VENTURE CAPITAL

When deciding whether to pursue venture capital, the entrepreneur should first determine whether the new business will meet the criteria used by most venture capitalists. The entrepreneur must then decide whether the pros outweigh the cons.

Investment Criteria

Generally, a venture capitalist will want to invest a substantial amount of money, usually $1 to $3 million or more. However, as costs to bring many products to market decrease, an increasing number of funds and groups of individuals will do seed investing for a new startup at a level of $1 million or less.

Venture capitalists are usually looking for an enterprise with the potential to grow to a significant size quickly and to generate an annual return on investment in excess of 40% over a period of three to five years. Venture capitalists need to target that rate of return to realize the compounded annual returns of at least 20% expected by their investors.

VCs tend to avoid investing in companies they view as slow growth or that have business models that are not scalable. Such companies are often called "lifestyle businesses," because they provide a regular income and particular lifestyle to the founders but not the investment returns a venture capitalist would want. If an entrepreneur is looking for a longer time horizon in order to grow the business at a slower pace and that minimizes the risk of failure—a factor that should be discussed with any investor—the enterprise may not be suitable for venture capital.

Venture capitalist firms often prefer to invest at a particular stage of development: *seed* (raw startup), *early stage* (product in beta testing or just being shipped), *later stage* (product is fully developed or is being sold and generating revenue), or *mezzanine* or *growth* (the financing round before an anticipated initial public offering). Although there is a greater risk of failure when investing in a "promising company at its infancy and bet[ting] on its growth," early-stage investors often earn the best returns.[2]

Most venture capitalists specialize in particular industries. A priority area of focus has been the information technology industry, which includes companies focused on computer software and hardware, digital media, e-commerce, advertising technology, social media, and mobile and virtual reality technology. The second largest concentration of venture capital investing has been in life sciences companies, including those focusing on biotechnology, genetics, medical devices, diagnostics, and therapeutics. Although venture capital investment remains most concentrated in these two fields, VCs are financial investors seeking an optimal rate of return, and to this aim they have invested successfully in many other areas, such as alternative and renewable energy, telecommunications, consumer products, retail, new composite materials, and business services.

Pros and Cons of Financing with Venture Capital

Even if a new venture fits the criteria for a VC financing, the entrepreneur must still weigh the pros and cons of a VC financing. As discussed briefly in Chapter 7, venture capital financing can be an attractive funding source for a number of reasons. Venture capital may allow the entrepreneur to raise all the necessary capital from one source or from a lead investor who can attract other investors. In contrast, family, friends, and angels are often unlikely to make substantial follow-on investments. This could leave the business high and dry if it requires additional capital in the future to survive or grow.

Venture capitalists understand the challenges of startups and have often had experience growing a company to an initial public offering, a sale of the business, or another liquidity event. In addition, experienced venture capitalists have a large network of contacts on whom to draw to help the company succeed. Venture capitalists can often provide valuable assistance in recruiting other members of the management team and in establishing high-level contacts among potential key customers and potential partners. Venture capitalists are also often excellent board members, lending their judgment and support to help the startup entrepreneur navigate tricky issues facing the company. As cash is fungible, the "value-adds" provided by VCs often become a determinative factor in a venture capitalist being chosen over another source of capital, including other venture capitalists, to lead an investment into a startup company.

Being "venture-backed" by a prominent fund can give a startup a certain cachet, which can open doors to more favorable debt financing and other resources. Venture-backed firms tend to raise more money, grow more quickly, secure more patents, and have substantially higher market shares than companies not backed by venture capital.[3] Ninety percent of new entrepreneurial businesses that do not attract venture capital fail within three years. This contrasts with a 33% failure rate for venture-backed companies.[4] Venture-backed firms also perform significantly better after they go public than similar nonventure-backed firms.[5]

The advantages of VC financing can come at a cost. First, venture investors are more sophisticated negotiators and may drive a harder bargain on the pricing and terms of their investment than friends or family. Family, friends, and angels may be willing to pay a higher price (i.e., to accept a higher valuation of the company at the time they invest), and they tend to require less onerous investment terms and conditions than venture capitalists. Unfortunately, they often bring little else to the table. Second, venture investors may be more likely to assert their power in molding the enterprise than more passive investors. Third, venture investors may be more interested than passive investors in replacing the management team (including the founders) or taking control of the enterprise if the initial team stumbles.

In short, venture capitalists may demand a lower valuation and tougher terms, but good VCs bring many intangibles that can help the company grow faster and be more successful. Hence this crucial funding decision is sometimes referred to as the choice between "dumb money" and "smart money."

13.2   FINDING VENTURE CAPITAL INVESTORS

Of the various approaches to finding venture capital investors, the practice of sending an unsolicited business plan or pitch deck to a venture capital firm is almost certainly a formula for failure. Venture capitalists receive dozens of such submissions each week, with very few being read thoroughly, if at all, and even fewer leading to financing.

A better way to get a venture capitalist's attention is to arrange an introduction by someone who knows the venture capitalist. If, for example, the entrepreneur has friends who have obtained venture capital financing, they may be able to provide the introduction. Similarly, individuals working at universities, government labs, and other entities that license technology to venture-backed companies may have connections worth pursuing. Accountants, lawyers, and bankers who do business with venture-backed companies also are good sources for introductions.

A critical step in raising venture capital is to engage a business lawyer who works primarily in the venture capital field. Although many lawyers may have done a venture capital deal, fewer than a dozen law firms nationwide truly specialize in representing venture-backed companies. Most of these law firms have a significant presence in northern California's Silicon Valley, often with branch offices located in other cities with a strong entrepreneurial presence, such as Austin, Texas; Boston, Massachusetts; Boulder, Colorado; New York City; San Diego, California; and Seattle, Washington.

In choosing a law firm, an entrepreneur should ask for information about the venture funds that the law firm has formed, the number and identity of venture funds the firm has represented in investments, and the venture-backed companies the firm represents. A law firm that specializes in this area will have substantial lists of these clients readily available, whereas a less experienced firm may speak in generalities or may reference only one or two relationships.

A firm that specializes in this area will also have experienced lawyers to provide in-depth information and advice and to ensure that negotiations with the venture capitalists go smoothly. Although deal making in the venture capital industry is not rocket science, it is a bit "clubby," and so it helps to have an attorney who knows the club rules. VCs may question the judgment of founders who select inexperienced counsel.

Because the most experienced firms represent venture capitalists as well as venture funds, it is likely that the entrepreneur's lawyer, or the law firm, may have represented, or may be currently representing, the venture capitalist in other matters. The legal code of ethics requires that the attorney disclose his or her firm's involvement in other transactions to both parties and obtain appropriate consents. An entrepreneur may wish to explore with the attorney his or her relationships with the venture capitalists to whom the entrepreneur is being introduced.

Because attorneys in this industry work with a large number of venture capitalists, they should be able to introduce the entrepreneur to those venture capital firms and individual partners who would be most appropriate for a particular deal. It would not make much sense to present an Internet deal to a venture capitalist who specializes in medical device companies.

Before pitching a deal to a VC, the entrepreneur should review the firm's website, which will usually contain detailed information about their investment professionals, their portfolio companies, and their investment philosophy. Many individual partners at venture capital firms maintain blogs, which provide insight into the partner's investing strategies and histories and often include examples of how the partner deals with various business challenges. In addition, there are a number of independent print and electronic sources of information on the venture industry. Websites such as VentureBeat.com, CBinsights.com, and Crunchbase.com contain information about different firms and partners, as well as their portfolio companies. An entrepreneur may also wish to consult such industry publications as *Venture Capital Journal* and reports from information-gathering organizations such as Dow Jones VentureSource and Thomson Reuters.

13.3 PITCHING TO A VENTURE CAPITALIST

Often, an entrepreneur begins the process of seeking venture capital by preparing a business plan or pitch deck, although many deals have been done without a written plan.

Business Plans or Pitch Decks

In years past, an entrepreneur would prepare a formal business plan before seeking an investment. (Business plans were discussed in Chapter 7.) More recently in the venture capital community, business plans have been almost entirely replaced by the pitch deck. The *pitch deck*, also sometimes called the investor deck, is typically prepared on a program like Microsoft PowerPoint and conveys the key components of a traditional business plan, but in a format that relies more on graphics and visuals than on heavy text. It describes the product or service concept and the opportunity for investors. Typically, the deck includes sections describing the industry, the market, the means for producing the product or delivering the service, the competition, the novelty of this product or service or its superiority over existing products or services, the marketing plan, the proprietary position that will provide barriers to entry by competitors (such as patents), and the strengths of the management team. Certain decks may also include projections and the assumptions on which they are based, if appropriate for the type of startup company.

Most venture capitalists will focus on the viability of the concept, the size of the opportunity, and the quality of the management team. To the extent that there are holes in the team (e.g., the team has great technical talent but no experienced managers, or vice versa, or the team lacks a strong sales or operations lead), the entrepreneur should acknowledge these weaknesses in follow-up discussions with venture capitalists and ask them for assistance in finding the right people. Multiple successful VCs have said that the three most important factors in making an investment are "people, people, and people." The right team can fix a flawed concept, but a flawed team cannot get a brilliant concept to market.

Venture capitalists comment that certain weaknesses appear repeatedly in the decks they review. Common pitfalls include:

> ➢ *The deck does not include the necessary elements.* The deck should concisely describe (1) the market; (2) the unmet need in the market; (3) the compelling solution offered by the entrepreneur; (4) the strategy for connecting the need, the solution, and the customers; (5) the technology or other proprietary aspects of the solution that will give this venture an edge over the competition; (6) the experience of the team that demonstrates that the plan can be implemented; and (7) how much money is being raised and what the company plans to accomplish with the funding.

> ➢ *The deck is too long.* Most venture capitalists have little tolerance for reading more than 15 or 20 slides in a deck. Details such as financials, press mentions, biographies, schematics, and market analysis can be shortened, eliminated (for now, but presented later to those really interested), or moved into supplemental appendices for the most interested reader.

> ➢ *The deck is poorly organized.* A poorly organized deck suggests that the team may be incapable of taking on the larger task of organizing a company. Often, the deck will serve as a basis for a live presentation to the venture capitalists. Therefore, the "flow" of the deck should be consistent with an entrepreneur telling a compelling story to an investor about why his or her startup represents a large opportunity.

> ➢ *The deck is unbalanced.* The deck should not be overly focused on one area at the expense of others. For example, sometimes decks drafted by engineers devote substantial space to explaining the technology in minute detail but fail to adequately describe the market, the competition, or the strategy for connecting the customer with the product.

> ➢ *The deck lacks focus.* Many decks call for a company to pursue multiple opportunities simultaneously in multiple markets.

The more complex the story, the harder it is to sell to venture capitalists. Great opportunities are conveyed in few words. VCs will want to know that an entrepreneur can prioritize and focus on the best opportunity. The other opportunities can be discussed later or highlighted in live conversations with prospective investors.

> *The opportunity is too small.* Many good business opportunities are too small for venture investors. Although other investors might be willing to put up $2 million to grow a company into a $25 million business with net income of 10% of sales in five years, these returns are too low to interest most venture capitalists.

Courtship Process

Once introductions are made, venture capitalists will follow up with meetings if they are interested in investing. This begins a courtship process that typically takes two to three months. For this reason, it is a good idea to engage a number of venture capitalists in discussions simultaneously, rather than serially. Many venture capital funds hold weekly internal meetings to discuss the status of various prospects. Generally, venture capitalists will be quick to let a company know if they are interested.

As a part of this courtship, the venture capitalists will perform due diligence. *Due diligence* in the context of venture financing is the process whereby venture capitalists examine a company's concept, product, potential market, team, financial health, and legal situation. Due diligence is typically conducted by venture capitalists, lawyers, and consultants with financial and technical expertise. Often a VC will send a technical or industry expert to meet with the entrepreneur and take a close look at the technology or concept. The venture capitalist may also talk with potential customers to help gauge the size of the potential market for the product or service. These meetings generally involve sharing a great deal of strategic information with the potential investor. Most experienced VCs will not agree to sign a nondisclosure agreement for discussions about a potential investment into a startup, so the entrepreneur should be sure to ascertain whether the VC or his or her fund has any portfolio companies that are or may soon be competitive with the new company.

As the courtship continues, the entrepreneur should also perform due diligence on the venture capitalist. Much information can be gathered conversationally. Appropriate questions include:

- ➢ In what other companies within this industry has the venture fund invested?
- ➢ What deals has this particular VC completed?
- ➢ Are there any other companies in the venture fund's portfolio that would be competitors?
- ➢ On what boards does the VC sit?
- ➢ What is the expiration year of the fund that will be making the investment?
- ➢ Will the VC be willing and able to participate in the next round of financing?
- ➢ Are there other venture capital firms that the VC thinks should be invited into the deal?
- ➢ Would the VC be willing to work alongside other VCs with whom the entrepreneur is already in discussions?
- ➢ How has the VC handled management changes in the past?
- ➢ Are there any founders in the venture fund's portfolio who were pushed aside or pushed out?
- ➢ What is the time horizon for this investment?
- ➢ What happens if there is no exit event providing liquidity (such as an initial public offering or sale of the company) by that date?
- ➢ What rate of return does the VC need to earn on this investment?

The entrepreneur should ask the venture capitalist to provide introductions to founders of other companies in which he or she has invested and then should contact those founders to obtain insight on the kind of partner the venture capitalist is likely to be. In a very real sense, choosing a venture capitalist is like choosing a business partner. Thus, it is imperative that entrepreneurs do their research thoroughly to get comfortable that the VC under consideration will be a good partner.

The Advantages of Having Multiple Venture Investors

If it is possible to attract and accommodate more than one venture capitalist in a round, it can be to the company's advantage to do so. Although working with more than one venture investor may be a bit more complicated, it does increase the network of resources available to the company. In addition, another venture capitalist may be able to serve as a counterbalance if the entrepreneur and the first venture capitalist end up at loggerheads on an issue.

Most venture capitalists can partner effectively with other venture capitalists. Some venture capitalists, however, will not participate in a deal unless they are the only investor or the only lead investor, generally in order to maintain a certain degree of control.

From the **TRENCHES**

The founder of a traditional multimedia company bootstrapped her company into a leader in its nascent industry. The company, which had been financed by family and friends, had modest earnings. With the growth of the Internet, the founder decided to raise $2.5 million in venture capital to expand the operation into cyber-space. By chance, she was introduced to a VC who had just set up a new fund for Internet investing. Due to the demands of running her business, the founder had little time to devote to fund-raising. Because her discussions with the VC were going so well, she decided not to seek introductions to any other venture capitalists.

After weeks of negotiation, they agreed on a valuation, and the VC sent over a term sheet. Unbeknownst to the founder, the VC was previously employed in the banking industry, and he had only recently moved into the bank's venture fund, which did only mezzanine investing (the financing round before an antici-pated public offering). The term sheet the VC presented looked more like a com-plex loan deal than a venture deal, due both to his background in banking and to the focus of mezzanine-round investors on protecting against the downside (given the limited upside of a mezzanine deal). It took more than five months to con-clude a deal with the VC, and the ultimate deal contained highly unusual down-side protection for the VC's fund.

Comment: Although the VC had the right industry focus for the company, an inquiry about his experience would have revealed that he was the wrong investor for this stage of investment. Had the founder pursued multiple investors and selected a more appropriate venture capitalist, she would have saved time and been able to negotiate a less onerous deal.

When raising money during a subsequent round of venture capital, the company will want to be able to tell new investors that the prior-round venture capital investors are interested in maintaining or increasing their stake. Typically, the lead venture capitalist in the prior round will allow the new investors to take the lead in negotiating with the company the price and other terms of the stock to be sold in the subsequent round. Once the price is set, the lead investors from the prior round will indicate how much stock they will buy. If there is more than one venture capitalist in the initial round, the company may stand a better chance that at least one of the existing investors will invest in the next round and be viewed as "supportive" of the company, a very important signal to future investors. Also, if there are several venture investors in the initial round, the entrepreneur is more likely to have an ally who can coax further investment from the group if the company underperforms.

A recent phenomenon is for large venture capital funds to invest much smaller amounts than they would traditionally invest in early-stage companies. Their goal is to get an early look into a potentially "hot" startup company. While potentially attractive for a startup company, a savvy entrepreneur will understand the potential risks, including that the failure of one of those large venture capital funds to seek to lead a subsequent round or even to participate could send a negative signal to new incoming investors.

13.4 DETERMINING THE VALUATION

Once a venture capitalist indicates that his or her firm is ready to make the investment, the discussion will quickly turn to valuation. In essence, this is a discussion of price: How much will the venture capitalist pay and for what percentage of the company?

Pricing Terminology

The venture capitalist often communicates his or her offer in an arcane shorthand that can be confusing to the uninitiated. For example, a venture capitalist might say:

> ➤ "I'll put in $2 million based on three pre-money"
> ➤ "I'm thinking two-thirds based on three pre-; that will get you to five post-"
> ➤ "I'm looking for two-fifths of the company post-money, and for that I'll put up the two" or
> ➤ "It's worth $3 million pre-money, and I want to own 40% of it after we close."

What does all this mean?

Each of the preceding statements is a different way of expressing exactly the same proposal. The venture capitalist is willing to invest $2 million in the company. The terms *pre-money* and *post-money* refer to the valuation that is put on the company before and after the investment. The venture capitalist is proposing that the company is worth $3 million before the investment of $2 million and is therefore worth $5 million immediately after the investment. The ownership share being requested is an amount equivalent to 66% of the equity based on the pre-money number (i.e., $2 million/$3 million), which will be 40% of the company measured immediately after the closing of the deal (i.e., $2 million/$5 million). When calculating the number of shares outstanding, an investor may insist that the calculation be done on a *fully diluted basis*. This means that the number of outstanding shares would include shares issuable upon the exercise of options (as discussed below) and the conversion of convertible notes. To ensure there is no misunderstanding, it is advisable to ask what dollar amount is to be invested and what percentage of the equity the investor expects to own following the deal.

If the investor knows the number of shares the company has outstanding, the investor may give the entrepreneur a per-share price. It is relatively easy to translate valuations based on share prices into pre- and post-money company valuations, and vice versa. For example, if 6 million shares are outstanding, the company will need to issue 4 million shares at $0.50 per share for a venture capitalist to invest $2 million and end up owning 40% of the company.

If the percentage the investor wants to own after the deal closes is known, the following two equations can be used to calculate the number of shares that will need to be issued:

(1) Shares outstanding post-money

      = Shares outstanding pre-money divided by one minus the percentage to be owned by investor post-money

(2) Shares to be issued

      = Shares outstanding post-money minus shares outstanding pre-money

Accordingly, if 6 million shares are outstanding pre-money and the venture capitalist wants to end up owning 40% of the company, then 6 million divided by 60% (i.e., 1 minus 0.40) tells us that 10 million shares need to be outstanding after the offering. Therefore, the company will need to issue 4 million new shares.

Negotiating Price

Often there is some negotiation of price. A venture capitalist may ask what valuation the company is seeking or may volunteer a ballpark figure for pricing. Valuing a company is never easy. It is especially difficult with a startup that has little or no operating history. Venture capitalists will often base their valuations on management's own projections and on deals done in the industry by other companies. Obtaining information on comparable companies that have received venture financing can help the entrepreneur establish an appropriate valuation. Additional factors that influence valuation, especially in the early stages, include supply and demand (popular deals will often get done at higher valuations), the strength of the management team, the strength of the intellectual property assets, and existing user or revenue traction. Often, a company will seek a valuation that is determined by how much funding it needs in order to reach its next target milestone and be in a position to raise its next round of financing. It then extrapolates a valuation based on the dilution it is willing to bear (i.e., if a company needs $2 million and is willing to give investors 25% of the company in the financing, it implies an $8 million post-money valuation).

Effect of Shares Reserved for Employee Option Pool and Exercise of Convertible Notes

Most early-stage venture capital deals include an option pool reserve calculated as part of the pre-money valuation in an amount anywhere between 15% and 20%, depending on the company's anticipated near-term hiring needs. The entrepreneur should understand how the reservation of shares for future stock issuances to employees will affect the price per share paid by the venture capitalist and their resultant ownership stake. For example, if the venture capitalist's offer of $2 million is for 40% of the company's outstanding stock on a fully diluted basis and there are 1 million shares reserved for issuance upon exercise of employee options, then the reserved shares are added to the 6 million shares already outstanding when calculating the post-money valuation and thus the percentage owned by the investor after the deal closes. So in effect the investor is saying that there are 7 million shares outstanding or reserved (not 6 million). Therefore, under the formulas set forth above, the venture capitalist would be entitled to 4.667 million shares (not 4 million) for the $2 million investment. Applying the formulas:

$$11.667 \text{ million} = \frac{7 \text{ million}}{1 - 0.40}$$

$$4.667 \text{ million} = 11.667 \text{ million} - 7 \text{ million}$$

As a result, the investor will end up owning roughly 43.75% (not 40%) of the 10.667 million shares outstanding upon closing of the deal (4.667 million shares issued to investors divided by total of 10.667 million shares outstanding postclosing [6 million shares already outstanding plus 4.667 million new shares issued to investors]).

If this is not what the entrepreneur has in mind, the company should propose that the 1 million reserved shares not be taken into account in the valuation. If they are not, then the venture capitalist will be issued 4 million shares, as we calculated above. In that case, the holders of the 6 million old shares and the venture capitalist holding the 4 million new shares will jointly bear the dilution for the 1 million reserved shares in a ratio of 60/40, rather than having the holders of the 6 million old shares bear all of the dilution.

Similarly, certain investors may include shares issuable upon exercise of convertible notes in the calculation of outstanding shares. It may not seem fair to entrepreneurs that the venture capital investor will not bear any of the dilution for reserved shares to be issued in the future, but most early-stage venture capital deals are done on that basis at least for the shares in the employee option pool.

Choosing among Firms

When the entrepreneur is confident that an offer is about to be made, or immediately after an offer is made, he or she will want to inform the other potential venture capitalists and ask for offers from any that remain interested. Provided that they have had a chance to do some due diligence and to discuss the investment with their colleagues within the fund, other venture capitalists who are interested in the deal will generally put their valuation offers on the table fairly quickly once they know that a company has received an offer from another firm. These valuations may differ substantially, and the entrepreneur may attempt to use the higher offers to persuade others to pay a higher price or to obtain other favorable terms.

The venture capital firm willing to pay the highest price is not necessarily the firm that the entrepreneur should most want in the deal. Another venture capitalist who is not willing to pay quite as much may be a better partner in growing the business or in attracting investors for future rounds. Some firms are better than others at standing behind an entrepreneur who stumbles. The entrepreneur should undertake due diligence in the form of reference checks to determine who the best partners might be. Also, terms other than price can be critically important and can differ greatly from deal to deal (as further discussed below). Although many entrepreneurs are tempted to try to maximize the pre-money valuation when deciding on a venture capital firm, experienced entrepreneurs recognize that their goal is to maximize the valuation of their stake on exit and not necessarily the valuation in any particular round.

 From the **TRENCHES**

Dan Nova, a general partner at Highland Capital, had just finished negotiating a term sheet when the entrepreneur stood up and said, "I'm getting screwed but I guess I have no choice. I'll sign your term sheet." Nova immediately walked away from the deal, not wanting to begin a relationship with an entrepreneur who evidenced that degree of mistrust and acrimony.

An entrepreneur who has more than one offer should be pleased and should move quickly to choose the investors and finalize the deal. Indeed, if the entrepreneur is extremely comfortable with the venture capitalist with whom he or she has been primarily negotiating, the entrepreneur may decide not to shop the offer to other venture capitalists after reviewing the initial offer but instead simply proceed to a closing.

Although it may seem like a good idea to get multiple suitors into a room to negotiate the price, this approach should be resisted. Those offering the higher valuation have little incentive to talk the lower offerors into offering more, and the lower offerors may convince those willing to pay a higher price that they are paying too much.

The final price will depend on whom the entrepreneur wants to have in the deal, how much money needs to be raised, and the non-price terms. For tax purposes and reasons of fairness, shares are not sold to different investors in the same round for different prices.

Once the valuation is agreed upon, it is unusual to revisit the issue, unless there is a material adverse change in the business before the closing or material adverse information is discovered. Although most venture capitalists will not attempt to renegotiate the price absent those kinds of developments, there are always some who feel that all items are negotiable before the deal is closed. Being able to avoid these types of partners is another reason to do due diligence.

Even though the most important issue in these negotiations will be price, some of the most time-consuming and difficult negotiations may involve the other terms and conditions of the investment, many of which revolve around governance and control of the company after the deal closes. Any entrepreneur who thinks these so-called nonmonetary terms are best left to the lawyers because they will not affect the entrepreneur's own financial return is sorely misguided.

13.5 RIGHTS OF PREFERRED STOCK

While most new companies have just one type of stock—common stock—upon their formation, once a company receives a venture financing investment it will almost always have two types of stock: common stock and preferred stock. Common stock is typically held by the founders, employees, and sometimes service providers. It does not have any "bells and whistles" special features.

Preferred stock, on the other hand, is typically issued to investors in exchange for their investment in the company. As described in the remainder of this chapter, preferred stock can have special features that provide rights and protections to preferred holders. Each new round of investment typically constitutes a new series of preferred stock. Historically, the company's first round of preferred stock was called "Series A Preferred Stock," followed by Series B Preferred Stock, Series C Preferred Stock, and so on. Increasingly, companies are choosing to start with a "Series Seed Preferred Stock" (also called "Seed Series") round before the "A" round. The different series of preferred stock within a company are usually distinguished from each other by differences in the price and in the bells and whistles attached to each series.

Regarding price, both the entrepreneurs and the investors hope that the progression of the company causes the price of the preferred stock to increase each time a new series is offered, because that means the company is gaining value. In contrast to that situation, which is called an *up round*, if a preferred series is offered at the same price as the previous series, it is called a *flat round*. If the preferred series is offered at a lower price than the previous series, it is called a *down round*. Down rounds are viewed negatively because they indicate that the company is losing, not increasing in, value. In addition to an absolute reduction in an investor's equity, they may also lower public opinion of the company and perhaps even adversely affect the customer base for the company's product or service.

From the TRENCHES

A number of startups faced lower valuations in early 2016 than in previous years, raising the likelihood for down rounds. For example, Foursquare, an app proclaiming that it can "find the best places to eat, drink [and] shop," raised $45 million in a new round of financing in early 2016. Its valuation in the 2016 round was about half of the $650 million valuation for its $35 million round in 2013. Dropbox, a service that allows documents to be stored online and "shared and synchronized"

(continued)

among different computers and different users, has also seen a reduction in its valuation. In 2014, Dropbox was valued at $10 billion, but it was valued by at least one investor in early 2016 at half of that amount. It has not, however, had to raise money in a down round.

One reason cited for the lower valuations is that the startups may have "got[ten] ahead of themselves" and taken longer than originally anticipated to achieve their "towering expectations." In some cases, the startups may "grow into" their valuations over time without the need for a down round. In others, however, down rounds may be unavoidable given the company's need for additional cash to grow.

Sources: Farhad Manjoo, *Dropbox May Not Be LeBron James, But It is Still in the Game*, N.Y. Times (Feb. 3, 2016), http://www.nytimes.com/2016/02/04/technology/dropbox-may-not-be-lebron-james-but-it-is-still-in-the-game.html; Mike Isaac, *Foursquare Raises $45 Million, Cutting Its Valuation Nearly in Half*, N.Y. Times (Jan. 14, 2016), http://www.nytimes.com/2016/01/15/technology/foursquare-raises-45-million-cutting-its-valuation-nearly-in-half.html.

Regarding the bells and whistles, the degree of difference of the preferred stock's features from round to round will depend upon both the investor syndicate composition and the performance of the company. New investors joining the syndicate, a decline in the company's performance, or a change in market conditions all can lead to demands for more investor-favorable features in subsequent rounds of preferred stock. One of the chief reasons VCs seek special features on their preferred stock is for downside and sideways protection (both are discussed below).

As explained in Chapter 4, for tax reasons, most venture funds are precluded by their pension-fund and other tax-exempt limited partners from investing in a tax pass-through vehicle, such as an S corporation, a limited partnership, a general partnership, or a limited liability company. Therefore, when venture capitalists make an investment, it is almost always in preferred stock of a C corporation.

Most of the nonprice terms of the deal will relate to rights that attach to the preferred stock. These rights will be spelled out in the company's certificate of incorporation (or the certificate of determination of preferences for companies with authorized blank check preferred stock) and in one or more contracts.

Traditional preferred stock issued by large, publicly traded companies carries a preference on liquidation, pays a higher dividend than common stock, and is often set up to be redeemed on a certain date. It is usually not convertible into common stock, and it is often nonvoting. In many ways, it functions like subordinated debt.

Venture capital preferred stock is a very different beast. It does have a preference on liquidation. It also has a dividend preference but traditionally dividends are payable only if and when the directors declare them. Given the need to preserve cash, investors will not expect a startup to declare dividends. Venture capital preferred stock is convertible at any time at the election of the holder and automatically converts upon the occurrence of certain events. It votes on an as-if-converted-to-common basis and may have special voting rights with respect to the election of directors and certain other events. It may have a mandated redemption provision, requiring the company to buy back the stock at a set price on a given date in the future if the investor requests. Even if it does have a redemption provision, however, the ability of a startup company to make the redemption is often far from certain.

Downside and Sideways Protection

Over the years, a number of bells and whistles have been added to the preferred stock issued to venture capitalists. At first, these changes were made to differentiate it from the common stock and to bolster the argument that it has a higher value for tax purposes. As explained in Chapter 5, this distinction allows the common stock to be sold to the founders and employees at a much lower price than the preferred stock. Many features were later added to increase the rights and protections provided to the preferred investors in the event that the company ran into difficulty.

When negotiating the rights and privileges afforded the holders of preferred stock, entrepreneurs should keep in mind that if all goes well and the venture performs as projected, the venture capitalists will convert their preferred stock into common stock (upon an initial public offering or, in some cases, upon a successful sale of the company). Upon conversion, most of the bells and whistles go away. As a result, if the company is successful, all the protective devices will have had little or no effect on the return to the founders and the other holders of common stock. But, if the company declines in value or moves *sideways* (i.e., earns only a modest return on capital invested), then the venture capitalists will not convert their preferred stock and will rely on their rights and preferences to augment their return. Unfortunately for holders of common stock, this nonconversion reduces their share of the pie.

In a down market, such as existed following the burst of the dot-com bubble and again in 2008 and 2009, many investors tend to seek better protection against falling valuation. It is, however, still the case that new money sets the terms of each new round of investment. As a result, the new investor may require the investors who participated in earlier rounds to give up many of their protective provisions and preferences as a condition of the new investment.

Many seasoned venture capitalists will tell you that no investor has ever made any significant money from these downside or sideways protection features and will argue that they receive far too much attention in the negotiation of a venture deal. Under this line of reasoning (which an entrepreneur should embrace in the negotiations), once the valuation is set, the preferred stock needs to have only a liquidation preference and a dividend preference (but only if dividends are declared). The preferred stock should otherwise function as common stock so that all investors are on essentially the same terms going forward. By having all shareholders aligned in this manner (sometimes referred to as ensuring that the founders and VCs sit on the same side of the table), the entrepreneur and the outside investors will focus only on what will create value for the company rather than on special circumstances that may afford one or the other greater leverage or returns. If the preferred stock gets special rights and downside protection, the stock begins to look like debt rather than equity. If it functions like debt, the argument goes, it should have a fixed return (like a loan) rather than the unlimited upside of equity in a high-growth venture.

Other venture capitalists will argue that the special rights granted holders of the preferred stock are necessary because the investors are putting up most of the cash for the enterprise and will not be managing company affairs on a day-to-day basis. If there are difficulties down the road, the preferred investors may need to assert certain rights to protect their investment from mismanagement or abuse by the founders, who hold common stock.

This debate over which rights the preferred stock requires and whether these rights will create misalignment in the shareholders' incentives as the company goes forward often arises as the various terms of the investment are discussed and negotiated.

Entrepreneurs should bear in mind that most venture capitalists have completed far more venture investment deals than have the entrepreneurs with whom they negotiate. It helps to have an adviser who has seen dozens of these transactions from different perspectives. An entrepreneur should also be skeptical about any term that is described as "standard." What is "standard" for one venture fund may be unusual for another. If the investor cannot explain why the term is important to him or her in the context of the deal, then it should probably be changed.

Given that a new enterprise might likely need subsequent rounds of financing, the company, as well as the investors themselves, must also consider how the rights granted to first-round investors will affect negotiations with investors in subsequent rounds. It is highly unusual for investors in a subsequent round to accept fewer rights than were granted in a prior round. Therefore, many seasoned early-stage venture capitalists have a preference for providing only relatively modest protections and rights to the preferred stock. Otherwise they may soon find themselves bearing the burden of these special terms to the extent they set a precedent for future financings.

The next sections of this chapter review the typical rights sought by venture capitalists investing in preferred stock. The discussion begins with the simplest type of deal and then proceeds with an outline of the bells and whistles that may be added and the reasons raised for and against such additions.

Liquidation Preference

The *liquidation preference* provides that upon a liquidation or dissolution of the company, or upon any sale of the business or sale of substantially all of the company's assets, the preferred shareholders must be paid some amount of money before the common shareholders are paid anything. In the simplest case, the preference amount is equal to the amount initially paid for the stock. (More commonly, the liquidation preference amount is equal to the purchase price plus all accrued and unpaid dividends, as discussed in the next section.)

For example, if Series A Preferred is sold to the investors at a price of $0.50 per share, it will be given a liquidation preference of at least $0.50 per share. This means that if the preferred shareholders invested $2 million for 40% of the company, then the first $2 million to be distributed to shareholders will go to the preferred shareholders. The remainder will then go to the common shareholders. If the company is liquidated at a high enough price, then the amount the holders of the preferred would receive if they converted to common may be higher than the liquidation preference. In such a case, it would make sense for the holders of the preferred stock to convert to common stock immediately prior to the liquidation. For example, if the company is to be liquidated for $9 million, the preferred shareholders would be better off converting to common stock and abandoning their liquidation preference, because 40% of $9 million is $3.6 million, which is greater than the $2 million liquidation preference.

Dividend Preference and Cumulative Dividends

Typically, the preferred stock will earn a dividend at some modest rate (4% to 8% per annum), when and if declared by the board of directors of the company. In most cases, the venture capitalist does not expect the dividend to be declared; nevertheless, this provision bolsters the argument for tax purposes that the preferred stock is worth more than the common stock purchased by the founders at a lower price.

Often the liquidation preference will equal the original purchase price plus any accrued and unpaid dividends. If no dividends are declared, then adding accrued dividends to the liquidation preference will have no effect on the distribution of proceeds. In some deals, however, there will be a mandatory annual (or quarterly) dividend that, if not paid, will cumulate (a *cumulative dividend*). Usually, the sole purpose of this cumulation is to build up the liquidation preference over time so the preferred investors receive some rate of return on the investment ahead of the common shareholders if the company does not do well. If the company does well and the preferred stock converts to common stock (on a public offering or a sufficiently high-priced sale of the company if the preferred is nonparticipating), the cumulative dividend provision will generally have no impact on returns. Rather than having dividends cumulate (which may require an accounting footnote of explanation), the same objective is achieved by having the liquidation preference increase annually by some rate (often 4%, 6%, or 8% per annum but sometimes higher). This latter approach is rarely seen in practice.

The venture capitalist who seeks either a cumulative dividend or an increasing liquidation preference will argue that the hard-money investors are entitled to receive a preferential rate of return before the common shareholders are paid on their very cheaply priced common stock. In response, the legally astute entrepreneur may want to point out that this transaction is not a loan, which would represent a guaranteed senior rate of return and no other upside. Thus, the entrepreneur will argue, all the investors should be focused on what brings the greatest value for the company, rather than on creating a situation in which some investors may push to sell the company because a particular deal provides a better return on their series of stock than available alternatives. The entrepreneur should also explain that although the common stock may have been sold cheaply, it is as "hard dollar" as the preferred stock when the value of the "sweat equity" of the founding team is taken into account.

Participating Preferred

Another typical twist on the liquidation preference concept is called participating preferred. If an investor holds *participating preferred stock*, then after the preferred stock is paid its liquidation preference, it also receives its pro rata share of what remains as though the preferred stock had converted to common stock. If the preferred shareholder is not participating, all proceeds in excess of the liquidation preference would go to the common shareholders.

The investor's argument here is similar. If the founders have paid only pennies for their stock (as is typically the case) and the preferred investors have paid hard dollars, then there is a range of prices for the company at which the preferred stock would earn a small or even zero internal rate of return on the investment, while the common shareholders who paid little for their stock could earn huge internal rates of return.

For example, if the company is sold after five years for $8 million and the preferred stock converts into common stock to get its $3.2 million return (40% of $8 million) on its $2 million investment, then the venture capitalist's internal rate of return is only about 9.8%, which is a disappointment in a venture portfolio. The founder team, on the other hand, which may have paid less than $100,000 for its common stock, is able to split the remaining $4.8 million for a large return. So, the argument goes, the preferred shareholders should both receive their preference and be allowed to participate in the common stock share. Thus, with participating preferred, the investors would receive their original $2 million investment back (plus any cumulative dividends) and then would receive 40% of the remaining $6 million of sales proceeds, for a total payout of $4.4 million. The common shareholders would receive the $3.6 million remaining.

Founders can become quite emotional about this issue because the holders of common stock have invested not just their cash but also what may be years of sweat equity in building the company. The entrepreneur can argue that the preferred shareholder is trying to double dip and should either take its preference or convert into common. If the preferred shareholder is to participate, one could argue, then the founders should receive back pay at the market rate.

One compromise is to "cap" the participation right. Caps are often set at an amount equal to two to three times the preferred holders' original investment. For example, with a three-times cap, the preferred holders are entitled to receive their liquidation preference (including any accrued cumulative dividends) and to share the remaining proceeds pro rata with the common shareholders up to the point where they have received an aggregate of three times their original investment. If the preferred holders would be entitled to more than the capped amount if they converted into common, then they will forgo their liquidation preference and convert. In other words, if the company is a home run, then the holders of the preferred will convert it to common and share the sale proceeds on a pro rata basis with the common shareholders with no cap on

their upside return. But if the company is only moderately successful, the preferred investors will want both their liquidation preference *and* a share of the remaining proceeds.

As described above, one of the more effective arguments that
an entrepreneur can make to an early-stage investor requesting
participating preferred is that it creates a negative precedent.
If investors in future rounds also get fully participating preferred
stock, the early-stage investor may be nearly as impaired as the
entrepreneur sitting under the weight of a senior participating
preferred. As a result, many experienced early-stage investors
actually prefer not to have participating preferred and instead
opt for the more "plain vanilla" nonparticipating preferred.

The percentage of deals with participating preferred tends to
be higher in a challenging funding environment. For example,
59% of deals tracked by the law firm Cooley LLP had some degree
of participating preferred in 2009, the year of the "great reces-
sion," while only 26% of deals in 2014 had participating preferred
stock.

Rights of Subsequent Series

When a subsequent series of preferred stock is issued, the company will need to address whether one series will be paid before
the other in a liquidation or whether all series will be treated
equally (in legal terms, *pari passu*). The new money has the greatest negotiating leverage for being paid out first (otherwise it may
not invest), but to maintain good relations among preferred investors, to win the backing of the existing shareholders, and to set the
precedent for the next round, the new investors may consent to
having payouts to the preferred be *pari passu* among all series.

Redemption Rights

Some venture investors will ask for the right to force the company
to repurchase (i.e., *redeem*) its stock at some point in the future
(a *redemption right*, less commonly called a *put option*). The investors may argue that they are minority shareholders and need
some mechanism to ensure that they will have a way to exit from
the investment in the future. In asking for a redemption right, the

venture capitalists are concerned that if the company does not perform well enough to complete a public offering or consummate a sale at an attractive price, they may have no effective way to achieve any liquidity.

Although redemption requests seem reasonable on their face—and are sometimes granted—they can cause difficulties for companies both in raising future rounds of capital and in meeting redemption requirements. If a redemption right is granted, the next round of investors may be legitimately concerned that the money they are putting into the company may be used to redeem the earlier-round investors rather than to grow the company. Also, once a redemption right is granted, it is likely that future investors will want one as well.

The company can argue that no redemption rights should be given and that the investors should rely on the judgment of the board of directors on liquidity matters. The board will seek a liquidity opportunity for all investors but should not be forced into making a poorly timed decision because of a looming redemption deadline. Another strong argument against redemption rights is that they may turn out to be meaningless if the company lacks the cash to fulfill its obligations. Of course, a counterargument is that if they are so meaningless, then there is no harm in granting them.

Duration   If redemption rights must be granted, the entrepreneur will want to push them as far into the future as possible. Redemption rights that kick in only after seven years are not unusual. Similarly, the actual payment of the redemption price should be spread over two or three years to reduce the impact on the company's cash flow. The period in which the investors can actually request redemption should be limited so that the threat to cash flow is not an ongoing concern. Any redemption rights should terminate upon an initial public offering.

Redemption Price   The redemption price is another matter for negotiation. Often venture capitalists will want the stock to be redeemed at its liquidation preference plus any accumulated but unpaid dividends. If the sole purpose is to give the investors liquidity, however, an argument can be made that the redemption price should be based on the fair market value of the company's stock at the time of redemption (which may be less than the

From the **TRENCHES**

One San Francisco Bay area venture fund is particularly fond of redemption rights and insists on them in every deal. The fund does a fair amount of investing outside the technology industry, where it is less likely to run into companies with advisers who are familiar with typical venture deals. In one such deal, the venture capitalists requested a redemption right that kicked in after three years at a price equal to twice the initial investment. The venture capitalists explained that, without the redemption right, they would receive an internal rate of return of less than 25%, which would be deemed a poor investment in the venture industry. In addition, they argued that the company should be willing to honor their request because its own projections showed a much higher rate of return. The entrepreneurs responded that they had no doubt that the company was a good long-term investment but that they could not accurately predict every bump in the road toward success. The company could not take the risk of being caught in a cash-short position if the venture capitalists exercised the redemption right at an inopportune time. After much haggling, the parties agreed to a redemption right at any point after the seventh year for the then fair market value of the stock as determined by an appraiser.

investment plus unpaid dividends, but could also be significantly higher if the company is successful). If the company and the investors cannot agree on the fair market value, it may be determined by an appraisal process, which the entrepreneur will argue should apply appropriate discounts for any lack of liquidity of the stock and the lesser value of a minority interest. In practice, redemption rights most often provide for the redemption price to be set at the liquidation preference amount (often the original price paid by the investor), plus any accrued but unpaid dividends.

Conversion Rights

Venture capitalists usually are given both optional and automatic conversion rights.

Right to Convert   Holders of preferred stock in venture deals normally have the right to convert their preferred stock into common stock at any time. The ratio at which preferred stock is converted into common stock is typically determined by dividing the initial purchase price of the preferred stock by a number called the *conversion price*, which is adjusted upon certain events. Initially, the conversion price is equal to the purchase price of the preferred stock, so each share of preferred stock converts into one share of common stock.

Automatic Conversion The preferred stock is usually automatically converted into common stock upon certain events. Typically, these events are the vote of some specified percentage of the preferred stock or an initial public offering that meets certain criteria. The company would like the preferred stock to convert as soon as possible to eliminate its special rights and to clean up the balance sheet for the initial public offering.

Often an affirmative vote of a majority or a supermajority of the preferred stock is required to force an automatic conversion of all of the preferred stock. A high-threshold requirement makes it easier for a group of investors to block a conversion. The entrepreneur should favor a simple majority or as small a super-majority vote as possible and should resist giving one investor the right to block a conversion if the other investors believe a conversion would be in the company's best interest. Of course, if there are only a few investors, or if one investor holds a majority of the preferred stock, then it will be difficult to avoid having at least one investor whose vote will be required for a conversion.

The criteria for automatic conversion on an initial public offering generally include the following: (1) the offering must be firmly underwritten (i.e., the underwriters must have committed to placing the entire offering, rather than adopting the best-efforts approach common in penny stock offerings) and (2) the offering must raise a certain amount of money for the company. There is sometimes the additional requirement that the offering price exceed a certain minimum (e.g., three to four times the conversion price of the preferred stock).

Effect of Conversion on Rights Upon any conversion of the preferred stock, most of the rights associated with it (i.e., liquidation preference, dividend preference, antidilution protection, special voting rights, and redemption provisions) cease to exist. Some contractual rights, such as *registration rights* (the right to force the company to register the holder's stock), usually survive. Others, such as *information rights* (the right to certain ongoing financial information about the company) and *participation* or *preemptive* *rights* (the right to buy stock issued by the company in the future), will often terminate upon an initial public offering.

Antidilution Provisions

Antidilution provisions are designed to protect an investor's percentage ownership share in a company. There are several types.

Structural Antidilution   Any equity issuance to another person can be considered dilutive to existing shareholders because it reduces their percentage ownership stake. All shareholders are customarily entitled to protection against the dilution caused by certain types of issuances. For example, when common stock is issued as a stock dividend, a pro rata dividend is given to each common shareholder, not just to some of them.

Preferred stock is also customarily given antidilution protection against stock dividends, stock splits, reverse splits, and similar recapitalizations. The conversion price is adjusted to ensure that the number of shares of common stock issuable upon conversion of the preferred stock represents the same percentage of ownership (on a converted-to-common basis) as existed prior to the stock dividend, stock split, reverse split, or recapitalization. For example, when there is a five-to-one stock split, the conversion price is reduced to one-fifth of its prior amount. Thus, if the conversion price was $1.25 prior to the split, it will be $0.25 after the split. In this way, the number of shares of common stock issuable upon the conversion of the preferred stock increases proportionately with the effect of the split. Structural antidilution provisions are important for the common as well as the preferred shareholders.

 From the **TRENCHES**

Financial Performance Corp. issued warrants that entitled the investors to purchase 1,698,904 shares of common stock at a price of $0.10 per share. The company effected a five-to-one reverse stock split, thereby reducing the number of common shares outstanding to one-fifth of the original number outstanding. As a consequence, each shareholder owned one-fifth of the original number of shares with the value of each share increased fivefold. Because the company failed to include structural antidilution provisions in the warrant, the New York

(continued)

Court of Appeals ruled that the investors were entitled to exercise their warrants for the original number of shares at the original price. So, without changing the aggregate cost of exercising the warrant, the warrant became issuable for five times the percentage of the company originally contemplated, thereby distorting the ownership structure to the disadvantage of the shareholders who did not hold warrants. This could have been avoided by a properly drafted antidilution provision.

Source: Reiss v. Fin. Performance Corp., 764 N.E.2d 958 (N.Y. 2001).

Structural antidilution protection from stock dividends, stock splits, and reverse splits is the most basic kind of antidilution provision and is nearly always included in venture capital financings. When venture capitalists say they want protection against dilution, they may be referring to this basic type of protection, but they probably also have in mind some of the more complex provisions such as those discussed below.

Right of First Refusal and Participation and Preemptive Rights
Another type of antidilution provision is called a right of first refusal or a participation or preemptive right. A *right of first refusal, participation right,* or *preemptive right* entitles any shareholder to purchase its pro rata share in any subsequent issuance to ensure that the shareholder can maintain its percentage ownership. In venture deals, this type of provision, if adopted, is usually a contractual right that terminates upon an initial public offering. In its most extreme form, a participation or preemptive right can require the company to give the venture group a right of first refusal on all shares to be issued in subsequent offerings, not merely a right to acquire sufficient shares to maintain their pro rata ownership interest.

Although a pro rata participation right appears reasonable on its face, in many circumstances in which a company may want to issue shares, it would not make sense to require the company to first offer them to every current investor. For that reason, if this right is included, it usually exempts stock issued to employees, directors, consultants, strategic partners, those providing leases or loans to the company, and acquisition targets.

Waiting for a right-of-first-refusal time period to expire (or soliciting waivers of such rights) can be time-consuming and can delay or prevent the closing of a deal. An entrepreneur may want to avoid giving up the company's flexibility to choose to whom it sells stock in the future. For example, the company may want to bring in a new venture capitalist or corporate investor but may find that, due to the exercise of participation rights, there is not enough stock to meet the new investor's minimum investment criteria. Also, investors without participation rights who want to be invited to buy in future rounds have an incentive to remain on good terms with the company. Finally, a participation right, if exercised by a large shareholder, may force other investors either to buy into the offering or to risk losing control of the company.

Price-based Protection   One could argue that the two types of anti-dilution provisions discussed above (protection from stock splits and the like, and the right to participate in future offerings) should be sufficient protection for an investor. Nevertheless, most venture deals feature a third type of antidilution protection known as price-based protection. *Price-based protection* gives the venture capitalist a benefit if stock is issued in subsequent financing rounds at a lower share price than the investor paid.

The theory behind price-based protection is that the valuation of a company at the time venture capitalists purchase stock is open to debate, and the investors are entitled to a price adjustment if they overpaid. As it is impractical to give back a portion of the venture capitalists' money, the investors should be entitled to a large percentage of ownership of the company to make them whole.

Full Ratchet   The simplest form of price protection (although by no means the fairest) is called full-ratchet antidilution protection. If the venture capitalist has *full-ratchet antidilution protection*, then if any stock is sold at a lower price per share in a subsequent round, the ratio for converting the preferred stock into common stock is adjusted so that an investor in the higher-priced earlier round gets the same deal as it would have gotten had the purchase been made in a subsequent lower-priced round. The mechanics of the adjustment are straightforward: the conversion price of the prior round is reduced to the purchase price of the new round.

Consider this example. Acorn Enterprises issues Series A preferred stock based on a pre-money valuation of $9 million. The investors pay $3 million for a 25% ownership interest (resulting in a post-money valuation of $12 million). Assuming that there are 4.5 million shares of common stock outstanding, the Series A investors will purchase 1.5 million shares at $2.00 per share. The shares convert into common stock based on the original price, so $3 million of preferred stock at $2.00 per share will convert into 1.5 million shares of common stock. It is therefore said to initially convert on a one-to-one basis.

Business does not go according to plan. When Acorn tries to raise another $2 million, it finds that it can obtain a pre-money valuation of only $10 million. It may seem counterintuitive that the second round could have a valuation lower than the post-money valuation of the first round, but it does happen. Typically, this situation occurs when (1) the earlier round was overvalued, (2) external events dampen the prospects of the relevant industry, or (3) the business has not met the projections in its plan.

The second-round Series B venture capitalists buy their preferred stock at $1.67 per share (the $10 million pre-money valuation divided by the 6 million total shares already outstanding). At this valuation, the second-round investors will receive 1.2 million shares of Series B Preferred stock for the $2 million second-round investment. After the first and second rounds, the capitalization will be as set forth in Table 13.1.

The Series A venture capitalists will be none too pleased to have paid a higher price per share for their Series A stock than the Series B investors paid. If the Series A investors have

TABLE 13.1   Capitalization Table with No Antidilution Protection

	Number of Shares	Number of Shares Fully Diluted[a]	Percentage of Company
First Round			
Common	4.5 million	4.5 million	75.00%
Series A	1.5 million	1.5 million	25.00
Second Round (with no adjustment for dilution)			
Common	4.5 million	4.5 million	62.50%
Series A	1.5 million	1.5 million	20.00
Series B	1.2 million	1.2 million	16.67

a. The number of shares on a fully diluted basis refers to the number of shares of common stock that would be obtained upon conversion or exercise of all outstanding securities into common stock.

full-ratchet antidilution protection, their conversion price will be reset to the lower sale price of the Series B stock. The result will be as though the Series A investors made their purchase at the most recent price so the Series A investors will be able to convert the Series A stock they purchased for $3 million into 1.8 million shares of common stock. As a result of the lower-priced dilutive issuance, additional common stock will be issued to the Series A investors upon conversion of their preferred stock, and the capitalization will be as set forth in Table 13.2.

Full ratchet may appear simple and fair on its face, but it is rarely used for more than a brief period of time. It is widely viewed as unfair for three reasons. First, it pushes most of the dilution onto the common shareholders. Second, the Series B investors end up buying less of the company than they bargained for, which can push down their price even further and lead to more dilution and more adjustments. Third, and perhaps most unfairly, all of the Series A stock is repriced regardless of the size of the issuance of Series B stock.

Although the ratchet formula is used much less often than the weighted-average formula discussed next, a ratchet may be appropriate under some limited circumstances. For example, if a venture capitalist uncovers a fact in due diligence that suggests that a company is overvalued and may need a cash infusion sooner than was anticipated, then the company might agree to a ratchet for 6 or 12 months to give the investors some assurance that the company will not immediately need to conduct a subsequent financing at a lower price per share than they paid (a *down-round financing*). Similarly, if some foreseeable event may occur within the next year that will have a dramatic effect on valuation

TABLE 13.2	Capitalization Table with Full-Ratchet Protection		
	Number of Shares	**Number of Shares Fully Diluted**	**Percentage of Company**
Second Round (with full-ratchet protection)			
Common	4.5 million	4.5 million	60.00%
Series A	1.5 million	1.8 million	24.00
Series B	1.2 million	1.2 million	16.00

From the **TRENCHES**

Some argue that liquidation preferences, and similar investor protections such as full ratchet antidilution provisions, drive up valuations, particularly among companies desirous of the "unicorn" moniker awarded to companies valued at more than $1 billion. Many startups agree to give investors such rights to guarantee that they will receive a specific minimum amount in certain liquidation events, or receive additional share protection upon other events, making the investors more comfortable with a higher valuation. The rights come at a risk for the startups, however: "Higher valuations create higher expectations, and failure to meet them can set off a downward spiral and a forced sale." Other negative effects can materialize if, for example, more funding is required when market conditions are less favorable and the company's valuation is lower. Raising money in such a down round has been referred to as a "major Silicon Valley no-no in terms of perception." Others point out that certain liquidation preferences can "bolster the returns" of the venture capitalist firms by "as much as 10 times [a]ll at the expense of the founders."

One partner at a law firm indicated that the frequency with which such provisions are becoming part of the investment agreement may mean that there is "more risk and uncertainty in the market" and that valuations may be getting too high. If the so-called "unicorn bubble" pops, employees and founders will be adversely affected. Employees with common stock may see their investments drastically decreased as liquidation preferences and antidilutive provisions kick in, causing potential liability for boards of directors if they sell the company without carefully considering the impact on the common shareholders.

Sources: Steven Davidoff Solomon, *Expect Some Unicorns to Lose Their Horns, And It Won't Be Pretty*, N.Y. TIMES DEALBOOK (Jan. 19, 2016), http://www.nytimes.com/2016/01/20/business /dealbook/expect-some-unicorns-to-lose-their-horns-and-it-wont-be-pretty.html; Sarah Frier & Eric Newcomer, *The Fuzzy, Insane Math That's Creating So Many Billion-Dollar Tech Companies*, BLOOMBERGBUSINESS (Mar. 17, 2015), http://www.bloomberg.com/news/articles/2015-03-17/the-fuzzy -insane-math-that-s-creating-so-many-billion-dollar-tech-companies; Steven Davidoff Solomon, *The Risk of a Billion-Dollar Valuation in Silicon Valley*, N.Y. TIMES DEALBOOK (Sept. 22, 2015), http:// www.nytimes.com/2015/09/23/business/dealbook/the-risk-of-a-billion-dollar-valuation-in-silicon -valley.html?_r=0.

(such as the issuance of a patent), the venture capitalists may seek a ratchet as protection in case the event does not occur and more money must be raised at a lower valuation. Also, investors in a mezzanine round might be concerned that a down-round financing will be necessary if the public market window closes. They too might seek a ratchet for a limited period. In such cases, when the ratchet period expires, the weighted-average method would typically apply.

Weighted Average   Today, the vast majority of venture deals use a weighted-average antidilution formula, which attempts to calibrate the repricing based on the size and price of the dilutive round. *Weighted-average antidilution* sets the new conversion price of the outstanding preferred stock as the product of (a) the old conversion price multiplied by (b) a fraction in which (1) the numerator is the sum of (x) the number of shares outstanding before the issuance plus (y) the quotient of the amount of money invested in this round divided by the old conversion price and (2) the denominator is the sum of (x) the shares outstanding before the issuance plus (y) the shares issued in this round. Algebraically, where *NCP* is the new conversion price, *OCP* is the old conversion price, *OB* is the number of shares outstanding before the issuance, *MI* is the amount of money invested in the current round, and *SI* is the number of shares issued in the current round. The weighted-average formula adjusts the conversion price based on the relative amount of the company that is being sold at the lower price.

$$NCP = OCP \times \frac{OB + \dfrac{MI}{OCP}}{OB + SI}$$

Applying this formula to the example above, the new conversion price is calculated as follows:

$$NCP = 2.00 \times \frac{6 \text{ million} + \dfrac{2 \text{ million}}{2.00}}{6 \text{ million} + 1.2 \text{ million}}$$

$$NCP = \$1.944$$

Under weighted-average antidilution, the capitalization table for the example given earlier would be as set forth in Table 13.3. No longer does the Series A stock convert on a one-to-one basis; each share of Series A stock now converts into 1.029 shares of common ($2.00/1.944) based on the new conversion price.

The weighted-average formula is fairly standard in venture capital financings, but there are some variations. The most common variation involves how options are counted—whether as issued or unissued common stock. Although counting the options adds the same amount to both the denominator and the numerator in the weighted-average formula, including them broadens the

TABLE 13.3	Capitalization Table with Weighted-Average Protection		
	Number of Shares	Number of Shares Fully Diluted	Percentage of Company
Second Round (with weighted-average protection)			
Common	4,500,000	4,500,000	62.13%
Series A	1,500,000	1,542,860	21.30
Series B	1,200,000	1,200,000	16.57

base so that it absorbs more dilution and keeps the conversion price from falling as quickly. Often shares reserved for options already granted are counted, but those reserved for future grants are not. This issue is a minor negotiating point, however, as it tends to have a negligible effect unless the option pool is unusually large.

Carve-Outs   Certain issuances will often be *carved out* from the price-based antidilution provisions. These often mirror those exempted from the participation rights discussed earlier in this chapter. For example, companies usually anticipate hiring additional members of the management team and offering them stock options with an exercise price below the price per share paid by the investors for their preferred stock. Over time, other members of management may need to have their incentives refreshed with additional stock options (especially following dilutive venture rounds). For this reason, options to be granted under stock option plans and other equity arrangements with employees are generally excluded from the price-based formula. Occasionally, there is a cap on the aggregate amount of stock that a board can allocate under this carve-out (typically between 10% and 30% of the stock for equity incentive programs) without obtaining the approval of the investors. Similarly, any outstanding rights to purchase shares at a lower price granted prior to the issuance of the preferred stock are usually excluded, as are shares of common stock issued upon conversion of preferred stock into common stock.

Pay to Play   Some venture capitalists and entrepreneurs like to add a *pay-to-play provision*, whereby holders of preferred stock lose the benefit of price-based antidilution if they fail to buy their pro rata share of any subsequent down round. An investor who does not participate at least pro rata in a down round would automatically convert into a different series of preferred stock that is identical to the original series in all respects except that it receives no price-based antidilution protection, or, in some more punitive versions of the provision, the investor's preferred stock would convert into common. Pay-to-play provisions are intended to encourage all investors to step up and help the company in difficult times and to penalize those that do not; therefore, entrepreneurs generally support them, as do some venture capitalists who are concerned about the reliability of their co-investors. In practice, pay-to-play provisions are relatively uncommon, having been used in less than 4% of 540 venture financings completed by Cooley LLP in 2014.

Voting Rights

The preferred stock issued to a venture capital investor votes on most matters on an as-converted-to-common basis (i.e., one vote for each common share into which the preferred can be converted). On most matters, the preferred and common shareholders vote together as one class.

Protective Provisions There may be certain actions for which the company must obtain approval from the holders of preferred stock voting as a separate class, even if the preferred stock represents a minority of the outstanding shares. The required vote is usually a majority, but sometimes a larger percentage of votes in favor is required to make it easier for a particular investor or group of investors to block an action. There is often a prohibition on the issuance of any security senior to (or even on a par with) the existing preferred stock, as well as provisions prohibiting adverse changes in the liquidation preference, dividend rights, conversion rights, voting rights, or redemption rights of the preferred shareholders without their consent (even though all of these rights might be considered to fall within the general corporate law restriction on adverse change to the preferred shareholders).

Another common protective provision requires approval of the preferred shareholders before the company can redeem stock, other than redemptions provided for in the certificate of incorporation and repurchases from departed employees, consultants, and directors pursuant to the contractual arrangements made when they bought their stock. Sale of the company and any increase in the authorized number of shares of stock may also require approval. If there is an agreement on how the board is to be elected, changes in the number of directors or the designation of who elects a stated number of directors may also require approval by the preferred shareholders.

Certain preferred investors may try to expand the number of items requiring their approval to include the types of matters often found in bank loan covenants, such as investing in or acquiring any other enterprise; establishing subsidiaries; incurring certain levels of indebtedness; making loans to others; and exceeding certain levels for capital expenditures. Generally, the company should vigorously resist such provisions. Rather than delaying such matters by requiring a shareholder vote, the investors should rely on the company's board of directors to do what is prudent.

When investors control a larger percentage of a particular series of preferred stock than of the preferred stock as a whole, they may want these protective provisions to require the separate approvals of holders of a majority of their series of preferred stock. Avoiding a series vote is generally in the company's best interest because doing so will give the company greater flexibility and lessen the likelihood that any single investor will have blocking power. Even if certain investors end up with blocking power, the fewer who have this power, the better it is for the company.

Board Elections   As discussed in Chapter 6, the board of directors is charged with overseeing the management of the company's business affairs. The board appoints the officers to carry out board policies and handle day-to-day operations. In America's version of shareholder democracy, as reflected in the corporation laws of the 50 states, the shareholders elect the board to run the company. At the same time, the shareholders are permitted to vote on a limited number of matters (e.g., amendments to the certificate of incorporation, decisions about selling the business, certain merger transactions, and dissolution). Control of the company is exercised by the persons with the power to elect the board of directors and by the directors themselves. Because the board has the power to select and remove corporate officers, including founders, composition of the board is a key corporate governance issue for entrepreneurs.

Generally, the lead venture capitalist in a round will expect a board seat. At the time of the first venture round, the founders will often retain a majority of the company's equity and be permitted to elect a majority of the board. If the round involves only one venture fund, it is not unusual for it to request two board seats. Sometimes other participating venture capitalists will also want a board seat. As the number of venture investors increases over time, the board can become too large and may quickly become dominated by financial investors.

Usually, the founders and the investors will enter into a voting agreement or will designate in the certificate of incorporation that the holders of a certain number of seats are to be elected by the common shareholders (or by the founders), that another number of seats are to be elected by the preferred shareholders, and that the balance is to be elected by all shareholders together. Control of the board is likely to shift over time as subsequent financings occur.

The founders may wish to establish from the outset that they want to be able to look to the board as a repository of business experience and advice. To this end, the founder group may decide to limit itself to just one or two founders on the board, with one or two seats reserved for venture investors and one or two seats reserved for industry leaders who are respected by the venture capitalists and the founders, and are often independent from each group. With this type of board composition, no one group controls the board, and the board can focus on the best interest of the company rather than the best interest of any particular group. (Chapter 6 discussed board composition issues in more detail.)

Milestones

Sometimes venture capitalists will require the company to achieve certain goals (*milestones*) within a specified time. These milestones

From the **TRENCHES**

There is a big difference between agreeing that specific directors will be elected by the holders of common stock and agreeing that specific directors will be elected by the founders. Investors at one venture-backed company were feuding with the founders about the direction of the company, including the role of certain members of senior management. The certificate of incorporation and the voting agreement each called for the election of a director by the holders of common stock. The investors held a significant majority of the company, but they did not hold any common stock. Because the director was to be elected by the holders of the common stock (rather than by the founders), the investors were able to convert some of their preferred stock into common stock and elect a candidate of their choice to the board seat. The founders were surprised, as they believed the investors would not be willing to give up their liquidation preference or the various other protections and rights afforded by their preferred stock in order to gain control of the board.

might include reaching certain stages in product development or attaining certain levels of sales or profitability. Milestones arguably protect the venture capitalist from overvaluing the company to a greater degree than price-based antidilution provisions. Sometimes the achievement of milestones will trigger an obligation by the venture capitalist to make a follow-on investment in the company at a previously determined price per share. In some cases, if the company fails to meet the milestones, the conversion price of the venture capitalist's preferred stock may be adjusted downward, thereby increasing the venture capitalist's ownership of the company. In unusual circumstances, an investor may suggest that control of the board should shift to the investors if the management team fails to achieve the milestones.

The company should resist any milestones that would result in a change of control. Business is filled with risks, and the unexpected can occur. When that happens, the company will have enough to worry about without the added distraction of dealing with different groups trying to use the company's difficulty to their own advantage. Although milestones associated with subsequent rounds of investment are not quite as onerous, they too may cause misalignment of incentives among shareholders. For example, certain investors may want the company to fall short so that they will be relieved of a further investment obligation (or, more likely, be in a position to purchase stock more cheaply or renegotiate the deal). Similarly, milestones that trigger ownership adjustments put the venture capitalist and the founders on different sides of the table, which is not conducive to a healthy business partnership. Also, failed milestones create a track record of failure by the company's management, which could negatively impact future financing efforts. Finally, milestones of any kind in a deal may distort the behavior of the entrepreneur, who may focus too much on the milestone and not enough on actions or expenditures that might otherwise be in the best interest of the business. For these reasons, many venture capitalists avoid using milestones.

Registration Rights

Entrepreneurs and VCs and their lawyers will devote a fair amount of discussion to the subject of registration rights. A *registration right* is the right to force the company to register the holder's stock with the Securities and Exchange Commission (*SEC*) so that it can be sold in the public markets. This is one way that venture capital investors seek to ensure that they will eventually be able to exit their position as a shareholder in a private company and obtain cash for their investment.

It is not always easy for venture capitalists to sell their shares, even if a company does go public. Often when a company goes public, the underwriters are unwilling to permit existing shareholders to sell in the initial public offering, as such sales can adversely affect the marketing of the stock being sold by the company to raise capital. The ability of shareholders to sell their stock without registering the transaction depends on whether they are an affiliate of the company. An *affiliate* is an officer, director, or owner of more than 5% to 10% of the outstanding shares. Because venture capitalists are often directors of their portfolio companies and often own more than 10% of the outstanding shares, they are almost always affiliates. If an affiliate of the company has held unregistered stock for more than six months and the company is public at the time the shareholder wants to sell, then the holder is generally permitted to sell a limited amount of stock (up to the greater of 1% of the outstanding stock of that class or the average weekly trading volume in the preceding four weeks) in any three-month period under SEC Rule 144. Affiliates must also comply with Rule 144's information and manner of sale requirements. If the selling shareholder is not an affiliate of the company (and has not been an affiliate for the three prior months), then it can freely resell any shares that it has owned for at least six months if the company is public; if the company is privately held, then the nonaffiliate must have held the shares for at least one year. In either case, the nonaffiliate can resell without regard to volume or manner of sale requirements in Rule 144. If the holder is an affiliate or has held the shares for less than the applicable period, but cannot meet the requirements of Rule 144 (e.g., because the company is a private company and so does not meet Rule 144's public information requirements), then it may need to register the shares to exit from the investment. Similarly, if the shareholder has not held the shares for the applicable period or wishes to sell more than is permitted by Rule 144, then registration may be required.

Types of Registration Rights   Venture investors are likely to request three types of registration rights: demand rights, S-3 rights, and piggyback rights.

Demand Right   A *demand right* is a right to demand that the company file a registration statement on SEC Form S-1 to sell the holder's stock. The company uses this form for an initial public offering; it requires a prospectus with extensive information about the company and the offering. (We discuss initial public offerings in detail in Chapter 17.) A company generally will want to limit this right, as it can be expensive and time-consuming. It can also adversely affect the company's own capital-raising plans. Generally, the investor group will receive only one or two demand rights, with limits on when they can be exercised.

Entrepreneurs should especially resist granting demand rights that can be used to force the company to go public. The argument is that if the board has determined that the company is not yet ready, its management team should not be forced to find underwriters, do the road show required for the offering, and try to make the offering successful. (As we discuss in Chapter 17, during the *road show*, the company's managers and investment bankers travel around the country and make presentations to potential investors.) The investors may seek such a demand registration right, arguing that an initial public offering may be their only path to liquidity, especially if the founders are content with the lifestyle afforded by running a successful private company.

S-3 Right An *S-3 right* allows the investor to force the company to register the investor's stock on Form S-3. This form is part of a simpler procedure that can be used by most companies that have been public for at least 12 months with a *public float* (market value of securities held by nonaffiliates) of at least $75 million. Form S-3 permits the registration statement to incorporate by reference information already on file with the SEC, so the preparation of the registration statement is simpler, less time-consuming, and cheaper than the preparation of a Form S-1 registration statement. The S-3 rights granted to venture capitalists tend to be unlimited in quantity, but they are available only once or twice per year and may expire at some point.

Piggyback Right A *piggyback right* is the right to participate in an offering initiated by the company. Piggyback rights are generally subject to cutback or elimination by the offering's underwriter if the underwriter determines, based on market conditions, that a sale by shareholders will adversely affect the company's capital-raising effort. The venture capitalist will seek rights that may not be completely cut back except in connection with the company's initial public offering. Piggyback rights granted to venture capitalists are generally unlimited in number but often expire three to five years after the company's initial public offering or after the venture investors have sold a certain percentage of their shares. Unless the rights expire, the company must notify all holders of the rights every time the company has a public offering and the rights might require the company to include a portion of the holders' shares in the offering.

Information and Visitation Rights

Holders of significant blocks of preferred stock may be granted the rights to receive certain information, such as monthly financial statements, annual audited financial statements, and the annual budget approved by the board. Information rights should expire upon an initial public offering, when the investors will be able to rely on SEC filings. In addition, with an increasing number of strategic investors participating in traditional venture capital transactions, many companies also seek to exclude potential investors that are competitors of the company from receiving information rights.

Some investors may seek more expanded rights, such as (1) the right to review the company's auditor's letter to management concerning the audit of the financial statements and any weaknesses in internal controls and (2) to make on-site inspections and inquiries of officers or employees and to observe board meetings (*visitation rights*). Generally, these additional rights should be resisted or limited to only those investors with very large stakes in the company. They can be disruptive to the company's operations and conflict with the board's performance of its duties. Investors who maintain good relations with the company will be able to obtain sufficient information to monitor their investment without placing undue burdens on the startup company.

Rights of First Refusal and Co-Sale Rights

Venture capitalists often ask the founders to give them rights of first refusal and co-sale rights. A *right of first refusal* gives the investors the right to buy shares that the founders propose to sell to a third party, other than transfers for estate planning purposes. A right of first refusal allows the investors to increase their stake if the founders want to sell and gives them the power to prevent the introduction of a new investor into the company.

A *co-sale right* (sometimes called a *tag-along right*) gives the investors a contractual right to sell some of their stock alongside a founder if the founder actually sells stock to a third party. Mechanically, a co-sale right usually gives the investor the right to replace a portion of the stock the founder planned to sell with the investor's stock or to require the founder to use a portion of the proceeds of the founder's sale to purchase shares from the investor. A co-sale right thus protects the investors from a situation in which the founder transfers control of the company by selling his or her stock to another person. In such a circumstance, the investor is looking for the opportunity to consider exiting as well. Founders may insist on exceptions to co-sale rights to permit a

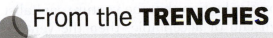

From the **TRENCHES**

One venture fund learned the hard way the merits of a co-sale right. The fund led a $2 million financing of a company that distributed toys and video games. The key founder had successfully resisted any effort to subject his shares to vesting. He argued that the company was more than two and a half years old and that he had already earned his shares. He also persuaded the venture capitalist that it was fundamentally unfair to put restrictions on his right to transfer his shares. As a result, his shares were fully vested and freely transferable. He also argued successfully that a co-sale right was not needed, because he had no reason to transfer his shares: the shares represented most of his net worth and the company could not succeed without him. Within 12 months of the closing, the entrepreneur transferred his shares to a competitor for more than $1 million and left the company. The company was unable to compete effectively without the entrepreneur, particularly given the large stake owned by the competitor, and the venture capitalist's investment became virtually worthless.

sale of a small amount of their stock for liquidity purposes (e.g., for estate planning purposes, to make a down payment on a house, or to pay college tuition) as well as carve-outs for dispositions upon death or upon termination of employment.

Drag-Along Rights

Many investors will request *drag-along rights*, which give the investors the right to force shareholders, including the founders, to sell their shares on the same terms and conditions on which the board of directors and a specified percentage of the investors have decided to sell their shares. Founders should vigorously resist granting drag-along rights or at least try to require their approval of the transaction before a drag-along right would apply or to provide that the rights not be exercisable for a substantial period of time or both. Otherwise, the founders may be forced to sell their shares before they have had a reasonable period of time to grow the company into a successful enterprise.

Relationship between Price and Rights of the Preferred Stock

Experienced venture capitalists are acutely aware of the economic value of the rights and preferences of the stock they agree to buy.

If an entrepreneur insists on a valuation that the venture capitalist considers to be at the high end of acceptable, then the venture capitalist may agree to the price but insist on tough terms, such as board control, participating preferred with no cap, cumulative dividends, mandatory redemption rights exercisable at an early date, and full-ratchet price protection. Although these rights may have little effect if the company does very well, they can dramatically reduce the amount payable to the holders of common stock when the company is only a modest success. Legally astute entrepreneurs understand the very real financial implications of these so-called nonprice provisions.

13.6 OTHER PROTECTIVE ARRANGEMENTS

Other protective arrangements include subjecting the founders' shares to vesting, reserving shares for employee stock options, and no-shop provisions.

Founder Vesting

Venture capitalists will usually insist that the founders subject some or all of their stock, and all the common stock to be sold to employees, to a vesting schedule if they have not already done so. As explained in Chapter 5, the vesting schedule is usually four years, with cliff vesting for the first year and then monthly or quarterly vesting for the next three years. The company typically has the right to repurchase the founder's unvested shares at cost if the founder leaves the company. If the vesting schedule is not put in place until the venture round closes, the founders may want to commence the vesting period on an earlier date, such as the day the founders first acquired stock or began working on the project. Investors do not always agree to this, which is the reason many founders voluntarily subject their shares to vesting at the time of the company's formation.

Founders may try to protect themselves from arbitrary termination by requesting that vesting be accelerated in the event the founder is terminated without cause or quits for a good reason (such as a substantial diminution of responsibilities). Most

From the **TRENCHES**

A potential venture investor in a medical device company asked that the founders, who had no vesting on their shares, agree to four-year vesting. The founders balked, pointing out that they had transferred their technology to the company and, once the venture round closed, could lose everything if they were fired by the board. As an alternative, the founders proposed that they receive a royalty from the company for their technology, with the royalty rate to decline ratably as the shares became vested. The venture capitalist accepted this compromise.

venture capitalists will resist granting acceleration, arguing that if the board determines that the founder should be replaced, then the company will need the unvested shares to help attract a replacement. If the founder is an experienced entrepreneur whose services are in high demand, however, the investors may agree to some acceleration. In those cases, it becomes very important to ensure that the definitions of termination "for cause" and of quitting "for good reason" are crafted carefully. Sometimes, vesting may be accelerated in the event of a change of control or, more commonly, upon a termination without cause within a limited period following a change of control.

83(b) Elections Employees who purchase stock subject to repurchase should file a Section 83(b) election with the Internal Revenue Service (*IRS*). As explained in Chapter 5, a *Section 83(b) election* allows the stock to be taxed at the time it is acquired (when there is no tax, assuming the employee paid fair market value) rather than on the date it becomes fully vested (when the stock may have increased dramatically in value over the original purchase price). The 83(b) election must be filed within 30 days of the purchase. It is extremely important that the election be filed on time; a missed or late filing can result in a very large tax bill for the employee at a time when the stock is not liquid. The IRS recently clarified that placing a repurchase restriction on shares at the time of a financing would not give rise to taxation as the shares vest, but founders should consult with their counsel at the time the vesting restriction is imposed to determine whether an 83(b) election is required.

Creation of Employee Stock Option Pools

As discussed in Chapter 5, at the earliest stages of a company's existence, founders typically receive common stock rather than options. Soon thereafter, many companies set up stock option plans as additional equity incentives for employees. Chapter 5 addressed various aspects of employee option plans.

When calculating the valuation of the company, venture investors will often want to reserve a certain percentage of the company for future equity incentives to new and existing employees. If the company does not have sufficient shares in its option plan to cover the amount to be granted over a 12- to 24-month period, the investor will ask the company to increase the size of the pool prior to the financing. As explained earlier in this chapter, calculating a pool increase as part of the pre-financing capitalization of the company reduces the price per share paid by the investors. Therefore, venture-backed companies generally reserve somewhere between 10% and 30% of the stock (measured on a postfinancing basis) for this purpose, depending on anticipated hiring needs. The number of shares in a company's option plan is typically reevaluated and re-adjusted at each round of venture financing. As discussed in Chapter 5, options generally vest over three, four, or five years (although credit is sometimes given in the initial grant for prior service to the company).

No-Shop Provisions

Many venture investors will want the founders to agree to a *no-shop provision*, whereby they agree not to negotiate with any other investors for a period of time following the signing of the term sheet. Their logic is that they do not want to go through the time and expense of performing detailed due diligence on the company and hiring counsel to review and negotiate the specific deal documents, unless they believe that the founders are committed to doing a deal on the terms set forth in the term sheet. The venture investors do not want to get close to completion of the deal only to have the founders tell them that they have identified another venture firm that is willing to invest at a slightly higher valuation, leaving the initial investors with the choice to either raise their price or lose the deal. An agreement by the company to "take itself off the market" evidences a commitment to do the deal outlined in the term sheet.

Just as it is important for entrepreneurs to assess whether a prospective venture capital investor would be a good business partner, the entrepreneurs should demonstrate to the investors that they will be good business partners as well. Even if the entrepreneurs are not contractually prohibited from shopping the deal, continuing to negotiate potential deals with other investors after agreeing to a term sheet is a bad idea. It will reflect poorly on the entrepreneurs, not only with the investor who agreed to the term sheet but even with the other investors, who are left to wonder whether they can trust the entrepreneurs to honor their future commitments.

 Putting It into **PRACTICE**

Recognizing that Genesist, Inc. required additional equity capital to grow, Alexei and Piper met with attorney Sarah Crawford to discuss venture capital funding. The company had successfully validated the technology and filed a preliminary patent application, but it needed to purchase a license for aspects of its manufacturing process, continue to test various resins, and try different manufacturing configurations before filing its final patent applications. Alexei and Piper figured that Genesist was worth about $2.4 million and would need only about $800,000 in an initial round. This would result in 25% ownership by the venture capitalists. Sarah suggested bumping that figure up to $1,000,000 to reflect unanticipated delays and expenses and to allow a venture capitalist to buy nearly 30% (29.67%) of the company. Alexei and Piper agreed, particularly in light of their earlier miscalculation of cash needs. Also, they hoped that some of the extra money could be used to buy out Bart Cooperman, who had become dissatisfied with his $50,000 investment during Genesist's earlier financial crisis. Sarah liked this idea, because it meant that the new investors would be able to purchase Series A Preferred stock rather than a Series B, thus simplifying the capital structure.

(continued)

Alexei and Piper had already prepared a pitch deck for Sarah's review. They worked with Aaron Biegert to pull together all of the company's material agreements and information on its technology, so that once an investor was selected, the investor could proceed quickly with its due diligence investigation.

Sarah suggested approaching Palm Drive Equity Partners, a venture capital group looking for opportunities in the 3D printing and manufacturing industry, which she thought would be a good investor. Sarah told Alexei and Piper that she was obligated to disclose that her firm had represented Palm Drive in the past and would continue to do so in the future. She said that she personally had not represented Palm Drive in any venture capital financings and assured Alexei and Piper that her firm would not represent Palm Drive in any business relating to Genesist. Sarah told Alexei and Piper that she would understand, however, if they wanted to seek other representation for the transaction. After discussing it privately, the founders indicated that they were comfortable with Sarah continuing to represent Genesist, and they asked Sarah to contact Palm Drive on their behalf.

Sarah set up an initial meeting between Alexei and Piper and one of Palm Drive's managing partners who had relevant operating experience in the 3D printing and manufacturing industry. That meeting went well, and Alexei used the opportunity to discuss his thoughts on valuation and to sound out Palm Drive on such issues as its vision for the company, its willingness and ability to step up for other rounds, its assessment of the company's weaknesses, and its ability to assist the company in addressing those weaknesses. Alexei and Piper also performed their own due diligence investigation of Palm Drive, keeping in mind that Palm Drive was not just a source of needed capital but was about to become their partner in one of the most important undertakings of their lives.

After several more successful meetings, including breakfasts with all three Palm Drive general partners, Palm Drive agreed to invest in Genesist, pending a satisfactory due diligence review. Alexei, along with Sarah and Aaron, then met with a partner of Palm Drive and its counsel to hammer out a term sheet.

After much negotiation, the two parties agreed on a term sheet that reflected the $2.4 million pre-money valuation that Alexei was seeking. (A sample venture capital term sheet is set forth in "Getting It in Writing" at the end of this chapter.) Palm Drive agreed to use $50,000 of its investment to purchase Bart Cooperman's convertible note, which would then be converted into the new Series A Preferred Stock to be issued by

(continued)

Genesist, at a price per share reflecting the 20% discount to the Series A price per share.

Prior to the meeting, Sarah had suggested to Alexei that they might negotiate a provision that would allow Genesist, with Palm Drive's permission, to bring in another venture firm for up to $300,000 of the $1,000,000 financing. She had said that he might want to talk to a few other firms and to select one to be another voice in the investor group. Alexei had responded that he and Piper were comfortable with Palm Drive being the only investor because of the rapport they had established with the Palm Drive partners. Sarah pointed out that other venture funds could still be part of the next round.

During negotiations with Palm Drive, all parties agreed that the board would consist of five directors. The voting agreement specified that the holders of the Series A Preferred Stock, voting as a class, would elect two directors. The current holders of the common stock (Alexei, Piper, and Empire State Fabrication Inc. (*ESF*)) would also elect two directors, one of whom would be Alexei. The second management director was to be chosen by a vote of the common shareholders. The fifth seat was to be filled by an independent director, preferably someone with significant experience in the 3D printing and manufacturing industry. The voting agreement specified that the fifth director had to be approved by a majority of both the common and the preferred shareholders, with each class holding a veto.

Alexei instructed Sarah to draft and circulate documents for closing the transaction. Although the attorneys for Palm Drive, Sarah, and the principals were able to reach agreement on the documents within three weeks, Palm Drive did not complete its due diligence until a month after the principals had agreed to the term sheet. As no problems were found, Palm Drive proceeded to invest $1,000,000. Table 13.4 shows Genesist's capitalization table as of the closing date.

After the Genesist board members were elected, Alexei and Piper began to work closely with Palm Drive's two designated board representatives to make sure they were kept in the loop on activities at the company. Alexei planned to brief Palm Drive's representatives prior to board meetings so that board discussions could be as productive as possible and surprises could be kept to a minimum. Palm Drive would play a critical role in helping the company raise money in subsequent rounds, and Alexei's and Piper's relationship with the Palm Drive board representatives was central to the success of their partnership.

After using a portion of the proceeds from the Series A round to acquire a favorable license for certain aspects of Genesist's manufacturing process, Alexei and Piper next turned to issues surrounding the protection and exploitation of Genesist's intellectual property.

(continued)

TABLE 13.4	Genesist, Inc. Capitalization Table					
	Genesist, Inc. Series A Capitalization Table					
Shareholder Name	Common Stock	Option Pool Increase	Series A (Note Conversion)	Series A (Cash)	Total Outstanding Shares Fully Diluted	Percentage Ownership Fully Diluted
Alexei Perlitz	500,000				500,000	24.67%
Piper Mao	350,000				350,000	17.27
ESF	150,000				150,000	7.40
Investors						
Palm Drive Equity Partners			37,118	564,193	601,311	29.67
Option Pool						
Allocated (two directors)	20,000				20,000	0.99
Unallocated	80,000	325,328			405,328	20.00
Total	**1,100,000**	**325,328**	**37,118**	**564,193**	**2,026,639**	**100.00**

Getting It in **WRITING**

SAMPLE VENTURE CAPITAL TERM SHEET

Genesist, Inc.
Sale of Series A Preferred Stock
Nonbinding Summary of Terms

Issuer:	Genesist, Inc. (the "Company").
Amount of Financing:	An aggregate of $1,000,000. Following the investment, the Series A Preferred will represent 29.67% of the fully diluted shares of the Company, including shares reserved for the employee option pool as set forth below.
Type of Security:	601,311 shares of Series A Convertible Preferred stock (the "Series A Preferred"), initially convertible into an equal number of shares of the Company's Common Stock (the "Common Stock").
Price:	$1.68382 per share (the "Original Purchase Price").
Valuation:	The Original Purchase Price is calculated on the basis of a pre-financing valuation of $2.4 million and the number of fully diluted outstanding shares of the Company prior to the investment (including shares reserved for the employee option pool as set forth below).
Purchaser:	Palm Drive Equity Partners, L.P. for $1,000,000, as follows: $950,000 will be invested directly in the Company; and $50,000 will be used to buy out an existing convertible promissory note, which will be converted into Series A Preferred at the Closing.
Anticipated Closing Date (the "Closing"):	January 11, 2017.

Terms of Series A Preferred Stock

Dividends:	The holders of the Series A Preferred will be entitled to receive cumulative dividends in preference to any dividend on the Common Stock at the rate of 7% of the Original Purchase Price per annum, when and as declared by the Board of Directors. The Series A Preferred will participate pro rata in dividends paid on the Common Stock.
Liquidation Preference:	In the event of any liquidation or winding up of the Company, the holders of the Series A Preferred will be entitled to receive in preference to the holders of the Common Stock an amount equal to the Original Purchase Price plus any accrued but unpaid cumulative dividends (the "Liquidation Preference"). After the payment of the Liquidation Preference to the holders of the Series A Preferred, the remaining assets will be distributed ratably to the holders of the Common Stock and the Series A Preferred until the holders of Series A Preferred have received a

(continued)

	total liquidation amount per share equal to two times the Original Purchase Price, plus any declared but unpaid dividends. All remaining assets will be distributed ratably to the Common Stock. A merger, acquisition, or sale of substantially all of the assets of the Company in which the shareholders of the Company do not own a majority of the outstanding shares of the surviving corporation will be deemed to be a liquidation.
Conversion:	The holders of the Series A Preferred will have the right to convert the Series A Preferred, at any time, into shares of Common Stock. The initial conversion rate will be 1:1, subject to adjustment as provided below.
Automatic Conversion:	The Series A Preferred will be automatically converted into Common Stock, at the then applicable conversion price, (i) in the event that the holders of a majority of the outstanding Series A Preferred consent to such conversion or (ii) upon the closing of a firmly underwritten public offering of shares of Common Stock of the Company with a total offering of not less than $20,000,000 (before deduction of underwriters' commissions and expenses).
Antidilution Provisions:	The conversion price of the Series A Preferred will be subject to a weighted-average adjustment to reduce dilution in the event that the Company issues additional equity securities (with customary exceptions) at a purchase price less than the applicable conversion price. The conversion price will also be subject to proportional adjustment for stock splits, reverse stock splits, stock dividends, recapitalizations, and the like.
Redemption at Option of Investors:	Commencing on the fifth anniversary of the Closing, at the election of the holders of a majority of the Series A Preferred made within 90 days of such anniversary, the Company will redeem the outstanding Series A Preferred in three equal annual installments. Such redemption will be at the Original Purchase Price plus any accrued and unpaid dividends.
Voting Rights:	The Series A Preferred will vote together with the Common Stock and not as a separate class except as specifically provided herein or as otherwise required by law. Each share of Series A Preferred will have a number of votes equal to the number of shares of Common Stock then issuable upon conversion of such share of Series A Preferred.
Board of Directors:	The size of the Company's Board of Directors will be changed to five. For as long as at least 300,000 shares of Series A Preferred remain outstanding, the holders of the Series A Preferred, voting as a separate class, will be entitled to elect two members of the Company's Board of Directors. The holders of the Common Stock will be entitled to elect two directors. The fifth director must be approved by the holders of a majority of the Common Stock and a majority of the Series A Preferred, each voting separately.
Protective Provisions:	For as long as at least 300,000 shares of Series A Preferred remain outstanding, consent of the holders of a majority of the Series A Preferred will be required for any action that (i) alters or changes the rights, preferences, or privileges of the Series A

(continued)

	Preferred; (ii) increases or decreases the authorized number of shares of Series A Preferred or Common Stock; (iii) creates (by reclassification or otherwise) any new class or series of shares having rights, preferences, or privileges senior to or on a parity with the Series A Preferred; (iv) results in the redemption of any shares of Common Stock (other than pursuant to employee agreements); or (v) results in any acquisition of the Company, other corporate reorganization, sale of control, or any transaction in which all or substantially all of the assets of the Company are sold.
Information Rights:	For as long as an Investor continues to hold shares of Series A Preferred or Common Stock issued upon conversion of the Series A Preferred, the Company will deliver to the Investor audited annual and unaudited quarterly financial statements. As long as an Investor holds not less than 120,000 shares of Series A Preferred (a "Major Investor"), the Company will furnish the Investor with monthly financial statements and will provide a copy of the Company's annual operating plan within 30 days prior to the beginning of the fiscal year. Each Major Investor will also be entitled to standard inspection and visitation rights. These provisions will terminate upon a registered public offering of the Company's Common Stock.
Registration Rights:	*Demand Rights:* If Investors holding a majority of the outstanding shares of Series A Preferred, including Common Stock issued on conversion of Series A Preferred ("Registrable Securities"), request that the Company file a Registration Statement for at least 30% of the Registrable Securities, or a lesser percentage if the anticipated aggregate offering price to the public is not less than $20,000,000, the Company will use its best efforts to cause such shares to be registered; provided, however, that the Company will not be obligated to effect any such registration prior to the fourth anniversary of the Closing. The Company will have the right to delay such registration under certain circumstances for up to two periods not in excess of 90 days each in any 12-month period.
	The Company will not be obligated to effect more than two registrations under these demand right provisions. In addition, it will not be obligated to effect a registration (i) during the 90-day period commencing with the date of the Company's initial public offering or (ii) if it delivers notice to the holders of the Registrable Securities within 30 days of any registration request of its intent to file a registration statement for an initial public offering within 90 days.
	Company Registration: The Investors will be entitled to "piggyback" registration rights on all registrations of the Company or on any demand registrations of any other investor subject to the right, however, of the Company and its underwriters to reduce the number of shares proposed to be registered pro rata in view of market conditions. If the Investors are so limited, however, no party may sell shares in such registration other than the Company or the Investor, if any, invoking the demand registration. Unless the registration is with respect to the Company's initial

(continued)

public offering, in no event will the shares to be sold by the Investors be reduced below 25% of the total amount of securities included in the registration. No shareholder of the Company may be granted piggyback registration rights that would reduce the number of shares includable by the holders of the Registrable Securities in such registration without the consent of the holders of a majority of the Registrable Securities.

S-3 Rights: Investors will be entitled to up to two demand registrations on Form S-3 per year (if available to the Company) as long as such registered offerings are not less than $1 million.

Expenses: The Company will bear registration expenses (exclusive of underwriting discounts and commissions) of all such demands, piggybacks, and S-3 registrations (including the expense of a single counsel to the selling shareholders, which counsel will also be counsel to the Company unless there is a conflict of interest with respect to the representation of any selling shareholder or the underwriters otherwise object).

Transfer of Rights: The registration rights may be transferred to (i) any partner or retired partner of any holder that is a partnership, (ii) any family member or trust for the benefit of any individual holder, or (iii) any transferee who acquires at least 100,000 shares of Registrable Securities; provided the Company is given written notice thereof.

Termination of Rights: The registration rights will terminate on the date five years after the Company's initial public offering.

Other Provisions: Other provisions will be contained in the Investor Rights Agreement with respect to registration rights as are reasonable, including cross-indemnification, the period of time in which the Registration Statement will be kept effective, and underwriting arrangements.

Participation Rights: Each Investor will have the right in the event the Company proposes to offer equity securities to any person (subject to customary exceptions) to purchase its pro rata portion of such shares (based on the number of shares then outstanding on an as-converted and as-exercised basis). Such right of participation will terminate upon an underwritten public offering of shares of the Company.

Purchase Agreement: The investment will be made pursuant to a Stock Purchase Agreement reasonably acceptable to the Company and the Investors, which agreement will contain, among other things, appropriate representations and warranties of the Company, covenants of the Company reflecting the provisions set forth herein, and appropriate conditions of closing, including an opinion of counsel for the Company. The Stock Purchase Agreement will provide that it may only be amended and any waivers thereunder may only be made with the approval of the holders of a majority of the Series A Preferred. Registration rights provisions may be amended or waived solely with the consent of the holders of a majority of the Registrable Securities.

(continued)

Employee Matters	
Employee Pool:	Prior to the closing, the Company will reserve shares of its Common Stock representing 20% of its fully diluted capital stock following the issuance of its Series A Preferred for future issuances to directors, officers, employees, and consultants.
Stock Vesting:	Unless otherwise determined by the Board of Directors, all stock and stock equivalents issued after the Closing to employees, directors, and consultants will be subject to vesting in accordance with the vesting provisions currently in place under the Company's stock option plan.
	The outstanding Common Stock currently held by Alexei Perlitz and Piper Mao (the "Founders") will be subject to similar vesting terms provided that the Founders shall be credited with 12 months of vesting as of the Closing, with their remaining unvested shares to vest monthly over 3 years.
Proprietary Information and Inventions Agreements:	Each officer and employee of the Company will enter into reasonably acceptable agreements governing nondisclosure of proprietary information and assignment of inventions to the Company.
Right of First Refusal and Co-Sale Agreement:	The shares of the Company's securities held by the Founders will be made subject to a right of first refusal and co-sale agreement (with certain reasonable exceptions) with the holders of the Series A Preferred such that they may not sell, transfer, or exchange their stock without first offering to the Company and then to each holder of Series A Preferred the opportunity to purchase such stock on the same terms and conditions as those of the proposed sale and unless each holder of Series A Preferred has an opportunity to participate in any sale to a third party on a pro rata basis. This right of first refusal and co-sale will not apply to and will terminate upon the Company's initial public offering.
Other Matters	
Finders:	The Company and the Investors will each indemnify the other for any finder's fees for which either is responsible.
Legal Fees and Expenses:	The Company will pay the reasonable fees, not to exceed $30,000, and expenses of one special counsel to the Investors.

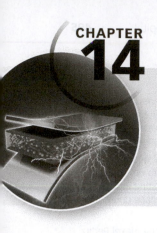

Intellectual Property and Licensing

ntellectual property (*IP*) rights can create barriers to entry; foreclose certain substitute products or services; generate brand equity; promote customer loyalty; and support premium prices for innovative products, services, and ways of doing business. Indeed, a startup's intellectual property rights can be decisive in a David-versus-Goliath battle with a much larger incumbent, as happened when Stac Electronics successfully sued Microsoft for patent infringement.[1] IP rights are also often a key driver of mergers and acquisitions involving both large and small firms.[2] As a result, the ability to manage intellectual property effectively is a valuable strategic capability.[3]

At the same time, "[i]f the innovation is no more than a clever and complex assembly of relatively available technologies, then no wall of patents could keep opponents out."[4] Firms need to create an "ongoing stream of innovation in response both to consumer need for cheaper or more differentiated products or for what Apple co-founder Steve Jobs was a genius at anticipating: products customers did not realize they needed until they saw them."[5]

Moreover, entrepreneurs need to make informed decisions about what to protect and what to put in the public domain. "Providing products and services widely and for free may at times have greater value to the company and society than the natural legal instinct to protect and limit access to them."[6] As CBS Television's Executive Vice President and General Counsel Jonathan Anschell explained, "in the world of new media if you lock it down, you don't get the kind of user-generated content that is such an important component of the new media."[7] Although Apple Inc. has continued to maintain proprietary integrated software and hardware for its computers, it greatly increased the appeal of its iPhones and iPads by making it easy for independent software developers to write applications that run on the Apple iOS. In contrast, Research in Motion (*RIM*), the inventor of the first widely commercialized smartphone, the BlackBerry, maintained a closed system, which left RIM "ill equipped for a world in which phones and tablets are platforms for the whole app ecosystem" and in which its customers shifted from the managers in firms' IT departments to consumer/employees encouraged by their employers to "Bring Your Own Device."[8]

All businesses need to take precautions to avoid violating others' intellectual property rights. Even unintentional violations can result in time-consuming and costly litigation and lead to the demise of an entire product line. Although Shawn Fanning, the founder of Napster, had created an innovative and highly popular technology for sharing music files peer-to-peer, his failure to successfully navigate the law of copyright led to the demise of his firm.[9] In contrast, Bram Cohen, founder of BitTorrent and creator of a revolutionary way to transfer large data files across the Internet, carefully avoided encouraging anyone from using his technology to infringe others' copyrights. When they did, he worked with Warner Brothers and other content providers to take down infringing material.[10]

Protecting intellectual property assets (and knowing when to forgo protection) and avoiding infringement of others' rights require entrepreneurs and their employees to be proactive to prevent missteps. Experienced counsel can provide guidance, but the ultimate responsibility for crafting and executing the firm's IP strategy rests with the company's management team. This chapter will give the entrepreneur an important leg up in meeting these challenges.

We begin with a discussion of trade secrets. Broad classes of information are protectable as trade secrets, but entrepreneurs must take concrete steps to preserve confidentiality in order to benefit from the law's protections.

Next, we address copyright law, including its application to computer software and the digital distribution of music and other original content. The discussion then moves to patents, the form of intellectual property that can protect novel inventions ranging from drugs to drones to database architectures.

This chapter also presents the basics of trademarks and service marks, which are important legal protections for logos, brand names, slogans, and other identifying symbols. We also discuss the use of domain names in a company's Internet address and protection for trade dress, the visual appearance of a product or its packaging.

We then outline the steps companies should take to ensure that they own the intellectual property created by their employees and describe the provisions commonly included in employee proprietary information and inventions agreements. Finally, we present an overview of key business and legal issues for transactions involving intellectual property. This discussion includes both licenses and acquisitions of intellectual property rights in the course of larger transactions, such as the purchase of an entire business, as well as the use of open-source software.

14.1   TRADE SECRET PROTECTION

Most businesses have important confidential information that helps them to compete in the marketplace. Once competitors gain access to these company secrets, their value is often diminished or even destroyed. The law of trade secrets is designed to protect business secrets and may afford important rights in instances where patent and copyright protection is not available.

What Is a Trade Secret?

The federal Defend Trade Secrets Act (*DTSA*),[11] enacted in 2016, defines *trade secrets* broadly to include all forms and types of "financial, business, scientific, technical, economic, or engineering information, including patterns, plans, compilations, program devices, formulas, designs, prototypes … programs, or codes, whether tangible or intangible, and whether or how stored, compiled, or memorialized physically, electronically, graphically, photographically, or in writing" if (1) the owner has taken reasonable measures to keep the information secret and (2) the information derives actual or potential independent economic value from not being generally known to, and not being readily ascertainable through proper means by, another person who can derive economic value from its disclosure or use.[12] The DTSA supplemented existing state laws,[13] many of which are based on the Uniform Trade Secrets Act (*UTSA*). The UTSA provides that a trade secret is "information, including a formula, pattern, compilation, program, device, method, technique, or process," that (1) derives actual or potential independent economic value from not being generally known to, and not being readily ascertainable by proper means by, other persons who can obtain economic value from its disclosure or use and (2) is the subject of efforts that are reasonable under the circumstances to maintain its secrecy.[14] Under both federal and state law, a trade secret is protected for as long as the relevant criteria are met.

Broad Types of Information Are Protectable Sales and marketing plans, customer lists and data, software, computer files, manufacturing techniques, formulas, recipes, research and development results, survey information, sales data, secrets embodied in products, circuits on computer chips, and almost any other type of information can qualify as a trade secret as long as the information provides the business with some competitive advantage from not being generally known. Thus, it is crucial to think in the broadest possible terms when assessing what information may qualify as a trade secret. The biggest risk is failing to take appropriate measures to protect less obvious forms of trade secrets and thereby losing trade secret protection.

Information Must Not Be Generally Known or Discoverable Information that is generally known or discoverable through proper means by competitors cannot constitute a trade secret. Thus, trade secret protection does not extend to information that is in the public domain or is otherwise generally available to customers or competitors. This includes information contained in a company's own product and promotional materials (even technical specifications) that are distributed to the public. It also includes information that is disclosed by mistake, such as when a document is left on top of a desk in plain view of a visitor to the company's offices, or when an employee on a cell phone or talking with a colleague in an elevator is overheard by a customer. In addition, trade secret protection is unavailable for information that competitors or others obtain through legitimate reverse engineering of a hardware product. (*Reverse engineering* is the process of deconstructing a product and examining its inner workings.) Thus, once a product containing trade secrets is released for sale, trade secret protection is often lost. However, if the trade secret cannot be ascertained from examination of the product, then release of the product will not cause the loss of trade secret protection. In addition, prototypes and information destined for public release can still be protected as trade secrets before they are released.

Even when trade secrets become public in violation of the owner's rights, once they are public, they cease to be trade secrets. This is true even though the owner is entirely innocent. Damages may be available, but winning them requires victory at trial, which is never a certainty. Even with a victory at trial, court-awarded damages may not provide full compensation for the harm to the business. If the wrongdoers are unable to pay the damages, there may be no effective remedy. Thus, an entrepreneur's best course is to take steps to prevent both improper and inadvertent trade secret disclosures. A trade secret protection program should form the centerpiece of this effort.

Reasonable Efforts Must Be Taken to Maintain Secrecy   Simply stated, a court will not protect trade secrets unless the owner does also. It is not necessary to take every conceivable precaution, but the owner must make reasonable efforts under the circumstances. In assessing reasonableness, courts examine the value of the information, the resources available to the company to protect its trade secrets, the difficulty and expense required for a competitor to develop the information on its own, and how broadly the information is known, both inside and outside the company. Elements of a sample trade secret protection program are discussed below.

Enforcing Trade Secret Rights

The DTSA created a private federal civil action for trade secret misappropriation. Claims can be brought in federal court as long as certain jurisdictional requirements are met.[15] The UTSA and similar state legislation provide a state law remedy enforceable in state courts. If a firm suspects that trade secret rights may have been violated, it is prudent to contact an attorney immediately.

Both federal and state law prohibit the improper disclosure and use of trade secrets by others. *Improper means* of acquiring trade secrets include theft, misrepresentation, bribery, breach of contract, computer hacking, and espionage. In addition, improper disclosures include disclosures that violate a duty of confidentiality owed to the owner of the trade secret.

A duty of confidentiality may arise because an employee, customer, consultant, independent contractor, banker, or other person has signed a *nondisclosure agreement* (also referred to as a *confidentiality agreement*) with the trade secret owner, in which the person to whom trade secrets are disclosed promises not to disclose them to others or to use them. A duty of confidentiality may also arise by operation of law, that is, merely because of a person's status as an officer, director, or employee of a company owning the trade secret. When a person discloses or uses a trade secret in violation of a duty of confidentiality, the trade secret owner can use the courts to protect its trade secret rights. Note, however, that if no duty of confidentiality exists, legal protections generally will not be available, unless the secret was obtained by improper means (such as theft). Thus, confidentiality agreements are critical.

Trade secret disputes most often arise when an employee leaves a company to join a competitor and is suspected of taking or using valuable competitive information belonging to the former employer. For example, suppose that a recent hire in a medical equipment firm brings to her new job a presentation she created for her former employer that outlines an as-yet-undisclosed marketing strategy for a new diagnostic medical instrument. Even if the new hire merely intends to show her new boss the presentation to demonstrate her skill in creating effective presentations, her actions may well constitute misappropriation of her former employer's trade secrets. If the new employer uses that information, then it too may be liable for misappropriating a trade secret if it knows or has reason to know that the ex-employee was violating a duty of confidentiality when she discloses the information. As discussed in Chapter 2, if an employee's new job inevitably requires the employee to use the trade secrets of the prior employer, certain courts will invoke the *inevitable disclosure doctrine* to preclude the employee from working in areas of overlap for some period of time.[16]

Violations of trade secret rights, both inadvertent and intentional, are common and are often costly. Legal relief can include a court order preventing disclosure or use of the trade secret information, money damages, and, in some cases, punitive damages and attorneys' fees. Remedies under the DTSA also include, in extraordinary circumstances, *ex parte* seizure orders that allow seizure of property to prevent propagation or dissemination of the trade secret.[17] When a person obtains trade secrets through the unauthorized use of a computer linked to the Internet, both the government and the owner of the misappropriated trade secrets can bring a civil action under the Computer Fraud and Abuse Act.

Concerns regarding trade secret theft by hackers, employees, and companies, especially involving theft by or sale to foreign governments, have led to more frequent criminal prosecutions of suspected wrongdoers under the federal Economic Espionage Act. If a person obtains trade secrets through the unauthorized use of a computer linked to the Internet, then the U.S. government can also bring a criminal action under the Computer Fraud and Abuse Act.

Establishing a Trade Secret Protection Program

Taking reasonable steps to protect trade secrets is legally necessary to secure the protection provided by the trade secret laws. Developing a program to protect company secrets usually makes good business sense as well. The company's trade secret policies should be in writing, be made available to all employees and contractors, and be discussed thoroughly with every employee and contractor who has access to trade secrets. In the end, knowledgeable and conscientious employees are the most important line of defense against trade secret disclosure.

An experienced attorney should help develop the trade secret protection program, but ultimately the entrepreneur is responsible for seeing that all employees and contractors honor the program. The plan should be comprehensive but not so complex and burdensome that employees or contractors refuse to implement it or are unable to do so. What constitutes a reasonable trade secret protection program that meets the legal standard necessary to enforce trade secret rights will vary from business to business. An entrepreneur in a startup business need not take the same precautions as IBM. Again, an attorney can help craft a balanced, effective plan that meets the legal requirements for a particular business.

Although every business's circumstances are different, trade secret protection programs will generally include most of the following elements.

Identify Trade Secrets The program should include guidance as to what constitutes a trade secret. The head of a small business is likely to be aware of many, but not all, of the company's important trade secrets. Employees and contractors must also shoulder responsibility for helping to identify a company's trade secrets. The trade secret protection plan should spell out general categories of information that are likely to be particularly important to the business. For a software company, this could be source code, sensitive computer files, and documentation; for a telemarketing company, it could be customer data. In addition, the plan should include appropriate catchall categories, such as any information that is not known outside the company and might have value to competitors.

The plan should require employees to mark all documents that contain trade secrets as "Confidential." However, it is important not to try to treat all company information as trade secrets. If every document is marked "Confidential," a court is likely to conclude that the company is not taking the notion of confidentiality seriously and may refuse to grant any trade secret protection, even for those items that truly are confidential.

Secure Employee Commitment Securing employee commitment to protecting trade secrets is essential. Employees are the biggest source of trade secret disclosure, both accidental and otherwise. Steps to achieve employee commitment include the following.

Preemployment Clearance When hiring an employee away from a competitor, it is important to stress that no trade secrets from the former employer are to be used on the job or shared with others in the company. In sensitive cases, an applicant should be required to sign an agreement to that effect as part of the recruiting process. The employer should make sure that the new employee has not brought paper or electronic files or documents or computer discs, key drives, or smartphones containing trade secrets to the job. The employer should require representations to this effect in the employee's employment or nondisclosure agreement. It is also prudent to review any employment or nondisclosure agreement that the new employee had with the former employer. Finally, conducting a broad search for a new hire to fill a vacant job, rather than merely offering the position to a designated employee of a competitor, can help show that a new hire was not singled out with the specific intent to acquire trade secrets from his or her former employer.

Nondisclosure Agreements   Many authorities consider nondisclosure agreements to be the single most important element in a company's trade secret protection program. In brief, a nondisclosure agreement contains a promise by the employee to avoid unauthorized use or disclosure of the company's trade secrets and to use care to prevent unauthorized use and disclosure from occurring. In addition to strengthening the employer's legal rights, the agreement impresses upon the new employee the seriousness with which the company guards its trade secrets.

Although a nondisclosure agreement may be a stand-alone document or be included in a more comprehensive employment agreement or an inventions assignment agreement, it is usually preferable for companies to include the nondisclosure obligations in a standard employee proprietary information and inventions agreement. We discuss proprietary information and inventions agreements further below.

Middle- and upper-level management, engineers, technical employees, secretaries, janitors, clerks, and all others with access to trade secrets, even as only an incidental part of their jobs, should be required to sign a nondisclosure agreement before beginning work and as a condition of employment. Experience suggests that most new employees will readily sign a nondisclosure agreement. If an employee was not required to sign a nondisclosure agreement as part of the hiring process, the employer should offer some consideration (e.g., a cash payment) other than just continued employment in exchange for the employee's agreeing to sign such an agreement later. Otherwise, the agreement may not be binding on the employee.

Noncompetition Agreements Some companies use noncompetition agreements (also called *covenants not to compete)* to prevent employees who leave the company from using trade secrets and other sensitive information on behalf of a competitor. The key advantage of a noncompetition agreement is that it avoids the often difficult task of proving that a former employee actually stole and used trade secrets to help a competitor. For example, a former employee might use general knowledge of a company's long-range strategic plans to design a strategy for his or her new company. In such a case, proving that the former employee actually divulged trade secrets in designing the new strategy might be virtually impossible. As discussed in Chapter 2, a noncompetition agreement prohibits the former employee from working on competing products for a designated period of time. Typically, noncompetition agreements have a limited duration, often one to three years.

The chief difficulty with noncompetition agreements is that in some states, including California, such agreements are generally unenforceable (except when executed in connection with the sale of a business, as discussed more fully in Chapter 2). Even the states that generally do enforce noncompetition agreements often have state-specific laws governing them and their courts may have different standards for determining whether the restrictions in the agreements are reasonable, in terms of scope, geographic area and duration. In addition, some employees may refuse to sign a noncompetition agreement. If a noncompetition agreement is desired, however, experienced counsel should draft the contract to maximize the likelihood that it will be held to be fully enforceable.

Employee Education The company should provide all employees with basic information about the company's trade secret protection program. Periodic reminders in newsletters and at companywide functions will remind employees of the need to protect trade secrets. For example, Synopsys, Inc., a Silicon Valley software firm, created a sinister-looking caricature of a spy and put it up on walls and in newsletters as a vivid reminder of the importance of trade secret protection. Company executives even performed a brief skit at a companywide meeting to show how easily sensitive information can accidentally be divulged. Educational efforts should also stress to employees the dangers of improperly using others' trade secrets. Companies should require employees to acknowledge annually all of the company's policies, including its trade secret program. Unintentional trade secret disclosures are common, and employee education is key to safeguarding confidential information.

Preclearance of Engineers' and Scientists' Speeches and Publications Scientists and engineers are often justifiably proud of their new discoveries and eager to share their findings with colleagues. To avoid inadvertent disclosures of trade secrets, technically oriented companies should have a policy of reviewing and clearing engineers' and scientists' speeches and publications in advance. (Disclosures in publications and speeches may also have implications for the company's patent rights, which is another reason why review of such material is critical.)

Exit Interview/Exit Agreement Employers should conduct exit interviews to ensure that departing employees recognize, and agree to abide by, their duty to refrain from disclosing or using any of the company's trade secrets. The current employer should admonish departing employees not to take or retain any materials or files containing trade secrets. Personal files, computer discs, smartphones, and other items that employees wish to remove should be inspected for company trade secrets, and the company should confirm with employees that all such materials have been deleted from hard drives at their home and from their personal laptop computers and other digital devices and from storage in the cloud. Companies should try to obtain written confirmation of these matters from departing employees. If the departing employee never signed a confidentiality agreement, this becomes even more important. If an employee is leaving to work for a competitor, the company should consider having its lawyer send a letter to the new employer, informing it that the employee had access to valuable trade secrets and warning it against using any trade secrets that may be brought into its possession by the new employee.

Other Protective Measures Other recommended measures to protect trade secrets include the following:

➤ Mark as "Confidential" documents that contain trade secrets, including, for example, PowerPoint presentations, proposals, marketing plans, source code, and design and specification documents.

➤ Disclose confidential information within the company only on a need-to-know basis.

➤ Keep confidential information on-site whenever possible.

➤ Use appropriate passwords and security codes to protect sensitive computer files.

➤ Encrypt email and other sensitive electronic transmissions.

➤ Restrict employees from sending sensitive company information to their personal email accounts.

➤ Maintain a clean-desk policy and lock offices and file cabinets.

➤ Protect prototypes and other physical products that contain trade secrets.

➤ Avoid the discussion of sensitive topics when visitors are present, on cell phones and other unsecured telephone lines, in emails that are not secure or may be inappropriately retransmitted, and in public, especially in airplanes, elevators, restaurants, restrooms, and other places where competitors could possibly be present.

➤ Train employees regarding appropriate and inappropriate uses of social media at work with respect to company trade secrets.

➤ Advise employees to use extra caution at trade shows, scientific conferences, and professional gatherings, where competitors are almost always present and the temptation is great to boast about new but confidential developments at informal social gatherings (especially in bars).

➤ Use appropriate information systems security (e.g., two-factor authentication for log-ins) to protect against hacking or other cyberattacks and periodically audit those security measures for adequacy.

➤ Use a shredder or otherwise destroy discarded confidential information before putting it in the trash.

➤ Prohibit personal software and personal computer files at work.

➤ Keep records of what software was checked out to whom and when.

➤ Use appropriate precautions when employees are working at home or away from the office, and when employees are allowed to use their own personal devices for work purposes.

➤ Use security software that can lock, disable, or destroy data remotely on a misplaced device, and train employees to report lost or stolen laptops or smartphones immediately.

➤ Restrict the ability to access, copy, or print confidential computer files without authorization.

➤ Inform employees in writing that work computers and work phones may be monitored without further notice or cause.

➤ Include information about trade secret protection in employee handbooks.

Although many of these precautions cost little, many companies fail to implement them, often with unpleasant consequences. Particularly in today's digital world, in which most information is maintained and transmitted in electronic form, the risk of loss of trade secrets is high, whether from negligent use of email, computer files, smartphones, laptop computers, social media platforms, or storage media or from intentional theft or corporate espionage. Trade secret cases have become increasingly common, requiring companies at all stages of development to be vigilant.

Dealing with Outsiders   A trade secret protection program should also include precautions for dealing with outsiders, such as independent contractors and potential investors.

Nondisclosure Agreements   Before disclosing confidential information to consultants, independent contractors, potential investors or business partners, and other outsiders, a company should require them to sign a nondisclosure agreement. Without such an agreement, these persons may have no duty to refrain from disclosing or using a company's trade secrets. (For an example of such a provision, see Section 4.1 of Appendix 8.1, "Sample Independent Contractor Services Agreement," in "Getting It in Writing" located on the companion website for this title at www.CengageBrain.com.)

Building Security   Security measures may range from steps as simple as keeping unattended doors locked, maintaining a visitor sign-in log, and providing employee escorts to steps as elaborate as providing fully guarded and electronically protected access. In addition, many of the suggested employee precautions noted above can also help to prevent inadvertent leaks to outside visitors.

International Considerations

Although most industrialized countries provide some protection for trade secrets, trade secret laws differ from country to country. The preceding discussion covers only U.S. trade secret law. In our global economy, it is increasingly likely that confidential business information will be used or maintained abroad. Companies need to be cognizant of security measures when employees are traveling on business and when establishing offices abroad. In that event, the company should consider retaining foreign counsel. An experienced U.S. attorney can help determine whether the often considerable expense of hiring a foreign attorney is justified and may be able to provide referrals. In addition, sharing information with foreign countries or foreign nationals can be affected by U.S. export control laws. Advice of experienced U.S. counsel may be needed for compliance with such laws.

14.2 COPYRIGHTS

Copyrights are critical to companies operating in the software, publishing, journalism, movie, entertainment, music, multimedia, and online industries, among others. Copyrights are also important to artists, writers, musicians, photographers, and architects. Indeed, virtually all businesses have some materials that can be protected through copyright law. This is especially true today when most businesses have a presence on the Internet. A company's website is a copyrightable work. New developments in copyright law concerning the potential liability of companies distributing devices that are capable of infringing use by others also make this an important area of law for many new businesses.

What Is a Copyright?

A *copyright* gives the owner of an original work of authorship the exclusive legal right to obtain certain economic benefits from the work. In particular, the copyright owner has the exclusive rights to (1) reproduce copies of the work, (2) develop derivative works based on the copyrighted work, (3) distribute copies of the work, (4) perform the work publicly, and (5) display the work publicly. For example, the owner of a copyright for a book or a piece of software has the exclusive right to create later editions, versions, or sequels to the work. Generally, if another person reproduces or distributes copyrighted material without permission or exercises any of the copyright owner's other exclusive rights without permission, the copyright owner can obtain legal relief for copyright infringement.

What Can Be Protected by a Copyright?

Copyrights protect a wide range of works. In addition to protecting books, works of art, musical recordings, magazines, plays, certain characters, dramatic performances, and movies, copyrights can also protect many other forms of creative work, including certain graphic designs,[18] software, webpages, advertisements, photographs, video games, instruction manuals, sales presentations and client proposals, labels, diagrams, architectural drawings, financial tables, and pitch decks.

Copyrights also protect derivative works and some compilations. A *derivative work* is a work that is based on another work. Derivative works can include adaptations and modifications of previous works, such as a translation of the original work into another language.

Facts are not copyrightable. A database or other compilation of facts is protected in the United States only if the author used

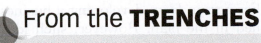
From the **TRENCHES**

"Holy copyright law, Batman!"—so began Judge Sandra S. Ikuta's opinion holding that DC Comics' Batmobile character was protected by copyright. DC Comics, the original creator of the Batmobile character, sued Mark Towle, alleging that the Batmobile replicas he created infringed DC's copyright. Towle sold these replicas for about $90,000 each. The court held that the Batmobile character was entitled to copyright protection because (1) it had "'physical as well as conceptual qualities'"—the Batmobile appeared graphically in comic books, as a three-dimensional car on TV and in the movies, and was not a "mere literary character"; (2) it was "'sufficiently delineated'" to be recognizable as the same character whenever it appeared—it was always equipped with high-tech gadgets and weaponry, was typically bat-like in appearance, and included "'consistent, identifiable character traits and attributes'"; and (3) it was "'especially distinctive'" in that it had a unique and recognizable name, was Batman's "loyal bat-themed sidekick," and was not "merely a stock character." Because DC Comics had the exclusive right to authorize the creation by others of derivative works based on its Batmobile character, DC Comics was entitled to sue for infringement of its underlying work.

Source: DC Comics v. Towle, 802 F.3d 1012 (9th Cir. 2015), *cert. denied*, 136 S. Ct. 1390 (2016).

some degree of originality and creativity in selecting and presenting the information.[19] For example, a selective listing of high-quality auto repair shops sorted by geographic location might have some copyright protection in the United States, although the individual names of the shops themselves would not be copyrightable. Even if a factual compilation is not eligible for copyright protection, the compiler may be able to require the purchaser of the database to agree by contract not to reproduce the information contained in the database. Importantly, the European Union provides broader protection of databases than does the United States.

Copyrights Do Not Protect Ideas

Copyright cannot be used to protect an idea or a certain way of performing some function; copyright protects only the particular way the idea is expressed in a tangible medium of expression (such as printed on paper, recorded on tape, or coded on a disc). For example, this book is protected by copyright, but the ideas contained in it are not. A business plan may be copyrighted, but that does not prevent another person from developing a business that uses the ideas contained in the plan. However, such ideas may be protectable as trade secrets if appropriate steps are taken to keep them confidential.

If an idea and the way it is expressed are inseparably bound, the idea and the expression are said to *merge,* and no copyright protection is available. For example, the maker of a karate video game cannot obtain a copyright on the karate moves made by the action figures in the game because the expression of the karate moves in the video game is inseparable from the moves performed in actual karate. The "H" pattern for a manual transmission cannot be copyrighted because it is inseparable from the basic functioning of the gearshift pattern employed in most manual transmissions.

In practice, it can be very difficult to separate an idea from its tangible expression, so the degree of protection afforded by a copyright is often hard to predict with precision. In general, the more ways an idea can be expressed, the more likely the work is to be copyrightable. For example, a court held that the use of the "+" sign to indicate addition in a computer spreadsheet program is not copyrightable because there really is no other logical and feasible way to express the notion of addition on a computer keyboard. On the other hand, a basic literary plot such as love triumphing over adversity is capable of so many unique expressions that many different stories expressing the same basic idea can be copyrighted. Litigation between Oracle and Google over Java application programming interfaces (*APIs*) resulted in a federal appeals court ruling that the structure, sequence, and organization of the Java APIs are eligible for copyright protection.[20]

Fair Use

Even if material does qualify for copyright protection, the law permits others to make limited use of copyrighted materials, including making copies for certain purposes, under the doctrine of fair use. *Fair use* purposes include criticism, comment, news reporting, scholarship, and research. Under the copyright statute, four factors are considered to determine whether a use is fair use: (1) the purpose and character of the use (including whether it is commercial or not), (2) the nature of the copyrighted work (factual or creative; published or unpublished), (3) the amount and substantiality of the portion used, and (4) the effect of the use upon the potential market or value of the copyrighted work. Whether an unauthorized use of a copyrighted work constitutes protected fair use is fact-specific. In very general terms, though, if the use is transformative—if it adds new insights and understandings to the copyrighted work and is a use which has a different purpose than the purpose of the original work—it is more likely to qualify as a fair use. On the other hand, if it is commercial and diminishes the value of the copyright to the owner, the use is less likely to qualify as a fair use.

Courts sometimes interpret the fair use exception quite broadly. For example, one court held that using another's drawings of film frames of the assassination of President Kennedy in a book qualified as fair use because the public interest was served by making available factual information about the assassination. The U.S. Supreme Court held that the use of the copyrighted song "Pretty Woman" in a parody by rap group 2 Live Crew was fair use as long as the parody used no more of the lyrics and music of the original work than was necessary to make it recognizable.[21] In 2013, a court held that use of artist Derek Seltzer's drawing "Scream Icon" in a video by rock band Green Day constituted fair use because the use was transformative and caused no harm to the value of Seltzer's work.[22] Because fair use is highly fact-specific and can be expensive to defend, even if the defendant ultimately prevails, entrepreneurs should always consult with counsel before using others' original works.

Many commercial uses of copyrighted information are not permitted under the doctrine of fair use. For example, Kinko's Graphics Corp. violated the copyrights of Basic Books, Inc. and other publishers when it copied without permission and sold portions of copyrighted works selected by professors to be used in student course readers. Even though the copied materials were used for educational purposes, the court rejected Kinko's fair use claim, noting that Kinko's involvement was for the purpose of obtaining profits.[23] Similarly, the copying of articles in scientific and technical journals by a scientist at Texaco, Inc. for his own files was held not to be fair use.[24]

From the **TRENCHES**

As part of its Library Project program, Google, Inc. scanned more than 20 million books in their entirety. Even though approximately 4 million of the scanned books were protected by copyright, Google did not obtain permission from the copyright holders to make the digital copies. After analyzing the scans, Google created an index that allows users of its Google Books search engine to enter a word or phrase and generate a list of books that include the word or phrase, as well as a "limited viewing" of text. Ten percent of all pages are "blacklisted," and no user can access all of the "snippets" (the horizontal segments of about an eighth of a page in which the word or phrase is used). The Authors Guild, along with several individual plaintiffs, sued Google for copyright infringement.

The U.S. Court of Appeals for the Second Circuit held that each of the four statutory fair use factors supported a finding of noninfringement. The court found that making digital copies of books to provide a search function was transformative—Google copied the books so it could make available "significant information *about those books*" that would be useful to a searcher, and the "snippet" function added to the "highly transformative purposes" of identifying books that were useful to the searcher. Google's overall profit motivation (present even though revenues did not flow directly to it from Google Books) was not enough to outweigh this transformative purpose. The nature of the copyrighted work favored fair use because Google "transformatively provides valuable information about the original" and did not "replicat[e] protected expression in a manner that provides a meaningful substitute for the original." The amount and substantiality of the portion of the original work used also favored fair use. Even though Google made an unauthorized digital copy of the entire book, the public did not have access to the entire copy through either the search function or the "snippet" function. The "fragmentary and scattered" nature of the snippets provided, at most, an aggregate 16% of a book's text. The court did note, however, that if the snippet view produced a "coherent block" of 16% of a book, a "very different question" would be raised. The court also found that the "snippet" view did not harm the value of the copyrighted original, as it did not result in "widespread revelation of sufficiently significant portions of the original as to make available a significantly competing substitute." Accordingly, making a complete digital copy of the books to provide the public with the Google Books search and snippet view functions was fair use and did not infringe the copyrights in the works.

Source: Authors Guild v. Google, Inc., 804 F.3d 202 (2d Cir. 2015), *cert. denied,* 136 S. Ct. 1658 (2016).

Reverse Engineering Copying unprotectable aspects of a work, such as facts and ideas, does not constitute infringement. Given the nature of computer code, however, if a competitor wishes to identify the unprotectable elements in a software program, it sometimes must copy and then decompile the object code. Copying and reverse engineering a computer program for this purpose is fair use.[25]

Similarly, in a case involving Sony PlayStation games, a court ruled that it was fair use for a company to decompile Sony's software program in order to create a new program that allowed the games to be played on a Macintosh computer. The court reasoned that the new program did not merely take the place of the Sony program but transformed it into something new and different.[26]

However, many software products are distributed via license, and the license terms often contain prohibitions on reverse engineering. Whether such provisions are enforceable is not yet clear, as the law continues to evolve.

In addition, the Digital Millennium Copyright Act (*DMCA*) prohibits circumventing access-control mechanisms and thus could limit a developer's ability to reverse engineer. Although the DMCA contains an exception for reverse engineering necessary to achieve interoperability, it is not yet clear how broadly or narrowly courts will apply this exception. Before implementing any reverse engineering program, a company should consult with experienced legal counsel.

Duration of Copyrights

A key advantage of copyrights is that protection typically lasts far longer than is needed for most commercial uses. The copyright for an individual creator lasts for the life of the creator plus 70 years. For a work made for hire (discussed below), the duration is 95 years from the year of publication or 120 years from the year of creation, whichever period is shorter.

Requirements for Obtaining Copyright Protection and Suing for Copyright Infringement

To be eligible for copyright protection, a work of authorship must meet three basic requirements. First, the work must be fixed in a tangible medium of expression (e.g., written on paper, saved on a computer disc or hard drive, or recorded on tape). Almost any medium from which the idea can be retrieved will qualify.

Second, the work must be original; that is, it must have been created by the author claiming the copyright. The work does not need to be unique, novel, or of high quality. Third, the work must contain some minimal level of creativity. The standard of creativity required is quite low—no particular merit is required. Thus, the white pages of the telephone directory would not qualify but the "Yellow Pages" with ads and text displayed would. Directions for how to use a beauty product displayed on a product label could also qualify. Thus, almost any original work of authorship developed for a business can qualify for copyright protection.

No action is required to obtain copyright protection. It arises automatically when an original work of authorship is first fixed in a tangible medium of expression. Nevertheless, the copyright owner should take steps to reinforce copyright protections. It is always advisable to display a copyright notice, even though it is not legally required. This puts others on notice that the work is copyrighted and can prevent a third party from attempting to avoid liability by asserting innocent infringement. This notice should be in the form of the word "Copyright" or a "c" enclosed in a circle (©), followed by the name of the author and the year of publication; the phrase "All rights reserved" may be added. The notice should be displayed prominently.

Notably, a wide range of photos, artwork, music, written text and other works is readily accessible on the Internet. Even though these materials frequently are not accompanied by a copyright notice, they are likely protected by copyright law. Thus, it cannot be assumed that the copyright owner is permitting the copying, distribution, or other use of these works without explicit permission. Some copyright owners are vigilant in policing and demanding significant payments for unauthorized use of their works. Entrepreneurs should determine in advance whether they have the right to use any material that could be subject to copyright protection.

To pursue an infringement suit in the United States, the owner of the copyright must have registered it with the Register of Copyrights in Washington, D.C. Registration of a copyright is a relatively simple and inexpensive procedure and should be considered for any significant works of authorship. Registration requires filing a copy of the work, which is available to the public, but special rules may be invoked to help protect the confidentiality of trade secrets or other valuable information revealed in the material deposited.

Although the right to sue can be secured by registration after an infringement occurs, statutory damages and attorneys' fees are available only if the copyright is registered before the infringement occurs or within three months of the date that the work is first published. Statutory damages are remedies provided by the Copyright Act and currently are limited to $30,000 per work infringed for ordinary infringement of each copyrighted work and $150,000 per work infringed for each willful infringement. Statutory damages are typically sought when the actual damages suffered are less than these amounts or are very difficult to prove in court. Because a startup often cannot prove actual damage given its short operating history, the availability of statutory damages becomes particularly important. A plaintiff who made a timely copyright registration can seek actual damages or statutory damages but not both. Sometimes the actual damages awarded in copyright cases can be much greater than these statutory amounts.

Proving Copyright Infringement

Direct proof that a work was copied is not required to prove copyright infringement. All that is needed is a showing that the alleged infringer had access to the copyrighted work and that his or her work is substantially similar to the copyrighted work. To make it easier to prove that software was copied, programmers often embed useless pieces of software code within a program; if another program contains the useless code, it is almost certain that the original code was copied.

In cases other than literal copying, determining whether protected expression was copied can be highly fact-specific and costly to litigate. A company should contact an experienced attorney immediately if infringement of an important copyright is suspected.

There are three basic types of copyright infringement—direct, vicarious, and contributory. A person may also be liable for inducing another to infringe.

Direct Copyright Infringement   *Direct copyright infringement* occurs when a person, without the consent of the copyright holder and outside the scope of fair use, violates at least one exclusive right granted to the copyright holder. For example, if a person buys a video game, burns a copy, and sells that copy, he or she has directly infringed the copyright owner's exclusive right to copy, distribute, and sell its copyrighted program. Similarly, if a company uses copyrighted music or art on its website without permission from the copyright owner, the company will be liable for direct infringement.

Vicarious Copyright Infringement   A person is liable for *vicarious copyright infringement* if it both has the right and ability to supervise or control a direct copyright infringement and has a direct financial interest in the infringement. For example, swap meet organizers who created and administered a market where they knew bootleg music was being sold could be liable for vicarious infringement even though the sellers paid a flat fee for admission, not a percentage of their sales proceeds.[27]

Contributory Copyright Infringement   Contributory copyright infringement occurs when a person, with knowledge of another's infringing activity, induces, causes, or materially contributes to the infringing conduct of another. For example, if a company creates and maintains a website and it knows or should know that users are using the site to post and download games without the consent of the copyright owners, then the company may be liable for contributory infringement.

Inducing Copyright Infringement by Others   Even if a person does not control the infringing acts of a third party or directly contribute to them, it may still be liable if it induced the infringement. In particular, a person who distributes a device or provides a service "with the object of promoting its use to infringe copyright, as shown by clear expression or other affirmative steps taken to foster infringement, is liable for the resulting acts of infringement by third parties."[28] Because Grokster promoted users' ability to use its software to share copyrighted music for free through decentralized, peer-to-peer networks, it was liable for inducing others to infringe. Importantly, Grokster did not incorporate any filtering

From the **TRENCHES**

Napster, a wildly popular startup, enabled users to search its centralized index of songs to share MP3 music files with each other (so-called peer-to-peer sharing). As Napster's user base expanded rapidly, the major record labels sued, alleging that Napster both vicariously infringed their copyrights and contributed to its users' direct infringement. Napster argued that it did not infringe the labels' copyrights because, as in the landmark Sony Betamax case, its technology was capable of "substantial noninfringing uses." In the earlier case, the U.S. Supreme Court had held that Sony did not engage in contributory copyright infringement when it sold its Betamax video recorders. Although Betamax made it possible for users to copy copyrighted movies, the Court concluded that "time shifting"—users' ability to record a program broadcast on television and play it back at a later time—was fair use. Napster also argued that it did not directly copy any copyrighted songs—all MP3 files were owned and possessed by its users.

The U.S. Court of Appeals for the Ninth Circuit rejected Napster's arguments and ordered it to remove from its directory every title to which a record company could establish a legitimate copyright. The injunction essentially crippled Napster, slashing its user base and forcing it to convert to a paid subscription service.

Sources: A&M Records, Inc. v. Napster, Inc., 239 F.3d 1004 (9th Cir. 2001); Sony Corp. v. Universal City Studios, Inc., 464 U.S. 417 (1984).

or other tools designed to diminish the potential for infringement. This suggests that courts, when evaluating whether a product (which, e.g., allows users to make copies of copyrighted movies for use on multiple devices) violates the copyrights of others, will consider whether the distributor took technological and promotional steps to discourage infringing uses. Any company creating a technology, online or off-line, that can be used to infringe copyright needs to understand the potential for secondary copyright infringement liability and avoid encouraging others to use the technology to infringe the copyrights of others. Early legal advice on this issue may prove invaluable.

Ownership of Copyrights and Works Made for Hire

As a general rule, the creator of a work is the initial owner of the copyright. However, under the doctrine of *works made for hire*, the employer owns works created by its employees within the scope of their employment. Courts consider the following nonexhaustive list of factors to determine whether, under the general common law of agency, an individual is an employee:

> ➢ Does the hiring party have the right to control the manner and means by which the work is accomplished?
> ➢ May the hiring party assign additional projects to the individual?
> ➢ Who provides the instrumentalities and tools required to perform the work, the hiring party or the worker?
> ➢ Where is the work to be done (e.g., on-site or at worker's place of business)?
> ➢ Is the work part of the hiring party's regular business?
> ➢ What is the manner of payment (e.g., weekly or in a lump sum)?
> ➢ How is the individual classified for tax purposes?
> ➢ Does the hiring party provide any employee benefits to the individual?

If the individual is determined to be an employee, that individual's activities will fall within the scope of employment if (1) it is of the kind the employee was employed to perform; (2) it occurs primarily within the authorized time and space parameters; and (3) it is performed, at least in part, by a purpose to serve the employer. Because it is not always clear whether a worker is an employee or an independent contractor and whether an employee is acting within the scope of his or her employment, employers should require both employees and independent contractors to sign an agreement specifying their intentions and relationship and assigning to the employer any rights they may have in their works, including any copyrights.

If the court finds that the creator of the work was an independent contractor, not an employee, then, absent a work-made-for-hire agreement or an express assignment of the copyright, the creator (not the employer) will be granted the copyright ownership of the work. For example, the U.S. Supreme Court held that the sculptor owned the copyright to a sculpture he created, not the organization that commissioned it.[29] The sculptor had used his own tools, worked in his own studio, had only one project that lasted a short period of time, and had total discretion in hiring and paying assistants. As the owner of the copyright, the sculptor was free to make additional copies of the sculpture.

Copyright ownership disputes can often arise between parties when their relationship is not clear, particularly in circumstances involving musical compositions, trade catalogs and pamphlets, pictorial illustrations, scientific and technical writings, photographs, works of art, and translations of foreign literary works. The company that pays for work created by an independent contractor will own the work as a work made for hire only if (1) there is a written agreement that states that the work is a work made for hire and (2) the work falls into one of nine legal categories of specially commissioned works made for hire (none of which expressly includes computer software). Because not all copyrighted works fit within the statutory categories of works made for hire, independent contractors are typically asked to sign agreements assigning to the company that hires them all their rights to any works they produce during their service and the copyrights related thereto. (See, e.g., Section 4.6 of the "Sample Independent Contractor Services Agreement," set forth in Appendix 8.1, "Getting It in Writing," located on the companion website for this title at www.CengageBrain.com.) A copyright assignment is particularly crucial for works, such as computer software, that do not clearly fall within one of the nine listed categories. Without a written assignment, the independent contractor will own his or her works, and the party that paid for them may be entitled to only a single copy or to make only limited use of the works. Moreover, the independent contractor, as the owner of the works, would be free to license or sell them to competitors of the hiring party, or to make other uses that could harm the hiring party.

Copyrights in Cyberspace: The Digital Millennium Copyright Act

The Digital Millennium Copyright Act (*DMCA*) was enacted in 1998 to provide copyright protection for books, music, videos, software, and other creative works transmitted in digital form over the Internet. Modifying the statutory scheme for licensing sound recordings, the DMCA sets forth a number of specific conditions—including the payment of royalties to SoundExchange, an organization representing record labels and recording artists—that an Internet music service must satisfy to qualify for a statutory license to webcast sound recordings.

As noted above, the DMCA makes it a crime to circumvent technological antipiracy measures designed to control access to a copyrighted work. It also outlaws the manufacture, distribution, or sale of technologies and devices that enable consumers to circumvent these measures. The DMCA also makes it illegal to intentionally remove or tamper with certain "copyright management information," including data identifying the title of a copyrighted work, the author, and the copyright owner, or to provide false copyright management information. The DMCA does, however, permit the cracking of copyright protection devices to conduct encryption research, to test computer security systems, and to access products to achieve interoperability. Armed with the DMCA's legal protections and the criminal penalties it provides, copyright owners have stepped up their development of technology-based protection schemes designed to control the flow and use of copyrighted content.

Equally important, the DMCA contains certain safe-harbor provisions that protect online service providers from copyright infringement liability when they innocently store or transmit infringing materials posted by their users. Protection against such claims is critical to the ability to offer, for example, a service that permits users to upload and share material subject to copyright protection. Several of the safe-harbor provisions require that the service provider take active steps to qualify, such as (1) registering designated agents with the Copyright Office, (2) following specified notice and take-down procedures to remove infringing materials, (3) adopting and reasonably implementing a policy for terminating users who are repeat infringers, and (4) taking steps to inform users of the policy. In addition, a service provider must accommodate and not interfere with "standard" technical measures used by copyright owners to identify and protect copyrighted works. Given the DMCA's many limitations and exclusions, entrepreneurs should seek the advice of qualified counsel to assess whether, and how, the Act may affect their business.

International Issues

Unlike most other forms of intellectual property protection, U.S. copyrights are generally valid overseas through a treaty—the Berne Convention for the Protection of Literary and Artistic Works (usually referred to as the Berne Convention)—signed by most major countries. Parties to the Berne Convention agree to provide holders of foreign copyrights the same protection a national would have if the work were copyrighted in that country. This means that the duration and scope of copyright protection in other countries might not be the same as in the United States. The World Intellectual Property Organization Copyright Treaty, which entered into force in 2002, extends the Berne Convention copyright protection to computer and electronic databases. The treaty also imposes on each ratifying nation the obligation to provide legal protection and effective legal remedies to combat the circumvention of copyright protecting measures and the removal of digital rights management information. Nevertheless, enforcing copyrights in other countries may be far more difficult and costly than enforcing them in the United States. In some countries, it may not be practical to use the courts to enforce copyright, requiring a degree of creativity. Microsoft Corporation was successful in persuading Italian officials to take more aggressive action against the sellers of counterfeit software after it pointed out that the illicit sellers were not paying Italian taxes on their sales.[30]

14.3 PATENTS

Patents can provide powerful protections for inventions and give young businesses the right to exclude others, even the largest competitors, from using their inventions. Patents can also give a new business instant prestige and quick revenues from licensing fees, and they may make it easier to raise venture capital. Obtaining a patent is often a complex and costly undertaking, however. Thus, it is important for entrepreneurs whose business involves the creation of new products, compositions of matter, articles of manufacture, or processes to understand the basics of patent law so they can make informed decisions.

As the U.S. Supreme Court explained, "patent law reflects 'a careful balance between the need to promote innovation' through patent protection, and the importance of facilitating the 'imitation and refinement through imitation' that are 'necessary to invention itself and the very lifeblood of a competitive economy.'"[31] So the government does not grant these exclusive rights readily.

Patents are generally granted country by country. There are exceptions to that general principle, though—for example, it is possible to file a common patent application in the European Union (*EU*) and there is movement toward creating an EU-wide court to handle patent cases. Moreover, many countries have entered into treaties whereby a party who files a patent application in Country A on Date X will be deemed to have filed an application in Country B as of Date X as long as an application is filed in Country B within a specified period, often ranging from 6 to 18 months after Date X.

Violating another's patent rights, even innocently, can result in large damage awards or settlement amounts, as well as significant legal fees. In 2014, after "years of protracted and often bitter litigation," medical-device maker Medtronic announced it would pay more than $1 billion to Edwards Lifesciences to settle patent disputes over transcatheter heart valves.[32]

Patents can also be used defensively as bargaining chips in patent disputes. If Company A claims that Company B's product violates Company A's patent, then ideally Company B can defend itself by establishing: (1) Company B is not infringing Company A's patent; (2) Company A's patent is invalid; and (3) Company A is violating one of Company B's patents. This can result in a cross-licensing agreement whereby each party is permitted to use the other's patented technology, sometimes on a royalty-free basis.

Often technology companies will incorporate their patented inventions into their products. So-called *nonpracticing* or *nonoperating entities* (or more negatively, "patent trolls") are in the business of generating royalty income solely by purchasing and enforcing patents. Some innovators—in particular, many large, established enterprises in the electronics and software spaces— have sought to make patent enforcement more difficult for nonpracticing entities. Others, however, including certain universities, large pharmaceutical companies, and emerging medical-device companies, believe that they need the law to provide strong patent protection in order to protect their product offerings and newly developed technologies from competitors and others who might choose to appropriate their ideas without paying meaningful royalties. Public interest in these issues has driven numerous judicial and legislative changes in the law, the most significant being the enactment of the America Invents Act (*AIA*) in 2011. Among other things, the AIA shifted the United States from a first-to-invent to a first-to-file jurisdiction (with a few twists), and it created new procedures within the U.S. Patent and Trademark Office (*USPTO* or *PTO*) to challenge the validity of patents, as described later in this chapter.

One note of caution: patent law is a subspecialty within the legal specialty of intellectual property and is particularly complex and technical. Even within the subspecialty of patent law, attorneys often focus on a single industry, such as biotechnology, software, or telecommunications. If patent issues arise, a company should consult a patent attorney familiar with the industry in which the company competes. The following discussion presents an overview that will help entrepreneurs assess when to contact patent counsel and make it possible for them to work with patent counsel more efficiently.

What Is a Patent?

A *patent* granted in the United States is an exclusive right granted by the federal government that entitles the inventor or patent assignee to prevent anyone else from making, using, selling, or offering to sell the patented invention in (or importing it into) the United States for a specified period of time. A patent does not give its respective owner the right to use the patented invention, simply the right to exclude others from using or selling it. Other countries have similar, but not identical, definitions.

Types of Patents

There are two main types of patents: utility patents and design patents. (Patents for certain types of asexually reproduced plants are a third type. For example, certain genetically modified seeds can be protected by plant patents.[33])

Utility Patents   The range of useful, novel, and nonobvious inventions that can be protected by a utility patent is broad. As the U.S. Supreme Court famously remarked, Congress intended patentable subject matter to "'include anything under the sun that is made by man.'"[34] As discussed more fully below, a *utility patent* can cover a machine, such as a machine for making auto parts, or a process, such as the process for filling an aerosol can or fabricating a computer chip. Utility patents can also protect articles of manufacture, such as an intermittent windshield wiper or a plastic paper clip. They can also cover nonnaturally occurring compositions of matter, such as a new chemical compound or a formula for mouthwash. Human-made microorganisms are also patentable, but naturally occurring living organisms, including organs and genes, are not. Improvements to any of these types of inventions can also be protected with a utility patent, provided the improvements are useful and nonobvious.

Design Patents   A *design patent* can be used to protect ornamental (as opposed to useful) designs. Design patents can protect the shape or appearance of items, such as computer icons, furniture, or a pair of running shoes. Design patents have become more popular in recent years.

Courts use the *ordinary observer test* to determine whether a design patent has been infringed.[35] Under this test, "if, in the eye of an ordinary observer, giving such attention as a purchaser usually gives, two designs are substantially the same, if the resemblance is such as to deceive such an observer, inducing him to purchase one supposing it to be the other, the first one patented is infringed by the other."[36]

Requirements for Obtaining a Utility Patent

Not all new inventions or discoveries qualify for utility patent protection.

Patentable Subject Matter   To be patentable, the invention must fall within a class of patentable subject matter: machine, process, article of manufacture, or composition of matter. If an invention falls into one of these categories, it typically qualifies as patentable subject matter. (Guidance on patent subject matter eligibility is available on the PTO website.[37])

There are, however, important exceptions to what constitutes patentable subject matter. Examples of nonpatentable subject matter include natural phenomena (e.g., photosynthesis), abstract ideas (e.g., mathematical algorithms, basic financial transactions, and methods of organizing human behavior), and laws of nature (e.g., $E = MC^2$). When an invention potentially falls within one of these enumerated exceptions to patentable subject matter, it must be determined whether the invention, as defined by the patent claims, is directed to an enumerated exception and, if so, whether some other innovative aspect of the invention makes the invention patentable.

Importantly, implementing a mathematical algorithm or method of organizing human activity in a conventional computer system will not confer patentability on an otherwise nonpatentable concept. For example, in 2014, the U.S. Supreme Court struck down patents on software and computer systems for mitigating settlement risk.[38] The Court ruled that the concept of mitigating settlement risk was an unpatentable abstract idea and that implementing that idea within a generic computer was not sufficient to confer patentability. This decision resulted in the invalidation of various issued patents related to certain software and business methods.[39]

Nor will using conventional techniques to isolate a naturally occurring gene sequence render that sequence patentable even if the gene sequence is never found isolated in nature. For example, Myriad Genetics could not patent the precise location and sequence of two human genes it discovered—BRCA1 and BRCA2—even though Myriad was the first to isolate these gene sequences and to establish that mutations in these genes can substantially increase the risk of breast and ovarian cancers.[40] The fact that finding and isolating the BRCA1 and BRCA2 genes required substantial investment and scientific effort did not render the gene sequences "new."[41] As a result, Myriad could not preclude others from selling physicians their own, much cheaper, diagnostic test kits to detect mutations in the BRCA1 and BRCA2 genes. In contrast, complementary DNA (cDNA), that is, synthetic DNA sequences, are patentable because they are human-made.[42]

The law governing patentable subject matter is evolving, and any entrepreneur facing issues of this type should retain competent counsel to assist with analysis and the development of related intellectual property strategies. The same is true for potential funders.

Useful   The invention must be useful. This is rarely a problem because most companies will not invest the time and expense of seeking a utility patent for a useless invention.

Novel   The invention must be novel. For patent applications filed on or after March 16, 2013, an invention is considered *novel* if, subject to certain exceptions, it has not been patented, described in a printed publication, publicly used, put on sale, or otherwise made available to the public anywhere in the world before the effective filing date of the application for the claimed invention. The focus is on when an application for a patent was filed and what information was available to persons skilled in the art prior to that filing date. In contrast, for patent applications filed before March 16, 2013, greater emphasis is placed on the date of invention, as opposed to the application filing date. For those applications, an invention is considered novel if, among other things, (1) it was not previously known or used by others in the United States; (2) it was not previously patented or described in a printed publication anywhere in the world; (3) it was not described in an issued patent filed before the invention; and (4) it was not publicly used or offered for sale in the United States more than one year before the filing of a patent application seeking to claim it.

One-Year "Grace Period" for U.S. Patent Filings   In the United States, unlike most other countries, an inventor has a one-year "grace period" within which to file a U.S. patent application following the inventor's disclosure of an invention, including the inventor's public use of the invention or offering the invention for sale. The grace period makes it possible for inventors in the United States to disclose and test an invention in commerce before determining whether to invest in the preparation and submission of a related U.S. patent application. Inventors must bear in mind, however, that independent activities of third parties, such as third-party patent filings, may preclude patent awards when an inventor delays his or her own filing in reliance on the U.S. "grace period."

Absolute-Novelty Requirements Outside the United States To the extent that an enterprise may seek international patent rights, as opposed to just U.S. patent rights, it will be important to ensure that all relevant patent applications are filed before the invention is disclosed publicly because most other countries do not have a grace period. Thus, in those countries, *any* publication or public disclosure of the invention before filing may result in a loss of patentability in those countries. This is often referred to as the *absolute novelty requirement* for patentability.

For example, if a scientist presents a technical paper describing a patentable invention at a conference in an absolute-novelty country before a patent application has been filed, the invention may no longer be patentable in that country. Disclosing the invention anywhere in the world is enough to prevent the invention from being patentable in most European countries, unless the inventor filed a U.S. patent application prior to disclosure and filed a European patent application within one year after filing the U.S. application.

Thus, to preserve foreign patentability, it is usually best to file a U.S. patent application before allowing any public disclosure, offering for sale, or sale of the invention. As discussed next, filing a provisional patent application in the United States can be an effective and relatively inexpensive way to preserve patentability for up to a year before filing a full-bore patent application.

Effect of Filing a Provisional Patent Application Publication or sale of an invention after the filing of a U.S. provisional patent application will not preclude patentability in the United States or elsewhere as long as the inventor subsequently files a full patent application in a timely manner. A provisional patent application lasts for 12 months after the application filing date, but it cannot be extended. A provisional patent application need not contain everything found in a nonprovisional application and typically will not include a detailed set of patent claims. As a result, it is generally faster and cheaper to prepare than a full patent application.

It is important to understand, however, that when a provisional patent application will be used to provide support for later claims, the application will need to (1) include sufficient disclosure (i.e., description and drawings) to teach a person of ordinary skill in the technical area how to make and use the claimed invention and (2) contain sufficient written description to demonstrate that, as of the provisional filing date, the inventor(s) actually possessed the claimed invention. Other aspects of provisional patent applications are discussed below.

Nonobvious Even if an invention is novel, it is not patentable if a person of average skill in the field would have the ability to build on the prior art and reach the same result. Thus, an obvious combination or extension of previously existing technology is not patentable, regardless of whether that technology is actively used today or is patented.[43] This *nonobvious requirement* prevents public knowledge from being converted into monopolized information and makes it possible for others to build on that knowledge. The possible motive others might have to combine the prior art in the same way need not be the same as the patent holder's. Nor is it necessary for the prior art to be used strictly as primarily intended.

Establishing Ownership of Workers' Inventions

As with copyrightable works, it is important for the hiring party to obtain a written transfer of all ownership rights in inventions (an *assignment of inventions*) from employees and independent contractors. Absent a written agreement assigning any and all rights in their inventions to the employer, all employees and independent contractors (except those falling into the narrow category of employees "hired to invent") will personally own the patentable inventions they create. Obtaining such an assignment after a promising invention has been created will almost always be far more expensive and may even be impossible.

Resolving Competing Claims for a Patent: First-to-File (with a Twist for U.S. Patents)

On March 16, 2013, pursuant to the America Invents Act, the United States shifted from a "first-to-invent" country to a "first-inventor-to-file" country. At a basic level, this means that, for patent applications filed on or after March 16, 2013, if two inventors attempt to patent substantially the same invention, then any resulting patent will be awarded to the first inventor to file a patent application claiming that invention. This is similar to what has been done in Europe and virtually everywhere else in the world for some time. This change in the law makes it important for inventors in the United States to file their patent applications as soon as may be practicable.

Even though the United States now has a "first-inventor-to-file" system, it has not adopted an "absolute novelty" system of the type used in most other countries. As noted above, in the vast majority of countries other than the United States, any public disclosure of an invention prior to the filing of a patent application will preclude the issuance of a patent for that invention. In contrast, if inventors make a public disclosure of their invention in the United States, or if they offer that invention for sale in the United States, they will not be barred from filing patent applications for that invention in the United States, as long as the inventor does so within one year of the first public disclosure or offer for sale. Further, to the extent that a disclosure by a third party is derived from the inventor's disclosure, then that third party's disclosure will typically not bar the true inventor from filing a U.S. patent application or acquiring the U.S. patent for the true inventor's invention. Importantly, the grace period is generally not available if the third party that disclosed the invention information independently created the disclosed information.[44] Note that even if these exceptions to the first-to-file rule in the United States are available, they apply only to U.S. patents, not to patents in other countries. Thus, as one commentator put it: "While we do not now have a pure first to file system, anyone who relies on the existence of a grace period really is foolish in the extreme. File first. File often."[45]

Provisional Patent Application   As noted above, a provisional patent application makes it possible for the inventor to "put a stake in the ground" until the startup has the time and funds to prepare a full-bore patent application. In particular, a provisional patent application may be used to establish an early effective filing date for a subsequent nonprovisional patent application as long as the nonprovisional application is filed within 12 months after the provisional application. For example, if a preliminary patent application is filed on July 2, 2016, and the nonprovisional application is filed on June 30, 2017, then as long as the claims in the nonprovisional application are adequately supported by the disclosure of the provisional filing, the filing date for any patent issued pursuant to the nonprovisional application filed on June 30, 2017, will be deemed to be July 2, 2016.

Duration of Patents

Rights to utility and plant patents last for 20 years from the date of filing of the earliest related patent application. In the case of design patents, the term depends on when the application was filed. For design patent applications filed prior to May 13, 2015, the rights last for 14 years from the date the design patent is granted. For design patent applications filed on or after May 13, 2015, the duration is 15 years from the date the design patent is granted. After the patent protection period lapses, anyone can use the information in the patent or any published patent application to make or use the invention.

Patent rights can be extended beyond these periods only under special circumstances defined in the patent statute. These special circumstances include cases where examination of a patent application is delayed by the PTO.

Overview of Procedures for Obtaining a Nonprovisional Patent

The procedures for obtaining a nonprovisional U.S. patent are usually time-consuming and expensive.

The Application   The applicant must file a complex application with the PTO that describes the invention in detail. In some instances, the application must include a diagram or illustration of the invention, and the specification must set forth the best way (so-called *best mode*) contemplated of carrying out the invention.

The application must set forth in detail in highly stylized language the specific *claims* of the patent, that is, the precise elements of the invention for which patent protection is sought. In many instances, a claimed invention may have elements that by themselves are not patentable so certain elements would be excluded from the claims. Skill and experience are required to draft claims that are sufficiently broad to achieve meaningful protections yet narrow enough to withstand scrutiny from a patent examiner. Thus, an experienced patent attorney should prepare the patent claims. Because the inventor usually understands the novel aspects of the invention better than anyone else, entrepreneurs can often reduce legal costs by having the inventor work with patent counsel to prepare an initial draft of the patent claims.

Once the claims are drafted, it is beneficial to take a funnel approach when preparing the patent specification. In other words, the description should include both a broad description of the invention and specific narrower versions of it. This approach allows the applicant to have fallback positions in case the PTO finds the broader invention not patentable.

Confidentiality of Certain U.S. Patent Applications If the applicant requests nonpublication of the nonprovisional patent application at the time of filing and certifies that patent protection is sought only in the United States, the patent application remains confidential until the patent is issued; as a result, trade secret protection continues until the patent protection begins. If, however, the U.S. patent application has a foreign counterpart, then the USPTO will publish the nonprovisional application 18 months after it is filed.

Search for Prior Art Before filing a nonprovisional patent application, the applicant should conduct a search for prior art. *Prior art* refers to earlier inventions and publications that may undercut the applicant's claims that the invention is novel and nonobvious. Prior art includes both patented and nonpatented technology, whether incorporated in existing products or described in written materials. Searching for prior art is essential to avoid wasting time and money trying to patent an invention that is not novel. It also helps the inventor anticipate the PTO's response. The patent attorney uses the search results to craft the patent claims to avoid the prior art, and the patent examiner at the PTO uses them to help determine whether a patent should be issued.

Additionally, knowledge of the prior art is beneficial from a patent drafting perspective. If there is close art, the patent specification can include how the invention differs, and the benefits of the invention over the prior art.

The applicant is required to disclose in the patent application all material prior art of which it is aware. Although online databases can be accessed by anyone, it is usually advisable to have a professional search firm conduct the search. Failing to uncover prior art leads to wasted time and expense if the examiner (or a person challenging the patent's validity) later discovers relevant prior art that was missed in the search. Additionally, a patent can be rendered unenforceable in litigation if the applicant is aware of information material to patentability but fails to disclose it to the PTO during prosecution of the patent application.

The Patent Examination   Once the application is submitted, a patent examiner will be assigned to determine whether the invention is patentable. The patent examiner will conduct his or her own search for prior art and frequently will seek to modify the claims of the patent. Very few applications are approved without modification. This back-and-forth process between the applicant and the examiner (called *prosecution*) usually takes at least a year and often more than two years. Although patent examiners usually have some relevant training, many patent applicants have been frustrated by the unfamiliarity of examiners with pertinent technology and the slowness of the proceedings. Applicants should be prepared for frustrations and delays.

An inventor will often want to begin using or selling the invention before the patent application is approved to achieve time-to-market advantages. Even though a provisional patent application is not examined by the PTO, it enables use of the term "patent pending," putting third parties on notice that a patent may be forthcoming.

Costs   Patents usually represent a major expense for a small business. However, many patent attorneys will provide a free initial consultation to determine whether pursuing a patent application makes sense. Although a definitive answer to the question of patentability is unlikely to emerge from a single consultation (unless the answer is a clear no), the entrepreneur can usually get a better idea of whether it is practical to pursue the patent process further. When assessing whether a patent is worth the cost, it is important to remember that having a strong patent portfolio may make it easier to raise money from outside investors.

Patent office fees are based on an applicant's classification as a large entity, a small entity, or a micro entity, and on other factors including the number of claims. In general, to qualify as a *small entity* the patent applicant must be, as defined, a "person," "small business" (500 or fewer employees), or nonprofit organization, and it must not have assigned or licensed the patent rights to a large entity. To qualify as a *micro entity*, the applicant, in general, must qualify as a small entity; not be named on more than four earlier applications; not have a gross income in excess of a defined amount (approximately $161,000 as of January 1, 2016); and not have assigned or licensed any rights to a small or large entity that would not meet the income limit. Certain applicants who work at an institution of higher education may also qualify for micro entity status. Applicants not qualifying as a micro or small entity are considered a *large entity* and must pay the standard fees. As of January 1, 2016, the utility patent application filing fee for individuals not qualifying as a micro entity and for companies with no more than 500 employees was $70, with a utility search fee of $300, a utility examination fee of $360, and an additional fee of $480 payable if and when the patent is issued. The standard fees are, for the most part, halved for small entities; micro entities generally pay half of the small entity amount. An extra fee is charged for nonelectronically filed applications.

Attorney and search firm fees typically bring the total cost of filing an application, including government fees, to $15,000 or more, depending on the complexity of the application and the level of modifications sought by the patent examiner. In contrast, it is sometimes possible to file a preliminary application for less than $5,000.

Additional PTO fees are required over the life of the patent to keep it in force. Total lifetime PTO fees for a small entity currently amount to approximately $7,500; for large entities the total cost may be $25,000 or more.

Challenging the Validity of Patents

Competitors and others frequently challenge patents and seek to overturn them. Currently, the validity of patent claims can be challenged via *ex parte* reexamination in the Patent Office, *inter partes* review in the Patent Office, and proceedings before a federal district court. Each process offers its own unique set of strategic benefits and risks. Thus, the granting of a patent is not always the end of the story.

In proceedings before the Patent Office, patent claims are typically given their broadest reasonable interpretation, and they are not presumed to be valid. In contrast, claims may be construed more narrowly in district court proceedings and the presumption of validity applies. One, therefore, might assume that the PTO provides a preferred venue for challenging patent validity. In some cases, that is no doubt true, but in others, for example, where an invalidity position may be less clear, it may be advantageous to have that position addressed by a judge or jury.

In the case of *ex parte reexamination* by the PTO, the party challenging validity submits a request for reexamination to the PTO and, from that point on, is excluded from participating in the proceeding. In the case of *inter partes review* by the PTO, a patent challenger has an opportunity to respond to positions taken by the patent owner, but those responses can be limited. District court proceedings offer the greatest opportunity to participate in the process, but those proceedings are far more expensive and time consuming. For these reasons, anyone seeking to challenge the validity of a patent should engage counsel to assist with that process.

Patent Infringement

The unauthorized making, use, sale of, offering to sell, or importation of a patented item or process constitutes patent infringement. This is true regardless of whether the infringer was aware of the patent at the time of the infringement. Infringement can also occur if someone intends to induce another to infringe a patent or knowingly contributes to another's infringement. To prove induced infringement, a plaintiff must show that the alleged inducer knew of the patent at issue and knew that the induced acts were infringing. A belief by the alleged inducer that the patent is invalid is not a defense to induced patent infringement.[46]

Remedies If a company is found liable for patent infringement, a court can award an injunction[47] prohibiting import or sale of the infringing product, damages, and/or attorneys' fees.

An injunction, particularly when a company has invested and achieved successful distribution of a product, can be devastating. In a case involving eBay, the U.S. Supreme Court ordered courts to exercise discretion when considering whether to issue an injunction.[48] In his concurrence, Justice Kennedy suggested that injunctions might be particularly inappropriate when a nonoperating firm uses patents to extract exorbitant fees from an operating company or when a business process patent is at issue. Since the Supreme Court's *eBay* decision, grants of injunctions have dropped from "pre-*eBay* rates of 94%-100% to post-*eBay* rates of 73% for all patent owners and 16% for patentees that do not practice the patents they own."[49]

Courts can award substantial damages for patent infringement, including recovery of all profits earned with the infringing product. The damages analysis must be tied to the value of the claimed invention, however. Prior "rules of thumb," such as allocating 25% of profits to a patent holder, are not properly considered in a damages analysis.[50] If a patent holder seeks to use the full market value of an accused product as a royalty base, the holder must show that the claimed invention found in that product is the driver of consumer demand for that product[51] and not just one of hundreds or thousands of valuable features in a complex product.[52]

Courts can triple damage awards in "egregious" cases involving "willful, wanton, malicious, [subjectively] bad-faith, deliberate, consciously wrongful, [or] flagrant" misconduct, including infringement by "the 'wanton and malicious pirate' who intentionally infringes another's patent—with no doubts about its validity or any notion of a defense—for no purpose other than to steal the patentee's business."[53] Courts may also award the prevailing party attorneys' fees in "exceptional" cases.[54]

Under the American Inventor Protection Act of 1999, inventors can recover, as part of their damages, reasonable royalties from others who make, use, sell, or import the invention during the period between the date the patent application is published and the date the patent is granted (*preissuance, provisional rights damages*). This right may be invaluable during the formulation stage of new businesses and for independent inventors in need of funds. Inventors are entitled to royalties under this provision only when the invention as claimed in the issued patent is substantially identical to the invention claimed in the published patent application. Although the PTO generally publishes patent applications 18 months after the filing of the nonprovisional patent application, filers can request that their applications be published earlier. Early publication gives inventors rights to recover royalties as of an earlier date, namely, the date the application is actually published. Thus, it may, in some instances, be worth monitoring published applications as well as issued patents.

When Does It Make Sense to Pursue a Patent?

Because of the time and cost required to obtain a patent, the decision to file a patent application merits careful thought. Some experts suggest that, before seeking a patent, the entrepreneur first evaluate the core technologies that are key to the business's success. For a small business, technologies outside this core area are probably not worth the expense of patenting (unless the patent is being obtained for strategic reasons, as discussed below). Competitors frequently review patents with an eye to designing around a patent, that is, coming up with a functionally similar invention that does not legally infringe the patent's claims. Large companies can then use their superior sales and marketing resources to capture the market. As a result, if better-established competitors could review the patent for an invention and design and sell a different invention that would not infringe the patent but would still convey the same benefits, then a patent may be of little value. This is another reason why inventors should retain an experienced patent attorney to precisely tailor the claims of the patent.

Experts caution against overlooking improvements to existing inventions. If an improvement is nonobvious and otherwise meets the standards of patentability, the improvement itself can be patented. However, such a patent will give the inventor only the right to exclude others from using the improvement—not rights to practice the unimproved invention, if still under patent. Nevertheless, this right to the improvement provides a powerful negotiating chip when seeking a license to the earlier invention.

When deciding whether to seek patent protection, the entrepreneur should also consider other, less costly forms of protection. For example, trade secret protection may be adequate for some inventions, particularly those that involve a process employed in making a product rather than a product that is sold to the public. Unlike patents, however, trade secrets cannot protect against a competitor that independently develops similar technology, even through reverse engineering. Patentable software can also benefit from copyright protection. Consulting an experienced patent attorney, particularly one with knowledge of the field in which the patent is sought, is advisable to assess the best strategy in the face of these complicated trade-offs.

Strategic Aspects of Patents

Legally astute entrepreneurs consider ways to use patents (and other forms of IP) strategically. Patents often convey prestige, and they may promote the image of a technologically innovative company. The familiar phrase "Patent Pending" on a product can suggest an image of technical superiority that can be useful in marketing (even though a patent is not guaranteed, as the phrase suggests). A strong patent portfolio can also make it easier to raise money from venture capitalists and other outside investors who are looking for a proprietary technology that creates a barrier to others who might otherwise enter the market. As noted earlier, owning a portfolio of patents that can be cross-licensed gives a company something to trade in a patent dispute. There is also a growing marketplace for the sale of patents to both operating companies and nonoperating entities.

In one practice, known as *bracketing*, a company will systematically review patent issuances and seek to obtain patents on improvements to the issued patents. With its patent on the improvement, the company may seek either to exact a royalty-free cross-license from the company that holds the initial patent or to block use of the improvement altogether. In some instances, it may be worthwhile to pursue additional patents to block potential bracketers.

Even if a young company is successful in obtaining one or more patents, it is important to remember that a patent rarely will be enough to create an impenetrable barrier to entry by other firms. It may give the patent holder a head start, but usually that early lead will be sustainable only if the company keeps a stream of new inventions flowing through the pipeline. Additionally, a patent is only useful if it covers the technology the company intends to market and commercialize. Therefore, the company should make sure that it communicates the company's business objectives to its patent attorney, so that the invention that is actually patented is in fact the technology the venture intends to commercialize or license.

Learning from Competitors' Patents

Even if a company does not plan to file for patent protection, it may undertake a patent search to uncover competing technology and to reduce the risk of inadvertent patent infringement. If the search uncovers a competitor's patent for a different invention that achieves superior results, pursuing a patent may make little sense. If the patent for that superior technology is owned by a company that is not a direct competitor, however, then an entrepreneur may be able to negotiate a licensing arrangement, whereby the entrepreneur secures the right to use the invention for a noncompeting product. Competitors' patent filings can also provide clues about future product and development directions. Search results have even been known to spark creative ideas in the minds of inventors, helping them develop new noninfringing inventions. Indeed, that is the purpose of the patent system—to promote the useful arts by encouraging public disclosure of new inventions in exchange for the right to exclude others from making the invention for a limited period.

International Issues

U.S. patents do not protect inventions sold or used in foreign countries. They will, however, prevent any unauthorized person from importing a product into the United States that includes an invention protected by a U.S. patent.

Each country usually requires a separate patent filing, but the Patent Cooperation Treaty allows an inventor to file a single international patent application to preserve the right to seek patent protection in each contracting country. The inventor may file this application either with the national patent office or the International Bureau of the World Intellectual Property Organization. In addition, a single filing in the European Patent Office (*EPO*) can provide protection in the nations in the European Union, although issue fees are required by individual countries once the EPO grants a patent.

Costs to prepare and file a foreign patent currently average about $5,000 per country (excluding translation fees), assuming that a U.S. patent application has already been completed. Even if a patent is granted, foreign patents may be difficult or impossible to enforce in certain countries.

The decision whether to obtain foreign patents is an important strategic issue that should be discussed with a patent attorney before an invention is disclosed or sold. Even if the company has no plans for overseas sales or use of an invention, it may still be worth the considerable expense of obtaining foreign patents to block foreign competitors from gaining access to the invention.

Most foreign countries publish patent applications 18 months after the patent application is filed regardless of whether the applicant is filing for protection in more than one country. Given the time required to process a patent, the information contained in the patent application usually becomes public before the patent is issued. Once such information is public, trade secret protection is lost. Therefore, if a trade secret is required in order to practice an invention, it is beneficial to include the secret within a broader disclosure (e.g., a list of options), so that the company's competitors do not know which exact option the company employs.

14.4 TRADEMARKS

Trademark law helps to protect both trademark owners and consumers from the confusion that can result when different companies use the same or confusingly similar identifying marks, either intentionally or unintentionally. By identifying the source of a product, trademarks make it possible for a company to create and protect "brand equity," a reputation for consistent quality, reliability, innovation, performance, and value. Well-recognized brands, such as the name and symbol for Mercedes-Benz, boost sales and contribute to the bottom line. If a low-quality automaker could freely use the name "Mercedes," or something confusingly similar such as "Mircedes," or the familiar circled three-point-star hood ornament, consumers could be misled into thinking that they were buying a genuine Mercedes or a product of equivalent quality. Daimler AG's sales and reputation could deteriorate as consumers wrongly concluded that Mercedes-Benz had let its quality and performance slip.

Trademarks used in connection with a service business are called service marks. For example, "Visa" is a service mark relating to credit card services offered by Visa International Services Association. Because the principles and laws relating to service marks are virtually identical to those of trademarks, the remainder of this section should be read as applying to service marks as well.

Definition of a Trademark

A *trademark* is any word (or phrase), name, symbol, sound, or design that identifies and distinguishes one company's products from those made or sold by competitors. The U.S. Supreme Court has held that the universe of things that can qualify as a trademark should be viewed "in the broadest of terms."[55] For example, Coke and the tagline "It's the real thing" are both trademarks for cola soda from the Coca-Cola Company. The Nike swoosh is a trademark for shoes and other products produced by Nike, Inc. The distinctive NBC chime is a trademark of National Broadcasting Company, Inc. Distinctive colors can serve as a trademark when the public has come to associate them with a product, such as the color brown used on UPS trucks and uniforms. Luxury fashion designer Christian Louboutin has a trademark on its distinctive red soles on multichrome women's high-fashion designer footwear; it cannot, however, preclude competitors from making monochrome shoes with red uppers and soles.[56] Even scents, such as the floral scent of sewing thread, can serve as trademarks.

Trade Dress Trademark law can also protect *trade dress*, such as packaging or the shape/configuration of a product or a restaurant or store, when the trade dress indicates or identifies the source of the offering and distinguishes it from those of others.[57] For example, Coca-Cola has a trademark for the shape of its "old-fashioned" six-ounce bottle. Pharmaceutical giant Pfizer, Inc. has a trademark on the blue diamond shape of its Viagra tablets. Toolmaker Black & Decker won a $54 million verdict in a case against another toolmaker that used a black and yellow color scheme similar to that used on Black & Decker's DeWalt brand tools.[58] Black & Decker presented survey data showing that 100% of professional tradespeople and 85% of "serious do-it-yourselfers" identified DeWalt by name upon seeing a black and yellow power tool. Apple Inc. obtained trademark protection for "the minimalist design and layout of its retail stores comprised of 'a clear glass storefront by a paneled façade' and the signature 'oblong table with stools … set below video screens flush mounted on the back wall.'"[59]

Unregistered trade dress is not entitled to protection unless it is distinctive or has acquired secondary meaning, meaning that consumers associate the trade dress with a particular source of a product or service.[60] Even if a feature has acquired secondary meaning, however, it will not receive trade dress protection if the feature is functional rather than ornamental. If the owner of trade dress obtained a utility patent covering the trade dress, then the expiration of the utility patent is "strong evidence" that the design features claimed in it are functional and thus not entitled to trade dress protection.[61]

Trade Names A *trade name* is a business's formal, legal name, which typically must be registered with either local or state authorities. A company's trade name is most often also a trademark because the company typically uses its trade name in connection with its products and services. In fact, a company's trade name may well be the most important trademark it owns. For example, Apple is a trademark of the company whose trade name is Apple, Inc.

Establishing a Strong Trademark

There are multiple steps involved in establishing a strong trademark.

Select a Distinctive Mark   The first step is to identify a mark that is distinctive and thus will serve uniquely to identify the company in its field of business. The degree of protection available under trademark law is determined by how distinctive the trademark is: the more distinctive, the better. The basic idea is that marks that directly describe the company's product or service offering are not distinctive. For example, generic terms, such as *plane, software,* and *designer,* are not protectable trademarks for the products they describe. In contrast, distinctive marks uniquely identify the offering as emanating from a single company. Many business-people choose their own marks, but professional advice from advertising agencies or marketing firms may be worth the cost, particularly for consumer goods. Selecting strong trademarks early in the life of a business can help to ensure that those marks will not need to be changed later on, perhaps at great expense.

Inherently distinctive marks are the strongest form of trademark. These marks have no meaning within an industry before their adoption by a company in that industry. There are three main types of inherently distinctive marks. *Fanciful marks* include made-up words, such as "Exxon" for gasoline and "Kodak" for cameras. *Arbitrary marks* are real words that have nothing to do with the product category, such as "Apple" for computers. Note, however, that neither Apple nor Macintosh could be trademarks for a company that sells apples. *Suggestive marks* suggest something about the product but do not describe it. Examples include "Claritin" for allergy medicine and "Chicken of the Sea" for tuna.

Descriptive marks are not considered to be inherently distinctive. A mark that indicates characteristics of the product it identifies is a descriptive mark. Examples include "Rapid Seal" for a paint sealant and "cc: Mail" for an electronic mail program. Laudatory terms such as "Gold Medal" are also considered descriptive. Marks that indicate the geographic origin of the product, such as "California Lumber" and "Albany Roofing," are considered descriptive, as are marks derived from a proper name, such as "Hilton Hotels."

Descriptive marks are not immediately protectable but may become fully protectable once they acquire secondary meaning in the marketplace. *Secondary meaning* is acquired when a significant number of people come to associate the mark with a particular

company or product. For example, in 1995, Microsoft was successful in registering "Windows" as a trademark for its PC operating
system in part because the word had acquired secondary meaning;
consumers had come to associate Windows with Microsoft's
operating system and did not use it as a descriptive term for any
software that generated "windows" on a computer screen. If a dispute over the ownership of a descriptive trademark arises, it can
be expensive to establish the existence of secondary meaning in
court.

Respect Individuals' Right of Publicity When considering
whether to use an individual's name or image as a trademark or
in advertising, it is important to keep in mind that certain states
recognize that an individual may have the right to prevent commercial exploitation of his or her name or image. This "right of
publicity" is implicated, for example, when a company uses a
celebrity image to promote a product without authorization. An
attorney can provide additional advice about endorsement, attribution, and publicity issues.

Perform a Trademark Search The second step in acquiring a trademark is to perform a trademark search to ensure that someone
else has not already established rights in the proposed mark or
one confusingly similar to it in the relevant field of business. The
search should include both federal searches and state searches in
any states where business will be conducted and, since business is
increasingly conducted globally, also in those countries where the
business believes it will have significant commercial activity. Com-
puterized databases exist for conducting these searches. A Google
search can also be used to identify unregistered trademarks that
are still entitled to protection by virtue of use-based rights under
U.S. common law. A number of vendors also offer more comprehensive searches that cover various common law databases.

In many cases acquiring the related domain name will be
important, so trademark searches should include a search of
domain names, the addresses used to locate businesses online.
For many years, most businesses obtained and primarily used
".com" top-level Internet domain names to establish a company's
online business presence. As businesses have become more global,

many companies also use various country code top-level domains, such as ".eu" for European Union or ".fr" for France. Over time, the Internet Corporation for Assigned Names and Numbers has expanded the number of "generic" top-level domains available to include such terms as ".marketing," ".dance," or ".feedback." It remains to be seen how widely these additional domains will be adopted and used in the marketplace, but the availability of these alternatives underscores the need for companies to seek advice in developing a comprehensive domain name strategy for their online presence while selecting trademarks.[62]

Although it is not necessary to hire an attorney to conduct a trademark search, it is often a good idea. A preliminary search can generally be performed for less than $1,500. An attorney can usually have a full search performed and assess the risk that the proposed mark infringes confusingly similar marks for less than $4,500. At the very least, the entrepreneur should review online trademark databases and search the Internet, including the domain name registries. A careful search reduces the risk of infringing another's mark and can limit any infringement damages by helping to show that the infringing use was undertaken in good faith.

Create Rights in the Trademark   The third step is to create rights in the trademark in the United States by using the trademark in commerce. Attaching the trademark to goods for sale and using the mark in advertising and promotional materials constitute use. The use must be in good faith, meaning that the user must be unaware of anyone else with prior rights to the mark or a confusingly similar mark. Every user is deemed by the law to be aware of every valid federal trademark registration (and every valid intent-to-use application), so failure to conduct a proper trademark search is not a defense as long as the trademark is registered or any intent-to-use filing is followed by a timely filing of a trademark registration application and use of the mark in commerce.

In the United States, if the trademark is inherently distinctive, the first person to use the mark in interstate commerce becomes the owner unless another person filed an intent-to-use application before the first use of the mark in interstate commerce. In the latter case, as long as the person who filed an intent-to-use application ultimately uses the mark in commerce within the specified time period, the first to file will own the mark in the specified field of use. If the mark is a descriptive mark, using the mark merely begins the process of developing the secondary meaning necessary to create full trademark rights. For both inherently distinctive and merely descriptive marks, greater use generally leads to stronger rights as the mark becomes more closely identified with a single business. In most other countries, the first to file a trademark application owns the mark in connection with the goods and/or services covered by the application.

Register the Trademark Although mere use can establish rights to a trademark in the United States under common law, federal trademark registration on the Principal Register of the USPTO is strongly recommended for all eligible trademarks. Trademark registration application fees range from $225 to $375 per class of goods or services. The process of obtaining federal trademark registration can be complex, and it is usually advisable to consult with an experienced attorney before proceeding.

Descriptive marks are generally not eligible for registration on the Principal Register. This is yet another reason to avoid using them. However, separate filing procedures for descriptive marks do exist that can offer some protections. An attorney can provide additional advice about protecting descriptive marks.

Federal registration on the Principal Register is evidence of ownership that can be useful if the trademark is ever contested. Because everyone is presumed by law to be aware of a registered trademark, no infringing use of a registered trademark can be in good faith. This makes it easier to stop trademark infringers from using the mark and to collect damages. In addition, after five years of continuous use, the trademark can be declared incontestable, making it far more difficult to challenge. Finally, registration enables the owner to prevent importation of articles bearing the trademark.

An *intent-to-use application* gives the entrepreneur the ability to secure protection against imitators who may become aware of a new product name via a trade show or other promotional announcement made before the product launches and trademark rights from use begin to accrue. Once this application is filed, the owner secures the filing date as his or her priority date and thus will be able to prevent others from subsequently adopting or registering the identical mark for the same or similar goods. If the mark is approved, the owner has six months to begin using it; this initial period can be extended an additional 30 months if "good cause" for not using the mark is shown, giving the applicant a full three years to file the statement of use.

After a trademark application is filed, a trademark examiner at the PTO will search for prior filings of confusingly similar marks and will decide whether the trademark is sufficiently distinctive to qualify for trademark protection. The process can involve multiple communications with the Trademark Office and may consume many months after the initial filing. However, protection begins from the date the ultimately approved application was filed, so no loss of rights can occur during the application process.

After examination, the Trademark Office will issue a *notice of allowance* if the trademark is eligible for registration. Before a registration will issue, however, the owner must file a *statement of use* advising the Trademark Office that the owner has begun using the mark in business, for example, by shipping or selling a product in interstate commerce that has the mark affixed to it or its package or by providing a service under the mark to out-of-state consumers. As noted above, if the Trademark Office approves an intent-to-use application, the owner must generally begin using the mark within six months to preserve its rights; this initial period can be extended in six-month increments for up to 30 months if the owner shows "good cause" for not using the mark sooner.

Regulators impose additional requirements for trademark use and advertising on companies in certain fields. For example, the Food and Drug Administration (*FDA*) must approve the name of a proposed drug or therapy, and the Alcohol and Tobacco Tax and Trade Bureau must approve the labels and advertisements for alcohol products. Advice of counsel is critical to understand whether additional requirements or regulations in addition to trademark requirements should be satisfied to ensure the successful launch of a new product or service.

Loss of Trademark Rights

Federal trademark registration currently lasts for 10 years, but the owner must prove continued use (or in limited circumstances, an "excusable nonuse") between the fifth and sixth years. If the required showing of use is met, the registration can be renewed indefinitely in increments of 10 years. Once a trademark has been obtained, however, the owner must take certain steps to ensure that the trademark rights are not lost. A trademark will be deemed *abandoned* if the owner ceases use of it with no intent to resume use; failure to use a trademark for three years will create a presumption of abandonment. Trademark protection can also be lost if a trademark loses its distinctive association with its manufacturer or distributor and becomes a *generic noun* for a product. "Escalator," "thermos," and "aspirin" were all once trademarks; they lost their protected status because their owners failed to police their use.

Trademark Infringement and Dilution

To prove trademark infringement, the trademark owner must prove, among other things, a likelihood that the allegedly infringing mark could create confusion in the minds of potential customers. Such a showing is easy in the case of competing counterfeit goods displaying another's trademark. If the marks are not identical, however, determining whether another's mark is confusingly similar is a highly subjective factual matter that can be expensive and time-consuming to prove in court. If infringement can be proved, remedies may include a court order barring the infringer from using the infringing mark and the assessment of damages.

Holders of *famous marks*, that is, registered marks that have become strongly associated with a particular company, can prevent others from using marks that would dilute the value of the famous mark. *Dilution* involves using another's trademark on goods or in connection with services or as a trade name if the use is likely to cause harm to the reputation of the mark's owner (*tarnishment*) or is likely to lessen the distinctiveness of the mark (*blurring*). Under certain circumstances, owners of famous marks will be able to prove dilution more easily than trademark infringement, which requires showing the likelihood of consumer confusion. The owner of a famous mark can successfully establish trademark dilution even if (1) there is no likelihood of consumer confusion between the two marks, (2) the subject marks do not commercially compete with one another, and (3) the famous mark owner has not actually suffered economic harm as a result of the third party's trademark use. For example, Tiffany & Co. could likely successfully sue to stop a tire manufacturer from using "Tiffany" as a trademark for its tires, even though the average consumer would not confuse Tiffany jewelry with Tiffany tires.

Permissible Use of Another's Trademark

Not all uses of another's trademark result in trademark infringement. The United States, for example, permits the use of another's trademark without permission in a way that does not result in dilution or a likelihood of confusion. For example, Ocean Spray was permitted to describe its cranberry juice as "sweet-tart" without violating Sunmark's rights to the *Swee*TART candy.[63]

Fair Use Defense Under certain circumstances, a third party's use of another's trademark to describe the third party's own goods or services may constitute noninfringing *fair use*. For example, in the United States, it is permissible to use the third party's mark when comparing one's own products or services with those sold by the third party. Fair use also permits, under certain circumstances, the use of another's trademark when advertising that one's product is compatible with a product from another company. Courts also sometimes permit the use of another's trademark for the purposes of parody, art, or speech.

International Issues

As with patents, trademark protection in the United States does not prevent the adoption and use of the mark outside the United States. Trademarks must be registered in each country where protection is sought, and the protections granted vary among jurisdictions. Certain foreign governments appear to be treating trademark infringement very seriously so founders of companies expecting to do business globally should consult with trademark counsel well in advance.

As discussed above, the United States gives priority to the first to *use* the trademark (except when an intent-to-use application is filed before another person uses the mark). In contrast, most other countries give priority to the first to *file* an application to register the mark. Trademark owners expanding into international markets therefor run the risk of encountering third parties who may enjoy superior rights to the same trademark in a particular country. Many well-known brands have found themselves the victims of trademark piracy when the company failed to protect the mark abroad and another firm registered it there first. Early registration in foreign countries is therefore important for companies planning to offer products or services abroad. An experienced IP attorney can provide entrepreneurs advice about protecting trademarks outside the United States.

The *Community Trade Mark* (also known as the *CTM*) is a single application process that, when issued as a registration, covers all European Union Member States. As the EU expands (or, after Brexit, contracts), so too will the coverage of existing CTM registrations. Companies doing business in three or more EU countries may want to consider registering key trademarks under the CTM system as it can result in significant cost savings compared with filing for individual national registrations in multiple EU member jurisdictions.

The *Madrid Protocol* is a centralized mechanism by which trademark owners can obtain national trademark rights in multiple select jurisdictions. Although it is subject to certain limitations, the Madrid Protocol system covers 97 countries and can offer significant cost savings over individual national filings.[64]

Although English is often cited as the global language of commerce, trademark holders planning to expand into foreign markets should also be aware of the potential to obtain trademark registrations for translations or transliterations of their trademarks in a local language or alphabet, such as Arabic, Chinese, or Cyrillic. For example, although Pfizer "owns Wai Aike (万艾可), a transliteration of Viagra that has no meaning in Chinese," Pfizer "does not own the best-known name for Viagra in China, *Weige* (伟哥) or Great Older Brother."[65] As Professor Chow explains:

> Obtaining a Chinese-language trademark before the English-language mark becomes public and the Chinese media subjects it to transliterations should allow the brand owner to establish its own Chinese-language transliteration for its English-language trademark and to exercise greater control over how the brand is presented in China.[66]

14.5 DOMAIN NAMES AND CYBERSQUATTING

Domain names are given on a first-come, first-served basis with no field-of-use restrictions. There is only one Ford.com, for example, although both Ford Motor Company and the Ford Modeling Agency might own the registered trademark "Ford" for use in connection with cars and trucks and for modeling services, respectively. In addition, even if only one firm owns a trademark, having a trademark does not automatically translate into a right to use the mark as a domain name or necessarily mean that the mark owner can stop someone else from using the identical mark as a domain name.

Seizing on the opportunity created by a system that gave domain names to the first to apply, *cybersquatters* registered domain names containing trademarks and then tried to sell them at exorbitant prices to the owners of the trademarks. In response, Congress passed the Anticybersquatting Consumer Protection Act of 1999, which made it illegal for a person to register or use a domain name, with a bad-faith intent to profit from the name, if the domain name is (1) identical or confusingly similar to a distinctive trademark or (2) identical or confusingly similar to or dilutive of a famous trademark.

The Internet Corporation for Assigned Names and Numbers (*ICANN*) has established an arbitration procedure (the Uniform Domain-Name Dispute-Resolution Policy or *UDRP*) that many domain name registries follow. The UDRP is a relatively fast and inexpensive way to pursue a cybersquatter who has registered a ".com," ".net," or ".org" domain name or one of the many country-code domains (e.g., ".au" for Australia, ".ch" for Switzerland, and ".de" for Denmark). Domain names determined to have been registered and used in bad faith can either be canceled or transferred to the successful mark owner or complainant. Notably, neither injunctions nor awards of damages or attorneys' fees are available in UDRP proceedings.

ICANN's Internationalized Domain Names program permits members of the global community to use domain names in their native language or script. An attorney can provide additional advice about protecting trademarks in foreign languages both online and off-line in light of these developments.

14.6 EMPLOYEE PROPRIETARY INFORMATION AND ASSIGNMENT OF INVENTIONS AGREEMENTS

As explained earlier, all employees at all levels of the company should be required to sign a detailed proprietary information and inventions agreement, sometimes called *nondisclosure* and *assignment-of-inventions agreements*. (The same is true of independent contractors with access to proprietary information or responsibility for creating original works or inventions.) Such agreements both provide broad protection for the company's proprietary information (including trade secrets) and ensure that the company will be entitled to all rights and title that a worker may have to inventions created or even conceived of during the period of employment.

Nondisclosure and Nonuse of Proprietary Information

The nondisclosure provisions should obligate the employee to refrain from unauthorized disclosure and unauthorized use of the company's proprietary information. The agreement should also state that the obligation to refrain from unauthorized use or disclosure of the company's proprietary information continues indefinitely after the employee terminates his or her employment with the company.

A company may also wish to include the following provisions in its nondisclosure agreement:

➤ A broad definition of proprietary information

➤ A commitment not to disclose or use third-party proprietary information, including information from joint venture partners or previous employers

➤ An agreement that precludes the employee from participating in business activities other than those activities that the employee is performing for the company

➤ A commitment to return all company materials upon termination of employment with the company, including any embodiment of proprietary information, such as notes or electronically recorded information

➤ An acknowledgment that signing the nondisclosure agreement does not breach any other agreement that the employee may have with other entities

➤ An acknowledgment that employment with the company is at will, if applicable

➤ An agreement not to solicit coworkers for a defined period of time after leaving the company.

Assignment of Inventions

The assignment-of-inventions agreement should require the employee to assign to the company all rights to any invention that results from work performed for the employer as well as work that relates to the employer's current business or demonstrably anticipated research or development. Any invention made on the employer's time, or using the employer's materials, equipment, or trade secrets, should also be assigned to the company.

The assignment agreement should be as broad as the law allows. In some states, such as California, Minnesota, and Washington, statutes have carved out an exception for inventions unrelated to the employer's business that the employee develops on his or her own time and without use of the employer's material, equipment, or trade secrets; certain states require written notice of these restrictions. Such carve-outs should be expressly referenced in the agreement.

It is important to limit the employer's right to an employee's postemployment inventions to a reasonable period of time. This is another case of less is more. For example, one court held that an agreement assigning postemployment inventions to the former employer was valid and enforceable as it related to ideas and concepts based on secrets or confidential information of the employer because the former employee conceived of the inventions within one year after the termination of employment.[67]

In contrast, another court found a contract provision requiring an employee to assign to the former employer ideas and improvements conceived of by the employee within five years after termination of employment to be unreasonable and void as against public policy.

It is also important that the agreement include an actual assignment of the employee's inventions (e.g., "I hereby assign to the company....") rather than an agreement to assign (e.g., "I agree that I *will* assign to the company...."). Although this distinction may seem to be a mere technicality, it results in substantially different rights. An agreement to assign suggests that some further act is necessary to effect the assignment; as a result, the employee can allege, at some point in the future, that the actual assignment never took place.

Disclosure of Preemployment and Postemployment Inventions

The assignment-of-inventions agreement should require the employee to identify any preexisting inventions to which the employee claims ownership rights. This will help eliminate disputes regarding employee claims to ownership of an invention allegedly developed or conceived of prior to joining the company. To ensure that the company is aware of all inventions for which it may have an ownership right, the agreement should also obligate the employee to disclose, on a periodic basis, all of his or her inventions created or conceived of during employment, as well as those invented for a specified period of time after employment.

14.7 COMPARISON OF TYPES OF PROTECTION

As explained in this chapter, different types of intellectual property protection are available and appropriate in different settings. The advantages and disadvantages of the four basic types of protection are summarized in Table 14.1.

TABLE 14.1	Advantages and Disadvantages of Different Types of Intellectual Property Protection			
	Trade Secret	**Copyright**	**Utility Patent**	**Trademark**
Benefits	Very broad protection for sensitive, competitive information; very inexpensive	Prevents copying of a wide array of artistic and literary expressions, including software; very inexpensive	Very strong protection; provides exclusive right to make, use, and sell an invention	Protects corporate image and identity by protecting marks that customers use to identify a business; prevents others from using confusingly similar identifying marks
Duration	For as long as the information remains valuable and is kept confidential	For individual authors, life of author plus 70 years; for works made for hire, 95 years from year of first publication or 120 years from year of creation, whichever is shorter	20 years from date of filing the utility patent application	Indefinitely as long as the mark is not abandoned and steps are taken to police its use
Weaknesses	No protection from accidental disclosure, independent creation by a competitor, or disclosure by someone without a duty to maintain confidentiality	Protects only the particular way an idea is expressed, not the idea itself; apparent lessening of protection for software; hard to detect copying in digital age	High standards of patentability; often expensive and time-consuming to pursue (especially when overseas patents are needed); must disclose invention to public	Can be lost or weakened if not appropriately used and enforced; can be costly if multiple overseas registrations are needed
Required steps	Take reasonable steps to protect—generally, a trade secret protection program.	None required; however, notice and registration can strengthen rights	Detailed filing with U.S. Patent and Trademark Office, which performs a search for prior art and can impose hefty fees	Only need to use mark in commerce; however, filing with U.S. Patent and Trademark Office is usually desirable to gain stronger protections
U.S. rights valid internationally?	No. Trade secret laws vary significantly by country, and certain countries do not protect trade secrets at all.	Generally, yes	No. Separate patent examinations and filings are required in each country; however, a single international patent application can be filed with the national patent office or the World International Property Organization, and a single filing in the European Patent Office can cover a number of European countries.	No. Separate filings are required in foreign jurisdictions, and a mark available in the United States may not be available overseas. A single CTM filing can, however, cover a number of European countries.

14.8 LICENSING AGREEMENTS AND OTHER TRANSFERS OF INTELLECTUAL PROPERTY

Like most other forms of property, intellectual property rights can be bought, sold, and licensed. It is critical for entrepreneurs and inventors to understand which rights are being conveyed in a given transaction. For example, an *assignment* is typically used to transfer all of the current owner's interests in an item of intellectual property to a new owner (the *assignee*). In contrast, a *license* gives a person the right to do something he or she would not otherwise be permitted to do, but it does not transfer the related property rights. For example, a movie theater ticket is a license giving the holder permission to enter the theater. The party granting the license is called the *licensor*; the party receiving the license is the *licensee*.

Assignments

Assignments are typically used to transfer intellectual property when a company sells some or all of its assets to another company. Trademark assignments transfer not only the marks but also the goodwill symbolized by the marks.

Employment and independent contractor agreements routinely contain assignments that convey all rights to the intellectual property generated by the worker to the company funding the work. For example, an inventor wishing to sell a patent to a corporation will transfer all of his or her "right, title and interest" in the patent to the corporation through an assignment document. After the assignment, the inventor will have no rights to the patent, and the corporation can sue the inventor for infringement if he or she uses any elements of the patent.

Licenses

When an owner wishes to retain some rights to or control over its intellectual property, a license agreement is commonly used. Unlike assignments, licensing agreements grant limited, specified rights to use intellectual property. For example, an inventor who owns a patent that has uses in several different industries might license the rights to use the patent in the medical field to one company, license the rights to use it in the chemical industry to another, and retain for itself the rights to use the patent in all other fields. Because of their great flexibility, licenses are a popular way to obtain intellectual property rights.

For example, software developers will typically license, not sell, their software to the customer. The license agreement often contains many restrictions on how and by whom the software may be used. These restrictions can become extremely detailed. McDonald's licenses to its franchisees rights to its many trademarks, such as the "Golden Arches" and "Big Mac," but the licenses provide that McDonald's can hold the franchisees to rigorous quality standards and take back the rights to use the trademarks if the franchisees use them improperly. Indeed, to protect the rights to its trademarks, the owner must police their use by others who are licensed to use them. Imagine the damage to McDonald's reputation if a franchisee were to operate a dirty restaurant with McDonald's trademarks displayed prominently throughout.

Licensing revenue can be significant, particularly in the technology field. For example, Microsoft reportedly earns more than $2 billion a year from its mobile device patents.

Key Terms in Licensing Agreements

The potential variety and complexity of licensing agreements are limited only by the ingenuity and business needs of the parties. Agreements can range from a few pages to several hundred pages in length. Because license agreements are very flexible, the entrepreneur should take an active role in structuring the arrangements.

Patent, trademark, and copyright licenses all have differing provisions that are of particular importance to each type of intellectual property. What follows is a very brief overview of key considerations common to many intellectual property licenses.

Specification of What Is to Be Licensed The *specification* sets forth the precise description of the intellectual property covered by the license. In a license agreement, the specification may be termed "Licensed Technology or Licensed Trademarks," for example. The licensee does not obtain rights to anything not included in the specification. Developing the specification can be straightforward, but traps abound. The licensee must be sure that the license conveys all rights the licensee needs to meet its business objectives. For example, are all necessary trademarks conveyed? If a developer of multimedia products licenses the rights to use scenes in a movie, does the license include the right to use the accompanying music in the soundtrack? Major issues in many software license agreements are whether the license includes improvements or enhancements to the licensed technology made by the licensor after the license agreement is signed and whether these will be provided to the licensee free of charge or require payment of an additional fee.

Scope of License The *scope* of the license describes what the licensee may do with the licensed intellectual property and spells out any limitations on the rights granted in the licensed intellectual property. Scope is the most important provision in many license agreements. Matters to address include the following:

➤ Is the license exclusive or nonexclusive? If the license is exclusive, the licensor cannot grant the same rights to another licensee, or exercise those rights itself.

➤ Is the license limited to certain geographic regions? To particular markets or products?

➤ Does the license include the right to modify or improve the licensed technology? To sublicense it to others? To share the license with affiliated corporations?

➤ How long does the license last?

➤ Does the license set performance criteria such as minimum sales requirements that, if not met, result in a termination of the license?

➤ On what terms, if any, may the license be renewed?

These and many other limitations on the use of the licensed intellectual property are contained in the scope-of-license provision.

Licensors must be careful to restrict the licensing of valuable rights to only those rights that the licensee truly needs. Otherwise, revenue opportunities may be lost. For example, if a licensor grants to a distributor exclusive rights to sell a patented invention throughout the United States, but the distributor has no operations in the Southwest, then the licensor may lose revenues that could have come from granting a separate license to a Southwestern distributor.

The licensee must also consider what rights it needs to meet its objectives, both now and in the future. For example, geographic restrictions can impede future growth. If the license does not cover improvements to the licensed technology made by the licensor, the licensee could end up with a right to obsolete technology. Lawyers can craft careful language to implement a deal, but the managers themselves must also carefully consider the appropriate scope of the license.

Payments   Payments are most often in the form of up-front lump sums, installment payments, royalties, or some combination of these. Sometimes a licensor will accept equity in the licensee in exchange for the license grant. Royalties can be based on many different measures, including unit sales, percentage of gross revenues, or percentage of profits. Careful consideration must be given to how royalties are calculated because the method chosen will affect licensee behavior. For example, a license based on the number of units sold will give the licensee an incentive to sell fewer units but at a higher price than would be the case under a percentage-of-gross revenues calculation. Similarly, basing royalties on a percentage of profits may require specifying exactly how profits are to be calculated because financial accounting principles allow for some leeway, especially in such areas as allocation of overhead across products. Many agreements include minimum royalty payments and sliding-scale royalties, under which the per-unit royalties decrease as sales increase.

Representations, Warranties, and Indemnification   The licensee wants to be sure that the licensor actually possesses all the rights to be transferred to the licensee and that performing the agreement

From the **TRENCHES**

A producer of boxing videos signed license agreements with five top former heavyweight champions, including Muhammad Ali, to use film footage of the boxers in a video. Each license included in the boilerplate a so-called *most-favored-nations clause*. Under this clause, if the producer agreed to an improved financial deal for any one of the boxers, the producer would have to offer the same deal to each of the other boxers. Sometime later, Ali's representatives negotiated a highly favorable deal that gave him 20% of the revenues from the video. When the other boxers learned of this deal, they each invoked the most-favored-nations clause, obligating the producer to pay each of the five boxers 20% of the revenues from the video. This left the producer with none of the revenues.

will not infringe the rights of any other person. The licensee also wants to ensure that the licensor is not bound by any restrictions that prevent it from carrying out its obligations under the license agreement. The *representations and warranties* set forth the licensor's assurances regarding these (and many other) matters.

In computer software licenses, the *indemnification* provisions commonly require the licensor to defend the licensee against claims by third parties that the licensed software infringes the third parties' intellectual property rights and to pay any resulting damages and costs. Licensors are often reluctant to give unlimited indemnification, especially for patent infringement, which can happen innocently. As a result, the indemnification provisions may specify a maximum total amount that can be recovered. The obligation to indemnify may terminate after a stated period of time, or it may continue for the same period as the license.

Similarly, the licensor will often demand representations, warranties, and indemnification from the licensee. For example, a licensor may demand assurances that the licensee is financially sound and is not under any contractual or other restrictions that could prevent it from performing its duties under the license agreement. These provisions are also intensely negotiated.

Covenants *Covenants* are promises by a party to the license agreement to do (or not do) certain things. For example, in a trademark license, the licensee must agree to use the trademarks in ways that maintain their value as symbols of goodwill for the business. In a patent license, one party will usually promise to make the additional payments, including maintenance fees, necessary to keep the patents in force for the term of the agreement.

Rather than requiring a party to make an absolute promise to do something, covenants sometimes require the party to use reasonable or best efforts to accomplish a task. Such covenants are frequently used when the party making the promise does not have complete control over the outcome. For example, a party may be required to use its best efforts to obtain patent protections in certain foreign jurisdictions. Because the party cannot force the patent examiners to issue the required patents, the party will not have breached the covenant if it did everything legally possible to obtain the patents.

Both the licensee and the licensor should be aware, however, that many courts interpret "best efforts" literally and will require a party under a *best-efforts obligation* to use extraordinary and costly measures if necessary to achieve the promised result. A *reasonable-efforts standard* requires the party to operate with diligence but introduces an element of cost-benefit analysis into the determination of whether the party has lived up to its promise. Extreme care should be exercised before undertaking any best-efforts obligation.

Importance of Due Diligence when Transferring or Licensing IP Rights

Although a well-crafted technology-sale (or assignment) agreement or license can provide many protections, it is no substitute for thoroughly investigating the technology and the other party to the transaction—*due diligence* in legal jargon. The amount of due diligence necessary is dependent upon the type of transaction; the representations, warranties, and indemnities provided; and the financial condition of the licensor and licensee. For example, if IBM gives full indemnification for any intellectual property problems, the licensee will have less need to conduct extensive due diligence. However, if a small, unknown company provides the same full indemnification for any intellectual property problems, the licensee should generally do sufficient diligence on the licensor to determine whether it has the assets to stand behind the indemnification. If it does not, suitable guarantees from principals in the licensor firm may be desirable, albeit difficult to secure.

A company acquiring technology (and other IP rights) must investigate whether the seller or licensor actually has all the rights in the property that the agreement requires it to transfer. Sometimes another party (such as an inventor, a prior employer of the inventor, or another licensee) may have rights to the technology that the seller or licensor has no right to transfer or that prevent the seller from transferring the technology. The acquiring company should also analyze whether the patents, trademarks, and copyrights to be conveyed fully cover all technology that is truly important to the acquirer. Too often a buyer or licensee will assume that just because a company has secured a number of patents, that company fully owns and has protected all its key technologies. Frequently, this is not the case. By searching public records, such as the USPTO databases, a party can verify the status of many intellectual property rights.

The financial condition and reputation of the seller or licensor should also be investigated. This is particularly important if the relationship is expected to last for a long period of time. A licensor should also thoroughly investigate the licensee and analyze the licensee's financial strength, reputation, and future prospects. This is particularly important when the licensee is required to pay royalties based on the level of sales and when the payments are to be made over a number of years. The potential licensor should also examine the licensee's technological and marketing capabilities to develop and sell products using the technology, as well as the strength of the licensee's desire to exploit the technology. An ill-equipped or undermotivated licensee is unlikely to generate substantial royalty revenue.

The Critical Importance of Skilled Human Capital

When acquiring or licensing IP rights, the entrepreneur must carefully evaluate the role played by the individuals—inventors, technicians, and others—who work with and understand the technology being acquired or licensed. Skilled individuals are often key to making an acquisition of technology competitively successful. Technical experts can help bring products to market quickly and can improve and enhance the acquired technology to meet new market pressures. Acquiring the rights to a patent, for example, without securing the services of the inventors may be next to worthless if the inventors' experience and expertise (so-called *tacit knowledge*) are necessary to exploit the technology.

As a result, companies acquiring technology will frequently hire the key personnel involved in its development. Often these individuals are asked to sign employment or consulting agreements with the acquiring company to ensure that their knowledge will be available to their new employer for a specified period of time. Keeping them happy and motivated is crucial. EMC Corporation's very successful acquisition of VMware was attributable in part to Boston-based EMC's willingness to permit the VMware team to remain in Silicon Valley, California.[68]

14.9 SPECIAL ISSUES ASSOCIATED WITH SOFTWARE LICENSES, OPEN-SOURCE SOFTWARE, AND ONLINE TERMS OF USE

Transactions involving computer software and online terms of use can raise issues not present in other IP transactions.

Software Licenses

Except for custom-produced software, virtually all software is licensed, not sold outright. Software license agreements come in many varieties: end-user, distribution, beta, development, VAR (value-added reseller), and others. Licensing permits the program's owner to retain important controls over the software's use and transferability. In addition, software vendors usually use license agreements to limit their warranties and liabilities.

Most mass-market software is sold without a signed license agreement under what are known as shrink-wrap licenses. *Shrink-wrap licenses* are included with the software along with a statement to the purchaser that by opening the software packaging (i.e., tearing off the shrink-wrap), the purchaser agrees to be bound by the terms of the included shrink-wrap license agreement. A more sophisticated version—the *click-wrap license agreement*—requires the user to indicate acceptance of the license agreement by clicking on an "I Accept" icon (or typing words to that effect) before being able to download or install the program. The U.S. Court of Appeals for the Seventh Circuit upheld a shrink-wrap license prohibiting resale of a database contained on a CD-ROM even though the database itself was probably not copyrightable.[69]

On the other hand, one appellate court refused to enforce a license agreement for software available for downloading on the licensor's website when the license agreement was available for viewing on the website (via a link at the bottom of the page), but the user was not required to indicate acceptance of the license agreement before downloading.[70] The most prudent course is to require the user to take some affirmative step, such as clicking "I Accept," to evidence acceptance of the terms of the license agreement. Licensors should continue to seek appropriate legal advice when implementing mass-market license programs.

Under the Uniform Computer Information Transactions Act (*UCITA*), which as of mid-2016 had been adopted only in Maryland and Virginia, most mass-market software licenses, such as shrink-wrap and click-wrap licenses, are enforceable as long as they meet certain requirements. Vendors in jurisdictions where UCITA has been adopted should give this statute consideration.

Open-Source Software

According to a 2015 survey, open-source software has become a pervasive and key element of innovation: 78% of respondents reported that their companies utilize open-source software in their operations and 66% reported that they incorporate open-source code in the software they develop for their customers.[71] *Open-source software* is typically distributed in source code form (rather than in binary, compiled form) under a license that gives the licensee broad rights to use, copy, distribute, and modify the licensed software. The software can be embedded in software products or physical products, such as phones or machines. It is frequently distributed at no charge or for a nominal charge although providers may charge for support subscriptions or other services. In addition, as explained below, it can come with substantial strings on the users' right to patent any software or products that incorporate the open-source code.

Many companies provide open-source products, including Apple, Google, and Microsoft. For example, Google announced in

2015 that it was making its TensorFlow machine learning system open-source code. This "machine-learning software," a branch of artificial intelligence, is geared toward researchers working with very large quantities of data in fields ranging from "protein folding to crunching astronomy data."[72]

Although open-source software can save a company time, work, and money in its development efforts, entrepreneurs should be cautious when utilizing open-source code. Several problems can arise, especially for entrepreneurs who plan to incorporate the open-source code in their products.

First, open-source software is typically distributed without warranty or support from the developer. Thus, the entrepreneurs must either be confident that they will be able to fix bugs in the software and support it or be prepared to purchase support separately, perhaps from someone other than the licensor. The absence of warranties also means that if the open-source software is not, in fact, owned by the licensor and infringes the intellectual property rights of a third party, the entrepreneur may have to stop using the software, defend against any infringement claims, and possibly pay damages for infringement, without any recourse against the provider. Due diligence becomes especially important if the open-source software has no ready substitutes and will be important to the operation of the entrepreneur's product, or if the startup's customers will demand warranties or support covering the open-source code.

Second, entrepreneurs must carefully examine the license terms for the open-source software. Certain open-source licenses require that the licensee distribute as open-source (and therefore not patent) any software based on or incorporating the licensed open-source code. If not part of the entrepreneur's business model, this result could have serious adverse effects. To comply with the license terms, the entrepreneur would have to make copies of his or her software freely distributable and make the source code available for examination and use by anyone, including competitors.

Many open-source programs are available under "dual licensing" models, in which the software (or sometimes a portion of the software) is available for free as open source or for a fee under a more traditional software license. Thus, entrepreneurs

From the **TRENCHES**

Notwithstanding the prevalence of software and products with embedded open-source code, many companies have limited or inadequate processes to verify and document their developers' use of open-source software and their compliance with applicable licenses. As one might expect, unmonitored use of open-source code can negatively affect the price that acquirers are willing to pay for a business. For example, IBM significantly reduced the price it paid for Think Dynamics after discovering the target's code violated several open-source licenses.

Programs such as protexIP from Black Duck Software offer companies a way to monitor their use of open-source code. The protexIP program flags open-source code in a client's software, identifies the licensing requirements for that code, and reports any potential licensing conflicts. By searching for the essential characteristics of open-source code, protexIP is able to recognize open-source code components even when copyright notices have been removed, variable names have been changed, or the code has been otherwise intentionally disguised. With potential problems identified, the technical and legal teams can work to either comply with the applicable licenses or substitute noninfringing code.

Source: Constance E. Bagley & David Lane, Black Duck Software, Harv. Bus. Sch. Case No. 806-121 (2006).

considering using open-source code in a product should check to see whether a license with more traditional terms, including warranties, is available.

Because open-source code is easily downloaded by developers, one challenge for entrepreneurs is tracking and controlling use of open source by its engineers. Firms should educate engineers about open-source licensing and establish a policy requiring management approval before open-source code is incorporated into a product.

Online Terms of Use

All firms doing business online need to carefully consider and craft agreements, called *terms of use,* that protect the content of the website and/or set forth the rules users must comply with when they engage in activities facilitated by the website. These terms will be critical to enforcing the business's rights vis-à-vis users and third parties. The enforceability of these agreements is an evolving area of the law but will depend in large part on the manner in which the terms are presented to the user and whether the presentation is such that users are given clear notice and an express means to indicate assent. As with terms buried in a clickwrap agreement, courts are far less willing to enforce obscure or difficult-to-find terms. Entrepreneurs should seek legal advice to prepare terms appropriate to the nature of their business.

 Putting It into **PRACTICE**

As noted in Chapter 2, Alexei's prior employer Empire State Fabrication Inc. had previously assigned to Genesist all its rights to the Genesis T-2000 (*GT*) technology in exchange for equity. Genesist now had to act promptly to strengthen and protect its intellectual property rights.

Genesist filed a copyright registration for the GT technology software and the accompanying documentation soon after publication. Registering the copyrights was inexpensive but made it possible for Genesist to recover statutory damages and possibly attorneys' fees if its copyrights were infringed. This was particularly important because Genesist's lack of an operating history would make it very difficult to prove actual damages. Genesist's counsel had already filed intent-to-use trademark applications for the protection of the names "Genesist," "Genesis T-2000," and "GT V-Brackets" and acquired the "Genesist.com" and "GenesisT2000.com" domain names. In addition, a friend of Piper's who was an active member of the American Institute of Graphic Artists had started work on possible logos.

Genesist set up a basic trade secret protection program. Attorney Aaron Biegert drafted a standard proprietary information and inventions agreement, which Genesist required Alexei, Piper, and all other Genesist employees to sign. To ensure that the agreements were supported by adequate consideration, Genesist paid all existing employees a $100 bonus in exchange for signing the documents. Genesist required all future employees to sign the agreements as a condition of being hired.

Alexei asked potential investors and others with whom any key technologies were to be shared to sign nondisclosure agreements. When the venture capitalists refused to sign, Alexei and Piper took a different tack. They refrained from describing any key proprietary facets of the technology until discussions reached a serious stage with Palm Drive Equity Partners, at which point the experts hired to examine the GT technology on Palm Drive's behalf agreed to sign a nondisclosure agreement.

Alexei and Piper then met with Sebastian Mathias, a patent attorney in Sarah's firm specializing in software and materials science patents, to consider whether the GT technology contained any patentable inventions. Sebastian used a well-known search firm to determine whether

(continued)

there was any relevant prior art. Sebastian, Alexei, and Piper carefully evaluated all of Genesist's technology and the prior art and concluded that three separate inventions appeared to be patentable. Alexei also reviewed the findings of the patent search for helpful ideas about possible enhancements. Even if Genesist had not pursued a patent, the novelty of the invention suggested that Genesist should undertake a patent search to ensure that the GT technology did not violate anyone else's patent rights.

Because the GT technology had sales potential overseas, Sebastian discussed the advisability of filing patent applications in key foreign countries. Alexci and Piper decided to file applications in Canada, Japan, Mexico, England, and the European Union. They also decided to seek trademark protection in those jurisdictions. In developing their funding requirements, Alexei and Piper budgeted for the considerable expense of obtaining the U.S. and foreign patents. They knew that having patents pending and protected marks would help in fund-raising efforts.

After Alexei and Piper had developed plans for a working prototype, they began the lengthy patent application process. Although they prepared a draft of the description of the inventions and the prior art, Sebastian drafted the claims sections after explaining to them that the claims section was the most legalistic and stylistic part of the application.

Once the patent and trademark applications were filed, Genesist released the GT V-Brackets for commercial distribution. Sales were brisk. The major automobile manufacturer that had beta tested the brackets announced that it would be installing them on all its new and pre-owned trucks and automobiles. In addition, The Go Boys, a major distributor of car parts for do-it-yourselfers, agreed to stock the brackets in its stores nationwide.

The PTO published the patent applications 18 months after filing. After a colleague forwarded the applications to Dom LaFrance, the Chief Science Officer of Scheer Medical Devices, Dom told CEO Shirley Scheer that Genesist's process for rapidly "growing" complex shapes made of various materials might enable heart surgeons implanting stents to open blocked arteries to customize the stent to the patient in the operating room. Shirley then reached out to Piper to discuss the possibility of licensing Genesist's technology to create customized medical devices. Although both Piper and Alexei saw the potential for using the Genesist technology for medical devices, they knew that the company did not have the capacity to navigate the path to approval of a novel medical device by the Food and Drug Administration. Nor did Genesist have the distribution system needed to commercialize a medical device. So a licensing arrangement with a seasoned medical-device firm like Scheer Medical looked like an attractive way to capture the value of the technology in the medical-device space.

(continued)

After signing a confidentiality agreement and having its experts review Genesist's technology, including its trade secrets, Scheer Medical offered to pay Genesist $100,000 for a three-year option to license Genesist's technology for medical use if and when Genesist's patents issued. The license would be global and coterminus with the patents underlying any aspect of the technology incorporated into medical devices of any sort. The applicable royalty would be calculated as follows: 1% of net profits from the sale of medical devices in any country where such sale would, but for the license, otherwise infringe a licensed Genesist patent that has issued in such country. Shirley proposed that the $100,000 would be fully refundable, at Scheer Medical's option, if the patents did not issue within 35 months after publication of the patent applications. Otherwise, the $100,000 would be applied to the royalties payable under the license.

After reviewing the proposed licensing arrangement with Alexei, Sarah and Sebastian, Genesist made the following counteroffer: In exchange for $100,000, Genesist would grant Scheer Medical a three-year option to license Genesist's technology for use in the manufacture of stents to be implanted in humans in the United States, Canada, Mexico, England, and the European Union. Because Scheer Medical was not currently distributing medical products in any other countries, Sebastian encouraged Alexei and Piper to limit the license to those countries. Genesist would agree to use reasonable efforts to prosecute the patents for the Genesist technology applicable to the manufacture of stents in humans. If the patents did not issue within 35 months after publication of the patent applications, then Genesist would refund $50,000 and retain the remaining $50,000 with no further obligations to Scheer Medical. For its part, Scheer Medical would agree to use best efforts to obtain approval of stents utilizing the Genesist technology by the FDA and the appropriate regulatory authorities in Canada, Mexico, and the European Union. The applicable royalty would be calculated as follows: 20% of net sales of stents manufactured using methods or compositions claimed in any licensed Genesist patent or patent application. The license would be coterminus with the applicable patents but would expire if the royalties paid to Genesist after FDA approval of the first product incorporating any aspect of the Genesist technology were less than $5 million in the first 12-month period following FDA approval or less than $10 million in any subsequent 12-month period.

Knowing that Genesist's technology held promise not only for stents but also for artificial heart valves and arteries, Scheer Medical sought to expand the scope of the license to all medical devices used in any part of the human cardiovascular system. In exchange for Genesist's agreement to extend the scope of the license, Scheer Medical agreed to Genesist's

(continued)

proposed royalty arrangement but insisted that its obligation to obtain FDA and other regulatory approval be limited to commercially reasonable, not best, efforts. Genesist agreed to that change and, at Scheer Medical's request, reduced the amount it would retain if the relevant patents did not issue from $50,000 to $35,000.

Although counsel for both Genesist and Scheer Medical took the lead drafting the option and license agreements and hammering out some of the more legalistic terms, the principals on both sides had to resolve a number of other business terms, including the geographic scope of the license, funding and management of global clinical trials, and the parties' rights to improvements to the Genesist technology during and after the term of the agreement. Alexei and Piper knew that it was important for them to remain active in the negotiations both to resolve all the open items and to strengthen their relationship with Shirley, Dom, and the other members of the Scheer Medical team who would be responsible for commercializing the Genesist technology. After six weeks of intense negotiations, Genesist and Scheer Medical signed the option agreement, which attached as an exhibit the licensing agreement that both parties agreed to execute if Scheer Medical exercised its option to license any aspect of the Genesist technology for use in a cardiovascular medical device.

Three patents for key elements of the GT technology were issued about 23 months after the applications were filed. Soon thereafter, Scheer Medical exercised its option to license the Genesist technology, and both parties signed the license agreement that had been attached to the option agreement. Sebastian continued to work with the patent examiner to secure a composition-of-matter patent covering one of the resins used in the manufacture of Genesist's GT V-Brackets. The trademark filings were also proceeding to completion. With the three patents and the licensing agreement in hand, Alexei, Piper, and the Genesist board of directors turned to the matter of deciding how best to expand Genesist's global business.

15

Going Global

G iven the continued growth of online sales and cross-border workers and partnering opportunities, startup companies in the United States need to consider how to harness these international resources for product development, manufacturing, localization, and sales to obtain a competitive edge. Proper planning can save significant time and expense and result in the creation of an international structure that is appropriate and scalable enough to support the company's current and future activities.

This chapter looks at some of the key issues and decisions management needs to consider when developing a U.S. business with a global reach. (Chapter 14 discussed international intellectual property (*IP*) protection and product licensing in detail.) We begin by identifying the most common forms of foreign business entity available for U.S. companies conducting business overseas, including whether a U.S. company will be required to establish a "business presence" due to the level or nature of its business activities in the overseas country. Given the importance for even small, early-stage companies of understanding how various structures will be taxed overseas, we outline key tax-planning considerations. The chapter continues with a more detailed examination of corporate issues to consider, including set up, management structure, and overseas hiring and employment concerns when establishing a presence overseas. Although we focus primarily on the establishment of one or more overseas subsidiaries, much of the discussion of ownership and control, IP protection, and financing applies equally to other business forms available to U.S. companies for their international operations, such as branch offices or the establishment of a separate joint venture with a foreign partner. The chapter also identifies certain issues to consider when appointing a foreign distributor or sales agent, then concludes with a discussion of various ways to mitigate risks when conducting business overseas.

15.1 SELECTING THE BEST OVERSEAS PRESENCE: REPRESENTATIVE OFFICE, BRANCH, SUBSIDIARY, OR A HYBRID APPROACH

Businesses can gain access to vendors, suppliers, and customers in foreign markets in a variety of ways, ranging from direct sales or licenses to end users (with no physical presence in the foreign country) to the acquisition of or merger with an existing foreign company. Just as with the initial startup of the U.S. business, certain forms of business entity may be more appropriate than others. Indeed, the structure of the U.S. business will often influence the international structure. For example, if a flow-through entity is used for U.S. tax-planning purposes, any foreign operations must be considered in light of that structure.

A threshold question to consider when choosing a form of business entity overseas is whether the country in question restricts foreign ownership. A few jurisdictions do not permit foreigners to own 100% of a business, often depending on the specific industry or sector of the business concerned; in that case, a local partner who will own a substantial or even majority stake in the enterprise may be necessary. Other countries place restrictions on the sectors in which a foreign company can invest. In each case, these restrictions raise additional issues, such as the foreign company's control over day-to-day operations, its strategic changes or acquisitions, and the financing of the local operation.

Subject to any limitations of foreign ownership, the three main choices of entity for an overseas operation are usually a liaison or representative office, a branch, or a subsidiary. A hybrid structure may also be available in certain countries. Each entrepreneur is driven by many factors and objectives when expanding internationally but, by and large, the options available and their respective benefits are outlined in Table 15.1.

TABLE 15.1	Risk Levels and Benefits of Various Methods of International Expansion	
Risk	**Method**	**Benefits**
High ⬆	⇨ Merger with or acquisition of foreign business	• Opportunity for rapid expansion • Accelerated market growth
	⇨ Subsidiary	• 100% ownership = 100% reward • Quality control over intellectual property • Strategic and operational control
	⇨ Joint venture entity	• Shared cost = shared risk • Diverse contributions by joint venture partners • Access local knowledge and resources
	⇨ Outsourcing	• Leverage expertise in low-cost jurisdiction • Nimble—quick to set up or terminate • Build, operate, transfer (*BOT*) lowers the risk; only acquire operation once successful
	⇨ Distributor, reseller, or sales agent	• Reduced up-front costs • Tap into local expertise • Access "value-added" local input
Low ⬇	⇨ Direct to end-user (sales or licenses)	• Easiest starting point • Little or no foreign presence required

It is important to keep in mind that the corporate structure, like the business itself, will need to grow and adapt as the company becomes more successful, expands its operations into additional countries, and hires employees in those countries. Thus, one objective is to craft a corporate structure that is flexible enough for future growth.

Representative Office

A *representative office* (sometimes referred to as a *rep office* or *liaison office*) is a minimal business presence. It is often the simplest overseas presence to set up, but local laws usually impose severe limitations on what it can do. A representative or liaison office is typically allowed to liaise between operations in the foreign country and U.S. headquarters and to conduct market research and analysis, but it usually cannot conduct commercial business activities or become involved in revenue-generation activities. This could mean, for example, that the representative office can help identify sales leads, but these leads must be directed to the parent for the negotiation of all key contract terms and the ultimate decision of whether to enter into a contract with the foreign customer. It is essential that the U.S. parent not merely "rubber stamp" a sale whose terms have been wholly negotiated by the representative office. The representative office will usually be required to register with local governmental authorities, make annual tax or financial filings, and regularly renew business licenses.

Branch

A *branch* is a local office of the U.S. parent company. It is legally a part of the U.S. parent and not a separate legal entity. As a result, any assets or liabilities associated with the business of the overseas branch form a part of, and are recorded in the financial statements of, the U.S. parent. Formalities for a branch registration vary but usually include an application to the relevant corporate regulatory authority. The application often includes copies of the U.S. parent company's charter documents and copies of its latest financial statements, which are filed with the relevant regulator and are very often available in a public registry. Financial statements for subsequent financial years may also be publicly filed. This can be important in determining whether or not to open a branch, particularly for privately held U.S. companies that are not required to publicly disclose financial information in the United States.

To avoid this public disclosure and to contain the liabilities associated with an expansion in the overseas country, it may be preferable to incorporate a separate subsidiary in the relevant country, or to consider the "hybrid" option described later in this chapter. That way, only the financial statements of a subsidiary company are publicly disclosed. In addition, a branch will normally need to produce financial statements for the branch business, separate from the U.S. company of which it forms part, for the purpose of calculating local corporate taxes; consequently, a second set of financial statements, with a separate accounting system, may be needed if a branch is set up.

Subsidiary

By incorporating a *subsidiary* in a different country, a separate legal entity is established. The overseas subsidiary has its own assets, liabilities, business, and employees. Subject to the overall tax structuring objectives of the U.S. parent, in-country customers may deal directly with the local subsidiary, although the U.S. parent may well be the owner of the IP and may also provide certain central services (discussed later), at least initially.

Establishing an overseas subsidiary signals that the U.S. parent has made a long-term commitment to that country that will often enhance the credibility of the parent in the local market. This may be particularly important in jurisdictions such as Japan, where business relationships are usually expected to last for many years, or in China, where revenue-generating activities will typically require the setting up of a subsidiary, known as a wholly foreign owned entity or *WFOE* (commonly pronounced "WOOF-ee"). For any operation that is likely to grow and develop into a significant overseas business, handling functions such as local sales and marketing, technical or customer support, or localization of products, a subsidiary will often make sense. At the very least, a subsidiary offers limited liability. If the foreign business fails or suffers unexpected liabilities (such as a lawsuit), the assets and liabilities of the subsidiary are segregated from those of the rest of the group, including the U.S. parent, as long as proper corporate formalities are observed.

Hybrid Approach

Emerging companies in the United States often consider a hybrid structure to separate their overseas activities from the U.S. parent. They set up a new U.S. subsidiary (which we will call the *International Sub*), which in turn hires employees in various overseas countries and sets up one or more representative offices or branches, depending on the nature and type of activities conducted by the employees in each country. The key benefit of the hybrid structure is that the revenue-generating operations of the U.S. parent (i.e., sales to customers) are in a separate legal entity from the company employing the overseas employees (the International Sub). The International Sub is the "employer" of overseas workers, and its activities are limited to marketing, business

From the **TRENCHES**

A New York web-based advertising company decided to open four branch offices in key locations in Europe to establish a direct sales force staffed by local employees. Management believed that branch offices would be simpler, cheaper, and quicker to set up than subsidiaries.

Within the next 12 months, advertising sales in Europe had accelerated and the branch offices were becoming self-supporting and profitable. As a result, the company decided to establish wholly owned subsidiaries in several European jurisdictions to demonstrate its long-term commitment to Europe, which had become its second largest market, and to deliver services via locally domiciled entities.

Because the various branches were legally part of the U.S. parent company, the transition to standalone entities in France, Germany, Italy, and the United Kingdom required the incorporation of four new subsidiaries, and the assignment and transfer to each new subsidiary of the branch's assets and liabilities pursuant to detailed asset-transfer agreements. The company also had to pay taxes associated with the transfer of each branch's assets, along with filing fees and, in some cases, local notary fees. In retrospect, management acknowledged that although an initial branch office was a simple way to "dip their toes" into the European market, the firm should have moved to local subsidiaries in its key markets earlier in the expansion process.

development, and other presales activities. This hybrid structure may be a particularly attractive and practical approach when the U.S. company is likely to have a small number of employees in several countries, because it avoids the need to set up new subsidiaries in each and every country, which can be expensive and time-consuming for management. As discussed further below, using the International Sub to hire overseas employees can also help minimize the risk of the U.S. parent being deemed to have created a permanent establishment in an overseas country, thereby exposing its revenues to local corporate taxes. The appropriateness of a hybrid structure will be affected by the types of goods or services involved, the U.S. parent company's tax objectives, and the rules in the foreign countries in which overseas employees are based. As with other forms of overseas expansion, expert tax advice will be required, especially as countries implement the intercompany transfer pricing reforms resulting from the Organisation for Economic Co-operation and Development's (*OECD*'s) base erosion and profit shifting (*BEPS*) review.[1]

In the hybrid approach, the International Sub registers branches or representative offices in the foreign countries where its employees are hired, as and when required. An intercompany arrangement between the U.S. parent and the International Sub allows the parent to purchase overseas marketing and support services from the International Sub, often on a cost-plus basis. The liabilities associated with the foreign employees are kept within the International Sub, and it is the International Sub (not the U.S. parent) that would file financial statements and make other disclosures overseas when it sets up branches or representative offices. Figure 15.2 depicts a typical hybrid structure.

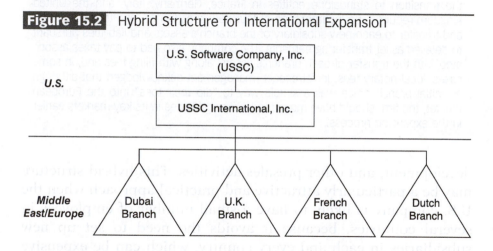

Figure 15.2   Hybrid Structure for International Expansion

15.2 INTERNATIONAL TAX PLANNING

Corporate tax rates vary enormously from country to country, as do employment, value-added, sales, and other indirect taxes. Thus, it is important to ensure that a flexible and tax-efficient structure is in place throughout the life of the company. Accordingly, legally astute entrepreneurs and their advisers evaluate the U.S. and local tax implications of conducting business activities overseas at the outset, then they revisit the structure on a regular basis and adjust it as needed in response to changing tax laws and tax rates in both the United States and overseas. When subsidiaries are created in certain countries, it may be appropriate to set up an intermediate holding company, sometimes in an offshore country, to afford maximum flexibility for future tax-planning purposes.

Employee Taxes and Withholding

Employees are normally subject to the domestic tax regime of their own countries, and their employer is typically responsible for withholding income taxes and social security from their salary payments. Social security deductions can be significantly higher outside the United States, especially in countries where medical, disability, retirement, maternity/paternity, and other benefits are provided by the state. A small company may want to subcontract payroll and tax administration to a qualified local payroll provider or accounting firm to allow foreign technical staff or sales employees to concentrate on their core areas of expertise.

The Effect of Creating a Permanent Establishment on Corporate Taxes

When considering the tax implications of selling goods or services in a foreign country, entrepreneurs should always determine whether their business activities or those of their agents constitute a permanent establishment in that country for tax purposes. If a U.S. company is deemed to have a *permanent establishment (PE)* in another country, it will be liable for corporate taxes under the domestic tax regime of the relevant country on the business profits derived from activities there. With corporate tax rates or tax withholding obligations ranging from 0% up to 50% or more, the magnitude and impact of the tax regime in a particular country may determine whether the U.S. company wants to establish a presence there at all.

Each country has different rules concerning the level and type of activity that trigger a PE. Just one employee working from home, a single agent or consultant, or even a local server handling customer emails may be sufficient to trigger a PE or to require the U.S. company to register with the local corporate authorities.

Tax authorities will often look behind the title of the operators to determine what types of activities are, in fact, being conducted in the overseas office, and they will base their assessment of whether a PE exists on that analysis. So, for example, even if the U.S. company calls its in-country sales staff "independent contractors," if the workers are deemed to be employees under the local employment laws, then their presence may be sufficient to trigger a PE in that country. The method of calculating "taxable profits" and the types of permissible corporate deductions also vary from country to country.

Fortunately, the negative impact of foreign corporate taxes is mitigated by several factors. First, a U.S. tax credit for taxes paid overseas will often reduce, at least partially, U.S. taxes. Second, corporate tax rates are often staggered, with relatively low rates applicable to the revenues generated by smaller businesses. Third, a new subsidiary will almost always incur initial startup costs, so it may generate significant net operating losses (*NOLs*), or their local equivalent, to offset any local corporate tax liabilities for the first few years. It is critical to obtain professional international tax advice before setting up foreign subsidiaries, hiring employees or contractors overseas, or launching foreign operations with a foreign business partner.

Using an International IP-Development Company

U.S. companies that generate significant revenues from licensing technology developed by the U.S. company or from the sale of products based on that technology often consider establishing an IP-holding company in a low-tax jurisdiction to co-own the group's IP as part of their international corporate structure. The IP-holding company acquires the non-U.S. rights to the company's existing IP, and it enters into cost-sharing arrangements with the U.S. company under which both the U.S. company and the IP-holding company jointly pay for future development of the IP. In this structure, the U.S. parent makes sales to customers in the United States, and the overseas IP-holding company makes sales to customers located outside the United States. The goal of this approach is to shift profits from sales outside the United States from a relatively high-tax jurisdiction (the United States) to a company in a low-tax jurisdiction, such as Switzerland, the United Kingdom, Luxembourg, or Ireland. The profits from the overseas sales by the IP-holding company remain offshore (perhaps for further expansion or development outside the United States) and are normally taxable in the United States only if repatriated there.

These structures are complex, involving significant professional costs for accounting and tax planning, and they are subject

From the **TRENCHES**

One type of tax transaction that has increasingly received negative press and political pushback is a "corporate inversion," whereby a U.S. corporation moves its tax residence to a country with a lower corporate tax rate without actually relocating the company's operations. This is typically accomplished by merging the U.S. company with or acquiring a smaller non-U.S. company. The goal is to avoid both the higher U.S. corporate tax rates and the U.S. regulations requiring a U.S. corporation to pay tax on all its repatriated earnings, regardless of where they are earned. In April 2016, the U.S. Treasury Department issued formal tempo- rary regulations that made it harder for companies to invert and limited the eco- nomic benefits of inversions. Several days later, U.S. pharmaceuticals giant Pfizer cancelled its proposed $160 billion merger with Ireland-based Allergan. The rules were finalized in October 2016.

Sources: Press Release, U.S. Dep't of the Treasury, Fact Sheet: Treasury Issues Inversion Reg- ulations and Proposed Earnings Strippings Regulations (Apr. 4, 2016), https://www.treasury .gov/press-center/press-releases/Pages/jl0404.aspx; Nathan Bomey & Kevin McCoy, *$160 Billion Pfizer, Allergan Inversion Scrapped*, USA Today (Apr. 6, 2016), http://www.usatoday .com/story/money/2016/04/06/pfizer-allergan-inversion-merger-canceled/82692716/; Press Release, U.S. Dep't of the Treasury, Treasury's Issues Final Earnings Stripping Regulations to Narrowly Target Corporate Transactions That Erode U.S. Tax Base (Oct. 13, 2016), https://www.treasury .gov/press-center/press-releases/Pages/jl0580.aspx.

to scrutiny by the U.S. Internal Revenue Service. For example, ownership of all IP and related resources needs to be verified, documented, and valued, and a transfer-pricing study must be completed to help determine the appropriate IP buy-in value to be paid by the new IP-holding company and the future IP- development cost-sharing arrangements. Nevertheless, if a signifi- cant portion of the venture's revenue will ultimately be derived from non-U.S. customers, the structure is worth considering at an early stage.

Tax Registrations

Once a branch or foreign subsidiary is established, it must register with the relevant employment tax and social security authorities as an employer at the national level and often at the regional or local level (or both). A U.S. company with an overseas subsidiary, or a branch with a PE, is also required to register for corporate tax pur- poses. In addition, a company may need to register for purposes of collecting value-added taxes if certain minimum thresholds for supplies of goods or services are met. (A *value-added tax* (*VAT*) is a consumption tax on the value added to a product or service at each stage in the production chain.) Even if the VAT thresholds are not met in the first few months of operation, early registration may be desirable to permit the new business to account for and possibly reclaim "input" taxes paid on purchases during the startup phase. Generally, if input taxes exceed the VAT charged by the business on sales to customers, the business may be entitled to claim a VAT refund. Many jurisdictions have similar sales or use taxes, such as the *goods and services tax* (*GST*) in Australia, which, as of mid-2016, imposed a 10% tax on most goods, services, and other items sold or consumed there.

Failure to register with the relevant local tax authorities in a timely manner can have serious adverse consequences for the business. These can include not only late registration fees and fines or penalties for noncompliance, but also the lost management time required for remedial action.

15.3 ESTABLISHING A FOREIGN BUSINESS PRESENCE

Entrepreneurs often find the formalities for establishing an overseas presence detailed, time-consuming and costly, particularly in civil-law countries, which generally require more extensive filings and registrations than the United States, including the notarization of key documents before a civil-law notary. Adequate time for the registration or incorporation process needs to be scheduled into the expansion plan. Planning ahead is therefore key.

Setting Up the Foreign Entity

Setting up a representative office, branch, or subsidiary usually requires mandatory filings and authorizations, including registration as a business and registration with the relevant tax and social security authorities. The obligation to register the local entity is usually triggered as soon as business is conducted or within a month of commencing business, but, in some countries, the entity must register before undertaking any business activity at all.

From the **TRENCHES**

In light of tremendous overseas demand for its web security software, a privately held software company in California decided to set up various research and development (*R&D*) and sales subsidiaries in Europe and Asia to accelerate product development and establish a direct sales force. The U.S. vice president (*VP*) for sales persuaded the company's chief executive officer (*CEO*) that the VP's college buddy, Bud, who ran a consulting business in Hong Kong, was the "right guy" to set up and oversee operations in China and Southeast Asia.

Bud and his colleagues started sending out offer letters and negotiating lease terms in Shanghai, Guangzhou, and Seoul. Not satisfied with certain of Bud's plans and budgetary reports, the CEO asked his U.S. advisers whether they agreed with Bud's assessment that the company could "stay under the radar" and neither register a business presence nor pay taxes in China and Korea despite having hired workers and making customer sales in both countries.

The company's advisers explained that the proposed R&D and sales activities could not be conducted in China without setting up a local wholly foreign owned enterprise, which required approvals from various Chinese government agencies, including the State Administration for Industry and Commerce and the Ministry of Commerce, as well as local authorities. Failure to complete the required processes and registrations exposed both the company and its officers to significant liabilities, potentially jeopardizing the company's ability to conduct business in China. The advisers raised similar concerns in relation to Korea. The company eventually obtained the proper approvals, but with more delay and at a higher cost than would have been the case had the company worked with locally qualified advisers from the outset to craft and implement the proper structure.

Even the establishment of a small sales and marketing office overseas is likely to trigger requirements for registration, filing, or other formalities. The firm will need to hire a local lawyer to draft the necessary documents and complete the forms in the local language. It is essential that the U.S. company fully understand what is being said and filed concerning its proposed business activities in the relevant country so local lawyers should be asked to prepare bilingual documents in English and the local language so that the U.S. parent, as well as its U.S. legal, accounting, and tax advisers, can review them. If unlicensed agents are used to make these filings, the U.S. company should ensure that the agent is drawing upon locally qualified tax, legal, and accounting resources when needed, particularly when filings are being made in a foreign language to overseas government regulators and tax authorities.

Registration of a branch will normally require the U.S. company to translate its charter into the local language. A subsidiary will require the local equivalent of a certificate of incorporation and bylaws. The time needed to register a branch or incorporate a subsidiary varies considerably from country to country and can be as long as two to three months. Initial setup costs will include the registration fees, notary fees (in civil-law countries), professional fees to prepare the documents and, for subsidiaries, the contribution of the initial equity (discussed below).

Selecting the Corporate and Business Names

The U.S. parent will usually want to use its own name and trademarks abroad. Often it is possible to search company name registers in other countries in advance to check whether the name is available. China, Singapore, India, and certain other countries require preclearance or preregistration of the proposed corporate name as part of the incorporation process. In most cases, the company name can be reserved pending incorporation of the local subsidiary or a branch registration.

If the parent's name is already registered and used by a local company as its corporate name in the foreign country, it may still be possible to register and use the parent's name as a business name there, as long as the companies are in different lines of business and use of the parent name does not infringe a local trademark. Using the same or a similar business name where both companies are in the same line of business may expose the new subsidiary and its U.S. parent to trademark infringement as well as the local equivalent of misrepresentation claims or similar business torts. Professional advice from the company's trademark and branding advisers will be needed before proceeding.

Even if registration of the local business name is not mandatory, it may well be worth registering it to prevent anyone else from registering or using the company name in that region. Indeed, even if the U.S. parent is not yet ready to establish a business in a particular country, it could consider setting up a company there as a preemptive move to protect the corporate name and prevent others from registering a company with the same name.

Periodic Filings and Payment of Franchise Fees

Most countries will require some form of annual or periodic filings for a local branch or subsidiary, and/or the payment of franchise fees or their equivalent, as do states in the United States. Many countries will also require the annual filing of financial statements, which may need to be audited by public accountants regardless of whether the U.S. parent conducts an audit. Financial statements filed by foreign subsidiaries or branches are often available through searches of public registries; in Europe, they will typically disclose the identity (but not the financial information) of the U.S. parent.

15.4 OWNING AND OPERATING AN OVERSEAS SUBSIDIARY

Owning and operating an overseas subsidiary subjects the U.S. company to a different set of legal, tax, and accounting rules, which bound the choices available to the managers of both the parent and the subsidiary.

Shareholding Structure

A threshold question is whether local law requires more than one shareholder to set up a subsidiary in the country of choice. Brazil, India, and many other countries require private companies to have two, five, or even seven shareholders. Because the subsidiary will usually be wholly owned by the U.S. parent, at least from an economic perspective, any additional shareholders required by local law must be carefully selected. Ideally, any additional shareholders will be companies within the U.S. company's group. Sometimes it may be desirable to have a nominee shareholder for company law or tax-planning purposes. *Nominee shareholders* usually are the record, but not the beneficial, owners of equity in the subsidiary. Thus, they hold the subsidiary shares on behalf of the U.S. parent and are not entitled to an economic interest in the subsidiary. The ideal nominee may be an independent professional adviser who is under a contractual or fiduciary duty to act in accordance with the U.S. parent's instructions. If employees of the U.S. parent act as nominee or secondary shareholders, there is always the danger that they will leave the company, perhaps under unhappy circumstances, such as a layoff. If that happens, then tracking them down and getting them to transfer "their" shares to replacement nominee shareholders can prove difficult. Another alternative is to have an inactive U.S. subsidiary company, whose sole purpose is to act as an additional shareholder in a foreign subsidiary when local law requires more than one shareholder to incorporate. If the U.S. company anticipates creating a number of foreign subsidiaries as its global business expands, then using a group subsidiary company as an additional shareholder is often a cost effective structure.

From the **TRENCHES**

A promising software company decided to set up subsidiaries in Europe and Asia. The U.S. vice president for sales persuaded his friend Claude, who lived in France, to become the vice president for European sales. "Don't worry," said Claude. "I'll set up the company and deal with hiring and premises. It'll be my baby." Because all the incorporation documents, filings, leases, and the like for the French subsidiary were in French, Claude did not bother to send them back to the United States. He did, however, give monthly email updates on the European operations.

The business quickly blossomed and the subsidiary hired a significant sales force. Fifteen months later, when U.S. auditors reviewed the books in Paris, they discovered that Claude and several of his senior managers were all shareholders in the French subsidiary. The U.S. parent owned a bare majority of the shares and could not make key corporate decisions without the French shareholders' support. When questioned, Claude replied, "I have always taken equity in operations I run in France—you never said we could not hold shares." Protracted negotiations between the U.S. parent and French management ensued, resulting in significantly higher compensation and severance packages for the entire French team.

Comment: Had the U.S. parent been more involved in the initial steps, worked closely with local counsel and the French managers, and insisted on English translations of the key documents, it could have avoided this scenario. Under certain circumstances, it may be appropriate to give local management equity compensation in the parent company as an incentive, but it rarely, if ever, makes sense to issue local managers shares in the local subsidiary: when local managers leave or move on, it can be very difficult in many jurisdictions for the parent to retrieve the former managers' shares of the subsidiary, and external shareholders in a subsidiary are potentially problematic if the U.S. parent company is being acquired.

Use of Shelf Corporations

A fast and cost-effective way to establish a subsidiary in many common-law countries (such as the United Kingdom and Ireland) and in certain civil-law countries (such as Luxembourg) is to purchase a shelf company—that is, a private company set up in advance by lawyers or company formation agents but left "on the shelf," neither transacting business nor incurring any liabilities, until needed. Ownership of shelf companies can be transferred to the U.S. parent in a matter of hours or a day, with a minimum of formality because the company already exists. The U.S. parent receives the initial equity (usually just one or two shares of stock) and appoints its own directors. The company name is changed at the same time, and the subsidiary is immediately ready for business. Shelf companies are not available in all countries and even if they are, they can cost more than simply incorporating a new company, so it is wise to check their suitability in the country concerned.

Capitalization

The minimum capitalization for an overseas subsidiary can be significant. For example, many civil-law countries in Europe (including Germany and Switzerland) require a minimum share capital for private companies of up to €25,000 (approximately $28,000), which must be deposited in a blocked bank account before the local notary can incorporate the subsidiary. Similarly, before establishing a subsidiary in China, it is necessary to determine the total amount of investment into the WFOE, which must be sufficient to establish the WFOE and fund its startup operations (e.g., rent, wages, and other expenses). There are also rules determining how much of that investment can take the form of debt, rather than equity. In some locations, a minimum investment amount may be required. For example, in mid-2016, the minimum registered capital for a WFOE in the Shenzhen free trade zone was RMB 5 million (approximately $766,500). Although not usually significant, capital tax on the issuance of stock in new subsidiaries may be payable to the local government in certain countries.

Most common-law countries have minimal share capital requirements. For example, one share and initial capitalization of as little as GBP 1 is sufficient to incorporate a private company in the United Kingdom. A more significant equity stake may none-theless be required to give the local subsidiary credibility with local customers, vendors, or suppliers, or be required for tax-planning purposes.

Registering to Do Business Outside the Place of Incorporation

Once a subsidiary is established in a particular jurisdiction, additional registrations may be required in other regions or territories within the country where business will be conducted. This is the same or similar to a "qualification to do business" required in various states in the United States for corporations doing business outside their state of incorporation. For example, if a subsidiary is set up in Ontario, Canada, but will have an office and employees in British Columbia, then the subsidiary would be required to make an extra-provincial registration with the authorities in British Columbia before conducting business in that province. In contrast, a subsidiary in Australia is registered with the Australian Securities and Investment Commission (*ASIC*) and nominates the state in which it will be registered. Once registered with ASIC, the company can conduct business anywhere in Australia.

Corporate Governance

The U.S. parent needs to find the right balance between controlling and delegating authority to the management of the foreign subsidiary, which will often be staffed by personnel with a greater understanding of the local market. At least in the early years, adequate parental oversight of the subsidiary's operations is vital to ensure a successful operation and the protection of the U.S. company's brand, image, and reputation. Some of the most difficult problems to correct are those created by unsupervised overseas subsidiaries that have run amok due to inadequate monitoring and control from U.S. headquarters.

The laws governing corporate governance and decision making overseas can vary significantly from the procedures used in the United States. As a result, the structure and role of the decision-making bodies of a foreign subsidiary may vary substantially from those of the U.S. parent. For example, local "managers" may as a matter of local law have decision-making capabilities on behalf of the local operation. It is therefore critical for the management of the U.S. parent to understand what it can and cannot control.

Board of Directors When selecting the board of directors, or other decision-making body, and granting certain titles to local personnel, it is important to understand what, if any, authority the various positions and titles bestow on local managers. Certain countries require one or more local directors, meaning nationals or permanent residents of the country concerned. Board meetings may be mandatory and must sometimes be held within the country of incorporation. Local law may not permit telephonic board meetings or action by written consent; thus, U.S. directors may be required to physically attend board meetings.

Registered Office and Local Company Secretary A registered office in the country of incorporation and a local company secretary are usually required. In the early days of the subsidiary, it may make sense to outsource the bookkeeping and company secretarial function to a local bookkeeper or professional adviser, who can also provide the registered office address for the subsidiary.

Instituting Internal Controls The managers of the U.S. company should ensure that the overseas subsidiary has instituted appropriate internal policies and controls concerning financial reporting, product quality, legal compliance, and other matters. For example, subsidiaries owned or controlled by U.S. entities should have clear policies prohibiting bribery of government officials, which can be particularly troublesome in certain countries, such as China and Russia, where many customers in those markets may be state-owned enterprises. To limit the parent's liability for the debts and other obligations of the subsidiary, it is important for any U.S. managers directly involved in operating the subsidiary to act with their subsidiary "hat" on, for example, in their capacity as an officer or director of the subsidiary.

Works Councils Many countries in Europe will require or permit "works councils" or other employee representatives to participate in certain corporate decision making, sometimes even in moderately small enterprises. Generally, employers must permit the establishment of works councils or other forms of employee representation once the business employs a certain number of people (e.g., 50 or more employees in France and 5 or more in Germany).

A works council will include one or more employee representatives who will be involved in significant decisions or strategic changes to the subsidiary's business. Companies must usually provide information to the worker representatives before decisions are made. In some instances, a company must also consult with the works council or another representative body before implementing changes, particularly those affecting individual employees or the number or location of its workers. Employee involvement or consultation is also likely to be triggered by a sale or merger of the U.S. parent company, which can raise issues if the obligation to consult with employees is triggered before the sale or merger transaction has been announced by the U.S. parent company.

Periodic Filings and Payment of Fees   As noted above, most countries will require subsidiaries incorporated there to make annual or periodic filings; they may also require the payment of franchise fees. Because local subsidiaries may often be staffed with only sales and marketing personnel, at least in the early years, it is important for the U.S. parent to ensure that key local documents and government notifications are directed to a competent adviser so that timely action can be taken. The penalty for noncompliance with local filings can range from a fine to director or officer personal liability and mandatory dissolution of the company for continued delinquency.

15.5 HIRING WORKERS OVERSEAS

Expansion overseas is often spearheaded by an experienced sales or marketing professional. Sometimes local agents or consultants will help establish the business, particularly where there are language barriers. Nevertheless, it is still essential for the U.S. parent to understand the employment environment in the foreign country. Failure to do so can lead to problems on many fronts. Increasingly, U.S. startups have workers in both the United States and overseas, requiring compliance with employment, tax and IP regimes in whichever country the worker is located.

When Does Hiring Abroad Create a Business Presence?

As noted earlier, before hiring workers abroad, the U.S. parent must consider whether having workers in a given country will trigger (1) the need for either a branch registration or incorporation of a subsidiary under local laws or (2) constitute a permanent establishment for tax purposes, requiring the local business to complete and file local tax returns and pay corporate taxes in the country on sales or business generated there. The tests used to make these two determinations are similar, but each aspect requires due consideration.

Characterizing Workers as Employees Versus Independent Contractors

As in the United States, simply calling a worker an "independent contractor" and paying him or her a gross amount are often insufficient to avoid characterization as an employee. Most countries have their own test for deciding who is an independent contractor and who is an employee. Individuals who devote all or substantially all of their time working for a single company, take direction on when and how to perform their role from U.S. management, have company email and business cards, and are otherwise integrated into the operations of the U.S. company in the same way as U.S. employees may be characterized as employees under local law, irrespective of what the worker is called in any agreement with the employer. Failure to withhold and pay over employment taxes or social charges on wages can lead to fines and penalties.

Recruiting Foreign Nationals

Recruiting foreign nationals can be a minefield if it is not handled properly. The U.S. company should consult in-country employment law advisers as part of the process. Recruiting methods used in the United States may not be legal or culturally appropriate elsewhere. More importantly, the U.S. parent needs guidance on the market rates of compensation, customary and statutorily required employee benefits, and other employer responsibilities in the country concerned. Otherwise, the first few employees may receive excessive compensation packages, including both the employee benefits that the U.S. employer makes available to U.S. personnel and various benefits that purportedly are standard or customary in the overseas country (e.g., "every sales representative here gets a new company car every year").

No Employment at Will Outside the United States

Regardless of whether an employee is hired by the U.S. parent or a local entity, the employer must understand that the U.S. doctrine of employment at will does not apply to employees serving outside the United States (including U.S. expatriate employees sent to subsidiaries overseas, who as a general rule will be entitled to the minimum levels of protection and benefits afforded all employees under the local laws of the host country). This is especially true in Europe, where most countries have legislation that is *extremely* favorable to employees when compared with U.S. employment laws. In these nations, firing or removing an employee can be an expensive and time-consuming process that distracts attention from other aspects of the business.

Procedures for Termination and Severance Pay

Several consequences flow from the fact that employees based overseas are not terminable at will.

Notice Before terminating an employment relationship, both the employer and the employee must give notice of termination of employment in accordance with applicable minimum notice requirements. These requirements may be embodied in an employment contract or, in certain countries, in a nationally applicable collective-bargaining agreement. Or they may be determined by statute or local custom in the industry. If times are tough and the subsidiary needs to significantly reduce its workforce, U.S. management needs to appreciate that notice periods overseas can be weeks, if not months. Although some countries permit payment in lieu of notice, that is not always the case. More important, the termination process itself will be fundamentally different from that used in the United States.

Consultation   Many countries require the employer to consult with the employees who potentially will be affected before giving them notice of termination. Indeed, in certain countries, the employer is prohibited from selecting specific employees for termination ahead of a formal consultation and termination process that is meant to use various selection criteria to identify which employees will be terminated. The effect of collective-bargaining agreements or works councils also need to be taken into account in any consultation or termination process. Failure to follow local due process requirements can result in hefty liabilities for the employer.

Permissible Grounds for Termination   Civil-law countries often permit terminations only in very narrowly defined circumstances, and the consent of a local court or employment authority may be required before a termination becomes effective. Again, failure to follow set procedures can result in the employee receiving greater termination compensation and/or becoming entitled to reinstatement. In certain European countries, the termination is null and void unless the appropriate procedures have been followed.

If the subsidiary is terminating more than a few employees, a more elaborate and formal process will often be required. For example, an employer in France may have to submit a formal social plan setting forth the basis of the terminations to the local court or tribunal before notice of termination may be sent to employees. In most European countries, the termination process is likely to take several months if a significant number of layoffs are involved.

Severance Pay   When employees are laid off due to redundancy, severance pay may be required by contract and/or statute or local laws and customs. The amounts can be significant, based on length of service, local laws, and other factors.

Documenting the Employment Relationship

When a company hires overseas, proper documentation is essential.

Avoiding the Inadvertent Creation of a Binding Employment Relationship with the U.S. Parent   Sometimes a U.S. company may need to act quickly to set up a local entity as a sales office to take advantage of a great business opportunity. As a result, the U.S. parent may want to initiate the hiring process before the new sales team is on the ground. Managers in the United States should use care when communicating with candidates and potential employees in foreign countries, because even emails back and forth between the U.S. management team and potential candidates may include sufficient information to establish a legally binding employment contract between the U.S. parent and the overseas individual.

To avoid this, the parent should make certain that the local subsidiary is set up before any offers are made. A duly authorized officer of the subsidiary should sign all offer letters and employment agreements so that the subsidiary—and not the U.S. parent—is deemed the employer. If the parent signed the offer letter or employment agreement, then it is technically the employer and it will be necessary to formally document a transfer of the employee to the local subsidiary, which may require the employee's consent.

The goal here is to avoid a *dual employment problem*, whereby overseas employees have the benefit of the mandatory employee protection laws in their home country and, at the same time, may have a cause of action against the U.S. parent if they are dismissed. If it is essential to get an offer letter to a foreign employee before the foreign business presence is registered, the offer letter should expressly provide for the transfer of employment to the foreign subsidiary once established.

Written Employment Terms   All employees in Europe and in most other parts of the world have written terms of employment, either in the form of an employment agreement or a detailed offer letter. In addition, employment relationships in civil-law countries are governed by labor codes and, in some countries, collective-bargaining agreements (*CBAs*) covering specific industries or business sectors. The terms of the applicable CBA will typically apply to the employment relationship, which often catches unaware a U.S. employer making its first few hires in countries like Italy or France. The terms of an employment contract normally may not be less favorable to the employee than the requirements set forth in the CBA. Moreover, the CBA may incorporate employment terms and conditions over and above what is set forth in the employment contract. Legislation enacted in the European Union (*EU*) usually requires the employer to give each employee certain written information, generally including the start date, job title and description, place of work, salary and benefits, details of the grievance/disciplinary procedure (if any), and so forth. For most countries in Europe, it will be sufficient to use a standard form or template, which can be amended as needed for new hires. More senior personnel will expect to negotiate individual employment agreements, with tailor-made employment terms, severance, and termination provisions. A properly drafted document must be prepared by experienced employment counsel in the country where the employee resides. The use of U.S.-style offer letters, even as a precursor to a formal written employment contract, should be avoided when hiring employees in Europe.

Mandatory Employee Benefits

Most countries, other than the United States, require employers to provide certain mandatory employee benefits or at least make them available. A number of European countries require a minimum of five or six weeks of vacation in addition to public holidays, which is significantly more generous than employee vacation allowances in the United States. This is merely the starting point, as more senior or experienced personnel may expect even more time off. Other government benefits, such as medical, disability, pension, and maternity/paternity leave, are often compulsory and funded by social security taxes. Certain countries allow a range of benefits to be provided either by the state or through private companies.

Negotiating Employment Benefits

Given the multiple variations and complexities involved in providing employee benefits to employees outside the United States, managers of both the U.S. parent and the subsidiary need to understand the local employment rules and environment when negotiating employment arrangements. For example, the relative cost of cars, cell phones, and even housing can make employees overseas much more interested in these benefits than in, for example, medical insurance, especially when the government of the country where the employee works covers most medical costs and services. Moreover, certain benefits may be heavily taxed, especially in Europe, so it is important to understand the employment and tax environment in which these negotiations take place.

Stock Options and Other Forms of Equity Compensation   Before granting stock options and other forms of equity compensation to overseas employees, the U.S. parent must carefully examine all the requirements imposed by local laws and evaluate the benefits to the employer and employees of granting options in light of the regulatory and compliance burdens imposed. Certain countries have an outright prohibition on the grant to local employees of stock options in U.S. companies, either due to regulatory requirements, foreign exchange restrictions, or securities laws. Even if a country permits equity compensation as part of an employment package, it is often not a particularly incentivizing or tax-efficient benefit. Because employee stock option plans have historically been designed and implemented under the auspices of the U.S. tax laws, these plans are unlikely to meet other countries' requirements for beneficial tax treatment, for either the employee or the employer-subsidiary. Indeed, a number of countries tax the underlying gain in equity awards at the employee's highest marginal income tax rate. Thus, even in countries where stock options are available, they are not as common as in the United States.

In many countries, the obligation to pay taxes and make social security payments is triggered when the employee exercises the stock option, with the tax calculated based on the difference between the exercise price and the fair market value of the stock at the time of exercise. Certain countries, however, may tax the employee upon grant of the option, upon vesting, or upon sale of the underlying stock, based on the value of the benefit to the employee at that time. Thus, before granting any options to overseas employees, it is important to determine both when tax and social security payments will be due and how they will be calculated; otherwise, employees could find themselves liable for significant tax or social security bills in the year the benefits are given, even if the options have not vested and will not provide liquidity for tax bills if the U.S. parent is a private corporation.

The employer is normally required to deduct and pay the relevant amount of tax. Social security payments on the benefit can also be significant for both the employee and the employer-subsidiary. U.S. companies should be wary of requests to send the documentation for option grants to an address outside the overseas employee's country of residence or to issue options to service companies purportedly owned by the employee as well as other nonstandard methods that may be motivated by a desire to avoid compliance with local laws and tax-reporting requirements.

In a very limited number of countries outside the United States, it may be possible to "qualify" the stock option plan under local tax laws. This purpose of qualifying or receiving tax approval of a U.S. option plan is to give local employees in the foreign country the best available tax treatment of the benefit afforded under the option, both upon grant and exercise of the option, and again upon sale of the underlying stock. Again, advice from a locally qualified adviser is needed to determine the most appropriate form of equity award for employees of a foreign subsidiary. For example, it may not be cost-effective to grant or qualify options if the company has only a small number of employees in the relevant country.

Another alternative is to issue options under the U.S. plan without qualifying the plan under local laws. This will usually have the effect of creating nonstatutory options (or their local equivalent) even when the category of employee and number of options would ordinarily qualify for the favorable tax treatment afforded incentive stock options (*ISOs*) in the United States. It is almost always advisable to modify the form of option agreement before awarding options to overseas employees to remove references to ISOs or tax benefits that do not apply to the overseas grant. This helps make it clear that the grant of an option is discretionary and does not form part of the foreign employee's annual remuneration package. Such a modification is often necessary not only to satisfy local tax or employment requirements but also to address foreign exchange issues and to comply with local securities laws.

Before offering employee options or stock outside the United States, the company must determine whether registration of the options or the underlying stock is required under local securities laws or an exemption from registration is available. An exemption is often available when the company grants options to a small number of employees, generally not more than 50 but sometimes limited to just a few individuals. Local securities law and tax advice from a tax or employment lawyer qualified to advise on the laws of the country where the employee is resident is essential when structuring an option program for employees in multiple jurisdictions.

A U.S. parent wishing to grant options to employees overseas has several choices. Almost certainly, the U.S. parent will want to grant options at the parent company level, rather than at the subsidiary level. Granting employee options to acquire stock in the subsidiary is unlikely to be attractive to U.S. investors because ownership of the foreign subsidiary would be diluted once the options were exercised. They would also create valuation difficulties because the subsidiary would have to be valued on a standalone basis. Just as a parent company should not grant external shareholders equity in the foreign subsidiary (except in the few countries where this is required for regulatory purposes), a U.S. company should not grant options to acquire shares in the foreign subsidiary.

Data Protection and Employee Privacy

As indicated in Chapter 10, EU directives on data protection and privacy, which have been implemented through legislation enacted by each Member State of the EU, govern the collection, use, and processing of personal data concerning not only consumers but also employees. This includes employees' salaries, equity compensation, tax payments, and medical information. Further restrictions prevent the transfer of such data outside the EU to countries that do not have comparable restrictions on the use of personal data. The United States is such a country. This means that personal employee data may not be transferred to the United States unless a data protection policy is in place *and* compliance with EU data privacy and security laws is met.

Data privacy requirements in Europe continue to evolve. As a first step, a U.S. company setting up subsidiary operations in Europe will need to consider (1) establishing a data protection policy that is appropriate for the nature, type, and location of its overseas operations; (2) registering with the local data protection registrar, commissioner, or the equivalent; and (3) complying with current local laws when collecting, storing, using or processing personal data, especially if the U.S. company intends to send such data back to the United States. Failure to do so exposes the company to fines and other compliance measures; it may also give terminated employees additional claims against the company.

Employee Inventions and IP Assignments

As noted in Chapter 14, it is customary and good practice, particularly for technology companies, to obtain assignments of inventions and other intellectual property rights from employees in the United States. Is such a mechanism needed or valid overseas? Many countries have legislation providing that inventions and IP produced by employees are automatically the property of the employer. However, each country is different, and the form of proprietary information and assignment-of-inventions agreement (*PIAA*) used in the United States may be inadequate or, worse, invalid in certain countries. Accordingly, entrepreneurs should always discuss appropriate mechanisms to secure and protect IP ownership with local professional advisers.

It is typical in certain countries to include IP assignment and employee confidentiality provisions in the main body of the employment agreement entered into by the local subsidiary and the employee. If the employee also signs a U.S. form of PIAA document with the U.S. parent company, this may cause confusion as to which company actually owns the IP/technology rights developed by the employee—the subsidiary or the parent.

Even when appropriate IP assignment agreements are executed at the start of the employer–employee relationship, they may not be completely adequate to ensure that IP created after the initial agreement is signed vests solely in the employer without further action by the employer and/or the employee. For example,

Germany requires employers to make payments to "inventors" of patentable inventions.

Regulations Governing U.S. Expatriate Personnel

A U.S. parent company will often want one of its own senior managers to head up the newly created overseas subsidiary, and there are many benefits in this approach. The U.S. expatriate can keep the U.S. parent apprised of factors affecting the local market, including new opportunities, threats, and competitor actions. The U.S. expatriate can also educate the local team in the ways and culture of the U.S. business.

U.S. expatriate employees will usually need work permits or visas both for themselves and any dependents residing with the employee overseas. The time required to obtain a visa varies enormously from country to country and should be built into the time line for the establishment and operation of the new subsidiary.

Usually, the expatriate's employment terms will need to be modified to produce an expatriate package. In addition to a hardship or overseas allowance, the expatriate may need housing and travel allowances and a mechanism for tax equalization; the latter is needed because the expatriate will usually be paying taxes in the foreign country on income earned there while remaining liable for U.S. taxes on worldwide income. The length of time the expatriate spends in the foreign country will normally determine whether the individual is required to pay local employment taxes and social security. Although the length of time will vary from country to country, six months is often a good rule of thumb for the dividing line. Local and specialized tax advice is needed, however, as the method of calculating the relevant time spent in-country will vary depending on the jurisdiction. As with corporations, the bilateral tax treaties between the United States and most other countries will often allow credit to be given in one jurisdiction for taxes paid in another.

All U.S. citizens employed by a U.S. employer or by an entity controlled by a U.S. employer are protected by the U.S. antidiscrimination and other civil rights laws described in Chapter 8 even if they work outside the United States. (All employees working in the United States are also protected by these U.S. laws regardless of their nationality.) It is, therefore, important to ensure that both the U.S. parent and its subsidiaries have adequate policies and procedures in place dealing with employment discrimination and sexual harassment. Policies must obviously cover both U.S. and local regulatory requirements and should be reviewed from time to time to ensure they are kept current.

15.6 DISTRIBUTORS, VALUE-ADDED RESELLERS, AND SALES AGENTS

To expand sales geographically or to develop additional channels of distribution, a U.S. company operating overseas may work with one or more distributors, value-added resellers, or sales agents as an alternative to, or in addition to, its direct sales and marketing team.

It is important to distinguish between a *distributor* or *reseller* (who purchases goods from the U.S. parent or its overseas subsidiary and then sells them to customers and end users) and a *sales agent* (who locates potential customers and passes on sales leads to be accepted and fulfilled by the U.S. parent or subsidiary). Many countries have legislation protecting sales agents and, to a lesser extent, distributors. It is important to be clear in any agreement with a foreign intermediary whether the relationship is one of a distributor or a sales agent, because the roles are very different, as are the laws and consequences applicable to each. This is a particularly technical and highly regulated area in Europe, where local, country-specific advice should be sought before a U.S. company enters into a reseller or sales agent agreement.

The advantages of a sales agent include the ability of the U.S. company to retain more control over the terms of sale, including price. There is a risk, however, that the agent's activities on behalf of the U.S. company could create a permanent establishment of the U.S. company for tax purposes. Another downside of appointing a commercial agent in the EU is the agent's right to receive lump-sum payments upon termination of the agreement and certain other protections guaranteed by legislation passed throughout the EU in accordance with the European Commercial Agents Directive. The legislation is designed to protect independent commercial agents, who are often individuals rather than companies, whose livelihoods can be severely jeopardized if a manufacturer takes away their ability to generate sales once they have built up a book of business. It provides that certain terms and protections automatically apply to commercial sales agents, notwithstanding what the agreement with the manufacturer provides. For example, independent commercial agents are entitled to indemnities or mandatory compensation upon termination of the sales agency, which can be the equivalent of up to several years' worth of commissions in certain countries. A non-EU company cannot avoid these requirements by including a choice-of-law provision in its agreement with an agent operating in the EU by specifying that their relationship will be governed by non-EU law.[2] The company can, however, and should establish an agreement with the sales agent that is detailed, covers mandatory legal terms in the sales agent's country, and minimizes termination payments to the maximum possible extent. Crafting such an agreement, determining whether the European laws governing sales agents apply to a particular situation, and evaluating the impact of European antitrust laws on a commercial arrangement all require local advice as the laws and court decisions in this area continue to evolve in the various countries within the EU.

Care must also be taken with the terminology used to describe a distributor's or sales agent's "Territory." The "European Union" currently includes 28 countries, with Great Britain voting in 2016 to withdraw from the EU and other countries waiting to join. European law generally places restrictions and prohibitions on the creation of exclusive territories within the EU because they can interfere with the operation of a common market. "Asia" is also open to a wide interpretation, as is "EMEA" (a term that refers to Europe, the Middle East, and Africa, but is subject to wide interpretation because it does not specify exactly which countries are covered).

15.7 INTERNATIONAL INTELLECTUAL PROPERTY ISSUES

As discussed in Chapter 14, a young company's key assets are often its intellectual property. It is, therefore, essential that entrepreneurs understand how to protect their IP in global markets and put a strategy in place early on to manage and control those assets in the international arena. Thus, even if the entrepreneur plans to start selling in Europe, for example, and is unlikely to have a physical presence in Asia for some time, protecting the IP assets on a global basis should be considered early on.

Before commencing any business overseas (whether using distributors or by establishing a more formal business presence such as a subsidiary), the U.S. company should consider the adequacy of IP laws and protections in that country. This is particularly critical if computer source code or other fundamental IP assets are likely to be transferred or made available to the subsidiary or third parties in that country. For countries where IP protection is inadequate or timely redress through the courts for infringement is not available, the U.S. company may want to think long and hard about the appropriate business model for that country and make adaptations from the U.S. model as needed.

In addition, even if a startup may not be entering certain geographic markets immediately, it may be appropriate to commence trademark applications overseas for key product and business names being registered as trademarks in the United States and, at the same time, apply for company names (or business name registrations) for the local subsidiary. Otherwise, a company may lose the brand equity it has generated while marketing in the United States if it has to use different names in certain markets to avoid violating another's trademarks or confusing customers. In Europe, the Community Trade Mark (*CTM*) may be appropriate and has the advantage of requiring just one application to potentially cover all of the Member States of the EU. We discussed IP and trademark protections in detail in Chapter 14.

15.8 FUNDING FOREIGN OPERATIONS

Although the establishment of the Euro-Zone has reduced some of the previous foreign exchange headaches in Europe (at least before Brexit, the United Kingdom's referendum to leave the EU), several issues must still be considered when funding an overseas business operation.

Initial Capitalization and Funding

As noted earlier, certain countries have significant minimum capital requirements for the incorporation of a subsidiary. In addition, if the company is tackling a new market and building its overseas network, cash may be flowing out of the United States until the subsidiary is generating revenue and thus self-sufficient. Consideration should be given to the following items when preparing the initial budget for incorporating the subsidiary and funding its operations in the first 6–12 months of business.

> ➤ ***Initial Capital Structure***. What will be the initial capital contribution? Cash? Does the country permit other tangible property, IP, or services to form part of the initial capital contribution? Does the U.S. company want to contribute IP or other valuable assets to a separate subsidiary entity overseas?

> ➤ ***Minimum Capital Requirements.*** Will the legal minimum capital be sufficient initially, or will regulators, customers, suppliers, or potential partners expect or require a higher amount?

> ➤ ***"Thin Capitalization."*** If working capital comes from bank borrowing, many countries require a balance of debt to equity in order for the interest on the debt to be deductible. A ratio of 1:1 may be required, so debt levels may need to be backed by equity from the U.S. parent. Careful tax planning with an international tax adviser will be needed to ensure compliance with these requirements.

> ➤ ***Working Capital.*** The new subsidiary may need substantial economic support in the first few months or even years, depending on the time to market for the local product and other factors, such as competition or other barriers to entry in the local market. Will the U.S. parent fund the initial startup and growth, or will some or all of the funding come from bank borrowing, either in the United States or through a local facility? If the latter, the parent company may have to guarantee the local subsidiary's debt if the subsidiary does not have adequate assets to secure the facility.

> ➤ ***Intercompany Arrangements.*** The functions performed by the local subsidiary will determine the basis upon which financial support from the U.S. parent is needed. For example, if a sales and marketing subsidiary is set up in Europe and will perform the limited role of finding sales opportunities to refer back to the U.S. parent to make the sale, the European subsidiary

would likely be financed under a cost-plus arrangement. When there is a *cost-plus arrangement*, the U.S. parent company compensates the European subsidiary for its presales and marketing efforts by paying the employment and related expenses of the subsidiary (the "costs"), together with a small markup on those expenses (the "plus"). The relevant markup will depend on the sophistication of the services provided by the subsidiary, and the tax requirements of the country involved.

Establishing Local Bank Accounts

Expanded overseas operations may need a working capital facility and a local bank account to pay local creditors and to handle payroll and related employee expenses. As with most aspects of operating overseas, formalities for setting up an account vary from country to country, but a few guiding principles apply in any jurisdiction.

When financing the local subsidiary, the U.S. parent needs to balance the need for flexibility with control over local expenditures. It is often appropriate to have signatories from the United States (particularly for board members) as well as local signatories, although the parent may want to ensure that checks or transfers above a certain monetary amount require dual signatures. The bylaws (or their equivalent) of the local subsidiary might also establish a mechanism for board approval of significant expenditures above a certain preset limit, and it is wise for the U.S. parent to establish and enforce internal company policies and approval procedures to tightly control overseas spending.

Many countries, especially in Europe, have anti-money-laundering (*AML*) regulations that require banks to investigate a new customer before opening a bank account. AML compliance can require disclosure to the foreign bank of detailed information on the U.S. parent company, its directors, and shareholders.

Bank signatories should be checked and updated at least once a year. The process of appointing or removing bank account signatories can be fairly formal, requiring board authorization, notarization or the production of various identification documents. If key people have left the operation, the subsidiary may not appreciate the inadequacy of its bank instructions until an urgent business need requires immediate action.

Financing International Sales

Both the U.S. parent and the local subsidiary need to consider how sales to customers in diverse parts of the globe will be financed. Although checking the creditworthiness of potential customers may be relatively easy in the United States or Western Europe, in many countries such information is simply not available, is unreliable, or is prohibitively expensive to obtain. It is not unusual for a U.S. company beginning to make international sales to require prepayment from new customers or distributors, at least until a course of dealings over several months or years gives the U.S. company confidence in the creditworthiness of the overseas party.

Letters of Credit   Even if a customer's credit standing can be checked prior to a sale, it may still be necessary to establish a reliable method of payment to ensure that the U.S. parent or its subsidiary receives payment promptly for goods shipped to the customer. In the absence of a reliable track record with the customer or prior dealings with businesses in a particular region, the best way to ensure reliable and prompt payment is to use letters of credit (*L/Cs*). There are two types of letters of credit. One type is usually referred to as a "documentary letter of credit" or just a "letter of credit"; the other is called a "standby letter of credit."

Documentary letters of credit are frequently used to secure payment for goods in international transactions. The overseas purchaser of the goods (known as the *applicant*) enters into a contract with the issuing bank (usually in its own country). The bank issues an L/C in favor of the seller (either the U.S. parent or its local subsidiary) as *beneficiary*. The L/C provides for payment of the purchase price by the issuing bank to the beneficiary upon delivery to the bank of specified documents (often the bill of lading issued by the carrier of the goods to the seller). A typical L/C requires the beneficiary to present a *clean bill of lading* to the bank, meaning one with no notations indicating defects or damage to the goods when they were received for transportation to the purchaser. Upon presentation of the relevant documents, the bank makes payment to the seller/beneficiary.

The key purpose of an L/C is to allow the issuing bank to pay based solely on the presentation of specified documents without requiring (or permitting) the bank to examine any underlying facts, including compliance by the purchaser or the seller with the terms of their sales contract. The sale of goods pursuant to an L/C therefore involves two contracts: one between the seller and the purchaser, and a second between the issuing bank and the seller. Absent proof of outright fraud, the issuing bank must pay the beneficiary even if, for example, the buyer asserts that the goods are defective. In such a case, the buyer must then sue the seller for breach of contract to recover the purchase price paid to the seller by the bank.

It is customary for sellers to require irrevocable L/Cs when dealing with unfamiliar parties. An *irrevocable L/C* can be amended or canceled only with the consent of the beneficiary (usually the seller) and the issuing bank.

A *standby letter of credit* requires payment only if the purchaser of the goods (or the recipient of services) has failed to perform its obligations under the sales or service contract, that is, to pay for the goods purchased or the services rendered. Payment by the issuing bank under a standby letter of credit is usually conditional upon a brief statement (in the precise language provided in the standby letter of credit) that the purchaser is in default and that the seller/beneficiary is therefore entitled to payment from the issuing bank. As with regular L/Cs, the issuing bank cannot inquire into the underlying transaction or assert defenses against payment the purchaser might have vis-à-vis the seller or service provider (other than blatant fraud). The bank must generally pay within seven business days following presentation of the specified documents.

Both types of L/Cs cost money. In an ongoing relationship, the purchasing customer usually presses for more favorable payment terms, including the possibility of substituting a guaranty for the L/C. Letters of credit are generally governed by Article 5 of the Uniform Commercial Code, although the parties may elect to be governed by a set of rules published by the International Chamber of Commerce.[3]

15.9 LEASING PROPERTY, ACQUIRING EQUIPMENT, AND SETTING UP OPERATIONS

Entrepreneurs need to take various factors into account before leasing or acquiring property in another country and before setting up operations.

Leases

Signing a lease—even a short-term or temporary one—for property in another country may, in certain situations, trigger the creation of a permanent establishment in that country, so the timing of the signing should be coordinated with the overseas expansion plans and tax-planning objectives. In some parts of the world, acquiring space can be enormously expensive. For example, in many parts of Europe, leases tend to be much longer than is customary in the United States. Doing some homework and investigation up front will avoid unpleasant surprises later.

Several different types of property may be available for lease. Many major cities have "serviced" or executive offices available, where a U.S. startup can rent the space it needs initially and also receive administrative support, such as reception, switchboard, and security services. This type of arrangement might be helpful for the first few months, until the local sales and marketing operation has the critical mass to take on its own office space and associated personnel.

Because a subsidiary will usually have minimal assets to begin with, overseas landlords may require the parent company to guarantee the subsidiary's obligations under the lease, particularly for longer leases in which the total rental obligation may exceed the financial resources of the subsidiary for the foreseeable future. The financial obligations under these guaranties are often worded broadly and can cover all conceivable costs and expenses associated with the property, not just the rent and service charges. As a result, the lease guaranty could itself become a significant contingent liability for the U.S. parent.

Acquiring Equipment

The new business overseas will also need equipment, which is often sourced in the local country. Supply times may not be as short as in the United States, so entrepreneurs need to plan accordingly. This is also true of technology and communications links. Although the EU and many parts of Asia have services comparable to those available in the United States, this is not necessarily the case in other parts of the world. If the subsidiary needs fast Internet connections and a state-of-the-art communication system properly integrated with the head office in the United States, additional planning and extra time are necessary to obtain the telecom links and services from the local suppliers (many of which may be state-run enterprises or monopolies).

Ensuring the Adequate Supply and Distribution of Products

Another element to consider when establishing an overseas office is whether there will be an adequate supply of products and associated components, manuals, and literature, which can be affected by the local roads and other transportation infrastructure. Additional distribution channels may also be necessary to ensure reliable and timely distribution of products. This may involve the appointment of independent distributors or resellers, to be selected and overseen by the new local subsidiary or to assist it in achieving broader sales coverage in certain territories or regions. All agreements with distributors, resellers, or sales agents should be negotiated with the full knowledge of and input from the U.S. parent so that any new arrangements, especially those made on an exclusive basis, dovetail with existing agreements covering sales or supply.

Obtaining Tax and Other Governmental Incentives

If the overseas subsidiary is a manufacturing center as well as a sales and marketing site, it may be possible to obtain investment incentives, tax breaks, or other forms of financial assistance from the regional or national government. These incentives are often offered to attract new business to rural or depressed areas— locations that may not be the most suitable for technology businesses. Incentives are often not available if the company has already started building a facility or setting up an operation, so entrepreneurs should look into this possibility early on if incentives or grants are expected to be key to financing the new operation. Also, it is important to clearly understand the terms of the grant or incentive, which are often linked to the number of jobs created by the project. If economic conditions require a reduction in the workforce, some or all of the grant may become immediately repayable to the government or regional agency.

15.10 U.S. SUPPORT FOR OVERSEAS OFFICES AND FACILITIES

A U.S. parent company will invariably provide some central services and support to its overseas offices, even when they are well established and relatively self-sufficient. The best practice is to formalize these arrangements at an early stage by putting them in writing. Intercompany agreements serve a variety of useful functions, from providing proper accounting and tax treatment for intragroup transactions to enabling both parties to budget for additional services to or from the other. These agreements typically spell out what sale, supply, and support arrangements will be provided for the overseas businesses and how the cost of these services will be calculated and adjusted from year to year. In addition, smaller subsidiaries can often piggyback on the U.S. parent's greater bargaining power with suppliers and vendors. Typical services supplied or procured by the home office include some or all of the following:

> ➤ Sales and marketing support and coordination
> ➤ Advertising/public relations (launch and ongoing)
> ➤ Pricing policies
> ➤ Technical support
> ➤ Administration and human resources
> ➤ Accounting and treasury
> ➤ Other support services (such as strategic planning, legal services, and supply chain management).

Regardless of whether the U.S. parent provides significant services directly to its overseas subsidiaries, the parent will have ongoing responsibilities with respect to their business. These include overseeing their corporate governance and ensuring that all subsidiaries are current with their filings, registrations, and tax returns in the relevant jurisdictions. Periodic responsibilities will include involvement in acquisitions, joint ventures, or strategic partnering, which affect the group as a whole and not just the local subsidiary involved.

The U.S. business will also need to review other aspects of the overseas operations, such as risk management. Adequate local insurance coverage and suitable corporate policies should be an integral part of the business from day one. U.S. managers and senior personnel will often be sent abroad to assist in running overseas operations and those personnel will need to be rotated at appropriate intervals.

Formal accounting and audit policies must be in place to ensure that the U.S. parent can properly supervise the financial and accounting activity of the subsidiary. This is especially important if the parent company is a public company or will shortly become one.

Finally, the U.S. parent should also be mindful of U.S. legal requirements regarding export control and the restriction of exports to certain countries and certain businesses/individuals. In particular, U.S. companies need to exercise caution when appointing distributors in one country with a "territory" that encompasses additional countries. Consider, for example, a distributor in Dubai or elsewhere in the United Arab Emirates (*UAE*), with a territory covering the "Middle East." There are several countries in that region where U.S. companies cannot do business, so it is vital for the U.S. company to educate the distributor concerning the applicable U.S. restrictions. The U.S. company must also comply with the antibribery and record-keeping requirements imposed by the U.S. Foreign Corrupt Practices Act (*FCPA*) (discussed in Chapter 11) and similar local legislation, which prohibit bribery or similar payments to foreign officials and impose criminal sanctions for violations. Regulators in the United States and other countries continue to aggressively pursue violations of their antibribery laws, and the fines and penalties can be staggering. For example, in 2016, the U.S. Securities and Exchange Commission (*SEC*) announced a global settlement that required VimpelCom Ltd., a telecommunications provider, to pay $167.5 million to the SEC, $230.1 million to the U.S. Department of Justice (*DOJ*), and nearly $400 million to Dutch regulators to resolve violations of the FCPA.[4] Eight years earlier, German manufacturer Siemens AG resolved FCPA and related charges with the DOJ, the Munich Public Prosecutor's Office and the SEC with multiple guilty pleas and the payment of $1.6 billion in fines, penalties, and disgorgement of profits.[5]

In addition, companies must be cognizant of the reach of other U.S. laws. Courts in the United States apply a "presumption against extraterritoriality," which means that, generally, unless there is a clearly expressed congressional intent to the contrary, a federal law is presumed to apply only domestically. In 2016, the U.S. Supreme Court clarified the geographic scope of the Racketeer Influenced and Corrupt Organizations Act (*RICO*),[6] holding that its prohibitions against certain (but not all) of its substantive predicate acts (specific federal criminal statutes) apply outside the United States, but its private right of action provision does not overcome the presumption against extraterritoriality. As a result, a private RICO plaintiff must allege and prove a domestic injury.[7]

 # Putting It into **PRACTICE**

As Alexei and Piper tested their designs and moved into production, they received interest from their initial customers in the United States to ramp up production of the GT V-Brackets for automotive manufacturing facilities outside the United States. In particular, establishing a manufacturing source in Asia was key to securing larger, longer term contracts with several U.S. automotive industry suppliers, with whom the U.S. car giants maintained global, just-in-time supply contracts.

Even though Alexei thought that having a significant outsourced manufacturer in Asia would secure the longer term contracts being discussed with their U.S. customers, Piper worried that their resources in California would be stretched too thinly to monitor and oversee such a significant outsourcing arrangement across the Pacific. In response, Alexei cautioned that if Genesist could not scale its business and manufacturing capabilities to cover the main automotive manufacturing sites around the globe, its current U.S. customers would simply look for similar 3D manufactured products from its overseas competitors.

Alexei and Piper discussed the matter with board members Keith Tinsley and Sue Quinn, after which Keith walked the team through various alternatives and the decision points to consider regarding overseas manufacturing. He recounted his own experience transitioning a fundamentally R&D-focused domestic business into a full-fledged operational company with the roll-out of manufacturing in several facilities across key locations internationally. After investigating the matter for several months on their own, soliciting more advice from Keith and Sue, and being introduced by Keith to the heads of several international

(continued)

outsourced manufacturing companies, Alexei and Piper identified Additive Manufacturing Private Limited (*AMPL*) in India as the most suitable outsourced 3D manufacturing partner. AMPL had a new manufacturing facility in Bangalore, which focused on the 3D manufacture of aerospace parts and military equipment. Keith had worked with its management team in his prior companies and had recommended AMPL to other U.S. companies for whom he had provided consulting services via Fast-Print Consulting. Alexei and Piper trusted Keith's recommendation and were pleased with the positive feedback they received from other U.S. companies that had worked with AMPL. Nonetheless, they still felt they needed hands-on monitoring and assessment of AMPL's production of the brackets because Genesist and AMPL would be jointly developing and refining the manufacturing systems based on the Genesis T-2000 technology. It was agreed that Anil Chopra, an Indian citizen by birth who was one of the first employees at Genesist, would relocate to India to head a small Genesist team to assist with the knowledge transfer to AMPL and the development of the novel manufacturing process. Anil was not only very familiar with the Genesis T-2000 technology, but he also brought a decade of clean room manufacturing experience to Genesist's fledgling manufacturing operations. AMPL agreed that Genesist personnel would work with the AMPL operational team to establish the manufacturing line with an 18-month implementation schedule.

As a first step, the Genesist board decided to establish a simple, wholly owned subsidiary in India to be called Genesist India Private Limited (*GIPL*). GIPL would both employ Anil and the expected three or four local hires and be the vehicle to receive the Indian government grants and R&D assistance the Indian team was seeking to enhance the manufacturing applications of the Genesis T-2000 technology. Attorney Sarah Crawford connected the Genesist team with excellent local counsel in Bangalore, who handled the incorporation of Genesist India Private Limited. She also introduced Alexei, Piper, and Anil to local bankers and accounting advisers. Local counsel advised that Indian law required the Indian subsidiary to have two shareholders. After discussion with the board and Sarah, Alexei and Piper agreed that Genesist should incorporate a simple, wholly owned subsidiary in the United States to act as the second shareholder in the Indian subsidiary. Forming the new U.S. subsidiary to act as a second shareholder also made sense given Genesist's plans to expand soon to Latin America for additional global manufacturing to support automotive contracts and potential aircraft manufacturers. Like India, many Latin American countries required two shareholders to form a subsidiary there.

The local counsel advised that Genesist India Private Limited could be set up with a minimal share capital because its employee and

(continued)

associated expenses would be paid by the U.S. parent company under a cost-plus intercompany services agreement. After Anil relocated to Bangalore, Alexei and Piper were named directors of Genesist India Private Limited, with Anil as the third director to meet the requirement that Indian companies have at least one Indian resident on the board of directors. Ninety percent of the GIPL shares were issued to Genesist, Inc. and ten percent to Genesist's new U.S. subsidiary.

With input from Piper and Alexei, Anil hired three local manufacturing engineers to help him with the AMPL outsourced manufacturing contract. Local counsel prepared the necessary employment documentation, after consulting with Sarah. Piper visited Bangalore once a quarter during the 18-month implementation schedule. She and Alexei also received feedback on an ongoing basis from Anil concerning the manufacturing ramp-up in India. There were some bumps in the road, but by the first anniversary of the set-up in India, the quality and quantity of products in production were looking good, and the solid resources in India opened doors for Alexei and Piper to pitch for additional contracts supplying dozens of automotive-parts manufacturers in Asia. While keeping a close eye on the operations in India, Alexei and Piper continued to consider other ways to grow both the business and the technical staff.

CHAPTER 16

Buying and Selling a Business

For many early-stage companies, selling the company or buying another company (a *business combination*) may be the most effective method of accessing capital, establishing strategic relationships, and offering increased liquidity to the acquired company's shareholders. Entering into a business combination can involve many complex issues, however. These include tax and securities law considerations; the treatment of employees and their benefits; and the integration of the combined companies after the transaction is completed. Entrepreneurs should carefully consider the structure and potential implications of a proposed transaction and review them with experienced counsel before agreeing to any business combination.

This chapter begins by discussing many of the issues an entrepreneur should consider when deciding between a sale of the company and an initial public offering. We then identify types of acquirers and describe general requirements for business combinations, including shareholder approval, board approval, and the fiduciary duties of directors and controlling shareholders. The chapter then discusses typical forms of business combinations, including asset purchases, acquisitions of stock and other equity, and mergers, and the advantages and disadvantages of each for the acquirer and target company and their shareholders. Next, we review pricing issues and types of consideration as well as the tax, securities law, accounting, and antitrust issues that frequently arise in connection with the purchase or sale of a business. The chapter describes the process for a typical merger, from due diligence and the memorialization of the basic terms of a transaction in a letter of intent or a term sheet, through the negotiation of the principal terms of a definitive merger agreement, to the closing of the transaction. We also discuss some of the typical terms in a merger agreement and conclude by addressing common post-closing issues.

Rather than buying or selling a business, an entrepreneur may decide to buy a franchise (such as a Best Buy store) or to sell franchises of the entrepreneur's business model and trademarks (such as franchises of a tax planning service). We discuss the definition of "franchise" and summarize the rules governing franchising in Appendix 16.1, "Franchising a Business," which is available on the companion website for this title at www.CengageBrain.com.

16.1 BUSINESS COMBINATIONS VERSUS INITIAL PUBLIC OFFERINGS

To obtain liquidity for shareholders, a company can either pursue a business combination or an initial public offering (*IPO*). Business combinations are a much more common method of obtaining liquidity for shareholders of private companies than IPOs, particularly if a company is experiencing slow but steady growth or operates in an industry not currently favored by the investment community. We discuss initial public offerings and their pros and cons in detail in Chapter 17.

Advantages of Business Combinations Compared with IPOs

The sale of a company for cash or for the stock of another company can offer several advantages not available with an IPO. In a cash sale, the shareholders of the target company obtain immediate liquidity, and the value of the consideration paid for their shares is fixed. (For purposes of this discussion, *target company* refers to the entity whose assets or stock is being sold or which is being merged with the acquirer or a subsidiary of the acquirer in a transaction that will result in control being shifted from the target company's shareholders to the acquirer.) Even business combinations involving the sale of the target company for stock of the acquirer are less subject to the risks associated with changing stock market conditions than IPOs. IPO "windows" can open and close with little warning, which may prevent the completion of the IPO or adversely affect the price at which stock can be publicly offered by the company or sold by shareholders after the offering is completed. In addition, through an agreement referred to as a *lockup agreement*, underwriters of an IPO typically require most shareholders to agree not to sell or otherwise transfer their shares for at least six months after completion of an IPO, resulting in additional constraints on shareholder liquidity and added exposure to market fluctuations.

In a stock-for-stock combination with a public company, market risk is not eliminated entirely, however. The degree of risk will, in part, depend on whether the shares being issued will be freely tradable or restricted for some period of time by the securities laws or by contract. Lockup agreements may still be required, particularly if the target company shareholders are receiving a significant portion of the buyer's stock. However, if the buyer is a more established public company, its market price is usually less volatile than that of a newly public company. In addition, unless precluded by a lockup agreement with the buyer, shareholders can often reduce their risk by selling stock or engaging in other activities that would be precluded by a typical lockup agreement with the underwriters of an IPO. Perhaps most importantly, a business combination may enable a company to avoid the costs and pressures of being a public company, including meeting or exceeding revenue and earnings estimates on a quarterly basis and communicating with and owing duties to a large number of shareholders.

Disadvantages of Business Combinations Compared with IPOs

A less positive feature of a business combination is the potential limitation on the upside return for the target company's shareholders. First, the price paid per share by an acquirer may be less than the target company could obtain in a public offering. Second, in an IPO, the target company's shareholders' *upside* (potential profit) is determined solely by the performance of the

From the **TRENCHES**

A publicly held semiconductor manufacturer considered acquiring a small privately held company whose principal asset was technology that could be applied in the public company's business. Although the public company acknowledged that it might be possible to develop the technology for use in other industries, the public company did not necessarily intend to develop this potential, which was far removed from its core competencies. As a result, it was not willing to factor this potential into the calculation of the purchase price. The public company was also unwilling to structure a transaction that would allow the private company to develop the technology in other industries. The founders of the privately held company were faced with the choice of completing a transaction at a lower valuation than they thought their company was worth or continuing on their own while they sought to consummate a transaction with investors or another company that shared their vision for the development of their technology. Ultimately, the founders of the privately held firm decided not to enter into a business combination with the semiconductor firm.

target, whereas in a business combination the target shareholders' upside is determined by the performance of the acquirer's stock when the consideration is stock, or is capped at the purchase price when the consideration is cash.

16.2 TYPES OF ACQUIRERS

It is important for an entrepreneur to consider the different types of acquirers and the role that an acquirer will play in the target company after a business combination is completed. Of particular importance are the acquirer's long-term vision for the target company and the allocation of control of the combined entity. Two types of acquirers—financial acquirers and strategic acquirers—would likely have different priorities. Often a financial acquirer's priority will be to fulfill the target company's potential for short-term financial return and as a consequence, the long-term vision of the target company may be sacrificed. This shift in priority may become manifest through a reduction in staff or research and development programs. In contrast, although strategic acquirers will often control the day-to-day operations of the target company, they will generally share its long-term vision. As a result, they may be less likely to take actions simply to increase the target's short-term financial value.

Although some acquirers may be interested in a mid-stage company, potential acquirers often surface near the time that a company is ready to proceed with an IPO because acquirers are aware that once a company is public, they will likely be required to pay a premium over the public market price to induce the target company's board of directors to approve the transaction.

16.3 FORMS OF BUSINESS COMBINATIONS

Business combinations can take three basic forms: asset acquisitions, stock acquisitions, and mergers.

Asset Acquisitions

In an *asset purchase*, the acquiring company purchases some or all of the target company's assets and assumes some or all of its liabilities. Figure 16.2 outlines the steps taken to accomplish an asset purchase and the result.

Advantages and Disadvantages of an Asset Purchase   Acquirers often prefer to purchase assets instead of stock. From the perspective of target companies and their shareholders, on the other hand, an asset sale is generally not as favorable as a sale of stock or other equity.

Ability to Pick and Choose Assets and Liabilities   By purchasing assets, the acquirer can purchase only those assets that it wants to acquire and agree to assume only specified liabilities of the target company. As a result, the acquirer may be able to avoid the expense of purchasing unwanted assets and reduce the risk of assuming most unknown liabilities. Conversely, when selling assets, the target company may be forced to retain significant known or unknown liabilities.

An acquirer can never totally eliminate the risk of being saddled with some of the target company's liabilities. Even though the acquisition agreement will almost always limit the acquirer's assumption of liabilities to those expressly set forth in the agreement, certain federal and state laws may override the parties' contractual limitations. For example, in some states, if the acquirer buys a business and continues selling the same products as the

Figure 16.2   Asset Acquisition

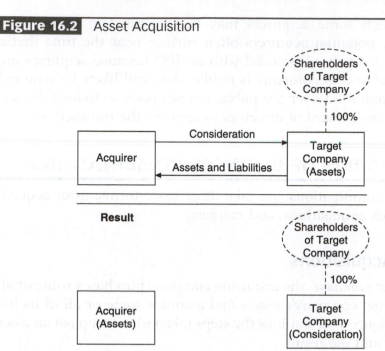

target company, the acquirer will be liable for defects in products sold by the target company *before* the acquisition. (Successor product liability was discussed further in Chapter 10.) As a result, liabilities may be imposed on an acquirer that were unknown or unquantifiable by either the acquirer or the target company at the time of the transaction.

Need for Target Company Shareholder Approval and Entitlement to Dissenters' Rights   If the target company does not sell all, or substantially all, of its assets, then the completion of the asset purchase should not require approval by the target company's shareholders or give rise to dissenters' rights for the target company's shareholders (discussed in Section 16.7). As a result, certain asset purchase transactions can be completed very quickly and without the possibility of additional payouts to the target company's shareholders.

If, however, the target company is selling all, or substantially all, of its assets, then the corporate laws of most states require both the target company's board of directors and the holders of a majority of its shares to approve the principal terms of the asset purchase-and-sale agreement. The need to secure shareholder approval can, at the very least, delay the closing of the transaction. It can also create uncertainty as to whether the target company will be able to obtain the necessary shareholder approval. In addition, the shareholders of the target company entitled to vote on an asset sale they oppose may have dissenters' rights.

Third-Party Consents May Be Required Contracts and permits (including real estate or equipment leases, technology licenses, and environmental or other governmental permits) often are either a part of, or fundamental to, the value of the assets being purchased in an asset acquisition. Many contracts and permits contain *anti-assignment* provisions, which prohibit assignment to third parties, or restrict the transfer of the related rights, without the consent of the other party to the contract or the issuer of the permit. If, as is usually the case, some or all of the target company's contracts and permits are critical to the acquired business then, as a practical matter, the acquirer will be unwilling to consummate the transaction unless the assignment to the acquirer is approved in advance.

Often it is not difficult to obtain third-party consents, especially if the acquirer is economically sound and is not a competitor of the other party to the contract. Obtaining consents takes time, however, so it can delay the closing of an asset purchase.

Sometimes the other party may refuse to grant its consent for business reasons that are unrelated to the proposed transaction. For example, if the target company has a below-market lease, then the lessor will usually elect to prohibit assignment so that it is free to lease the property to a new tenant at the higher market rate. The need to procure a third-party consent may also give that party sufficient leverage to condition its consent on the acquirer's willingness to accept terms that are less favorable than those in the target company's original contract or permit. In addition, the request for third-party consents may force disclosure of the proposed asset sale to outside parties earlier than the acquirer and target company desire.

Tax Treatment An acquirer doing an asset purchase may obtain a beneficial *step-up* (increase) in the tax basis of the acquired assets to reflect the purchase price of the assets (as compared with inheriting their historic tax basis in the hands of the target company, which is normally the result when stock is purchased). The stepped-up tax basis of the assets can then be amortized by the acquirer over the applicable tax depreciation lives of the assets (including intangible assets like goodwill), thereby potentially providing significant tax savings to the acquirer, as discussed further below. If, however, the purchase price for the acquired assets is less than their historic tax basis (which is unusual, but can occur), then the asset purchase will instead result in a reduction or *step-down* in the tax basis of the acquired assets, which will potentially be less favorable for the acquirer from an income tax perspective.

If the consideration a target company organized as a C corporation receives in an asset purchase transaction is distributed to its shareholders, then the transaction will result in double taxation of any gain on the sale (unless it is structured as a tax-free reorganization): first at the target company level (unless the target company has sufficient available net operating losses to offset such gain) and then at the shareholder level when the consideration is distributed to the company's shareholders. Double taxation will often reduce the net after-tax proceeds of the sale for the target company's shareholders relative to a stock sale. (C corporations were discussed in Chapter 4.)

Bulk Sales Laws   Certain states have *bulk sales laws*, which contain very specific requirements that can work to protect both an acquirer and creditors of the target company, including taxing authorities. If the target company fails to comply with the applicable bulk sales laws, however, then the acquirer may find itself liable to the target company's creditors.

Bulk sales laws are typically triggered when a target company is selling a significant portion of its business or assets out of the ordinary course of business, but they usually apply only to the sales of certain types of assets in designated transactions. Among other things, they require the target company to give notice to its creditors before completing certain sale transactions.

Stock and Other Equity Acquisitions

In an equity acquisition, the acquirer purchases all of the target company's outstanding shares of stock (or other form of equity,

Figure 16.3 Stock Acquisition

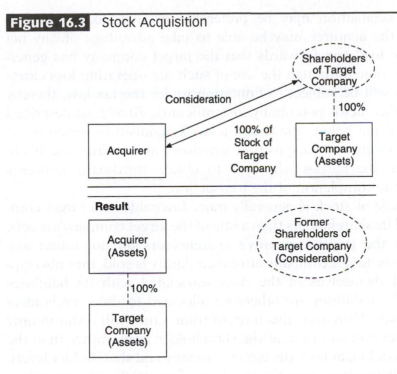

if the target company is not a corporation) from the target's share-holders. (For convenience, we will use "stock acquisitions" to include all types of equity acquisitions, including acquisitions of the members' equity interest in a limited liability company, and "shareholders" to include all types of equity holders.) Figure 16.3 (above) outlines the steps involved and the result.

Parties to Stock Purchase Agreement Technically, it is often not necessary for the target company to be a party to a stock purchase agreement because the acquirer is buying stock directly from the target company's shareholders. As a practical matter, however, the acquirer will often require the target company to be a party so the target company can (1) make representations and warranties regarding the target company and its business and operations and (2) agree to certain covenants relating to the operation of the target company's business in the period from the signing of the stock purchase agreement to the completion of the transaction.

Advantages and Disadvantages of Stock Acquisition An acquirer may favor a stock acquisition because the acquirer is assured of obtaining all the assets owned by the target company. In addition, a stock acquisition may be preferable from a tax perspective because the acquirer may be able to take advantage of any net operating loss carryforwards that the target company has generated over time (although the use of such net operating loss carryforwards will be subject to limitation under the tax law, thereby making this factor potentially insignificant). Finally, as described in more detail below, the use of a stock acquisition structure, as opposed to an asset acquisition structure, may reduce the likelihood that the parties will need to obtain third-party consents prior to the completion of the transaction.

The sale of stock is generally more favorable to a target company and its shareholders than a sale of the target company's assets. Although the target company's shareholders do not retain any assets of the target company after their equity is sold, they also typically rid themselves of the risks associated with its liabilities (unless the liabilities are otherwise allocated to the shareholders by contract). Moreover, this form of transaction will result in only a single level of taxation, at the shareholder level, rather than the double taxation, at both the target company and shareholder levels, commonly resulting from the purchase of assets of a C corporation.

Automatic Assumption of Liabilities of Target Company The acquirer will, by virtue of its ownership of the target company following the completion of the transaction, assume and be liable for all of the target company's liabilities, whether known or unknown, fixed or contingent, unless the liabilities are otherwise allocated to the target company's shareholders by contract. As a result, acquirers must perform extensive due diligence (a process described below) to attempt to confirm the extent of any possible exposure to such liabilities before the transaction is completed.

The acquirer can try to limit its exposure by having a separate subsidiary acquire the equity of the target company, but in such a case the acquirer must ensure compliance with all corporate formalities so that there will be no basis for piercing the corporate veil. This may be impracticable if the acquirer plans to integrate its operations with those of the acquired company. In addition, if the acquirer plans to dividend up money or property to the parent firm, then it must also comply with all state law restrictions on the payment of dividends.

Need for Unanimous Approval from the Target Company's Share-holders and Use of Second-Step Mergers Another disadvantage of an acquisition structured as a stock sale, which affects both the acquirer and the target company, is the need to obtain unanimous approval of the sale from the target company's shareholders. Because the acquirer is buying the target company's stock directly from the shareholders themselves, the acquirer may need to negotiate with and make concessions to minority shareholders who would not necessarily have the same leverage in a merger transaction. These negotiations can significantly delay and even derail the completion of the transaction. Therefore, a stock purchase is typically used only when a target company's shareholder base is small and unified in support of the proposed transaction. Otherwise, most acquirers will use a merger structure rather than buy stock.

If an acquirer that elected to structure the acquisition as a stock acquisition is unable to acquire all of a target company's securities directly from the target company's shareholders, it may be able to acquire the balance in a second-step merger. Under the laws of most states, the holders of a majority of a corporation's equity can call a shareholder meeting and seek approval of a merger of the target company with either the acquirer or a subsidiary of the acquirer. The board of directors of the target company owe (and the majority shareholders may owe) a fiduciary duty to the minority, so the board and the acquirer should ensure that the terms of the "freeze-out" merger are procedurally and substantively fair to the minority.

If the acquiring corporation holds 90% or more of the outstanding shares of a target company's stock, many states (including California) allow the completion of a merger without the approval of the target company's shareholders. In such a transaction, called a *short-form merger,* the acquiring corporation can effect the merger through a resolution of its board of directors and by filing the specified certificate with the target company's state of incorporation. For California corporations, if the acquirer owns more than 50% but less than 90% of the target company's shares, then, as a practical matter, the acquirer may not be able to eliminate the minority in a second-step merger if there is any substantial minority opposition.

From the **TRENCHES**

In July 2014, Herman Miller, Inc., a manufacturer of classic midcentury furniture, entered into a stock purchase agreement with Design Within Reach, Inc. (*DWR*), a contemporary furniture retailer. The agreement stated that DWR had 7,500,000 shares of common stock authorized, of which 6,624,470 shares were outstanding on the date of the agreement. Pursuant to the agreement, Herman Miller acquired approximately 83% of DWR's common stock for approximately $155 million. After two individuals contributed additional DWR shares to Herman Miller's acquisition vehicle, DWR was then merged into a newly formed subsidiary of Herman Miller in a short-form merger.

Shortly thereafter, in December 2014, two former DWR shareholders sued, claiming that the merger never occurred because DWR had made certain "technical mistakes" when it did a purported 1 for 50 reverse stock split in 2010. (In a reverse stock split, the number of outstanding shares are decreased by the ratio.) That transaction was intended to reduce the total number of authorized common and preferred shares of DWR stock from 31.5 million to 630,000. The plaintiffs claimed that DWR did not follow Delaware law when purporting to effect the split because DWR did not provide prompt notice that the purported reverse split and a related amendment to the certificate of incorporation had been approved by nonunanimous written consent of shareholders. The plaintiffs also asserted that they did not receive notice of the purported split until discovery in this suit. The suit also alleged that the minority shareholders did not receive required notices when DWR had sold numerous shares of new stock in multiple issuances since 2010, which increased the amount of DWR outstanding stock to more than the number of shares authorized by the certificate of incorporation. As a result, plaintiffs alleged, Herman Miller never acquired the 90% of DWR stock needed to effectuate the short-form merger.

The DWR defendants acknowledged that certain "defective corporate acts," including the purported reverse stock split, occurred, but they asserted that the defects were remedied under applicable provisions of Delaware state law and that the merger was, therefore, valid. One media source reported that the suit "could, in theory," result in the rescission of the merger.

Comment: This situation underscores the importance for any acquirer of equity to have counsel review the stock books of the target company as well as all minutes of meetings of the board and the shareholders to ensure that all corporate formalities have been satisfied.

Sources: Michael J. de la Merced, *Design Within Reach Merger Never Happened, Lawsuit Claims*, N.Y. TIMES DEALBOOK (June 7, 2016), http://www.nytimes.com/2016/06/08/business/deal-book/design-within-reach-merger-never-happened-lawsuit-claims.html?emc=edit_dlbkam_20160608&nl=dealbook&nlid=68481898&ref=dealbook; Herman Miller, Inc., Current Report (Form 8-K) (July 28, 2014), art. 2.3, http://investor.shareholder.com/mlhr/secfiling.cfm?filin-gID=66382-14-40; Almond v. Glenhill Advisors LLC, C.A. No. 10477-CB (Del. Ch. Nov. 20, 2015), http://a.fastcompany.net/asset_files/-/2016/06/08/DWR_HM_FastCo.pdf.

Third-Party Consents Usually Not Required Upon the completion of a stock purchase transaction, the target company continues to exist and the only immediate change is in the ownership of its capital stock. As a result, there is no actual transfer of the target company's contracts or permits to the acquirer. Accordingly, under the laws of most states, the parties will not be required to obtain third-party consents for a sale of stock unless there are specific contractual provisions requiring consent to a change of control of the target company.

Tax Treatment A sale of stock will result in only a single level of taxation—at the shareholder level—rather than the double taxation (at both the target company and the shareholder levels) commonly resulting from the purchase of the assets of a C corporation. A stock purchase may also be preferable to an acquirer from a tax perspective because the acquirer may be able to take advantage of any net operating loss carryforwards that the target company has generated over time. However, because the use of the target company's net operating loss carryforwards are subject to limitation under the tax law, this factor is potentially insignificant.

Mergers

In a *merger*, two corporations combine into one surviving corporation. The surviving company will, by operation of the applicable state merger statute, assume all of the rights, assets, and liabilities of the disappearing company. The completion of a merger requires the approval of the board of directors of each of the combining companies. Under certain circumstances, as described above, approval of the shareholders of the combining companies may also be required.

Types of Mergers A merger will generally take one of three forms. In a *direct* or *forward merger*, the target company merges directly into the acquirer and does not survive the merger as a separate entity. This is depicted in Figure 16.4.

The other two forms, a forward triangular merger and a reverse triangular merger, use a wholly owned subsidiary of the acquirer to effect the merger. In a *forward triangular merger*, the

Figure 16.4   Direct Merger

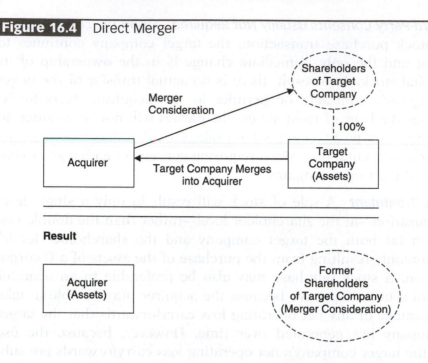

target company merges directly into a subsidiary of the acquirer and does not survive the merger. The subsidiary ends up with all of the assets and liabilities of the target company. This is depicted in Figure 16.5.

In a *reverse triangular merger,* a subsidiary of the acquirer merges with and into the target company, and the target company survives the merger as a wholly owned subsidiary of the acquirer. This is depicted in Figure 16.6. A reverse triangular merger is a commonly chosen structure. A sample term sheet for the acquisition of a privately held corporation by a public company utilizing a reverse triangular merger can be found in "Getting It in Writing" at the end of this chapter.

Advantages and Disadvantages of Mergers   As with purchases of assets and stock, there are various advantages and disadvantages of mergers.

No Need for Unanimous Target Company Shareholder Approval   The principal advantage of a merger transaction over a stock purchase is that typically there is no need to obtain the unanimous

Figure 16.5   Forward Triangular Merger

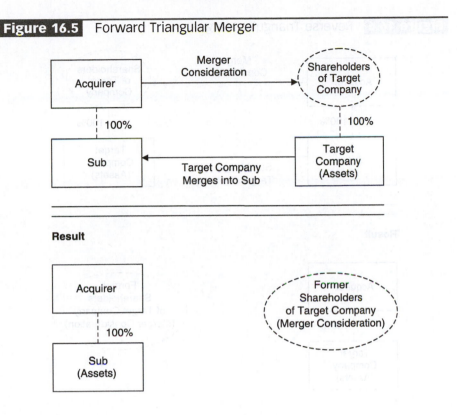

Result

approval of the target company's shareholders. Unless the target company's certificate of incorporation provides otherwise, completion of a merger requires approval by target company shareholders holding at least a majority of the outstanding capital stock. If the target company has more than one class of stock or more than one series of preferred stock, then each class or series, voting separately, may have to approve the merger. This significantly reduces the ability of recalcitrant minority shareholders to block or delay the completion of the proposed transaction.

Flexibility   The variety of available merger structures provides the parties with significant flexibility to structure a transaction that (1) shields the acquirer from direct exposure to the target company's liabilities, (2) optimizes the tax treatment for both the acquirer and the target company's shareholders, and

Figure 16.6   Reverse Triangular Merger

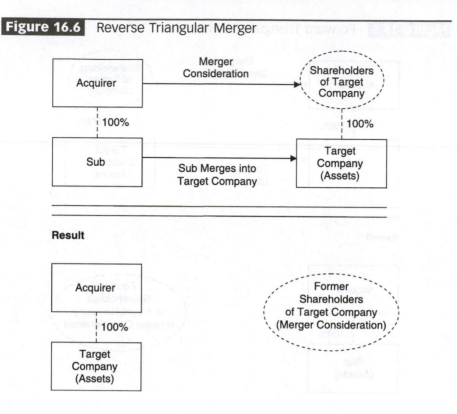

---

(3) reduces the possibility of third-party interference in the transaction.

Insulation from Direct Exposure to Target Company's Liabilities   A triangular merger involving a subsidiary of the acquirer insulates the acquirer's assets (other than the value of its stock in the subsidiary) against liabilities of the target company.

Need for Shareholder Approval from Acquirer's Shareholders   In addition, unless the transaction requires a change in the acquirer's certificate of incorporation or the acquirer is a publicly traded company and the transaction involves the issuance of a substantial amount of the acquirer's stock (generally 20% of an acquirer's outstanding shares at the time of the merger, depending on the rules of the listing or exchange on which the acquirer's stock is traded), the use of a subsidiary may obviate the need for the acquirer to obtain approval from its shareholders. In certain states, such as California, however, the acquirer's shareholders must approve the merger if the acquirer is issuing a substantial amount of stock, regardless of whether a subsidiary is used in structuring. Although the shareholders of the subsidiary must approve a triangular merger, this is a mere formality because the acquirer corporation owns all of the subsidiary's capital stock.[1]

Need for Third-Party Consents   Whether the parties will need to obtain third-party consents in a merger depends on how the transaction is structured. In a direct or forward triangular merger (in which the target company will not survive the merger and all of its assets and liabilities will be assumed by the acquirer or a subsidiary of the acquirer), the contracts and permits of the target company will be deemed to have been assigned or transferred to the acquirer. As a result, third-party consents are typically required. In contrast, in a reverse triangular merger, the target company continues to exist so there is no actual transfer of the target company's contracts or permits to the acquirer. In this structure, under the laws of many states, absent specific contractual provisions to the contrary, the parties will be required to obtain third-party consents for only those contracts or permits that require a consent to a change of control of the target company.

Shareholder Approval   The completion of a merger requires the approval of shareholders holding at least a majority of the outstanding capital stock of the target company. If the target has more than one class of stock or more than one series of preferred stock, then the merger may have to be approved by each class or series voting separately. To mitigate the risk that this vote will not be attained, the acquirer may seek to obtain voting agreements from a portion of the target company's shareholders at the time the merger agreement is signed. In mergers requiring approval by the acquirer's shareholders, the target company may seek similar voting agreements from certain of the acquirer's shareholders. The percentage of shares that can be covered by voting agreements and the type of shareholder from which voting agreements may be obtained can be limited by fiduciary duty case law in some states.[1]

16.4 PRICING ISSUES AND TYPES OF CONSIDERATION

In addition to determining how to structure the business combination, the parties must agree on the purchase price and the type of consideration to be used.

Purchase Price

Various formulations may be used to determine the purchase price. The simplest method is to set a *fixed dollar amount* that will be paid to the target company or its shareholders in cash at the closing of the transaction. Or the parties can agree on a *fixed number of shares* of the acquirer that will be distributed at closing.

Another method is to set a fixed dollar amount that is subject to a *postclosing adjustment*. An adjustment may be appropriate when there is a substantial period of time between the signing of the acquisition agreement and the closing of the acquisition or when the target company does not have audited financial statements. A postclosing adjustment may be based on an audit of the target company's financial statements on the closing date and may include, among other things, working-capital adjustments and earnings tests.

Alternatively, the parties may agree that a portion of the purchase price will be paid through an *earn-out* (also referred to as a *contingent payment*), in which a portion (or, rarely, all) of the purchase price is tied to events after the closing, including the ability of the acquired company to meet specified postclosing levels of earnings or to achieve certain milestones.

Earn-out arrangements can pose risks for both the target company and the acquirer. Because the acquirer will often control the management of the target company's business after the acquisition, the acquirer may be able, for example, to reduce the company's earnings by spending more during the earn-out period on research and development than the target company's management might have spent or by failing to use the same efforts to achieve the milestones that the target would have made. Even if the acquirer is not deliberately manipulating earnings or taking similar actions, the target company's shareholders might still sue the acquirer, claiming that the acquirer breached an implied covenant of good faith and fair dealing or a fiduciary duty to the target company's shareholders by not maximizing the payouts due under the earn-out. To mitigate these risks, the parties should be as explicit and detailed as possible in the acquisition agreement about the duties owed by the acquirer and the consequences of certain transactions.

Type of Consideration

An acquirer can buy assets or stock of a target company or effect a merger with the target company by paying cash, issuing stock, delivering promissory notes, or providing some combination of cash, stock, and promissory notes. (For convenience, we use "stock" in this section to include any securities issued by the acquirer.)

Cash Payment at Closing Cash will provide the target company and its shareholders with the least risk and the greatest liquidity. Except to the extent that the target company and its shareholders have agreed to indemnify the acquirer for breaches of the target company's representations and warranties (discussed below) or other matters or have entered into other ongoing contractual obligations, once the cash is delivered, there are no further obligations on the part of either party after the transaction is completed. However, a cash payment will result in an immediate taxable event for the target company or its shareholders.

Deferred Cash Payments or Promissory Notes The acquirer may also offer deferred cash payments or promissory notes for all or

 ## From the **TRENCHES**

The founders of the Pier 39 shopping and entertainment center on Fisherman's Wharf in San Francisco successfully used a complex earn-out formula to sell the company after a sharp spike in interest rates made it impossible to refinance their construction debt at an affordable rate. Because the center had just opened, it had no proven track record. The buyers offered to pay the fair market value of the 99-year lease for the property from the City and County of San Francisco, but that was far less than what the founders projected the center would be worth based on expected cash flow. To bridge the gap, the founders agreed to accept earn-out notes with a highly detailed definition of "net cash flow."

a portion of the purchase price. These methods of payment are particularly advantageous for an acquirer that wants the ability to reduce future payments by deducting any indemnification payments or other amounts that may be owed to the acquirer by the target company or its shareholders. To ensure payment, the target company will often seek to have the amount of anticipated future payments placed into an *escrow account*, as discussed below. Under certain circumstances, the target's shareholders (or, if the transaction is an asset sale, the target company) may be able to defer some of the tax on the gain attributable to deferred cash payments by using the installment-sale method of reporting gain in respect of the deferred cash. Note, however, that use of an escrow to secure the deferred payments will often preclude installment-sale reporting and require instead that the deferred amounts be taxable in the year of sale.

All Stock or Part Cash-Part Stock   The acquirer may offer the target company's shareholders all stock or a portion of the consideration in cash and a portion in stock. A combination structure helps reduce the shareholders' downside risk of accepting stock as consideration. It also provides the shareholders with some amount of immediate liquidity. Moreover, shareholders who receive stock may be entitled to receive tax-free treatment for the stock component of the consideration.

The number of shares to be used in an all-stock deal or in a part cash-part stock transaction may be calculated using a formula specifying a fixed cash amount, a fixed or floating exchange ratio for the acquirer's shares (with or without a collar), or any other combination thereof.

Fixed Exchange Ratio   The simplest pricing structure that the parties to a sale or merger can use is a fixed exchange ratio. An *exchange ratio* is the number of an acquirer's shares that will be issued in exchange for each share of the target company's equity securities. In a *fixed exchange ratio* structure, the exchange ratio is fixed at the time the acquisition agreement is executed so each party knows with certainty the exact number of shares that will be issued in the transaction. A different exchange ratio may be designated for the target company's common stock and its preferred stock.

Collar If the transaction will not close for some period of time after the acquisition agreement is signed, the parties will need to determine the effect, if any, of changes in the market value of the acquirer's stock between signing and closing. A fixed exchange ratio provides each party with certainty as to the exact number of shares that will be issued in the transaction. It does not, however, permit an adjustment if an acquirer's stock price declines (or increases) between the time that the acquisition agreement is signed and the closing.

Although not a major issue in a transaction involving the issuance of stock of a private company, a substantial decrease in the market value of the acquirer's public securities may jeopardize the willingness of the target company's shareholders to approve the business combination. Similarly, market price increases may result in the issuance by the acquirer of shares with a greater value than was anticipated at the time that the acquisition agreement was signed. To at least partially mitigate these effects, the parties may negotiate a *collar* that provides that if the stock price moves outside specified upper and lower market price limits, then the exchange ratio will be adjusted. If the price fluctuates but does not move outside the specified range, no adjustment to the exchange ratio is made.

Fixed Market Value Formula As an alternative to a fixed exchange ratio (with or without a collar), the parties may agree on a fixed market value formula, also referred to as a *floating exchange ratio formula*. With a *fixed market value formula*, the acquirer agrees to provide the target company's shareholders a fixed dollar amount of

From the **TRENCHES**

In the spring of 2000, when Bob Davis, the CEO of Internet pioneer Lycos, was negotiating the sale of Lycos to Spanish media giant Telefonica in exchange for stock in Telefonica's publicly traded Terra subsidiary, Davis insisted on a collar, which protected Lycos shareholders if Terra's stock price dropped by as much as 20%. After the Nasdaq sharply declined in the summer of 2000, this clause ended up being worth more than $1 billion in the deal price.

Source: Bob Davis, Speed Is Life: Street Smart Lessons from the Front Lines of Business 184 (2001).

its shares in exchange for each target company share, with the exact number of shares to be determined based on the market price or value of the acquirer's stock during a specified period prior to closing. If the acquirer's stock price declines in value, then the target company shareholders will receive a higher number of the acquirer's shares than may have been anticipated at the time of the signing so the dollar amount of the stock they receive is equal to the dollar amount specified in the acquisition agreement. Conversely, if the acquirer's stock price increases in value, then the target company's shareholders will receive fewer of the acquirer's shares than may have been anticipated, although the dollar value of the stock issued in the exchange will, as of the closing, be equal to the amount specified in the acquisition agreement.

To at least partially limit the potential fluctuations in the number of shares that may be required to be issued, the parties may negotiate a maximum number of shares that will be issued in the transaction, referred to as a *cap*, or a minimum number of shares that will be issued, referred to as a *floor*. If the number of shares needed to equal the specified dollar amount falls below the floor or rises above the cap, then the acquisition agreement may permit one or both parties to terminate the agreement and not close.

16.5 EFFECT OF A BUSINESS COMBINATION ON PREFERRED STOCK RIGHTS AND STOCK OPTIONS

A business combination can affect both preferred stock rights and stock options.

Effect on Preferred Stock Rights

Chapter 13 outlined the basic features of preferred stock typically issued by startups and the accompanying rights commonly provided. Although the specific characteristics of preferred stock issued by any given company will be determined by the terms set forth in the company's certificate of incorporation and bylaws, a business combination will typically trigger special rights for preferred shareholders. These may include liquidation and dividend preferences, antidilution protection, special voting rights, and

From the **TRENCHES**

After a privately held Internet company was unable to secure a new round of venture financing, it agreed to be acquired by a large publicly held corporation for $20 million in cash in a reverse triangular merger. Because the holders of the target company's preferred stock were entitled to receive a liquidation preference of $25 million upon the sale of the company, the common shareholders (comprising mainly the founders and employees holding options) were not entitled to receive any of the $20 million purchase price.

California law required approval of the transaction by the holders of a majority of both the common and the preferred shares, with each voting as a class. The acquirer was concerned that the common shareholders would vote against any transaction in which they would receive nothing for their shares. Moreover, the target company's employees, who were critical to the future success of the company's products, would probably be less motivated going forward if they received no equity compensation for their past and future efforts.

As a result, the acquirer demanded that the preferred shareholders reduce their liquidation preference so that $5 million of the purchase price could be allocated to the common shareholders. The acquirer also demanded that another $2 million be set aside in an employee retention pool, which would be payable over time to the employees if and when the target company met certain product development milestones. Faced with the prospect of not being able to secure the vote of the common shareholders and thus losing their last opportunity for a liquidity event, the preferred shareholders agreed to the acquirer's demands.

redemption provisions. For example, a liquidation preference may provide that, upon liquidation of the company (which may include a business combination), the preferred shareholders will receive the amount of their original investment and, possibly, a preferential return on their investment, including any accrued and declared but unpaid dividends, before the common shareholders receive anything from the transaction. In addition, the holders of participating preferred stock may, after converting their shares into common stock, share the purchase proceeds with the common shareholders and enjoy any other rights given to common shareholders in connection with the transaction.

Treatment of Stock Options

Another factor to consider when planning a business combination is the treatment of stock options. Under many stock option plans, a business combination in which the target company's shareholders receive cash consideration will trigger acceleration of the vesting of the employee stock options. This acceleration may give the option holders the opportunity to exercise their options in full prior to the business combination and receive fully vested shares of stock. In a cash transaction, the target company's option holders will generally choose to exercise their stock options to the extent that their options are *in the money* (i.e., to the extent that the consideration to be paid in the business combination exceeds the exercise price of the option). For example, if an employee has an option to purchase shares at $0.53 per share and the consideration to be paid in the transaction is $1.64 per share, those options are in the money, so the employee will probably choose to exercise. Colloquially, the opposite of "in the money" is *underwater*. Thus, if an employee has an option to purchase shares at $2.10 per share and the consideration to be paid in the transaction is $1.64 per share, that employee's options are underwater, making it unlikely that the employee will choose to exercise them.

The target company's stock option plan may provide that any party who acquires the target company in a stock-for-stock transaction must assume the target company's stock option plans on the same terms and conditions as are in effect immediately prior to the business combination. In that case, the options may be exercised after the business combination only for shares of the acquirer's common stock, based on the merger exchange ratio. Under some option plans, the target company's board of directors has the discretion to determine whether (1) the outstanding options will become vested when the business combination closes or (2) the acquirer will be given the alternative of assuming the stock option plan upon the closing of the transaction. As the treatment of stock options can change the number of shares of a target company's stock that are exchangeable in the transaction or the allocation of consideration between a target company's equity holders, or both, the acquirer and the target company should carefully review the target company's stock option plans to determine how the transaction will affect the companies and their shareholders and option holders.

Tax Considerations   Section 409A of the Internal Revenue Code of 1986 (the *Code*) and voluminous Treasury regulations promulgated under that section govern the tax treatment of stock options in business combinations. Section 409A can affect or even prevent certain methods of handling options in business combinations so it is important for the parties and their tax advisers to carefully consider the impact of Section 409A when structuring acquisitions.

16.6 TAX TREATMENT OF BUSINESS COMBINATIONS

Tax considerations (in addition to Section 409A of the Code) often dictate the form of acquisition in a business combination. An acquisition can be structured as a taxable purchase and sale of assets, a taxable purchase and sale of stock, a taxable merger, or a tax-free reorganization.

Although tax consequences are critical in determining the best way to structure an acquisition (including, most importantly, whether the transaction will be tax-free to the shareholders of the target company with respect to the stock portion of the consideration), other factors come into play as well and must be factored into each party's analysis. We discussed a number of them earlier in this chapter. For example, the acquirer may be unwilling to issue its stock in the transaction because of the dilutive effect on its earnings per share. Even if the acquirer would prefer to pay for the acquisition with stock, the target company may be unwilling to accept the market risk of receiving the acquirer's stock and instead insist on cash. Although the risks of negative fluctuations in the acquirer's stock can be mitigated through the use of collars and floating exchange ratios, the target company may still insist on a cash transaction. If, however, the acquirer is unable to borrow money or otherwise finance the transaction, its stock may be its only currency. Consequently, the parties must take into account both the tax implications of various structures and the nontax issues when negotiating the structure of the acquisition transaction.

Except as noted, the discussion below assumes that the target company is a C corporation. The discussion generally addresses the tax treatment only of the corporate parties to the business combination and the target company's shareholders, not holders of stock options.

Taxable Transactions

Taxable acquisitions can be structured as a taxable purchase and sale of assets, a taxable forward merger, a taxable purchase and sale of stock, or a taxable reverse triangular merger.

Taxable Purchase and Sale of Assets   In a *taxable purchase and sale of assets*, the target company must recognize gain on the difference between (x) the consideration (such as cash or stock) paid or provided by the acquirer for the assets, including the amount of any assumed liabilities, and (y) the tax *basis* of the assets sold (which is generally equal to the historic cost of the assets less depreciation). Thus, if a target company sells assets with a tax basis of $6 million for $8 million in cash, plus the acquirer's assumption of $2 million of the target company's liabilities, then the target company will be required to recognize a gain on the $4 million excess of purchase price over tax basis ($8 million plus $2 million minus $6 million). If the target company has available net operating losses to offset that gain, then it may incur no actual tax. If not, the resulting tax may significantly reduce the after-tax proceeds available for distribution to shareholders.

In an asset acquisition, the acquirer is often able to *step up* (increase) the tax basis of the assets acquired to an amount equal to the cash and other consideration paid and the liabilities assumed. This permits the acquirer to depreciate the acquired assets going forward based on the higher, stepped-up basis, thereby increasing the amount of depreciation deductions available and potentially decreasing the acquirer's tax liability. For example, if an acquirer pays $10 million for a target company whose assets had been depreciated to $6 million for tax purposes, the acquirer is eligible to take depreciation deductions based on the $10 million stepped-up tax basis rather than based on the preexisting $6 million tax basis that the assets had in the hands of the target company. The target company's net operating losses and other tax attributes are not transferred to the acquirer in a taxable asset purchase, however.

If the target company liquidates after a taxable asset sale, the target company's shareholders will face an additional level of tax, calculated based on the difference between each shareholder's tax basis for his or her shares (typically, the cost of those shares) and the amount of cash or other property distributed to the shareholder when the target company is liquidated. Gain or loss realized by the target company's shareholders in connection with a liquidating distribution will typically be a capital gain or loss.

Taxable Forward Merger A *taxable forward merger* of the target company into the acquirer is taxed the same as an asset sale followed by liquidation of the target company. Tax is imposed at both the corporate level and the shareholder level.

Taxable Purchase and Sale of Stock In a *taxable purchase and sale of stock*, the target company does not pay any tax, but its shareholders generally pay capital gains tax on the difference between the consideration paid by the acquirer for their stock and their basis for that stock. The tax attributes of the target company (such as net operating losses and tax credit carryovers) are generally preserved (in a limited sense), but the target company's basis in its assets remains the same as it was prior to the stock purchase. In other words, the acquirer does not receive a step-up (or step-down) in asset tax basis. Using the facts from the example in the section above entitled "Taxable Purchase and Sale of Assets," in a taxable purchase of stock the acquirer would be eligible to depreciate only $6 million of asset tax basis. In certain circumstances, the acquirer can make a *Section 338 election*, a *Section 336 election*, or a *Section 338(h)(10) election*, which permits the acquirer in a taxable stock purchase to achieve a step-up in asset tax basis.

Taxable Reverse Triangular Merger A *taxable reverse triangular merger* is taxed the same as a taxable stock purchase.

Choosing among Taxable Alternatives The interplay of the factors discussed above will determine the acquirer's choice of structure from a tax perspective. From the target company and its shareholders' viewpoint, whether a taxable asset sale or a taxable stock sale is preferable for tax purposes will turn on which alternative will produce the larger after-tax return. As noted above, gains on asset sales are generally taxed twice, first to the target company and subsequently to the target company's shareholders when the sale proceeds are distributed. This double level of taxation (in contrast to a sale of stock, which involves no entity-level tax) causes most taxable sales to be structured as stock sales, absent other factors.

Exceptions to this general rule include (1) sales by S corporations and limited liability companies (which generally pay no entity-level tax and so generally incur only a single level of taxation); (2) sales by corporations with operating losses, which can shelter the asset sale gain and so avoid or minimize corporate-level tax; and (3) transactions in which nontax considerations are particularly important, as described above. Each party must examine the facts and circumstances of the situation and its objectives to determine the optimal structure of a particular transaction from a tax perspective, recognizing that they must also factor in nontax factors.

Tax-Free Reorganizations

In addition to taxable purchases and sales of assets or stock and taxable mergers, an acquisition transaction can be structured as a tax-free reorganization. (The term is a bit of a misnomer; tax is not forgiven but merely postponed until a later taxable disposition of the acquiring company's stock.) In a *tax-free reorganization*, assuming the applicable tax law requirements for such treatment are met, stock of the acquiring company is exchanged for the stock or assets of the target company. Generally, the selling shareholders will not recognize gain or loss with respect to receipt of the acquiring company's stock until they sell that stock later in a taxable transaction. In certain types of tax-free reorganizations, the sellers may receive consideration in addition to stock; in that case, taxes are due immediately on the nonstock portion of the total consideration received. This taxable portion is called *boot*. The types of tax-free reorganizations include (1) a statutory merger, (2) a stock-for-stock exchange, (3) an exchange of stock for assets, (4) a forward triangular merger, and (5) a reverse triangular merger.

Statutory Merger (A Reorganization)   In a *statutory merger*, the target company disappears and, in order for tax-free treatment to apply, at least 40% of the consideration paid by the acquirer to the target company's shareholders must consist of the acquirer's

Figure 16.7 A Reorganization: Statutory Merger

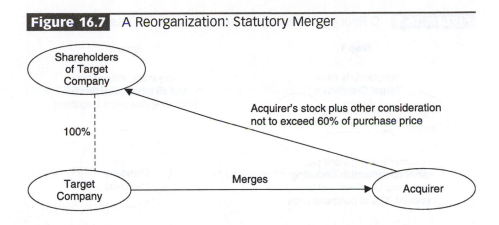

stock (called an *A reorganization* because it is described in Section 368(a)(1)(A) of the Code). This is depicted in Figure 16.7.

Stock-for-Stock Exchange (B Reorganization) In a *stock-for-stock exchange*, the acquirer exchanges solely its voting stock for target company stock, and the acquirer owns at least 80% of the stock of the target company following the acquisition (a *B reorganization*, described in Section 368(a)(1)(B) of the Code). This is depicted in Figure 16.8.

Exchange of Stock for Assets (C Reorganization) In an *exchange of stock for assets*, the acquirer exchanges its stock for all or substantially all of the assets of the target company; the target company is then liquidated, and the acquirer's stock is distributed to the target company's shareholders. To be tax-free, at least 80% of the consideration (including assumption of liabilities) paid by the acquirer must consist of its own voting stock (a *C reorganization*, described in Section 368(a)(1)(C) of the Code). This is depicted in Figure 16.9.

Figure 16.8 B Reorganization: Stock-for-Stock Exchange

Figure 16.9   C Reorganization: Exchange of Stock for Assets

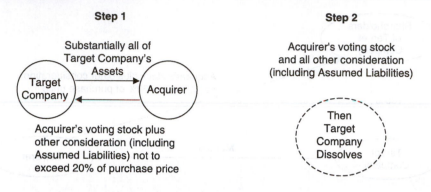

Step 1

Substantially all of
Target Company's
Assets

Target Company → Acquirer

Acquirer's voting stock plus
other consideration (including
Assumed Liabilities) not to
exceed 20% of purchase price

Step 2

Acquirer's voting stock
and all other consideration
(including Assumed Liabilities)

Then
Target
Company
Dissolves

Forward Triangular Merger   In a *forward triangular merger*, the target company is merged into a subsidiary of the acquirer. To be tax-free, at least 40% of the total consideration paid by the acquirer to the target company's shareholders must consist of the acquirer's stock (as described in Section 368(a)(2)(D) of the Code). Forward triangular mergers that qualify as reorganizations under Code Section 368(a)(2)(D) involve mergers into *corporate* subsidiaries of the acquirer. A forward triangular merger into a *limited liability company* (*LLC*) subsidiary of the acquirer is normally treated by the income tax law as a direct merger of the target company into the acquirer and is tested for reorganization qualification under the A reorganization rules described above. A forward triangular merger is depicted in Figure 16.10.

Reverse Triangular Merger   In a *reverse triangular merger*, a subsidiary of the acquirer is merged into the target company. To be tax-free, at least 80% of the consideration paid by the acquirer to the target company's shareholders must consist of the acquirer's voting stock, and the acquirer must obtain 80% control of the target in the transaction (as described in Section 368(a)(2)(E) of the Code). This is depicted in Figure 16.11.

Additional Requirements for Tax-Free Reorganizations   Although certain other requirements must also be met to achieve tax-free treatment of the stock consideration given to the target company's shareholders, the requirements set forth above are the primary ones.

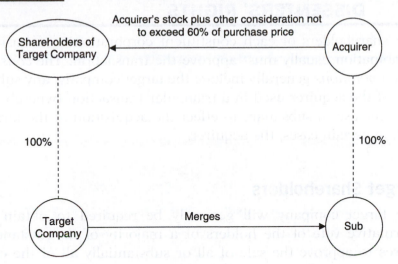

Figure 16.10 Forward Triangular Merger

Acquirer's stock plus other consideration not
to exceed 60% of purchase price

Shareholders of
Target Company

Acquirer

100%

100%

Target
Company

Merges

Sub

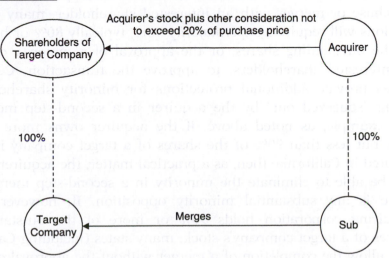

Figure 16.11 Reverse Triangular Merger

Acquirer's stock plus other consideration not
to exceed 20% of purchase price

Shareholders of
Target Company

Acquirer

100%

100%

Target
Company

Merges

Sub

16.7 SHAREHOLDER APPROVAL AND DISSENTERS' RIGHTS

The shareholders of each constituent corporation in a business combination usually must approve the transaction. The *constituent corporations* generally include the target company, any subsidiary of the acquirer used in a triangular transaction (whereby the acquirer uses a subsidiary to effect the acquisition of the target), and, in certain cases, the acquirer.

Target Shareholders

The target company will generally be required to obtain the affirmative vote of the holders of a majority of its outstanding shares to approve the sale of all or substantially all of the company's assets, a merger or consolidation, or any other extraordinary transaction. However, certain states and companies' charter documents may require a higher percentage to approve a transaction. In addition, some states and the charter documents of some companies may provide that the company must obtain the affirmative vote of a majority of the holders of a certain class or series of the company's stock in order to approve the transaction.

If the proposed transaction involves a stock purchase, asset purchase or merger with an interested shareholder, many jurisdictions will require a *supermajority* vote, typically 80% or higher of the outstanding shares, or the approval of a majority of the disinterested shareholders, to approve the transaction. Certain states provide additional protections for minority shareholders being "squeezed out" by the acquirer in a second-step merger. For example, as noted above, if the acquirer owns more than 50% but less than 90% of the shares of a target company incorporated in California, then, as a practical matter, the acquirer may not be able to eliminate the minority in a second-step merger if there is any substantial minority opposition. If, however, the acquiring corporation holds 90% or more of the outstanding shares of a target company's stock, many states (including California) allow the completion of a merger without the approval of the target company's shareholders. In such a transaction, called a *short-form merger*, the acquiring corporation can generally effect the merger through a resolution of its board of directors and by filing the specified certificate with the target company's state of incorporation.

Subsidiary Shareholders

When the parties structure the business combination as a triangular transaction, whereby a subsidiary of the acquirer purchases all or substantially all the assets or stock of the target company, or merges with the target company, the shareholders of the subsidiary must approve the transaction. This is a mere formality, however, because subsidiaries used in triangular transactions are virtually always wholly owned by the acquirer.

Acquirer Shareholders

Direct mergers of an acquirer corporation and a target corporation generally require the approval of shareholders holding a majority of the outstanding capital stock of the acquirer. Certain state corporate laws and companies' charter documents may require a higher percentage to approve a transaction. In addition, state laws and the charter documents of certain companies may provide that the company must obtain the affirmative vote of a majority of the holders of a certain class or series of the company's stock in order to approve the transaction.

Although the acquirer may be deemed to be a constituent party to the transaction under state law, most transactions that use a triangular structure do not require approval by the acquirer's shareholders unless the transaction requires a change in the acquirer's certificate of incorporation. If, however, the acquirer is a publicly traded company and the transaction (whether structured as a merger or a purchase of stock or assets) involves the issuance of a substantial amount of the acquirer's stock (generally, 20% of an acquirer's outstanding shares at the time of the merger), then stock exchange rules will generally require the acquirer to obtain the approval of its shareholders. Certain states, including California, also require the approval of the acquirer's shareholders if the business combination transaction involves the issuance of a substantial amount of the acquirer's stock, even if the acquirer is not a publicly traded company.

Dissenters' (Appraisal) Rights

To protect the right of the shareholders of the target company to receive the fair value of their stock in a business combination, most states provide some form of *dissenters'* or *appraisal rights*, which give opposing shareholders who meet the requirements for the exercise of such rights the right to receive cash equal to the fair market value of their target stock. Shareholders who exercise dissenters' rights may therefore be entitled to receive cash even when the transaction is structured as a sale of assets (or merger) in exchange for stock of the acquirer. Under certain circumstances, shareholders of the acquirer may also have dissenters' rights.

Dissenters' rights are generally only available to the holders of a class or series of securities entitled to vote on the business combination at issue. To exercise this right, shareholders must vote against the proposed transaction and give notice to the company that they have so voted and that they are demanding an appraisal of the fair value of their securities. Because fair market value is generally calculated without taking into account the effect of the merger or another transaction giving rise to the rights, the cash due the dissenting shareholders may be less than the acquisition consideration. If the company and the shareholders are unable to agree on a satisfactory amount, the shareholders can file a claim for appraisal in court. Courts often use discounted cash flow analysis to determine a company's going concern value and thus the fair value of its stock.

16.8   FIDUCIARY DUTIES OF THE BOARD AND CONTROLLING SHAREHOLDERS

Both directors and controlling shareholders must satisfy their fiduciary duties in connection with any business combination.

Fiduciary Duties of the Board

Generally, the board of directors of each constituent party to a business combination must approve the agreement governing the transaction. As explained in Chapter 6, under state and common law, directors have specific fiduciary duties to the corporation, including the duty of care and the duty of loyalty.

The *duty of care* requires that the board be fully informed prior to making the business decision to enter into the transaction. Therefore, prior to executing the agreement for the business combination, the respective boards will meet and discuss the terms of the proposed transaction. In addition, the companies' legal advisers will often explain the material legal terms of the transaction. The meeting may include a presentation from the target company's investment advisers regarding the fairness of the transaction and the delivery of a *fairness opinion* stating that the transaction is fair to the target company's shareholders from a financial point of view. The fact that the proposed acquisition of a public company is at a substantial premium over the trading price of the target's stock is not, taken alone, sufficient to justify accepting the offer, because the "intrinsic value" of its stock may be higher.[2]

The duty of loyalty requires that the directors from the respective boards refrain from any conduct that could injure their company or its shareholders or deprive the target company or its shareholders of any profit or advantage to which they are entitled. In other words, the directors must act in good faith and avoid transactions in which they have any personal or financial interest that is adverse to the interests of the company. If a director does have such an interest, certain procedures should be followed to ensure that the board, as a whole, is able to fulfill its obligations to the shareholders. The director may be required to abstain from voting on the transaction, to disclose his or her interests to the shareholders, or, in extreme circumstances, to delegate the evaluation and approval of the transaction to a special committee of directors who do not have such a personal or financial interest. As part of their duty of loyalty, directors of a Delaware corporation have a duty of candor, which means that they must disclose to the board of directors any material information they have that affects a board decision, particularly when the director has a personal stake in the outcome of that decision.

Although the board of directors must fulfill its fiduciary duties and carefully review the terms and conditions of the merger or purchase agreement, most, if not all, states provide that the board has satisfied its duties to the shareholders if the board acted on an informed basis, in good faith, and with the honest belief that the actions it was taking were in the best interests of the company. This presumption is called the *business judgment rule*. The business judgment rule may not apply if one or more of the directors have a financial or personal interest in the transaction.[3]

Courts will review the actions of directors opposing a takeover with *enhanced scrutiny* to ensure that any defensive tactics employed are proportional to the threat posed by the hostile bidder and reasonable in response to that threat.[4] In circumstances when a *sale of control* or *break-up* of a company is inevitable, the directors' role shifts from being "defenders of the corporate bastion" to "auctioneers" with an obligation to obtain the highest price reasonably available to the company's shareholders.[5] This duty is often referred to as the *Revlon duty* after the case of the same name, which first articulated this duty.[6] Revlon duties do not apply in most stock-for-stock transactions, unless the stock of the acquiring company is controlled by a single individual or a small group acting in concert.[7]

It is not always clear whether a board is subject to *Revlon* duties with respect to a particular transaction, and it is important to consult with counsel to ensure that the board is acting appropriately with respect to any business combination transaction. Prior consultation is critical when a target company is opposing unwelcome takeover advances or considering deal protection devices, such as lockups and breakup fees, which are discussed in Section 16.13 below.

Fiduciary Duties of Controlling Shareholders

Sometimes founders erroneously assume that as long as they have voting control of a company and have handpicked its directors, then they can dictate the company's affairs. In fact, controlling shareholders owe fiduciary duties to the controlled entity and cannot secretly seize for themselves opportunities belonging to that entity.[8]

From the **TRENCHES**

Conrad M. Black, the ultimate controlling shareholder of Hollinger International (publisher of *The Chicago Sun-Times*, *The Daily Telegraph* and *The Jerusalem Post*), violated his duty of candor when he concealed from Hollinger's board of directors Barclays' "intense interest" in acquiring the *Telegraph* and instead secretly negotiated a deal whereby Barclays agreed to buy from Black the holding company that held Black's Hollinger shares. Because the *Telegraph* constituted far less than half of Hollinger's assets, the Hollinger board had the power to sell that asset without seeking the shareholders' consent. Black violated his duty of loyalty when he failed to inform the Hollinger directors of the opportunity to sell the *Telegraph* and instead secretly rejected Barclays' offer and diverted that opportunity to himself.

Source: Hollinger Int'l, Inc. v. Black, 844 A.2d 1022 (Del. Ch. 2004), *aff'd*, 872 A.2d 559 (Del. 2005).

16.9 SECURITIES LAW REQUIREMENTS

If the consideration to be issued by the acquirer in a business combination includes stock or other securities, then the issuance of the securities must be in compliance with federal and state securities laws. As explained in Chapter 7, unless an exemption from registration or qualification is available, the issuer may have to register the securities with the Securities and Exchange Commission (*SEC*) under the Securities Act of 1933 (the *1933 Act*) and qualify them with the state securities commissions under any applicable blue sky laws. In addition, the shareholders of the target company may have restrictions on their ability to resell securities they receive in the business combination.

When a business combination entailing the issuance of stock requires a shareholder vote (such as a stock-for-stock merger or the sale of all, or substantially all the assets, of the target's assets for stock), the decision by the target company's shareholders to approve the transaction is considered tantamount to the investment decision that investors make when deciding to buy securities. As a result, the securities law analysis is similar in both contexts. Absent an exemption, business combinations involving the issuance of stock to public shareholders are often registered on SEC Form

S-4, which includes a combined prospectus and proxy statement. Postmerger companies and their shareholders must comply with securities laws on an ongoing basis. Chapter 17 discusses securities law compliance both in the context of initial public offerings and thereafter.

The target company and acquirer (and its shareholders if they are selling stock) are also subject to federal and state laws concerning fraud and misrepresentation in connection with the offer and sale of securities. The antifraud rules apply even if the transaction is exempt from registration and qualification. These laws, along with the contractual provisions of the merger agreement, will offer each party limited protection from fraud by the other party.

Federal Registration Exemptions

The exemptions that are available for the issuance of securities in a business combination are generally the same as those available in any private placement financing pursuant to Sections 3(b) and 4(a)(2) of the 1933 Act and SEC Regulation D, which provides certain safe harbors under these sections. As discussed in Chapter 7, these include purely intrastate offerings under Section 3(a)(11) and private placements under Section 4(a)(2). Although an acquirer may consider proceeding directly under Section 4(a)(2) of the 1933 Act if all of the target company's shareholders are able both to understand and to bear the risk of the investment, most acquirers will seek to qualify the transaction under the Regulation D safe harbors.

Regulation D An acquirer may issue up to $5 million of its securities pursuant to the exemption set forth in Rule 504 of Regulation D, without regard to the qualifications or number of the target company's shareholders. If the transaction involves the offering of more than $5 million of securities, then the acquirer will often seek to qualify for an exemption under Rule 506.

Rule 506 under Regulation D Meeting the requirements of Rule 506 can be more onerous in a business combination than when Rule 506 is used in a financing. In a financing, the issuer selects and agrees to each investor. In contrast, when attempting a business combination, the acquirer must work with a fixed group of the target company's shareholders, who may or may not meet the qualifications of Rule 506.

Under Rule 506, an acquirer issuing securities may offer an unlimited dollar amount of securities to any number of *accredited investors* and to no more than 35 unaccredited investors who, either alone or with a purchaser representative, are deemed to be sophisticated. A *sophisticated* investor is one who has enough knowledge and experience in financial and business matters to be capable of evaluating the merits and risks of the prospective investment. The acquirer will generally require the target company's shareholders to complete an investor questionnaire to determine which of the shareholders are accredited and whether those who are not accredited are nonetheless sophisticated. If one or more shareholders oppose the transaction and are unwilling to complete the investor questionnaire, and the acquirer is not otherwise able to reasonably verify the shareholder's accreditation or sophistication, then Rule 506 may not be available as an exemption for the transaction.

If a shareholder is neither accredited nor sophisticated, then Rule 506 requires that a purchaser representative be appointed for that shareholder. A purchaser representative must meet specific requirements set forth in Regulation D, and the shareholder must acknowledge that person as his or her representative. By agreeing to this representation, the shareholder becomes, in effect, sophisticated (albeit, not accredited).

Regulation D Information Requirements Acquirers offering securities pursuant to Rule 504 do not have to provide any particular information to the target's shareholders (although, as noted in Chapter 7, full disclosure is often prudent to avoid antifraud liability). If, however, (1) the transaction involves the issuance of more than $5 million of the acquirer's stock and (2) any of the target's shareholders is not an accredited investor, then Regulation D requires the acquirer to furnish the target company's shareholders with information regarding the securities and the business combination within a reasonable period of time prior to the closing of the transaction.

From the **TRENCHES**

A privately held software company negotiated its sale to a successful public company for $50 million of the acquirer's common stock. One of the conditions for consummation of the transaction was that the acquirer have available an exemption from registration of the shares under Rule 506. The target company's option plan included an early exercise program, which enabled employees to exercise their options prior to the vesting of the options. Many employees had done so, resulting in the target company's having approximately 100 shareholders.

The parties confirmed that approximately 70 of the target company's shareholders could be considered accredited investors for purposes of Rule 506. Of the remaining 30 shareholders, 22 could be considered sophisticated because of their educational background and investment experience. The remaining eight shareholders were not considered sophisticated for purposes of Rule 506 because they possessed neither the requisite educational background nor the investment experience.

The acquirer required these remaining eight shareholders to appoint the president of the target company as their purchaser representative. Seven of the eight shareholders were willing to do so; the remaining shareholder, who had been fired by the target company six months previously, refused to do so, thereby jeopardizing the whole transaction. Fortunately, one of the other officers of the company was able to persuade the former employee that, whatever grievances he might have against management, his refusal to appoint a representative was only hurting his friends who remained employed by the company. This disgruntled former employee also remained free to vote against the transaction if he believed it was not a good deal. He appointed as his purchaser representative one of the other shareholders, who was an accredited investor, and the transaction was consummated.

In particular, Rule 502 of Regulation D requires the acquirer to provide the target company's shareholders with information that is substantially similar to the information the acquirer would be required to provide if it were offering registered securities. The information required by Rule 502 is, however, limited to what is "material to an understanding of the issuer [the acquirer], its business and the securities being offered." The disclosure document containing this information is often referred to as an *information statement* or a *private placement memorandum*. We discussed this document in detail in Chapter 7.

Section 3(a)(10)   If the acquirer does not want to register the offering, but the offering does not qualify under Section 4(a)(2) of the 1933 Act or any of the exemptions provided by Regulation D, an alternative to registration may be available under Section 3(a)(10) of the 1933 Act. Section 3(a)(10) provides an exemption from the federal registration requirements for securities issued in business combinations when a duly authorized government agency has held a fairness hearing and approved the terms and conditions of the transaction. A particular advantage of proceeding under Section 3(a)(10) is that stock issued in the transaction to shareholders who were not affiliates of the target company is freely tradable and not subject to restrictions on resale.

The Section 3(a)(10) exemption is potentially quite useful, but, unfortunately, only a limited number of states (including California) provide a mechanism for fairness hearings. The states that do conduct fairness hearings generally require a nexus between the state and the parties to the business combination, such as having the target company incorporated in California.

Compliance with State Securities Laws

In addition to complying with federal securities laws, the acquirer must also comply with any applicable state securities laws. In general, the acquirer must comply with the blue sky laws of (1) the state where the acquirer has its principal place of business (and, if different, the state from which the offers will emanate), (2) the state where the target company has its principal place of business, and (3) the states where any of the target company's shareholders reside or have their principal place of business.

Protection from Fraud and Misrepresentation

The best way for a party to ensure that it is protected from fraud and misrepresentation in a business combination is to conduct a thorough due diligence investigation and to ensure that protective provisions are included in the acquisition agreement. The agreement will generally provide specific representations and warranties regarding the parties, and it may provide indemnification or other protection if the representations and warranties or covenants of a target company turn out to be false or misleading.

If, however, a party to the transaction believes that it has been misled by the other side, it may seek to go beyond the negotiated contractual protections in the acquisition agreement and bring an action for common law fraud or, if the transaction involves securities, a claim under Rule 10b-5 of the Securities Exchange Act of 1934. In either case, the plaintiff faces an onerous task since the standard of proof to show fraud or misrepresentation is high. Parties to a privately negotiated sale of securities may find broader rights of recovery under the antifraud provisions of applicable state securities laws.

From the **TRENCHES**

O. Randall Rissman owned two-thirds of the stock of Tiger Electronics, a toy and game company founded by his father. His brother Arnold owned the balance. After the brothers had a falling out, Arnold sold his shares to Randall for $17 million. Thirteen months later, Tiger sold its assets to toymaker Hasbro for $335 million. Arnold sued Randall, claiming that Randall had deceived him into thinking that Tiger would never be sold to a third party or taken public. Believing that his stock would remain illiquid and not pay further dividends, Arnold had sold his shares for whatever Randall was willing to pay. In his suit for securities fraud under federal law (with state law claims under supplemental jurisdiction), Arnold sought the extra $95 million he would have received had he retained his stock until the sale to Hasbro.

During the negotiation of the sale of his shares to Randall, Arnold asked Randall to represent in writing that Tiger would never be sold. Randall refused; instead, he warranted (accurately) that he was not aware of any offers to purchase Tiger and was not engaged in negotiations for its sale. Arnold and Randall also agreed that if Tiger were sold before Arnold had received all installments of the purchase price, then payment of the principal and interest would be accelerated. Arnold represented in the stock sale agreement that "this Agreement is executed by [Arnold] freely and voluntarily, and without reliance upon any statement or representation by Purchaser, the Company, any of the Affiliates or O.R. Rissman or any of their attorneys or agents...."

The court dismissed Arnold's securities law claims, reasoning that "[s]ecurities law does not permit a party to a stock transaction to disavow such representations-to say, in effect, 'I lied when I told you I wasn't relying on your prior statements' and then to seek damages for their contents." The court pointed out that Arnold could have avoided this result if he had negotiated an arrangement whereby he would accept less than what Randall was willing to pay unconditionally (say, $10 million) but receive an additional payment (or kicker) if Tiger were sold or taken public.

Source: Rissman v. Rissman, 213 F.3d 381 (7th Cir. 2000).

Restrictions on Resale Imposed by the 1933 Act

In a business combination in which the target company's shareholders receive stock issued pursuant to an exemption under the 1933 Act, other than under Section 3(a)(10), the stock is deemed to be *restricted* under the 1933 Act, that is, subject to restrictions on resale for a period of time. In addition, when affiliates of the target company receive stock in a business combination, that stock will also be deemed to be restricted. This is the case even when the stock has been registered under a registration statement filed with the SEC. Restricted securities may not be offered or sold by a target company's shareholders (until they cease to be restricted) unless they are subsequently registered under the 1933 Act or exempted from registration.

Exemptions under Rules 144 and 145 The most commonly relied upon exemption for the resale of restricted stock by the target company's shareholders is Rule 144 adopted by the SEC under the 1933 Act. As explained in Section 13.5 of Chapter 13, Rule 144 provides a safe harbor that often allows restricted securities issued by a publicly held company that provides current public information to be resold in the open market six months after the restricted stock is acquired, subject to certain volume and manner of sale requirements applicable to affiliates of the issuer. Shares issued by a private company that have been held by a seller for at least one year can be resold under Rule 144, subject to certain volume and manner of sale requirements applicable to affiliates of the issuer. Registered securities and securities offered pursuant to Section 3(a)(10) that are issued to a target company's stockholder who is or becomes an affiliate of the acquirer in a business combination are, pursuant to Rule 145 of the 1933 Act, deemed to be restricted and are subject to the resale limitations of Rule 144.

Registration Rights If the target company's shareholders receive unregistered or restricted securities, the acquisition agreement may require the acquirer to register the shareholders' resale of the stock at some later date, typically on a short-form Form S-3 registration statement. We discussed registration rights in detail in Chapter 13.

Contractual Restrictions on Resale

In addition to restrictions on resale resulting from federal and state securities laws, the resale of acquirer stock may be restricted by contractual obligations agreed to by all or some of the target company's shareholders. Such restrictions will generally be in the form of a *lockup* agreement, which prohibits the shareholders from transferring or selling the securities for a certain period of time after the closing of the transaction or prior to a public offering or another specified event.

16.10   ACCOUNTING TREATMENT

Under U.S. generally accepted accounting principles, companies must account for all business combinations under the acquisition method of accounting. Under the *acquisition method*, (1) all of the assets and liabilities acquired from the target company must be recorded on the acquirer's balance sheet at their fair value; (2) any excess of the purchase price over the fair value of the net assets acquired must be recognized as goodwill; and (3) all intangible assets with finite lives must be amortized over their estimated useful lives. Goodwill is not amortized and will generally remain on the acquirer's books unless it becomes *impaired*, that is, the acquirer determines that the fair value of the goodwill is less than its carrying amount. Goodwill must be tested for *impairment* annually and upon the occurrence of certain significant events. Once the value of the goodwill has become impaired, the carrying amount of the goodwill on the acquirer's balance sheet must be reduced to its current fair value. Reductions in goodwill are recorded as charges against income; as a result, they will reduce earnings.

16.11   ANTITRUST COMPLIANCE

Mergers and acquisitions are subject to potential review by U.S. and non-U.S. antitrust authorities.

U.S. Requirements

The U.S. Department of Justice (*DOJ*) and the Federal Trade Commission (*FTC*) act as enforcement agents for the federal antitrust laws. As part of this mandate, they are responsible for determining whether potential transactions (such as mergers, stock or asset acquisitions, investments, joint ventures, or grants of exclusive licenses) are likely to lessen competition in any given market.

Hart–Scott–Rodino Antitrust Improvements Act of 1976   Although the U.S. antitrust authorities evaluate all transactions they believe may raise competitive concerns, certain transactions, including many business combinations above a certain size, require the companies involved to comply with the federal notification and preclosing waiting period requirements set forth in the Hart–Scott–Rodino Antitrust Improvements Act of 1976, as amended (the *HSR Act*). The resulting waiting period, or periods in the case of transactions receiving greater scrutiny, provides these antitrust regulators with an important preclosing window to investigate (and challenge) transactions they believe may be anticompetitive.

 From the **TRENCHES**

In September 2014, General Electric (*GE*) and Electrolux announced Electrolux would acquire GE's appliance business in a $3.3 billion cash merger. Following the parties' submission of their HSR filings, and the resulting investigation, the Antitrust Division of the Department of Justice sued to block the deal, concerned that it would reduce competition, especially for consumers seeking to purchase lower-cost appliances and for contractors that install cooking appliances in the homes they sell. Four weeks into the trial, GE exercised its contractual right to walk away from the deal. Had the merger gone through, the merged company and Whirlpool would have controlled almost 80% of the range, stove and cooktop market, which the DOJ believed would have eliminated the direct competition between Electrolux and GE that has led to lower prices and higher quality for consumers.

Sources: Dep't of Justice, *GE and Electrolux Walk Away from Anticompetitive Cooking Appliance Merger Before Four-Week Trial Ends*, https://www.justice.gov/atr/division-operations/division-update-2016/ge-electrolux-walk-away-anticompetitive-appliance-merger (updated Apr. 5, 2016); Antoine Gara, *General Electric Receives $175 Million Fee for Terminating Appliance Unit Sale to Electrolux*, Forbes (Dec. 7, 2015), http://www.forbes.com/sites/antoinegara/2015/12/07/general-electric-receives-175-million-fee-for-terminating-appliance-unit-sale-to-electrolux/#494d86944361.

Jurisdictional Thresholds Transactions that do not exceed the $50 million (as adjusted) *size-of-transaction threshold* are not subject to the HSR Act notification and waiting period requirements. If the transaction exceeds the $200 million (as adjusted) size-of-transaction threshold, then HSR Act jurisdiction is satisfied without needing to consider the size-of-person test (although even then various technical exemptions may obviate the need to file). If the transaction is valued between the $50 million (as adjusted) and the $200 million (as adjusted) levels, then no HSR Act filing or waiting period is required unless the parties also satisfy a separate $100 million/$10 million (as adjusted) size-of-person test.

The size-of-transaction and other HSR Act jurisdictional thresholds are adjusted annually based on the prior year's percentage growth (or decrease) in the Gross National Product. The FTC typically publishes the adjusted thresholds in late January, and they take effect in late February. Beginning February 25, 2016, the $50 million (as adjusted) size-of-transaction threshold was $78.2 million; the $200 million (as adjusted) size-of transaction threshold was $312.6 million; the $100 million (as adjusted) size-of-person threshold was $156.3 million; and the $10 million (as adjusted) size-of-person threshold was $15.6 million.

When calculating the size of the transaction, the parties must follow the HSR Act's valuation rules, which focus not on the deal consideration but, when different, the total value of the voting securities and/or assets the acquirer will own as a result of the transaction. For example, a minority shareholder who is acquiring additional shares of an issuer has to value its entire posttransaction stake, and it must do so in a way that reflects the current value of its holdings by incorporating the fair market value of its existing holdings rather than using their cost basis. For these reasons, parties to transactions that initially might appear to be valued at less than $50 million (as adjusted) must ensure that they calculate the value of the transaction properly.

For private target companies, the value of a securities transaction in which the acquirer does not already hold any of the target company's voting securities will be the acquisition price, if that price has been set or can reasonably be estimated by the acquirer. Otherwise, the value of the transaction will be the fair market value of the stock, as determined within 60 calendar days prior to closing (or filing) by the acquirer's board of directors or its designee. (Note that no formal designation of authority to perform this valuation exercise is required when the acquirer's chief financial officer, or any of its financial officers with direct responsibility for the transaction, sets the value because they are automatically treated as de facto designees.)

The *size-of-person test* focuses on the annual net sales and total assets of both the specific buyer and the target and the companies or individuals standing above this buyer and target, in the chain of control (in what we'll call the "control group"). As a result, a very small target with annual net sales and total assets well below the relevant thresholds, when considered on a standalone basis, can still end up satisfying the smaller part of the size-of-person test, or even the larger $100 million (as adjusted) part of the test, if it is controlled by a large company or a very wealthy individual.

To satisfy the $100 million/$10 million (as adjusted) size-of-person test, one party (most commonly the acquirer) must, together with its control group, have either annual net sales or total assets of at least $100 million (as adjusted). In addition, the other party (typically the target) must, together with its control group, have either annual net sales or total assets of at least $10 million (as adjusted). An exception exists to this "either–or" approach when a target, together with its control group, is not engaged in manufacturing. In such cases, the threshold applied to the target is net sales of at least $100 million (as adjusted) or total assets of at least $10 million (as adjusted).

Required Filings and Fees If an HSR Act filing is required, both sides must submit filings. Filings are required even when the target company has no direct role in the reported acquisition (e.g., when a buyer is purchasing the target company's shares in the open market) or even when the target company actively opposes the transaction (as in the case of a hostile tender offer). The parties must disclose certain information and produce various documents regarding the filing parties and the proposed transaction. In addition, the acquiring party must pay a filing fee based on a three-tiered filing fee structure. Fees range from $45,000 to $280,000. Absent the parties agreeing otherwise, the acquiring party is responsible for paying the fee at the time of filing, but the parties to the transaction may agree to share or shift the obligation to pay the filing fee, either initially or by reimbursing the other party later. Effective August 1, 2016, the FTC raised the maximum civil penalty for violations of premerger filing notification requirements from $16,000 per day to $40,000 per day.

Waiting Periods   After making any required filings under the HSR Act, the parties will face a waiting period—during which time the transaction cannot close—that lasts for a specified number of days depending on the type of transaction (typically 30 calendar days for most transactions, including mergers, and 15 calendar days for cash tender offers), unless the reviewing agency (1) approves a request for early termination and cuts the waiting period short or (2) launches a formal investigation by issuing a "Second Request" demanding more information and materials about the parties, competition in the affected market(s), and the proposed transaction. The acquiring party may elect to *pull and refile*, that is, to voluntarily withdraw its HSR Act filing and submit an updated one, in order to give the regulators extra time to conclude their review. Although this triggers a second "initial" waiting period, it may obviate the need for a Second Request or at least resolve certain issues so that the Second Request can be more narrowly focused. Thus, a pull-and-refile may be appropriate if it appears that the regulators will be unable to resolve their concerns during the initial waiting period but are likely to conclude their investigation favorably if given a little more time. There is, however, always a risk that even after the additional delay of another "initial" waiting period, the regulators will still issue a Second Request if they are not comfortable allowing the transaction to close as the new waiting period is set to expire.

If the reviewing agency issues a Second Request, the waiting period does not start to run again until the parties have complied with the (typically very burdensome) request. As a practical matter, receipt of a Second Request often delays the transaction for at least three months, even if the transaction is likely to ultimately be approved. In transactions raising serious antitrust concerns, this delay can be even more substantial. For example, the FTC's investigation into the approximate $14 billion combination of Zimmer

Holdings, Inc. and Biomet, Inc., both companies in the musculo-skeletal health-care field, continued for almost a year after the parties received their Second Request. To alleviate concerns about the possible anticompetitive effects of the business combination, the FTC required the merged company to divest certain intellectual property, manufacturing technology, and product inventory.

Non-U.S. Requirements

Antitrust compliance issues can reach beyond the United States even when both parties to a business combination are U.S. companies. More than 90 jurisdictions worldwide have merger filing systems, and many of them require clearance prior to the closing of any transaction affecting competition in the jurisdiction. As a result, foreign filing analysis has become an increasingly important part of the regulatory landscape, particularly given the often detailed and jurisdiction-specific reporting associated with these non-U.S. filings. The increasing cooperation among international antitrust agencies puts a premium on a well-orchestrated approach to seeking antitrust approvals. When announcing its 2014 approval (with conditions) of Thermo Fisher's acquisition of Life Technologies, the FTC noted with approval the cooperation of regulators in Australia, Canada, China, the European Union (*EU*), Japan, and Korea with FTC staff.

Very large transactions (typically multi-billion-dollar business combinations) affecting competition in the EU may also require filing with the European Commission, a body that can impose its own requirements for approval, which are sometimes at odds with the stance taken by the U.S. antitrust regulators. For example, General Electric's 2001 proposed acquisition of Honeywell was approved by the U.S. authorities but blocked by the European Commission.

Although antitrust filings with the European Commission are relatively rare, filings with individual Member States within the EU and in the rest of the world are far more common.

16.12 THE MERGER PROCESS

In this section, we outline the steps involved in completing a merger. Although this discussion is focused on mergers, the process is generally similar for other forms of business combination.

Chapter 7 provided additional information concerning the purchase and sale of stock and related issues.

Overview of Steps

As a first step in a business combination, small teams from both the target company and the potential acquirer will generally meet for preliminary discussions of the business and financial aspects of the proposed transaction. Some companies will engage an investment bank to provide financial advice at this stage. Once the parties decide to engage in further discussions about the potential business combination, legal counsel will help prepare a confidentiality agreement regarding the confidential treatment of nonpublic information. They may also prepare an exclusivity agreement.

After the confidentiality agreement is in place, the parties will begin the due diligence review process, and management will begin strategic negotiations about the terms of the deal. The parties may prepare a letter of intent that outlines the principal terms of a transaction.

With guidance from management, legal counsel (generally, for the acquirer) will prepare a draft of the merger agreement, and the parties will negotiate the terms of the agreement. After the companies' respective boards of directors review the terms of the merger agreement and determine that the transaction is fair to the company and its shareholders, the agreement will be executed. Once the merger agreement has been executed, the companies will generally issue a joint press release announcing the terms of the transaction. The parties will also make any necessary governmental or other filings (such as any required filing under the HSR Act or the securities laws). If one or both of the parties are subject to the reporting requirements under the Securities Exchange Act of 1934, certain restrictions regarding disclosure will apply, and certain filings must be made with the SEC, depending on the type of transaction and its materiality to the parties. For example, a publicly traded constituent company may have to file a proxy statement with the SEC describing the transaction and soliciting approval from its shareholders.

The target company will set the date of its shareholders' meeting or begin soliciting written consents from the shareholders. If approval by the acquirer's shareholders is required, the acquirer

TABLE 16.12	Sample Merger Timeline			
Presigning Period	**Signing Period**	**Period between Signing and Closing**	**Closing**	**Postclosing Period**
• Parties execute confidentiality agreement and, potentially, exclusivity agreement. • Acquirer conducts presigning due diligence review. • Parties determine transaction structure. • Parties may execute letter of intent or term sheet. • Parties negotiate definitive merger agreement.	• Parties execute definitive merger agreement.	• Parties make necessary governmental filings and obtain consents and approvals. • Target company's shareholders (and potentially acquirer's shareholders) vote on transaction.	• Acquirer delivers consideration (stock, cash, or notes). • Target files agreement of merger with secretary of state.	• Parties publicly announce merger. • Parties make postclosing purchase price adjustments and assert potential indemnification claims. • Parties integrate businesses.

will set the date of its shareholders' meeting or begin soliciting written consents. After the target company shareholders (and, if necessary, the acquirer's shareholders) have approved the merger, and all necessary third-party consents and other approvals have been received, the parties will close the transaction, file a certificate of merger in the target company's state of incorporation, begin integrating the companies, and deal with any postclosing purchase price adjustments. Table 16.12 presents an example of a merger timeline.

Preliminary Documents

Confidentiality Agreements In the preliminary stages of a business combination, each party will generally require access to confidential, nonpublic information regarding the other party. To protect the confidentiality of this information and to prevent it from being misused if the merger negotiations break down, the parties will generally enter into a confidentiality agreement. Most confidentiality agreements set forth the parties' obligations regarding the use and disclosure of nonpublic information and various other related matters, including the return of confidential information if the merger is not completed. The parties should ensure that the confidentiality agreement is in place before they exchange any nonpublic information in the due diligence review or engage in discussions regarding their strategic plans and other nonpublic issues.

Exclusivity (or No-Shop) Agreements An *exclusivity agreement* (also called a *no-shop agreement*) limits the ability of a target company that is negotiating with a potential acquirer, or that has entered into a merger agreement with that acquirer, to solicit or encourage an acquisition proposal from any other company for a specified period of time. The target company typically also agrees not to provide another company interested in entering into merger negotiations nonpublic information or to participate in any potential merger-related discussions or negotiations with another potential acquirer.

The duration and specific terms of no-shop agreements will vary from deal to deal. Sometimes, a target company will enter into an exclusivity agreement while negotiating with a specific acquirer. A typical no-shop agreement entered into by a private target company before a merger agreement is signed restricts the target company for approximately one to two months. The merger agreement will usually also include a no-shop provision that replaces the presigning exclusivity agreement and precludes the target company from soliciting, providing information to, or negotiating with other bidders until the first transaction is submitted to the target company's shareholders for a vote.

Letters of Intent and Term Sheets In the early stages of negotiating a business combination, the parties will generally want to settle the key terms of the transaction. These terms may include an agreement on the price or the pricing formula, the form of acquisition, intended tax treatment, closing conditions, and employee issues. To memorialize these details, the parties may decide to enter into a *letter of intent* or prepare a *term sheet*.

A letter of intent or term sheet can help focus negotiations and make the process of finalizing terms for the merger agreement more efficient. A letter of intent or term sheet may also create a "moral" commitment that will influence a party's decision to propose a change in the terms of a transaction after a letter of intent is executed or the parties preliminarily agree on a term sheet. In addition, a letter of intent or term sheet will generally permit the parties to make any required filing under the HSR Act and to begin the HSR Act waiting period prior to the execution of the definitive merger agreement.

A letter of intent or term sheet can present a serious problem, however, if negotiations break down and one party tries to seek enforcement of the letter as a binding contract. If the document can be interpreted as binding, the terminating party may be liable to the other side even if a merger agreement is not executed. If the parties desire to enter into a letter of intent, it is important that the document specifically identify the terms that the parties intend to be binding and be explicit regarding the nonbinding nature of those that are intended to be nonbinding. The execution of a letter of intent may also complicate the disclosure obligations of a public company. A sample term sheet for the acquisition of a privately held corporation by a public company utilizing a reverse triangular merger can be found in "Getting It in Writing" at the end of this chapter.

Due Diligence

As in a venture financing (discussed in Chapter 13) or in preparation for a company's initial public offering (discussed in Chapter 17), due diligence is crucial in a business combination. Through this process, the acquirer examines the target company's business, financial condition, and legal affairs. Due diligence enables the acquirer to independently verify whether the target company's assets meet its expectations, to identify any required contractual or governmental consents, and to uncover any potential liabilities or issues that may make the merger unattractive. In addition, due diligence is often the best way to determine the true value of the target company to the acquirer.

In some acquisitions, generally those in which the acquirer's stock is offered as consideration, the target company may conduct a due diligence review of the acquirer. Usually, the target company's due diligence investigation will be less extensive than an acquirer's review.

Generally, the acquirer will provide the target company with a list of documents relating to the target company and each of its subsidiaries and predecessors that the acquirer wishes to examine. The acquirer will seek documents containing information concerning the following:

- ➤ General corporate matters, including charter documents and minutes of the board of directors and of shareholder meetings and actions by written consent
- ➤ The target company's capital stock and other securities, including any options or warrants as well as any stock splits or reverse stock splits
- ➤ Financial performance, including balance sheet and income statement
- ➤ Any indebtedness
- ➤ Taxes
- ➤ Significant contractual obligations and rights
- ➤ Employment matters
- ➤ Past, pending, or threatened litigation
- ➤ Intellectual property, including schedules of patents, copyrights, and trademarks
- ➤ Environmental issues and liabilities.

Gathering due diligence materials is time-consuming and can be challenging. Therefore, the requesting company should ensure that the due diligence request list is carefully tailored to reflect the specific terms of the transaction and the nature of the target company and its business.

Generally, the acquiring company will lead the due diligence investigation and allocate the review of certain information to its legal counsel and accountants. In addition, if investment bankers have been retained to deliver an opinion as to the fairness of the transaction to the target company or the acquirer and its shareholders, the investment bankers may wish to review certain information. As the due diligence materials are being reviewed and potential issues are uncovered, the reviewing teams should keep management fully informed. This information could be crucial to help management in the merger negotiations and may lead to the addition of representations and warranties or escrow, indemnification, or other protective provisions in the merger agreement to address potential liabilities. In addition, the due diligence review will be useful in preparing and analyzing the target company's disclosure schedule, discussed below. Finally, material issues uncovered during due diligence should be discussed with each party's board of directors to help the board fulfill its fiduciary obligations to make an informed decision regarding the transaction.

Sometimes, information uncovered during due diligence may prompt a party to abandon the proposed transaction. For example, if the founders of the target company appeared to have developed the desired technology while still employed by another company, this may raise significant doubt as to whether the target company actually owns that technology. Rather than risk facing a lawsuit from the founders' prior employer, the proposed acquirer may decide not to pursue the transaction.

16.13 THE MERGER AGREEMENT

The merger agreement sets forth the terms and conditions of the business combination; it governs the behavior of the parties prior to the closing of the merger; and it determines their rights and obligations after the closing. Although details vary, most merger agreements have a similar overall section structure: Introduction, Mechanics of the Transaction, Representations and Warranties, Covenants, Conditions to the Closing, Indemnification, Termination, Miscellaneous, and Disclosure Schedule and Other Exhibits. The agreement may also include deal-protection covenants and other ancillary agreements, which are often attached as exhibits. We discuss each of these below.

Introduction

The introduction sets forth the names of the parties, the date of the transaction, and often includes *recitals* (orientation statements that help a reader understand what the rest of the document will cover) and definitions.

Mechanics of the Transaction

The mechanics section is called different names depending upon the structure of the transaction, but it describes the securities being acquired, sets forth the purchase price or exchange ratio (including any earn-out or escrow provisions), and provides a description of the structure of the merger. The agreement may describe the treatment of outstanding stock options and the terms of any purchase price adjustment in this section or in a later section.

Representations and Warranties

Each party to the merger agreement will make *representations and warranties* to the other party regarding its business and financial condition. Representations and warranties serve three main purposes in a merger agreement. First, they are a method for obtaining disclosure about the contracting parties before the execution of the merger agreement. Second, they serve as a foundation for a party's right to indemnification (and, potentially, a common-law claim for fraud) if a party discovers after the closing that the other party has breached one or more of its representations or warranties. Finally, they provide a basis for conditions to the parties' obligations to close the transaction. We discuss indemnification provisions and closing conditions later in this section.

Representations and warranties about the business of a target company generally include information regarding the target company's organization; the accuracy of its financial statements; title to its assets; the absence of liabilities and legal proceedings; compliance with laws; tax and environmental matters; contractual obligations; and full disclosure of all facts necessary to ensure that the representations and warranties are not misleading. Unless the transaction is what can be described as a *merger of equals*, the representations and warranties of an acquirer are typically much less extensive than those of a target company, especially when the acquirer is paying cash. Representations and warranties can be absolute—such as "there is no pending legal proceeding and no person has threatened to commence any legal proceeding against the Target"—or they can be modified by a *knowledge qualifier*—such as "to the best of the Target's knowledge, there is no pending legal proceeding and no person has threatened to commence any legal proceeding against the Target." Because knowledge quali-fiers shift the risk to the acquirer that a representation or war-ranty may be untrue even though the target company believed it to be true, a target company will seek to include as many knowl-edge qualifiers as possible. An acquirer naturally will resist knowledge qualifiers because the damages resulting from an inac-curate representation are the same regardless of whether or not the target company knew of the problem.

An important part of the representations and warranties in most merger agreements is the information set forth in the accom-panying disclosure schedule. As discussed in detail later in this section, the disclosure schedule will usually include exceptions from a party's blanket representations and warranties.

Covenants

Covenants include the obligations of the parties to take, or refrain from taking, certain actions between the execution of a merger agreement and the closing of the merger. For example, a target company might agree to a covenant to operate its business in accordance with past practices; it might agree to use reasonable efforts to prosecute a patent for which an application has already been filed; it might agree not to borrow more than a specified amount of money without the approval of the acquirer; or it might agree not to give its employees large raises or option grants before the acquiring company takes over. The performance of all covenants, in all material respects, is often a condition to the other party's obligation to complete the transaction.

When the parties can obtain all necessary consents and approvals in advance, they can close the transaction promptly after signing the merger agreement, often called a *simultaneous sign and close*. In this event, the merger agreement generally will not contain covenants or conditions of the parties, resulting in a much simpler document than an agreement providing for a delayed closing. If the transaction will not close for some period of time after an acquisition agreement is signed (a *delayed sign and close*, which is common), then the merger agreement will contain both covenants as to the behavior of the parties prior to the closing and conditions to both parties' obligations to complete the transaction.

Target Board's Covenant to Recommend the Deal to its Shareholders
In transactions where the target company must hold a shareholder meeting to obtain shareholder approval for the transaction, the acquirer may want the target company's board to agree to recommend its deal to the target company's shareholders. If, however, a subsequent offer received by the target company is superior, the board needs the ability to make an honest recommendation to its shareholders. The directors of a corporation that has agreed to a transaction involving a change of control or the breakup of the company may, under certain circumstances, have a fiduciary duty to consider competing bids. As a result, the target company should request a *fiduciary out*, which permits the target board to take steps that might otherwise violate the no-shop covenant if, in the good-faith judgment of the target directors, the steps are necessary to fulfill their fiduciary duties.

Conditions to the Closing

If the merger will not be closed shortly after the merger agreement is signed by the parties, the agreement will contain conditions that must be satisfied before the parties are obligated to close the merger. These provisions are often of particular importance to the target company because tightly drawn closing conditions will reduce the likelihood that the acquirer will be able to withdraw from the merger. An acquirer may seek a closing condition that provides that the acquirer will not be obligated to close the transaction if it is not satisfied with the results of its due diligence investigation. In most circumstances, due diligence should be completed before a merger agreement is signed, however, so the target company should vigorously resist this closing condition. Otherwise, an acquirer can almost always identify a problem uncovered during the due diligence process that can serve as a justification for not closing the transaction. As a result, a diligence-based closing condition effectively converts a merger agreement into an option to acquire the target company.

Common closing conditions include the following:

➤ The representations and warranties made by the other party are true and correct as of the date of the merger agreement and the closing date.

➤ The covenants or obligations of the parties have been performed or waived.

➤ The transaction is in compliance with federal and state securities laws.

➤ Shareholder approval and third-party consents have been received.

➤ Any necessary governmental approval has been obtained.

➤ Key employees have entered into new employment agreements.

➤ There has not been any material adverse effect on the other party.

➤ If the acquisition is intended to qualify as a tax-free reorganization, opinions of counsel for the target company and the acquirer that the transaction will so qualify have been obtained.

When negotiating a merger agreement, the parties generally focus particular attention on two closing conditions. The first is the accuracy of the representations and warranties made by the parties as of the date of the merger agreement and as of the closing date. The second is the effect of events between signing and closing that have had, or could have, a material adverse effect on the target company.

Accuracy of Representations and Warranties   If a party's representations and warranties are incorrect as of the date of the merger agreement or as of the closing date, the other party often has the right not to close the transaction. To enable a target company to avoid a situation in which an acquirer uses trivial breaches of the target company's representations to walk away from the transaction, closing conditions related to the accuracy of representations and warranties often include materiality qualifications. Such qualifications provide that the acquirer will be required to close the merger unless the representations and warranties are not true and correct *in all material respects* as of the date of the merger agreement or the closing date or unless any inaccuracies in the representations and warranties as of the date of the merger agreement or as of the closing date have had or will have a *material adverse effect* on the target company.

Absence of Material Adverse Events   Typically, an acquirer will assume the business risks of a target company operating in the ordinary course of business during the time between signing and closing. However, the appropriate allocation of risk for an event outside the ordinary course of business that has had, or could have, a material adverse effect on the business or financial condition of the target company is often heavily negotiated.[9] From the target company's perspective, if the events causing a material adverse effect could have occurred as a result of the announcement of the merger, then the risk is more appropriately borne by the acquirer. Sometimes a target company may go further and take the position that the risk of any material adverse events should be borne by the acquirer because, once the merger agreement has been announced, the business community may view the target company as "damaged goods" that would have a lower value if it were to attempt a business combination with another party.

From the acquirer's perspective, the allocation of this risk to the target company is more appropriate because, at the closing of the merger, the acquirer expects to own the company it agreed to acquire, not a potentially damaged company. A possible compromise is for the parties to agree that certain events, such as those caused by the announcement of the transaction or by an adverse turn in the target company's industry or general economic conditions, will not alone, or collectively, constitute a material adverse effect. These exceptions must be carefully drafted, however, to ensure that the risks of a material adverse effect are properly allocated.

Indemnification

In a merger, the acquirer, or its subsidiary if a triangular structure is used, will assume all the liabilities of the target company by operation of law. To avoid this liability, an acquirer may require a target company that does not have publicly traded shares to provide indemnification with respect to any breach of the target company's representations and warranties in the merger agreement

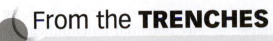

From the **TRENCHES**

Tyson Foods, Inc., the largest chicken distributor in the United States, sought to merge with IBP, Inc., one of the nation's largest beef and pork distributors, initially offering $26 per share. Tyson later raised its offer by $4 per share even though Tyson believed that IBP executives had lied to it, learned that IBP would need to take a one-time charge due to accounting fraud within a key business unit, and knew that IBP was going to drastically miss its earnings projections for 2000. The parties signed a merger agreement on January 1, 2001. The agreement was ratified by Tyson's board and shareholders soon thereafter.

During the first quarter of 2001, both companies struggled. IBP's profits suffered as the price of cattle rose, and Tyson's earnings fell 82%. By March, Tyson wanted to abandon the merger. To effectuate that desire, Tyson notified IBP that it was terminating the merger agreement. Each company filed suit—IBP to compel the merger and Tyson to prevent it.

Tyson argued that it was entitled to abandon the merger because IBP had suffered a material adverse effect "on the condition (financial or otherwise), business, assets, liabilities or results of [its] operations and [its] Subsidiaries taken as whole." Absence of such a material adverse change was a condition to Tyson's obligation to close the deal. Tyson cited IBP's poor performance and the fraud-related charge as evidence.

The court rejected this argument, ruling that a strategic acquirer, such as Tyson, with a long-term view of a merger should be excused from completing that merger on the basis of a material adverse effect only if unknown events occur that "substantially threaten the overall earnings potential of the target in a durationally-significant manner." The court deemed it "odd to think that a strategic buyer [like Tyson] would view a short-term blip in earnings as material, so long as the target's earnings-generating potential is not materially affected by that blip or the blip's cause." In addition, Tyson knew that IBP would miss its earnings projections for 2000 and knew about the fraud before it signed the merger agreement. The court viewed Tyson's desire to terminate the deal as a case of "buyer's regret," and it ultimately held that the merger must go forward. Soon after the decision, Tyson agreed to pay $2.7 billion for IBP, roughly $500 million less than the original deal.

Sources: In re IBP, Inc. S'holders Litig., 789 A.2d 14 (Del. Ch. 2001); Greg Winter, *After a Rocky Courtship, Tyson and IBP Will Merge*, N.Y. Times, June 28, 2001, at 6.

and potentially other identified liabilities. The provisions regarding indemnification raise many issues that are often among the most intensively negotiated in the merger agreement.

One indemnification issue is the extent to which a target company's shareholders should be liable for any potential indemnification. If the target company is owned by more than one shareholder, the acquirer will often request that the shareholders who are selling their shares of the target company's stock be held jointly and severally liable for any potential indemnification claims. However, a shareholder's exposure to this potential liability will usually be limited to his or her percentage ownership in the target company. Moreover, in certain situations, it may be more appropriate to impose different liability on different shareholders, depending on the representations made. For example, the shareholders may be held jointly and severally liable for representations regarding the target company but be held individually liable for any representations regarding their individual shares.

Another issue is the duration of the indemnification. In general, a target company will seek to limit the time during which a claim for indemnification can be made (often one year), while an acquirer may require that a target company's shareholders be responsible for certain matters, such as environmental liabilities or liability under previously filed tax returns, for longer periods of time.

To secure payment of any indemnification claim, an acquirer may require that a portion of the purchase price (whether in cash or shares of the acquirer's stock) be placed in *escrow* or *held back*. If an escrow is used, the release of the consideration from escrow will usually be tied to the expiration of the indemnification claim period set forth in the merger agreement, though the target company will often seek to provide for the release of the escrowed amount at an earlier time.

A target company will often seek limits on the indemnification obligations of its shareholders. One such limitation, called a *deductible* or an *excess liability basket*, sets a minimum amount of damages that must be exceeded before the target company's shareholders are liable to the acquirer. For example, if a contract provided for a $500,000 deductible and then the acquirer reached $600,000 in claims against the company's shareholders for misrepresentations or other liabilities, the acquirer would be permitted to recover only $100,000 and would forgo recovery of the first $500,000 in damages. An acquirer will often agree to the limit on indemnification but may insist on characterizing it as a *threshold* or a *tipping basket* (sometimes called a *dollar-one basket*) that will entitle the acquirer to recover all damages that are incurred once the threshold is crossed, not merely the amount over the deductible. In a recent contract for the sale of a distribution company for

$50 million, the contract provided for a $500,000 limitation on indemnification, just as in our example above. But this limit was structured as a tipping basket, which meant that once the claims exceeded $500,000, the acquirer was permitted to recover every dollar of claims, not just claims above the initial $500,000.

In addition to a deductible or threshold, a target company will generally seek to limit the maximum exposure of its shareholders to all or a portion of the purchase price. If the acquirer seeks an escrow of a portion of the purchase price, the target company's shareholders will likely try to limit their total exposure to the amount of the escrow.

Termination

Typically, a merger agreement may be terminated by a party if there is a material breach by the other party that would result in the failure of a closing condition. In addition, a merger agreement will generally provide that the agreement may be terminated by either party if the merger has not been completed by a specified date, if a court order has prohibited the merger, or if the required shareholder approval has not been obtained.

If the merger agreement is terminated without fault by either party, there will generally not be any further obligations under the agreement, although each party will usually have a continuing obligation to pay its own expenses and maintain the confidentiality of the other party's information. However, if the terminating party shows that a breach by the other party caused the termination, then certain rights and liabilities of the parties may remain in effect. In addition, in certain circumstances a break-up (or termination) fee may be payable.

Break-Up (or Termination) Fees One or both parties may agree in the acquisition agreement to pay a *break-up fee* (also called a *termination fee*) if the deal does not close under certain circumstances. The fee is often set at between 2% and 5% (or more) of the value of the transaction, and the amount of the fee and the payor may vary depending on the reason why the transaction was terminated. Most often break-up fees are payable in situations when the target company receives an acquisition proposal from an interloping party. Sometimes, break-up fees are negotiated in transactions involving special circumstances, such as antitrust risk. For example, AT&T paid Deutsche Telecom, the German parent of T-Mobile USA, a record break-up fee of $4 billion after U.S. antitrust regulators blocked AT&T's $39 billion merger with T-Mobile.[10]

Miscellaneous

A merger agreement or other acquisition agreement will almost always include a miscellaneous section, which includes items such as governing law, the procedure for amending the agreement, severability, counterpart signature pages, and other sections that typically address the contract itself.

The Disclosure Schedule and Other Exhibits

The merger agreement will typically include a disclosure schedule and certain ancillary agreements and other documents as exhibits.

Disclosure Schedule   A critical companion document to a merger agreement is the *disclosure schedule*, also known as the *schedule of exceptions*, which keys to the representations and warranties section of the agreement. The disclosure schedule is a mechanism for the target company to provide information with respect to the representations and warranties made in the merger agreement, either in the form of lists or exceptions. For example, the merger agreement will typically contain a representation that all material contracts of the target company are listed on the disclosure schedule (this is an example of a *listing rep* because it calls for a list of items). The corresponding section of the disclosure schedule would display that list of material contracts. Or the merger agreement might include a representation that there is currently no litigation pending against the target company. If in fact there *is* pending litigation against the target company, the corresponding section of the disclosure section would describe that litigation, thereby stating an exception to the representation made in the main agreement.

When properly completed, the disclosure schedule will provide a complete picture of the representations and warranties made in the merger agreement and can provide an acquirer with a valuable reference to help it complete a thorough due diligence review. The acquirer should review the disclosure schedule very carefully, however, because it may include both material and immaterial information. The acquirer will be deemed to have been given notice of all information included in the disclosure schedule and will generally lose its right to terminate the transaction or to postclosing indemnification for matters identified in the disclosure schedule.

A target company will typically deliver the final disclosure schedule when the merger agreement is executed. If the transaction will close some period of time after an acquisition agreement is signed, the target company may need to add information to the disclosure schedule between signing and closing to include developments that occurred after signing but prior to the closing date. The parties will need to determine the effect, if any, of this additional disclosure on both the closing condition related to the continued accuracy of the representations and warranties and the indemnification obligations.

Other Ancillary Agreements A business combination may also require the execution and delivery of various other documents, including shareholder voting agreements, a general release, employment contracts, and noncompetition agreements. They are often attached to the merger agreement as exhibits.

Shareholder Voting Agreements Even if the target company's shareholders are initially in favor of a given deal, they may change their minds if another acquirer subsequently proposes a more attractive transaction. To mitigate this risk, the acquirer may seek voting agreements (often including irrevocable proxies) from a portion of the target company's shareholders at the time the merger agreement is signed. Certain states may limit the percentage of shares that may be "locked-up" by voting agreements and the type of shareholder from which voting agreements may be obtained may be limited by fiduciary duty case law, at least in certain states.

General Release In certain transactions, an acquirer may be concerned that a target company has undisclosed liabilities to certain of its shareholders or third parties. One way to limit the risk of this liability is to have the shareholders or third parties enter into a general release, in which they agree to release the acquirer from any claims for known or potential liabilities that arise after the closing of the business combination. As with any contract, a general release must be supported by consideration, as discussed in Chapter 9.

From the TRENCHES

Faced with a low-ball hostile takeover offer by Omnicare, Inc., NCS Healthcare, Inc. (the target company) entered into merger discussions with Genesis Health Ventures, Inc., a potential "white knight" favored by the target's management. As a condition to making a substantially higher bid, the white knight insisted that the board of directors of the target company expressly agree to submit the merger of NCS Healthcare and Genesis Health to the NCS Healthcare shareholders for their approval. In addition, the white knight required two target directors who together controlled a majority of the target company's stock to enter into a voting agreement whereby they agreed to vote all their shares in favor of the merger of NCS Healthcare and Genesis Health Ventures. Neither commitment was subject to a fiduciary out.

Before the target company's shareholders could vote on the NCS Healthcare–Genesis Health merger agreement, Omnicare made another unsolicited offer to acquire the target company at a price that was higher than what the white knight had agreed to pay. Omnicare also filed suit against the target company and the white knight seeking an injunction to prevent the scheduled vote by NCS Healthcare's shareholders on the merger with Genesis Health.

The court granted the injunction, ruling that the protective devices were invalid and unenforceable. In the court's view, the combination of the required shareholder vote, the directors' voting agreement, and the omission of a fiduciary out clause "completely prevented the board from discharging its fiduciary responsibilities to the minority stockholders when Omnicare presented its superior transaction." The court explained that directors have a continuing obligation to execute their fiduciary responsibilities even after reaching an agreement to merge. They cannot contractually limit or preclude their fulfillment of that obligation. In this case, the three terms effectively made shareholder approval of the proposed merger of NCS Healthcare and Genesis Health a foregone conclusion and prevented the target company from considering an offer that better served its shareholders.

Source: Omnicare, Inc. v. NCS Healthcare, Inc., 818 A.2d 914 (Del. 2003).

Employment Agreements   An acquirer may decide that it is essential to retain key employees and members of a target company's management team, at least during the integration period following the closing of the transaction. For example, if members of the target company's technical staff have tacit knowledge necessary to exploit key technology, then their continued involvement may be critical. To assure retention, an acquirer may require that employment agreements with key personnel be secured prior to the signing of the merger agreement or provide in the merger agreement that the execution of such agreements is a condition to the obligation of the acquirer to complete the transaction. Although no contract can guarantee that personnel will remain with the target company after the merger is completed, employment agreements may give the acquirer more comfort. If an acquirer requires employment contracts as a condition to its obligation to close, the target company should seek to ensure that the employment arrangements are finalized before the acquisition agreement is executed and announced to reduce the possibility that negotiations with one or more employees could prevent the closing of the transaction. We provided general information concerning employment agreements in Chapter 8.

Noncompetition Agreements An acquirer may also want to secure noncompetition agreements from key personnel who may leave the target company and seek to compete directly with the surviving corporation. These agreements may be in the form of covenants not to compete in preexisting employment contracts or may be the subject of agreements entered into in contemplation of the business combination. We discussed postemployment restrictions and covenants not to compete in detail in Chapter 2.

16.14 THE CLOSING AND POSTCLOSING INTEGRATION

Immediately prior to the closing, the parties to a merger will typically exchange documentation, including officers' certificates attesting that certain conditions to the closing have been satisfied. At the closing, the parties will generally file a certificate of merger, articles of merger, or other required form of notification in the states in which the constituent companies are incorporated. Once such documentation has been filed, the merger will be complete, and the shares of the target company will generally be automatically converted into the right to receive the consideration offered by the acquirer.

One of the most crucial and often underemphasized components of a successful merger is the integration of resources and systems after the merger has been completed. Most often, the high-level merger negotiations will designate the executives and board members expected to serve postclosing, but only rarely will the discussions deal with integrating accounting practices, financial and operational systems, or management teams. The need to address employee or facility redundancy is also often neglected.

As a result, management and employees—and often clients, distributors, and suppliers—may receive little information about how the merger will affect their relationships with the company. This lack of communication, and the resulting rumors, can lead to lower employee morale, higher employee turnover, a reduction in customer trust, and other adverse results for the newly merged company. For these reasons, among others, it is crucial that merging companies understand that postmerger integration is as important to the success of the merger as any other key issue.

 From the **TRENCHES**

In 2004, EMC Corporation, a leading manufacturer of servers and other computer hardware for data processing, storage and security, and related software, acquired VMware, a small privately held software firm located in Silicon Valley, California, for $635 million cash. Led by founder Diane Greene, VMware had created innovative virtualization technology that made it possible for customers to run multiple operating systems on the same server, thereby increasing utilization rates and providing redundant storage of data. Understanding the importance of keeping Greene's tightly knit team together, and recognizing the cultural differences between Silicon Valley and Hopkinton, Massachusetts, where EMC was headquartered, EMC kept the VMware team in Silicon Valley.

By October 2015, when Dell Inc. announced its plan to acquire EMC for $67 billion, VMware's market capitalization was more than $33 billion. Thus, the 80% stake EMC retained after it spun off 20% of VMware's stock to the public was worth more than $26 billion. According to Christian Mohn, of EVRY Consulting, after Dell's acquisition of EMC, "VMware will continue to operate on its own, and do its own thing, much like it has been while being controlled by EMC." He went on to state, "My gut feeling is that VMware will be allowed to continue to innovate, and bring potentially disruptive technologies to market, even if it means its software will be competing with Dell hardware." The combination of Dell and EMC to form Dell Technologies, which closed on September 7, 2016, was the largest deal in tech history. Dell paid part of the $58 billion purchase price in cash and part in VMware tracking stock. Although analysts praised the deal, Ron Miller predicted that the "politics [of combining EMC and Dell] will likely be stunning and getting both companies moving as one is going to be a huge organizational challenge."

Sources: Constance E. Bagley, C.I. Knoop & C.J. Lombardi, EMC Corp: Proposed Acquisition of VMware, Harv. Bus. Sch. Case No. 806–153 (2006); Matt Brown, *Resurgent VMware Stock Pulls Value of Dell's EMC Acquisition Higher*, CRN (May 31, 2016), http://www.crn.com /news/virtualization/300080860/resurgent-vmware-stock-pulls-value-of-dells-emc-acquisition -higher.htm; Nick Martin, *What Does the Dell Takeover of EMC Mean for VMware?*, TECHTARGET (Oct. 2015), http://searchservervirtualization.techtarget.com/feature/What-does-the-Dell -takeover-of-EMC-mean-for-VMware; Ron Miller, *$67 Billion Dell-EMC Deal Closes Today*, TECHCRUNCH (Sept. 7, 2016), https://techcrunch.com/2016/09/07/67-billion-dell-emc-deal -becomes-official-today/.

From the perspective of employee compensation and benefits, a business combination presents many challenges, but it also offers the opportunity for improvements. Management of the merged company will need to determine the optimal way to bring together the various compensation and benefits programs of the combining entities. If an acquirer regularly does acquisitions, then it may have standardized this process and generally know how to integrate a new group of employees into the acquirer's workforce. For less experienced acquirers—particularly when the combining entities are of nearly equal size—the integration process will require careful analysis of each compensation and benefit program with an eye to what is optimal for the merged entity. This may require the maintenance of parallel programs, at least for the short term, to accommodate regional differences and geographic distance. One of the biggest challenges is to find the time, in the midst of frantic premerger activity, for the necessary analysis.

 Putting It into **PRACTICE**

About six months before Genesist hoped to launch its initial public offering, Piper attended a trade show in San Jose, California, where she met Dwayne Clark and Tomáš Tesluk, the founders of VaporIce. A two-year-old company based in Bismarck, North Dakota, VaporIce was experimenting with gas-to-solid and liquid-to-solid technologies that made it possible to make products derived from gas or liquid starting states stronger and more structurally sound. Dwayne and Tomáš explained that VaporIce's technology was not yet production ready but that they were testing a trial version of its Flexwater product in several locations throughout the Midwest. Piper quickly realized that VaporIce's prototype contained certain features that, if developed properly, could be incorporated into the manufacture of products utilizing the Genesis T-2000 technology with a minimum of modification and extra cost. Piper then invited Dwayne and Tomáš to fly out to the Bay Area the next Monday to meet with Alexei and the Genesist technical team for further discussions.

Toward the end of their daylong meeting the following week, Piper asked Dwayne how much it would cost to license VaporIce's technology on an exclusive basis. Dwayne responded that an exclusive licensing arrangement would preclude VaporIce from using its technology to

(continued)

manufacture its own products, leaving VaporIce totally dependent on the fortunes of Genesist. "What would you think about the possibility of acquiring VaporIce outright instead?" asked Tomáš. Alexei responded that the Genesist management team had considered that alternative but thought that integrating a North Dakota-based company into Genesist's existing operations would be too costly and divert scarce management resources from Genesist's main efforts at a critical time in the company's development. "Anyway," Alexei declared, "why would you be interested in selling your company before your product has even been fully developed? Don't you expect a higher return once you have a market-ready product?"

Dwayne then explained that VaporIce had encountered difficulties in obtaining a further round of venture financing to cover the company's expenses until Flexwater began to generate revenue. With very little money left from their last round of financing and little or no hope of raising additional money through a venture round or a commercial debt facility, Dwayne and Tomáš were faced with the reality that VaporIce might go out of business before Flexwater made it to market. Accordingly, they were willing to sell as long as they had the opportunity to continue working on the product with a company that shared their vision of Flexwater's potential. Although they understood that their dreams of a quick liquidity event would not be realized, they hoped that by combining with a better-funded company with bright prospects, they might reap a higher return on their investment in the long term.

Alexei and Piper thanked Dwayne and Tomáš for their presentation and told them that their team would caucus further on the possibility of acquiring VaporIce. As Piper walked down the stairs with them to show them the closest BART station going to the airport, she mentioned that she was concerned that even if the price were right, integration issues would still complicate the picture. "That should not be a problem," responded Dwayne. He and Tomáš were the major players in Flexwater, and they had already agreed to move to California if necessary. Trying to hide their excitement, Alexei and Piper agreed to get back to Dwayne within a week or two.

After discussing the opportunity further, the Genesist team confirmed Piper's belief that certain characteristics of the Flexwater prototype would greatly enhance the manufacture and performance of the GT V-Bracket and other products in the pipeline without adding significant development time or cost. Moreover, as several people noted, Dwayne and Tomáš were both clearly very talented and the personalities and visions of the two technical teams meshed well.

(continued)

Alexei next called a special meeting of the Genesist board of directors to discuss the prospect of acquiring VaporIce. The directors' initial response was less than enthusiastic. Although they did not dispute the benefits of the Flexwater technology, a majority of the members expressed concern that the acquisition would unduly divert management's attention from Genesist's own technology and products. At the meeting, the directors made it very clear that they would not approve a transaction that resulted in an additional office in North Dakota. After Alexei and Piper convinced the board that the technology was worth exploring further notwithstanding the integration issues, the board authorized them to continue examining the possibilities for a business combination with VaporIce.

Alexei scheduled a further meeting at VaporIce's offices in Bismarck between the T-2000 and the VaporIce technical teams. Before the meeting, Dwayne sent Alexei a confidentiality agreement, which he signed after Genesist's attorney Sarah Crawford reviewed and revised it so it did not preclude Genesist from pursuing any research and development it already had in the works. Alexei and Piper made sure to block off some of their own time to sit down with Dwayne and Tomáš in Bismarck to try to hammer out the integration issues that so concerned Genesist's board. The Genesist team came away from the Bismarck meetings more enthusiastic than ever. The members of the two technical teams had quickly established an excellent working relationship, sometimes finishing each other's sentences. Piper's chief concern going into the Bismarck meetings was that the development of the Flexwater technology would require the assistance of VaporIce personnel who would not want to leave Bismarck. In particular, after spending time with Regi Steitz, one of VaporIce's top engineers, Piper realized that Regi's continued involvement was essential to a successful acquisition. After spending a week in the Bay Area and discovering that one of her favorite former professors and several of her grad school classmates were now working at the University of California at Berkeley, Regi agreed to move if that was what it would take to get the deal done. Dwayne explained that the other seven people then employed by VaporIce would not leave Bismarck, but their responsibilities could be assumed by those willing to relocate as well as by current Genesist employees.

Alexei and Piper went back to the Genesist board and, after a full discussion of the pros and cons of the acquisition, the integration plans, the purchase price and other key terms of the deal, the board unanimously approved an offer to acquire VaporIce. The offer contemplated an acquisition of all the outstanding stock of VaporIce for approximately $5 million worth of Genesist common stock pursuant to a reverse

(continued)

triangular merger. In addition, Genesist would hire Dwayne, Tomáš, and Regi to work with the T-2000 technical team. Genesist would also extend an offer to another key technologist, Hank Jerritt. All four would be asked to sign noncompetition agreements in connection with the transaction and would receive benefits and option packages comparable to those offered to similarly situated Genesist employees. Alexei asked Sarah Crawford to prepare a term sheet reflecting these terms as well as the standard provisions typically included in a term sheet, such as the structure of the transaction and the need for a definitive agreement before the offer would become binding. After reviewing Sarah's draft and suggesting a few changes, Alexei emailed the term sheet to Dwayne and Tomáš and asked them to get back to him as soon as possible, which they did. Their chief concerns were the purchase price (the parties finally agreed on a $6 million purchase price) and the indemnification provisions. Dwayne and Tomáš explained that the business had been funded to date by their relatives and friends, as well as several of the local business leaders of Bismarck. The term sheet provided that the representations and warranties that VaporIce and its shareholders would be required to make in the definitive agreement would survive the closing of the transaction for a period of two years and that the sellers' indemnification obligations would be limited only by the amount of the purchase price each seller would receive in the transaction. In addition, 50% of the aggregate purchase price would be placed in escrow for two years. This was not acceptable to VaporIce's shareholders, because it meant that they would not know for two years what they would actually receive in the transaction.

Piper countered that given the nature of VaporIce, a small startup without much operating history, she was concerned that possible infringement claims arising from the creation and development of the Flexwater technology, as well as potential environmental contamination stemming from the disposal of chemicals used in the manufacturing process, might not surface until after Genesist had expended substantial sums of money and time and effort incorporating Flexwater into Genesist's product offerings. After some further back and forth, the parties agreed that all representations and warranties made by VaporIce would terminate one year after the closing of the transaction except for the representations dealing with intellectual property infringement, which would survive for 18 months. Moreover, the amount held in escrow would be the sole and exclusive remedy available to Genesist for breaches of these representations and warranties. Forty percent of the purchase price would be held in escrow for the first year after the

(continued)

closing; after that time, the escrow fund would be reduced to 20% of the purchase price. After reaching agreement on these issues, the parties established a schedule for conducting due diligence and negotiating definitive documents.

During the due diligence process, Genesist's attorneys discovered that VaporIce had approximately 55 shareholders. Further inquiry revealed that at least 25 were accredited investors, but it was unclear whether each of the remaining 30 investors possessed the requisite sophistication to satisfy the requirements of Rule 506 under Regulation D. Accordingly, Alexei explained to Dwayne and Tomáš that those investors not possessing the requisite sophistication would have to appoint a qualified person to act as their purchaser representative. Tomáš explained that he was an accredited investor with extensive investment experience and offered to act as purchaser representative on behalf of the unsophisticated investors, each of whom readily agreed to his appointment.

Unfortunately, not everything proceeded so smoothly. Hank Jerritt, whose role in the continuing development of the Flexwater product was more instrumental than even VaporIce had initially realized, balked at leaving Bismarck and relocating to San Francisco. A North Dakota native and retired Toyota engineer, Hank had returned to Bismarck after several years in Japan. He had missed his birthplace and was hesitant to again give up the slower pace of life in Bismarck. Coming home had also rekindled his interest in paleontology—an interest well served by the Badlands of western North Dakota, but not easily pursued in the Bay Area. Clearly then, some accommodations would have to be made with Hank if the transaction were to proceed.

After much internal discussion and further negotiation with Hank, the parties agreed that Genesist would hire Hank as a consultant who would work one week a month in the Bay Area and telecommute the rest of each month. Although this arrangement was not ideal for Genesist, Piper was hopeful that Hank could remain productive and be a valuable contributor to the product development efforts of the combined team from a distance. Hank assured her that he could and explained that he often worked separately from the main technology team at VaporIce to keep himself free to think of new directions for the company rather than having to troubleshoot the existing technology.

The final sticking point in negotiations was the type of Genesist capital stock to be issued in exchange for the outstanding equity of VaporIce. If Genesist issued $6 million worth of its common stock, the

(continued)

percentage interests of Genesist's existing investors would be substantially diluted because of the extremely low value of Genesist's common stock. On the other hand, Genesist did not wish to create an additional series of preferred stock issuable to VaporIce's existing shareholders and optionholders; if it did, the employees of VaporIce who were employed by Genesist would have the right to receive a better return on their options than the current Genesist employees. Alexei explained to Tomáš and Dwayne that if they received preferred stock, they would have greater rights than he and Piper had as founders if Genesist were sold for a price below the aggregate liquidation preferences of Genesist's preferred stock.

Dwayne saw the bind that Genesist was in, but he noted that, with the exception of a small number of outstanding shares held by him and Tomáš, none of VaporIce's employees owned stock. Instead, they all held unexercised options. Dwayne said that issuing preferred stock to these optionholders would not create any compensation issues because none of these employees would be working for Genesist. Moreover, Dwayne declared, he, Tomáš, Regi, and Hank were willing to terminate their existing VaporIce options in exchange for receiving Genesist options for common stock, provided that they were given credit in their vesting schedule for the time they had worked at VaporIce as well as a limited number of additional options to partly make up for the value they were ostensibly leaving on the table. Alexei readily accepted the offer, and the parties made plans to proceed with the closing of the transaction.

After obtaining the approval of the boards of both companies, the parties signed the definitive merger agreement. Within days of the execution of the definitive agreement, VaporIce mailed an information statement to its existing shareholders that explained the transaction, provided information concerning Genesist and VaporIce, and solicited the approval of the transaction by the shareholders. Ten days later, VaporIce had received sufficient written shareholder consents to satisfy the last condition to closing. The parties scheduled a closing date two days later. During the closing, the attorneys exchanged signature pages by email for all the relevant documents. When the attorneys were finally satisfied that everything was in order, the transaction closed. Alexei immediately called the newest members of the Genesist team with a heartfelt, "Welcome aboard! Now, back to work, everyone."

Getting It in WRITING

SAMPLE TERM SHEET FOR THE ACQUISITION OF A PRIVATELY HELD CORPORATION BY A PUBLIC COMPANY

CAVEAT TO THE READER: This form is intended only to serve as an example of a hypothetical term sheet. Every term sheet must be carefully tailored to reflect the specific terms of the transaction to which it relates; accordingly, it may be necessary to make substantial modifications to this form before it can be used in the context of any proposed transaction.

Term Sheet for Proposed Acquisition of Private Corp. by PublicCo, Inc.

This preliminary nonbinding term sheet sets forth certain key terms of a possible transaction involving PublicCo, Inc. and Private Corp. Neither this term sheet nor any action taken in connection with the matters referred to in this term sheet will give rise to any obligation on the part of PublicCo or Private Corp. to continue any discussions or negotiations or to pursue or enter into any transaction or relationship of any nature.

Parties:	PublicCo, Inc. ("Acquirer") Private Corp. ("Target") _____, _____, _____, and _____, who collectively hold approximately _____% of the outstanding common stock of Target on a fully diluted basis (the "Major Shareholders").
Acquisition of Outstanding Target Equity Securities:	Acquirer would acquire 100% of the outstanding equity securities of Target by means of a reverse triangular merger in which a newly formed subsidiary of Acquirer would be merged into Target (the "Transaction"). As a result of the Transaction, Target would become a wholly owned subsidiary of Acquirer.
Treatment of Outstanding Target Common Stock:	All outstanding shares of Target common stock would be exchanged for newly issued shares of Acquirer common stock in the Transaction. Any repurchase rights applicable to shares of Target common stock would remain in effect after the closing of the Transaction (the "Closing") and would become rights to repurchase the shares of Acquirer common stock issued in exchange for such shares of Target common stock.
Treatment of Outstanding Target Stock Options:	All outstanding Target stock options would be assumed by Acquirer in connection with the Transaction and would become options to purchase Acquirer common stock. The terms of the assumed stock options (including terms relating to vesting) would not change; there would be no acceleration of the vesting of unvested stock options.

(continued)

Purchase Price:	The aggregate value of the consideration (including all shares of Acquirer common stock and all options to purchase Acquirer common stock) to be provided by Acquirer to the holders of Target's outstanding equity securities in the Transaction would be _____ million dollars ($_____). For purposes of the Transaction, Acquirer common stock would be valued at the average of the closing prices of Acquirer common stock for the 20 consecutive trading days immediately preceding the Closing.
Voting Undertakings:	The Major Shareholders would agree to vote a total of _____ shares of Target, representing _____% of the Target's outstanding capital stock, in favor of the Transaction.
Tax Treatment:	It is expected that the Transaction would constitute a tax-free reorganization for U.S. federal income tax purposes.
Securities Law Matters:	Acquirer common stock to be issued in the Transaction would be issued in reliance upon the "Regulation D" exemption from the registration requirements of the federal securities laws.
Employment and Noncompetition Agreements:	Contemporaneously with the execution of the definitive agreement and plan of merger and reorganization relating to the Transaction (the "Merger Agreement"), certain key executives of Target would enter into employment agreements and one-year noncompetition agreements that would become effective as of the Closing.
Representations, Warranties, Indemnities, and Other Provisions:	In the Merger Agreement, Target and the Major Shareholders would make customary representations and warranties (which would survive the Closing) relating to the business, financial condition, contracts, liabilities, employees, and prospects of Target and would provide customary indemnities. A portion of the consideration to be provided by Acquirer in the Transaction would be held in escrow to secure Acquirer's rights of indemnity. The Merger Agreement would also contain customary covenants, closing conditions, and other provisions.
Transaction Expenses:	All legal fees and other expenses incurred on behalf of either party would be borne by the party that incurs such expenses, except that expenses of Target in connection with the Transaction would be borne by the shareholders of Target.
"No-Shop" Agreement:	Target would execute a 45-day exclusivity ("no-shop") agreement on or before the _____ day of _____ [month] in 20___.

CHAPTER 17

Going Public

F or many entrepreneurs, their company's *initial public offering* (*IPO*) is the realization of a dream. This first offering of the company's securities to the public represents recognition, and often validation, of the entrepreneur's vision as well as access to the capital that is often required for the company to achieve its potential. It can also create substantial wealth for the entrepreneur and the early investors, at least on paper.

By default, all companies start as private companies. Although the timing varies by industry, most companies decide to go public when (1) the company has reached the point at which its initial investors have invested the total amount of capital that they are willing to provide and are focused on *liquidity* (a return on their investment) or otherwise believe that the public capital markets will facilitate additional financing at higher valuations and (2) the company has made sufficient progress to make a public offering viable. Significant progress is generally measured by sustainable profitability and revenue growth or, in the case of life sciences companies, the achievement of other significant objectives or success metrics, such as technology adoption, partner validation, or positive results in clinical trials. The company may need significant additional capital for research and development, product launches, or working capital to fund revenue growth or expand business operations. As the company's valuation increases, however, the company may encounter difficulty in attracting new private investors, who would rather target earlier-stage companies with a lower valuation but greater upside potential. In addition, the demands, in particular on larger high-value technology companies, to create a mechanism for employee liquidity often push companies toward the public markets rather than toward less structured and legally complex private transactions.

This chapter first provides a brief history of IPO market conditions, then discusses matters to consider in deciding whether or not to become a public company, identifies certain advantages and disadvantages of being a public company, outlines several factors to consider in determining when a company is a good candidate for an IPO, and describes the participants in an IPO. A large portion of this chapter is then dedicated to the details of the public-offering process and the related documents for each step. We then discuss important post-IPO considerations and conclude with a summary of some of the key ongoing responsibilities of a public company and its board of directors, including a discussion of insider trading.

17.1 A BRIEF HISTORY OF MODERN IPO MARKET CONDITIONS

The ease with which a company can go public fluctuates, and those who follow the IPO market know that the only thing truly predictable is the unpredictability. Depending on market conditions, economic and political uncertainty, and other factors, IPO windows open and close, often quite abruptly. At times, hundreds of companies are in the IPO pipeline. At other times, there may be a slow series of months when only one or two companies go public. The ability of a particular company to go public is also often highly dependent on its industry. In large part as a result of macroeconomic conditions and a very volatile public market, only 59 companies successfully priced their IPOs during the first half of 2016.

During the dot-com craze that began around 1998 and continued through the spring of 2000, hundreds of Internet and other technology companies went public in a great IPO market. Many of these companies had more limited operating histories and more substantial losses than previous viable IPO candidates. This favorable momentum came to an abrupt halt shortly after the Nasdaq Composite Index reached its then height in March 2000. By May 2000, the IPO window had effectively shut, and a number of companies had to terminate their in-progress IPOs. The dismal IPO market continued through the stock market slide of 2001 and through 2002 and the first half of 2003, a period marked by economic uncertainty as well as external events, such as the tragic terrorist attacks of September 11, 2001.

In mid-2003, the IPO window began to reopen for life sciences, semiconductor, electronics components, and other technology companies. Drug development companies with drug candidates in later-stage clinical trials and other biotechnology companies were among the most active IPO market participants. As the life sciences IPO market picked up steam during 2004 and 2005, biotechnology companies with earlier-stage drug development candidates and companies with development-stage products completed successful IPOs. The IPO market for computer programming, data processing, and other technology companies also saw a significant resurgence in IPO activity toward the end of 2003 and during 2004 and 2005. IPO activity continued at a reasonable pace during various IPO windows in 2006 and then increased through 2007, with 282 IPOs being completed in 2007.

The IPO market significantly deteriorated in 2008 and 2009 as a result of the global credit and financial crisis, including the collapse of Lehman Brothers and other major financial institutions in late 2008. The years 2008 and 2009 represented the worst IPO markets in over a decade, as fewer IPO transactions were completed and less capital was raised than even during 2001 and 2002 (with only 51 completed IPOs in 2008 and 64 in 2009). The IPO pace increased in late 2009 and during the first half of 2010, particularly for the health-care technology, media, and telecommunications sectors.

In 2012, the Jumpstart Our Business Startups (*JOBS*) Act, which was designed to make it easier and less expensive for small companies to go and stay public, became law. The JOBS Act created a new category of issuer—the *emerging growth company* or *EGC*, which is any company that had less than $1 billion in total annual gross revenue in its most recently completed fiscal year. The JOBS Act provided EGCs with various benefits, including reduced financial statement requirements and compensation disclosures, temporary exemption from having their internal control over financial reporting audited as otherwise required by the

Sarbanes-Oxley Act of 2002 (*SOX*), the ability to submit draft registration statements to the Securities and Exchange Commission (*SEC*) on a confidential basis, and the ability to engage in *testing the waters* (*TTW*) communications with certain large institutional investors to gauge interest in the IPO. More than 85% of the companies that have completed IPOs since the enactment of the JOBS Act have qualified as EGCs. The Fixing America's Surface Transportation Act of 2015 (*FAST Act*) modified the JOBS Act to further relax the regulatory burden on EGCs and improve their access to capital.

The year 2015 was the slowest for IPOs since the JOBS Act was enacted, with only 185 companies going public. Private valuations were at an all-time high, and it was relatively easy for certain companies that might have otherwise gone public to access alternative private financing (some with very attractive valuations).

Historically, even in periods of significant IPO activity, there has been substantial price volatility. Many IPOs have ultimately concluded at offering prices below their initial price ranges. Except for a small minority of IPOs (such as Google, Facebook, and LinkedIn) that have experienced blockbuster post-IPO performance, post-IPO trading success has often been mixed.

17.2 IPO VERSUS SALE OF THE COMPANY

Partly because of the volatility of the IPO market, many entrepreneurs considering a public offering are also thinking about selling the company as an alternative to going public. Indeed, the sale alternative is a far more common path to liquidity, particularly for entrepreneurs with a company experiencing slow but steady growth or operating in an industry not currently favored by investment bankers. Especially when the IPO environment is challenging, certain companies may engage in "dual tracking," which means concurrently exploring a potential IPO and a potential sale transaction. Chapter 16 discussed business combinations and contracts for the sale of an enterprise, as well as the pros and cons of selling the company.

Potential buyers often surface about the time a company is ready to go public because they are well aware that once a company is public, they typically will have to pay a significant premium

From the **TRENCHES**

Founders of a biotechnology company with a potential drug product in clinical development and several preclinical programs faced a different dilemma after the company began the IPO process. The investment banks had initially advised the company that the public marketplace would value the outstanding shares at between $120 and $140 million and that the company could likely raise between $50 and $75 million. Subsequent drug-product failures, saturation in the life sciences IPO market, and poor post-IPO performance for other life sciences companies at the time the company hoped to go public prompted the investment bankers to decrease the proposed offering size to less than $30 million with the outstanding shares being valued at $60 to $80 million. Even though this would represent a substantial reduction in the pre-money value of the company, the founders believed the company would be able to raise more capital on better terms in the public market than could be obtained in a private financing from venture capitalists or other sources. Because the company did not have other viable near-term prospects to sell the company, the founders reluctantly went forward with the IPO at the lower valuation.

(often 20% to 30% over the public market price, or more) to induce the board of directors of the target company to approve the sale. A hot IPO market can also stimulate a hot acquisition market because buyers may fear they will lose the chance to get a company while it is still private. For example, a significant number of life sciences companies that had filed or submitted confidential draft registration statements to go public in recent years (but had not yet completed the IPO process) were acquired by large pharmaceutical companies seeking to augment their internal drug discovery and development capabilities with new drug candidates and additional drug discovery technologies.

17.3 ADVANTAGES AND DISADVANTAGES OF GOING PUBLIC

Going public offers a company certain advantages. A public offering of securities often allows a company to raise capital at a higher valuation than a private offering of its illiquid stock and provides a company access to broader financial markets to fund its capital requirements. Once the company goes public, it can use its stock instead of cash to acquire strategic technologies, products, or other businesses. The company will also have the benefit of public visibility. As long as the company is performing well and the market is receptive, the company can return to the public market to raise additional capital. A public trading market will also provide the company's early investors, employees, and option holders the opportunity for selling their shares and converting their "paper wealth" into more tangible fare.

Going public can also entail a significant number of disadvantages, however. As explained in more detail below, a public company must meet a host of legal obligations that are inapplicable to private companies, including significant disclosure obligations to hundreds of shareholders whom the entrepreneur and the board have never met—and will never meet. The company will forever be in the fishbowl of public scrutiny. In particular, since the adoption of SOX and implementation of other regulatory reforms, the costs and disclosure obligations of being a public company as well as the related public scrutiny have significantly increased, even in light of exemptions for EGCs and smaller companies. After every period of significant economic uncertainty, there tends to be increased regulatory reform that, while in recent years has been focused on economic stimulation and reducing the burden on public companies, has in the past been directed at additional disclosure and enhanced public scrutiny of company executives.

Disclosure requirements apply not only to a public company but also to its officers and directors, who must inform the marketplace of the amount of the company's stock they and their family own and of any sales, gifts, purchases, or other changes in ownership of that stock, including stock option grants and exercises. Officers and directors are also required to disclose certain business transactions with the company and its advisers, customers, and service providers as well as to provide substantial information about their background, experience, qualifications, and involvement in certain prior legal proceedings. Disclosure reforms also require the company to publicly report material developments on a more current basis (generally within four business days) and to provide more detailed information about executive compensation decisions, risk taking, board risk oversight, and other corporate governance matters.

Furthermore, the going-public process is expensive, often costing significantly more than $2 million in legal and accounting fees, printing costs, filing fees to the SEC, state securities filing fees, stock exchange or over-the-counter registration fees, compensation consultant fees, and increased premiums for directors' and officers' liability insurance. If the company has not had annual audits or interim reviews of its financial statements performed, or if it has recently completed acquisitions of other businesses, then accounting fees will be higher, and obtaining the requisite financials may lead to delays in the public offering process. Going public also consumes an enormous amount of management time during what is usually a crucial period for growing the business. Once public, the company will spend significantly more in legal, accounting, and printing expenses than in the past. For non-EGCs and companies that have lost their EGC status, these costs have significantly increased since the adoption of the Sarbanes-Oxley Act and other regulatory reforms that require tighter internal accounting and disclosure controls and procedures as well as greater transparency and disclosure regarding corporate governance, executive compensation, and other matters.

Other disadvantages of operating as a public company include increased liability exposure and pressure for short-term results. Although the JOBS Act reduced disclosure and compliance burdens for EGCs, EGCs are only entitled to these accommodations for at most five years after becoming a public company.

In addition, an entrepreneur contemplating a public offering in hopes of getting liquidity for his or her stock should be aware of likely restrictions on the sale of that stock, even if it is fully vested. These impediments to the sale of stock are discussed in detail near the end of this chapter in the discussion of post-IPO matters.

For all of these reasons, there are now approximately half as many public companies in the United States as there were in the mid-1990s, as the number of IPOs has been more than offset by the number of companies who have been taken private, been bought, or been delisted.

17.4 WHEN IS THE COMPANY A VIABLE IPO CANDIDATE?

When considering an IPO, the founders and the board must determine whether the company should pursue an immediate IPO or an alternative strategy, such as waiting until the company has made additional progress, so that it can potentially command a higher valuation in an IPO, or pursuing a merger with a private or public company. Factors to consider include the nature of the company's existing products and product pipeline; the strength and depth of the company's research, development, and management teams; the company's revenue growth and profitability (or path to profitability), particularly during soft IPO markets; the competitive landscape; the company's intellectual property portfolio and the proprietary nature of the company's technology, products, or business model; the strength of the public and private capital markets as well as the level of recent merger activity; the IPO activity for companies in the same industry or market; and the company's anticipated capital requirements.

The timing of an IPO is often dependent on conditions beyond the company's control, such as whether (1) the stock market is performing well, (2) the market is receptive to IPOs at the time, (3) the relevant industry is "hot," (4) major institutional investors have exceeded the proportion of their portfolios reserved for investment in the relevant industry or in IPOs generally, and (5) a competitor or other companies in the industry have announced disappointing financial or regulatory results that have caused the market to be wary of the industry as a whole. When faced with less than ideal conditions, some companies seek bridge financing from existing investors or venture lenders or mezzanine (later-stage) financing from new investors to raise enough capital to permit the company to wait until market conditions improve or product or revenue milestones are achieved. If bridge or other private financing is not available on acceptable terms and the IPO window closes, then the company may have to reevaluate its decision to go public and instead try to find a buyer for the company. Companies may be particularly challenged during periods of reduced levels of private financing activity and weaker merger and acquisition activity.

IPO market volatility, particularly in certain sectors (such as the biotechnology industry), makes it difficult for even experienced management teams to select the optimal time to go public. The IPO process is lengthy, involving intense scrutiny and multiple cycles of regulatory review with the SEC, and underwriters will not start marketing the offering until the regulatory process is substantially complete. As a result, advance preparation for a potential IPO is increasingly critical so companies can move quickly and efficiently to take advantage of open IPO windows.

17.5 PARTICIPANTS IN THE IPO PROCESS

A number of individuals contribute to a company's IPO process. The company's management plays a central role in the offering, guided by the underwriters, company counsel, underwriters' counsel, and the company's independent public accounting firm, referred to in this chapter as *auditors*. Together, they constitute the IPO's *working group*, whose primary task is the preparation of the prospectus (explained below). The financial printer and transfer agent play important roles as well. Each of these roles is explained in turn.

Company Management

The company's management, with the assistance of its counsel and auditors, works to ensure that the company has adequate corporate governance mechanisms to comply with the rules and regulations of the SEC and any stock exchange or market on which the company's shares are traded following the IPO. In anticipation of the IPO, it is critical that the company's management coordinate with its auditors and counsel well in advance of the IPO so that corporate governance and other legal and financial matters do not cause delay. Even a small delay in the offering may be the difference between a successful or unsuccessful (i.e., failed) offering, especially during times where there is significant market volatility.

Underwriters

The underwriters are typically investment banks whose role is to sell the stock to investors in the IPO. The lead underwriter (and there may be more than one lead) is called the book-running manager. The book-running manager actively participates in the drafting of the prospectus and is primarily responsible for the selling effort. It puts together the syndicate of investment banks that will participate in the offering (often with guidance from the company), organizes the road show and marketing meetings, and coordinates other matters relating to the marketing and sale of the securities.

Company Counsel

Retaining experienced counsel is extremely important to help the company prepare for, and navigate through, the complex IPO process. The lawyers for the company advise the company on corporate governance, disclosure, and compliance issues; coordinate the drafting of the registration statement; and shepherd the registration statement through the SEC review process. Company counsel also helps the company select and coordinate with other participants in the process, such as stock exchange representatives, the financial printer, and the transfer agent. Company counsel participates in the negotiation of the *underwriting agreement* (explained below) between the company and the book-running manager or managers, which covers numerous aspects of the offering, including the amount of the gross spread, discussed below.

Typically, company counsel will review the company's charter documents and legal records to determine what actions the company must or should take prior to becoming a public company. Company counsel also conducts a detailed review of the business, addressing any legal problems that may emerge and identifying items that require disclosure in the prospectus. Company counsel will also conduct a detailed review of corporate governance matters, including Sarbanes-Oxley compliance, the independence of the company's board and board committees, the role of the board chair or lead director, and executive compensation matters, to ensure the company complies with SEC rules and regulations and those of any exchange on which the company's shares will ultimately be traded. If the company has separate specialist counsel (e.g., intellectual property counsel or regulatory counsel), the specialists are generally asked to participate in discussions with the working group and to review sections of the prospectus in their area of legal expertise and, in some cases, to render an opinion to the underwriters regarding those sections. Companies operating in certain industries will be asked to engage such counsel if they have not yet done so.

Underwriters' Counsel

The lawyers for the underwriters participate on behalf of the underwriters in the prospectus drafting process and the due diligence effort and advise the underwriters on legal issues that arise. In part to shield their clients from potential liability for material misstatements or omissions in the preliminary or final prospectus, underwriters' counsel sometimes plays a "policing" role at drafting sessions, encouraging the inclusion of additional risk factors, toning down superfluous positive language, and challenging management to substantiate every arguably material statement in the prospectus. Given that an accurate preliminary and final prospectus is in the best interests of all participants, experienced company counsel will work closely with both management and underwriters' counsel to ensure that the language in each prospectus is satisfactory to both. Underwriters' counsel also coordinates the review of the underwriting arrangements by the Financial Industry Regulatory Authority (*FINRA*) and any filings required by state securities authorities. Completion of the FINRA filings requires the company to circulate a questionnaire to its officers, directors, and certain security holders who have acquired securities in the 180 days prior to the first confidential submission or filing for the IPO.

Underwriters' counsel also prepares the initial draft of the *underwriting agreement*, which is the agreement between the company and the underwriters that governs numerous aspects of the way the offering will be managed. The company and the underwriters typically reach general agreement on all major business points relating to the form of underwriting agreement prior to the initial confidential submission or filing of the registration statement with the SEC, and then the underwriting agreement is actually signed later when the deal is priced.

Auditors

The company's auditors provide accounting advice in connection with the offering and work closely with the company's chief accounting officer to prepare the sections of the prospectus relating to accounting issues and financial disclosure. Again, experience doing IPOs is critical. The auditors also address SEC comments related to accounting issues and prepare comfort letters. A *comfort letter* summarizes the procedures the auditors used to verify certain financial information in the prospectus and describes the scope of their review of the prospectus. The auditors typically prepare a draft of the comfort letter relatively early on in the IPO process and finalize it before the company prints the preliminary prospectus. The auditors deliver the final version of the comfort letter to the underwriters at the pricing of the IPO and deliver a *bringdown* comfort letter at the closing that explains any further procedures since the deal was priced.

Financial Printer

Generally, the prospectus is printed by a financial printer, which is a company that specializes in creating the customized documents that must be filed with the SEC. The printer must be experienced; able to produce a high-quality, timely, and accurate product; and able to respond quickly and cost-effectively to revisions prepared by the working group. For a typical IPO, a company should expect to spend around $300,000 (and often significantly more) to print several thousand preliminary prospectuses and about 2,000 final prospectuses. The company should obtain quotes from two or three reputable financial printers with extensive IPO experience.

Transfer Agent

The company will also need a *transfer agent*, which is typically a specialized stock transfer company or a commercial bank, to issue and effect transfers of the company's shares and to coordinate mailings to shareholders. The company may also need to select a banknote company to help design and then print the new stock certificates that will be issued to the shareholders after the public offering, although some transfer agents can assist with this.

17.6   PREPARING FOR THE IPO

Companies well-prepared to move quickly once the IPO process begins will be in the best position to control the IPO timing and minimize market risk, so a company's management and its lawyers work together on IPO preparations for weeks or months before the process "officially" begins. With the help of its lawyers, the company starts determining a strategy for the IPO, including evaluating the benefits of the JOBS Act and FAST Act and considering which to implement, and it attends to tasks such as beginning the preliminary due diligence process, assessing changing corporate governance needs, addressing restrictions on pre-IPO publicity, and even starting to draft key sections of the prospectus.

Preliminary Due Diligence Process

The due diligence process, which is explained in greater detail below, begins with the company and its lawyers ensuring the company records are in order, then organizing an electronic data room to facilitate the due diligence process. As part of this process, the company works with its auditors to address stock financial matters and any option valuation and pricing issues. It is important for the company to discuss any cheap stock or other option pricing issues (discussed below) with its counsel and auditors prior to the organizational meeting. A thorough review of these and other equity compensation matters will help ensure that any potential issues are identified and addressed as early as possible. This is also the time to address any missing or incomplete company records.

Regulators heavily scrutinize option pricing and dating practices. Accounting rules (such as Financial Accounting Standards Board Accounting Standards Codification (*ASC*) Topic 718, Compensation - Stock Compensation [formerly, FAS 123R]) have significantly changed the treatment of stock options for financial reporting purposes. Under ASC Topic 718, equity-based payments, such as stock options, generate a current charge to earnings based on their fair value. In addition, as explained in Chapter 5, equity awards will result in adverse tax consequences under Section 409A of the Internal Revenue Code if they are determined to be granted below fair market value. If the company has recently (i.e., within 12 months prior to effectiveness of the registration statement) granted stock options or otherwise issued stock at a price significantly below the IPO price, an additional charge to earnings to reflect the issuance of this so-called *cheap stock* may be required. The theory is that cheap stock issued to employees is actually additional compensation to the employees and should be accounted for as such. Cheap stock sold to nonemployees represents a *deemed dividend* (in effect, a built-in gain) to the purchaser. Cheap stock is often the subject of SEC comment on the prospectus. If the proposed charge is significant, it can jeopardize the offering because of its impact on the company's financial statements.

The company is well advised early in the IPO process to begin the preparation of a chronology of recent option grants and restricted stock grants with justification and the rationale behind the pricing. To minimize the risk of adverse consequences under Section 409A and avoid potential accounting issues with the SEC, companies that are contemplating an IPO should obtain periodic valuations from independent appraisers to assist the board in determining the fair market value of the company's stock for option granting purposes. Care should be taken to select a qualified and experienced independent appraiser who will utilize an appropriate valuation methodology and will take into consideration the appropriate valuation inputs (such as material developments in the company's business, new private financing valuations, market developments, and the like). The cost of these independent valuations has continued to decline as they have become more common and a greater number of third parties have begun providing stock valuation services.

Improprieties, such as backdating the option grant date, can lead to significant accounting and legal issues. They may also expose the company's directors and officers to liability. Chancellor William Chandler III of the Delaware Court of Chancery indicated that approving option grants that are *backdated* (falsely documenting that an option was granted on an earlier, more financially advantageous date), *spring-loaded* (timed to take advantage of positive news), or *bullet dodging* (timed to avoid the impact of negative news) without disclosing that information publicly violated the fiduciary duties that directors owe to shareholders.[1] Officers and directors involved in improper option-granting processes also face potential criminal liability.[2]

Changing Corporate Governance Needs

During the preparation period, the company also starts improving its infrastructure and internal controls in anticipation of operating as a public company, addressing the composition and independence of the board of directors and reincorporation in Delaware, if applicable.

Composition and Independence of Board of Directors In preparation for becoming public, a company should review both the composition of its board of directors and its board committees. Public investors will be concerned if the board does not include enough *outside* or *independent directors*, that is, persons who are not officers or employees of the company or its subsidiaries and who do not otherwise have a relationship with the company that could interfere with their exercise of independent judgment in carrying out their responsibilities. (We discussed independent directors and board composition in Chapter 6.) The securities laws, as well as the rules and regulations of Nasdaq, the New York Stock Exchange (*NYSE*) and other securities exchanges, require that a majority of the company's board consist of "independent" directors. These rules specify what it means to be "independent" and require the board to make an affirmative determination of a director's independence.

Board committees, such as audit, compensation, and nominating and corporate governance committees, become much more important once a company goes public. The duties of these committees are detailed toward the end of this chapter in the discussion of responsibilities of a public company and a board of directors, but it is wise for management to understand these requirements before starting the IPO process and to begin deciding who will serve in what capacities once the company is public.

Reincorporation in Delaware As explained in Chapter 5, many companies choose to incorporate in Delaware for a number of reasons. Accordingly, companies not already incorporated in Delaware frequently reincorporate there as part of the IPO process. Shareholder protection measures available in Delaware to reduce

 ## From the **TRENCHES**

In an IPO involving a company with several venture capitalists on its board of directors, Nasdaq challenged the board's determination that each of the venture capitalists on the board was independent. Although the venture funds affiliated with two of the directors had significant stock ownership positions in the company, the company argued to Nasdaq that the directors were clearly independent and had no relationship with the company other than through their board membership and the passive investment in the company's securities. All preferred shareholders' rights, including the right to the board seats, terminated upon the IPO. After several rounds of comments, Nasdaq accepted one director as independent but rejected the other because of the director's affiliation to the most significant equity holder who owned more than 20% of the company. Nasdaq permitted the company to rely on a temporary safe harbor that allowed the company to qualify for trading on Nasdaq so the IPO was completed with no delay. The company added additional independent members to its board of directors shortly following the IPO.

a corporation's vulnerability to hostile takeover attempts are often adopted at the same time. These measures are typically adopted by the shareholders in connection with an IPO because it is much easier to obtain shareholder approval of such measures as a private company prior to having a broad base of public shareholders and prior to being required to comply with the public company proxy rules and regulations.

Drafting Key Sections of the Prospectus

As described in detail below, companies with experienced counsel often get a jump start on the IPO process by beginning to draft key sections of the prospectus and collecting information for other sections of the prospectus that may require significant lead time. This allows a company to hit the ground running once the IPO process is officially launched and can save valuable time later.

Restrictions on Pre-IPO Publicity

Companies preparing for an IPO must be careful to avoid inappropriate publicity. Any publication of information or publicity effort made in advance of a proposed public offering that has the effect of conditioning the public mind or arousing public interest in the issuer or its securities, other than permitted TTW communications by EGCs, may constitute an impermissible offer to sell securities under federal securities laws. This type of impermissible activity during the *prefiling period* (the period before the registration statement is filed) is referred to as *gun jumping*. Gun-jumping violations, in addition to embarrassing the issuer and its underwriters, may delay the marketing of the securities because the SEC may refuse to declare a public offering registration statement effective until the effect of the violations has dissipated. Such violations may also result in criminal and civil actions against the issuer and the underwriters.

The company's communications are most significantly restricted during the prefiling period. For example, as a general matter, the company may not issue forecasts, projections, or predictions about its expected future performance. The SEC has created a safe harbor for most issuers that provides a bright-line period ending 30 days prior to the initial public filing of a registration statement, during which issuers may communicate (orally or in writing) without risk of violating the gun-jumping provisions as long as (1) the communication does not reference a securities offering, (2) the communication is made "by or on behalf of the issuer," and (3) the issuer takes reasonable steps within its control to prevent further distribution or publication of the information during the 30-day period immediately before the issuer files the registration statement. The only communication about the offering permitted during this 30-day period is a notice of proposed offering, the contents of which are narrowly prescribed by regulation. These notices are rarely used in connection with IPOs.

Other disclosures that may run afoul of the securities laws include marketing letters, press releases, speeches, interviews, presentations at seminars or conferences, articles in the financial press, uses of social media, and other forms of advertising. The company should remember that newspaper and magazine articles often have a long lead time. Thus, an article currently being researched and written may not be published until many months later, when the public offering process is in full swing. It can be particularly problematic when management quotes are later folded into a larger piece talking about the company's public offering.

Nevertheless, the company need not completely discontinue its normal public relations activities. It is generally permissible to continue advertising that is consistent with past practices, to send out customary reports to shareholders, and to make routine press announcements with regard to factual business developments.

 ## From the **TRENCHES**

Two Google founders granted *Playboy* an interview shortly before filing the IPO registration statement in mid-2004. The interview, in which the founders extensively discussed Google's business, was published shortly before the company proposed to price the offering. There was much speculation among securities analysts as to whether the SEC would delay the offering as a violation of the "quiet period" rules. Ultimately, Google was required to include a copy of the article in its prospectus and add risk factors in the prospectus advising potential investors that Google's involvement in the publishing of the article could be considered a violation of the 1933 Act and that Google potentially could be required to repurchase shares sold in the offering if it were determined to have violated such laws.

The company should consider setting up an internal control procedure to ensure that all public disclosures are properly reviewed and coordinated in advance. Counsel for the company and the underwriters should review all press releases and publicity, including product announcements, to be released for publication, broadcast, or distribution during the registration period. In addition, the company should establish a policy prohibiting employees, officers, and directors from recommending the company's securities, offering their opinions or forecasts regarding the company, or, without the advice of counsel, providing any information regarding the IPO. This can be particularly important in the age of widespread social media usage. Media surrounding a company in registration is routinely reviewed by the SEC.

The websites of companies in registration are also routinely reviewed by the SEC, so companies should be cautious about statements to their employees and information posted on their websites. The company website should be carefully reviewed and periodically scrubbed for information that would conflict with the registration statement or that could be perceived to be conditioning the market for the IPO or as an "offer" of the company's securities. The company should also review all hyperlinks to other websites and eliminate any that may be inappropriate. Hyperlinked third-party information arguably could be deemed to be part of the company's website.

17.7   THE IPO PROCESS

An IPO involves a series of steps.

Timing and Overview of Steps

Not including the preparation period described above, it typically takes a company around three to five months to complete an IPO. It is sometimes possible to accelerate that schedule. Conversely, the schedule is sometimes extended in the event of significant or difficult-to-resolve SEC staff comments, company transactions or events (such as an acquisition or a significant business development), or market developments during the process. Table 17.1

TABLE 17.1	Sample Summary Timetable for IPO of Emerging Growth Company

JANUARY

S	M	T	W	T	F	S
					1	2
3	4	5	6	7	8	9
10	11	12	13	14	15	16
17	18	19	20	21	22	23
24	25	26	27	28	29	30
31						

FEBRUARY

S	M	T	W	T	F	S
	1	2	3	4	5	6
7	8	9	10	11	12	13
14	15	16	17	18	19	20
21	22	23	24	25	26	27
28	29					

MARCH

S	M	T	W	T	F	S
		1	2	3	4	5
6	7	8	9	10	11	12
13	14	15	16	17	18	19
20	21	22	23	24	25	26
27	28	29	30	31		

APRIL

S	M	T	W	T	F	S
					1	2
3	4	5	6	7	8	9
10	11	12	13	14	15	16
17	18	19	20	21	22	23
24	25	26	27	28	29	30

MAY

S	M	T	W	T	F	S
1	2	3	4	5	6	7
8	9	10	11	12	13	14
15	16	17	18	19	20	21
22	23	24	25	26	27	28
29	30	31				

JUNE

S	M	T	W	T	F	S
			1	2	3	4
5	6	7	8	9	10	11
12	13	14	15	16	17	18
19	20	21	22	23	24	25
26	27	28	29	30		

Genesist, Inc.	Company
Representatives of the Underwriters	UW
Company Counsel	CC
Underwriters' Counsel	UC
Auditors	AU

January 4	Organizational meeting and due diligence session
January 4	Commence due diligence review
January 11	Distribute first draft of registration statement; circulate director and officer and 5% shareholder questionnaires and negotiated lockup agreements

(Continued)

TABLE 17.1 (continued)

Week of January 11	All-hands registration statement drafting sessions at CC; review draft underwriting agreement; review draft opinions and other key documents
Week of January 18	All-hands registration statement drafting sessions at CC
Week of January 25	All-hands registration statement drafting sessions at CC
Week of February 8	All-hands drafting sessions at the printer; substantially finalize draft underwriting agreement, opinions, and other key documents
February 12	Confidentially submit initial registration statement with SEC
Weeks of February 15 and 22	Prepare initial drafts of testing-the-waters and road show presentations
March 10	Receive initial comments from SEC
Weeks of March 14 and 21	Continue finalizing TTW presentation/road show presentation and preparing response to SEC comments
March 25	Confidentially submit pre-effective amendment number 1 responding to SEC comments
Week of March 28	Engage in TTW meetings
April 8	Receive additional comments from SEC
April 22	Initially publicly file registration statement responding to SEC comments and including first quarter financials
Weeks of April 25 and May 2	Finalize road show presentation; determine preliminary price range; submit price range letter to SEC; prepare preliminary prospectus
May 9	Clear SEC and FINRA comments; file charter amendment effectuating stock split; file and print preliminary prospectus
Weeks of May 9 and 16	Domestic and international road shows
May 25	Receive FINRA no-objections letter; SEC declares registration statement effective; pricing; sign underwriting agreement; prepare final prospectus
May 26	Commence trading; file and print final prospectus
June 1	Closing

sets forth a sample timetable and Table 17.2 depicts an illustrative timeline for an IPO by an emerging growth company.

The company chooses investment banks to act as underwriters for the IPO, holds an organizational meeting, and works together with the underwriters to complete the registration statement. Next, the company submits confidential drafts of the registration statement to the SEC, which provides comments for revision. The company revises the registration statement and submits an amended version to the SEC, which can

TABLE 17.2   **Illustrative IPO Timeline for Emerging Growth Company**

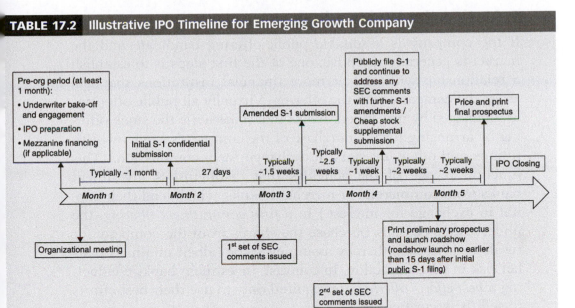

a. This timetable is subject to a number of factors such as timing of any mezzanine financing, availability of financials, extent to which issuer's counsel is up to speed and experienced in IPOs, nature of SEC staff comments, desired deal timing in light of upcoming milestones, holiday seasons, and the like.

b. The schedule also typically includes testing-the-waters meetings after the initial S-1 confidential submission.

either issue additional comments or accept the revised submission. When the company has addressed any additional comments and is ready to announce the upcoming IPO publicly, it files a preliminary prospectus. A preliminary prospectus is also known as the *red herring* because it contains a red legend mandated by the SEC on its front cover, warning of its preliminary and incomplete nature. The company and the underwriters then each work to create demand for the company's shares once they become public—the company by making presentations to potential investors on a road show, and the underwriters by building a "book" of purchase offers from its customers. The registration statement then becomes effective in its final form, which now includes the initial price at which the shares will be offered and the number of shares in the offering. The company's stock then commences trading on an exchange such as Nasdaq or the NYSE. Three days later, the deal "closes" and the company's shares are now available to the public to buy and sell. Each of these steps in the IPO process is explored in detail below.

Selecting the Underwriters

If the company is a suitable public-offering candidate and the market is generally receptive, one of the first steps is to establish a relationship with one or more financial institutions that will assist the company with the offering. Virtually all public offerings are managed by investment banks that *underwrite* the stock offering by arranging for the purchase of the company's stock by institutions and other investors in exchange for a commission. (This function is one of the activities that distinguishes investment banks from commercial or merchant banks, which lend their capital in exchange for interest.) In a *firm-commitment offering*, the underwriters actually purchase the shares from the company for resale to investors, thereby assuming some (albeit minimal) market risk in the transaction. In contrast, investment banks conducting a *best-efforts offering* are required only to use their best efforts to sell the securities.

In a typical firm-commitment offering, the underwriters buy stock from the company at a discount (typically 7% of the public-offering price, though for very large IPOs such as Facebook and Alibaba, it can be substantially lower than that) and then sell it to the public at the full price. The difference between the offering price to the public and the proceeds to the company is called the *gross spread*.

To choose investment banks to underwrite the IPO, companies will often hold what has come to be colloquially called a *beauty contest* or *bake-off* among a number of investment banks. In this process, each investment bank brings a team of people to make a presentation to the board of directors. The investment bankers often prepare and distribute elaborate bound materials (referred to as *books*). The books detail the strengths of the investment banking firm, its recent relevant IPOs, the post-IPO price performance of the companies it has taken public, and, perhaps most importantly, its preliminary views on how the market will value the company.

These valuations are typically based on past and projected future earnings and achievement of significant milestones (initially supplied by the company but massaged by the bankers before the presentation); the *price-earnings ratio* for revenue

From the **TRENCHES**

A Silicon Valley company invited six prestigious investment banks to engage in a bake-off for its IPO. Although all the firms made impressive presentations, the company was attracted to the winner for two principal reasons. First, the bank had the industry's best analyst, which the company felt was important both for completing the IPO successfully and for providing ongoing research reports about the company. Second, the bank had completed many deals as a co-manager but only recently had begun to be selected as a lead underwriter in the particular industry. The company's management felt that the bank, intent on building its reputation, would provide excellent service during the offering and make certain the deal attracted significant attention in an overcrowded market. The offering was wildly successful as the preliminary orders exceeded the shares available in the offering by several times.

generating companies (market price per share divided by earnings per share), or perhaps different relevant ratios or valuation metrics of comparable public companies (for instance, a ratio of market price to revenues for companies not yet profitable or the market capitalization of companies at similar stages of development if not generating revenue); and the strengths and weaknesses of the company compared with its competitors. Despite the similarity of approach, the valuations among investment banks can vary tremendously. Given the various criteria that are important to the company and the process, the bank with the highest estimated valuation of the company is not necessarily the best choice. Due to a number of factors, these estimated valuations may bear little or no relation to the valuation ultimately achieved, which is determined by the actual price at which a company's shares are actually sold in the IPO. Following the presentations, the company will select the underwriters who will act as *book-running manager* or managers, and typically any co-lead managers or co-managers (though these other banks are sometimes selected later in the IPO process).

Typically, the company will select several investment banks to act as book-running managers. Certain managers will be *active* (e.g., having a role as syndicate lead or stabilization agent for the securities) and others may be *passive* (helping to build the book of investors but little else). The other underwriters are typically known as *co-managers*. Sometimes there are mezzanine levels of bankers between the book-running managers and the co-managers, who are often known as *co-lead managers*. The company should seek underwriters that are willing to underwrite the offering on a firm-commitment basis (as opposed to best-efforts basis).

The role of the book-running managers is to position the company in the public market and to form a *syndicate* (a group of investment banks) to participate in the offering. The primary reasons for syndicating an offering are risk sharing, marketing, and responding to issuers' desires for multiple banks to be participants in their IPOs. The syndicate will comprise multiple underwriters that share both potential liability under the securities laws and the underwriting component of the gross spread. The syndicate may also include selling group members or dealers who do not share liability with the underwriters. Selling group members or dealers agree only to purchase a specific number of shares at the public-offering price less a selling commission (usually around 60% of the gross spread). Unless otherwise indicated, references in this chapter to underwriters mean the book-running managers.

To be effective, a book-running manager must be familiar with the company's industry and be capable of differentiating the company and its products or services from others in its industry. The company should evaluate the reputation, experience, and prestige of the underwriter in the relevant industry (including its recent relevant deal experience, pricing success, failed or aborted offerings, and the like); its level of commitment to the company's IPO as compared with other transactions it may have in its IPO deal pipeline; its ability to staff the offering appropriately with experienced and knowledgeable personnel; company management's impressions of the individual bankers who will shoulder the responsibility for the deal; the individual bankers' understanding and belief in the company's story; the bank's marketing strength (with some banks having deep retail, institutional and international distribution networks); the bank's preliminary valuation of the company; and the quality of its support after the public offering (e.g., the reputation and following of the bank's research analysts who cover the company and the company's industry, market-making capabilities, experience in mergers and acquisitions, ability to execute on a wide range of follow-on offerings post-IPO, and history of continuing to work with companies when they struggle post-IPO). If there are multiple book-running managers, they should have complementary strengths. For example, one might be stronger selling to institutional buyers, and another might have stronger retail distribution or a better-known analyst.

A related role of the investment bank is to provide analysts who publish ongoing research reports on the company's progress, which can foster investor interest after the offering. Companies in the IPO process must generally communicate separately with the book-running manager's investment banking team and its research analysts and comply with other procedures designed to avoid potential conflicts of interest within the banks. The SEC enacted these rules in 2003 in response to instances during the Internet boom where brokerage firms' research groups allegedly issued false and misleading analyst reports to garner more investment banking business. As a result, a presentation by the bank's top industry analyst of his or her five-year projections for the company, which used to be a highlight of the road show, is now a thing of the past.

Organizational Meeting

Although a company has likely been preparing for the IPO for weeks or months in advance and has already selected its underwriters, many people consider the *organizational meeting* to be the "official" launch of the IPO process. Also called the *all-hands meeting* or simply the *org meeting*, the organizational meeting is the first gathering of all of the key participants in the IPO. To help facilitate the IPO process, the underwriters typically prepare a time-and-responsibilities schedule setting out who does what and when those tasks must be completed and hand out this schedule at the org meeting. The participants spend the rest of this meeting discussing key considerations and strategies for the IPO. Table 17.3 is a sample agenda for the organizational meeting for an IPO by an EGC.

TABLE 17.3   Sample Agenda for Organizational Meeting for IPO of EGC

I. INTRODUCTION OF THE WORKING GROUP

   A. Management team, underwriters, issuer's counsel, underwriters' counsel, and auditor introductions

II. TIMELINE AND PROCESS DISCUSSION

   A. Preparation of registration statement and SEC review period

   B. Drafting sessions and due diligence

   C. Shareholder communications

      1. Piggyback registration rights

      2. Proposed lockup and FINRA questionnaires

      3. Proposed director and officer and 5% shareholder questionnaires

      4. Consents, notices, waivers, and approvals

   D. Board of directors' meetings

   E. Target confidential submission/initial public filing/offering timing

   F. Responding to SEC and FINRA comments

   G. TTW meetings/road show/distribution strategy/target launch date

   H. Discuss timing impact of important announcements, events, and business developments

   I. Other lead-time items (e.g., audit timing, board structure, and industry consents)

   J. Target pricing and closing dates

III. TRANSACTION OVERVIEW

   A. Size of offering

   B. Primary and secondary components

   C. General discussion of use of proceeds

   D. Option to purchase additional shares (greenshoe)

   E. Review existing shareholder list

      1. Registration rights

      2. Rule 144 restricted stock, stock option program

      3. Shareholder approval thresholds

      4. IPO participation rights

      5. Automatic preferred-stock conversion triggers

      6. Warrants

      7. Convertible notes

   F. Number of shares authorized

      1. Shares outstanding

      2. Any pending capital raises/acquisitions

      3. Any stock splits or reverse stock splits

   G. Lockup agreements with officers, directors, and shareholders and percentages to be obtained prior to confidential submission and launch

   H. Distribution objectives

      1. Institutional/retail, domestic/international

      2. Syndicate structure

TABLE 17.3 (continued)

I. Directed share program

J. Possibility of confidential treatment requests

K. Exchange listing venue

L. Proposed trading symbol

IV. REVIEW LEGAL ISSUES

A. Underwriting and lockup agreements, legal opinions, and analysis of major business issues to be resolved prior to first confidential submission

B. Outstanding claims/pending litigation

C. Loan agreement restrictions or other consents needed to offer the shares

D. FINRA and blue sky issues

E. Shareholder or other notes

F. Cheap stock

G. Stock options (grant practices, pricing, and the like)

H. Corporate governance compliance

　　1. Confirm appropriate board composition and independence

　　2. Confirm appropriate governance infrastructure

　　3. Board committees and committee charters

　　　　a. Board chair and/or lead independent director

　　　　b. Corporate governance policies (ethics, whistle-blower, insider trading, window-period, related-party transactions, and the like)

　　4. Executive compensation matters

I. Public company's charter and bylaws

J. Employment agreements

K. Board/Pricing Committee meetings

　　1. Preparation of resolutions and appropriate board authorizations

　　2. Pricing Committee appointment and approval

L. Directors' and officers' questionnaires

M. Disclosure of confidential agreements

N. Related-party and certain transactions disclosures

O. Required shareholder approvals and third-party consents, including customers and case studies

P. Expert opinions

Q. Transfer agent and registrar

R. Directors' and officers' liability insurance

S. Other matters that may require disclosure or discussion with SEC

V. DISCUSS FINANCIAL AND ACCOUNTING MATTERS

A. Audited financials

　　1. Review of significant accounting principles

　　2. Discussion of historical audits/auditors

　　3. Revenue recognition policy

TABLE 17.3 (continued)

B. Timing and availability of quarterly financials

C. Potential inclusion of pro forma financials

D. Tax issues

E. Acquisitions, divestitures, restructures, etc.

F. Cheap stock

G. Auditor comfort letters

H. Management letters

    1. Any special accounting issues (beneficial conversion, deferred compensation charges, etc.)

VI. DISCUSS PUBLICITY POLICY

  A. Quiet periods (prefiling, postfiling/pre-effective, postoffering periods)

  B. Control of information in press releases, conferences, interviews, and advertising

  C. Pending newspaper/magazine articles to be published

  D. Press releases, conferences, and other corporate announcements

  E. Communication with employees

  F. Interaction with research analysts

  G. Website review and policy

  H. Public relations/investor relations firms

VII. DISCUSS PRINTING OF DOCUMENTS

  A. Selection of financial printer and banknote company (if needed)

  B. Use of color, artwork, and pictures

  C. Volume requirements

VIII. DUE DILIGENCE REVIEW

  A. Management interviews

  B. Company history and consent strategy

  C. References for customer/supplier due diligence

  D. Detailed competitive analysis

  E. Regulatory and compliance matters

  F. Projected financials (e.g., revenues, earnings, backlog)

  G. Methodology and models for financial planning

  H. Product brochures, trade press, and other public relations materials

  I. Separate diligence with research analysts

  J. Intellectual property matters

  K. Material contracts and agreements

  L. Key partners, suppliers, distributors, contractors, etc.

  M. Pending or anticipated acquisitions or material agreements

IX. COMPANY MANAGEMENT PRESENTATION

X. CLOSING REMARKS AND NEXT STEPS

Due Diligence

Now that the IPO process is in full swing, the company, the underwriters, and their respective counsel conduct *due diligence* by assembling and reviewing vast amounts of information about the company and its business. The underwriters, their counsel, and company counsel ask numerous questions of the company's officers and key employees in order to understand thoroughly the company's business, its current products and services, the products and services under development, their markets or potential markets, and inherent risks of the business. The due diligence review often includes discussions with key customers, suppliers, collaborators, licensors, and other third parties important to the company's business; analysis of projections, business plans, and product strategy; a review of industry publications; analysis of pending litigation and an assessment of potential claims; a review of stock option practices and officer and director compensation; a review of environmental issues; and consultations with intellectual property counsel, regulatory counsel, technology advisers, and auditors. It also includes a thorough review of a very broad range of company records and documents, including minutes of board and shareholder meetings, stock records and related documentation, charter documents, shareholder agreements, any debt instruments, communications with auditors and regulatory authorities, any materials related to litigation, materials related to stock option and securities issuance, and all material contracts. This time-consuming process has three purposes.

The first purpose of due diligence is to uncover any problems or risks that need to be addressed in connection with the IPO. Due diligence also often reveals existing agreements or relationships that must or should be amended or terminated prior to the offering. These include agreements that grant certain shareholders rights to information, rights to participate in future financings, board observation rights, or other rights not appropriate for a public company. There might also be contractual or other provisions with third parties that could result in their having inappropriate leverage or claims.

The second purpose of due diligence is to determine what information needs to be included in the registration statement, which is typically being drafted concurrently with the due diligence process. A company should expect the unexpected here. Matters of personal and professional character (such as any prior arrests or bankruptcies of key company personnel) can become significant issues. The founders should discuss with counsel any and all issues, both real and perceived, that could affect the offering. The company must make sure that all participants are aware of the importance of complete candor in the due diligence process. It is critical that the information in the prospectus be complete and accurate and adequately highlight key risks associated with an investment in the company. A thorough due diligence process and appropriately crafted and qualified disclosure in the registration statement may minimize the SEC's requests for additional support or modification of disclosures and thereby expedite the SEC review process.

The third purpose of due diligence is to verify the accuracy of the information included in the registration statement. The company must be prepared to back up the claims it makes in the prospectus. Even if a statement is cast as opinion, such as the company's belief that it is an industry leader, the company must be able to demonstrate the reasonableness of this belief. Company counsel typically collects and organizes this information into a backup book. A *backup book* organizes the background information and materials that support many of the company's assertions and other factual matters contained in the prospectus. Items such as industry publications and market surveys are common forms of support for statements regarding market size and the company's position in the market. Companies are often required to obtain consent to use industry publications or customer case studies in the registration statement, which may take some lead time. The information collected in the due diligence process is useful in responding to the SEC staff if, as often happens, it asks for support for certain of the company's assertions.

 ## From the **TRENCHES**

A member of the management team of a company that was planning to go public failed to disclose early in the due diligence process adequate detail regarding correspondence with regulators that could adversely impact sale of the company's products. The underwriters withdrew their support for the offering just before the registration statement was due to be publicly filed as a result of credibility concerns. If the information had been disclosed in adequate detail early in the diligence process, the underwriters and the company together with their counsel could have worked together to modify the disclosure without it becoming an issue of credibility.

At the same time the company is engaged in the due diligence process with the underwriters, auditors and counsel, the company separately provides information to and meets with research analysts at investment banks to ensure that they have adequate information about the company and understand the company's business and "story." Because the underwriters at investment banks generally are not permitted to share information with their research analysts, the company must separately communicate with the research analysts in parallel with the broader due diligence process, except in joint due diligence sessions carefully chaperoned by underwriters' counsel following legally mandated procedures.

Registration Statement

Concurrently with the due diligence process, the working group for an IPO is drafting the registration statement. A *registration statement* is a document that a company must file with the SEC in order to offer new securities to the public. It includes a detailed selling document called a *prospectus*, which describes the company and its business and management as well as the terms of the proposed offering. In the case of an IPO by a U.S. company of its stock, the prescribed form for a registration statement is *Form S-1* (foreign private issuers may qualify for filing on Form F-1, which is substantially similar to a Form S-1). As part of the SEC's smaller reporting company regulatory relief and simplification rules implemented in early 2008, and as a result of the JOBS Act and FAST Act reforms, EGCs and certain other smaller companies qualify to provide somewhat less disclosure than standard IPO issuers. After receiving the registration statement from the company that wishes to offer securities, the SEC staff reviews it for compliance with SEC rules and reviews the substance and adequacy of the disclosure in the prospectus, which is the part of the registration statement that will be printed and distributed to the public.

EGCs may alternatively confidentially submit draft registration statements to the SEC for nonpublic review prior to an initial filing, which provides benefits such as protection of confidential information (including the fact that the company was considering an IPO) if the company later decides not to proceed with the IPO. Unlike registration statement filings with the SEC, confidential draft registration statements do not need to be signed by management or the company's directors and do not need to be accompanied by an auditor's consent. In addition, an EGC does not need to pay SEC registration fees until it first publicly files the registration statement. Almost all EGCs choose to make confidential submissions.

Contents of the Prospectus

The general contents of the prospectus are prescribed by applicable securities laws. Drafting the prospectus is a collaborative effort by company management, investment bankers, attorneys, and auditors. Company management can provide the most in-depth knowledge of the company itself, but the attorneys, investment bankers, and auditors have the experience needed to shape the prospectus into a form that will facilitate SEC approval and disclose all the information legally required, while also still serving as a marketing document to sell stock. The SEC requires that the company describe the company's business and provide other required disclosures in simple, straightforward "plain English" language. Generally, most prospectuses follow a fairly standard format: Box Summary, Risk Factors, Use of Proceeds, Management's Discussion and Analysis of Financial Condition and Results of Operations, Business, and Management. After other brief sections, the prospectus includes the company's Audited Financial Statements. Each of these components is discussed in turn.

After the table of contents and often several other minor sections, the prospectus typically begins with a short (e.g., 8- to 12-page) summary of the offering, referred to as the *Box Summary*, or simply the *Box*, which summarizes the key elements of the company's business, strategy and financial statements, and the terms of the offering.

Following the Box Summary is an extremely important section entitled *Risk Factors*, which alerts investors to the key risks, uncertainties, and challenges faced by the company. It is important that risks specific to the company be identified and clearly explained. Additionally, an IPO prospectus usually addresses other risks that make the stock particularly speculative. These include the absence of an extended operating history or profitable operations, the fact that the nature of the business is inherently risky, risks associated with operating as a public company, the dependence on a sole

From the **TRENCHES**

In 2015, Broadwind Energy Inc. and its former chief executive officer (*CEO*) and chief financial officer (*CFO*) settled accounting and disclosure charges brought by the SEC. The SEC alleged that the alternative energy company knew that a "deterioration" in its relationship with two significant customers had led to "substantial declines in the company's long-term financial prospects," including a "substantial impairment" of $58 million to intangible assets. Yet the company did not disclose this information to its investors in its registration statement or record the impairment charges until two months after its 2010 offering. The SEC alleged that the company shared the information with its auditors and investment bankers. Although the defendants did not admit guilt, the company agreed to pay a $1,000,000 penalty, and the CEO and CFO agreed to pay, in combination, approximately $566,000 in disgorgement and prejudgment interest as well as $125,000 in penalties.

Source: Press Release, SEC, SEC Charges Chicago-Area Alternative Energy Company for Accounting and Disclosure Violations (Feb. 5, 2015), https://www.sec.gov/news/pressrelease /2015-24.html.

supplier or particular customers, the uncertainties regarding technology or regulatory approvals, the uncertainty of proprietary rights, intense competition from more mature companies, and the lack of manufacturing or sales and marketing experience. The Risk Factors section is intended to be cautionary, not optimistic; it highlights potential risks and serves as important protection in the event of shareholder litigation. In the past two decades, the average length of the risk factors section has grown dramatically as expectations from both the SEC and the market have evolved. Experienced attorneys for both the company and the underwriters can provide valuable guidance as to what should be included in this section.

In fact, the underwriters and their counsel at times must exert great effort to convince the company's management to make the Risk Factors section in a prospectus as strong as possible. Management may believe that identifying all possible material risks will have a negative effect on the offering and feel that it amounts to trashing the company's business in a public document. The underwriters and their counsel also have an interest in having an effective marketing document, but they will want to make certain that all conceivable material risks are disclosed. This dynamic may lead to significant back and forth between the underwriters and their counsel on the one hand, and the CEO or

From the **TRENCHES**

After receiving several rounds of comments from the SEC staff requiring more detailed disclosure regarding use of its upcoming IPO's proceeds, a drug delivery company revised its prospectus to include more detailed disclosure regarding the amount of IPO proceeds it intended to use in connection with its principal clinical programs and other drug discovery and development efforts. Thereafter, the underwriters advised the company that they did not believe that market conditions would support an offering at the price range in the preliminary prospectus. Instead, they recommended that the company lower the range by approximately 30% to 40%. Because this significantly lowered the amount of proceeds to the company, the SEC required the company to provide a detailed analysis of whether the description of the use of proceeds was still accurate. If the lower proceeds had represented material changes, the SEC could have required recirculation of the preliminary prospectus and potentially delayed the offering. Because the company and its counsel had focused the detailed use of proceeds disclosure on the company's main programs (while providing more general disclosure with respect to its other programs), the company was able to convince the SEC staff that, even with the reduced proceeds, it was still going to have adequate proceeds from the offering to fund its principal clinical programs and the other main activities described in the prospectus. As a result, the offering was not delayed.

other members of the management team on the other, as each attempts to balance the need for robust risk factor disclosure against the desire to tell the company's story and sell the company's securities. In such circumstances, company counsel often serves as a mediator, crafting language that appropriately balances the interests of all parties.

The *Use of Proceeds* section describes how the company intends to use the proceeds of the offering in its business. The company should be able to support, by projections or otherwise, the proposed uses. The SEC staff may insist on fairly detailed discussions of the proposed uses of the funds, despite resistance from companies that do not have specific uses planned or that want to avoid specific commitments of specific amounts to the extent possible.

The *Management's Discussion and Analysis of Financial Condition and Results of Operations (MD&A)* section contains an analysis of the financial statements for at least the three most recent fiscal years and any applicable interim periods (unless the company has been in business for a shorter period of time). An EGC is required to provide financial statements for only the two most recent fiscal years and any applicable interim periods and may omit the earlier of the two years if it reasonably believes it will have provided an additional full year of annual financial statements by the time it commences its IPO. The MD&A analysis provides a year-to-year and period-to-period comparison, focusing on material changes and the reasons for those changes, as well as unusual or nonrecurring events that could cause the historical results to be a misleading indicator of future performance. The goal is to enable a reader to better understand the financial statements and financial condition of the company and known trends or uncertainties.

The MD&A section has been the subject of heightened SEC scrutiny. Although projections per se are not required, the MD&A section does require a forward-looking analysis of the effect of known trends, events, or uncertainties, including information that may not be evident on the face of the financial statements. As part of the MD&A, the company's historical and projected sources of funds for the business must be discussed, as well as off-balance sheet and related-party transactions, contractual obligations, and critical accounting policies. Although certain readers view the Risk Factors as the key section in the prospectus where the risks related to the business are disclosed, MD&A is often instrumental in understanding what could cause variability in the company's financial performance in the future and affect the company's business and stock price.

The *Business* section provides a narrative description of the company, its strategies and goals, products/services or products/services in development, technology, intellectual property, manufacturing, sales and marketing, regulatory matters, legal proceedings, and competitive landscape. Within certain limits, this section can be customized in terms of both presentation and substance. It often has easy-to-read diagrams, graphs, or charts. Potential risks, such as technological uncertainties, shortages of raw materials, timing of new product introductions, or reliance on sole suppliers, are often highlighted in this section to provide investors with balanced disclosure. This section reflects the tension between the need to provide complete disclosure of the material risks of the investment and the desire to describe the company in a manner that will make it attractive to investors, all without revealing sensitive or competitive information.

The *Management* section provides biographical information about certain officers, directors, and key employees. It also describes executive compensation, insider transactions, employee benefit plans, board committees, board independence, and other corporate governance matters. Disclosure of executive compensation is very comprehensive, and it must follow certain prescribed tabular formats designed to facilitate comparisons among companies. The SEC requires detailed disclosure of the policies and principles behind a company's executive compensation, including a detailed Compensation Discussion and Analysis, as well as disclosures of relationships between the board chair and management, the board's role in risk oversight and enterprise risk management, potential risks associated with compensation decisions, and director qualifications and diversity. The JOBS Act permits EGCs to take advantage of reduced disclosure obligations regarding executive compensation.

Other sections normally included in an IPO prospectus include *Special Note Regarding Forward-Looking Statements, Dividend Policy, Capitalization, Dilution, Selected Financial Data, Certain Relationships and Related-Party Transactions, Principal and Selling Shareholders, Description of Capital Stock, Shares Eligible for Future Sale, Material U.S. Federal Tax Consequences for Non-U.S. Holders, Underwriting, Legal Matters, Experts,* and *Where You Can Find Additional Information.*

The issuer must include *Audited Financial Statements* in a registration statement. Assuming the company has been in existence for the specified periods, these include balance sheets as of the end of the last two fiscal years and income statements for the three most recent fiscal years; however, as noted above, an EGC is required to include income statements for only the two most recent fiscal years and may omit the earlier of the two years in any confidential submission or public filing if it provides an additional full year of annual financial statements before it commences its IPO. Unaudited interim financial statements are required for offerings by non-accelerated filers that become effective 135 or more days after the end of the company's most recent fiscal year. A *non-accelerated filer* is (1) an issuer with less than a $75 million public float or (2) an issuer that does not meet other accelerated filer requirements. Most IPO candidates are non-accelerated filers. The number of days decreases to 130 in the case of *large accelerated filers* and *accelerated filers*, that is, issuers that have been filing reports with the SEC for 12 calendar months and meet other requirements. All financial statements must conform to generally accepted accounting principles (often referred to as *GAAP*) and to SEC accounting requirements.

The company need not but often does include photographs, illustrations, and graphs in the prospectus. Although color photographs or illustrations add to the cost of printing and require additional lead time, in some circumstances graphics can be important in helping readers understand the company's business and products. Photos of prototype products may be used in the prospectus, but the SEC staff has commented on the need to fully disclose them as prototypes in development. The SEC has also commented heavily on graphs and charts that provide forward-looking or summary information without appropriate qualification or explanation. In addition to saving on related costs, some issuers have elected to forgo front- and back-cover artwork to avoid the potential delay that can result from clearing the artwork through the SEC review process.

Liability for Misstatements in the Registration Statement

The securities laws regulating IPOs and other registered public offerings of securities are geared, in large part, toward ensuring that sufficient disclosure of relevant facts and information is made to permit potential investors to make informed investment decisions. To further this goal, Section 11 and Section 12 of the 1933 Act make certain persons associated with a registered offering of securities—including the company; the officers required to sign the registration statement (i.e., the chief executive officer, the chief financial officer, and the chief accounting officer); the directors and the named nominees for director; and the underwriters—civilly liable to the purchasers of the shares for any untrue statement of a material fact contained in a registration statement and for any failure to state a material fact required to be stated or necessary to make the other statements not misleading. Persons associated with the offering of securities also have potential civil liability for statements in the preliminary prospectus, the final prospectus, and in any free writing prospectus (discussed below). The auditors are liable for any material misrepresentation or omission in the financial statements. Liability may attach to other parties involved in the IPO process, such as law firms, based on their legal opinions rendered in connection with the IPO.

The company is strictly liable for any material misrepresentation or omission, regardless of the degree of care that was used in preparing the prospectus. A director or an underwriter may avoid liability by establishing that he, she, or it exercised due diligence; that is, that, after undertaking a reasonable investigation, such person reasonably believed the statement at issue to be accurate. This *due diligence defense* is technically available to officers as well, but it is much more difficult for officers to demonstrate that they would not have been aware of the inaccuracy or omission if they had exercised due diligence. Underwriters, directors, and officers are often named as defendants in Section 11 and Section 12 lawsuits, and even a successful defense is expensive, time-consuming, and unpleasant. Willful misrepresentations or omissions can also result in criminal prosecution, fines, and imprisonment.

Confidential Treatment of Material Agreements

Generally, all of the company's material contracts must be filed as exhibits to the registration statement. These filings are public documents, and copies can be obtained by anyone, usually over the Internet. However, when documents contain information that could harm the company's legitimate business interests if disclosed (or the interests of relevant third parties), the company can seek to protect the information from public disclosure. In response to a narrowly framed request, the SEC may grant confidential treatment, for a limited number of years, of select portions of the agreements, such as royalty rates, payment amounts, volume discount rates, proprietary technical data or chemical compounds, and fields of research. A copy of the exhibit with the confidential portions carefully redacted (excised) will then be available to the public. Requests for confidential treatment must be cleared with the SEC prior to effectiveness of the IPO. Prolonged negotiation with the SEC, or a third party who might be affected by such disclosure, may delay this clearance and thus delay the offering. As a result, it is advisable early in the IPO process for companies to identify contracts that contain information the company desires to redact and to coordinate with the parties to those contracts regarding the specific redactions to be submitted to the SEC for approval.

SEC Staff Comments

When a company pursuing the IPO process finishes a draft of its registration statement, it submits the registration statement to the SEC for comments. The draft will be substantially complete, but the final IPO price and certain other terms of the offering are omitted and replaced with placeholders because they are yet to be determined. This draft with the omitted information is called a *preliminary prospectus*.

The SEC usually provides comments to a registration statement within approximately 27 days after receipt of the initial confidential submission or public filing; during extremely busy periods, however, the comments may be delayed. The company responds to the SEC's staff comments by publicly filing its registration statement with the SEC for the first time or by confidentially submitting another registration statement, along with a corresponding response letter addressing each of the SEC's comments, often within a week or two after receiving the comments (or sometimes sooner if the company is pursuing an aggressive time line and depending on the complexity of the comments). That submission is typically reviewed by the SEC examiner within two weeks after receipt. In addition, the SEC's staff often sends the company additional comments in a subsequent comment letter. These comments are typically focused on a narrower set of issues or concerns than those expressed in the initial comment letter. The company then responds to the additional comments, sometimes within several days (once again, depending on how aggressive the time line is and the complexity of the comments). The additional information supplied by the company in amendments to its original registration statement are called *pre-effective amendments* because the registration statement has not yet been declared effective by the SEC. In most IPOs, the issuer publicly files multiple registration statements (or pre-effective amendments related thereto) or files multiple confidential submissions to respond to SEC comments, particularly when the initial comments are numerous or broad in nature. Once the SEC has no additional comments, the SEC examiner will indicate that the SEC will accept an acceleration request from the company and the book-running manager or managers to declare the registration statement effective. While the company is publicly filing or confidentially submitting its registration statements (or pre-effective amendments thereto), the underwriters and the company, with input from their respective counsel, are finishing preparation of the road show, and EGCs are often engaging in TTW communications to determine interest in the offering. The underwriters will generally not actually commence the road show until the SEC review process is complete or very near completion. Moreover, EGCs are required to wait at least 15 days from the date that the registration statement is initially filed publicly with the SEC before starting their road show.

Listing on Stock Exchanges, 1934 Act Registration, and Compliance with Blue Sky Laws

Each stock exchange has its own listing requirements, which must be satisfied for a company to be listed on that exchange. Underwriters typically recommend that companies apply to list their shares for trading on an exchange, such as the Nasdaq Global Market (*Nasdaq-GM*) (formerly the Nasdaq National Market), concurrently with the public offering. When stock is traded on the Nasdaq-GM, brokers and traders are able to obtain real-time trading information. Listing on the Nasdaq-GM is generally viewed as preferable to listing on the Nasdaq Capital Market (formerly the Nasdaq SmallCap Market) because more information is available for Nasdaq-GM companies and they are followed by more analysts and investors. The standards for being listed on the Nasdaq-GM are generally more stringent than those for the Nasdaq Capital Market, and they include financial as well as corporate governance requirements. Early-stage companies may have difficulty meeting the Nasdaq-GM listing requirements. A special appeal process is available to permit the company to present additional facts to support its application. Alternatively, if the company satisfies the listing requirements of the NYSE, or the different requirements of the NYSE MKT LLC (formerly known as the American Stock Exchange), the company may apply and be approved for listing there.

To list its stock on the Nasdaq-GM, the company must file an application and satisfy specified criteria. It is important to begin the application process as early as possible. As part of its Nasdaq-GM listing application, the company must select a unique trading symbol, which is often four letters. A company should reserve its proposed trading symbol as early as possible in the IPO process to ensure its availability.

Trading on the Nasdaq-GM or another securities exchange requires the company to register the class of securities being listed under the Securities Exchange Act of 1934, as amended (the *1934 Act*), which subjects the company and its officers and directors to certain additional securities law requirements. (We summarize a number of the requirements imposed by the 1934 Act, including periodic public reporting, in Section 17.11 below.) Company counsel usually files to register the company under the 1934 Act at about the time the preliminary prospectus is filed. Registration under the 1934 Act takes effect simultaneously with the effectiveness of the registration statement for the offering, which occurs just prior to the pricing of the offering and the commencement of trading.

The company must also comply with the securities or blue sky laws of each state in which shares are offered or sold except to the extent that such state laws are preempted by federal law. Blue sky qualification is usually handled by underwriters' counsel. The fees and expenses incurred in this process are typically paid by the company, sometimes subject to a cap on applicable attorneys' fees. Federal preemption enables a company that is listed for trading on the Nasdaq-GM or certain other exchanges to avoid time-consuming merit review by state regulators (whereby regulators evaluate the fairness of the terms of the offering) and eliminates the need for any preoffering state filings.

FINRA Review Process

FINRA reviews IPOs to ensure that the underwriting terms and arrangements are not unfair or unreasonable and that there are no underwriter conflicts of interest. FINRA will review the underwriting discount to be received by the underwriters as well as other items of value received by the underwriters within the 180 days preceding the date of the initial confidential submission or public filing of the registration statement through 90 days following the effectiveness of the registration statement or commencement of trading and may require companies to place limits or caps on such compensation. If an underwriter has a conflict of interest in connection with an IPO—for example, where 5% or more of the proceeds of the IPO will be used to repay a credit facility for which the underwriter is the lender—FINRA may require that a qualified independent underwriter (*QIU*) participate in the offering. FINRA may also require that companies disclose certain information regarding underwriting compensation and other material underwriter relationships in the prospectus.

Underwriters' counsel must make filings with FINRA within one business day after each SEC filing or confidential submission. These filings disclose documents and information relating to the IPO's underwriting arrangements, including copies of the registration statement and all amendments, the underwriting agreement, and any engagement letters. Underwriters' counsel will typically send questionnaires as early as possible in the IPO process to the company, its officers, directors and certain significant shareholders, as well as to all of the underwriters, to assist in determining which FINRA rules are applicable and to gather information to make the required FINRA filings. (The questionnaires themselves are not submitted to FINRA.)

FINRA must provide its clearance by issuing a *no-objections letter*, and notify the SEC of this, before the SEC will declare the registration statement effective and the company may sell its securities to investors, even if the company has otherwise cleared comments with the SEC. As it can be a gating item, FINRA issues should be identified and potential QIUs appointed upfront to avoid unnecessary offering delays.

The Road Show

The road show generally commences immediately or shortly after the preliminary prospectus is printed and filed with the SEC. The *road show* consists of a series of meetings with potential investors in major cities throughout the United States (and sometimes Europe and Asia) during a one and a half- to two-week period. During this series of informational meetings, company management makes presentations about the company, its business, and its strategy. The meetings are set up for large audiences and are often followed by one-on-one meetings with certain potential investors. Increasingly, media pieces, such as a short video demonstrating how a company's product works, are being integrated into the road show activities. The material presented in the road show should be consistent with, and generally should not include, any arguably material nonpublic information that is not contained in the prospectus, and no written materials other than the preliminary prospectus should be distributed to the potential investors. The company typically posts the road show materials on the Internet as well. Issuers doing electronic road shows must file the road show presentation with the SEC or make it electronically available to the public over the Internet on their company's website or a road show compilation site such as www.retailroadshow.com. An issuer and the underwriters have potential liability for statements made in the preliminary prospectus distributed on the road show as well as for information in any free writing prospectus provided to potential investors. A *free writing prospectus* is a written (including electronic) communication that constitutes an offer of securities but does not meet the statutory requirements for a prospectus; a free writing prospectus is not considered part of the registration statement. In an IPO, written sales literature and other free writing prospectuses can be used only if preceded by a preliminary prospectus, and they generally must be filed with the SEC when they are first used. As a result, it is important for the company and the underwriters to carefully review not only the registration statement and final prospectus but also the preliminary prospectus, the road show materials, and any potential free writing prospectuses.

Testing-the-Waters Communications

The JOBS Act permits EGCs to engage in oral and written TTW communications with large institutional investors to solicit preliminary indications of interest at any time before or after confidentially submitting or publicly filing a registration statement and prior to the launch of the road show. The SEC typically asks to see copies of the TTW materials used in such meetings, even if they are not distributed. As with road show presentations, these materials should generally only include information that is in or derivable from the registration statement. As noted above, companies typically wait until they have at least initially submitted the registration statement prior to commencing TTW communications, in part to ensure consistency in the company's "story" presented at TTW meetings with the information to be included in the final prospectus. The more complex the company's story, the more important are the TTW meetings. For example, TTW meetings are nearly universal for life sciences companies whose stories are largely dependent upon complex science and intellectual property rights.

Postfiling Publicity

After the registration statement is filed but before it is declared effective by the SEC, the company is in the *registration period*, or *waiting period*, during which the company may offer its securities for sale but may not actually sell them. The offer of securities must be made by means of the preliminary prospectus or through oral communications. Therefore, great caution must be taken during this time to avoid engaging in written communications that could be deemed "offers" to potential investors other than permitted TTW communications by EGCs. Near the end of this period, the company and the underwriters will conduct the road show. Antifraud provisions of the securities laws still apply, and selective disclosure of material not included in the prospectus is problematic.

Industry conferences are typically extremely important opportunities for the company to meet the investment community. These conferences are often planned long in advance, and invitations to present at them are often intensely coveted. Companies should carefully discuss participation in these conferences with counsel and the underwriters during the registration or waiting period. In certain

From the **TRENCHES**

In June 2011, the cofounder and executive chair of Groupon told *Bloomberg* in an interview that Groupon would be "wildly profitable." The company subsequently filed an amendment to its registration statement disclaiming the statement and asserting that investors should not consider it in making an investment decision. In August 2011, Groupon's cofounder sent an email to employees rebutting criticisms against Groupon, which was leaked to the press. The company was required to amend the registration statement to include a copy of the email as well as add a risk factor advising investors not to consider the email in isolation.

Sources: Groupon, Inc., SEC Comment Letter re Registration Statement on Form S-1, pt. 4 (June 29, 2011); *Can Sending an Internal Email Become a Gun-Jumping Nightmare?*, BLANK ROME LLP (Sept. 28, 2011), http://www.lexology.com/library/detail.aspx?g=3f3ebf04-6ee0-45a1-a343-ccc82213c0bb.

cases, a company may go forward with previously arranged conference presentations subject to certain conditions being met (e.g., the preliminary prospectus is available at the conference, and no other written or electronic materials are given out because they would be considered offering materials not included in the prospectus; the presentation is consistent with the road show presentation; and the company does not participate in one-on-one or breakout sessions). In other cases, a company may be advised to not participate in these conferences to avoid potential issues with the IPO.

Posteffective Period

The 25-day period after effectiveness of the registration statement is called the *posteffective period*. During this period, sales of the securities can begin, and the final prospectus is delivered. Distribution of other written literature is permitted, provided that it is accompanied or preceded by a prospectus. It is also traditional for the underwriters to run a "tombstone advertisement" (typically an ad surrounded by a black box border consisting of plain black text on a white background with no graphics other than perhaps the company's logo) in the financial press to announce the commencement of the sale of the securities. This tombstone advertisement is governed by both regulation and custom.

Even though the offering may be complete from the company's perspective once the closing has occurred, dealers are still required to deliver a prospectus during the 25-day posteffective period. If material developments do occur during this period, it may be necessary to supplement, or sticker, the prospectus to reflect the new developments or, in some cases, to file a posteffective amendment with the SEC. As a result, issuers are encouraged to remain generally cautious with respect to non-ordinary course publicity matters until the expiration of the 25-day posteffective period.

Delayed or Terminated Offerings

Frequently, the IPO process is delayed or terminated. An IPO may be delayed for various reasons, including a temporary downturn in the stock markets or the IPO climate; the need to incorporate another quarter's financial results into the prospectus; material developments, such as an acquisition, that must be completed and incorporated into the prospectus to permit adequate disclosure; regulatory problems in the case of highly regulated industries, such as medical devices and biotechnology; a need for liquidity that requires a company to complete a concurrent private placement during the IPO process; a significant change in company management; or the inability of the bankers to generate sufficient interest in the company's stock during the road show to adequately fill the book and ensure that the offering will be sold. In many cases, a company will leave its registration statement in confidential submission or on file, wait or take action as required to be in a position to continue the offering, and then go forward. Offerings are most frequently delayed (1) before responding to SEC comments and confidentially submitting or publicly filing an amendment to the registration statement; (2) before printing the preliminary prospectus; and (3) in the case of an undersubscribed offering, at or near the completion of the road show. If the company and its bankers decide to terminate the IPO process, then the company asks the SEC to withdraw its registration statement and continues corporate life as a private company.

Determination of Stock Price and Offering Size

At the end of the road show, the managing underwriters advise the *pricing committee* of the company's board of directors of the number of shares and the price at which the underwriters are willing to purchase the IPO shares. The number of shares and the price generally depend on market conditions and demand for the issuer's stock. When demand is soft, the size of the IPO may be reduced and the price per share may be lower than the range described in the preliminary prospectus. If this is the case, the issuer generally will be required to file additional pre-effective amendments lowering the price range before the SEC will declare the registration statement effective. When there has been volatility in the capital markets or a relatively soft IPO market, pricing IPOs within the price range in the preliminary prospectus has been more difficult, making additional pre-effective amendments more common. In addition, challenging market conditions have prompted a number of issuers' insiders to purchase shares in the IPO to support the offering.

Although underwriters often prefer the company's offering price to be more than $10 and less than $20 per share (a price that is often backed into by means of a stock split that is effectuated shortly before the printing of the preliminary prospectus, as discussed below in "Putting It into Practice"), the offering price and the size of the offering vary and will ultimately be determined by the demand for the company's stock in the IPO, as well as negotiations between the company and its underwriters. The preliminary valuation is reflected in a *price range* set forth on the cover of the preliminary prospectus, such as "$14–$16 per share," for example.

The valuation of the company takes into account numerous factors, including market conditions, the performance of comparable companies in the industry, past and projected financial performance, product and technology position, the management team, the potential for growth, and new products in development. As noted above, the book-running manager or managers will have proposed a preliminary valuation of the company at the outset of the IPO process. Additional due diligence by the underwriters' financial analysts and revisions to the company's financial models will take place before the registration statement is publicly filed and before the preliminary prospectus is printed. Moreover, because an IPO takes at least several months, continued developments in the company's business and financial results from new fiscal periods, as well as other developments and events, can also significantly impact valuation. This may result in a valuation in the preliminary prospectus that is materially different from the initially proposed valuation.

The final offering price is usually set after the SEC review process is completed (i.e., the SEC has declared the registration statement effective) and just before the company and the underwriters sign the underwriting agreement. The final price is based on the market and the reaction to the offering, as reflected in potential investors' nonbinding indications to the underwriters of intent to purchase shares (commonly referred to as the *underwriters' book*). Typically, underwriters like a book to be several times the offering size so that the offering is "oversubscribed." Many underwriters try to price the shares below the price at which they predict the stock will trade in secondary trading after the initial sale by the underwriters (the *target price*) to give the stock room to move up in the aftermarket. This *IPO discount* varies, and increased volatility of and other challenges related to the stock market have sometimes resulted in an offering price far below the value the underwriters expect the aftermarket to put on the stock.

The size of the offering is based on various factors, including the company's capital needs, dilution to existing shareholders, the level of *public float* (the value of the shares held by investors other than officers, directors, and 10% shareholders) needed to achieve an active trading market and to provide liquidity for existing shareholders, market receptivity, and the proposed price per share. Factors such as a challenging market environment often result in the need for existing investors to purchase a substantial portion of the IPO shares to support the deal. Moreover, the underwriters are typically granted an option to purchase additional shares at the IPO price, called the *greenshoe*. This option typically gives the underwriters the right to purchase an amount of additional shares equal to 15% of the amount originally offered within 30 days after the offering commences.

If the underwriters want to sell more shares than the company is willing to sell or if the underwriters otherwise believe that the offering will support the sale by insiders and other existing shareholders, the underwriters may invite certain shareholders of the company to offer a portion of their shares for resale as part of

From the **TRENCHES**

The relationship between the IPO price and subsequent trading prices is anything but predictable. Amgen, one of the most successful biotechnology companies in history, remained at (and even below) its IPO price for several years before going on to give investors extraordinary returns. In the Google IPO completed in August 2004, the price range was reduced several days before pricing from between $108 and $135 per share to between $85 and $95 per share; the deal ultimately priced at $85 per share. The Google shares traded up approximately 18% on the first day of trading, climbed to close to $200 per share by the end of 2004, and traded above $750 per share in 2016. VA Linux Systems, Inc., a maker of computer products based on the Linux operating system, broke an IPO record in 1999 when its IPO shares, which were priced at $30 per share, climbed as high as $320 on its first day and closed the day at $239.25. Two years later, the VA Linux stock traded at less than $1 per share.

the IPO. In addition, certain shareholders may have registration rights entitling them to sell shares in the offering pursuant to agreements entered into with the company at the time of their initial investment. (Registration rights were discussed in more detail in Chapter 13.) These registration rights usually either are waived or do not apply to an IPO or can be limited if the underwriters do not want to include selling shareholders because they believe that an offering limited to company shares is optimal or that management or significant investors may be perceived as bailing out if they make substantial sales. The inclusion of selling shareholders in an IPO has become less common in recent years, although there are notable exceptions—the selling shareholders sold more than $450 million of Google shares in its IPO, and only selling shareholders (including the U.S. Treasury) sold shares in the General Motors IPO.

Pricing, Commencement of Trading, and Directed Shares

After the SEC review process is completed, the company and its underwriters will each request that the SEC declare the registration statement effective by submitting a request for acceleration. The underwriters and the company's board of directors (or more typically, a subcommittee of the board acting as a pricing committee) then negotiate the final price, usually after the stock market has closed on the day before the offering is to commence. This actual price may or may not be within the price range set out on the cover page of the preliminary prospectus. The company may reject the price proposed by the underwriters and elect not to proceed with the offering, although this rarely happens. What does happen with some frequency, particularly in challenging IPO markets, is that the price per share is lower than the price range on the cover of the preliminary prospectus. If this is the case, the issuer may be required to file additional pre-effective amendments before the SEC will declare the registration statement effective. If the price reduction materially changes the disclosure in the preliminary prospectus, the SEC may delay the offering and require the company to recirculate a new preliminary prospectus with the reduced price and other related changes in the disclosure. (*Recirculation* involves circulating the revised version of the preliminary prospectus to all persons who received a copy of the earlier version; it is often called for if material changes are made to the preliminary prospectus.) On the flip side, a very well received IPO may result in a price per share that is higher than the price range on the cover of the preliminary prospectus and/or an increase in the number of shares offered. Depending on the circumstances, this is accomplished by either a pre-effective amendment to the registration statement, a short form 462(b) registration statement generally allowing for a 20% upsize of the previously registered offering without the need for new SEC review, a free writing prospectus or verbal conveyance by the underwriters of the upsized offering to investors prior to confirming their orders. Once the registration statement has been declared effective, the deal is priced, and the underwriting agreement between the company and the underwriters is signed, trading in the stock will commence, usually on the Nasdaq-GM, NYSE or other exchange, depending on where the stock is listed. Trading typically commences the morning after the pricing.

Sometimes a portion of the shares to be sold is set aside by the underwriters and sold to purchasers specifically identified by the company. These shares are called *friends and family shares*, or *directed shares*. These transactions occur at the same time as the sales through the underwriting syndicate. Making directed shares available can be an effective way to permit persons and entities with which the company or its management has a relationship to participate in the offering and be part of the excitement. In large part due to the complexity of running these programs and the less common extreme jump in the price at which stocks first trade after being priced in an IPO, in recent years, directed share programs have become less frequent.

If a company promises directed shares to customers or sells stock or issues warrants to customers shortly before an IPO at a price substantially below the IPO price, the SEC staff may become concerned that the company's reported revenues from those customers are overstated. The staff may require explicit disclosure of the sales to customers and, in extreme cases, may require the company to write down its revenues to reflect the portion of the amount paid that is attributable to the cheap stock. The SEC may also take the position that the company is gun jumping, that is, inappropriately conditioning the market prior to an IPO by making offers to prospective purchasers without delivering a valid preliminary prospectus, which may lead to potential delays in the offering.

The Closing

The offering is not *closed* (consummated) until the stock is transferred and the related funds are received. The closing usually takes place on the third business day after trading has commenced. This is often referred to as closing in "T+3." For offerings that price after the close of markets (which is normally the case), this means the closing typically takes place on the fourth business day after pricing.

17.8   RESTRICTIONS ON RESALES OF SHARES AFTER AN IPO

After an IPO, the sale of shares by employees and other shareholders may be restricted under lockup agreements or by the securities laws or both. We discuss the 1934 Act's ban on insider trading, which applies to sales and purchases of both registered securities and securities exempt from registration, in Section

17.9, and the ban on short-swing trading of securities of a company registered under the 1934 Act (a sale and purchase or a purchase then sale within a six-month period by an officer, director, or shareholder owning more than 10% of the issuer's stock) in Section 17.10.

Lockup Agreements

In the days and weeks after an IPO, everyone involved in the deal wants the company's stock price to be well-supported so that it rises, or at the very least does not fall. The possibility of having additional shares of the company's stock come onto the market after the IPO creates a very significant risk for the underwriters, the company, and the investors. Referred to as the *overhang*, an excess supply of shares in the marketplace can substantially depress stock prices. The sale of shares by insiders may also be perceived negatively by investors and the market and substantially depress stock prices. Therefore, as a condition to the offering, underwriters typically require all of the company's officers and directors and substantially all other shareholders, including all employees of the company, to sign *lockup agreements* restricting their ability to sell any of their shares for a specified period of time (subject to certain exceptions), generally 180 days from the effective date of the IPO. Investors usually agree in advance to sign such a lockup at the time of their initial investment. Most underwriters believe that unless the company secures lockups for at least approximately 95% of the shares (and often with *no* significant holders remaining outstanding), an IPO could be jeopardized. Because of the risk, the underwriters are typically reluctant to initially publicly file the registration statement, let alone market an IPO, until sufficient lockup agreements have been obtained. In light of the initial confidential review process for EGCs, and to protect the confidentiality of the deal, underwriters sometimes agree with EGCs to obtain lockups only from directors, officers, their affiliates, and major shareholders prior to the initial confidential submission, with lockups for the remainder of the shareholders to be obtained immediately following the initial public filing of the registration statement.

Regulatory Restrictions on the Resale of Unregistered Stock and Stock Owned by Affiliates

Neither common stock issued to founders, employees, or others prior to an IPO in an offering not involving the public (*restricted stock*) nor common stock issued when preferred stock is converted to common stock may be resold in the open market unless either the shares to be resold are registered under the 1933 Act or there is an applicable exemption from registration. In addition, *affiliates* of the issuer (i.e., officers, directors, or certain significant shareholders) are restricted in their ability to resell even shares that were initially issued in a registered offering. Restrictions on resale are designed in part to prevent promoters and others who control an issuer from evading the securities registration requirements by issuing stock to themselves then distributing it to the public without adequate disclosure. They are also designed to prevent persons who buy certain unregistered shares from promptly reselling them without bearing the risk of that investment or providing adequate disclosure to the purchasers.

The nature of the restrictions on resale generally vary depending on (1) whether the seller is an employee who received the stock pursuant to an employee compensation plan; (2) how long the shareholder has owned the shares to be sold; (3) whether the seller is, or has been within the preceding three months, an affiliate of the issuer; and (4) whether the company is registered under the 1934 Act and has filed all required periodic reports on a timely basis. Although venture capitalists will, as discussed in Chapter 13, normally have registration rights, most resales are made pursuant to exemptions from registration (under Rule 701 or Rule 144 under the 1933 Act) or, in the case of shares issued post-IPO to employees, in offerings registered by the company on SEC Form S-1 or Form S-8.

Resales of Employee Shares Under Rule 701　Subject to any lockup agreements, employees who are not affiliates of the issuer may generally rely on the Rule 701 exemption to resell shares that were issued to them prior to the IPO under written compensatory plans as long as 90 days have elapsed since the IPO. Employee shares held by affiliates may also be sold 90 days after the IPO pursuant to Rule 701, subject to the volume limitations in Rule 144 described below.

Registration of Post-IPO Issuances Pursuant to Employee Plans and Resales of Such Shares After the IPO, stock issued pursuant to employee plans is generally registered with the SEC on Form S-8. As a result, such shares are unrestricted and freely tradable.

Rule 144 Exemptions for Resales of Restricted Stock Both affiliates and nonaffiliates must generally sell restricted stock that was not issued under employee plans or for compensatory purposes only in compliance with Rule 144 under the 1933 Act. Rule 144 generally requires that the securities be held for at least six months (the required *holding period*) after purchase and be sold in limited quantities (*dribbled out*) through brokers or market makers (the *manner-of-sale restrictions*). *Rule 144's volume limitations* restrict the amount that may be sold in a three-month period to the greater of 1% of the outstanding shares and the average weekly trading volume in the preceding four weeks. A *Form 144 notice* must be filed with the SEC when the order to sell is placed, and these filings are publicly available. If, however, the selling shareholder is (1) not an affiliate (and has not been one within the three months preceding the date of sale) and (2) has held the restricted stock to be resold for more than one year, then that person may sell his or her shares under Rule 144 without complying with the manner-of-sale or volume restrictions or the Form 144 filing requirement as long as the company is current in filing the periodic reports required by the 1934 Act.

Rule 144 and Rule 701 Exemptions for Resales by Affiliates Sales by affiliates must generally meet all the requirements of Rule 144 even if the affiliate is selling stock acquired on the open market that was previously registered or was initially issued in an offering to the public. If, however, the affiliate is selling previously registered shares, stock initially offered to the public or stock acquired pursuant to an employee plan that has been registered on a Form S-8 registration statement, then the affiliate is not required to meet Rule 144's holding period requirement. In addition, as noted above, an affiliate-employee selling stock acquired pursuant to an employee compensation plan may rely on Rule 701 and resell 90 days after the IPO (subject to any lockup) as long as the seller complies with Rule 144's volume limitations.

17.9 BAN ON INSIDER TRADING

The 1934 Act and SEC Rule 10b5-1 prohibit *insider trading*, defined as the purchase or sale of any security (registered or exempt from registration) on the basis of material nonpublic information about that security or the issuer in breach of a duty of trust or confidence owed (1) the issuer of that security or its shareholders or (2) the source of the information.[3] Failure to comply with the laws against insider trading may subject the individual (and perhaps the company as well) to both civil and criminal liability, including penalties of three times the profit or avoided loss on a transaction, fines of up to $1 million (up to $2.5 million for entities), and prison sentences. In addition, if the SEC can prove that an individual willfully violated insider trading laws, the violator can be imprisoned for up to 20 years in addition to paying fines of up to $5 million ($25 million for companies or partnerships). The determination that an act is "willful" does not turn on the violator's knowledge of the law; rather it turns on the violator's awareness that the insider was either engaging in a wrongful act or enriching himself or herself to the detriment of another. During the period from mid-2013 through mid-2016, the SEC charged more than 230 individuals with insider trading. Regulators use very sophisticated tracking devices and databases, including social media, to identify potential violators.

Traditional Theory of Insider Trading

Directors, officers, employees, accountants, attorneys, and consultants are considered *insiders* of the company they serve because they have a fiduciary duty to that company and its shareholders. *Temporary insiders* include investment bankers and rating agencies. Under the *traditional theory of insider trading*, insiders and temporary insiders in possession of material nonpublic information about the issuer must either disclose it before trading in that company's securities (which is often not feasible for a variety of reasons) or refrain from trading. Thus, the legal prohibition on insider trading severely limits when insiders and temporary insiders may legally sell or purchase company stock without risk.

Even the sales or purchases of small amounts of stock by insiders and temporary insiders may lead to significant scrutiny by public investors and regulatory bodies, such as the SEC and FINRA. For example, an attorney was indicted for trading in the securities of his client at a time when he had nonpublic information about a pending merger. The resulting $14,000 profit could not have been worth the subsequent pain. He resigned from his firm and reportedly pled guilty to one count of insider trading, a felony charge with a maximum 10-year prison term.

Tipping   Insiders and temporary insiders are also prohibited from disclosing material inside information to others who might use the information to their advantage when trading in the company's securities (*tipping*). Both the person who discloses the information (the *tipper*) and the person who receives it (the *tippee*) may be liable. In fact, the tipper may be held liable for the profits or losses avoided by the tippee even if the tipper does not share in the profits or losses avoided.[4] Insiders and temporary insiders should therefore be extremely cautious with respect to any circumstance that might, particularly with the benefit of hindsight, create the appearance of insider trading or any other impropriety.

Often, testimony concerning what the insiders or tippees thought or knew, or later claimed they thought or knew, may not provide a successful defense when, in hindsight, their personal securities transactions created the impression that they were in fact taking advantage of undisclosed information about the issuer to the detriment of the shareholder on the other side of the trade.

For example, assume that a director, who is also a partner in a venture capital firm, knows that the company has won a significant unannounced contract. The director-partner does not communicate this information to anyone, but another partner in the venture capital firm, based entirely on public information, purchases securities of that company. Shortly thereafter, the company's securities increase substantially in value. Because it would be possible for an objective fact finder to conclude, based on appearances, that the director-partner had tipped the non-director-partner, the partners and the firm could have significant exposure to litigation and potential liability for insider trading, even though they have not in fact violated the law. Accordingly, persons with special relationships with insiders of a company (including family members) are well advised to check with the insider before trading in the company's stock to make certain that the insider is not in possession of material nonpublic information about the company.

Company Liability for Insider Trading by Employees

Under certain circumstances, an employer can be liable for insider trading violations by its employees. The Insider Trading and Securities Fraud Enforcement Act of 1988 (*ITSFEA*) provides that any controlling person who knew or recklessly disregarded the fact that a controlled person was likely to engage in acts constituting an insider trading violation and failed to take appropriate steps to prevent such acts before they occurred may independently be liable for a civil penalty of up to the greater of $1 million or treble (triple) the controlled person's profits or avoided losses resulting from the violation. This penalty provision theoretically would permit a court to assess a company a penalty of $1 million even if the insider trading by the employee involved only a few thousand dollars.

Adopting a written policy prohibiting insider trading can reduce the company's exposure for controlling-person liability. A well-drafted policy educates employees on the law of insider trading and establishes internal procedures to safeguard against both intentional and unintentional illegal trading. In the event that an employee does violate the law, the policy and related procedures reduce the risk that the company itself will be liable under the ITSFEA.

Most companies go beyond a simple insider trading policy applicable to all employees and adopt an additional policy limiting the times when directors, officers, and principal shareholders can sell or purchase stock. These so-called *window-period policies* typically prohibit the person from trading in the company's stock during a specific period, such as a period commencing two to four weeks before the end of a quarter (depending on the type of company and industry sector) and extending until 48 to 72 hours after the company has released its earnings report for that quarter (which usually occurs three or four weeks after the quarter has ended). The company usually retains the right to close the trading window early or not open it at all if there is undisclosed information that would make trades by insiders inappropriate. The company can provide an exception to this policy, as well as to its insider trading policy, for trades properly conducted under Rule 10b5-l plans discussed below. Many companies also adopt a *pre-clearance policy* that requires officers and directors to clear any proposed transaction with the company, in part so that the proper insider reports (discussed below) can be timely filed.

The purpose of these policies is to protect the company from being sued because an officer or director traded stock at a time when the insider might have known how the quarter was going to turn out and the market did not. Defending such lawsuits takes management time and company resources, and the suits can bring ill repute to the company. In addition, the fact that insiders are trading can require the company to disclose pending developments (such as sensitive merger negotiations, major mineral finds, or clinical trial results) that the company might otherwise legally be entitled to keep quiet. Furthermore, if insiders sell substantial amounts of stock shortly before the company announces disappointing earnings, unhappy shareholders, who acquired stock prior to the announcement of the bad news and the ensuing drop in the stock price, will often sue the company for securities fraud and cite the insiders' sales as evidence that the insiders intentionally misled the market so they could sell their stock at an artificially high price. A window-period policy lessens the possibility of such lawsuits and makes it easier to get them dismissed.

Insider Trading Safe Harbor for Preexisting Arrangements or Blind Trusts

Rule 10b5-l, promulgated by the SEC under the 1934 Act, provides that a trade will be deemed to be made on the basis of material nonpublic information if the person making the trade was aware of the information at the time of the trade unless the insider has taken specific measures to come within the safe harbor set forth in Rule 10b5-l(c). There are two ways to make trades under the safe harbor. First, an individual may, at a time when he or she has no material nonpublic information, adopt a *Rule 10b5-1 plan* that expressly authorizes trades in the future by (1) entering into a binding contract to make the trades, (2) instructing another to make the trades on his or her behalf, or (3) adopting a written plan for making trades. (Although the first two methods can be oral, written documentation is important to help validate when and under what terms the contract was entered into or the instructions given.) The contract, instruction, or plan must be specific as to the amount of shares and the price and trading date, or it must include a formula or other specific manner of determining the amount, price, and trading date. An insider using this method must not engage in hedging or any other activity designed to mitigate the risk of the trades; the insider must also be acting in good faith and not pursuant to a plan or scheme to evade the insider trading restrictions.

Alternatively, an insider may permit another person to make trades at his or her sole discretion. Because the insider does not make the "investment decision," the trade will not be made on the basis of any material nonpublic information the insider might have. This empowerment of another to make trades is often referred to as a *blind trust*. The person actually making the trades on behalf of the insider may not, however, be in possession of any material nonpublic information at the time of the trades. If he or she is, then the person trading would violate the insider trading rules. The insider is also required to implement reasonable policies and procedures to prevent the trader from obtaining such information and to ensure that the trader will not trade if he or she does obtain such information.

Written 10b5-1 plans have become increasingly common in recent years. They can be an effective mechanism for insiders to obtain some liquidity and diversify their company holdings without running afoul of the insider trading laws. Yet, even though utilizing 10b5-1 plans can provide additional protection to insiders, the public still may react adversely to sales by insiders during periods when the stock is not performing well. In addition, trades effected under such plans can still be scrutinized by shareholders or regulators if they believe the insider was in possession of material nonpublic information when the plan was adopted or at any time the plan is amended.

Illegal Trading by Employees Based on Information Belonging to Employer

In addition to the bans on insider trading in the 1934 Act, the mail and wire fraud statutes make it illegal for an employee to trade the securities of any company based on material nonpublic information belonging to the employer. Thus, if an employee of Company A knew that her employer would be announcing a major recall of a key product, it would be illegal for her to buy stock in Company A's main competitor before the recall was publicized.

17.10 LIABILITY FOR SHORT-SWING PROFITS

Section 16(b) of the 1934 Act also affects trading by certain insiders. It provides for the automatic recovery by a company registered under the 1934 Act of any profits made by executive officers, directors, and greater-than-10% shareholders on securities purchased and sold, or sold and purchased, within a six-month period (*short-swing trading*). Section 16(b) is mechanically applied and liability is imposed regardless of the trader's possession of, or intent to use, or actual use of, material nonpublic information. Professional plaintiffs' attorneys monitor the trading reports required to be filed by executive officers, directors, and greater-than-10% shareholders pursuant to Section 16(a) for indications of short-swing trading violations. Thus, even if a company might be tempted to ignore the short-swing trading of its insiders (which itself could constitute a breach of fiduciary duty by the board of directors), insiders who have violated the strictures of Section 16(b) will still be pursued in shareholder derivative suits.

Complex rules exist for the attribution to insiders of purchases and sales by persons and entities related to insiders for the purposes of Section 16(b). In addition, the shares bought or sold within a six-month period need not be the same as the shares sold or bought. For example, a sale by an officer on January 1, 2017, of stock acquired when he founded the company in 2000 could be matched with a purchase by that person's spouse on March 30, 2017, even though the officer had held the shares 17 years before selling them and even if neither spouse knew the other was trading. As a result, all the profit on that trade could be recoverable.

17.11 ONGOING RESPONSIBILITIES OF A PUBLIC COMPANY AND ITS DIRECTORS AND OFFICERS

The realities of being a public company include heightened disclosure obligations to the public and corporate governance requirements to which a private company is not subject. The increased disclosure obligations include the requirements to file current and periodic reports, insider reports, and disclosure requirements related to communications with analysts. The company's new governance obligations include procedures for shareholder votes (including the distribution of proxy statements), responsibilities of directors and officers, and the constitution and charter of certain board committees. We address each of these obligations in turn.

Current and Periodic Reports

Once public, the company will be required to file certain current and periodic reports with the SEC. The company must also comply with the notification and filing requirements of the exchange that lists its shares.

Annual Report on Form 10-K The annual report on Form 10-K (*10-K*) provides a summary and update of information about the company and its management substantially similar to that contained in the company's prospectus. The due dates for filing annual reports on Form 10-K and quarterly reports on Form 10-Q vary depending on the size of the issuer's *public float* (the value of its publicly traded stock).[5] For 10-Ks, they range from 90 days for companies with a public float of less than $75 million (*non-accelerated filers*) to 60 days after the end of the fiscal year for companies with a public float of $700 million or more (*large accelerated filers*). The 10-K includes, among other things, a description of the company's business for the preceding fiscal year; a discussion of risk factors; a description of the company's disclosure controls and procedures as well as its internal controls over financial reporting (once a public company is required to include this disclosure); information regarding management, executive compensation and various corporate governance matters and policies (most of which is generally incorporated by reference to the proxy statement that is filed in preparation for the company's annual meeting of shareholders); audited financial statements; and an MD&A section relating to the periods covered by those financial statements. A newly public company is also required to make disclosures in its periodic reports (on Form 10-K or the quarterly report on Form 10-Q) concerning how the proceeds from its IPO have been used and how much remains.

Section 404 of SOX sets forth the requirements for the description of the company's disclosure controls and procedures and its internal controls over financial reporting. Both management and the outside auditor must provide assessments. Complying with SOX is expensive. A 2016 survey found that the yearly internal costs of complying with SOX (excluding the cost of the external audit) averaged about $1.11 million for public companies, $1.44 million for private companies planning for an IPO, and $1.38 million for private companies.[6] Newly public companies that are not EGCs generally must fully comply with Section 404 by their second annual report.

Quarterly Report on Form 10-Q   The report on Form 10-Q (*10-Q*) is filed with the SEC after the end of each quarter. (The due dates range from 45 days after the end of the quarter for non-accelerated filers to 40 days for large accelerated filers.) The 10-Q includes summary unaudited quarterly financial statements, an MD&A section covering those results, risk factors, and certain other specified disclosures, such as information concerning new developments in legal proceedings, disclosure and internal controls, an update with respect to use of IPO proceeds during the quarter, any stock repurchases during the quarter, and any shareholders' actions taken during the quarter.

Form 8-K   A report on Form 8-K (*8-K*) is intended to supplement the normal annual and quarterly filing requirements when material events occur that should be brought to the prompt attention of the investing public, including any of the following:

➤ Entry into or termination of a material agreement

➤ A merger, a change in control, a sale of significant assets, or other exit or disposition transaction

➤ Bankruptcy

➤ Certain results of operations

➤ Creation of direct financial obligations or obligations under off-balance sheet arrangements

➤ Costs associated with exit or disposal activities or material impairments

➤ Notice of delisting or failure to satisfy listing conditions

➤ Unregistered sales of securities or material modifications to stockholder rights

➤ A change in accountants

➤ Management's conclusion that previously issued financial statements or audit reports or reviews should not be relied upon because of an error

➤ Departure or election of principal officers or directors

➤ Compensatory arrangements of certain officers

➤ Amendments to certificate of incorporation or bylaws or change in the fiscal year

➤ Amendments or waivers to the company's code of ethics

➤ Results of matters submitted to a vote of security holders

➤ Certain other material disclosures.

With certain exceptions, companies must file current reports within four business days following the date of the event giving rise to the reporting obligation.

Safe Harbor for Certain Forward-Looking Statements

Federal legislation makes it easier for companies to protect themselves from litigation concerning certain disclosures made after an IPO by creating a safe harbor for certain oral and written forward-looking statements, such as projections, forecasts, and other statements about future operations, plans, or possible results. For a company to be protected, the statement must disclose that it is forward-looking and that the company's actual results may differ materially. In addition, the company must, in the case of a written statement, provide a detailed discussion of the factors that could result in a discrepancy and, in the case of an oral statement, refer the audience to a readily available written statement that contains such a discussion. Courts have found this safe harbor and companies' properly worded and specifically tailored cautions regarding forward-looking statements to be a defense to various claims of inaccurate or misleading disclosures. Careful crafting of forward-looking statements is critical, however, and should be discussed thoroughly with counsel.

Effects of Current and Periodic Reporting Requirements on the Company

The current and periodic reporting requirements, together with the need to issue press releases and deal with securities analysts and public shareholders, add significant pressure to achieve short-term results at the expense of long-term goals. As a result, they may limit the flexibility of management and the board of directors in making strategic corporate decisions and long-term investments. The company and its directors and officers also face increased potential liability as a result of their fiduciary responsibilities to public shareholders and their disclosure obligations. The current and periodic reporting requirements also bring additional costs to a public company in the form of increased legal, accounting, and printing expenses. The company may also need to hire additional management personnel to handle its expanded reporting and other obligations, as well as to manage the company's public and investor relations strategies.

Insider Reports Concerning Beneficial Ownership of Company Stock

Another disclosure requirement of public companies is attributable not to the company itself but rather to its executive officers and directors. Executive officers and directors of public companies are subject to a number of reporting requirements designed, among other things, to provide the investing public with information regarding their holdings and trading activity in the securities of the companies by which they are employed or on whose boards they serve. Section 16(a) of the 1934 Act, for instance, requires that each executive officer and director of a company involved in an IPO file a Form 3 detailing his or her beneficial ownership of the securities of that company. They typically file Form 3s at the same time the public offering becomes effective. Newly appointed directors and executive officers each must file a Form 3 within 10 days of their election. All executive officers and directors must file a Form 4 within two business days after the day in which a change in their beneficial ownership of their company's stock occurs, including purchases and sales of the company's stock, gifts, and transfers to trusts. A Form 5 must be filed to report certain transactions that should have been reported previously on Form 4 or that were eligible for deferred reporting. The Form 5 is due 45 days after the company's year end. Finally, the company must disclose in its 10-K whether any officer or director failed to file the required reports in a timely manner. It should be noted that, for purposes of these reporting requirements, complex rules exist regarding who is deemed to be the beneficial ownership of securities. Under certain circumstances, securities owned by another person, such as a minor child living with the officer or director, may be attributed to the insider.

The SEC has the power to seek substantial monetary fines from individuals and entities that violate these laws of up to $150,000 ($725,000 for entities) per violation for violations that both involve fraud or reckless disregard of the law and also result in, or create a substantial risk of, substantial losses to others or a substantial gain to the individual involved. In the past, the SEC has taken the position that a new violation occurs each day a filing is late or is not corrected.

Avoiding Selective Disclosure and Violations of Regulation FD: Communications with Analysts, the Press, and Investors

Discussions with market analysts, who write reports following the progress of the company and generally keep the public informed of business developments, are inherently risky. No information given to an analyst or reporter is ever truly off the record. Casual or ill-considered disclosure of material nonpublic information can lead to shareholder lawsuits and SEC investigations for securities fraud and insider trading, as well as a violation of Regulation FD discussed below. Although it is important to maintain good relations with analysts and the press, it is also critical to avoid selective disclosure of material information. *Selective disclosure* is the release of material information to one or more individuals without its simultaneous release to the public generally.

Regulation FD and Corrective Steps   *SEC Regulation FD* (Fair Disclosure) is designed to prevent and regulate selective disclosure and to reinforce a company's obligations to keep the public informed in a fair and evenhanded manner. Regulation FD restricts a company's senior officers, and others who regularly communicate with analysts or investors, from selectively disclosing material nonpublic information to securities market professionals (such as investment advisers or analysts), as well as to shareholders when it is reasonably foreseeable that the shareholders will trade on the basis of such information. If a selective disclosure of material nonpublic information is intentional, the information must simultaneously be broadly disseminated to the general public. If a selective disclosure is unintentional, the company must broadly disseminate the information within the later of 24 hours from the selective disclosure and the commencement of the next day's trading.

As a result, with few exceptions, such as when the recipient agrees to "embargo" and not use the information until it is made public, the senior officials of companies are required to broadly disseminate any material information they discuss with a small group of investors or investment professionals. This broad dissemination can take the form of a press release, a Form 8-K filing, properly noticed conference calls or Internet broadcasts, or any other method that is reasonably designed to provide broad nonexclusive distribution of the information to the public. Although a company has flexibility in determining what is reasonable, it may be liable in a suit by the SEC if (1) it knows, or is reckless in not knowing, that information selectively disclosed is both material and nonpublic; (2) it fails to promptly disseminate the information to the public; or (3) its methods of communication are not reasonably designed to prevent illegal selective disclosure. Individuals responsible for selective disclosure in violation of Regulation FD may also be liable, either as the direct violators or as aiders and abettors. Although only the SEC is empowered to sue for violations of Regulation FD, affected shareholders may sue under Section 10(b) of the 1934 Act if the selective disclosure constitutes illegal tipping by an insider under Rule 10b-5.

The SEC has cautioned that an official who engages in a private discussion with an analyst seeking guidance about earnings estimates "takes on a high degree of risk under Regulation FD."[7] Sometimes the combination of spoken language, tone, emphasis, and demeanor at a private meeting may be enough to constitute the disclosure of material nonpublic information. In most cases, however, it is permissible to provide general background information to analysts and the press or to fill in incremental details regarding a matter that has been disclosed in all material respects. The theory is that a company should be able to selectively disclose bits of information that would in themselves be immaterial to a "reasonable investor" deciding whether to buy, sell, or hold the company's securities even though, when combined with other information gathered from sources outside the company, the recipient of those "bits" could create a "mosaic" of information that becomes material when pieced together.

Strategic Compliance Management In an attempt to avoid selective or premature disclosure problems, many companies observe a consistent no-comment policy with respect to certain material undisclosed corporate developments, such as acquisitions. Being proactive and cooperating with regulators to promptly remedy violations of Regulation FD may reduce the likelihood that regulators will charge the company instead of just the individuals involved. For example, even though the SEC charged the former vice president of investor relations of the energy company First Solar Inc. with violating Regulation FD after he told about 20 analysts and institutional investors in separate phone conversations that the company would not be receiving a certain government loan guarantee before the company disclosed the information to the public, the SEC elected not to charge the company due to its "extraordinary cooperation."[8] The SEC noted that the company (1) had a disclosure committee that focused on compliance with Regulation FD; (2) immediately discovered the selective disclosure and issued a press release the next morning disclosing the loss of the loan guarantee before the stock market opened; and (3) self-reported the selective disclosure to the SEC. The individual did not admit liability but paid a $50,000 fine.[9]

Whenever material developments occur or the company becomes aware of rumors circulating in the marketplace, the company should always consult with counsel to determine whether a press release or other public disclosure is appropriate. If the company becomes aware that there has been a leak of material non-public information, it is prudent for that company to instruct its employees and directors not to trade until the information has been publicly disclosed.

Liability for an Analyst's Report   If an analyst provides an inaccurate projection regarding a company, it is generally considered to be the analyst's assessment and not the company's unless the company confirms the information or otherwise becomes *entangled* in the analyst's report. Companies should always consult carefully with counsel whenever they are tempted to comment on an analyst's report. Disclaimers, warnings, and generalities can reduce the risk if the company decides to comment.

However, any spokesperson talking to analysts must understand that, if he or she comments on projections and forecasts, even if only by confirming or reaffirming prior financial guidance, the company may be held liable if the projections prove incorrect or if the analyst uses the information to engage in trading before the information is released to the public. The comments or any other communication could also be a violation of Regulation FD. Generally, the safest course is for the company not to comment.

Effect of Proxy Rules

In addition to the heightened disclosure obligations discussed above, public companies also face different governance requirements than they did when they were private. For example, the process for conducting a shareholder vote is very different in a public company versus a private company. A company registered under the 1934 Act must comply with the SEC proxy rules when soliciting a shareholder vote or consent. (A *proxy* is a written [or electronic] power of attorney giving another person, often an officer of the company in an uncontested election, the authority to vote the shares owned by the giver of the proxy as directed on the form.) Generally, these rules require public companies to send a proxy statement to each shareholder of record in advance of every shareholders' meeting. The proxy statement must set forth detailed information regarding the company's management, including information regarding related-party transactions and significant detail regarding executive compensation and corporate governance matters, and the matters to be voted on. For example, a proxy statement relating to the election of directors must include a detailed report of the compensation committee (or the full board, if there is no such committee) that summarizes and analyzes executive and director compensation for the year and explains how executive compensation was determined and the relationship between pay and performance. Furthermore, the company must conduct an evaluation of risks associated with the company's compensation structure that could have an adverse effect on the company and disclose any such risks in its proxy statement. It must also include a graph comparing performance of the company's stock against a broad-based index and an industry-group index. A company must also include a detailed summary of various other corporate governance matters and discuss policies and procedures that are in place to address committee structures and responsibilities, board risk oversight, board diversity, ethics and whistle-blower policies, and other governance matters.

Management is also required to include certain shareholder proposals in the proxy statement and put them to a vote of the shareholders. In some cases, such as a shareholder vote on a merger, the company must submit the proxy statement and the form of proxy to the SEC for review and comment prior to submission to the shareholders. Because of the filing and other procedural requirements applicable to proxy solicitations, the company should plan all meetings of shareholders well in advance.

Directors' Responsibilities in a Public Company

Because directors have a fiduciary relationship to both the company and its shareholders, they are bound by the duties of loyalty and care imposed by the law of the state where the company is incorporated. These duties are applicable to directors of all companies, whether public or private, and were discussed in Chapter 6.

Directors' Liability for Securities Claims   Companies and their officers and directors are subject to damage claims for securities fraud under the antifraud rules if their current, quarterly, or annual disclosures to the SEC and the public are inaccurate in any material way. Similarly, the securities laws make it unlawful for any person to solicit proxies in contravention of the rules and regulations of the SEC. In this context, directors may be held liable if they knew, or through the exercise of due diligence should have known, that a proxy solicitation issued on their behalf contained material false or misleading statements or omissions. Beyond required disclosures, it is possible to incur liability for securities fraud in connection with the issuance of misleading press releases, reports to shareholders, speeches, or other communications that could be expected to reach investors and trading markets. In addition, directors and officers are prohibited from purchasing and selling their company's equity based on material nonpublic information (as discussed in Section 17.9) and during company *blackout periods* (whenever insiders have been instructed not to trade) or outside of any designated trading windows. Any profits gained from such transactions are subject to disgorgement.

Indemnification and Liability Insurance for Directors   Under the laws of most states, companies have broad and flexible powers to indemnify directors who are made parties to proceedings and incur liability by reason of their status as directors. Delaware law generally provides broader powers and flexibility to companies to indemnify their directors, officers, employees, and agents than does the law in other states. The case law regarding the interpretation of indemnification provisions is also more extensive in Delaware than in other states. For example, Delaware permits companies to eliminate monetary liability even for gross negligence, whereas California law requires directors to remain liable under certain circumstances for acts or omissions that constitute an unexcused pattern of inattention or reckless disregard of their duties. In addition, companies may acquire directors' and officers' (*D&O*) liability insurance. Most companies secure D&O liability insurance prior to completion of an IPO or consider increasing the company's current coverage while still a private company.

Board Committees in a Public Company

Another governance requirement for public companies relates to the committees of its board of directors. SOX requires public companies to have audit committees comprising only independent members.[10] SOX also effectively requires that the audit committee include a *financial expert* familiar with accounting and auditing principles.[11] The audit committee, which reviews the company's independent auditors and evaluates the company's accounting system and internal controls, plays a critical oversight role in preventing and detecting fraudulent financial reporting. The audit committee is required to submit a report with the company's annual proxy statement detailing its independence and activities. Audit committee members are (1) required to be financially literate, (2) subject to a more stringent definition of independence, and (3) often referred to as having to be "super-independent." Most companies also form a nominating and corporate governance committee comprising independent members to identify and evaluate board candidates and to oversee board committees, shareholder communications, and other corporate governance matters. Companies that are required to comply with complex regulatory schemes, such as biotechnology and diagnostics companies, sometimes also form compliance committees to review and approve various compliance matters.

Both the New York Stock Exchange and Nasdaq require listed companies to establish a compensation committee, which is responsible for overseeing the company's compensation plans and programs; approving compensation decisions and strategies; and evaluating any material risks that could adversely impact the company. Additionally, a committee composed of at least two nonemployee directors generally must administer most of the company's employee stock plans if the company intends to take advantage of the favorable treatment afforded those plans by certain exemptions from liability for short-swing trading under Section 16 of the 1934 Act, discussed earlier in this chapter. The SEC's proxy rules require a report from the compensation committee (or the full board if there is no such committee) in the proxy statement explaining how the compensation of the company's executive officers was set. Public EGCs are exempt from the requirement to include a report from the compensation committee in their proxy statements for five years or until they become a large accelerated filer or otherwise cease to be an EGC.

The NYSE also requires a nominating committee comprising only independent directors to identify and evaluate board candidates. The nominating committee (sometimes called the nominating and corporate governance committee) often oversees board committees, shareholder communications, and other corporate governance matters as well. Nasdaq gives its listed firms the option of either forming a nominating committee or having a majority of the independent directors nominate candidates for director.

 Putting It into **PRACTICE**

Soon after the successful product launch of the GT V-Bracket and related products, Alexei and Piper met with the other Genesist directors to decide whether to proceed with an IPO or to sell the company. They knew that Genesist would need additional funds to accelerate its growth and continue to leapfrog over its competitors. The directors felt that it would be relatively easy to find a buyer for the company, given the enormous interest in the company's 3-D manufacturing technology. In fact, two customers had already made unofficial overtures. But the directors also felt that Genesist had a huge potential for growth that would not be reflected even in the IPO price, much less the price they would be able to command as a pre-public company. They also concluded that the current IPO environment was generally favorable: the choppy IPO window that existed the prior year appeared to be stabilizing and companies in the high-tech manufacturing industry were successfully completing IPOs. In fact, a 3-D printing company that had gone public in the preceding quarter was performing very well in the IPO aftermarket, especially when compared with other available alternatives such as an exit through a

(continued)

merger or acquisition or a private financing. In addition, corporate counsel Sarah Crawford had confirmed that Genesist would qualify as an EGC and could therefore submit its registration statement confidentially and take advantage of reduced SEC disclosure and compliance requirements. In the end, the directors were unwilling to cap the potential upside of an IPO by selling Genesist for cash or by taking stock in a larger company whose stock price would be determined in large part by the performances of businesses other than Genesist's. They were also excited by the challenge of taking Genesist to the next level of growth as an independent company. After due consideration, the board unanimously decided to proceed with an IPO.

Once the board reached this decision, Alexei assembled a team of investment bankers, lawyers, and accountants. The first step in picking an investment banking firm was to update and assemble a corporate profile to present to potential underwriters. This consisted of a business plan, marketing literature, and audited yearly and unaudited quarterly financial statements for the previous two and a half years as permitted by the JOBS Act. Next, with the help of Sarah, Alexei compiled a list of suitable and likely candidates for underwriters. He wanted to consider firms with (1) expertise in and commitment to companies in Genesist's industry; (2) track records of successful IPOs that also performed well in the aftermarket; (3) broad and experienced sales forces with deep ties to the investor community; (4) respected analysts who were likely to support the company by providing research reports to the investment community in the future; (5) histories of providing support and services to companies post-IPO, even when those companies struggled; and (6) no conflicts of interest. The list of potential underwriters included firms that had expressed interest in the company in the past as well as others that were likely to be receptive to the company. Sarah Crawford and other experienced securities counsel at her firm were helpful in providing leads and introductions.

Well in advance of the first organizational meeting, Alexei and Piper met with Sarah and the company's auditors to determine whether there were any corporate housekeeping, corporate governance, or financial cleanup items that could affect the timing or success of the offering. They discussed the composition of Genesist's board of directors and board committees as well as Genesist's stock option practices and the pricing of option grants over the preceding 18 months. Fortunately, Genesist's corporate secretary had kept an accurate record of all stock option grants together with the documentation supporting the determination of fair market value. They had also, upon Sarah's advice, been utilizing a reputable independent valuation firm to perform American Institute of Certified Public Accountants (AICPA) compliant stock

(continued)

valuations in connection with securities issuances and option grants over the past 18 months. The group also discussed the current infrastructure and some additional key hires that the company would need to consider bringing on to prepare for operating as a public company, including additional finance and accounting staff. They also considered adding independent directors with skills and industry experience complementary to that of the existing members of the board to add greater diversity of experience and background and allow the company to satisfy applicable board independence requirements. Sarah suggested that Alexei and Piper reserve a trading symbol as soon as possible. After discussing it with their board, management selected "GENS" as the trading symbol. Sarah's senior associate Aaron Biegert then reserved the symbol with the Nasdaq Global Market.

At the organizational meeting, attended by Alexei and Piper on behalf of Genesist, Sarah and Aaron as company counsel, representatives of the underwriters, underwriters' counsel, and the auditors, the participants aired and thoroughly discussed a wide range of pre-IPO issues. By discussing these issues up front, the group was able to develop a realistic timeline for the IPO.

In addition to disclosure and timing issues, the Genesist working group discussed a number of other important issues at the organizational meeting. These included the size of the offering, the price range, a required stock split, the percentage of shareholders required to sign lockup agreements, reincorporation in Delaware, and the anti-takeover provisions they would likely include in the certificate of incorporation and bylaws. They also considered which JOBS Act provisions to take advantage of as well as other corporate governance matters, including the need for additional independent outside directors. Fortunately, Sue Quinn, Piper's former accounting professor, had agreed to continue to chair the audit committee, satisfying the requirement for a financial expert. The group also addressed a wide variety of due diligence, publicity (including the timing of TTW meetings), and securities law issues. Then, and for the bulk of the day, the various executive officers and key employees of Genesist introduced themselves, and each gave a 30-minute presentation on his or her respective area of responsibility. Alexei and Piper had reviewed the content of the presentations with the officers in advance. At a minimum, they wanted them to include an overview of the business, a review of the intellectual property portfolio, a description of significant corporate partners and strategic relationships, and a review of the company's current financial condition and projections. A highlight was a demonstration of the company's 3-D manufacturing system in action.

After the organizational meeting, underwriters' counsel delivered to Genesist and company counsel a standard but broad due diligence

(continued)

request to get the formal due diligence process under way. The company, with guidance from Sarah, had already set up an electronic data room with its financial printer and had compiled a significant amount of backup material to support various statements it would be making in the registration statement. The underwriters and their counsel also scheduled a number of due diligence calls, including financial, regulatory, intellectual property, and accounting matters as well as pending and threatened litigation. They also set up a call with the audit committee chair, as well as calls with certain key customers and strategic partners of the company.

Company counsel produced the first draft of the registration statement, which the company had decided to submit confidentially, with significant input from Alexei, Piper, and other members of the management team. Alexei and Piper had prepared the first draft of the Business section, making it specific to their business but also including language based on several sample prospectuses Sarah had provided to them. The underwriters also provided input on the content they felt they needed from a marketing perspective. Because all prospectuses have a particular style and tone with which Alexei and Piper were unfamiliar, Sarah substantially revised the Business section to address certain standard points and to put the disclosure into "plain English." Once the first draft was completed and distributed, the working group met for a series of all-hands meetings. The dates for these meetings had been confirmed at the organizational meeting and took place at the offices of Sarah's law firm. Concurrently with these meetings, Sarah finalized the forms of lockup agreements, the FINRA questionnaires, and the director, officer and 5% or greater shareholder questionnaires with the underwriters' counsel. Aaron circulated them for completion and signature by the company's officers, directors, and shareholders. Underwriters' counsel and Sarah also took the lead, with input from their clients, to substantially finalize all major business points in the underwriting agreement that had been produced by underwriters' counsel soon after the organizational meeting. Underwriters' counsel also worked with Sarah, intellectual property counsel, and regulatory counsel to substantially finalize their respective legal opinions.

Once the draft registration statement had progressed sufficiently, a smaller group met at the financial printer's offices to finalize the document and submit it confidentially to the SEC. Alexei had chosen a printer early in the process based on competitive bids and the recommendations of the underwriters and counsel. Given the SEC requirement that all documents, including confidential submissions, be transmitted to the SEC electronically, it was important that Genesist retain an experienced financial printer that could meet the company's tight proposed schedule.

(continued)

At the same time the registration statement was submitted to the SEC, Sarah submitted a request to the SEC for confidential treatment with respect to several of Genesist's key customer, collaboration, and license agreements. Aaron and the company had discussed the required redactions with the applicable counterparties to these agreements ahead of time. By the time the company confidentially submitted the initial registration statement, underwriters' counsel had reviewed all the documents in the e-data room; the company had addressed all due diligence requests and produced backup material; all officers, directors, employees, and 1%-or-greater shareholders (who collectively owned approximately 80% of the outstanding stock) had executed lockup agreements (to preserve the confidentiality of the IPO, the underwriters agreed that the company would obtain the remaining lockups immediately after the initial public filing); and counsel had substantially finalized all major business points in the underwriting agreement and legal opinions.

After the company confidentially submitted the registration statement, Alexei, Piper, and other members of the management team turned their attention to corporate and corporate governance matters that had to be handled prior to the closing of the offering. For example, the company needed to undertake a shareholder mailing to obtain written shareholder consents to adopt new charter documents to take effect immediately prior to the IPO. These included shareholder authorization of reincorporation in Delaware, a stock split, and certain other modifications to the company's charter and shareholder agreements to waive certain rights related to the proposed offering.

The underwriters worked with Alexei and Piper and their team to develop the TTW and road show presentations and schedule. They carefully coordinated with legal counsel to make certain the TTW and road show presentations complied with applicable securities laws. The underwriters told them that they expected that the TTW meetings would commence following the second confidential submission of the registration statement (assuming they could successfully respond to most SEC comments in the first amendment), and that the road show would commence 15 days following the initial public filing of the registration statement. The bankers told Alexei and Piper to expect to spend approximately a week and a half on the road show, making their presentation 20 to 30 times in as many as 15 different U.S. cities. (The road show would have been even longer if trips to Europe or Asia had been included.) In addition to the invitation-only live meetings, they made appropriate arrangements to have the electronic version available to the public on the Internet.

After approximately 27 days, the SEC staff provided comments on the initial registration statement, which had been submitted

(continued)

confidentially. At this point, the working group reassembled at the printer to prepare the first amendment to the registration statement to respond to the comments. The group believed that certain of the SEC's comments were not clear or reflected a misunderstanding on the part of the SEC staff. In those cases, the company explained in a supplemental letter to the SEC why the company believed that the registration statement should not be revised in response to those comments. A number of the comments related to accounting matters, and Alexei obtained from the auditors a realistic estimate of the time they needed to revise any numbers, draft additional disclosures, and prepare any required supplemental response. In addition, the group assembled certain supplemental information that the SEC had requested so that it could determine whether other comments were appropriate.

After confidentially submitting the amended registration statement, Alexei and Piper expected one or more additional sets of comments from the SEC, each of which would probably require another amendment to the registration statement, which the company intended to submit confidentially until almost all the SEC comments were cleared. While waiting for SEC comments, the company and the underwriters held TTW meetings with large institutional investors to gauge interest in the IPO. The company received the next "round" of comments two weeks after confidentially submitting the first amendment, which were very light. The company and the underwriters were then satisfied that they had addressed substantially all of the SEC comments, so the company decided to go ahead and file the registration statement publicly. The initial public filing, which also included new financial statements and relevant information regarding the company's most recently completed quarter, was signed by Alexei as CEO, the CFO as chief accounting officer on behalf of the company, as well as all of the company's directors. It also included an executed consent of the auditors to inclusion of their opinion. The company then waited 15 days to commence the road show, during which time the board met with the underwriters and approved a preliminary price range for the offering and the company obtained executed lockup agreements from nearly all of the remainder of its shareholders. The company also submitted a "cheap stock" letter to the SEC, in which it disclosed the preliminary price range, described its option grants in the preceding 12 months, and articulated the rationale for the discrepancies between the grant date fair values and the preliminary price range. In addition, the company prepared an amendment to the registration statement, which included a preliminary prospectus disclosing the preliminary price range. Alexei and Piper worked with the underwriters and counsel to finalize the road show presentation, and videorecorded the presentation to be posted

(continued)

on the Internet. The company also prepared to file its charter amendment effectuating a stock split and ran the stock split throughout the preliminary prospectus as needed. Shortly before the 15 days were up, the company received a third "round" of comments from the SEC, comprising two straightforward requests for clarifying disclosure that the company was able to incorporate into the preliminary prospectus. After the required 15 days had elapsed, the company filed its amended charter, printed the registration statement amendment containing the preliminary prospectus, and commenced the road show. Alexei and Piper met separately with key industry analysts to introduce themselves and tell Genesist's "story." Although one of the analysts asked for a copy of Genesist's five-year projections, Alexei (after consulting with Sarah) refused to provide them. The SEC confirmed shortly thereafter that the SEC had no further comments to the registration statement, and the underwriters and the company completed the road show. At the end of the road show, FINRA, at the underwriters' request, notified the SEC examiner that it had completed its review and had no objections to the underwriting terms and arrangements for the offering. The company then requested that the SEC declare the registration statement effective. This was done by means of a letter filed electronically with the SEC. As required, the underwriters joined in the request with their own letter.

On the day the offering was declared effective, the underwriters set up a telephonic conference call after the close of the market with company management, the pricing committee of the board (which the board had previously established), and company counsel. The underwriters first congratulated Alexei and Piper and the rest of the Genesist team on a successful road show, and they then proposed the final size of the offering, the offering price, and the underwriters' gross spread (commission). Alexei wanted to try to negotiate the offering price with the underwriters, so he came to the meeting armed with the latest information about Genesist's competitors, particularly recent trends in their stock prices and price-earnings ratios. Two of the underwriters had given Alexei and Piper some indication of their preliminary pricing numbers, and the founders had done their best prior to the call to justify increasing these numbers to a level where they still believed there would be an appropriate jump in the price in the after-market. Because Genesist was considered "hot," they were able to negotiate a slightly higher offering price than first proposed. The company agreed to pay the underwriters a standard 7% gross spread. Once the deal was struck, the underwriting agreement was executed and the auditors delivered their comfort letter that same day.

Trading commenced the following morning. The company and the underwriters and their respective counsel prepared the final prospectus

(continued)

with the final pricing information, and the company then filed it with the SEC. The underwriters and the auditors utilized the final prospectus to produce the bring-down comfort letter.

The offering closed three business days following the commencement of trading. At the closing, the parties executed and delivered numerous documents and addressed a variety of logistical issues related to the closing. Fortunately, both company and underwriters' counsel were experienced and well prepared, and they facilitated a smooth and relatively painless closing process.

After the offering closed, Alexei invited Sarah to visit the company to meet with the other members of the executive management team to set up procedures to implement the company's insider trading and window-period policies, the SEC and Nasdaq-GM compliance procedures, and the investor relations strategy. Sarah then spoke to the employees about the implications for them of owning stock in a public company and the applicable restrictions on trading. She also provided an overview of periodic and current filing obligations, selective disclosure matters, and corporate governance requirements.

After Sarah finished, Alexei and Piper addressed the employees. They thanked them for their long nights and weekends of toil to commercialize the Genesis T-2000 technology, moving it from the lab to the customer. The original members of the team recounted the dark days before venture financing, when Genesist's creditors were hounding the company and it almost failed. Finally, Alexei and Piper spoke of the future. Genesist had made remarkable progress from the time when it was merely a dream of its founders, but now it was time for the next stage. The challenges of entrepreneurship had been met, and the challenges of building Genesist into a successful and enduring public company lay ahead. "But first," Alexei declared, "let's break out the champagne and the fresh-squeezed orange juice—it's time to celebrate. A new era for Genesist has begun!"

Notes

Preface

1. Bianca Male, Aimee Groth & Alison Griswold, *Founders and VCs Reveal 25 Books Every Entrepreneur Should Read*, Business Insider (Oct. 16, 2013), http://www.businessinsider.com/books-entrepreneurs-should-read-2013-10?op=0#the-entrepre-neurs-guide-to-business-law-by-constance-bagley-and-craig-dauchy-18. In 2010, Bloomberg Business named Chris Dixon the savviest angel investor in tech. *Columbia Alumni: Chris Dixon*, Columbia U., http://entrepreneurship.columbia.edu/pride/chris-dixon/ (last visited Nov. 16, 2016).

2. Male, Groth & Griswold, *supra* note 1.

3. Press Release, Fed. Trade Comm'n, Mobile Advertising Network InMobi Settles FTC Charges It Tracked Hundreds of Millions of Consumers' Locations Without Permission (June 22, 2016), https://www.ftc.gov/news-events/press-releases/2016/06/mobile-advertising-network-inmobi-set-tles-ftc-charges-it-tracked.

4. *See* Constance E. Bagley, *Winning Legally: The Value of Legal Astuteness*, 33 Acad. Mgt. Rev. 378 (2008); Constance E. Bagley, *The Value of a Legally Astute Top Management Team: A Dynamic Capabilities Approach*, *in* The Oxford Handbook of Dynamic Capabilities (David J. Teece & Sohvi Leih eds., 2016).

5. *See* Constance E. Bagley, Mark Roellig & Gianmarco Massameno, *Who Let the Lawyers Out?: Reconstructing the Role of the Chief Legal Officer and the Corporate Client in a Globalizing World*, 18 U. Pa. J. Bus. L. 419 (2016).

6. Bagley, *The Value of a Legally Astute Top Management Team*, *supra* note 4.

7. Cade Metz, *Artificial Intelligence Is Setting Up the Internet for a Huge Clash with Europe*, Wired (July 11, 2016), http://www.wired.com/2016/07/artificial-intelligence-set-ting-internet-huge-clash-europe/.

8. *Id.*

9. *See* The White House, Non-Compete Agreements: Analysis of the Usage, Potential Issues, and State Responses 3 (May 2016), https://www.whitehouse.gov/sites/default/files/non-competes_report_final2.pdf.

10. *See* Lewis v. Epic Sys. Corp., 823 F.3d 1147 (7th Cir. 2016) (noting that Section 7 of the NLRA protects collective legal processes and renders unenforceable contract provisions purporting to waive employees' access to such remedies); Morris v. Ernst & Young, LLP, 834 F.3d 975 (9th Cir. 2016) (noting that the employment agreement required employees to pursue legal claims against the employer only through arbitration and "arbitrate only as individuals and in 'separate proceedings'").

11. David J. Teece, *Explicating Dynamic Capabilities: The Nature and Microfoundations of (Sustainable)*

Enterprise Performance, 28 Strategic Mgmt. J. 1319 (2007).

Chapter 1   Taking the Plunge

1. *See* Howard H. Stevenson & David E. Gumpert, *The Heart of Entrepreneurship*, Harv. Bus. Rev., Mar.–Apr. 1985, at 85.

2. Patrick J. McGinnis, The 10% Entrepreneur: Live Your Startup Dream Without Quitting Your Day Job (2016).

3. Sandra L. Kurtzig, CEO: Building a $400 Million Company from the Ground Up 2–3 (1994).

4. *See* Stevenson & Gumpert, *supra* note 1.

5. Eric Ries, The Lean Startup: How Today's Entrepreneurs Use Continuous Innovation to Create Radically Successful Businesses (2011).

6. Michael E. Porter, Harvard Bus. Sch., Shared Value Leadership Summit, Shared Value and Strategy 10 (May 12, 2015), http://www.hbs.edu/faculty/Publication%20Files/Michael%20Porter%20-%20CSV%20and%20Strategy%20presentation_5c6accd5-94ac-444c-ac01-24772ce95bfa.pdf [hereinafter Leadership Summit]; Inst. for Strategy & Competitiveness, Unique Value Proposition, Harv. Bus. School, http://www.isc.hbs.edu/strategy/creating-a-successful-strategy/Pages/unique-value-proposition.aspx (last visited July 28, 2016).

7. Michael E. Porter, Competitive Advantage 3 (1985).

8. William A. Sahlman, *Some Thoughts on Business Plans, in* The Entrepreneurial Venture (Sahlman et al. eds., 2d ed. 1999).

9. Leadership Summit, *supra* note 6, at 10.

10. *Id.* at 7.

11. Michael E. Porter, Competitive Strategy: Techniques for Analyzing Industries and Competitors 3–33 (1980).

12. *Id.*

13. Joseph A. Schumpeter, Capitalism, Socialism and Democracy (1942).

14. Clayton M. Christensen, The Innovator's Dilemma: The Revolutionary Book That Will Change the Way You Do Business 23 (2011).

15. *See* Kirsten Korosec, *It's Lag or Lead Time for General Motors*, Fortune (Oct. 5, 2015), http://fortune.com/2015/10/05/its-lag-or-lead-time-for-general-motors/.

16. Lee E. Preston & James E. Post, Private Management and Public Policy: The Principle of Public Responsibility 12 (1975).

17. Constance E. Bagley, *What's Law Got to Do with It?: Integrating Law and Strategy*, 47 Am. Bus. L. J. 587 (2010).

18. Preston & Post, *supra* note 16, at 4.

19. 558 U.S. 310, 454 (2010).

20. Frederick W. Smith, the founder of Federal Express, stated that the hub-and-spoke system "was all made possible because the government began to deregulate ... much of which we induced." Edited excerpts of Interview by Dean Foust with Frederick Smith, *Fred Smith on the Birth of FedEx*, Bloomberg Business (Sept. 19, 2004), http://www.bloomberg.com/bw/stories/2004-09-19/online-extra-fred-smith-on-the-birth-of-fedex.

21. *See* David J. Teece, *Explicating Dynamic Capabilities: The Nature and Microfoundations of (Sustainable) Enterprise Performance*, 28 Strategic Mgmt. J. 1319, 1319 (2007).

22. Jay B. Barney, *Resource-Based Theories of Competitive Advantage: A Ten-Year Retrospective on the Resource-Based View*, 27 J. MGMT. 643 (2001).

23. *See* Teece, *supra* note 21, at 1319.

24. *See id.* at 1319-20.

25. HERNANDO DE SOTO, THE MYSTERY OF CAPITALISM: WHY CAPITALISM TRIUMPHS IN THE WEST AND FAILS EVERYWHERE ELSE 6 (2000). *See also* CONSTANCE E. BAGLEY, WINNING LEGALLY: HOW TO USE THE LAW TO CREATE VALUE, MARSHAL RESOURCES AND MANAGE RISK 27 (2005) ("In the absence of law and order, property rights, and enforceable contracts, 'few people will habitually take risks to improve on what they currently have.'").

26. As Nobel laureate Douglass C. North explained, institutions "are made up of formal constraints (rules, laws, constitutions), informal constraints (norms of behavior, conventions, and self imposed codes of conduct), and their enforcement characteristics." Douglass C. North, Economic Performance through Time, Prize Lecture, The Sveriges Riksbank Prize in Economic Sciences in Memory of Alfred Nobel 1993 (Dec. 9, 1993), http://www.nobelprize.org/nobel_prizes/economic-sciences/laureates/1993/north-lecture.html. He continued, "If institutions are the rules of the game, organizations and their entrepreneurs are the players." *Id.*

27. *See generally* Constance E. Bagley & Christina D. Tvarnø, *Promoting "Academic Entrepreneurship" in Europe and the United States: Creating an Intellectual Property Regime to Facilitate the Efficient Transfer of Knowledge from the Lab to the Patient*, 26 DUKE J. COMP. & INT'L L. 1 (2016).

28. *See* Constance E. Bagley, *Winning Legally: The Value of Legal Astuteness*, 33 ACAD. MGT. REV. 378 (2008); Constance E. Bagley, *The Value of a Legally Astute Top Management Team: A Dynamic Capabilities Approach*, in THE OXFORD HANDBOOK OF DYNAMIC CAPABILITIES (David J. Teece & Sohvi Leih eds., 2016).

29. Attributed to French Prince Charles Maurice de Talleyrand or French Prime Minister Georges Clemenceau by ERIC VON DER LUFT, GOD, EVIL, AND ETHICS 7 (2004).

30. MARSHALL B. CLINARD & PETER C. YEAGER, CORPORATE CRIME 20 (1980).

31. Joseph DeSimone, *What if 3D Printing Was 100x Faster?*, TED (Mar. 19, 2015), https://www.ted.com/talks/joe_desimone_what_if_3d_printing_was_25x_faster/transcript?language=en.

32. *Id.*

33. *Id.*

34. *Id.*

35. *Id.*

36. *Id.*

37. *Id.*

38. *Id.*

39. *Id.*

Chapter 2 Leaving Your Employer

1. Lamorte Burns & Co. v. Walters, 770 A.2d 1158 (N.J. 2001).

2. *Id.*

3. Vibra-Tech Eng'rs, Inc. v. Kavalek, 849 F. Supp. 2d 462 (D.N.J. 2012).

4. Reeves v. Hanlon, 95 P.3d 513 (Cal. 2004).

5. ABC Trans Nat'l Transport, Inc. v. Aeronautics Forwarders, Inc., 379 N.E.2d 1228 (Ill. App. Ct. 1978).

6. Abel v. Fox, 654 N.E.2d 591, 597 (Ill. App. Ct. 1995).

7. Gibson v. Neighborhood Health Clinics, Inc., 121 F.3d 1126 (7th Cir. 1997).

8. Lake Land Emp't Grp. of Akron, LLC v. Columber, 804 N.E.2d 27 (Ohio 2004).

9. Fifield v. Premier Dealer Servs., Inc., 993 N.E.2d 938 (Ill. App. Ct. 2013).

10. Alex Sheshunoff Mgmt. Servs., L.P. v. Johnson, 209 S.W.3d 644 (Tex. 2006).

11. WellSpan Health v. Bayliss, 869 A.2d 990, 997 (Pa. Super. Ct. 2005) (citing Pa. Funds Corp. v. Vogel, 159 A.2d 472, 476 (Pa. 1960)).

12. Jones v. Deeter, 913 P.2d 1272 (Nev. 1996).

13. Weber v. Tillman, 913 P.2d 84 (Kan. 1996).

14. DCS Sanitation Mgmt., Inc. v. Castillo, 435 F.3d 892, 897 (8th Cir. 2006).

15. Coventry First, LLC v. Ingrassia, No. Civ. A. 05-2802, 2005 WL 1625042 (E.D. Pa. July 11, 2005).

16. CAL. BUS. & PROF. CODE § 16601 (providing a limited exception to California's general prohibition against noncompetition agreements to protect an acquired business's goodwill). *See, e.g.,* Alliant Ins. Svcs., Inc. v. Gaddy, 72 Cal. Rptr. 3d 259 (Ct. App. 2008) (finding a five-year noncompete agreement enforceable in connection with a stock purchase agreement).

17. FLIR Sys., Inc. v. Parrish, 95 Cal. Rptr. 3d 307 (Ct. App. 2009); Whyte v. Schlage Lock Co., 125 Cal. Rptr. 2d 277 (Ct. App. 2002).

18. *See* PepsiCo, Inc. v. Redmond, 54 F.3d 1262 (7th Cir. 1995).

19. *Schlage Lock Co.*, 125 Cal. Rptr. 2d 277.

20. *See, e.g.,* Manuel v. Convergys Corp., 430 F.3d 1132 (11th Cir. 2005).

21. *Id.*; Advanced Bionics Corp. v. Medtronic, Inc., 59 P.3d 231 (Cal. 2002).

22. D'Sa v. Playhut, Inc., 102 Cal. Rptr. 2d 495 (Ct. App. 2000).

23. *See, e.g.,* Maw v. Advanced Clinical Commc'ns, Inc., 846 A.2d 604 (N.J. 2004).

24. *See, e.g.,* MAI Sys. Corp. v. Peak Comput., Inc., 991 F.2d 511 (9th Cir. 1993) (holding that a customer database was a protectable trade secret).

25. Defend Trade Secrets Act of 2016, Pub. L. No. 114-153, 130 Stat. 376. This act amends the Economic Espionage Act of 1996.

26. PepsiCo, Inc. v. Redmond, 54 F.3d 1262, 1270 (7th Cir. 1995).

27. Whyte v. Schlage Lock Co., 125 Cal. Rptr. 2d 277 (Ct. App. 2002).

28. 18 U.S.C. §§ 1831–1832.

29. Tom Huddleston, Jr., *Court Sentences U.S. Businessman to 15 Years in DuPont Espionage Case*, FORTUNE (July 10, 2014), http://fortune.com/2014/07/10/walter-liew-sentenced-15-years-dupont/.

30. Beth Winegarner, *Ex-DuPont Engineer Gets 2.5 Years for Trade Secrets Theft*, LAW360 (Aug. 26, 2014), http://www.law360.com/articles/571212/ex-dupont-engineer-gets-2-5-years-for-trade-secrets-theft.

31. Cliff Joseph, *The Whole World in Her Handheld*, INDEPENDENT (UK), 2000 WLNR 5916673 (Mar. 20, 2000). *See also* Candida G. Brush, Patricia G. Greene & Myra M. Hart, *From Initial Idea to Unique Advantage: The Entrepreneurial Challenge of Constructing a Resource Base*, 15(1) ACAD. MGMT. EXECUTIVE 64 (2001).

32. Michelle Kessler, *Palm Buys Handspring in Deal Valued at $169M*, USA TODAY (June 5, 2003), http://usatoday30.usatoday.com/money

/industries/technology/2003-06-04
-palm_x.htm.

Chapter 3 Selecting and Working with an Attorney

1. Constance E. Bagley, *The Value of a Legally Astute Top Management Team: A Dynamic Capabilities Approach*, in THE OXFORD HANDBOOK OF DYNAMIC CAPABILITIES (David J. Teece & Sohvi Leih eds., 2016).

2. *See* Constance E. Bagley, Mark Roellig & Gianmarco Massameno, *Who Let the Lawyers Out?: Reconstructing the Role of the Chief Legal Officer and the Corporate Client in a Globalizing World*, 18 U. PA. J. BUS. L. 419, 456–60 (2016). *See also* ANTHONY T. KRONMAN, THE LOST LAWYER: FAILING IDEALS OF THE LEGAL PROFESSION xiv (1993).

3. For a discussion of ways to mitigate the possible conflict of interest, see ABA Standing Comm. on Ethics and Prof'l Responsibility, Formal Op. 00-418 (2000).

4. *See* COOLEY GO, https://www.cooleygo.com/.

5. 17 C.F.R. pt. 205.

6. Case C-550/07 P, Akzo Nobel Chems. Ltd. v. Eur. Comm'n, 2010 E.C.R. I-08301.

Chapter 5 Structuring the Ownership

1. Constance E. Bagley & Richard H. Koppes, *Leader of the Pack: A Proposal for Disclosure of Board Leadership Structure*, 34 SAN DIEGO L. REV. 149 (1997).

2. Katie Benner, *Airbnb and Others Set Terms for Employees to Cash Out*, N.Y. TIMES (Aug. 10, 2016), http://www.nytimes.com/2016/08/12/technology/airbnb-and-others-set-terms-for-employees-to-cash-out.html.

3. *See generally* MYRON S. SCHOLES ET AL., TAXES AND BUSINESS STRATEGY: A PLANNING APPROACH (5th ed. 2014).

Chapter 6 Forming and Working with the Board

1. JOHN L. WARD, CREATING EFFECTIVE BOARDS FOR PRIVATE ENTERPRISE 4 (1991).

2. *Quoted in* Robert Stobaugh, *Voices of Experience: Part One—How Boards Add Value in Small Companies*, DIRECTOR'S MONTHLY, Feb. 1996, at 3.

3. INVESTOR RESPONSIBILITY RESEARCH CENTER, BOARD PRACTICES/BOARD PAY 116 (2005). For additional information on issues pertaining to boards of directors for startup entities, see Suren G. Dutia, *Primer for Building an Effective Board for Growing Startup Companies*, EWING MARION KAUFFMAN FOUND. (May 2014), http://www.kauffman.org//media/kauffman_org/research%20reports%20and%20covers/2014/05/primer_for_building_an_effective_board.pdf.

4. J.L. Ward & J.L. Handy, *A Survey of Board Practices*, FAM. BUS. REV., Sept. 1988, at 289.

5. *See* NAT'L ASS'N OF CORP. DIRS. BLUE RIBBON COMM'N ON DIR. PROFESSIONALISM, REPORT OF THE NACD BLUE RIBBON COMMISSION ON DIRECTOR PROFESSIONALISM (2001).

6. HONG KONG EXCHANGES & CLEARING LTD., CONSULTATION CONCLUSIONS, BOARD DIVERSITY, PRINCIPLE A.3 BOARD COMPOSITION 19 (Dec. 13, 2012), https://www.hkex.com.hk/eng/newsconsul/mktconsul/Documents/cp201209cc.

7. NOTE, PRINCIPLE A.5.6 NOMINATING COMMITTEE. *Id.* at 20.

8. *See* Jim Fisher, *Studies Show Women Are Better Entrepreneurs, Board Members and Managers*, WOMEN2.0 (May 1, 2014), http://women2.com/2014/05/01/studies-show-women-better-entrepreneurs-board-members-managers/; Tekla Perry, *Getting Tech Women*

on Board (Boards of Directors, That Is), IEEE (July 24, 2015), http://spectrum.ieee.org/view-from-the-valley/at-work/startups/getting-tech-women-on-board-boards-of-directors-that-is; Brande Stellings, Opinion, *Female Board Members Are Good For Business*, N.Y. TIMES (Apr. 1, 2015), http://www.nytimes.com/roomfordebate/2015/04/01/the-effect-of-women-on-corporate-boards/female-board-members-are-good-for-business.

9. *See* MYLES L. MACE, DIRECTORS: MYTH AND REALITY 112–15 (1986).

10. *See* NAT'L ASS'N OF CORP. DIRS. BLUE RIBBON COMM'N ON DIR. PROFESSIONALISM, *supra* note 5; BUSINESS ROUNDTABLE, PRINCIPLES OF CORPORATE GOVERNANCE - 2012 (2012), http://businessroundtable.org/sites/default/files/BRT_Principles_of_Corporate_Governance_-2012_Formatted_Final.pdf; AMERICAN BAR ASSOCIATION COMMITTEE ON CORPORATE LAWS, CORPORATE DIRECTOR'S GUIDEBOOK (4th ed. 2004).

11. *See* Constance E. Bagley & Richard H. Koppes, *Leader of the Pack: A Proposal for Disclosure of Board Leadership Structure*, 34 SAN DIEGO L. REV. 149 (1997).

12. Directors' duties are discussed in more detail in CONSTANCE E. BAGLEY, MANAGERS AND THE LEGAL ENVIRONMENT: STRATEGIES FOR THE 21ST CENTURY 610–23 (8th ed. 2016).

13. Stroud v. Grace, 606 A.2d 75, 84 (Del. 1992). *See also* Shell Petroleum, Inc. v. Smith, 606 A.2d 112, 113 n.3 (Del. 1992) (holding that an understatement of the value of oil and gas reserves by roughly $1 billion was both material and violated the duty of disclosure the directors and majority shareholders owed the minority in a freeze-out merger as it affected their decision whether to exercise appraisal rights).

14. Smith v. Van Gorkom, 488 A.2d 858 (Del. 1985).

15. Jones v. H.F. Ahmanson & Co., 460 P.2d 464 (Cal. 1969).

16. *See* BAGLEY, *supra* note 12, at 620–21.

17. *In re* Caremark Int'l Inc. Derivative Litig., 698 A.2d 959 (Del. Ch. 1996).

18. Hanson Trust PLC v. ML SCM Acquisition, Inc., 781 F.2d 264, 276 (2d Cir. 1986). The court found that the directors accepted Goldman Sachs' conclusion that the prices of the optioned assets were fair, without ever inquiring about the range of fair value. Had the directors so inquired, and had Goldman Sachs revealed that they had not investigated the range of fair value as such, the directors might have then discovered that the prices represented lower valuations than their own experienced business judgment would allow them to approve. *Id.* at 276. Even though the court found "no fraud, no bad faith and no self-dealing" by the independent directors, it ruled that when directors' "'methodologies and procedures' are 'so restricted in scope, so shallow in execution, or otherwise so *pro forma* or halfhearted as to constitute a pretext or sham,' then inquiry into their acts is not shielded by the business judgment rule." *Id.* at 274 (citation omitted).

19. *See In re* Caremark Int'l Inc. Derivative Litig., 698 A.2d 959 (Del. Ch. 1996).

20. Sarbanes-Oxley Act of 2002, Pub. L. No. 107-204, 116 Stat. 745, § 301.

21. BUSINESS ROUNDTABLE, *supra* note 10, at 7–10.

22. *See, e.g.,* Graham v. Allis-Chalmers Mfg. Co., 188 A.2d 125, 130 (Del. 1963) ("[I]t appears that directors are entitled to rely on the honesty

and integrity of their subordinates until something occurs to put them on suspicion that something is wrong").

23. *In re* Walt Disney Co. Derivative Litig., 906 A.2d 27, 65 (Del. 2006).

24. Desimone v. Barrows, 924 A.2d 908, 935 (Del. Ch. 2007).

25. *In re* Citigroup Inc. S'holder Derivative Litig., 964 A.2d 106, 126 (Del. Ch. 2009). *See also* Espinoza v. Dimon, 807 F.3d 502 (2d Cir. 2015) (after concluding that the JPMorgan board's investigation of the "London Whale" derivatives trading scandal, which ultimately resulted in more than $6 billion of losses, was "exhaustive" and not "half-hearted," the court upheld under Delaware law the dismissal of a shareholder derivative suit seeking to recover damages from JPMorgan's directors, including CEO Jamie Dimon). Without admitting wrongdoing, JPMorgan agreed to pay $150 million to settle a separate class action lawsuit against the corporation itself, in which various pension funds alleged that the bank had mislead them about the risk of derivatives trading. Kat Greene, *JPMorgan Inks $150M Deal in 'London Whale' Investor Row*, Law360 (Dec. 18, 2015), http://www.law 360.com/articles/740291/jpmorgan -inks-150m-deal-in-london-whale -investor-row.

26. Ward & Handy, *supra* note 4.

27. *See* Martin Lipton & Jay Lorsch, *A Modest Proposal for Improved Corporate Governance*, 48 Bus. Law. 59, 71 (1992).

28. Peter Drucker, *The Bored Board*, Wharton Mag., Fall 1976, at 19.

29. For an excellent discussion of ways to get the most out of a board, see Jay W. Lorsch, Pawns or Potentates: The Reality of America's Corporate Boards 169–93 (1989).

30. Nat'l Ass'n of Corp. Dirs. Blue Ribbon Comm'n on Strategy Development, Report of the NACD Blue Ribbon Commission on Strategy Development (2014). *See also* Nat'l Ass'n of Corp. Dirs. Blue Ribbon Comm'n: Report of the NACD Blue Ribbon Commission: The Board and Long-Term Value Creation, Executive Summary (2015) (noting that SEC leaders, Delaware courts, and institutional investors have "all commented on the board's critical role in ensuring that company operations and business strategies promote the creation of long-term value").

31. Jeffrey Pfeffer, The Human Equation: Building Profits by Putting People First 5 (1998).

32. Ward, *supra* note 1; Eric Ries, The Lean Startup: How Today's Entrepreneurs Use Continuous Innovation to Create Radically Successful Businesses (2011); Charles A. O'Reilly III & Jeffrey Pfeffer, Hidden Value: How Great Companies Achieve Extraordinary Results with Ordinary People (1999).

33. Eugene Zuckert, *quoted in* Charles A. Anderson & Robert N. Anthony, The New Corporate Directors (1986), at 2.

34. Pfeffer, *supra* note 31, at 4–5.

35. *See generally* Jeffrey Pfeffer, Leadership BS: Fixing Workplaces and Careers One Truth at a Time (2015).

36. Richard C. Breeden, Restoring Trust: Report to The Hon. Jed S. Rakoff, the United States District Court for the Southern District of New York on Corporate Governance for the Future of MCI, Inc. 50 (Aug. 2003), http://www.law.du.edu /images/uploads/restoring-trust.pdf.

37. For a more detailed discussion of the role and responsibilities of the board's compensation committee,

see Nat'l Ass'n of Corp. Dirs. Blue Ribbon Comm'n on the Compensation Comm., Report of the NACD Blue Ribbon Commission on the Compensation Committee (2015).

38. *See* Nat'l Ass'n of Corp. Dirs. Blue Ribbon Comm'n on CEO Succession, Report of the NACD Blue Ribbon Commission on CEO Succession (2000).

39. *See* Nat'l Ass'n of Corp. Dirs. Blue Ribbon Comm'n on Performance Evaluation of Chief Executive Officers, Boards, and Directors, Report of the NACD Blue Ribbon Commission on Performance Evaluation of Chief Executive Officers, Boards, and Directors 19–46 (1995).

Chapter 7   Raising Money and Securities Regulation

1. Mueller v. Sullivan, 141 F.3d 1232, 1235 (7th Cir. 1998).

2. For a discussion of business plans, see William A. Sahlman, *Some Thoughts on Business Plans*, *in* The Entrepreneurial Venture 138 (Sahlman et al. eds., 2d ed. 1999) and Stanley R. Rich & David E. Gumpert, *How to Write a Winning Business Plan, id.*, at 177.

3. The text reflects the amendments to Rule 147 and the enactment of new Rule 147A, approved by the SEC on October 26, 2016, and effective 150 days after publication in the *Federal Register*. Exemptions to Facilitate Intrastate and Regional Securities Offerings, Securities Act Release No. 10,238, Exchange Act Release No. 79,161 (Oct. 26, 2016), https://www.sec.gov/rules/final/2016/33-10238.pdf. An issuer's *principal place of business* is "the location from which the officers, partners, or managers of the issuer primarily direct, control and coordinate the activities of the issuer." *Id.* at 2, 22.

4. The standards for determining whether an issuer is "doing business" in a given state are set forth in Rules 147(c)(2) and 147A(c)(2). *Id.* at 26–32.

5. As the SEC explained:

New Rule 147A thereby will permit issuers to engage in general solicitation and general advertising of their offerings, using any form of mass media, including unrestricted, publicly-available Internet websites, so long as sales of securities so offered are made only to residents of the state or territory in which the issuer is resident.

Id. at 17.

6. The text reflects the SEC's October 26, 2016 amendments to Rule 504, effective 60 days after publication in the *Federal Register*. *Id.* at 2, 76. The SEC has repealed Rule 505, effective 180 days after publication in the *Federal Register*. *Id.* at 2, 83.

7. Under Rule 504(b), "No general solicitation or advertising is permitted unless the offering is registered in a state requiring the use of a substantive disclosure document or sold under a state exemption that permits general solicitation or advertising so long as sales are made only to accredited investors." *Id.* at 88 n.337.

8. *See* 17 C.F.R. 230.506(d).

Chapter 8   Marshaling Human Resources

1. Paul Farhi, *Roger Ailes Resigns as CEO of Fox News; Rupert Murdoch Will Be Acting CEO*, Wash. Post (July 21, 2016), https://www.washingtonpost.com/lifestyle/style/roger-ailes-resigns-as-ceo-of-fox-news-rupert-murdoch-will-be-acting-ceo/2016/07/21/816c1dc4-4f80-11e6-a422-83ab49ed5e6a_story.html; John Koblin, *Gretchen Carlson, Former Fox Anchor, Speaks Publicly About Sexual Harassment Lawsuit*, N.Y. Times (July 12, 2016),

http://www.nytimes.com/2016/07/13
/business/media/gretchen-carlson
-fox-news-interview.html. Former
anchor Gretchen Carlson claimed
that Roger Ailes had told her, "I
think you and I should have had a
sexual relationship a long time ago,
and then you'd be good and better
and I'd be good and better"; that he
had talked about her body while she
complained to him about sexual
harassment at the station; and that
he had "labeled her a 'man hater'"
and told her she needed to "learn
to 'get along with the boys.'" *Id.* In
addition to denying her charges,
Ailes asserted that he had not
renewed Carlson's television contract because of poor ratings. *Id.*

2. *See generally* JAMES N. BARON &
    DAVID M. KREPS, STRATEGIC HUMAN
    RESOURCES: FRAMEWORKS FOR GENERAL
    MANAGERS (1999).

3. Noam Scheiber, *Growth in the 'Gig
    Economy' Fuels Work Force Anxi-
    eties*, N.Y. TIMES, July 13, 2015, at
    A1.

4. *See* JEFFREY PFEFFER, COMPETITIVE
    ADVANTAGE THROUGH PEOPLE: UNLEASH-
    ING THE POWER OF THE WORK FORCE
    (1995).

5. *See* Barry A. Colbert, *The Complete
    Resource-Based View: Implications
    for Theory and Practice in Strategic
    Human Resource Management*, 29
    ACAD. MGMT. REV. 341 (2004).

6. News Release, U.S. Dep't of Labor,
    Judge Finds Ohio-Based Cascom
    Inc. Liable for Nearly $1.5 Million
    in Back Wages, Damages to
    Employees Misclassified as Inde-
    pendent Contractors (Aug. 29,
    2013), http://www.dol.gov/news
    room/releases/whd/whd20131807.

7. In *Nationwide Mutual Ins. Co. v.
    Darden*, 503 U.S. 318 (1992), the
    U.S. Supreme Court provided a
    list of 13 nonexclusive factors to
    weigh when determining whether
    a person qualifies as an employee

under the Employee Retirement
Income Security Act of 1974.

8. The IRS provides basic guidance
    about employee classification on
    its website. Information for busi-
    nesses is available at https://www
    .irs.gov/businesses/small-business
    es-self-employed/independent
    -contractor-self-employed-or
    -employee (last updated July 7,
    2016). Information for charities
    and nonprofits is available at
    https://www.irs.gov/charities-non
    -profits/exempt-organizations
    -independent-contractors-vs-employ
    ees (last updated Mar. 19, 2016).

9. *See, e.g.*, Nationwide Mut. Ins. Co.
    v. Darden, 503 U.S. 318 (1992).

10. *See* FedEx Home Delivery v. NLRB,
    563 F.3d 492, 497 (D.C. Cir. 2009).

11. *See, e.g.*, Vizcaino v. Microsoft
    Corp., 173 F.3d 713 (9th Cir.
    1999); Vizcaino v. Microsoft
    Corp., 97 F.3d 1187 (9th Cir.
    1996), *aff'd on reh'g*, 120 F.3d
    1006 (9th Cir. 1997) (10,000
    Microsoft software testers and wri-
    ters of technical manuals were
    found to be employees for pur-
    poses of participation in Micro-
    soft's benefit plans, even though
    the workers had signed contracts
    stating that they were independent
    contractors responsible for their
    own federal taxes and benefits).
    Microsoft ultimately paid $97 mil-
    lion to the misclassified workers.

12. *Board Issues Decision in Browning-
    Ferris Industries*, NAT'L LABOR RELA-
    TIONS BD. (Aug. 27, 2015), https://
    www.nlrb.gov/news-outreach/
    news-story/board-issues
    -decision-browning-ferris-indus
    tries.

13. *Id. See also Joint Employment
    Under the FLSA and MSPA*, U.S.
    DEP'T OF LABOR, http://www.dol.-
    gov/whd/flsa/jointemployment.
    htm (last visited Aug. 17, 2016)
    (providing guidance on the

definition of joint employers for purposes of both the Fair Labor Standards Act and the Migrant and Seasonal Agricultural Worker Protection Act).

14. Daniel Fisher, *Controversial NLRB Ruling Could End Contract Employment As We Know It*, For- bes (Aug. 27, 2015), http://www .forbes.com/sites/danielfisher/2015 /08/27/nlrb-declares-browning-ferris -a-joint-employer-whos-next/.

15. *Id.*

16. *Id.*

17. Sun Young Lee, Marko Pitesa, Ste- fan Thau & Madan M. Pillutla, *Dis- crimination in Selection Decisions: Integrating Stereotype Fit and Inter- dependence Theories*, 58 Acad. Mgmt. J. 789, 789 (2015).

18. *See* Brett McIntyre, *All the Rage: Is Your Business Going to be in Trouble with the EEOC?*, Business.com (Dec. 1, 2015), http://www.business.com /human-resources/all-the-rage-the -top-5-litigation-trends-for-the-eeoc/.

19. EEOC Decision Appeal No. 0120133080, 2015 WL 4397641, at *5 (July 16, 2015).

20. *What You Should Know About EEOC and the Enforcement Protec- tions for LGBT Workers*, EEOC, https://www.eeoc.gov/eeoc/news room/wysk/enforcement_protect ions_lgbt_workers.cfm (last visited July 26, 2016).

21. *EEOC v. Abercrombie & Fitch Stores, Inc.*, 135 S. Ct. 2028 (2015).

22. 42 U.S.C.A. § 2000e-2(a)(1).

23. 42 U.S.C.A. § 2000e-2(m).

24. 42 U.S.C.A. § 2000e-5(g)(2)(B).

25. *See* Townsend v. Lumbermens Mut. Cas. Co., 294 F.3d 1232, 1241 (10th Cir. 2002) (explaining that a pretext instruction to the jury is required when a "rational finder of fact could reasonably find the defendant's explanation false and could 'infer from the fal- sity of the explanation that the employer is dissembling to cover up a discriminatory purpose.'").

26. Price Waterhouse v. Hopkins, 490 U.S. 228, 251 (1989), *superseded in part by statute*, Civil Rights Act of 1991, § 107(a), 42 U.S.C. § 2000e- 2(m).

27. *See, e.g.*, Azimi v. Jordan's Meats, Inc., 456 F.3d 228 (1st Cir. 2006) (jury found that employee was subjected to an "offensive work environment that was hostile" to his race, religion or ethnic origin. The employee, a Muslim immi- grant from Afghanistan, claimed he was subjected to disparaging remarks about his religion, an attempt by a coworker to shove pork into his mouth, and other offensive conduct).

28. Meritor Sav. Bank, FSB v. Vinson, 477 U.S. 57 (1986).

29. Faragher v. City of Boca Raton, 524 U.S. 775 (1998). The *Faragher* Court explained that Title VII does not prohibit "'genuine but innocuous differences in the ways men and women routinely interact with members of the same sex and of the opposite sex'" and also noted that "'simple teasing,' offhand com- ments, and isolated incidents (unless extremely serious)" are not discriminatory changes in the terms and conditions of employ- ment. *Id.* at 788. Similarly, in *Bur- lington Northern & Santa Fe Railway v. White*, 548 U.S. 53, 68 (2006), the Court explained that "those petty slights or minor annoyances that often take place at work and that all employees experience" are not actionable under Title VII.

30. Matthew Goldstein, *Bridgewater Hedge Fund Settles Harassment Claim That Described a 'Caldron of Fear,'* N.Y. Times DealBook (Aug. 10, 2016), http://www.nytimes.com

/2016/08/11/business/dealbook
/bridgewater-hedge-fund-sexual
-harassment-claim.html; Lucinda
Shen, *Sexual Harassment Suit
Calls World's Largest Hedge Fund a
"Cauldron of Fear and Intimida-
tion,"* FORTUNE (July 27, 2016),
http://fortune.com/2016/07/27/ray
-dalio-bridgewater-associates/. As
part of a settlement, Bridgewater
waived the noncompete clause in
Tarui's employment contract,
allowing him to move to Kohlberg
Kravis Roberts & Co., a private
equity firm. *Id.*

31. Oncale v. Sundowner Offshore
Servs., Inc., 523 U.S. 75, 80
(1998) (quoting Harris v. Forklift
Sys., Inc., 510 U.S. 17, 25 (1993)
(Ginsburg, J., concurring)).

32. Lockard v. Pizza Hut, Inc., 162
F.3d 1062 (10th Cir. 1998).

33. Faragher v. City of Boca Raton,
524 U.S. 775 (1998).

34. *Id.*

35. Pa. State Police v. Suders, 542 U.S.
129, 138 (2004) (quoting Burling-
ton Indus., Inc. v. Ellerth, 524
U.S. 742, 765 (1998)).

36. Univ. of Tex. Sw. Med. Ctr. v. Nas-
sar, 133 S. Ct. 2517 (2013).

37. Wilson v. Sw. Airlines Co., 517 F.
Supp. 292 (N.D. Tex. 1981).

38. *See* St. Cross v. Playboy Club,
Appeal No. 773, Case No. CFS
22618-70 (N.Y. Human Rights App.
Bd., 1971) (dicta); Weber v. Playboy
Club, Appeal No. 774, Case No. CFS
22619-70 (N.Y. Human Rights App.
Bd., 1971) (dicta).

39. Gross v. FBL Fin. Servs., 557 U.S.
167 (2009).

40. Anderson v. Consol. Rail Corp.,
297 F.3d 242, 249 (3d Cir. 2002).

41. If, after terminating an employee
based on illegal age discrimination,
the employer learns that the
plaintiff has violated work rules
and establishes that the violation
would have been a legitimate
basis for termination, then the
employer will be liable for back
pay from the date of termination
to the date the evidence of
employee wrongdoing was discovered, but neither reinstatement
nor front pay would be proper.
McKennon v. Nashville Banner
Publ'g Co., 513 U.S. 352 (1995).

42. Smith v. City of Jackson, Miss.,
544 U.S. 228 (2005).

43. *Id.*

44. *See, e.g.,* Oubre v. Entergy Operations, Inc., 522 U.S. 422 (1998).

45. 42 U.S.C.A. § 12102(4)(A).

46. ADA Amendments Act of 2008,
§ 2(b)(5), Pub. L. No. 110-325,
122 Stat. 3553.

47. 42 U.S.C.A. § 12102(4)(E)(i)(I).

48. 29 C.F.R. § 1630.2(i)(2).

49. Bragdon v. Abbott, 524 U.S. 624
(1998).

50. Chevron U.S.A., Inc. v. Echazabal,
536 U.S. 73 (2002).

51. 29 C.F.R. § 1630.2(r).

52. Waddell v. Valley Forge Dental
Assoc., 276 F.3d 1275 (11th Cir.
2001).

53. Pernice v. City of Chicago, 237
F.3d 783 (7th Cir. 2001).

54. *See, e.g.,* Vandenbroek v. PSEG
Power Conn. L.L.C., No. 3:07-cv-
869, 2009 WL 650392 (D. Conn.
Mar. 10, 2009), *aff'd,* 356 F. App'x
457 (2d Cir. 2009).

55. *See generally* Civil Rights Act of
1866, 42 U.S.C.A. § 1981; Equal
Pay Act of 1963, 29 U.S.C.A.
§ 206(d); Title VII of the Civil
Rights Act of 1964, 42 U.S.C.A.
§§ 2000e–2000e-17; Age Discrimination in Employment Act of
1967, 29 U.S.C.A. §§ 621-634;
Older Workers' Benefit Protection
Act of 1990, 29 U.S.C.A. § 623;

Vietnam Era Veterans' Readjustment Assistance Act of 1974, as amended, 38 U.S.C.A. § 4212; Rehabilitation Act of 1973, 29 U.S.C.A. §§ 701-797; Uniformed Services Employment and Reemployment Rights Act of 1994, 38 U.S.C.A. §§ 4301-4335; Immigration Reform and Control Act of 1986, Pub. L. No. 99-603, 100 Stat. 3359 (codified as amended in scattered sections of U.S.C.); Americans with Disabilities Act (*ADA*) of 1990, as amended by the ADA Amendments Act of 2008, 42 U.S.C.A. §§ 12101-12213, as amended by Pub. L. No. 110-325, 122 Stat. 3553; Civil Rights Act of 1991, Pub. L. No. 102-166, 105 Stat. 1071 (codified in scattered sections of U.S.C.); Family and Medical Leave Act of 1993, as amended by the National Defense Authorization Act for Fiscal Year 2010, 29 U.S.C.A. §§ 2601-2654 & Pub. L. No. 111-84, 123 Stat. 2190; Genetic Information Nondiscrimination Act of 2008, Pub. L. No. 110-233, 122 Stat. 881.

56. For additional information on employers' obligations with respect to immigration status and employment eligibility, see U.S. CITIZENSHIP & IMMIGRATION SERVS., HANDBOOK FOR EMPLOYERS, GUIDANCE FOR COMPLETING FORM I-9, http://www.uscis.gov/sites /default/files/files/form/m-274.pdf (rev. Apr. 30, 2013).

57. Kern v. Dynalectron Corp., 577 F. Supp. 1196 (N.D. Tex. 1983), *aff'd*, 746 F.2d 810 (5th Cir. 1984).

58. Courts have ruled that certain federal employers may be exempt from the FLSA's overtime requirements when another statute grants discretion to set wages notwithstanding the FLSA. *See* Jones v. United States, 88 Fed. Cl. 789, 792 (2009).

59. *Final Rule: Overtime*, DEP'T OF LABOR, https://www.dol.gov/whd /overtime/final2016/ (last visited July 26, 2016). *See also* 29 C.F.R. § 541.600.

60. Lydia DePillis, *Why Wage and Hour Litigation Is Skyrocketing*, WASH. POST (Nov. 25, 2015), https://www.washingtonpost.com /news/wonk/wp/2015/11/25/people -are-suing-more-than-ever-over -wages-and-hours/.

61. *Id.*

62. Workers' compensation may not preclude a suit for discrimination based on disability. For example, a Connecticut court permitted an injured construction worker to sue the employer for unlawful discrimination on the basis of physical disability after presenting evidence that the employer told him before he was laid off that it did not want to incur the cost of providing him health insurance. Tyler v. Woodco, LLC, No. CV146023102S, 2015 WL 897775 (Ct. Super. Feb. 13, 2015).

63. Whole Foods Mkt, Inc., 363 N.L.R.B. 87 (2015).

64. *See, e.g.*, MCPc Inc. v. NLRB, 813 F.3d 475 (3d Cir. 2016) (holding that a policy prohibiting employees from disseminating confidential information was overbroad because it could be interpreted by rational employees as inhibiting or prohibiting protected wage discussions). Thus, an employee who made statements during lunch with coworkers about what another employee was paid, and its impact on a staffing shortage, was engaged in a concerted activity for which he could not be fired. The employee could, however, be fired if he had obtained the confidential material improperly or lied about how he had accessed the information.

65. Jada A. Graves, *The Top Cyberloafing Activities of a Distracted Office Worker*, U.S. NEWS (Mar. 21, 2013),

http://money.usnews.com /money/careers/articles/2013/03 /21/the-top-cyberloafing-activities -of-a-distracted-office-worker? page=2.

66. Blakey v. Continental Airlines, Inc., 751 A.2d 538 (N.J. 2000).

67. *See, e.g.,* Muick v. Glenayre Elecs., 280 F.3d 741 (7th Cir. 2002).

68. *See, e.g., In re* Asia Global Crossing, Ltd., 322 B.R. 247, 257 (Bankr. S.D.N.Y 2005).

69. *See Muick,* 280 F.3d 741.

70. GC 15-04, REPORT OF THE GENERAL COUNSEL CONCERNING EMPLOYER RULES, can be accessed at the NLRB's website: https://www.nlrb .gov/reports-guidance/general -counsel-memos.

71. Stengart v. Loving Care Agency, Inc., 990 A.2d 650 (N.J. 2010).

72. *Id.* The court concluded that the employer's policy had not unambiguously stated that personal emails are company property. The court indicated in dicta, however: "Because of the important public policy concerns underlying the attorney-client privilege, even a more clearly written public policy manual—that is, a policy that banned all personal computer use and provided unambiguous notice that an employer could retrieve and read an employee's attorney-client communications, if accessed on a personal, password-protected email account using the company's computer system—would not be enforceable."

73. *See generally* Linda Abdel-Malek, *HIPAA Privacy Rules Impact Employers,* N.Y.L.J., May 14, 2001, at 5.

74. *See* Robert C. Bird, *Rethinking Wrongful Discharge: A Continuum Approach,* 73 U. CIN. L. REV. 517, 542 (2004).

75. Horn v. New York Times, 790 N.E.2d 753, 756 (N.Y. 2003).

76. Green v. Ralee Eng'g Co., 960 P.2d 1046 (Cal. 1998) (citing Tameny v. Atlantic Richfield Co., 610 P.2d 1330 (Cal. 1980)).

77. McLaughlin v. Gastrointestinal Specialists, Inc., 750 A.2d 283 (Pa. 2000). *Cf.* Oliveri v. U.S. Food Serv., No. 3:09cv921, 2010 WL 521126 (M.D. Pa. Feb. 9, 2010) (suggesting that federal courts may view federal statutes as a source of Pennsylvania public policy under certain circumstances).

78. Suchodolski v. Mich. Consol. Gas Co., 316 N.W.2d 710 (Mich. 1982); McNeil v. Charlevoix Cty., 772 N.W.2d 18 (Mich. 2009) (recognizing public agencies as a source of public policy).

79. Rocky Mountain Hosp. & Med. Serv. v. Mariani, 916 P.2d 519 (Colo. 1996).

80. 18 U.S.C.A. § 1514A(a).

81. 18 U.S.C.A. § 1513(e).

82. *See, e.g.,* Abraham v. Cty. of Hennepin, 639 N.W.2d 342 (Minn. 2002); N.Y. LAB. LAW § 740 (McKinney).

83. Fortune v. Nat'l Cash Register Co., 364 N.E.2d 1251 (Mass. 1977).

84. The federal EB-5 program, which has been renewed through September 2016, allocates 10,000 visas each year to foreign investors who invest $500,000 in a real estate project in targeted areas (and $1,000,000 in other locations) that will create a minimum of 10 jobs. The investors and their families are eligible for the visas, and the program reduces the time it takes to obtain legal U.S. residency to about two years. EB-5 investors generally are willing to accept smaller returns than more traditional investors. Andy J. Semotiuk,

Where Are We Going with the EB5 Program and Investor Immigration to the United States, Forbes (Dec. 17, 2015), http://www.forbes.com /sites/andyjsemotiuk/2015/12/17 /where-are-we-going-with-the-eb5 -program-and-investor-immigra tion-to-the-united-states/#12ff 08354693; Jonathan O'Connell, *Buying Visas with Investments Is Big Business. And Congress Is Taking Notice,* Wash. Post (June 28, 2015), https://www.washington post.com/news/digger/wp/2015/06 /28/buying-visas-with-investments -is-big-business-and-congress-is -taking-notice/; Julie Satow, *Want a Green Card? Invest in Real Estate,* N.Y. Times (May 15, 2015), http://www.nytimes.com /2015/05/17/realestate/want-a -green-card-invest-in-real-estate .html?_r=0.

85. Typically, the issue of whether parties have agreed to arbitrate a particular dispute is a question to be decided by a court not an arbitrator. Thus, "a court may order arbitration of a particular dispute only where the court is satisfied that the parties agreed to arbitrate *that dispute.*" Granite Rock Co. v. Int'l Bhd. of Teamsters, 561 U.S. 287, 297 (2010).

86. Gilmer v. Interstate/Johnson Lane Corp., 500 U.S. 20 (1991).

87. Circuit City Stores, Inc. v. Adams, 532 U.S. 105 (2001).

88. Rent-A-Center, West, Inc. v. Jackson, 561 U.S. 63 (2010); *see also* Circuit City Stores, Inc. v. Adams, 279 F.3d 889 (9th Cir. 2002); Armendariz v. Found. Health Psychcare Servs., Inc., 6 P.3d 669 (Cal. 2000).

89. *Rent-A-Center, West, Inc.,* 561 U.S. 63. The dissent argued that "when a party raises a good-faith validity challenge to the arbitration agreement itself, that issue must be resolved before a court can say that he clearly and unmistakably intended to *arbitrate* that very validity question" and that it was necessary for a court to resolve the merits of an unconscionability argument to determine whether a valid arbitration agreement exists. *Id.* at 82.

90. Preston v. Ferrer, 552 U.S. 346 (2008) (holding that an arbitration agreement can validly limit an employee's right to seek adjudication of employment claims by an administrative agency); *see also* Pearson Dental Supplies, Inc. v. Turcios, 229 P.3d 83 (Cal. 2010).

91. EEOC v. Waffle House, Inc., 534 U.S. 279 (2002) (holding that a mandatory arbitration agreement between an employer and an employee did not preclude the EEOC from prosecuting statutory antidiscrimination violations).

92. The California Supreme Court ruled that courts can vacate arbitration awards if the arbitrator made a clear legal error that deprived an employee of a hearing on the merits of an unwaivable statutory employment claim, holding that in such case the arbitrator exceeds his or her powers. *Pearson Dental Supplies, Inc.,* 229 P.3d 83. Especially in light of several recent pro-arbitration decisions by the U.S. Supreme Court, other courts may be more arbitrator-friendly.

93. Kristian v. Comcast Corp., 446 F.3d 25 (1st Cir. 2006).

94. *Mandatory Class Waivers Struck Down by 9th Circuit,* Fisher Phillips (Aug. 22, 2016), http://www.- lexology.com/library/detail.aspx? g=9b97603a-430d-4f9f-b98d- 855ea6817af9.

95. Lewis v. Epic Sys. Corp., 823 F.3d 1147 (7th Cir. 2016) (noting that Section 7 of the NLRA protects collective legal processes and renders

unenforceable contract provisions purporting to waive employees' access to such remedies).

96. Morris v. Ernst & Young, LLP, No. 13-16599, 5:12-cv-04964 (9th Cir. Aug. 22, 2016) (noting that the employment agreement required employees to pursue legal claims against the employer only through arbitration and "arbitrate only as individuals and in 'separate proceedings'").

97. Pub. L. No. 111-148, 124 Stat. 119 (2010).

98. *See Small Business Health Care Tax Credit and the SHOP Marketplace*, I.R.S., http://www.irs.gov/uac /Small-Business-Health-Care-Tax -Credit-and-the-SHOP-Market place (last reviewed or updated Jan. 6, 2016).

99. *See Choosing a Retirement Plan: 401(k) Plan*, I.R.S., http://www.irs .gov/Retirement-Plans/Choosing-a -Retirement-Plan:-401(k)-Plan (last reviewed or updated Dec. 15, 2015); *Retirement Topics, 401(k) and Profit-Sharing Plan Contribution Limits*, I.R.S., http://www.irs.gov /Retirement-Plans/Plan-Participant, -Employee/Retirement-Topics -401k-and-Profit-Sharing-Plan -Contribution-Limits (last reviewed or updated July 28, 2016).

100. *See generally* Constance E. Bagley, *Risky Business: Understanding and Reducing Employer Risk*, in 10 ADVANCES IN THE STUDY OF ENTRE-PRENEURSHIP, INNOVATION AND ECO-NOMIC GROWTH 123–66 (Gary Libecap, ed., 1998).

101. For an excellent discussion of good hiring practices, see PIERRE MOR-NELL, HIRING SMART (1998).

102. David Sumner & Andrea Fox, *Simple Measures Help Smaller Firms Reduce Risk Efficiently*, CORP. COUNSEL WKLY (BNA), Apr. 14, 2010, at 120.

103. *Id.*

Chapter 9   Contracts and Leases

1. Constance E. Bagley, *Winning Legally: The Value of Legal Astute-ness*, 33 ACAD. MGMT. REV. 378, 383–86 (2008).

2. Constance E. Bagley, *The Value of a Legally Astute Top Management Team: A Dynamic Capabilities Approach*, in THE OXFORD HANDBOOK OF DYNAMIC CAPABILITIES (David J. Teece & Sohvi Leih eds., 2016).

3. Apple Comput., Inc. v. Microsoft Corp., 709 F. Supp. 925 (N.D. Cal. 1989); Apple Comput., Inc. v. Microsoft Corp., 717 F. Supp. 1428, 1430–32 (N.D. Cal. 1989).

4. 717 F. Supp. 1430–32.

5. Apple Comput., Inc. v. Microsoft Corp., 799 F. Supp. 1006 (N.D. Cal. 1992).

6. Texaco, Inc. v. Pennzoil, Co., 729 S.W.2d 768 (Tex. Ct. App. 1987).

7. RESTATEMENT (SECOND) OF CONTRACTS § 87 cmt. b (1981).

8. Zimmerman v. McColley, 826 N.E.2d 71 (Ind. Ct. App. 2005).

9. Wickham & Burton Coal Co. v. Farmers' Lumber Co., 179 N.W. 417 (Iowa 1920).

10. Dahl v. HEM Pharms. Corp., 7 F.3d 1399 (9th Cir. 1993).

11. Harriman v. United Dominion Indus., Inc., 693 N.W.2d 44 (S.D. 2005).

12. Laura Poppo & Todd Zenger, *Do Formal Contracts and Relational Governance Function as Substi-tutes or Complements?*, 23 STRAT. MGMT. J. 707, 708 (2002).

13. *Quoted in* S. Macauly, *Non-Con-tractual Relations in Business: A Preliminary Study*, 28 AM. SOC. REV. 58–59 (1963).

14. Illinois, New York, and Washing-ton have not enacted the UETA, but each of them has laws recog-nizing electronic signatures and

governing certain other aspects of electronic documents.

15. Unif. Elec. Transactions Act § 7 U.L.A. (1999).

16. Roger Edwards, LLC v. Fiddes & Son, Ltd., 245 F. Supp. 2d 251 (D. Me., 2003), *aff'd in relevant part by* 387 F.3d 90 (1st Cir. 2004) (applying Maine law).

17. *In re* Cafeteria Operators, L.P., 299 B.R. 411 (Bankr. N.D. Tex. 2003).

18. *See* Campbell v. Gen. Dynamics Gov't Sys. Corp., 407 F.3d 546 (1st Cir. 2005).

19. Fed. Commc'ns Comm'n, In the Matter of Rules and Regulations Implementing the Telephone Consumer Protection Act of 1991, FCC 12-21, https://apps.fcc.gov/edocs_public/attachmatch/FCC-12-21A1.pdf (released Feb. 15, 2012). The FCC noted that the E-SIGN Act defines an electronic signature as "an electronic sound, symbol, or process attached to or logically associated with a contract ... and executed ... by a person with the intent to sign the record." *Id.* at 14, n.93.

20. Melford Olsen Honey, Inc. v. Adee, 452 F.3d 956, 963 n.9 (8th Cir. 2006).

21. Drafting Dispute Resolution Clauses–A Practical Guide can be accessed at the AAA's website, which also includes links to information on drafting clauses involving international cases. *See* https://www.adr.org/aaa/ShowPDF?doc=ADRSTG_002540 (last visited Aug. 23, 2016).

22. Circuit City Stores, Inc. v. Adams, 279 F.3d 889 (9th Cir. 2002).

23. AT&T Mobility LLC v. Concepcion, 563 U.S. 333 (2011).

24. *CFPB Proposes Rule Prohibiting Class Action Waivers and Requiring Reporting of Arbitration Information*, King & Spaulding (May 11, 2016) http://www.kslaw.com/imageserver/KSPublic/library/publication/ca051116a.pdf.

25. Raffles v. Wichelhaus, 159 Eng. Rep. 375 (Ex. 1864).

26. Wood v. Boynton, 25 N.W. 42 (Wis. 1885).

27. Murdock & Sons Constr., Inc. v. Goheen Gen. Constr., Inc., 461 F.3d 837 (7th Cir. 2006).

28. Hoffman v. Red Owl Stores, Inc., 133 N.W.2d 267 (Wis. 1965).

29. The Environmental Protection Agency has issued guidance outlining the steps that must be taken to comply with its "All Appropriate Inquiries" rule. The steps include, among others, hiring an environmental professional; conducting a site assessment; interviewing prior owners; reviewing records; and visually inspecting facilities. 40 C.F.R. § 312.20. *See* Constance E. Bagley, Managers and the Legal Environment: Strategies for the 21st Century 459 (8th ed. 2016).

Chapter 10   E-Commerce, Sales, and Consumer Privacy

1. E-commerce figure derived from U.S. Census Bureau, E-Stats 2014: Measuring the Electronic Economy (June 7, 2016), http://www.census.gov/content/dam/Census/library/publications/2016/econ/e14-estats.pdf.

2. Walton v. Bayer Corp. (*In re* Yasmin and Yaz (Drospirenone) Mktg, Sales Practices, & Prods. Liab. Litig.), 692 F. Supp. 2d 1012 (S.D. Ill. 2010), *aff'd by* 643 F.3d 994 (7th Cir. 2011).

3. U.C.C. § 2-104(1).

4. *See, e.g.*, ProCD, Inc. v. Zeidenberg, 86 F.3d 1447 (7th Cir. 1996) (upholding a software licensing shrink-wrap agreement under UCC. The ProCD software box stated that the software came with

restrictions listed in "an enclosed license," which was encoded on the CD-ROM disks (and in the printed manual) and which appeared on the user's screen each time the software ran. The court explained that ProCD therefore "proposed a contract that a buyer would accept by *using* the software after having an opportunity to read the license at his leisure. This [the plaintiff] did. He had no choice, because the software splashed the license on the screen and would not let him proceed without indicating acceptance.").

5. Specht v. Netscape Commc'ns Corp., 306 F.3d 17 (2d Cir. 2002).

6. UNCITRAL, Model Law on Electronic Signatures (2001), http://www.uncitral.org/uncitral/en/uncitral_texts/electronic_commerce/2001Model_status.html (last visited Aug. 16, 2016).

7. *Id.*

8. UNCITRAL, United Nations Convention on the Use of Electronic Communications in International Contracts (2005), Status As At: 16-08-2016, https://treaties.un.org/pages/ViewDetails.aspx?src=TREATY&mtdsg_no=X-18&chapter=10&clang=_en (updated as of Aug. 16, 2016).

9. *Id.*

10. The 18 countries that have signed CUECIC are Central African Republic, China, Colombia, Honduras, Iran, Lebanon, Madagascar, Montenegro, Panama, Paraguay, Philippines, Republic of Korea, Russian Federation, Saudi Arabia, Senegal, Sierra Leone, Singapore, and Sri Lanka. The Congo, Dominican Republic, Honduras, Montenegro, Russian Federation, Singapore, and Sri Lanka have ratified, acceded to, or accepted the convention. *Id.*

11. *See* U.C.C. § 2-315.

12. UNCITRAL, United Nations Convention on Contracts for the International Sale of Goods (1980), http://www.uncitral.org/uncitral/en/uncitral_texts/sale_goods/1980CISG.html (last visited Aug. 16, 2016).

13. As of August 2016, 85 countries had ratified, acceded to, or accepted CISG. *Id.*

14. *See, e.g.*, Branham v. Ford Motor Co., 701 S.E.2d 5, 16 (S.C. 2010) (holding that in a product design defect action, the plaintiff must present evidence of a reasonable alternative design and show how it would have prevented the product from being unreasonably dangerous. The plaintiff must also include cost, safety, and functionality considerations affecting such alternative design).

15. Austin v. Will-Burt Co., 361 F.3d 862 (5th Cir. 2004).

16. Eastman v. Stanley Works, 907 N.E.2d 768 (Ohio Ct. App. 2009).

17. LaPaglia v. Sears Roebuck & Co., 531 N.Y.S.2d 623 (App. Div. 1988).

18. Ariz. Rev. Stat. Ann. § 12-683(1).

19. Tenn. Code Ann. § 29-28-105(b).

20. Colo. Rev. Stat. Ann. § 13-21-403(a).

21. Geier v. Am. Honda Motor Co., 529 U.S. 861 (2000).

22. Riegel v. Medtronic, Inc., 552 U.S. 312 (2008).

23. Wyeth v. Levine, 555 U.S. 555 (2009).

24. PLIVA, Inc. v. Mensing, 564 U.S. 604 (2011). In the wake of this decision and the decision in *Mutual Pharmaceutical Co. v. Bartlett*, 133 S. Ct. 2466 (2013), the Food and Drug Administration proposed regulations that would "create parity" with respect to the requirements for updating labels for new safety information for generic

and brand-name drug companies. In 2016, the FDA announced that it would delay a decision on the labeling until 2017.

25. Dep't of Justice, Remarks as Prepared for Delivery by Attorney General Eric Holder at the Press Conference Announcing Criminal Charges and Deferred Prosecution Agreement with Toyota Motor Corporation (Mar. 19, 2014), http://www.justice.gov/opa/speech /remarks-prepared-delivery-attorney -general-eric-holder-press-confer ence-announcing.

26. *Privacy: Feeling Pressure from Legislators, Firms Are Turning to "Privacy Officers,"* 7 Electronic Com. & L. Rep. 92, 93 (Jan. 30, 2002).

27. Privacy professionals can help the management team determine which types of information are collected and how data are used, stored, and secured. Int'l Ass'n of Privacy Prof'ls, A Call for Agility: The Next-Generation Privacy Professional 19 (2010), https://www .huntonprivacyblog.com/uploads /file/IAPP_Future_of_Privacy.pdf.

28. The responsibilities of privacy professionals vary by organization, but typically include developing privacy strategy; analyzing existing, and anticipating new, regulations; training employees; measuring compliance; ensuring accurate incident reporting; assessing risk; and developing, administering, and amending privacy policies. *Id.* The International Association of Privacy Professionals, which has 20,000 members from more than 80 countries, assists companies in managing and protecting data and offers certification as an international privacy professional, manager or technologist. *Id.*

29. *See Privacy: Feeling Pressure from Legislators, supra* note 26, at 93.

30. Identity theft is a federal crime, 18 U.S.C.A. § 1028(a)(7), and it violates a number of state laws as well.

31. Corona v. Sony Pictures Entm't, Inc., No. 14-CV-09600, 2015 WL 3916744 (C.D. Cal. June 15, 2015).

32. Jonathan Stempel, *Home Depot Settles Consumer Lawsuit over Big 2014 Data Breach*, Reuters (Mar. 8, 2016), http://www.reuters.com /article/us-home-depot-breach -settlement-idUSKCN0WA24Z.

33. *Id.* In 2015, the U.S. Court of Appeals for the Seventh Circuit ruled that hundreds of thousands of Neiman Marcus credit card holders, whose credit card data were put at risk after hackers breached the high-end department store's computer systems, could sue for the future harm they would suffer as a result of the "increased risk of future fraudulent charges and greater susceptibility to identity theft." Remijas v. Neiman Marcus Grp., 794 F.3d 688 (7th Cir. 2015), *reh'g denied*, No. 14-3122 (7th Cir. Sept. 17, 2015). The court rejected the argument that the alleged future injuries were speculative and not impending, holding that the plaintiffs were not required to wait to sue until the hackers actually committed identity or credit card theft because there was an "objectively reasonable likelihood" that such harm would occur. *Id.*

34. *See, e.g.,* Cal. Civ. Code § 1798.29 (requiring prompt disclosure of any consumer data breach).

35. *In re* Toys R Us, 1 Privacy & Security L. Rep. 48 (Jan. 14, 2002) (Toys "R" Us, Inc. agreed to pay the State of New Jersey $50,000 for allegedly obtaining and transmitting personally identifiable information about consumers who accessed its websites in violation of the New Jersey Consumer Fraud Act).

36. Norberg v. Shutterfly, Inc., 152 F. Supp. 3d 1103 (N.D. Ill. 2015).

37. *See* Theodore F. Claypoole, *Privacy and Social Media*, Bus. L. Today (Jan. 2014), http://www.american bar.org/publications/blt/2014/01 .html.

38. Individuals can report identity theft on the IdentityTheft.gov site, which describes identity-theft warning signs, explains what to do if notified of a data breach, outlines steps individuals should take if their identity has been stolen, and includes sample letters and tips for dealing with tax-related and medical-related identity theft. The FTC's Business Center guidance can be accessed at www.ftc.gov/tips-advice/business -center/guidance; guidance on security-related issues is included in Start with Security: A Guide for Business (2015), https://www .ftc.gov/tips-advice/business-cen ter/guidance/start-security-guide -business.

39. 15 U.S.C.A. § 45(a)(2).

40. Wyndham Worldwide Corp., a hotel enterprise, unsuccessfully challenged the FTC's authority to sanction it for security failures that led to the hacking of the company's computer networks, thereby compromising more than 619,000 consumer credit card account numbers. FTC v. Wyndham Worldwide Corp., 799 F.3d 236 (3d Cir. 2015) (holding that the FTC has authority under Section 5 to take action against companies whose inadequate cybersecurity results in consumer harm). *See also* Marc H. Perry, FTC v. Wyndham: *Recent Developments and Implications*, Law360 (Apr. 8, 2015), http://www .law360.com/articles/640783/ftc-v -wyndham-recent-developments -and-implications.

41. *In re* Eli Lilly & Co., 67 Fed. Reg. 4963-02 (Feb. 1, 2002); *In re* Eli Lilly & Co., 2002 FTC LEXIS 3 (Feb. 1, 2002). *See also* Press Release, FTC, ChoicePoint Settles Data Security Breach Charges; to Pay $10 Million in Civil Penalties, $5 Million for Consumer Redress (Jan. 26, 2006), https://www.ftc .gov/news-events/press-releases /2006/01/choicepoint-settles-data -security-breach-charges-pay-10 -million (consumer data broker ChoicePoint pays $10 million in civil fines and $5 million in consumer redress to settle FTC charges that it improperly sold private information concerning 163,000 individuals to subscribers it did not properly screen).

42. *Lax Security Could Bring FTC Enforcement Under 'Unfair' Practices Section of FTC Act*, 72 U.S.L.W. 2744 (June 8, 2004).

43. Gina Stevens, Cong. Research Serv., R43723, The Federal Trade Commission's Regulation of Data Security Under Its Unfair or Deceptive Acts or Practices (UDAP) Authority, Summary (2014), https://www.fas .org/sgp/crs/misc/R43723.pdf.

44. Press Release, FTC, Two Data Brokers Settle FTC Charges that They Sold Consumer Data Without Complying with Protections Required Under the Fair Credit Reporting Act (Apr. 9, 2014), https://www .ftc.gov/news-events/press-releases /2014/04/two-data-brokers-settle -ftc-charges-they-sold-consumer -data.

45. 15 U.S.C.A. §§ 6501-6506.

46. 15 U.S.C.A. § 6502(b)(1)(A)(ii).

47. Gramm-Leach-Bliley Financial Services Modernization Act, Pub. L. No. 106-102, 113 Stat. 1338 (1999) (codified as amended in scattered sections of 12 and 15 U.S.C.), and related regulations.

48. 15 U.S.C.A. § 1681-1681x.

49. Health Insurance Portability and Accountability Act of 1996 (HIPAA), Pub. L. No. 104-191, 110 Stat. 1936 (1996), and related regulations.

50. 15 U.S.C. §§ 6151-6155. More information is available on the FTC website at https://www.donot-call.gov. and https://www.ftc.gov/tips-advice/business-center/guidance/qa-telemarketers-sellers-about-dnc-provisions-tsr (last visited Aug. 16, 2016).

51. Mainstream Mktg. Servs., Inc. v. FTC, 358 F.3d 1228 (10th Cir. 2004).

52. 15 U.S.C. §§ 7701-13.

53. CAL. BUS. & PROF. CODE § 22947–22947.6.

54. 18 U.S.C. §§ 2510–22.

55. 15 U.S.C. § 45.

56. European Commission Press Release Statement /16/1403, Joint Statement on the Final Adoption of the New EU Rules for Personal Data Protection (Apr. 14, 2016), http://europa.eu/rapid/press-release_STATEMENT-16-1403_en.htm. Regulation (EU) 2016/679 repeals General Data Protection Regulation, Directive 95/46/EC.

57. In a highly controversial decision, the European Court of Justice ruled in 2014 that Google could be ordered to delete links between search results and corresponding webpages if they contain personal information that should be deleted to protect an individual's "right to be forgotten." Google Spain SL v. Agencia Espanola de Proteccion de Datos (AEPD), Case No. C-131/12 (E.C.J. May 13, 2014). The ruling was predicated on the determination, among others, that when personal data is "inadequate, irrelevant or no longer relevant, or excessive" when weighed against the reason why the information was initially processed and the amount of time since the processing, the right to be forgotten can be asserted.

58. The full text of the agreement and related documents can be accessed on the International Association of Privacy Protection website, https://iapp.org/media/pdf/resource_center/eu_us_privacy_shield_full_text.pdf.pdf (last visited Aug. 16, 2016).

59. Mark Scott, *Europe Approves New Trans-Atlantic Data Transfer Deal*, N.Y. TIMES (July 12, 2016), http://www.nytimes.com/2016/07/13/technology/europe-eu-us-privacy-shield.html; *see also* Laura De Jong, *European Union: European Commission Adopts EU-US Privacy Shield*, MONDAQ (Sept. 6, 2016), http://www.mondaq.com/x/524412/data+protection/European+Commission+Adopts+EUUS+Privacy+Shield).

60. *EU-US Privacy Shield Framework Formally Adopted*, GOODWIN (Aug. 11, 2016), http://www.goodwinlaw.com/viewpoints/2016/08/08_11_16-eu-us-privacy-shield-framework-adopted/.

61. S.C. Johnson & Son, Inc. v. Clorox Co., 241 F.3d 232 (2d Cir. 2001).

62. Morgan v. AT&T Wireless Servs., Inc., 99 Cal. Rptr. 3d 768 (Ct. App. 2009), *reversed in part on unrelated grounds*, 2013 WL 5034436 (Cal. Ct. App. Sept. 13, 2013).

63. *See, e.g.*, Auto Europe, LLC v. Conn. Indem. Co., 321 F.3d 60 (1st Cir. 2003).

64. *In re* Campbell Soup Co., 77 F.T.C. 664 (1970).

65. 16 C.F.R. § 255.

66. *See* FTC, THE FTC's ENDORSEMENT GUIDES: WHAT PEOPLE ARE ASKING 21 (May 2015), https://www.ftc.gov/system/files/documents/plain-language/pdf-0205-endorsement-guides-faqs.pdf. The FTC updated

this "questions and answers" section of its Endorsement Guides in 2015 to include more detailed information about marketing and social networking sites.

67. Midler v. Ford Motor Co., 849 F.2d 460 (9th Cir. 1988).

68. UNCITRAL, Model Law on Electronic Commerce with Guide to Enactment 1996 with Additional Article 5 *bis* as Adopted in 1998, http://www.uncitral.org/pdf /english/texts/electcom/05 -89450_Ebook.pdf; UNCITRAL, Model Law on Electronic Signatures with Guide to Enactment 2001, http://www.uncitral.org/pdf /english/texts/electcom/ml-elecsig-e .pdf.

69. *See generally* ORGANIZATION FOR ECONOMIC CO-OPERATION AND DEVELOPMENT [hereinafter OECD], GUIDELINES FOR CONSUMER PROTECTION IN THE CONTEXT OF ELECTRONIC COMMERCE 2000, http://www.oecd.org/sti/consumer/ 34023811.pdf; OECD, CONSUMERS IN THE ONLINE MARKETPLACE: THE OECD GUIDELINES THREE YEARS LATER 2002, http://www.oecd.org/officialdocu-ments/publicdisplaydocumentpdf/? doclanguage=en&cote=dsti/cp (2002)4/final; OECD, THE ECONOMIC AND SOCIAL IMPACTS OF ELECTRONIC COMMERCE: PRELIMINARY FINDINGS AND RESEARCH AGENDA (1999).

70. Various studies are available at the "E-Commerce, Studies" section of the Hague Conference on Private International Law's website, at http://www.hcch.net/index_en.php? act=progress.listing&cat=9 (last visited Aug. 16, 2016).

71. The text of the convention, as well as the parties bound by the convention, can be accessed at https:// www.hcch.net/en/instruments/con-ventions/full-text/?cid=98 (last visited Aug. 16, 2016).

72. Int'l Shoe Co. v. Washington, 326 U.S. 310, 316 (1945).

73. *See, e.g.,* GTE New Media Servs., Inc. v. Bellsouth Corp., 199 F.3d 1343 (D.C. Cir. 2000); *see also* Trintec Indus., Inc. v. Pedre Promotional Prods., Inc., 395 F.3d 1275 (Fed. Cir. 2005).

74. *See, e.g.,* Zippo Mfg. Co. v. Zippo Dot Com, Inc., 952 F. Supp. 1119 (W.D. Pa. 1997); *see also* Gather, Inc. v. Gatheroo, LLC, 443 F. Supp. 2d 108 (D. Mass. 2006).

75. *See, e.g.,* iAccess, Inc. v. WEBcard Techs., Inc., 182 F. Supp. 2d 1183 (D. Utah 2002); *see also* High Maintenance Bitch, LLC v. Uptown Dog Club, Inc., No. C07-888Z, 2007 WL 3046265 (W.D. Wash. Oct. 17, 2007).

Chapter 11 Operational Liabilities, Insurance, and Compliance

1. Constance E. Bagley, *Winning Legally: The Value of Legal Astuteness,* 33 ACAD. MGMT. REV. 378 (2008).

2. Clohesy v. Food Circus Supermarkets, Inc., 694 A.2d 1017 (N.J. 1997).

3. *See* Posecai v. Wal-Mart Stores, Inc., 752 So. 2d 762 (La. 1999) (explaining the four different approaches courts apply in determining when a crime is foreseeable, exposing a business to liability for crimes perpetrated by third parties against its customers).

4. Otis Eng'g Corp. v. Clark, 668 S.W.2d 307 (Tex. 1983).

5. Lett v. Collis Foods, Inc., 60 S.W.3d 95 (Tenn. Ct. App. 2001).

6. Faverty v. McDonald's Rests. of Oregon, Inc., 892 P.2d 703 (Or. Ct. App. 1995).

7. *See, e.g.,* Secs. Inv'r Prot. Corp. v. BDO Seidman, LLP, 222 F.3d 63 (2d Cir. 2000) (explaining that a plaintiff may be able to establish a relationship that "approach[es] that of privity" if three elements

are satisfied, but that it is a "heavy burden" to do so).

8. *See, e.g.,* McCamish, Martin, Brown & Loeffler v. F.E. Appling Interests, 991 S.W.2d 787 (Tex. 1999) (concluding that party who entered into settlement agreement with lender, which could not be enforced after lender was declared insolvent, could bring suit against lender's attorneys for representing that agreement would be enforceable).

9. *See, e.g.,* Heupel v. Jenkins, 919 N.E.2d 378 (Ill. App. Ct. 2009).

10. *See, e.g.,* McIntyre v. Balentine, 833 S.W.2d 52 (Tenn. 1992).

11. Wallace v. Stringer, 553 S.E.2d 166 (Ga. Ct. App. 2001).

12. Ford v. Revlon, Inc., 734 P.2d 580 (Ariz. 1987).

13. *See, e.g.,* Kearney v. Salomon Smith Barney, Inc., 137 P.3d 914 (Cal. 2006) (California law prohibits the secret recording of telephone calls by broker in Georgia speaking with client in California).

14. Hilary M. Goldberg, Melanie Stallings Williams & Deborah Cours, *It's a Nuisance: The Future of Fracking Litigation in the Wake of Parr v. Aruba Petroleum, Inc.,* 33 Va. Envtl. L.J. 1, 11–12 (2015).

15. *See* Restatement (Second) of Torts, § 222A illus. 2 (1965).

16. Brass v. Am. Film Techs., Inc., 987 F.2d 142 (2d Cir. 1993).

17. Texaco, Inc. v. Pennzoil, Co., 729 S.W.2d 768 (Tex. App. 1987).

18. Korea Supply Co. v. Lockheed Martin Corp., 63 P.3d 937 (Cal. 2003).

19. *See, e.g.,* Conseco Fin. Servicing Corp. v. North Am. Mortg. Co., 381 F.3d 811 (8th Cir. 2004) (former employer awarded $3.5 million in compensatory damages and $7 million in punitive damages from new employer after former employees took trade secrets from prior employer, causing former employer to lose business as a result of new employer's use of the trade secrets).

20. State Farm Mut. Auto. Ins. Co. v. Campbell, 538 U.S. 408, 416, 424-25 (2003).

21. 15 U.S.C.A. § 1.

22. *Id.*

23. 15 U.S.C.A. § 15.

24. Press Release, Dep't of Justice, Five Major Banks Agree to Parent-Level Guilty Pleas (May 20, 2015), https://www.justice.gov /opa/pr/five-major-banks-agree -parent-level-guilty-pleas.

25. *Id.*

26. James Titcomb, *Barclays Handed Biggest Bank Fine in UK History Over "Brazen" Currency Rigging,* Telegraph (May 20, 2015), http:// www.telegraph.co.uk/finance /newsbysector/banksandfinance /11619188/Barclays-handed-big gest-bank-fine-in-UK-history-over -brazen-currency-rigging.html.

27. Leegin Creative Leather Prods., Inc. v. PSKS, Inc., 551 U.S. 877 (2007). The Antitrust Division of the Department of Justice and the FTC have issued a proposed update to the agencies' 1995 Antitrust Guidelines for the Licensing of Intellectual Property which will, among other updates, incorporate (1) the Court's holding in *Leegin Creative* that rule of reason analysis should be applied to price maintenance in intellectual property licensing agreements, and (2) the Court's holding in *Illinois Tool Works, Inc. v. Independent Ink, Inc.,* 547 U.S. 28 (2006), that owning a patent does not support a presumption of market power. Public comments on the proposed guidelines were due in September 2016. *Antitrust Agencies Release*

Update to IP Licensing Guidelines for Comment, Cooley LLP (Aug. 17, 2016), https://www.cooley .com/news/insight/2016/2016 -08-16-antitrust-agencies-release -update-to-ip-licensing-guidelines -for-comment.

28. Constance E. Bagley, Winning Legally: How to Use the Law to Create Value, Marshal Resources, and Manage Risk 213 (2005).

29. United States v. Microsoft Corp., 253 F.3d 34 (D.C. Cir. 2001).

30. Robert A. Guth & Mark Boslet, *Microsoft, Sun Announce Details of Collaboration*, Wall St. J., May 16, 2005, at B4.

31. European Commission Press Release IP/09/745, Antitrust: Commission Imposes Fine of €1.06 bn on Intel for Abuse of Dominant Position; Orders Intel to Cease Illegal Practices (May 13, 2009), http://europa.eu/rapid/press-release _IP-09-745_en.htm.

32. Press Release, Fed. Trade Comm'n, FTC Approves Modified Intel Settlement Order (Nov. 2, 2010), https://www.ftc.gov/news-events /press-releases/2010/11/ftc -approves-modified-intel-settlement-order. For an inside account of Advanced Micro Devices's 2005 decision to sue Intel for anticompetitive behavior, see Hector Ruiz, Slingshot: AMD's Fight to Free An Industry From The Ruthless Grip Of Intel (2013).

33. Press Release, Intel, AMD and Intel Announce Settlement of All Antitrust and IP Disputes (Nov. 12, 2009), http://www.intel.com /pressroom/archive/releases/2009 /20091112corp_a.htm.

34. United States v. Bestfoods, 524 U.S. 51, 66 (1998).

35. *See* Nurad, Inc. v. Hooper & Sons Co., 966 F.2d 837, 843 (4th Cir. 1992).

36. The Phase 1 assessment requirements include interviews with past and present owners and operators; reviews of historical information and government records; visual inspection; commonly known or reasonably ascertainable information; an assessment of the relationship of the purchase price to the fair market value of the property, if it were not contaminated; and an assessment of the degree of obviousness of the presence or likely presence of contamination.

37. Press Release, Dep't of Justice, BP Exploration and Production Inc. Pleads Guilty, Is Sentenced to Pay Record $4 Billion for Crimes Surrounding Deepwater Horizon Incident (Jan. 29, 2013), https://cfpub .epa.gov/compliance/criminal_ prosecution/index.cfm?action=3& prosecution_summary_id=2468.

38. Timothy M. Phelps, *Record $20-billion Fine for BP in 2010 Gulf Spill: Where the Money Will Go*, L. A. Times (Oct. 5, 2015), http://www .latimes.com/nation/la-na-bp-gulf -20151006-story.html.

39. U.S. Senate Committee on Banking, Housing, and Urban Affairs, Foreign Corrupt Practices and Domestic and Foreign Investment Improved Disclosure Acts of 1977, Senate Rep. No. 95-114, (May 2, 1977), https://www.justice.gov /sites/default/files/criminal-fraud /legacy/2010/04/11/senaterpt-95.

40. *Id.*

41. *Id.*

42. The Department of Justice and the Securities and Exchange Commission guide A Resource Guide to the U.S. Foreign Corrupt Practices Act can be accessed at https://www. justice.gov/sites/default/files /criminal-fraud/legacy/2015/01/16 /guide.pdf (last visited Aug. 22, 2016).

43. Press Release, Dep't of Justice, Avon China Pleads Guilty to Violating the FCPA by Concealing More Than $8 Million in Gifts to Chinese Officials (Dec. 17, 2014), http://www.justice.gov/opa/pr/avon-china-pleads-guilty-violating-fcpa-concealing-more-8-million-gifts-chinese-officials.

44. Ed Beeson, *Mead Johnson Pays SEC $12M to Settle FCPA Claims*, Law360 (July 28, 2015), http://www.law360.com/articles/684272/mead-johnson-pays-sec-12m-to-settle-fcpa-claims.

45. Hester Plumridge & Laurie Burkitt, *GlaxoSmithKline Found Guilty of Bribery in China*, Wall St. J. (Sept. 19, 2014), http://www.wsj.com/articles/glaxosmithkline-found-guilty-of-bribery-in-china-1411114817.

46. *Id.*

47. 18 U.S.C.A. §§ 1341, 1343, 1349.

48. Durland v. United States, 161 U.S. 306, 313 (1896).

49. *See* 18 U.S.C.A. § 1519.

50. *See, e.g.,* United States v. Stewart, 433 F.3d 273 (2006) (Martha Stewart was convicted not for insider trading but for lying to a federal investigator).

51. 18 U.S.C.A. § 1513(e) (applies to private and public companies). As explained in Chapter 8, the Sarbanes-Oxley Act also (1) prohibits public companies from retaliating against whistle-blowers who provide information concerning federal securities fraud, accounting violations, and other financial crimes and (2) gives aggrieved employees a private civil right of action to sue for reinstatement and damages. 18 U.S.C.A. § 1514A.

52. *See* United States v. Zolin, 491 U.S. 554, 562–63 (1989).

53. 18 U.S.C.A. § 1030.

54. United States v. Valle, 807 F.3d 508, 511–12, 524 (2d Cir. 2015).

55. *See id.* at 511–12, 524.

56. *Id.* at 527 (citing WEC Carolina Energy Sols. LLC v. Miller, 687 F.3d 199, 206 (4th Cir. 2012)).

57. 18 U.S.C. §§ 1831–1839.

58. Defend Trade Secrets Act of 2016, Pub. L. No. 114-153, 130 Stat. 376.

59. Florian Beerli, *5 Reasons to Purchase Product Recall Insurance*, PropertyCasualty360 (July 15, 2014), http://www.propertycasualty360.com/2014/07/15/5-reasons-to-purchase-product-recall-insurance?page_all=1.

60. *Cost of Data Breaches Increasing to Average of $3.8 Million, Study Says*, Reuters (May 27, 2015), http://www.reuters.com/article/2015/05/27/us-cybersecurity-ibm-idUSKBN0OC0ZE20150527.

61. *Id.*

62. *A Look at CGL Coverage for Data Breaches*, Jere Beasley Rep. (Apr. 2, 2015), http://www.jerebeasleyreport.com/2015/04/a-look-at-cgl-coverage-for-data-breaches/.

63. *Id.*

64. *Id.*

65. Natalie Lehr & Tom Quy, *Cyber Insurance: The Last Line of Defense or Frontline Offense*, Ins. J. (Feb. 9, 2015), http://www.insurancejournal.com/magazines/features/2015/02/09/356337.htm.

66. *Id.*

67. This 10-step program is drawn from Constance E. Bagley, Winning Legally: How to Use the Law to Create Value, Marshal Resources, and Manage Risk 50-86 (2005), and Constance E. Bagley, *The Value of a Legally Astute Top Management Team: A Dynamic Capabilities Approach, in* The Oxford Handbook of Dynamic Capabilities (David J. Teece & Sohvi Leih eds., 2016).

68. Press Release, Goldman Sachs, Goldman Sachs Announces a Settlement in Principle with the RMBS Working Group (Jan. 14, 2016), http://www.goldmansachs.com/media-relations/press-releases/current/announcement-14-jan-2016.html; Tom Schoenberg & Michael Moore, *Goldman Says U.S. Mortgage Settlement to Cost $5.1 Billion*, Bloomberg (Jan. 14, 2016), http://www.bloomberg.com/news/articles/2016-01-14/goldman-says-it-will-settle-u-s-mortgage-probe-for-5-1-billion.

69. Bagley, *supra* note 67.

70. Max H. Bazerman & Michael D. Watkins, Predictable Surprises: The Disasters You Should Have Seen Coming, and How to Prevent Them (2008).

71. *See generally* Benjamin W. Heineman, Jr., The Inside Counsel Revolution: Resolving the Partner-Guardian Tension (2016), for an excellent discussion of the roles of general counsel and chief compliance officers in corporate compliance programs.

Chapter 12   Creditors' Rights and Bankruptcy

1. Quadrant Structured Prods. Co. v. Vertin, 115 A.3d 535, 546 (Del. Ch. 2015) (referencing N. Am. Catholic Educ. Programming Found., Inc. v. Gheewalla, 930 A.2d 92 (Del. 2007)) (holding that there is "no legally recognized 'zone of insolvency' with implications for fiduciary duty claims").

2. *In re* Trafford Distrib. Ctr., Inc., 431 B.R. 263, 290 (Bankr. S.D. Fla. 2010) (referencing *In re* Toy King Distribs. Inc., 256 B.R. 1 (Bankr. M.D. Fla. 2000)).

3. Bank of Am. Nat'l Trust & Sav. Ass'n v. 203 N. LaSalle St. P'ship, 526 U.S. 434 (1999).

Chapter 13   Venture Capital

1. Paul Graham, *Announcing the Safe, A Replacement for Convertible Notes*, Y Combinator (Dec. 6, 2013), blog.ycombinator.com/announcing-the-safe-a-replacement-for-convertible-notes.

2. Katie Benner & Michael J. de la Merced, *Top Start-up Investors Are Betting on Growth, Not Waiting for It*, N.Y. Times (Mar. 13, 2016), http://www.nytimes.com/2016/03/14/technology/top-startup-investors-are-betting-on-growth-not-waiting-for-it.html (survey by CB Insights revealed that 15 of the top 20 venture capitalists worldwide invested in startups in their early financing rounds, with only a few investing at a subsequent time).

3. Paul A. Gompers & Josh Lerner, The Money of Invention: How Venture Capital Creates New Wealth 5, 12 (2001).

4. *Id.* at 10–11.

5. *Id.* at 28.

Chapter 14   Intellectual Property and Licensing

1. Microsoft was ordered to pay $120 million in damages to Stac Electronics. Lawrence M. Fisher, *Microsoft Loses Case on Patent*, N.Y. Times (Feb. 24, 1994), http://www.nytimes.com/1994/02/24/business/microsoft-loses-case-on-patent.html.

2. *See* Kevin A. Hassett & Robert J. Shapiro, *What Ideas Are Worth: The Value of Intellectual Capital and Intangible Assets in the American Economy*, Sonecon, http://sonecon.com/docs/studies/Value_of_Intellectual_Capital_in_American_Economy.pdf (last visited Aug. 18, 2016).

3. Constance E. Bagley, *The Value of Legally Astute Top Management Teams: A Dynamic Capabilities*

Approach, in THE OXFORD HANDBOOK OF DYNAMIC CAPABILITIES (David J. Teece & Sohvi Leih eds., 2016).

4. Margaret A. Peteraf, *The Cornerstones of Competitive Advantage: A Resource-Based View*, 14 STRAT. MGMT. J. 179, 187 (1993).

5. Bagley, *supra* note 3.

6. Constance E. Bagley, Mark Roellig & Gianmarco Massameno, *Who Let the Lawyers Out?: Reconstructing the Role of the Chief Legal Officer and the Corporate Client in a Globalizing World*, 18 U. PA. J. BUS. L. 419, 467 (2016).

7. *Quoted in* Gillian K. Hadfield, *Legal Infrastructure and the New Economy*, 8 I/S J.L. POL'Y FOR INFO. SOC'Y 1, 4 (2012).

8. James Surowiecki, *BlackBerry Season*, NEW YORKER (Feb. 13 & 20, 2012), http://www.newyorker.com /magazine/2012/02/13/blackberry -season.

9. *See* Paul Maidment, *The Rise and Fall of Shawn Fanning's Napster*, FORBES (May 27, 2003), http:// www.forbes.com/2003/05/27 /cx_pm_0527bookreview.html.

10. Constance E. Bagley & Reed Martin, BitTorrent, Harv. Bus. Sch. Case No. 806-169 (2006).

11. Pub. L. No. 114-153, 130 Stat. 376 (2016).

12. 18 U.S.C.A. § 1839.

13. Patrick J. Coyne, *What You Should Know About the Defend Trade Secrets Act*, LAW360 (June 27, 2016), http://www.law360.com /articles/806201/what-you-should -know-about-the-defend-trade -secrets-act.

14. Uniform Trade Secrets Act with 1985 Amendments, http://www. uniformlaws.org/shared/docs /trade%20secrets/utsa_final_85.pdf (last visited Aug. 18, 2016).

15. The DTSA amended the Economic Espionage Act of 1996, Pub. L. No. 104-294, 110 Stat. 3488 (1996) (codified as amended at 18 U.S.C. §§ 1831–1839).

16. *See, e.g.*, PepsiCo, Inc. v. Redmond, 54 F.3d 1262 (7th Cir. 1995) (precluding marketing director privy to PepsiCo's plans for marketing its sports drink and instant tea products from working on the marketing of Quaker Oats' Gatorade and Snapple products for six month after leaving PepsiCo).

17. 18 U.S.C.A. § 1836(b)(2)(A)(i).

18. *See, e.g.*, Varsity Brands, Inc. v. Star Athletica LLC, No. 10-2508, 2014 WL 819422 (W.D. Tenn. Mar. 01, 2014), *vacated*, 799 F.3d 468 (6th Cir. 2015), *cert. granted in part*, 136 S. Ct. 1823 (2016).

19. Feist Publ'ns, Inc. v. Rural Tel. Serv. Co., 499 U.S. 340 (1991).

20. Oracle Am., Inc. v. Google Inc., 750 F.3d 1339 (Fed. Cir. 2014), *cert. denied*, 135 S. Ct. 2887 (2015). A jury subsequently concluded that Google's use of Oracle's APIs was nevertheless permitted as a fair use under copyright law, and Oracle has vowed to appeal this decision. Joe Mullin, *Google Beats Oracle– Android Makes "Fair Use" of Java APIs*, ARS TECHNICA (May 26, 2016), http://arstechnica.com/tech -policy/2016/05/google-wins-trial -against-oracle-as-jury-finds -android-is-fair-use/.

21. Campbell v. Acuff-Rose Music, Inc., 510 U.S. 569 (1994).

22. Seltzer v. Green Day, Inc., 725 F.3d 1170 (9th Cir. 2013).

23. Basic Books, Inc. v. Kinko's Graphics Corp., 758 F. Supp. 1522 (S.D.N.Y. 1991).

24. Am. Geophysical Union v. Texaco, Inc., 60 F.3d 913 (2d Cir. 1994).

25. Sega Enters. Ltd. v. Accolade, Inc., 977 F.2d 1510 (9th Cir. 1992).

26. Sony Comput. Entm't, Inc. v. Connectix Corp., 203 F.3d 596 (9th Cir. 2000).

27. Fonovisa, Inc. v. Cherry Auction, Inc., 76 F.3d 259 (9th Cir. 1996).

28. MGM Studios, Inc. v. Grokster, Ltd., 545 U.S. 913 (2005).

29. Cmty. for Creative Non-Violence v. Reid, 490 U.S. 730 (1989).

30. *See, e.g.,* Steve Lohr, *Pirates Are Circling the Good Ship Windows 95,* N.Y. TIMES (Aug. 24, 1995), http://www.nytimes.com/1995/08/24/business/pirates-are-circling-the-good-ship-windows-95.html (noting that Microsoft has made the "most aggressive push to thwart software pirates" and that Microsoft, and other software companies, fought for better copyright protection for software abroad, resulting in Italy enacting software protection legislation).

31. Halo Elecs., Inc. v. Pulse Elecs., Inc., 136 S. Ct. 1923, 1935 (2016) (quoting Bonito Boats, Inc. v. Thunder Craft Boats, Inc., 489 U.S. 141, 146 (1989)).

32. Larry Huston, *Medtronic to Pay Over $1 Billion to Settle Patent Litigation with Edwards Lifesciences,* FORBES (May 20, 2014), http://www.forbes.com/sites/larryhusten/2014/05/20/medtronic-to-pay-over-1billion-to-settle-patent-litigation-with-edwards-lifesciences/.

33. *See, e.g.,* Bowman v. Monsanto Co., 133 S. Ct. 1761 (2013); J.E.M. Ag Supply, Inc. v. Pioneer Hi-Bred Int'l, Inc., 534 U.S. 124 (2001) (discussing rights of holders of patents on genetically modified seeds).

34. Diamond v. Chakrabarty, 447 U.S. 303, 309 (1980).

35. Egyptian Goddess, Inc. v. Swisa, Inc., 543 F.3d 665 (Fed. Cir. 2008).

36. *Id.* at 670 (quoting Gorham Co. v. White, 81 U.S. 511, 528 (1871)).

37. U.S. PATENT & TRADEMARK OFFICE, 2014 INTERIM GUIDANCE ON PATENT SUBJECT MATTER ELIGIBILITY, http://www.uspto.gov/patent/laws-and-regulations/examination-policy/2014-interim-guidance-subject-matter-eligibility-0 (last modified July 20, 2016).

38. Alice Corp. Pty. Ltd. v. CLS Bank Int'l, 134 S. Ct. 2347 (2014).

39. WilsonElser, *Hope for Computer-Related Patents–Alice Corp. v. CLS Bank,* NAT'L L. REV. (June 24, 2015), http://www.natlawreview.com/article/hope-computer-related-patents-alice-corp-v-cls-bank.

40. Ass'n for Molecular Pathology v. Myriad Genetics, Inc., 133 S. Ct. 2107 (2013).

41. The Supreme Court's approach in *Myriad Genetics* is similar to its rejection of the copyrightability of compilations of facts that are not organized in an original manner in *Feist Publ'ns, Inc. v. Rural Tel. Serv. Co.,* 499 U.S. 340 (1991). In that case the Court rejected the "sweat of the brow" doctrine, whereby the creator of difficult to assemble facts should be rewarded just for the effort required to gather them.

42. *Myriad Genetics,* 133 S. Ct. 2107.

43. KSR Int'l Co. v. Teleflex Inc., 550 U.S. 398 (2007).

44. Gene Quinn, *A Simple Guide to the AIA Oddities: First to File,* IP WATCHDOG (Sept. 11, 2013), http://www.ipwatchdog.com/2013/09/11/a-simple-guide-to-the-aia-oddities-first-to-file/id=45104/.

45. *Id.*

46. *Supreme Court Rejects Good-Faith Belief in Invalidity as a Defense to Induced Patent Infringement,* COOLEY LLP (May 2015), https://www.cooley.com/supreme-court-rejects-good-faith-belief-in-invalidity-as-defense-to-induced-patent-infringement.

47. eBay Inc. v. MercExchange, L.L.C., 547 U.S. 388 (2006).

48. *Id.*

49. Ryan T. Holte, *The Misinterpretation of* eBay v. MercExchange *and Why: An Analysis of the Case History, Precedent, and Parties*, 18 CHAP. L. REV. 677, 677, 682 (2015).

50. LaserDynamics, Inc. v. Quanta Comput., Inc., 694 F.3d 51, 66-70 (Fed. Cir. 2012).

51. *Id.*

52. Lucent Techs., Inc. v. Gateway, Inc., 580 F.3d 1301, 1332 (Fed. Cir. 2009).

53. Halo Elecs., Inc. v. Pulse Elecs., Inc., 136 S. Ct. 1923, 1932 (2016).

54. Octane Fitness, LLC v. ICON Health & Fitness Inc., 134 S. Ct. 1749 (2014).

55. Qualitex Co. v. Jacobson Prods. Co., 514 U.S. 159 (1995).

56. Christian Louboutin S.A. v. Yves Saint Laurent Am. Holding, Inc., 696 F.3d 206, 228 (2d Cir. 2012).

57. Two Pesos, Inc. v. Taco Cabana, Inc., 505 U.S. 763 (1992) (holding that trade dress is protectable under the Lanham Act, Pub. L. No. 79-489, 60 Stat. 427 (1946) (codified at 15 U.S.C. §§ 1051-1127)). The restaurant Two Pesos infringed Taco Cabana's trade dress when it copied the design, decor, and product offerings of the popular Taco Cabana restaurants. In addition to awarding damages, the judge ordered Two Pesos to display for one year a prominent sign in front of each of its restaurants acknowledging that it had unfairly copied Taco Cabana's restaurant concept.

58. Bill Donahue, *Black & Decker Wins $54M in DeWalt Trade Dress Battle*, LAW360 (Oct. 5, 2015), http://www.law360.com/articles/711130/black-decker-wins-54m-in-dewalt-trade-dress-battle.

59. Julia Anne Matheson & Whitney Devin Cooke, *Is Your Store Design Unique? Trademark It*, FINNEGAN.COM (July 17, 2013), http://www.finnegan.com/resources/articles/articlesdetail.aspx?news=cec05725-e298-4d22-8025-521e46e99ea0.

60. Wal-Mart Stores, Inc. v. Samara Bros., Inc., 529 U.S. 205 (2000).

61. TrafFix Devices, Inc. v. Mktg. Displays, Inc., 532 U.S. 23, 29 (2001).

62. ICANN NEW GENERIC TOP-LEVEL DOMAINS, https://newgtlds.icann.org/en/ (last visited Aug. 18, 2016).

63. Sunmark, Inc. v. Ocean Spray Cranberries, Inc., 64 F.3d 1055, 1060 (7th Cir. 1995).

64. *WIPO-Administered Treaties, Madrid Protocol*, WORLD INTELLECTUAL PROPERTY ORGANIZATION, http://www.wipo.int/treaties/en/ShowResults.jsp?country_id=ALL&start_year=ANY&end_year=ANY&search_what=C&treaty_id=8 (last visited Aug. 18, 2016).

65. Daniel Chow, *Lessons from Pfizer's Disputes over Its Viagra Trademark in China*, 27 MD. J. INT'L L. 82, 83 (2012) (citations omitted).

66. *Id.* at 82.

67. Armorlite Lens Co., Inc. v. Campbell, 340 F. Supp. 273 (S.D. Cal. 1972).

68. Constance E. Bagley et al., EMC Corporation's Proposed Acquisition of VMware, Harv. Bus. Sch. Case No. 806-153 (2006).

69. ProCD, Inc. v. Zeidenberg, 86 F.3d 1447 (7th Cir. 1996).

70. Specht v. Netscape Commc'ns Corp., 306 F.3d 17 (2d Cir. 2002).

71. *2015 Survey Results - The Future of Open Source*, NORTHBRIDGE, http://www.northbridge.com/2015-future-open-source-survey-results.

72. Steve Lohr, *Google Offers Free Software in Bid to Gain an Edge in Machine Learning*, N.Y. TIMES (Nov.

9, 2015), http://bits.blogs.nytimes
.com/2015/11/09/google-offers-free
-software-in-bid-to-gain-an-edge-in
-machine-learning/?_r=0.

Chapter 15 Going Global

1. Press Release, OECD, OECD Announces Further Developments in BEPS Implementation (July 11, 2016), http://www.oecd.org/ctp /oecd-announces-further-develop ments-in-beps-implementation. htm.

2. Case C-381/98, Ingmar GB Ltd. v. Eaton Leonard Techs. Inc., 2000 E.C.R. I-9305; Accentuate Ltd. v. Asigra Inc., [2009] EWHC 2655 (QB).

3. *See* CHARLES DEL BUSTO, ICC GUIDE TO DOCUMENTARY CREDIT OPERATIONS FOR THE UCP 500 (1994); INT'L CHAMBER OF COMMERCE, INTERNATIONAL STANDBY PRACTICES—ISP 98 (1998). *See also* INT'L CHAMBER OF COMMERCE, INCOTERMS 2010: ICC OFFICIAL RULES FOR THE INTERPRETATION OF TRADE TERMS (2010).

4. Press Release, SEC, VimpelCom to Pay $795 Million in Global Settlement for FCPA Violations (Feb. 18, 2016), https://www.sec.gov/news /pressrelease/2016-34.html.

5. Press Release, SEC, SEC Charges Siemens AG for Engaging in Worldwide Bribery (Dec. 15, 2008), https://www.sec.gov/news /press/2008/2008-294.htm.

6. 18 U.S.C. §§ 1961–1968.

7. RJR Nabisco, Inc. v. European Cmty., 136 S. Ct. 2090 (2016).

Chapter 16 Buying and Selling a Business

1. *See, e.g.*, Omnicare, Inc. v. NCS Healthcare, Inc., 818 A.2d 914 (Del. 2003).

2. Smith v. Van Gorkom, 488 A.2d 858, 874-75 (Del. 1985).

3. The business judgment rule is discussed in detail in CONSTANCE E. BAGLEY, MANAGERS AND THE LEGAL ENVIRONMENT: STRATEGIES FOR THE 21ST CENTURY 610–17 (8th ed. 2016).

4. Unocal Corp. v. Mesa Petroleum Co., 493 A.2d 946 (Del. 1985).

5. Revlon, Inc. v. MacAndrews & Forbes Holdings, Inc., 506 A.2d 173, 182 (Del. 1986).

6. *Id.*

7. Paramount Commc'ns, Inc. v. Time Inc., 571 A.2d 1140, 1150 (Del. 1990) (holding that a merger agreement that does not "constitute a 'change of control'" does not "trigger *Revlon* duties"; further, a change in control does not exist when before and after "the merger agreement was signed, control of the corporation existed in a fluid aggregation of unaffiliated shareholders representing a voting majority—in other words, in the market"); Paramount Commc'ns Inc. v. QVC Network Inc., 637 A.2d 34, 46-47 (Del. 1994) (finding that *Revlon* duties apply when a fundamental change of corporate control occurs, such as could occur in a stock for stock merger when one of the companies is privately held, or when there is a "control block of stock in the hands of a single shareholder or a group with loyalty to each other." When, however, the shares of both companies in a stock-for-stock merger are widely held, so there is a "fluid aggregation of unaffiliated stockholders both before and after the merger," there is no *Revlon* duty to maximize short-term shareholder value.) (internal citations omitted).

8. *See, e.g.*, Perlman v. Feldmann, 219 F.2d 173 (2d Cir. 1955); Jones v. H.F. Ahmanson & Co., 460 P.2d 464 (Cal. 1969).

9. *See* Robert T. Miller, *Canceling the Deal: Two Models of Material Adverse Change Clauses in Business Combination Agreements*, 31 Cardozo L. Rev. 99 (2009).

10. David Benoit, *Verizon Wireless Deal Comes with Biggest Breakup Fee Too*, Wall St. J. Blog (Sept. 3, 2013), http://blogs.wsj.com /moneybeat/2013/09/03/verizon -wireless-deal-comes-with-biggest -breakup-fee-too/.

Chapter 17 Going Public

1. Ryan v. Gifford, 918 A.2d 341, 355–56 (Del. Ch. 2007); *In re* Tyson Foods Consol. S'holder Litig., 919 A.2d 563, 592–93 (Del. Ch. 2007).

2. Jesse M. Fried, *Options Backdating and Its Implications*, 65 Wash. & Lee L. Rev. 853 (2008).

3. Under the misappropriation theory, adopted by the U.S. Supreme Court in *United States v. O'Hagan*, 521 U.S. 642 (1997), individuals can be liable for insider trading even if they have no fiduciary relationship with the company in whose stock they trade if they secretly trade on the basis of material nonpublic information in violation of a duty of trust and confidence owed the source of that information. Thus, a lawyer at a law firm representing Grand Met in its hostile takeover of Pillsbury violated Section 10(b) and Rule 10b-5 (as well as Rule 14e-3) when he bought options to buy Pillsbury stock before Grand Met announced its takeover bid. *Id.*

4. For example, Maher Kara, an investment banker at Citigroup, gave his older brother Michael material nonpublic information concerning pending mergers and acquisitions involving Citigroup's clients. Without Maher's knowledge, Michael passed this information along to others, including his friend and Maher's brother-in-law Bassam Salman. Salman then secretly traded on the basis of this information. After regulators caught on, Maher and Michael pleaded guilty and testified against Salman at his trial for conspiracy and insider trading. Maher stated that he intended to confer a gift on his brother Michael and that he expected Michael to trade on the basis of his tips. Michael testified that Salman knew that Maher was the source of the information Michael was passing on to Salman. The U.S. Supreme Court unanimously upheld Salman's conviction in *Salman v. United States*, 137 S. Ct. 420 (2016). Even though neither Maher nor Michael received any pecuniary benefit from Salman's trades, the Court held that it was enough that the original tipper Maher intended to give a gift to his brother Michael and that Michael's tippee Salman knew that Maher had given the information to Michael in breach of Maher's duty of trust and confidence to Citigroup and its clients.

5. SEC, *Fast Answers*, https://www .sec.gov/answers/form10k.htm (last modified June 26, 2009).

6. Terry Sheridan, *Financial Services Spend More than $1M Annually on SOX*, AccountingWEB (Aug. 2, 2016), http://www.accountingweb .com/aa/law-and-enforcement /financial-services-spend-more -than-1m-annually-on-sox.

7. Selective Disclosures and Insider Trading, Securities Act Release No. 7881, Exchange Act Release No. 43154, Investment Company Act Release No. 24599, 17 C.F.R. pts. 240, 243, 249 (Aug. 15, 2000).

8. Press Release, SEC, SEC Charges Former Vice President of Investor Relations with Violating Fair

Disclosure Rules (Sept. 6, 2013), https://www.sec.gov/News/Press Release/Detail/PressRelease /1370539799034.

9. *Id.* In 2010, Office Depot and its chief executive and chief financial officers settled claims that they had violated Regulation FD by having investor relations staff call analysts to remind them of Office Depot's previously released cautionary language and other companies' public statements concerning the impact of the slowing economy on earnings. Edward Wyatt, *Office Depot to Pay $1 Million to Settle S.E.C.'s Fair Disclosure Charge*, N.Y. TIMES, Oct. 22, 2010, at B3. Although they did not admit or deny the SEC's findings, the CEO and CFO agreed to pay $50,000 each in penalties, and Office Depot paid $1 million. The Office Depot CEO resigned less than a week later, but an Office Depot spokesperson denied that his departure was due to the SEC fine. Marcia Heroux Pounds, *Office Depot Chief Steve Ödland Resigns in Wake of SEC Settlement Disclosure*, SOUTH FLA. SUN-SENTINEL (FT. LAUDERDALE) (Oct. 25, 2010), http://articles.sun-sentinel.com/2010-10-25/business/fl-office-depot-resign-20101025_1_steve-odland-office-depot-office-supply-industry.

10. Sarbanes-Oxley Act of 2002, Pub. L. No. 107-204, 116 Stat. 745, § 301.

11. *Id.* § 407. If the audit committee does not include a financial expert, the company must disclose that fact and explain why there is no financial expert on the committee.

Index